Innovations in Energy

Innovations in Energy

The Story of Kerr-McGee

John Samuel Ezell

UNIVERSITY OF OKLAHOMA PRESS
Norman

By John S. Ezell

Fortune's Merry Wheel: The Lottery in America (Cambridge, Mass., 1960)
The New Democracy in America: Travels of Francisco de Miranda in the United States, 1783–84 (ed.) (Norman, 1963)
The South Since 1865 (Norman, 1975)
Readings in American History (ed.), (Boston, 1976)
Innovations in Energy: The Story of Kerr-McGee (Norman, 1979)

Library of Congress Cataloging in Publication Data

Ezell, John Samuel.
  Innovations in energy.

  Includes bibliographical references and index.
  1. Kerr-McGee Corporation—History. I. Title.
HD9569.K4E93   338.7′66′550973   79–4737

Contents

Illustrations

Color

Black-and-White

Figures

Preface

At a time when the American people face $20-a-barrel crude oil and $1-a-gallon gasoline there is no doubt that the end of an era is at hand. Only the most blindly optimistic deny the existence of an "energy problem," and nostalgia for the golden age of cheap fuels has already begun. Consequently, much can be said in favor of a case study within the energy field which spans the years of abundance and scarcity. This, then, is such a story: the story of an oil company begun in the days of gushers and oil booms whose struggles and successes dramatically mirror the circular path from coal to oil, to uranium, and back to coal.

The history of Kerr-McGee should carry the subtitle "Only in America." Where else could two farm boys, devoid of financial resources or family power, dream of fame and fortune and make their dreams come true? One man had only his ambition and personality to contribute; the other, his on-the-job training. With borrowed money and inferior equipment they embarked on their great adventure. The scene was a state that was only twenty-two years old; the time was the eve of the greatest depression the world had known. So slight was the chance of success that the birth of the small firm went unnoticed even in the journals of the little town where it was formed.

But they were wiser than they knew. Through the fortuitous circumstance of being in the right place at the right time and with the knack of turning adversity into opportunity by taking chances no one else would, these two not only survived the Great Depression but also attained a modicum of prosperity. The oldest and least daring was then satisfied and chose to take his share and retire. The other, with greater objectives yet to be achieved, stayed on to pursue his dreams. He had the extraordinary good fortune eventually to attract a partner, also from a rural background, who brought both needed technical knowledge and the driving force so vital in creating a modern, diversified corporation.

The history of Kerr-McGee Corporation is basically a business biography of three men. Robert Samuel Kerr and James LeRoy Anderson were founders of the infant drilling company. Dean Anderson McGee was the genius who transformed it into an integrated energy concern of national status. It is a saga of drive and ambition with two dominant characteristics always present: the ability to attract men with special, needed talents at crucial stages in the development of the firm and the willingness to adopt innovative techniques in old fields and to enter new ones. As a result, in only fifty years time, an impressive list of firsts caused the small business and its leaders to vault into the top ranks of American industry.

The nature of the company's inception and the individuality of its leaders presented the author with special problems and challenges. In the early days management was only a few people, often family-related, and office support and staff were virtually nonexistent. This trait continued for many years after the embryonic stage—perhaps memories of the Depression played a role—with the result that the organization was possibly underadministered when compared to others of similar size. Furthermore, management owned most of the stock. Therefore, it was under slight obligation to explain its actions to outsiders, or even to record them.

While this situation obviously worked to the advantage of Kerr-McGee, it created difficulties for the historian. When the decision makers are few in number, hold positions for a long time, and are in close physical proximity, they do not write the usual number of memorandums, but simply "talk it out" informally. Even when Robert S. Kerr was in Washington, daily telephone calls and frequent visits kept him informed about the office in Oklahoma City. Thus explanations of how things happened all too often benefit from hindsight, and the circumstances surrounding major decisions are difficult to reconstruct.

Lawyer Kerr also had a propensity for establishing companies. Often these were not subsidiaries in the usual sense, but separate business entities, although management and stockholders commonly consisted of the same group. During the early years little, if any, differentiation was made between them as to their unique functions. It was almost as if whatever needed to be done became the responsibility of whichever company had the money or manpower to do it at that particular moment. Thus leases were taken out in the name of any one of four companies, or even segments of the management. At one time there existed the anomaly of a contract drilling firm owning production without the personnel to produce it. The researcher faces a cumulative situation where little "paper" was generated and corporate responsibilities were mingled and also modern policy calling for automatic destruction of files after a stated number of years.

The nature of this book consequently was influenced by the absence of an organized historical base and the certainty that much of the existing material would not be preserved. Since this may well be the only record of a remarkable story, some materials normally summarized have been included in full because of their value not only to the company record but also to future scholars in business and petroleum history. The goal has been to write a "traditional" history of a major corporate development with emphasis on the human elements who made it work.

Although Kerr-McGee does not have an established archives, and its internal organization actually works against the historian, Dean McGee himself has a sense of history. Without his support and encouragement this project would never have been possible. His backing likewise insured the author's access to every existing document. Consequently, gaps in documentation are not the result of material withheld or censored but rather the absence of the records themselves. Management, as well as all personnel, was uniformly interested and cooperative and carefully avoided any action that could be interpreted as an effort to influence the outcome of this study. Any errors of fact, or judgment, therefore are entirely those of the author.

The list of Kerr-McGee personnel who assisted is lengthy. Certain individuals, however, were so vital to this study that special mention must be made. In a category all her own is Elizabeth ("Bette") Brenz. Long-time editor of the _Kermac News_, she spent many years collecting and preserving materials on which a history of the company could be based. Of inestimable value were the taped interviews she so skillfully conducted with sixty-one individuals who played vital roles in the history of the corporation. These were the real beginning of the story.

Paul Puttroff and William Teague helpfully provided liaison with the numerous divisions and subsidiaries and received and answered numerous calls from the frustrated author. George Cobb spent hours patiently shedding light on subjects confusing to this layman. Others who are due sincere thanks for special assistance include Elizabeth Zoernig, R. J. Hefler, George Cochran, William Ewert, John Raunborg, Carter Dudley, C. M. Van Zandt, Earl Wiseman, William Long, Marvin Lacy, Austin Traverse, Robert ("Bob") Anderson, William Phillips, Bob Kiser, Charlotte Buchanan, and Patrick Petree. And to the dozens unnamed: you, too, my heartfelt gratitude.

Outside the corporation there were many others who graciously contributed time and information. The management of the First National Bank of Chicago and the personnel of its archives were uniformly cooperative in opening their records for research. The employees in several branches of the government of the state of Oklahoma dug out files for materials otherwise unavailable. My colleagues in the Western History Collections at the University of Oklahoma, especially Jack Haley and June Witt, cheerfully bore extra loads to free my time. Numerous county clerks in courthouses in Oklahoma, newspaper publishers, and oldtimers who recalled events on the main streets of Anadarko, Ada, and other oil-play locales, all helped in the search for the elusive background of the earliest days of the company. Relatives and personal friends of Robert Kerr and James Anderson provided details which fleshed out the picture of two young, struggling entrepreneurs. And, finally, long-time employees and oilmen in general were happy to talk over old times and "how it was done then."

Special mention must be made of three people who were an integral part of this undertaking: Savoie Lottinville, who acted as the link between the corporate, academic, and publishing worlds and who was always available for consultation; Josephine Tilson Gil, who made many helpful corrections and provided the masterfully typed manuscript; and Jean McLean Ezell, whose work is reflected on every page of this book.

Norman, Oklahoma   JOHN S. EZELL

Innovations in Energy

Chapter 1

Prologue

In America the decades after the Civil War were ones of readjustment and change. Even without the aftermath of war life was hard for most people, who had few of the comforts and conveniences that the twentieth century would eventually present. Indoor plumbing was known only to a few urban dwellers, and central heating was equally rare. All cooking stoves used coal or wood fuel. Illuminating gas, made also from coal, was available in about four hundred cities, but it was smelly and dangerous. Consequently whale-oil lamps and tallow or spermaceti candles were nearly universal. Coal also fueled the mills and plants of the rapidly expanding industrial society. Transportation was limited to steam-propelled ships and railways and horse-drawn vehicles driven over inadequate systems of roads.

Mankind, so far, had only limited sources of energy. One of these, the whale, was fast being eliminated by increasing demands for its by-products. It was imperative that a substitute be found for this prime source of illuminants and lubricating oil. Furthermore, the American dream of wealth now included finding ways to do things faster, easier, and more safely. To accomplish this, cheap and abundant sources of new energy were vital. The stage was set for a development which would revolutionize not only America, but also the world's way of life, forever.

It began with the digging of a shallow oil well in western Pennsylvania in 1859. The product was initially significant because it would be used to grease the axles of American industry. Later, and more important, it would be easily distilled into a superior fluid, kerosene, for illuminating, cooking, and heating. In the face of demand here and abroad, the only limit to its expanded use was availability. For more than a quarter of a century nearly all of the petroleum produced in this country came from the environs of Oil Creek, between Titusville and Oil City, Pennsylvania. This was the greatest oil-producing area in the world until 1895, with a peak of 30,053,509 barrels in 1882, and furnished nearly 83 percent of the world's supply during these years.

Paradoxically, as the demand for petroleum grew, output declined. Many predicted that the oil era would end with exhaustion of Pennsylvania's reserves. Oil seepages in other areas were known locally, to exist, and a few wells had been drilled, but their production was negligible. Because of differences in surface terrain some people, including oil men, believed that petroleum did not exist west of the Mississippi River, and one cynic announced that he would "undertake to drink all of the oil ever produced in that section." Fortunately not everyone accepted this, and in 1885 a significant new strike was made near Lima, Ohio. The mad influx that had characterized Oil City, Pennsylvania, was now repeated in Ohio. In 1895, with a production of 19,545,233 barrels, Ohio surpassed Pennsylvania.

The introduction of the internal-combustion engine around the turn of the century and successful experiments with the automobile in France opened unlimited uses for petroleum and its numerous by-products. In this country the Model T Ford motorized American life. Although first produced in 1908, the use of assembly lines for mass production allowed over 500,000 cars to be sold in 1916. By 1923 this total had risen to two million and four years later to an output of fifteen million. Furthermore, the price of this automobile, which had started at $825, was down to $260 in 1925.

By this time oil had moved from an amenity to a necessity of life. In the process it had created new multimillionaires such as the Rockefellers and the Mellons and fostered national scandals such as Teapot Dome. But more important were the thousands of new jobs and new businesses—large and small—which sprang up in its wake. Motorized vehicles for instance, demanded improved roads, but in return gave cheap, more effective transportation and communication. The United States quickly developed into a nation on wheels, and old barriers between rural and urban living crumbled. The more compact and versatile gasoline motors quickly replaced steam as the motive power for large engines, only in turn to be supplanted by the oil-driven diesel. Americans achieved the highest standard of living in the world, largely as the result of the use of petroleum in its many forms.

To keep pace with the increasing demand, the science and technology of production had also to change. The first holes were hand-dug in the same fashion as water wells. The greater depths where oil was found quickly doomed this slow and laborious approach. The first mechanical breakthrough came with the use of cable tools. A crude, wooden structure was erected over the spot to be drilled, and, using the technique of a pile driver, a heavy, pointed projectile on the end of the cable was dropped from a height, literally pounding a hole into the earth. Steam usually powered the winches that retrieved the bit from the hole in preparation for the next drop. As holes became deeper and bits became heavier, multiple boilers became common.

4

As great an improvement as this was, there were still shortcomings. Depth was still a limiting factor. Cable tools were slower than desired—painfully slow in hard-rock formations—and it was impossible to get a straight hole. By the early 1920's the new rotary rigs were common. By means of a metal drillstem and specially designed bits, a hole was bored into the earth. Drilling could now be a continuous process, except when testing or other work in the hole was necessary. Limiting factors were the need for power to turn the drill, the strength of the derrick, and the ability of the drill stem to withstand the twisting forces inherent in the greater length as the holes became deeper.

The search for new oil required unique kinds of men—men who were gamblers, willing to play hunches and risk everything. As in all gambles, the rewards could be enormous, but likewise the chance of winning was slight. The oil world bred a new kind of entrepreneur called the wildcatter. Usually unburdened by knowledge of geology, he was willing to look almost anywhere in search of the new El Dorado—in the lands across the Mississippi and Rockies, and even on Indian lands. Small discoveries of gas and oil in Kansas in the 1870's had sparked a minor interest there, and to the south in Indian Territory some believed that the presence of "oil springs" meant the mineral might be discovered in paying quantities. They pursued this hope, though whites, except those who were intermarried citizens, had no real rights in Indian Territory, and they could be forced out at any time by the tribal governments.

One early group that obtained permission to seek oil was the Chickasaw Oil Company, organized in Indian Territory in 1872. Difficult as it was to negotiate such permits with the various tribes, the creation of companies proved easier than finding oil in profitable amounts. Lack of local markets, problems of transportation, and resistance by the federal government to white intrusion kept drilling activity to a minimum. But other forces were at work to change the situation. During the 1880's whites began moving illegally into the western part of the territory where few if any Indians lived. The "Unassigned Lands" were officially opened by the United States government for settlement in 1889, and in 1890 Oklahoma Territory was created by Congress. The region occupied by the Five Civilized Tribes remained as Indian Territory.

The commercial production of oil in Kansas in 1892 again spurred new activity to the south. Still it was not until April 15, 1897, that the first commercial well was brought in, and Bartlesville became Indian Territory's first oil boomtown. By 1900 most of the internal problems which faced oilmen operating on Indian lands had been solved by federal limitations on tribal governments and by allotment of Indian lands to individuals. Oil activity flourished without restraint, and probably nowhere in the world has an area of similar size ever grown more rapidly. In 1890 the Twin Territories, which became the state of Oklahoma in 1907, had an estimated population of 300,000, mostly in Indian Territory. By 1900 this number had risen to nearly 800,000; by 1910 to 1,500,000; and by 1920 to slightly over 2,000,000.

Oil made its contribution to this growth. Although nothing was found to rival Texas' spectacular Spindletop Dome discovery in 1901, by 1905 the territories were producing approximately 25 percent of the Mid-Continent's oil. The discovery of Glenn Pool near Tulsa in November, 1905, soon propelled Oklahoma into regional supremacy, a position it held until dethroned by Texas in 1928. Between 1920 and 1926 the state supplied almost 1 billion barrels of petroleum worth 2 billion dollars and drilled 42,000 wells, of which 26,600 were producers. In 1926, it led the nation in annual output.[1]

Ironically, Oklahoma's success showed that production could on occasion outrun demand, and prices fluctuated as a result. Oil brought $3.50 a barrel in early 1920 but dropped as low as $1.00 by late 1923. The next year the price wavered between $2.00 and $1.25 but recovered to $2.29 by 1926. During this period there were no brakes on output except the few restraints that were self-imposed. Landowners, lease speculators, and most producers wanted to get all of the oil out of the ground at the earliest possible moment.[2]

Optimism prevailed in the young state. Lives disrupted by war and depression were finding paths that promised happier and more prosperous times for individuals and communities. Still frontiersmen at heart, these Oklahomans firmly believed that the hardships of pioneering were finally over. On January 1, 1926, on the eve of the twentieth year of statehood, only rosy clouds were on the horizon. The Boomers and Sooners were ready for a new era.

The *Watonga Republican*, which boasted that it had the largest circulation of any weekly in western Oklahoma, mirrored the rural optimism in 1926. January's news was characterized by headlines such as "Business Good the Past Year," "Bright Prospects For the Coming Year," and "Oil Game Exciting in Kingfisher County." Advertisements proclaimed Chevrolet trucks reduced in price to $395, and Harold Lloyd in *Girl Shy* could be seen at the local movie house for 10¢ or 25¢. In February an editorial reminded the readers that there were 192,000 farms in Oklahoma, 7,000 schools, and 2,500,000 (*sic*) people. Oklahomans had $432 million in bank deposits, and the previous year's crops had been worth $325 million. The state led the nation in petroleum and zinc production, and its citizens, with a bonded indebtedness of only $1.65 per capita, were better off than those of thirty-nine other states.

"Oklahoma Has a Birthday" the editor wrote in April: "Thirty-four years have passed since the opening of the Cheyenne and Arapaho Reservation of which Blaine County is a part. Broad fields and fine homes have now displaced prairie dog towns." In July an increase in local bank assets by $71,238.53 made the headlines. "State Record Reached in May Collections by State Auditor" and "President Makes Plea for Nation's Return to Spirit of 1776" were climaxed by "Oklahoma Farmers Prosper in 1926." Typical of

[1] Carl Coke Rister, *Oil: Titan of the Southwest* (Norman, University of Oklahoma Press, 1949), chaps. 2, 7, 10, 18.

[2] Lloyd E. Gatewood, "Oklahoma and Oil—Fifty Years of Ups and Downs," *Shell Shaker*, Vol. 21 (June, 1971), pp. 246–52; Roy M. McClintoch, "Oil in Oklahoma" (unpublished manuscript, Oklahoma State Historical Archives), p. 52.

the day and mood was the advertisement for the Fay Oil and Development Company, of Fay, Oklahoma: "Millions of Dollars Have Been Made in Oil—Millions More Will be Made. Will You Get Your Share?"

The more sophisticated *Daily Oklahoman* of Oklahoma City was equally sanguine. The year 1926 opened with the headlines "State Cotton Crop Increases 50 Per Cent in 5 Years," "Wewoka Field Wilcox Well Holds Up for 4,000 Barrels," and "Stocks Close Year with Broad Upturn." Two days later the newspaper announced "State Production Mounts Above Billion Mark in 1925," as Oklahoma livestock and crops brought in $402 million and mineral resources another $400 million. It was reported that Oklahoma City had paved 110 blocks of streets in 1925 and expected to pave a mile a month in 1926. During the rest of January readers were reminded that "Cotton Futures in Near Months Hold Above 20 Cents," that "Magnolia Gets 24,000 Barrel Well in Wewoka Field," and that California and Oklahoma were in a seesaw battle for first place in oil production. In December the story was still the same: "Banks Now Nearing Close of Sound Fiscal Year"; "Seminole Passes Panhandle to set Peak Record"; and "Oil Lease Brokers Are Flocking to Central Fields."

It was not surprising then that ambitious young men throughout the United States felt that their fortunes might also rise like the gushers and that Oklahoma was the place to be. One who did was James LeRoy Anderson, born September 29, 1884. In 1900 this sixteen-year-old boy ran away from the family's Blount County, Tennessee, farm to join an older brother in California, who was a salesman for an oil-field supply company. Jim got a job as a common laborer on a drilling rig, and, working in the Taft and Bakersfield fields, he learned the trade and saved his money.

About two years later Jim returned to Tennessee, reentered school, and graduated from Maryville Presbyterian College in 1906. Although documentation is scanty, it seems that he immediately returned to the oil fields, for in 1908 he was back in California working as a tool dresser and later as a driller on the cable rigs then in vogue. When the new rotary units were introduced, he worked his way up again from roughneck, to driller, to tool pusher. Apparently he followed the action from field to field, for in 1917 he was doing rotary work in Wyoming and in 1919 was head driller on a rig in Cement, Oklahoma. In 1921–22 he worked for an English firm in the British West Indies, but the next year oil, or romance, called him back to Oklahoma. In November he married a young schoolteacher, Mildred Kerr, whom he had met in 1919. Although he suggested that they go to Trinidad for a working honeymoon, the bride talked him into staying in the Oklahoma fields.[3]

Jim Anderson had gone to work as a tool pusher for J. D. Patrick. When

[3] Tapes and transcripts for all interviews cited are in the Public Relations Department, Kerr-McGee Corporation (hereafter cited as Public Relations Department). Interviews with Mildred Kerr Anderson, January 1, 1970, and James K. Anderson, July 28, 1971; Xerox of passport issued August 25, 1921; and unidentified obituaries in James K. Anderson file, Public Relations Department.

Patrick, a driller from south Texas, moved into the Anadarko, Oklahoma, area some time shortly after World War I,[4] Bert S. Dixon, cashier of the Anadarko National Bank and Trust Company, and his brother, William A. Dixon, obtained an interest in the Texan's activities. The Dixon brothers, who were also partners in the Anadarko Ice Company, soon purchased control of the bank, so in early 1923, when Patrick decided to return to Texas, they were in a position to take over his two rotary drilling rigs.[5] Needing someone to operate the units, the bankers turned to Jim Anderson and made him their superintendent.[6]

Thus the scene was set, waiting for the entrance of the next character in this story. Southeast of Anadarko, destiny was shaping the career of Jim Anderson's brother-in-law, Robert Samuel Kerr, born on September 11, 1896, in Indian Territory near Ada. He was the first son of parents who had moved from Texas to the Cherokee Nation in 1895 in search of a better life. Bob and his six brothers and sisters learned from experience the realities of living on a frontier. While the father took a variety of jobs to help support his large brood, the family farmed corn and cotton and had a small fruit orchard. Both parents had some formal education and were firmly convinced that education and hard work were the keys to success in any endeavor.

This passion for work and ambition for advancement rooted early in the oldest son. After finishing the equivalent of high school, Bob took a teaching position at a small country school to help his family and also to earn money for further education for himself. Although there was some parental pressure to become a minister, law and politics became his goal. After two years at East Central State College in Ada, he borrowed money to enter the University of Oklahoma in Norman. But his funds ran out after a year and he left school for the last time. A new job as a magazine salesman gave him contacts which he turned into an opportunity to become a clerk and messenger for a Missouri attorney and to read law on the side.

When the United States entered World War I, Robert S. Kerr won a commission as a second lieutenant in the field artillery. Although he served in France for nine months, he saw no combat. However, his military service was later to provide connections that were invaluable. After the war he returned to Ada, where in 1919 he married Reba Shelton and, using borrowed money, became a partner in the Kerr-Dandridge Produce House.[7]

[4] The Patrick Drilling Company was incorporated by Patrick and four other Anadarko citizens on April 16, 1918. The Dixons were not included. Oklahoma Secretary of State, "Corporation File."

[5] No legal or newspaper accounts of this transaction have been found, and contemporaries are uncertain whether Patrick sold out or the bank foreclosed on the rigs. The Patrick Drilling Company's registration was not canceled until December 15, 1930. Secretary of State, "Corporation File." See also interview with D. L. Brown, Sr., August 5, 1971.

[6] Interviews with Mildred Kerr Anderson; Neil Dikeman, president of the First State Bank of Anadarko, August 19, 1971; Quinton C. ("Pete") Walton, April 16, 1971; and Dixon employee R. E. ("Buck") Fowler, October 29, 1972. Fowler said of the Dixons: "They had money to do everything, anything they wanted to do, but they didn't want to do much. Just make money."

But again the course of his life was changed, for in November, 1921, a fire destroyed his business and left him $10,000 in debt. This catastrophe propelled him once more toward his youthful ambition: law. While his wife taught school to support them, Kerr resumed his studies in the local office of Judge J. F. McKeel. Probably because of a need for additional funds as well as his interest in the military, he joined the Oklahoma National Guard in 1921 as captain of Battery F 160th Field Artillery at a salary of sixty dollars a month.[8] He also became a charter member of the Ada post of the American Legion.

After passing the bar in 1922, he began a law practice which lasted about ten years. At the same time financial pressures and an inexhaustible supply of energy assured his participation in a myriad of activities. As a youth he had announced to his father that he wanted three things from life, in the following order: a family, a million dollars, and the governorship of Oklahoma. He had a wife and so began to work toward the other two goals. He had entered Democratic politics in early 1919, serving as a delegate to county and state conventions, as a precinct committeeman, and as an inspector for the election board.[9] Already he was in great demand as a speaker at all kinds of functions. With an eye to clients and future votes, he also cultivated his American Legion connection, becoming post commander in 1924, and judge advocate for the department of Oklahoma in 1925. At the same time ran for and was elected state commander.[10]

It was some of Bob's other activities which were to bring about his fortune, however. Oil had entered the Kerr family when his younger sister married Jim Anderson, but there is no indication that Bob had any early interest in the petroleum business other than the usual curiosity which accompanied stories of gushers and instant fortunes. However, in 1923, when oil was found at BeeBee, the little town where Kerr had formerly taught school and had friends, he saw a chance to make some money. Although his practice was bringing in about $125 a month, he and two close Ada friends, Merle O. Matthews and Byron Sledge, formed a partnership to buy and sell oil royalties. At first it was on a small scale at BeeBee, but later their operations expanded. Each partner owned a third of the business although they bought under the name of one or another of the three men. Sometimes they would buy royalties on credit and then sell enough to put them in the clear

---

[7] Bob's father at one time ran a store while the sons ran the farm, and as a youth Bob and his brothers peddled fruit and vegetables raised by the family. Jon H. Nabors, "Robert S. Kerr, Baptist Layman: A Study of the Impact of Religion and Politics on the Life of An Oklahoma Leader" (unpublished master's thesis, Department of History, University of Oklahoma, 1964); interviews with J. R. Kitchel, April 5, 1972, and Aubrey M. Kerr, April 28, 1971. Kerr's discharge is dated May 24, 1919. Robert S. Kerr scrapbooks, 1, Western History Collections, University of Oklahoma.

[8] He served as captain from 1921 to 1925 and as major from 1925 to 1929.

[9] T.P. Tripp, "Bob Kerr May Enter State Contest," *Harlow's Weekly*, December 9, 1933, p. 7.

[10] Kerr scrapbooks, 1.

financially. There is no real evidence that this sideline made a great deal, but it did give Bob Kerr his first taste of oil money, and he liked it.[11] Then in 1924, his wife and son died in childbirth, and it seemed that the first of his dreams was lost. But his brother Travis took a job with an oil-field supply firm, Lucey Products Corporation, and another strand of the future was slowly but surely being woven into his life.

Meanwhile, the Dixon brothers, for whom Jim Anderson worked, were having their own problems. With the improvement of rotary-drilling techniques, such equipment was much in demand in the early 1920's because of its efficiency and relatively low drilling cost in comparison to the old cable tools. But this demand, however, was followed by an over-all decline in drilling activity. In 1925 and 1926 many operators found themselves with idle equipment. Since drilling was a minor sideline with the banking brothers, they decided that they needed the services of someone who could secure contracts for their rigs.[12] They apparently mentioned their decision to their superintendent, Jim Anderson, and yet another thread of Bob Kerr's future tied into the pattern.

With his customary carefulness Jim thought it over. He decided that his brother-in-law Bob might just be the one the Dixons could use. Bob had remarried, this time to Gracye Breen, and additional financial pressures were besetting the young lawyer and dabbler in lease royalties. Jim's wife, Mildred, later recalled that when her husband asked about recommending her brother, "I didn't go overboard because . . . I'd lived with him long enough then to know if I go all out then he's going to go against it." Her tactics worked, for Bob was suggested as the contact man.[13]

Thirty-three years later Kerr and Anderson were to recapitulate that fateful meeting with the Dixons. On March 11, 1959, Jim wrote Senator Kerr:

"In my personal 'album of memory' I will always reserve a special place for the names of Bill and Bert Dixon: I consider them to be the 'founders' of my own success, in that they gave me a *start* by offering the opportunity to take my first faltering steps toward success."

In Jim's eyes a *Fortune* magazine article on Kerr had slighted his and the Dixons' roles in Kerr's success. He went on to say:

I have watched with a great deal of interest your rise to towering prominence; and, along with my interest, I have even felt a little personal pride in remembering and believing that my past affiliations with you may have contributed somewhat, how-

---

[11] Interviews with Aubrey M. Kerr and J. R. Kitchel.

[12] "Supplemental Information *re* A&K Petroleum Company Class A Common Stock." Probably issued in 1936 in connection with sale of that stock.

[13] Some secondary sources have suggested that the Dixon brothers first became acquainted with Kerr through some of his legal work, but there is no evidence to support this. It appears conclusive that the contact was through Anderson.

ever, slightly, toward achieving for you the successful conflagration of those burning fires of ambition in you, which were somewhat "frustrated" fires, back around the year 1925 when you and I drove in my car to the little town of Anadarko, Oklahoma. The return from that trip . . . marked the entrance of Bob Kerr into the oil business, from your modest law practice of the time; and I know that then, at least, it represented a considerable step upward in your almost perpendicular climb toward realization of your aspirations.[14]

Kerr responded eight days later with an apology for the omissions and added, "I told him [the author of the article] in minute detail how I joined you and Bert and Bill in the drilling company."[15]

Anderson was right. In 1925–26 the part-time position was undoubtedly an important step in Kerr's future. There is no formal evidence of the original financial arrangements,[16] but young Kerr immediately set out to learn more about the drilling business. Old-timers who had worked for the Dixons recalled their first contact with him. Buck Fowler, who ran one of the rigs while Anderson bossed the other, said that they were drilling near Maud, Oklahoma, in 1926 when Bob Kerr came out from Ada and announced that he was the new contact man and that he wanted to be around the rig and learn about drilling. He came over from Ada every day with his lunch in a paper sack and sat around and watched.[17] Bob never learned much about the technique, however, and eventually was willing to leave that aspect to others. But he did become an active and enthusiastic part of the new oil world.

In whatever business occupied his attention, Bob's long suit was personal contacts. Through his legal, political, and especially his military connections he was unusually well qualified as an agent for the Dixons and for his own interests. For example, one lucrative friendship was with Baird H. Markham. In 1923, Markham was appointed adjutant general of Oklahoma, and later served as commander of the Forty-fifth Division of the National Guard at a time when young Kerr headed the Ada unit. In 1926, Markham joined the Marland Oil Company of Ponca City, and when it merged with the

[14] James L. Anderson, Gainesville, Texas, to Robert S. Kerr, March 11, 1959. Xerox copy in KM/PR James K. Anderson file. For other evidence of Anderson's role, see Mildred Kerr Anderson interview and "Supplemental Information *re* A&K Petroleum Company. . ."

[15] Robert S. Kerr, Washington, D.C., to James L. Anderson, March 19, 1959, in KM/PR James K. Anderson file, The article that caused this exchange was Daniel Seligman, "Senator Bob Kerr, the Oklahoma Gusher," *Fortune*, Vol. 59 (March, 1959).

[16] Both Jim and Bob had acquired an interest in the company by 1929. Whether they earned their interests in lieu of full salary or bought them is not clear. Jim's son, James K., related that the Dixons insisted that his father take part of his salary as an interest in the company or as an interest in the two steam drilling rigs. "He didn't want to do it, but they insisted." Later his father credited them with his financial success by making him take an interest in the rigs and by giving him financial responsibility. Interviews with James K. Anderson and D. L. Brown, Sr.

[17] Interview with R. E. ("Buck") Fowler.

Robert S. Kerr and James L. Anderson about the time that they worked for the Dixon brothers.

Continental Oil Company in 1928, he moved from treasurer to controller and finally became assistant to the president of Continental Oil.[18]

Too, the times were right. To Americans in general 1926 was a year of promise. The old war-born issues which so recently had torn the nation seemed safely in the past, while the new specters of depression and unemployment were only vague threats for the future. Six years earlier voters had cast their ballots for Warren G. Harding and a "return to normalcy." Then in 1924 a majority had opted to "keep cool with Coolidge." "Silent Cal" had promised to wipe out the scandals that had tainted his predecessor and that there would be no more foreign entanglements, although there would be cooperation with the new League of Nations to outlaw war and armaments. Most businesses were booming; only a few had bitter memories of the agricultural recession of 1920, when cotton skidded to five cents a pound and wheat to its lowest level in twenty-five years. Thus, on the eve of the nation's one hundred and fiftieth birthday, the average citizen was convinced that past struggles had been worthwhile and that the beginning of a golden age was near.

Conditions in Oklahoma were also favorable for Kerr's new involvement. The slow play of 1925 gave way to a renewed burst of enthusiasm as new strikes were made in rapid succession. Beginning with Earlsboro and Seminole City in March, 1926, the year was brightened by additional discoveries at Bowlegs, Crescent, Maud, and north Oklahoma City. Although the Dixon brothers' operation might be described as a two-horse outfit, there was work for everyone. One relatively small example of the opportunity for drillers was Earlsboro, which had 248 wells by November 1, 1927. Over all the state produced some 179,195,000 barrels of oil worth about $413,900,000.

And the future was even brighter. The Seminole City strike proved to be only a small part of what was to become Oklahoma's biggest field. Greater Seminole alone increased 1927 oil production by almost 100 million barrels. In June, 1928, the Oklahoma Geological Survey's oil-and-gas map of the state showed 39 counties with 324 fields of oil and gas and 8 with gas alone. Then on December 4, 1928, Indian Territory Illuminating Oil Company's #1 Oklahoma City well blew in. For an hour and a half it ran wild before it could be brought under control, and it produced 4,909 barrels of 40-degree-gravity oil in the first twenty-four hours. On this roaring note was opened the Oklahoma City field, destined to become a billion-barrel field in less than forty years.

Needless to say, these events had a profound effect on the Kerr, Anderson, and Dixon fortunes. On the basis of available evidence there seems to be no reason to doubt that the two drilling rigs were kept fully utilized. What apparently had been an informal arrangement among the three parties was formalized on February 4, 1928, when a charter for Dixon Brothers Incorpo-

---

[18] Interviews with Aubrey M. Kerr and Travis M. Kerr, December 16, 1969; Rex Harlow, *Successful Oklahomans* (Oklahoma City, 1927), pp. 220–29.

A Dixon rig in 1927, with rock bits in the foreground.

rated, with five hundred shares at $100 each, was filed with the Oklahoma secretary of state, showing the four men as incorporators.[19] Anderson personally oversaw the operation of one of the rigs and was undoubtedly occupied day and night with the problems of both units. Kerr, however, while serving as a contact agent for Dixon Brothers, still carried on his law practice in partnership with Lowery H. Howell of Ada. He also made many speeches on various topics and, as the records of the county clerk for Pontotoc County show, was active in buying and selling leases.

Since it can be assumed that the Dixons found the drilling business a profitable sideline, it is somewhat surprising that less than a year later they approached their two partners with an offer to sell their 60 percent in-

[19] Secretary of State, "Corporation File."

terest.[20] It is possible only to speculate on the reason for this, for there are simply not enough records in existence. It is known that both of the Dixons were having health problems and that Bert's wife died in February, 1929,[21] but the real reason was probably economic. There is no question that Bert, the dominant brother, was a hardheaded businessman. By late 1928 a glut on the crude-oil market forced prices down, and the larger producers at Seminole began trying to cut back. The Oklahoma City field only added to the oversupply. Then, too, the Dixon steam rigs were old, wearing out, and could not drill deep enough for some of the newer fields. The low price of $30,000 that they put on their 60 percent share of the business confirms their awareness of all these situations.

The offer was apparently made sometime near Christmas of 1928. Aubrey Kerr recalled that all the Kerr children and their families had gathered at father W. S. Kerr's home in Ada and that the possibility of buying out the Dixons was discussed. It was pointed out that Continental Oil had some leases adjoining those the Dixons were currently drilling and, if Markham could get his company to give the Kerrs a contract, it could be the start of their own business.[22] But money was the big problem, for neither Bob nor Jim had much. Bob Kerr later wrote Anderson:

I told him [a writer for *Fortune*] in minute detail . . . how, when the time came for us to buy them out, that you furnished the Five Thousand Dollars that was paid down to them, and how I then borrowed Five Thousand from Lew Wentz to give us some cash and a basis for getting additional money for payroll and otherwise in connection with the drilling of the original well for I.T.I.O. [Indian Territory Illuminating Oil Company].[23]

So the deal was made: $5,000 in cash and a $25,000 mortgage based primarily on hopes and expectations. In the future Senator Kerr would always use the date, although technically incorrect, of February, 1929, for the beginning of the eventual Kerr-McGee Corporation. The simple partnership was drawn up by lawyer and brother, Aubrey Kerr. Father Kerr and sister Mildred kept the set of accounting books which was the initial purchase by the Anderson & Kerr Drilling Company. This was followed by a desk and typewriter, which were placed in the elder Kerr's home.[24] They discussed bringing Travis Kerr into the business, but, as Travis later recalled, the decision was that, since he was on a salary and had an expense

[20] At this time Anderson and Kerr each had a 20 percent interest.

[21] *Anadarko American-Democrat*, March 18, 1925, February 6, 1929; *Anadarko Tribune*, December 27, 1928, January 24, 1929.

[22] Interview with Aubrey Kerr.

[23] Robert S. Kerr to James L. Anderson, March 19, 1959. Lew Wentz was an Oklahoma oilman and a good friend of Mrs. Robert S. Kerr's family.

[24] Aubrey Kerr (May 24, 1972) believed that contracts with Markham may have served as a basis for the loan and/or mortgages. The company from which the current corporation descended was not formed until November, 1932. Interviews with Aubrey M. Kerr and Mildred K. Anderson; "Supplemental Information *re* A&K Petroleum. . ."

account from Lucey Products, he should wait to see if the fledgling enterprise was going to make it. George T. Sims, the first cable-tool superintendent and a friend of Anderson, remembered how Anderson told him that he and his brother-in-law were "figgering on buying the tools that belonged to the Dixon brothers" and that, when they got a contract north and west of Ada, he was hired. Apparently most of the Dixon employees went with the new management, for as late as January 1, 1947, there were seven who had been with the company for seventeen years.[25]

Anderson & Kerr Drilling was only one of dozens, if not hundreds, of small oil-related firms in Oklahoma in 1929. It was so unremarkable that the newspapers of Ada made no mention of its birth, and several years passed before even the oil journals acknowledged the company's existence. In the absence of records, its early struggles to survive can only be imagined. What is known is that Kerr stayed in Ada, practiced law, and was active in lease speculating and in seeking drilling contracts.[26] Anderson, who had earlier moved his family to Oklahoma City, looked after the actual drilling operations. According to old-timers at least one of the two rigs was at Maud when Anderson and Kerr took over, and the other was shortly to be at Tonkawa. During the first few months they also apparently drilled at Earlsboro and around Seminole before moving into the new field at Oklahoma City in July of 1929. Kerr wrote that their first contract was with I.T.I.O., but he may have been referring only to Oklahoma City. Aubrey Kerr remembered an early one with Continental Oil by which Bob made a deal with Markham to drill a well and, if they hit, to keep drilling as long as they were needed. But it was in Oklahoma City that the young partnership was to find its foundations for success.

[25] Cable tools were still used to "finish" a hole and were often considered as part of one rig; thus Anderson and Kerr probably bought two steam rotary rigs and two sets of cable tools. Interviews with Travis M. Kerr, D. L. Brown, Sr., George T. Sims, June 17, 1971; Loyal Edwards, June 17, 1971; and Q. C. Walton and George Kitchel, June 17, 1971. For a list of the original employees see *Kermac News*, Vol. 1 (January, 1947), p. 1.

[26] The Pontotoc County clerk's records show 18 transactions for 1929, 5 for 1930, and 2 for 1931 that seem to involve oil. A number of these involved Matthews and Sledge, and 3 included Anderson.

Chapter 2

Oklahoma City: Anderson & Kerr Drilling Company 1929–31

Oklahoma City was the focus of attention for everyone in the oil business. The *Daily Oklahoman* was not about to allow any of its readers to overlook that fact. On December 30, 1928, under the headline "Oil Stimulates Growth," it reported 21 new business buildings and 1,150 new homes. Because of the "probability of continued oil development," real-estate men were unwilling to forecast the growth for 1929, but the *Oklahoman* predicted that the "proving . . . of the Oklahoma City oil field probably will usher in more than a dozen new major business structures, plans for which are under discussion. . . . Between 25,000 and 40,000 new citizens are expected next year in Oklahoma City as a result of our rich oil and gas fields and general prosperity."

During February, 1929, the paper noted with pride that Oklahoma City had experienced seventeen consecutive months in which building permits totaled $1 million per month. January alone had seen $19,230,303.04 in new capital invested in state businesses, and incorporation papers had been granted to 170 local and 47 foreign corporations. In June it reported the Standard Statistics Company of New York's findings that Oklahoma City transacted the largest volume of business in the nation and that Oklahoma was the most prosperous state in the West-South-Central area. The onset of the Great Depression in October was reported briefly under the caption "Business Men Are Unnecessarily Troubled by Crash of Stocks"; November and December editions carried the good word of "All Business Records Smashed by City" and "City Fund Surplus of $300,000 Is Seen by Auditor for Fiscal Year," because income was above all estimates of revenue.

One of the two rigs bought by James L. Anderson and Robert S. Kerr from the Dixons in 1929.

December's news brought more reassurances. The approximately eight thousand workers lured to Oklahoma City by the discovery of oil had not caused unemployment problems; only a few of the unskilled were out of work. The *Daily Oklahoman* reported "New Industries Coming to City Assure Future," as businesses moved in to share cheap fuel and the general prosperity. Retail trade increased more than 5 percent in Oklahoma City, and the state was "Bullish Despite Stock Market Slide." Governor William J. Holloway stated: "Business in Oklahoma has not been caught in the throes of stock market turmoil as that in so many other states. To be sure the effect of the market is felt but not sufficiently to rock the stable condition and businessmen are confident of a greater future." He was confident that the $40 million spent on rigs and equipment in 1929 for use within a fifty-mile radius of Oklahoma City indicated that oil development would keep business prosperous.

The end-of-the-year newspaper summaries were equally glowing, paying tribute to the oil industry. Over 361 firms had been established in Oklahoma City, and its population had swelled by over thirteen thousand new citizens. Under the caption, "Nation's Brightest Spot Right Here. Country Takes off Hat to Oklahoma," the *Daily Oklahoman* heralded the conclusion of the United States Chamber of Commerce "Nation's Business Survey." "Due primarily to the development of new oil fields, but also because the wheels of industry have kept turning with business brisk in all lines, Oklahoma, for the first month of the new year, occupied a large place in the brightest spot in the country."

The light of relative prosperity acted as a lodestar in attracting all kinds of people to Oklahoma City. As thousands poured in, shanty towns sprang up near the producing area, and the lobbies of hotels buzzed with the contagious excitement of promoters, lease vendors, and speculators. In 1925, Oklahoma City had a population of 120,458. After ITIO's discovery six miles south of town the southwestern metropolis started to grow. By 1930 the population was 189,389. The depression was no hindrance, and the chamber of commerce formulated a five-year building program designed to save the city from the predicted boomtown chaos. The owners of the Skirvin Hotel announced a 150-room expansion plan, and during 1930–31 a $15 million building campaign included two 33-story buildings: the First National Bank and Trust Company and the Ramsey Tower.

The city fathers moved with commendable haste. But the new oil field's rapid expansion was even faster. In a situation never before confronted by the oil business, a major field threatened to engulf a major metropolitan area as lease by lease it leapfrogged steadily northward. The first feeble efforts to use zoning laws to create limited drilling areas proved largely ineffective. In the words of one historian: "Derricks, slush pits, and steel and ground tanks invaded industrial and residential areas. Rigs reared their crown blocks in school yards, slush pits were dug on playgrounds, and storage tanks were built in alleys."[1]

[1] Carl Coke Rister, *Oil: Titan of the Southwest* (Norman, University of Oklahoma Press, 1949), p. 255.

Against this chaotic backdrop the small Ada firm of Anderson & Kerr made its entrance in July, 1929. The unregulated and unplanned way in which the field was developing proved to be one of the company's chief advantages. For example, the ITIO leases were so situated that it needed to drill at least 29 wells to protect its boundary lines, and it seems probable that Anderson & Kerr's first drilling contract in Oklahoma City was with them.[2] There was work for any operative rig, and while Anderson pushed the tools, Kerr operated from a hotel room seeking additional contracts, commuting to his home in Ada on weekends.[3] On September 12 there were 15 producing wells in the new field with a daily output of 67,507 barrels, and 19 more were drilling. By January 1, 1930, the totals had risen to 53 producing wells, 161 drilling, and 53 shut down for various reasons. As of March 10 there were 135 completed and 173 in various stages of completion.

Six months in the Oklahoma City field not only provided opportunities for the partners but also convinced them of the need to expand. A faint omen of the future occurred in May, 1930, when the partnership opened a filling station at 845 Southeast Twenty-ninth Street.[4] A second decision was to take advantage of Travis's position as sales manager for Lucey Products and buy two new, modern rigs. The depth of the field in Oklahoma City made one of their units unusable, causing a loss in contract opportunities.[5] All of this extra involvement made it obvious that Kerr could not carry on his part of the company's business alone. The inconvenience of having the office in Ada when most of the work, as well as the partners, were in Oklahoma City compounded his work load. Therefore a branch office was opened in Oklahoma City. A suite of three small rooms was rented at 343 Commerce Exchange Building, and T. W. ("Whit") Fentem, a cashier at the First National Bank of Ada, was hired as office manager. In September, 1930, Theresa Clark and Harry Caldwell made up the entire staff.[6]

With rising debts, strong competition, and four rigs to keep busy, there can be little doubt that Kerr's boundless energy was a vital asset. An unverified and undated story, but one which probably happened, illustrates his techniques at this time. Rex Hawks, a longtime friend and close associate of Kerr's, claimed to have heard Moss Patterson (the owner of the Oklahoma Transportation Company) tell the following story a dozen times at least. According to Patterson, he was at Woolaroc Ranch with Frank Phillips,

[2] Interviews with Quinton C. Walton, April 29, 1970, and April 16, 1971.

[3] Interviews with Walton and Mrs. T. W. Fentem, June 30, 1971; *Polk's Oklahoma City Directory, 1929.*

[4] Oklahoma City telephone directory, August, 1930; *Kermac News*, May, 1950, p. 2.

[5] See interviews with D. L. Brown, Sr., August 5, 1971, and Q. C. Walton and Travis Kerr, December 16, 1969.

[6] At this time the Ada office was 301–303 American Building. *Classified Buyers' Guide of Ada, Oklahoma, 1930–1931* (Springfield, Mo., n.d.), p. 32. For Oklahoma City see entry for Anderson & Kerr Drilling and the "yellow pages," telephone directory, August, 1930. Although they were not listed in Polk's Oklahoma City Directory for that year, Travis was shown as sales manager for Lucey Products. See also interviews with Mrs. T. W. Fentem and Foley Collins, June 11, 1971; *Kermac News*, Fall, 1951, p. 4.

founder of Phillips Petroleum Company, when a servant announced that
Bob Kerr wanted to see Mr. Phillips. Kerr introduced himself as part owner
of Anderson & Kerr Drilling Company and explained that his partner was
one of the most experienced production men and drillers in Oklahoma. The
company had decided it would like to drill some of Phillips' leases in the Ada
and Konawa area. Frank Phillips eventually agreed to let them drill a well
and called his office in Bartlesville to say he had given Anderson & Kerr the
contract. As Kerr was about to leave, he turned and said, "By the way, Mr.
Phillips, there's one little item I was about to forget." When asked what that
was, Kerr replied that he would have to borrow $20,000 to sink the well.
Phillips then "cussed a little while" and exclaimed, "You spend all this time
wanting the job and haven't got the money to drill it with." Kerr "hemmed
and hawed," but in the end Phillips called Bartlesville again and said, "Let
this damn man have $20,000 to drill this lease with."[7]

Lending credence to the above story was the fact that the first well drilled
on their own account was three and one-half miles east of Konawa. According to Rex Hawks, Kerr told him that while drilling for Phillips in this area he
discovered a farmer with forty unleased acres held back because he did not
trust the "oil crowd." Kerr talked the reluctant owner into a lease. It is
possible that Kerr was the original lessee as a result of his speculating
activities, but the right to drill was actually acquired by Anderson & Kerr on
January 4, 1930, from the Denver Producing & Refining Company for
$1,085.

As if his other ventures were not enough, Kerr was now determined to get
into the production end of the oil business as well. Probably he had dreamed
of being a producer ever since dabbling in leases during his early days in
Ada. At any rate, he assumed that production was the key to big money. The
initial gamble was on land belonging to a full-blood Seminole, Edmond
Morgan. The well was spudded on January 5, and apparently money was a
problem from the start. On January 14, Anderson & Kerr, a "copartnership," signed a contract with S. W. Wells and Watson B. Joyes of
Okmulgee whereby the latter pair would receive one-third interest in the
well in return for a contribution of acreage and "dry-hole" money. Wells and
Joyes had pledges of $4,000 from Gypsy Oil Company, $2,500 from Mid-
Continent Oil and Gas, $1,500 from Superior Oil, and $500 from Shaffer Oil
& Refining Company. If the well came in, Wells and Joyes would then bear
one-third of the expense of equipping and operating it.

The Konawa field had been opened in November, 1929. The producing
sands lay at depths of only 2,700 to 2,900 feet, and a well could be drilled in
fifteen to twenty days. On January 16, 1930, the *Konawa Leader* reported
that thirty-three derricks had been erected in the field—one of which was
Anderson & Kerr's. The first specific notice of what eventually became
Morgan #1 was taken in the January 30 issue. Three days earlier the boiler of
the Anderson & Kerr rig had exploded: "It is believed that cold water turned
in on a hot boiler was the cause. . . . The boiler proper was hurled a distance

[7] Interview with Rex Hawks, May 24, 1972.

of about 150 yards. The concussion of the explosion wrecked the dwelling house within forty feet of the boiler." Three legs were blown off the derrick, and it fell on the drillers, killing two and mangling two others. Travis, who had not yet joined the company, recalled that, about 10:00 P.M. on January 27, Bob called and asked him to drive with him from Ada to Konawa because they had had an explosion. "It sure did upset Bob," said Travis, who saw humor in the fact that a drunken Indian (Morgan, perhaps?) in the ruined house was unaware of the blast until they dug him out the next day. A new rig apparently was furnished by Denver Producing, with the stipulation that, if the well were successful, Anderson & Kerr would buy it.[8]

This was still not the end of Morgan #1. Trouble with the crew surfaced after the new derrick was erected. On February 11, 1930, Joyes wrote Kerr in Ada complaining that the boys on the well were not keeping a log: "We had to fake it for the first 500 feet. . . . All samples between 1280 and 1600 were all mixed up. Don't let this news get out else there may be a big holler. . . and [Superior] may crab about paying off if we are unfortunate and get a dry hole."

On February 13, the *Leader* reported that, shortly after drilling resumed, a crew member lost his hand in another accident and that workers began calling it the "Hoodoo Well." The next issue, a week later, informed the readers that the lease would be lost unless the well were completed by midnight of that date. It was a full week later before the *Leader* reported that the gamble had succeeded, but only after an unusual number of misfortunes and hours of hard labor.

The anticipated two weeks of drilling time had stretched into more than two months because, as the original drilling reports show, caving was a constant problem both before and after completion. By June the well was pumping about thirty barrels per tour (probably a twelve-hour shift). For the month of January, 1937, it made 614.21 barrels. In 1939 the oil company repurchased Joyes and Wells's interest for $3,750, and by 1965, when the average was only five barrels per day, cumulative production reached 110,177 barrels. Old-timers recalled that Kerr would never allow them to make any changes in this well, since it was his first. Finally, on September 12, 1969, Kerr-McGee transferred its interest in Morgan #1 with an adjoining lease to Oklahoma Gas and Electric Company for $75,000 to use in a reservoir.[9]

Accidents such as those at the "Hoodoo Well" were not uncommon at that

[8] *Konawa Leader* for dates cited; *Ada Evening News*, January 28, 1930; Travis Kerr interview; Lease Records file, "S-516 Morgan."

[9] The usual lease vests the holder, for a specified "primary" period, with exclusive rights to explore for and produce oil and gas that may be found under the lands covered by the lease. During such primary period if a specified amount of drilling is not done, the lease may be forfeited, or annual "delay" rentals must be paid the lessor. If drilling is done during the primary period and commercial production is found, the holder's rights are perpetuated for the life of the production from the lease. The Morgan well produced over 130,655 barrels before it was plugged on September 27, 1969, to make way for a new lake. *Kermac News*, October, 1969; Lease Records file, "S-516 Morgan."

Steam rigs often required multiple boilers. These were probably acquired from the Dixon brothers.

time. In a letter dated July 5, 1930, the partnership informed Messrs. Black, Sivils & Bryson of Bartlesville of the explosion on the Morgan lease and that the family of one of the dead roughnecks was suing for $75,000 to $80,000. The firm's insurance covered it only to $25,000 per man. The family had been offered $9,000 and funeral expenses. The writer then added, "We had an accident in the Oklahoma City field where we are running five rigs, in which a single man was killed." In this case the heirs were suing for $25,000, "but [we] expect their recovery will be $1500 to 2000."

There is no reason to believe that Anderson & Kerr was any less concerned with the welfare of its employees than any of its contemporaries. Yet, even allowing for lapses of memory and the tendency of old-timers to darken a picture to impress neophytes, by today's standards drilling was hazardous.

Steam rigs like the Konawa one, with three or four boilers hooked together and carrying 250 to 300 pounds of steam, were a special danger. The poor state of the art of accident prevention caused other tragedies. There were no hard hats, no chain guards, and, initially, no blowout preventers. It was not uncommon in high-pressure fields such as Oklahoma City for wells to blow out. The mud used was made by the crew, often from old red clay dug around the rig. Eddie Baxendale, a tool pusher, said of those days: "You didn't have anything to work with; you put bailing wire on any way you could to keep it running. It was a kind of sin not to keep a rig running. If it tore down, it was your own fault and you had to get it fixed."

Henry Pryor even saw these as the good old days: "Now if a little piece gets worn, they throw it away and buy something new and put on it. It just tears me up the way they operate now and the way we used to operate. . . . When I started in the field, we done everything. If we could save, we saved it."

And then there was always the personal factor. E. H. ("Jeep") Harvey, another drilling veteran, recalled: "We had no safety at that time. Yet we had very very few accidents. It seemed like that everybody kind of looked after each other." He "never did hear about anybody suing the company for accidents; they was just trying to get well as fast as they could and go back to work." Foley Collins probably had the typical rig man's attitude:

I worked for everybody, everybody except Buck Jackson. And Old Buck killed two or three men, and I was afraid of Buck. . . . He was just reckless, that's all. . . . I worked . . . a long time for old Duroc Johnson. . . . I saw Duroc come to the rig and he was so tight that he'd have to hold that rig to stand up, [but he] never drawed a drop of blood from a man.[10]

Although other wells were drilled in the Konawa and Asher fields, most of the work in 1930 was straight contract drilling in Oklahoma City. The drilling company furnished the men and equipment and got ten to twelve dollars a foot upon completion of the well. The employer provided the land, derrick, slush pits, fuel, pipe, casing, and other material. The contract was usually for about 6,500 or 7,000 feet. If the driller had bad results with his rig or twisted off his drill pipe, it was his hard luck. He either had to clean out the hole or skid his tools and drill a new one. At first it took between 100 and 120 days to sink a well, but in a year or so the time was halved because of new techniques and knowledge of the formations. At the same time, low oil prices and competition cut the footage rate by the same percentage. The men on the rig were not on salary, but were hired by the day for a specific well. All worked twelve-hour shifts, but their pay varied from job to job. George Sims recalled that, when he moved to Oklahoma City, he received $4 a day if the hole were dry and $6 if it produced. Eddie Baxendale said he got $6 a day on a wildcat well and $5 in the Oklahoma City field.

The relative success of Anderson & Kerr's drilling efforts and its new lines of business probably caused Kerr, the lawyer, to want more than the simple agreement which then existed. Consequently, on November 5, 1930, the partnership was dissolved, and two new domestic corporations were formed, both with offices at 343 Commerce Exchange Building. The first was Anderson & Kerr Drilling Company, to engage in the business of "Drilling and Producing Oil Wells." The authorized capital was $25,000, divided into 2,500 shares with a par value of $10 each. Its president was James L. Anderson of Oklahoma City, and the secretary and treasurer was

---

[10] For letters see Lease Records file "S-516 Morgan." See also interviews with O. L. ("Barney") Limes, July 12, 1970; Foley D. Collins, June 11, 1971; H. G. Kuhlman and E. H. ("Jeep") Harvey, April 15, 1971; Jacob Henry Pryor, undated; Eddie Baxendale, July 26, 1971; and Q. C. ("Pete") Walton.

Oklahoma City
Anderson & Kerr
Drilling Company
1929–1931

A typical drilling-floor scene in the 1930's. Note the absence of safety equipment.

Robert S. Kerr of Ada, Oklahoma. These two men plus T. W. Fentem were the directors. The stock was divided as follows: Anderson, 1,250 shares; Kerr, 1,249; and Fentem, 1. The second corporation was Anderson-Kerr, Incorporated, to engage in "Investments and Securities." It had the same authorized capital and division of shares, and the directors and officers duplicated those of the drilling company.[11]

The year which saw this infant drilling firm incorporated also saw Oklahoma, especially Oklahoma City, move into the national limelight. There seemed to be no limit to a field that boasted 350 producers without a single dry hole. In March, 1930, it was the scene of awe-inspiring spectacles such as the "Wild Mary Sudik," which blew out with a deafening roar, spouting an estimated 200 million cubic feet of gas and 20,000 barrels of oil per day. For eleven days the well reigned unchecked, while twice every day the famed radio commentator Floyd Gibbons went on the air to describe her antics to a listening world. There were other, less spectacular blowouts. On one occasion the North Canadian River caught fire and brought danger to the city's very doorstep.

With the huge volumes of oil produced in Oklahoma City, Seminole, and East Texas, it did not take a financial genius to see that this might be "too much of a good thing." The daily domestic demand for oil had been only 2,840,000 barrels per day in early 1930. The nation's production reached 5,030,000 barrels, making oil prices unstable. Consequently, on June 30 the Oklahoma Corporation Commission issued an order severely restricting production from the Oklahoma City field. The order withstood legal challenges, and the state's output for 1930 was some 37 million barrels less than that of the preceding year. Violations, plus production outside the state, caused the price to drop by the summer of 1931 to sixteen to twenty cents a barrel in Oklahoma City and ten cents in East Texas.

The growing distress of the Oklahoma oil producers increased problems for drillers. The latter had limited options if they wanted to stay in business: cut their profit margins, redouble their efforts to secure contracts, or try to get production of their own and hope to hang on until prices rose. Kerr and Anderson did all these things during 1931. In what was later to prove one of their shrewdest moves Bob's younger brother, Travis, was brought into the company on April 1. Travis recalled that at the time he was making $500 a month and expenses at Lucey Products Corporation, while the new job paid only $350 and the use of a secondhand car. His double assignment was to assist Bob in getting contracts and to secure credit for the hard-pressed firm. His former position as sales manager for Lucey Products in both the California and the Mid-Continent areas made him ideally suited for both responsibilities. He not only knew more oil men than Bob did but also was close to Lucey Products' president, a fact which allowed Anderson & Kerr to buy

[11] Both were incorporated for 20 years, but the latter was canceled on December 11, 1937, and the former on March 23, 1940. File numbers for the two corporations were 42335 and 42336. Oklahoma State Archives, "Office of Secretary of State."

"far exceeding their credit limit," a situation that became increasingly crucial.[12]

Furthermore, they took advantage of some unique characteristics of the period and the Oklahoma City field. Most of the land was held in small tracts, and it was soon obvious that the pool extended not only to the east side of the city, but also through it. At first, wells were drilled on city lots, although later rules specified only one well to each block. Speculators rushed to lease these small tracts, making orderly drilling impossible. Soon many small companies owned big wells drilled on financial shoestrings. Owners such as these were interested not in promoting orderly development or the eventual good of the industry but rather in getting their money out of their wells in the shortest possible time. Even the glut that forced down prices was no deterrent, for with unrestricted flow the small operator could pay for his well in a short time.

Two factors affected the fledgling firm of Anderson & Kerr. First, the hundreds of small companies and individuals were eager to drill before their oil was siphoned off by adjoining leases or before the falling price of oil made it unprofitable. Second was the hazard of drilling under existing conditions. Would-be entrepreneurs short of money for drilling capital were willing to hire Anderson & Kerr if they could pay with either an interest in the property or with a small sum of cash *and* a percentage in the lease. The partners' willingness to bargain placed them in the position of acquiring rights in a number of parcels.

As shown above, the Oklahoma City field was a tricky one. The drilling was in populated areas, and some of the major companies were reluctant to assume the liability of sinking and completing the wells. But Kerr and Anderson were willing to take financial risks as well as drill, and they assumed all legal responsibilities until the well was completed and tested— for a price or a share of the production.[13]

While town-lot drilling was dangerous, it had characteristics which could be turned to advantage. For example, the maximum acreage needed to drill was only a city block. Travis Kerr described the procedure as follows:

Bob would make a deal with Continental, Phillips, Denver Producing, and private individuals such as Harrison Smith. Bob would work out some deal to get a city block, then make a deal with someone and tell them, either you put up so much money and we'll get the block or we'll sell you an interest in the completed well for a stipulated sum (A&K gambled what profit it might have made had it been a straight drilling contract in acquiring an interest in the production). Since a lot of the deals in Oklahoma City were in semi-proven areas, we felt like it was more than a 50/50 chance of getting production.[14]

---

[12] Interviews with Travis Kerr and Aubrey Kerr, April 28, 1971; *Oil and Gas Journal*, February 19, 1931; *Kermac News*, January, 1947, p. 3.

[13] George Cobb interview, January 21, 1971. The emphasis on risk taking is also present in "The Rock Hound," *Forbes*, Vol. 86 (October 15, 1960), p. 21; "E. G. 'Ty' Dahlgren Calls on Robert S. Kerr," *Oil*, Vol. 20 (September, 1960), pp. 9–12; and Daniel Seligman, "Senator Bob Kerr, the Oklahoma Gusher," *Fortune*, Vol. 59 (March, 1959), pp. 136–38.

[14] Interviews with Travis Kerr and Elton ("Buster") Wooten, April 7, 1970.

One of the few extant contracts from this period was probably typical of many others. By an instrument dated September 2, 1931, Robert S. Kerr and J. B. Sledge (doing business as Kerr & Sledge of Ada) and Anderson & Kerr Drilling Company sold Continental Oil one-half share in seven-eighths interest in four leases they owned and in two others they had contracted to buy. Continental agreed to advance $150,000 for drilling costs, plus a sum up to a total of $75,000 for each producing well, and $60,000 for each nonproducer. Oil was found on all of these leases, and on December 1 an operating agreement was signed between Anderson-Kerr, Incorporated, and Continental whereby the latter would be the operator.[15]

The newspapers and trade journals normally did not indicate the driller's name when reporting a well. Thus the only wells known to have been sunk by Anderson & Kerr in 1931 were those in which they had an interest. Some eleven have been identified, seven of which were completed during that year. Its share varied with almost every venture, including 18/64 of 8/8, 3/8 of 7/8, 18.75 percent of 7/8, 1/2 of 7/8, 1/4 of 7/8, and 35/92 of 7/8. The outside companies involved included Harrison M. Smith, Denver Production & Refining, Dangail Oil & Gas, H. F. Wilcox Oil & Gas, Trans-Mississippi Oil, and Continental. Several of the wells were excellent producers: Roach #1 made 6,174 barrels of oil in less than six hours; Dambold #1 was gauged at 11,528 barrels in eight hours; Smith #1 flowed 9,162 barrels in six hours; and Metcalf #1 made 5,720 barrels in six and one-half hours.[16]

Other events occurred in 1931 to affect the firm. In May, H. H. Patton sold his interest in seven producing wells in Oklahoma City to a group which included Anderson & Kerr Drilling Company. In December, one of the blocks shared with Continental brought a lawsuit in which the judge held that the Oklahoma City School Board was entitled to one-sixth of the royalty in a well that adjoined the Shields School property. Although the school land was not part of the lease, it was in the drainage area of the well, which was estimated to have a potential production of 35,000 barrels per day.[17]

In 1931, Kerr and Anderson added the keystone, or apex, to the corporate structure they were erecting. On September 15, An-Ker, Incorporated, was chartered in Delaware for the purpose of "Oil Production" with Anderson & Kerr Drilling Company and Anderson-Kerr, Incorporated, as its wholly-owned subsidiaries. This new corporation had an authorized capital stock of 2,000 shares of no-par value. Its paid-up capital was 480 shares, valued at $48,000. Officers were James L. Anderson, president; Robert S. Kerr, vice-president and treasurer; and T. W. Fentem, secretary. The holders of

[15] The leases involved were St. Louis, Warsaski, Black, Volk, Shields, and Metcalf. Lease Records file, "Contract File #24."

[16] The wells and dates of completion (all in 1931) were Hile (January 25), Woodson (February 3), Foote (March 20), Roach (May 28), Dambold (August 11), H. Smith (December 1), and Metcalf (December 1). For additional reference to Anderson & Kerr wells see *Oil and Gas Journal*, Vol. 30 (January 22, March 19, 26, April 2, 16, 23, May 21, 28, June 4, 11, July 23, August 13, October 8, 15, 22, 29, November 5, 26, and December 3, 10, 17, 1931).

[17] *Oil and Gas Journal*, Vol. 30 (May 28, 1931), p. 26; *ibid.* (December 31, 1931), p. 24.

the paid-up capital were Anderson and Kerr with 240 shares each, for which each had paid 1,200 shares of Anderson & Kerr Drilling and a like amount of Anderson-Kerr, Incorporated. One of the first acts of this new entity was to purchase 95 percent of the stock of Blackhawk Drilling Company for $300 from T. W. Fentem, Floyd C. Dooley, and N. C. Smith.[18]

Some of the optimism and financial success of their various ventures can be seen in the unaudited consolidated statement of Anderson & Kerr Drilling and Anderson-Kerr, Incorporated, on September 24, 1931. The term "optimistic" must be used because among the assets listed, totaling $1,814,355.47, the "accounts receivable" were set at $280,678.99. These were based largely on oil payments, that is, oil yet to be produced and vended at an undetermined price. For example, one entry for $50,000 reads, "This account represents oil payment to be made out of one-fourth of the first oil produced and sold from the Kammerdeiner Well #1." Another $178,000 was given as the value of stocks that were probably taken in as partial payment for drilling. Equally speculative was over $800,000 assigned to leases, with the value of each being based on production potential. Thus some $1,275,000.00 of the accounts receivable largely represented future hopes versus $158,756.97 "Cash on Hand or in Banks." Total liabilities, not counting capital stock, were listed at $141,037.00.[19]

Despite the chaotic conditions of the oil business in Oklahoma in 1931, the partners told themselves that they had a surplus of $1,416,024.27. The optimism of their report belied the fact that the price of oil per barrel had dropped from ninety-five cents to eighteen cents before Governor William H. Murray of Oklahoma, on August 4, declared a state of emergency and martial law. All prorated wells were closed "until the price hits one dollar." So serious was the problem that, before the year ended, Oklahoma, Kansas, and Texas had joined in an eighteen day shutdown of all production, and as of December 31, Oklahoma had produced some thirty-six million fewer barrels of oil than it had in 1930, with a corresponding loss of income.

Even if the consolidated statement was rosier than hard economic facts justified, Kerr and Anderson had reason to be proud. From a two-man partnership, with assets of $50,000 and debts of $30,000, in less than three years they had become a recognized drilling firm, had become producers in their own right, and had taken at least two minor steps (production and marketing) toward becoming an integrated oil company. It seems probable that at the end of 1931 they had more than the original four drilling rigs—their statement gives the figure of $230,170.19 for "Drilling Tools, Trucks, etc." Bob, with his sanguine disposition, faced the future undaunted by the deepening economic depression around him. But Jim, who was older and

[18] State Archives of Oklahoma, "Statement of Foreign Corporation"; "Origin of Kerr-McGee Oil Industries, Inc. Stock Ownership by Grayce B. Flynn," attached to a letter from S. B. Robinson to Arthur Anderson & Co., dated July 5, 1966, in Public Relations files. Some old-timers recall receiving paychecks drawn on Blackhawk Drilling Company.

[19] "Consolidated Statement Anderson & Kerr Drilling Company and Anderson-Kerr, Inc. September 24, 1931," in Public Relations files.

more conservative by nature, undoubtedly had moments when he wondered whether they were not getting into too many things at once and moving faster than their resources would justify. After all, as he wrote Kerr in 1959:

When all has been said, Bob, I find in FORTUNES article at least one definition of our separate desires and capabilities which perhaps reads truer than the average reader will probably notice, and may be more indicative of the "codes" and "efforts" summarizing our separate endeavors: I am content to have it said in print that : —"Anderson had a 'nose for oil' and an ability to drill cheaper than his competitors" (for I have never been discontent with my "little destiny" as an oil driller); even while viewing all these years your—, "talent for separating investment capital from its owners."[20]

[20] James L. Anderson to Robert S. Kerr, March 11, 1959. Kerr personally had been honored in March by being appointed a special justice of the Oklahoma State Supreme Court by Governor W. J. Holloway to hear a case involving the location of the county seat for Pottawatomie County. *Daily Oklahoman*, March 18, 1931.

Chapter 3

The Birth of a New Corporation: The A&K Petroleum Company 1932

In the course of American history 1932 is not remembered as a happy year. During its gloomy days everyone found it difficult to believe that "only a business recession" was causing their woes, and even Republican spokesmen were beginning to realize that the economy was not reacting to traditional stimuli. President Hoover had earlier concluded that economy, a balanced budget, and adherence to the gold standard were not enough to bring about recovery. Instead, federal funds and authority must be used on an unprecedented scale. Banks and industry were the first beneficiaries, for Hoover believed that their recovery would in turn bring relief to all. In line with this approach of aid from the top the lending power of the federal land banks was increased, and a system of home-loan banks was established. The major effort went into the Reconstruction Finance Corporation, with initial assets of $1.5 billion for loans to banks, insurance companies, railroads, and local self-liquidating projects.

But the filtering-down process proved painfully slow. In the spring of 1932, unemployed veterans marched on Washington demanding immediate and full payment of soldiers' bonuses, only to be evacuated by federal troops. Unemployment continued to mount: five million in 1930, nine million in 1931, and thirteen million in 1932. People who had never known unemployment lost their jobs, used up their savings, cashed in their life insurance, and relinquished mortgaged homes and farms. Even the middle class was not spared. Tramps abounded, panhandlers plied the streets, once prosperous factories were closed or produced at reduced rates, stores lacked customers, luxury businesses went bankrupt, and new automobiles became a rarity.

The Great Depression unquestionably ruined the Republicans. The Democrats in the election of 1932 had only to harness the national grudge and let it pull them to victory. The overwhelming Democratic majority indicated a demand for change. Any Democratic candidate probably could have won.

Even the buoyant frontier optimism in Oklahoma had worn thin by 1932. Until then oil had dulled the sharp edge of the depression for the state, especially Oklahoma City, but this industry was itself in a precarious condition. Governor Murray's drastic actions of the preceding summer had not raised the price of oil to $1.00 a barrel. But by October troops had been withdrawn and field control lifted, and wells operated on a 5 percent allowable. On April 11, 1932, the price of Oklahoma oil did reach $0.92 but turned down once more because of increases in Texas production and in the number of Oklahoma producers who were violating their allowables. Once again, on June 6, martial law was proclaimed, and meters were installed in an effort to choke off the hot oil. Free-for-alls between militiamen and field workers were not uncommon, nor was tear gas spared. Nevertheless, the December price was $0.69 and unstable on the downward side. Paradoxically, the state's total production for the year declined by some 28 million barrels, but the financial return rose $19 million over 1931 sales.

During this period the Kerr brothers were beating the bushes for customers for their rigs. No records have been found that shed any light on this aspect of their business, although Eddie Baxendale, who joined an Anderson & Kerr drilling crew in March, 1932, said that they were doing contract work in the Capitol Hill area of Oklahoma City and that on some of these wells they received part of the production as payment.[1] As noted earlier, it is easier to identify the wells in which Anderson & Kerr was part or sole owner. The increase in the number of such wells during 1932 probably meant the drilling was more on its own account to keep the rigs and crews busy and that Kerr was attempting to build up production. The first part of this supposition is strengthened by the fact that the firm was active outside Oklahoma County on several occasions. Lack of reports in newspapers and trade journals makes it impossible to be sure, but indications are that Anderson & Kerr had interests in some twelve wells drilled during 1932 in the Oklahoma City field and in three or four drilled in Seminole and Pottawatomie counties.

Of these ventures the listings suggest that they were the sole owner in approximately six: three in Oklahoma City, two in Seminole County, and one in Pottawatomie County. It should be remembered, however, that on some occasions in Oklahoma City the driller was technically the owner only in initial stages. In only a few of the shared wells is it possible to determine who the other owners were and what fraction Anderson & Kerr had. Four such wells were with Continental (1/2 of 7/8), and one each with Anderson-

---

[1] Interview with Eddie Baxendale, July 26, 1971.

Prichard (9/40 of 7/8), Trans-Mississippi Oil, W. M. Gallagher (9/40 of 7/8), and Harrison Smith.

Although production was strictly limited or not allowed at all, test-flow or estimated-potential figures are available. For example, three of the possible four wells in Seminole and Pottawatomie counties were dry. On the other hand, some of the Oklahoma City wells were huge even by modern standards. As a case in point, in the deals with Continental the wells produced 1,375 barrels of oil in one hour and 27 million cubic feet of gas per day (Black #1); 35,000 barrels per day (St. Louis #1); 1,761 barrels of oil in two hours and 20 million cubic feet of gas per day (Shields #1); and 8,510 barrels of oil in four hours and 91 million cubic feet of gas per day (Volk #1). The firm had no dry holes in this field, and the other wells were similar in production.[2]

During 1932, Anderson & Kerr Drilling Company ran into a problem which became common as drilling approached the limits set by the city council. Property owners appealed a favorable ruling by a city board to permit the company to drill near the junction of Grand and Byers avenues and were upheld by the district court. Anderson & Kerr then applied for a *supersedeas* bond allowing the firm to proceed while it, in turn, appealed. Under the heading "Objection to Town Lot Wells," the *Oil and Gas Journal* reported that this attempt to drill was barred by the state supreme court: "The Anderson-Kerr Drilling Co. was refused a permit to drill a well in the 300-foot border zone which extends around the U-7 drilling zone until the merits of the company's appeal can be passed on."[3]

Drilling contracts and lawsuits were not the only things on management's mind. Office space had become cramped. When the First National Bank Building was completed early in the year, Kerr and Anderson's three companies became one of the first tenants.[4] They occupied five rooms, two used for accounting, on the twentieth floor. Travis later recalled the first Christmas party in their new home. The eleven people in the Oklahoma City office drew names for an exchange of gifts limited to a dollar each. "Everybody got tight; I'd have a little snopps around in my office, and Bob would have Coca-Cola there in his office."[5]

The most significant development of the year, however, was the decision to change the corporate structure once more. Two things made this imperative: first, the need for additional financing; second, the oil production had grown so much that it could no longer be handled as an adjunct to any one of the three existing companies. As Travis said, it was easier to sell the public on investing in an oil company than to sell an interest in a drilling rig. Also,

[2] Information concerning Anderson & Kerr wells is found in *Daily Oklahoman*, January 3, 7, 10, 24, February 7, 21, March 6, 13, 1932; *Oil and Gas Journal*, January 14, 21, February 4, 11, 18, March 17, 24, 31, April 7, 14, 21, May 19, June 2, 16, 23, 30, July 14, 28, August 4, 25, September 1, 8, 22, October 13, November 10, and December 1, 22, 1932.

[3] *Oil and Gas Journal*, Vol. 31 (July 21, 1932), p. 45. The final outcome was not noted.

[4] *Polk's Oklahoma City Directory, 1932*, "Oil Producers and Shippers."

[5] *Polk's Oklahoma City Directory, 1932* indicates the offices were on the twenty-third floor. Interview with Travis Kerr, December 16, 1969.

Bob's whole aim in acquiring production was to have an oil company. The official reason was that, "In 1932 the size of these holdings developed the need for a corporate structure to permit public financing for further development of their properties." On November 7, C. S. Peabbles, L. E. Gray, and L. H. Herman of Wilmington, Delaware, filed a certificate of incorporation with the Delaware secretary of state to incorporate the A&K Petroleum Company. The new firm proposed to deal in oil, gas, and mineral leases on lands containing "petroleum, asphaltum, mineral gases, metals, ores, coal and other minerals and mineral substances, to prospect, search and explore for petroleum, natural gas, asphaltum, ores, coal, metals, minerals, and mineral substances" and to drill, produce, and sell such products. It further proposed to own and sell machinery connected therewith, and to issue and deal in stock. The new corporation would be empowered to issue 400,000 shares of common stock, at $5.00 par value, divided into two classes: 125,000 class A and 275,000 class B.[6]

On November 9, 1932, the incorporation was approved, establishing the legal forebear of the Kerr-McGee Corporation. (The corporation, however, celebrates 1929 as its date of origin.) On the same day the incorporators met and elected Harrison M. Smith, James L. Anderson, and Travis M. Kerr of Oklahoma City, Robert S. Kerr and C. H. Rives of Ada, F. M. Porter of Ardmore, and Lloyd Maxwell of Chicago, Illinois, as directors and empowered them to issue stock to the full amount provided for in the certificate of incorporation.

Since Bob Kerr, with Anderson's consent, undoubtedly chose these men, the background of the outside directors is interesting. Rives was president of the Oklahoma State Bank of Ada and a longtime personal friend; Porter was an oilman and vice-president in charge of production of the Wirt Franklin Petroleum Corporation. Smith was a dealer in oil payments and had been a partner in some of the Oklahoma City wells with Anderson & Kerr. The connection with Maxwell, who served for only one year, is less clear, but apparently he was president of Roche, Richerd & Cleary, a Chicago advertising agency.[7]

On November 10 the directors met at the Anderson & Kerr offices, 2009 First National Building, Oklahoma City, to formalize the corporation. Robert S. Kerr was chosen as president and treasurer; James L. Anderson, executive vice-president and secretary; Lloyd Maxwell, vice-president; and T. M. Fentem, assistant secretary and assistant treasurer. Their only other business was to approve and adopt the forms for class A and B stock certificates. On November 14 a request to do business in the state of Oklahoma was filed with the secretary of state. The following day a special stockholders' meeting was called. Only the two Kerrs and Anderson were present; the rest voted by proxy. Shares represented on this occasion were R. S. Kerr, Anderson, and T. M. Kerr, fifty shares each of class B; Rives,

[6] Travis Kerr interview; "Supplemental Information *re* A&K Petroleum Company, Class A Common Stock"; A&K Petroleum Company "Minute Book," 1 (pages unnumbered).

[7] A&K "Minute Book," 1; Oklahoma Secretary of State, "Statement of Foreign Corporation."

Porter, and Smith, one-thousand shares each of class B; and Maxwell, two-thousand shares of class B.

The A&K Petroleum stockholders unanimously authorized the acquisition of certain interests in oil and gas leases in Oklahoma City from Anderson-Kerr, Incorporated, and Anderson & Kerr Drilling. They also agreed to assume the accounts payable of the two companies. In return A&K would issue 275,000 shares of class B and 5,000 of class A to An-Ker, Incorporated, the only stockholder of the other two companies. To get money to fund the accounts payable and for operating expenses, Travis moved that they authorize a public offering of 120,000 shares of class A at $5.00 each. The motion was unanimously approved. A special meeting of the board the same day instructed management to qualify this stock for sale in the state of Illinois.

There were now four business entities. Only two of them, however, had any real significance in Kerr-McGee history. These were Anderson & Kerr Drilling, which owned and operated the rigs and still had some production, and A&K Petroleum, with most of the producing properties. Initially, most activities were carried on through the drilling firm, since it was the largest company in terms of employees, revenues, and equipment. A&K Petroleum became the vehicle for financing and expansion.

Until this time Bob Kerr had maintained his home and a company office in Ada. With his growing oil interests centered in Oklahoma City, his drilling firm and law offices in Ada became less important. After the creation of A&K Petroleum he moved his family to Oklahoma City and apparently closed out the drilling office in Ada, although he remained an inactive partner in the law firm for many years.[8]

The first significant notice taken of Kerr and Anderson and their expanded business came in late 1932 or early 1933. It took the form of a long article in what was probably a vanity publication put out by an Oklahoma City advertising firm. Entitled *The Oklahoma City Oil Field—In Pictures*, the lead story dealt with the "A and K Petroleum Company." The tone is so flowery and the adjectives so lavish that extensive quotation is warranted:

The dynamic industry and invincible courage of James L. Anderson and Robert S. Kerr, who recognized and seized an unprecedented opportunity in the Oklahoma City oil field's discovery, built the A&K Petroleum Company from a lone but extremely active string of drilling tools to its present powerful station as controlling owner of sixteen producing wells.

Even business vision and rare executive genius are responsible for the well-nigh miraculous development of this concern, whose properties are now valued at millions of dollars and whose expansion involves industrial romance of almost fictional character. So substantial was the foundation and so sturdy the structure of this company that even a period of world-wide chaos and depression has failed to impair its integrity or impede its prosperous progress.

The author continued his saga of how Anderson and Kerr ("son of Okla-

[8] Interview with Aubrey Kerr, April 28, 1971; *Ada Evening News*, November 16, 1932; *Daily Oklahoman*, March 19, 1933. The first Kerr home was at 420 East 14th Street.

Table 3.1. Corporate Structures Involving Robert S. Kerr
and James L. Anderson, 1928–32

February 4, 1928
Dixon Brothers Incorporated
Incorporators: Anderson, Kerr, B. S. and W. A. Dixon
Shares: 500 at $100 each

1929
Anderson & Kerr Drilling Company
(a copartnership)

November 5, 1930
Anderson & Kerr Drilling Company
Capitalization: 2,500 shares at $10 each
Stockholders: Anderson, 1,250 shares; R. S. Kerr, 1,249; T. W. Fentem, 1
Directors: Anderson, R. S. Kerr, and Fentem
Officers: Anderson, president; R. S. Kerr, secretary and treasurer

November 5, 1930
Anderson-Kerr, Incorporated
Capitalization, stock, officers, and directors same as Anderson & Kerr Drilling Company

September 15, 1931
An-Ker, Incorporated
Authorized capital stock: 2,000 shares, no par value
Paid up capital stock: 480 shares valued at $48,000
Stockholders: Anderson, 240 shares; R. S. Kerr, 240 shares
Officers: Anderson, president; R. S. Kerr, vice-president and treasurer; Fentem, secretary
Wholly owned subsidiaries: Anderson & Kerr Drilling Company and Anderson-Kerr, Incorporated

November 7 –10, 1932
A&K Petroleum Company
Shares: 400,000 (125,000 class A and 275,000 class B) at par value of $5.00
Directors: H. M. Smith, Anderson, and T. M. Kerr of Oklahoma City; R. S. Kerr and C. H. Rives of
    Ada; F. M. Porter of Ardmore; and Lloyd Maxwell of Chicago
Officers: R. S. Kerr, president and treasurer; Anderson, vice-president and secretary; Maxwell,
    vice-president; and Fentem, assistant secretary and assistant treasurer
Stockholders: R. S. Kerr, Anderson, and T. M. Kerr, 50 shares each of class B; Rives, Porter, and
    Smith, 1,000 shares each of class B; and Maxwell, 2,000 shares of class B

homa's soil") plunged into the "seething turmoil of the world's greatest oil field." Being "level-headed and far-sighted," they were "quickly" hired to drill wells, "very speedily" acquired additional equipment, and consequently "won fortune practically overnight." The "quick recognition of their unusual managerial ability" resulted in lucrative contracts. As a result, the company "now enjoys ownership of incalculably rich interests jointly with the Continental and other major operators." The firm had "jealously safeguarded its reputation, which it holds priceless." Anderson, who personally supervised and controlled the drilling department, was described as being without peer in skill and experience in the Mid-Continent Field. Kerr, who administered the business department, was well known throughout the industry for his success as an executive. "Thus," the article concluded, "the company's affairs are promoted smoothly and economically while it continues to expand without sensation but with soundness and surety."

There were also pictures and additional adjectives for these two. Robert S. Kerr was described as one "who ranks high among the successful younger executives of the oil operating enterprises in the Mid-Continent Field. His business sagacity is largely responsible for A&K's intrenched position as an outstanding oil producer and operator." Anderson, popularly known as "Jim," acquired his knowledge "through actual experience on the derrick floor. Although phenomenally successful financially he continues to work hard, and has the confidence and respect of his field force." As a member of Anderson and Kerr Drilling Company, "who are among the best known, and certainly the most capable drilling contractors in the southwest," Jim had drilled two of the biggest wells in the Oklahoma City field for the (R. A.) McArthur Oil Company and was "looked upon as part of the McArthur organization."[9]

Since the nature of any organization reflects the character of its leaders, a more discriminating look should be taken at Robert S. Kerr and James L. Anderson, both individually and collectively. Certainly, Bob Kerr, the "front man," was initially the leader and during his lifetime the dominant force. A member of his family once said: "Anytime he comes in and sits down, that's the head of the table. And he's always been that way." Aubrey remembered that even as a child working in the fields Bob had been the "strawboss," and that only Lois, who was two years older, could order him around. Travis, who was six years younger, said, "I loved Bob not only as a brother but sort of like a father."

Bob stood about six feet three inches and weighed around 250 pounds. Despite his size he was not athletic, aside from fishing, but took pride in being an orator and bookworm. He never drank and smoked only while in military service. But he loved to eat, especially candy and soft drinks. He was religiously inclined, refused to steal watermelons as a child, and early in life became a Sunday-school teacher. Nevertheless, he had a large store of salty stories and loved card games of all sorts. Travis recalled a poker game in which the two brothers won enough money to acquire an oil lease. Dean Terrill, later legal counsel to A&K, remembered that in the early days after the directors' meetings pitch and gin rummy were means by which Kerr often recouped the expense money paid to out-of-town members! J. R. Kitchel, a friend from Ada days, said, "The only vice he had was he loved to play cards . . . and was a good card player."

[9] The exact date of this publication has not been determined. Two different editions have been found, but both contain the same cover and front material. Obviously the version used could not be from the date indicated: Jack Lance, Inc., comp., *The Oklahoma City Oil Field—in Pictures* (Oklahoma City, January, 1931), pp. 11–12, 39.

From his mother he inherited wit and a cheerful disposition, but this was buttressed by his father's tenacity and determination to succeed. Kerr personally gave him much of the credit for his achievements:

My father often impressed on me the secret of the success of John D. Rockefeller. . . . It was the ability to associate with him men of far greater ability than he had, and with them he established a community of interest, and for them he provided the opportunity to achieve success for themselves while they were contributing to his. I have followed that formula all my life.

He gave similar advice to his own children. Robert S. Kerr, Jr., remembered being told "Boys, be careful what you start. You might succeed." Bob Kerr started a lot of things. And he succeeded. As a contact man and later a politician he had all the necessary social traits: booming voice, a ready smile, a commanding presence, and great powers of persuasion. Although he never finished college, his mastery of detail was remarkable. Senator Paul Douglas of Illinois, himself a university professor, once said of him, "I regard the Senator from Oklahoma as probably having the highest I.Q. in the Senate." He was also a determined optimist: Sam Rayburn of Texas characterized him by saying, "Bob Kerr is the kind of man who would charge hell with a bucket of water and believe he could put it out."

A man of extraordinary vigor, both mental and physical, Kerr was a ruthless debater and wily back-room manipulator. The columnist Jack Anderson, who was no friend of his, wrote: "He loved life, but he loved victory even more than life, and whether in politics, at the poker table, or in the oil fields, he played to win. . . . He bulldozed anyone who obstructed his will, horse-traded with anyone he could not bulldoze." *Newsweek*, August 6, 1962, said of the man who was then known as the "Uncrowned King of the Senate": "Not only does Kerr have power but he exercises it—through cajolery, wheedling, invective, threatening, and bludgeoning." But the secret of his success was: "He always finds some way to make your interest his interest. People find they need him more than he needs them. He has a way of getting people obligated to him on a due bill for collection later."

After Kerr's death his fellow Oklahoman, Carl Albert, read this evaluation into the *Congressional Record*:

Some people thought that Bob Kerr pushed too hard. He was like a great engine powered by super fuel as he drove to every task. . . . He never worried about finesse. He could accomplish almost any task he undertook by main strength—by sheer weight of his intellect, by his rock-like determination, and his vast energy. . . .

He was the center of everything that he undertook. Those who worked with and for him were not only coworkers and employees, they were disciples. To be an active part of the Kerr organization was a way of life to hundreds of people. He commanded the most devoted loyalty from those closely associated with him.

As might be expected, his co-workers in business viewed him in different ways. Most of the men in the field seldom saw him. Foley D. Collins, one of the original employees, remembered Bob at a rig on only two or three occasions. He recalled a time when Kerr had asked a question of a crew member and that later the man had asked Collins, "Who was that inquisitive son of a gun out here a while ago?" When told it was Bob Kerr, he replied, "Was that him? I wouldn't have talked like I did if I'd known that was Bob Kerr." Collins's own opinion was that "Bob Kerr had never been around old laboring men a workin' and he didn't understand their trouble," but he did admit that Kerr was good in dealing with the companies for which they drilled.

Jim Anderson also had some problems with his partner. In a letter which scolded Kerr for a lack of humility—that quality "has now been relegated in you to the mere coincidence of having been born in a log cabin"—he spoke of Kerr's "burning fires of ambition." After the fact there was near-unanimous agreement about what Kerr's main contributions to the company had been. First of all, he had the ability to pick good men. Then, after he left active management for politics, there was his complete faith in the future, complete confidence in his own ability, and in the ability of his associates, to accomplish things. A later president of the company, F. C. Love, said that Kerr's value lay in his imagination, his willingness to take risks, and the fact that he was always pushing, "which undoubtedly caused the company to grow somewhat faster than it otherwise would have grown."

A member of his Board of Directors, Guy C. Kiddoo, echoed this sentiment. According to him, Kerr's greatest contribution was his "abiding, steady, substantial confidence" in the ability of his employees, his belief that the company had no way to go but up, and his "consistent optimism that things would go well." This faith was also singled out by Dean McGee as Kerr's principal contribution after 1942, adding that this was an asset every business could use. A typical, and often repeated, story related to a call Kerr made from Washington to inquire of McGee what was going on. When told they were building a drilling rig, Kerr replied that they should build two or even, three![10] Some employees, however, believed that, if it had not been for McGee, Kerr probably would have gone broke because he would become so enthusiastic in his projects that he "couldn't see how they could go wrong." In retrospect another important factor was Kerr's desire to own more than a drilling company. Consequently, he was eager for the firm to grow as fast as it could and did not stunt it by cashing in his profits. As he often said, he would rather have a little piece of a large pie than all of a small one.

Bob Kerr furnished the optimism and the "talent for separating investment capital from its owners." But it was his brother-in-law Jim Anderson, with his "nose for oil" and ability to drill cheaper than his competitors, on whom the company depended for the sum total of its technical knowledge. Even Travis, who had worked for a supply house and was later to take over the drilling department, said that Jim taught him what little he knew about drilling. Anderson was twelve years older than his partner but physically much like him. He was just short of six feet two inches tall and weighed two

[10] "Making Money Make Money," *Forbes*, November 1, 1962, p. 32.

hundred pounds. While his frame was not as massive as Bob's, he was broad-shouldered, with curly black hair, and was generally considered a man's man. Whereas Bob was genial and smiling, Jim's son, James K., remembered that, when his father "wanted to look mean, he could look like the devil, himself."

If few of the field men knew Bob Kerr, all of them knew Anderson, and the impact that he made was lasting. J. R. Glover said that he was afraid of him and would hide from him, but that he was a "mighty fine man" and the "best guy in the world." Glover told about a man whose carelessness once had set fire to a rig, who announced to Anderson: "By God, I quit, you old son of a bitch. You aren't going to fire me." Anderson retorted, "If I don't, I'll whip you, just which ever you want," adding that he could fire the employee any time he wanted to, but "by God, he couldn't quit." When the man decided he was fired, Anderson then told the driller not to terminate him because the culprit had learned his lesson.

Eddie Baxendale said of Anderson:

Jim was one of the hardest men in the oil fields, but he was one of the best. What I mean, he expected you to work and work hard. . . . He'd come up and eat you out a little bit, but he'd pat you on the shoulder before he left. He was a dandy. . . . He knew what he was doing; he knew the oil business. . . . Lots of times . . . we'd get broke and before pay day we'd go down to the hotel and borrow $5.00 from him. He'd raise hell, but he'd give us the money. . . . He was a hard worker, and he expected you to work hard."

Eddie's brother, Norman, added, "But when the work was over, he just played as hard as he worked."

Foley Collins believed that "there never was a man better to his men" than Anderson. According to him Anderson would override Kerr when it came to advancing money to the men. Kerr would say, "Why, Jim, that man's not even a workin'!" Jim would answer: "I don't give a damn if he's not. If he didn't need the money, he wouldn't be up here."

Most of the men said, with only slight variations in their stories, that one could tell at a distance whether Jim was in a good humor. According to Collins, a cigarette was the tip-off: "If that cigarette was going around and around, boy, you'd better look out 'cause he's fixing to find somebody he could eat out. It didn't make him no difference who he come to." Collins also remembered a well that they drilled for Phillips Petroleum Company where Anderson ran Phillips's engineers off the site: "These school boys can't come out here and tell me how to drill a well. They've never drilled a well. They don't know nothin' about it." Bob Kerr had to pacify Phillips.

According to Henry Pryor Anderson called his own outbursts "hay-wired fits." Pryor said: "[I had] been fired and hired before I would get my clothes changed. But other than that he was a good man, and he'd do anything in the world for you." Just watch that cigarette. "Buck" Fowler, who had worked with Jim since the days of the Dixon brothers, characterized him as: "kind of a strange sort of fellow. . . . He was quick, quick on the draw. . . . He was liable to fire you today and hire you tomorrow." Harold Freeman remembered the cigarette as rolling "about 90 percent of the time" and that Anderson had a policy that a man worked nine years as a roughneck before he would consider him as a driller.

Jim Anderson was aware of his reputation for having a temper. In 1962 he wrote: "I will say this: I don't think I have ever knew a man that didn't have a temper that I could understand or respect. Also, I hate to see a fellow that never can admit he's wrong. If I ever was wrong, I'd be the first to admit it."[11] His son, whom he advised, "Never own a drilling rig," also felt his father's anger; he was even fired and rehired himself. James K. characterized his father as something of a loner, a rugged individualist with a tough exterior to hide the fact that underneath he was tender and compassionate. On the job there was no time for telling jokes or kidding around. Off the job, however, Jim excelled at both. The son felt that this double image was one of the reasons Jim had trouble getting along with people, especially those who worked for him. They admired and respected him for what he knew and the way he drove himself as well as his rig men. But they were afraid of him. He knew what needed to be done, how it should be done, and he expected them to do it. He would say, "This is the way it is," and he would expect his decision to be accepted. If it were not, he was always happy to fight, physically as well as verbally.

His wife, Mildred, who was fourteen years younger than Jim, was credited by the other Kerrs with keeping her husband in the company. He often would blow up and say, "The hell with the Kerrs." He seemed to feel that he was doing the work but that Bob and Travis were making more from it than he was. Mildred admitted that Jim's pride lay in his ability to drill, but he did not have Bob's ambition. Bob wanted a large company, and Jim wanted no more than he could personally look after. As Travis said: "Jim didn't like to cotton to these oil companies to get their business. But that's part of the public relations, making friends with the companies and their personnel."

Jim summed up his philosophy in a letter to Bob in 1959:

Mine has been a life of comparatively modest but gratifying (to me) satisfaction. As a matter of preference, I have chosen a life of private endeavor, unencumbered by the intrusion of the 'limelight' of either public recognition or support. I cannot honestly say that I envy you your successes, Bob, as they are not the ones I would have chosen for myself, even if I could have attained them."

Of the despised *Fortune* article he wrote that what really angered him was the statement that he "retired modestly," for he said: "I fully intend to go down shouting and shaking both fists, if ever I retire completely (to do so modestly would be a betrayal of every facet of my disposition!)."

Travis, born July 28, 1902, had the Kerr physical characteristics, although he was not as large a man as brother Bob. If possible, he had an even sunnier disposition. Even after he reached the top levels of management, most employees continued to call him by his first name, and he was considered "one of us." Foley Collins said that any man in trouble would go see Travis,

---

[11] James L. Anderson, Gainesville, Texas, to James K. Anderson, Midland, Texas, August 24, 1962. Xerox copy in J. L. Anderson file, Public Relations Department.

" 'cause Travis is a good hearted son of a gun." Norman Baxendale claimed that Travis knew all the men in the drilling department by their first names. J. C. Comer recalled that, although men were off the payroll between jobs, most of them just waited until the company got another contract. He said: "jobs weren't too far between as Travis was pretty good at getting them contracts. Lots of the older employees called him 'cousin' behind his back. Often Travis would have the well half drilled before the contract was written."

Travis probably did not object to being known as the family black sheep. As his brother Aubrey said: "Travis has done everything. He tried it all." Yet everyone liked him. Dean McGee said of him:" [He was a] real great fellow. I never saw anyone with a bigger heart or warmer personality." It was, of course, these very traits that made his contribution to the struggling company so important. People liked him and trusted him. Not only could he get credit from his former employers but his contacts with friends in the major oil companies were more extensive and, cumulatively, more valuable even than Bob's. Furthermore, he was modest about his own contribution: "You've got to be lucky. And I've been lucky. There was lots of luck involved in the development of the company. Even with all of Bob's ambition and foresight, and Mr. McGee's, if we hadn't been lucky we wouldn't be as great a company as we are. And we're lucky that we have so many good people working for the company." Ironically, Travis took more pride in owning the third greatest money-winning ($1,749,869) racehorse, Round Table, than in his association with a great company.[12]

A fourth person should be mentioned for his special contributions in this formative period, and that is T. W. ("Whit") Fentem, who began as office manager. Born in 1900, Fentem, a handsome man of average size, was reserved by nature but had a sly sense of humor and was respected by all with whom he worked. None of the other three men had the knowledge or the temperament to handle the multitude of business and financial chores associated with the four companies, which suffered from a chronic shortage of staff. In the days of perennial money shortages Fentem often found himself hard pressed to come up with the dollars to match Bob Kerr's optimism, and the wheeling and dealing that went on in an oil company operating on a shoestring must have given pause to this young man trained in banking. The most common stories concerning him give insight into both the condition of the company and Fentem's own personality. Wallace Wiggs, who went to work under Fentem in 1934, said that his boss would often hold up checks that the company had issued for payments "because he had something else in mind that had to be paid and the company didn't have the money."

D. A. Watkins, who joined his staff about fifteen years later, added another variation to the Fentem legend. He recalled an occasion when he received a check request for $100,000. Watkins knew the company did not

---

[12] All references to the Kerrs and Anderson not otherwise identified are in the interview files in Public Relations Department.

have anything near that amount in the bank—"probably not $10,000"—so he went to Fentem with the problem. Fentem laughed and said, "Well, I fooled thosé so-and-sos." He reached into his desk, pulled out three checks that totaled about $300,000 that he had held back from deposit. "I fooled them this time; I fooled those so-and-sos this time." Watkins believed that Fentem maintained "his little kitty" of money that management did not know about for times just such as this. There would be more occasions in later years when Fentem would be called on to perform his money-magic act.[13]

[13] Interviews with Wallace Wiggs, August 12, 1970, and D. A. Watkins, May 5, 1971.

Chapter 4

Depression Years
1933–1935

The fate of A&K Petroleum, as well as the other Kerr and Anderson ventures, was in the hands of four young men—only Anderson had reached his forties—when the full force of the Great Depression swept the nation in 1933. Unemployment was at its worst during the winter of 1932–33, with estimates of as many as seventeen million workers out of jobs. The vast and vaunted American economic machine shuddered virtually to a halt, as production in one important industry after another dropped to almost negligible proportions. In February fear that the financial structure was collapsing caused gold and other currency to go out of circulation at the rate of $30,000 a day. At the same time the automobile industry was so depressed that the governor of Michigan closed that state's banks. As the panic spread, other state executives quickly duplicated his move, and on March 6, President Franklin D. Roosevelt declared a national bank holiday. Despite all the efforts of the New Deal and its frantic "Hundred Days Congress," some 4,000 banks failed in 1933.

In Oklahoma also the depression was at its worst. The state's relief funds had long since been expended, and taxpayer resistance to collections became widespread. Although the 1933 legislature cut expenditures by one-third, the reduction came nowhere near closing the gap created by loss of revenues. Soon the state was issuing nonpayable warrants to its employees and debtors. The pressures were so great that Governor Murray used martial law to prevent the forced sale of homes and farms in eleven counties for nonpayment of taxes.

Oil, which had earlier been a bright spot in the state's economy, was now one of its major problems. Overproduction, falling prices, and "hot oil" continued despite hammer-handed efforts by the governor. In an effort to bring some stability, Murray again completely closed down the Oklahoma City field from March 4 to 14, 1933. Some permanent improvement came on April 10, 1933, when Oklahoma passed a proration law which was to become a model for other states. The National Recovery Act (June 16, 1933) and its petroleum codes gave the embattled Oklahoma oil industry some additional hope of stability in the future, and the National Guard was demobilized after almost two years of service. Nevertheless, oil prices and production yo-yoed with almost every hint of good or bad news, but prospecting continued to decline through most of the thirties. During 1933 oil sold between $0.25 and $1.08 per barrel. Despite all of this, the state's production was up 30 million barrels, but the net return dropped $17 million from 1932.

It was against this background that Bob Kerr began his travels to Chicago to try to peddle the 120,000 shares of stock authorized for sale in November, 1932. While he made the rounds of the Chicago investment firms, his headquarters was the cheapest room in the La Salle Hotel; his principal liquid diet was Coca-Cola; and his main eating place was Pixley & Ehlers, a "one-arm beanery" where the best buy was baked beans at 10¢ a plate. Dean Terrill, later legal counsel for A&K, related that "it was a source of some amazement and amusement to us when the Board of Directors occasionally met in Chicago long after those lean days, that Bob would frequently insist that some of us dine with him at Pixley & Ehlers."[1]

His success was as poor as his diet. Through brokers such as George Grant, Inc., Howard W. Elmore Company, and Larry Romaine, all of Chicago, he sold 1,102 shares at a par value of $5,510. But George Grant, the principal agent, turned in only $2,190 as cash collected. In 1934 the balance of accounts receivable for Grant's firm amounted to $8,081.57 and was considered uncollectable.[2] This experience must have shaken even Bob Kerr's perennial optimism.

Several official actions were taken by A&K Petroleum during 1933, probably to strengthen Kerr's bargaining position. In a special meeting in April the directors declared that proceeds of any future stock sold in Illinois would be applied toward retirement of outstanding notes and accounts payable and that any excess would be used to clear current oil obligations. They likewise agreed to restrict registration of the company's securities to those states approved by the secretary of state of Illinois. In June, Travis resigned as a director of A&K to permit the election of Harry Olson, a Chicago attorney. But the July resignations of F. M. Porter and Lloyd Maxwell brought him back to fill Maxwell's unexpired term, while Porter's

[1] Dean Terrill to Malvina Stephenson, June 19, 1963, in Dean Terrill file, Public Relations Department. See also Terrill's marginal note on first draft of Dean A. McGee's Newcomen speech "Evolution Into Total Energy" in Bette Brenz file, Public Relations Department.

[2] "A&K Petroleum Company Registration Statement" with Securities Exchange Commission, September 22, 1936.

seat was left vacant. A 12½-cent quarterly dividend was also declared for class A stockholders, but it too was a token gesture.[3]

Needless to say, the employees of Anderson & Kerr Drilling felt the financial pinch. Foley Collins remembered that, while the banks were closed, the company paid the men with "grocery books" and often had to borrow money to meet the payroll. J. R. Glover, a cousin of the Kerrs who went to work on Washington #1 that year, recalled a pay rate of four dollars for an eight-hour day and six dollars for twelve. O. L. ("Barney") Limes, troubleshooter and cable-tool man, said that Bob Kerr would come out to his rig and say: "We got some money coming in from Phillips. We are drilling a well for Phillips, and it will be in in a few days, and we'll give you a check." Eddie Baxendale remembered that sometimes the crew had to wait fifty or sixty days for their pay or until the well was completed. As a sidelight he added that, while he was drilling in Oklahoma City: "I used to see Old Cuckleburr Bill Murray, the Governor, with that Palm Beach suit he had, go up and down that dirt road. He'd walk from that Park Hotel, . . . and we'd see him walk by going back and forth each day." Perhaps the actual sight of the oilman's nemesis helped provoke the unspoken frustration.

The extent or location of the contract drilling is impossible to gauge. Probably most such work was in the Oklahoma City field, where wells were drilled so close together that, if the holes slanted, it was not clear whose land they were under. Old-timers vaguely remember drilling also in Stroud, Ada, Crescent, Anadarko, and Elk City. Only six new wells definitely carried the Kerr and Anderson names in 1933. Two of these were in Oklahoma County: Potts #1, with Harrison Smith, which was completed in January after a test produced 2,653 barrels in four hours, and the M.K.&T., which was begun in December. Four wells were drilled in Stephens and Seminole counties, apparently without success. About all that can be found about production during 1933 is that six of the company's Oklahoma City wells had July pipeline runs of 147,582 barrels and that the August net allowables for these wells were set at 121,092 barrels.[4]

The small amount of information available indicates that 1933 was at best a survival year for the partners' various undertakings. The effort to sell stock was a disaster, and even the gesture of paying quarterly dividends was misleading. Although $625.00 was declared between January 1 and July 1, 1933, nothing was actually paid. This undoubtedly was attributable to the fact that the current stockholders were all insiders, and oil and gas sales from December 1, 1932, to June 30, 1933, totaled only $59,087.19 for an earned surplus of only $5,739.90.[5]

One other series of events is worthy of mention, for it foreshadowed things to come. Despite his father's admonition that a politician should be

---

[3] Porter cited "conflict of interest" as his reason, while Maxwell gave none. A&K Petroleum Company "Minute Book," 1.

[4] *Oil and Gas Journal*, Vols. 31–32 (January 26), (March 2, 30), (July 13, 20), (August 17), and (December 14, 1933).

[5] "A&K Petroleum Company Registration Statement."

independently wealthy, Bob Kerr allowed it to be known that he was considering the race for lieutenant governor. Stories in the November 21 *Daily Oklahoman* and December 9 *Harlow's Weekly* of 1933 were similar enough to suggest they had been planted. Both pointed out that while Kerr did want to become governor eventually, he would not use the lesser office as a stepping-stone. He got as far as building up a limited state organization before changing his mind in January, 1934. Apparently he decided that the million dollars should come first.[6]

In 1934 political solutions seemed to be helping the economy, and national optimism slowly returned. The Dow-Jones stock averages moved upward, and the gross national product for that year increased by 20 percent. The National Recovery Administration's petroleum code was designed "to stabilize the oil industry upon a profitable basis" through regulation of prices, wages, working schedules, and the like. The actions of federal and state governments, plus a slight increase in consumption, combined to produce an improved outlook.

Oklahoma shared these gains, but not all of the old problems were eliminated. In hearings before a House subcommittee, an agent of the United States Department of the Interior charged that 400,000 barrels of hot oil had been run in Oklahoma in July, 1934, and a state proration umpire estimated that Oklahoma City had overproduced by 188,753 barrels during the same period.[7] Over all however, it was a better year for Oklahoma oilmen as most of their companies moved into the black. The rank and file also benefited, for between May, 1933, and July, 1934, employment in drilling and production increased 62.1 percent, and payrolls rose 74.7 percent.[8]

At Anderson & Kerr Drilling the changes were gradual. Although construction began on its first motor-driven rig, hiring was slow. Elton ("Buster") Wooten, who came in January, 1934, as a production clerk, remembered that there were only two departments, drilling and production, at that time. The former had about sixty employees and four or five rigs, all steam. In production there were three full-time employees and five to seven others who worked part-time, in addition to about twenty pumpers, switchers, and the like. The same recollection was shared by Jacob Henry Pryor, hired on February 1, for $0.55 an hour; "Buster" Kuhlman, who came in May, reported that there were only two tool pushers—Charlie Reno and Q. C. ("Pete") Walton—and that: "Jim Anderson was everywhere. He did not have a title. He was just part owner; he was our boss in the field, whereas Bob Kerr was in the office." Pete Walton added to this that they did not see much of Bob Kerr since he was "busy selling stock to keep going." Walton also remembered that he had to change to an eight-hour shift from his usual

[6] A number of letters on this subject are found in the Robert S. Kerr Collection, Western History Collections, University of Oklahoma, Box 1, folders 1 and 2.

[7] Rister, *Oil: Titan of the Southwest*, 265 n. 38.

[8] Some idea of the Depression's impact on Oklahoma City can be seen in the fact that between 1931 and 1934 real and personal property assessments dropped from $169,774,658 to $119,148,658, and assessments of public service companies from $31,392,103 to $24,401,360. *Chronicles of Oklahoma*, Vol. 47 (Summer, 1969), p. 181.

twelve-hour day. J. R. Glover was more specific in that the NRA cut their hours and raised their wages. Under its minimum-wage provisions, derrickmen and firemen got $4.50 a day and roughnecks $4.00. He also claimed that management generally met these rules by giving the same amount for the short day that previously had been paid for the longer one.

At this time there was still no clear-cut delineation of functions, or even personnel, between Anderson & Kerr Drilling and A&K Petroleum. An anecdote is perhaps indicative of how amateurishly the latter company was run. On August 20, 1934, Bob Kerr reported to the A&K board that he had received a letter from Harry Olson, the Chicago attorney who had been elected a director in June, 1933. The letter read in part: "I have just come across some literature in which my name is advertised as a director of your company. I have never accepted a directorship in the company, and if your literature carries my name, please discontinue same." The board chose to view this as a letter of resignation, which was accepted. A vote was taken not to fill the position, thus leaving only two outside directors.

Contract drilling picked up, at least in joint-interest wells. Anderson & Kerr Drilling records show that seven of these were completed in Oklahoma City during 1934. The most frequent partner was Director Smith's Trans-Mississippi Oil Corporation, but included among others the Watchorn Oil Company, Black Gold Petroleum, and Lynch & Sledge. Although Anderson & Kerr's ownership was usually 1/2 of 7/8ths, variations were wide. The wells were very productive; the Miller #1, for example, flowed 2,483 barrels in eight hours. Five additional wells were recorded in Oklahoma County in the name of one or the other of the Kerr and Anderson companies: one (the M.K.&T. #1) was successful, one was abandoned, and the fates of the other three remain unknown.

A search of the literature indicates at least twenty more wells in which Anderson & Kerr Drilling was involved. The *Oil and Gas Journal*, January 11, 1934, reporting leasing in Logan, Lincoln, Grady, Kingfisher, and Garvin counties, listed Anderson & Kerr Drilling as being one of the most active companies. In fact, it was Anderson & Kerr #1 Hull in Logan County which sparked interest in that location. On May 17 the publication indicated that the well had been completed at 355 barrels per day; then, on July 26, wrote "Another pool was opened in the first half of the year in Logan County by Anderson & Kerr in their No. 1-A Hull. . . . It produced 227 bbls. naturally in the first 24 hours." The company was also part owner in another venture, the James #1, drilled in Logan County during the year, and was noted as being involved with a fourth. Furthermore, the *Journal* in September named Anderson & Kerr Drilling as the contractor for a test hole some eleven miles from Pauls Valley.

Other counties furnished less successful stories. The company was involved in the dry Huckabee #1 in Lincoln County and in two wells in Garvin County. About the latter, the *Journal*, wrote on March 8, 1934, "No two wells in the state are being more closely watched than those of Anderson & Kerr and the Phillips Petroleum Company in Garvin County." Apparently both were unsuccessful, however. The same fate awaited a well in the Fittstown field, but the loss was offset by a very small producer in the

Earlsboro pool. Three additional counties were explored: Cleveland, Canadian, and Caddo. Under the headline "Experience Gained in Drilling Wildcat Well at Binger, Oklahoma, Adds to Drilling Techniques" the *Journal* reported that the Caddo well was drilled at the start by contract with Anderson & Kerr and made good progress until the owner died: "The hole below 7,500 feet was drilled with the equipment acquired from Anderson & Kerr, but the crews were under the supervision" of the Denver Producing & Refining Company.[9] Wells by "Kerr & Others" and "Kerr & Bisetts" in Creek and Tulsa counties were not further identified.

Over-all 1934 must have been an improvement for the Kerr and Anderson enterprises. Although no annual reports were issued, other sources indicate that between July 1, 1933, and June 30, 1934, their oil and gas sales reached $414,914.87, giving them a net profit of $152,095.49. From October 1, 1933, to July 1, 1934, dividends of $3,002.45 were declared, although only $502.45 of that amount ever left the A&K treasury.[10] The July, 1934, date should be noted, however, for the economy turned downward during the second half of that year.

Despite his decision not to run for political office, Bob Kerr was active in the governor's race of 1934. The Democratic candidate was his old friend oilman E. W. Marland, and he was introduced by Kerr in the statewide radio address which opened the successful campaign. The *Ada Daily Evening News* wrote that Kerr "was one of the original Marland supporters and it is generally thought throughout the state that he will be a prominent figure in the next administration."[11]

By 1935 some of the preceding year's optimism for a quick end to the depression began to wane. Vocal opposition to the New Deal became widespread, and its various programs came under attack in the courts. In May a unanimous decision of the U.S. Supreme Court destroyed the NRA and with it the various petroleum codes. To a large degree this loss was offset when Governor Marland quickly worked out a compact between the oil-producing states to replace federal controls. His success restored a degree of stability to the industry.

The depression was still very much in evidence, however, and jobs were eagerly sought. Harold Freeman, recently hired by Anderson & Kerr, related that at that company's Knox yard "you couldn't walk for people out there that were trying to hire out—for just one rig starting up." After a contract had been completed, the crews would be laid off "to save a dollar" and the truck drivers would tear down the rig and move it to the yard or another drilling location.

A problem unique to the Oklahoma City field, and therefore important to

---

[9] Citations for the preceding paragraphs are found in *Oil and Gas Journal*, January 11, 18, 25, February 1, 22, March 1, 8, 22, April 5, 12, 19, May 9, 17, 24, 31, June 7, 14, 21, July 5, 18, 26, August 3, 16, 30, September 13, 20, October 4, 11, 25, and November 8, 15, 22, 1934.

[10] "A&K Petroleum Company Registration Statement."

[11] Kerr scrapbooks, 1.

Kerr and Anderson, was that by 1935 drilling had reached the geographical limit allowed by existing law. It was the second-largest American oil field, covering some 11,000 acres, and possessing 1,713 wells. Moreover, the pool extended under the forbidden area which contained the state capitol complex, the University of Oklahoma Medical School, and some better residential areas. The oilmen wanted to continue their encroachment, but many citizens opposed it, and extension soon became a political issue.

The city council was inundated with petitions from both sides. The question of possible enlargement was compounded by where and how much land would be involved. Each group of oilmen had an area of principal concern—acreages with secured leases. Consequently the industry was far from agreement on any one plan and consequently offered conflicting petitions.[12] Organizations pro and con sprang up throughout the city and fought each other as well as their more obvious enemies. During the first three months of the year hardly a day passed that the *Daily Oklahoman* did not front-page the charges and countercharges. The following exchange was symptomatic of the confusion: In reply to a request by the East Side Development and Protective League that drilling be allowed on property that they represented, the East Side Property Owners Association argued that no extension should be granted at that time because it would result in depreciation and damage to their property and, in fact, to all property in the city. *But*, the association added, if the league's request were granted, it wanted to be "included if an extension is made."

The city planning commission at first came out with a long statement in opposition to any extension. From its point of view the results would mainly be bad. The probability was great that irreparable damage to property rental, income, and sales values would result. As tax assessments fell—"oil equipment carries no ad valorem tax"—other areas could face tax increases as a consequence. General depreciation and increased home insurance rates from the fire and explosion hazards would cost more than the revenue that oil would bring to anyone, except, of course, the oil companies. There was no guarantee where the expansion might stop. In short, the citizens had to decide "whether the City shall be turned into an oil field town, or be continued as a progressive commercial, financial, and cultural center."

This argument simply shifted the attention to the city council, which had the responsibility for the ultimate decision. It seemed likely that at least one of the proposals would be voted on, and a hot battle developed. Among those in favor of extension the feeling had grown that Phillips Petroleum Company was the real enemy and was using the East Side Development and Protective League as a front. Phillips was accused of using "freeze-out" tactics, and so the demand was made that the other petitions be given equal priority with the one alleged to represent Phillips' interest. The mayor was warned that he could be recalled unless this were done and that a court fight most certainly would follow a vote on the Phillips petition if it were consid-

[12] Plats showing the various proposals are found in the *Daily Oklahoman*, January 4, 21, 1935.

ered first. The city's legal department advised the council to submit *all* extension proposals at a single election. This would have covered nearly five hundred city blocks and 1,050 acres in the eastern part of the city.

The council voted six to two, however, for a referendum on the area identified with Phillips's interests. Opponents declared this unconstitutional, vowed vengeance against the supporting councilmen, and called for a boycott of Phillips products. The Negro Oil Protective Association promised three thousand negative votes in the election, reflecting the initial reaction of one portion of the east-side population on the matter.

On February 14, 1935, the *Daily Oklahoman* headlined its story "Move to Stop Oil Vote Fails." It reported: "Pro forces set up headquarters in the Commerce Exchange Building Wednesday. This group is headed by Bob Kerr of the Anderson-Kerr Drilling Company." Three days later, Kerr issued the following statement:

We are for conservative extension because we believe such extension will benefit Oklahoma City. . . . Extension will result in the expenditure of $17,700,000 in the city, and fully $3,000,000 of this will be spent for labor. Purchase of materials for development of the new zone will represent an expenditure of $11,900,000.

The new group, Associated Oil Industries of Oklahoma City, cooperated with the East Side Development and Protective League to put workers into every ward. The opposition, including the East Side Anti–Slush Pit League, could not unite its efforts, and when the votes were counted on March 5, 1935, extension passed, 13,527 to 9,994. Kerr congratulated the voters on bringing a "continuing boom" to Oklahoma City's development.[13]

Kerr's role in this election has become a part of his legend. As Dean Terrill, who joined A&K Petroleum the next year, pointed out, the company stood to benefit very little. It did not have the money to buy leases in the expanded area at the beginning of the extension fight and got in only later, and in a small way, when the best leases had been taken up by others.[14] What, then, motivated Kerr to spend his time and energy on a project which primarily benefited a rival oil company? Three authors have told essentially the same story: Kerr was approached to head the campaign by two officials of Phillips, Robert H. Lynn, vice-president in charge of the land and development department, and Kenneth S. Adams, an assistant to Frank Phillips. One writer, Marquis W. Childs, reconstructed the dialogue that follows: Adams: "Now. How much will we have to pay for your services?" Kerr: "Mr. Adams, I don't want you to pay me anything. I want a chance for my company to drill your wells." Whether or not there was any truth to this story, it is indisputable that Kerr's infant companies soon afterward established a relationship with Phillips Petroleum which made the difference

[13] Newspaper accounts of the extension fight can be found in the *Daily Oklahoman*, January 1, 3, 6, 8, 12, 15, 16, 21, 23, February 1, 2, 6, 10, 14–17, 19, 22, and March 5–6, 1935. *Oklahoma News*, February 15, 17, 19, 20, 27, March 1, 3, 4, 5, 6, 1935. *Capitol Hill Daily Beacon*, February 27, 1935.

[14] Telephone interview with Dean Terrill, April 27, 1970.

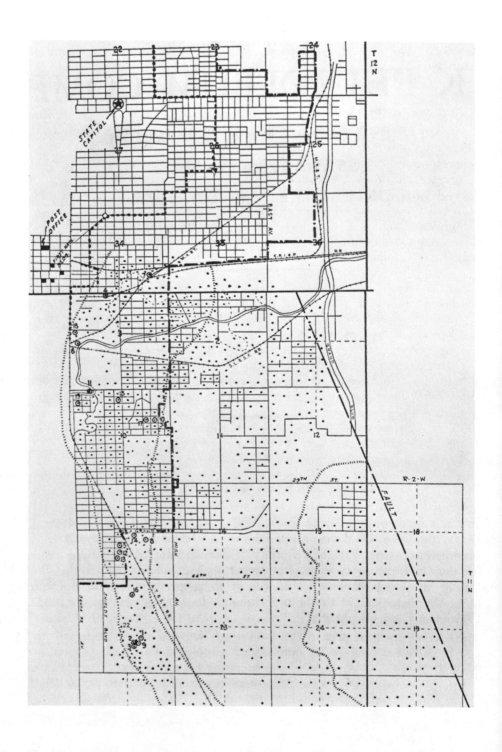

Oklahoma City oil field as of 1935, showing A&K wells. *Source: A&K Petroleum Company "Prospectus," June 4, 1935.* Legend for map appears at the top of page 53.

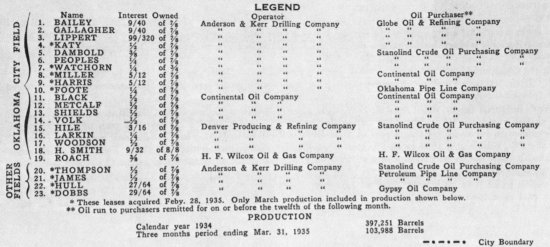

A & K PETROLEUM CO.
2009 FIRST NATIONAL BUILDING
OKLAHOMA CITY, OKLA.

LEGEND

	Name	Interest Owned	Operator	Oil Purchaser**
1.	BAILEY	9/40 of 7/8	Anderson & Kerr Drilling Company	Globe Oil & Refining Company
2.	GALLAGHER	9/40 of 7/8	" " " "	" " " "
3.	LIPPERT	99/320 of 7/8	" " " "	" " " "
4.	*KATY	1/2 of 7/8	" " " "	" " " "
5.	DAMBOLD	3/8 of 7/8	" " " "	Stanolind Crude Oil Purchasing Company
6.	PEOPLES	1/4 of 7/8	" " " "	" " " " "
7.	*WATCHORN	1/4 of 3/4	" " " "	
8.	*MILLER	5/12 of 7/8	" " " "	Continental Oil Company
9.	*HARRIS	5/12 of 7/8	" " " "	" " " "
10.	*FOOTE	1/4 of 7/8	" " " "	Oklahoma Pipe Line Company
11.	BLACK	1/2 of 7/8	Continental Oil Company	Continental Oil Company
12.	METCALF	1/2 of 7/8	" " "	" " "
13.	SHIELDS	1/2 of 7/8	" " "	" " "
14.	VOLK	1/2 of 7/8		
15.	HILE	3/16 of 7/8	Denver Producing & Refining Company	Stanolind Crude Oil Purchasing Company
16.	LARKIN	1/4 of 7/8	" " " "	" " " " "
17.	WOODSON	1/2 of 7/8	" " " "	" " " " "
18.	H. SMITH	9/32 of 8/8	H. F. Wilcox Oil & Gas Company	H. F. Wilcox Oil & Gas Company
19.	ROACH	3/8 of 7/8	Anderson & Kerr Drilling Company	Stanolind Crude Oil Purchasing Company
20.	*THOMPSON	1/4 of 7/8	" " " "	Petroleum Pipe Line Company
21.	*JAMES	1/2 of 7/8	" " " "	" " " "
22.	*HULL	27/64 of 7/8	" " " "	Gypsy Oil Company
23.	*DOBBS	29/64 of 7/8	" " " "	

OKLAHOMA CITY FIELD (1–19) · *OTHER FIELDS* (20–23)

* These leases acquired Feby. 28, 1935. Only March production included in production shown below.
** Oil run to purchasers remitted for on or before the twelfth of the following month.

PRODUCTION

Calendar year 1934	397,251 Barrels
Three months period ending Mar. 31, 1935	103,988 Barrels

—·—·—• City Boundary
— — — — Oil Zone Boundary

between rapid growth, stagnation, or possible death for the Kerr enterprises.[15]

In the meantime, until this alliance was established, the companies of Kerr and Anderson needed new financing immediately. They already had been forced to trade off some of their wells in the south end of the Oklahoma City field to keep going. Other wells were frequently placed with banks as security for funds to meet the payroll or to carry out drilling contracts. A February 28, 1935, balance sheet showed $106.66 in cash in the bank, current assets of $28,059.20, total assets of $1,607,770.43, and a total deficit of $117,517.28. Obviously a cash infusion was drastically overdue.

One A&K Director, Harrison M. Smith, had resigned "on advice of counsel" on January 25. The four remaining directors made a vitally important decision at their March meeting. Rives, Anderson, and the two Kerrs, recognizing the dire condition of the balance sheet, decided to propose an amendment of the articles of incorporation to allow an increase in the amount of stock that could be issued to a total of 250,000 class A and 550,000 class B at par value of $5.00. It was also proposed that class A receive up to $0.35 quarterly (a drop from $0.50) and that the corporation redeem class A at $5.50 a share or the holders convert to Class B. The technical side of

[15] Marquis W. Childs, "The Big Boom from Oklahoma," *Saturday Evening Post*, April 9, 1949, pp. 22ff.; Daniel Seligman, "Senator Bob Kerr, the Oklahoma Gusher," *Fortune*, March, 1959, pp. 136ff.; "E. G. 'Ty' Dahlgren Calls on Robert S. Kerr," *Oil*, September, 1960, pp. 9–12.

selling the new stock was handled by proposals to engage W. Earle Phinney & Company to market the new issue; Chapman and Cutler, a legal firm, to work out compliance with the Illinois securities laws; and Lawrence Scudder & Company to handle the accounting.

A special meeting of the A&K stockholders was called, and on April 2 the articles of incorporation were amended. This was a foregone conclusion, since of the 6,062 shares of class A and 275,000 of class B represented An-Ker, Incorporated, accounted for all but 1,062 shares of Class A. After approving the firms to conduct the stock sale, the stockholders appointed three new directors: W. Earle Phinney, the newly registered agent for A&K in Illinois and the sole member of the brokerage firm engaged to handle the stock sale; T. W. Fentem, office manager for the various Kerr and Anderson enterprises; and Stanley B. Catlett, law partner of Billy Kerr, the youngest of the Kerr brothers. Perhaps these additions lessened the "insider" image of the board, but in reality an executive committee, created earlier by the directors and composed of Anderson and the two Kerrs, made many of the decisions for the company.

In a further move to improve the corporate image, the new board moved on April 15 to enlarge the assets of A&K. A contract was approved with Anderson & Kerr Drilling to buy nine developed leases (five in Oklahoma City) and fifty-seven undeveloped holdings in eight Oklahoma counties for $259,519.01 and the assumption of certain contingent payments totaling $50,066.06. It also authorized Phinney to sell the shares remaining from the earlier authorization of 120,000. Since only 1,102 shares had been sold, most of the issue remained to be disposed of by this effort.

But new problems developed. In connection with the registration of the stock under the Securities Act, a dispute had arisen over the way depletion should be charged, so on May 20 the board proposed reduction of the par value of class B from $5 to $1, thus lowering capitalization by $1,100,000 to $305,510. This again called for stockholders' approval, which was voted later in May. [16] In July the board approved the creation of a sinking fund to be used to purchase and retire class A common stock and application of indebtedness owed by Anderson & Kerr Drilling to A&K Petroleum against the purchase of properties bought from it earlier. Later that month the board recommended that the certificate of incorporation again be amended to prohibit payment of dividends on class B stock and to limit the number of B shares to four-fifths the total of class A shares (this was apparently never ratified).

On August 2, W. Earle Phinney & Company contracted to sell 118,898 shares of class A stock for five dollars each in return for 15 percent of the sales or seventy-five cents a share. The issue was not underwritten in the usual sense, but was on an "agency," or "best efforts only," basis, for Phinney was "even more devoid of cash than was A&K Petroleum." In the words of Dean Terrill, a junior member of Chapman and Cutler, it would be up to "the combined efforts of that romanticizing underwriter, W. Earle Phinney, and

---

[16] Oklahoma Secretary of State, "Kerr-McGee *vs*. John Rogers," State Archives, folder 3.

Stock certificate for A&K Petroleum Company.

Bob Kerr to inspire the proprietors and salesmen of a number of small securities houses" finally to sell the stock to the public. In other words, an unknown one-man investment-securities firm would undertake to finance an equally unknown A&K Petroleum Company, assisted by the unproven Robert S. Kerr.

The next problem turned out to be a major one: getting approval of Illinois authorities to make sales in that state. That task fell to Dean Terrill, the young Chicago attorney. His job was to register the issue under the Securities Act of 1933 and get it qualified under the blue-sky laws of several states, especially Illinois. The task took several months, and it was unusually difficult to convince Illinois officials that A&K stock was worthy of being offered to residents of that state. Kerr and Terrill made repeated trips to Springfield, where it was finally cleared, according to Terrill, by "the persistence and persuasiveness of Bob Kerr." Years later Terrill often remarked that this was also the most difficult of the company's many public offerings to clear with the Securities and Exchange Commission.[17]

---

[17] Dean Terrill to Malvina Stephenson, June 19, 1963, in Dean Terrill file, Public Relations Department. See also Terrill's marginal note on the first draft of Dean A. McGee's Newcomen speech "Evolution Into Total Energy" in Bette Brenz file, Public Relations Department.

It was now possible for Phinney and Kerr to peddle the stock wherever they could. Kerr's personal scrapbook contains a gaudy ten-page pamphlet, backed in imitation black suede, with "Black Gold" embossed upon it in large gold letters. The title page is headed "Oil: A Discussion from an Investment Standpoint," and the bottom carries the notation that it was prepared by W. Earle Phinney & Co., June, 1935. The narration begins "A&K . . . Another Romance in Oil." The gist of the booklet can best be summarized by typical quotes: "When the Oklahoma City Oil Fields were a seething turmoil and excitement was at its zenith, James L. Anderson and Robert S. Kerr organized the Anderson & Kerr Drilling Company and united two necessary attributes for success—practical experience and executive ability."

James Anderson was "considered among the best in drilling skill and experience in the Mid-Continent field. Although he has made a phenomenal success financially, he continues to work hard and has the confidence and respect of all his field forces." At the same time, "industrial leaders of the Mid-Continent fields recognize Mr. Kerr as one of the outstanding executives in the oil industry." The "practical experience and business sagacity of these two men is largely responsible for A&K Petroleum Company's intrenched position as an outstanding producer and operator." The statement of assets was scarcely less glowing: twenty-three producing wells in Oklahoma—nineteen of these in the "renowned Oklahoma City Field"— and fifty-seven undeveloped leases in eight counties of the state.[18]

A prospectus was issued on June 4, announcing the terms of the offering: 118,898 shares of class A common at $5.00, with a $0.35 annual dividend. "So substantial was the formation of this Company that even a period of world-wide chaos and depression failed to impede its continuous progress. It is reasonable to assume that with this management the success of the A&K Petroleum Company seems assured." The reason given for the offering was that in the past "the Company has not had cash available in large sums with which to take advantage of opportunities to acquire interests in oil properties which appear to offer probabilities of good returns." There were 6,102 shares of class A and 275,000 shares of class B currently outstanding, with An-Ker, Incorporated, owning 5,000 A and all of the B.

A supplement was issued on September 27, 1935. It restated the total number of wells in which the company owned an interest from twenty-three to twenty-one—seventeen in Oklahoma City—and lowered the number of undeveloped leases from fifty-seven to forty-eight in nine counties in Oklahoma and Texas. All but 4 wells were owned in conjunction with other companies, such as Trans-Mississippi Oil, Watchorn Oil, Denver Producing and Refining, and Continental. All but one had been drilled by Anderson & Kerr Drilling Company, which was paid twenty-five dollars a month per well to operate them for A&K.[19]

In retrospect, money was not the most significant result of this endeavor. More important were the contacts made with the lawyer, Dean Terrill, and

[18] Kerr scrapbooks, 1.

the top management of Straus Securities Company of Chicago. This small firm, of which F. W. Straus was owner and J. D. Blosser president, played the major part in selling the stock issue, and these men were to perform many vital roles in the history of the company for years to come.

While Bob Kerr spent most of 1935 in Chicago, Travis Kerr and Jim Anderson were active in the field, attempting to give substance to the claims made by the company's salesmen. Work was slack in Oklahoma City, and only one well identified with A&K was drilled in Oklahoma County. Apparently seven others were unsuccessful in Garvin, Creek, Logan, Okfuskee, and Pontotoc counties. It is not surprising, therefore, that, on April 8, A&K sold the Oklahoma City "Volk lease" for $70,000 and an equal amount in future oil production.

Anderson & Kerr Drilling turned to neighboring states. An unsuccessful well was drilled in Rice County, Kansas, and Texas became the focus of a three-pronged attack. Notice had been taken by the *Oil and Gas Journal* on January 10, 1935, of the promising prospects of Anderson & Kerr's Gideon #1 in Collingsworth County, Texas, but on March 14 the journal announced that the well had been given up for dry, despite the estimate of 3 million feet of gas per day. The drilling firm was more successful, however, when a wildcat sunk by their first power-driven rig was the discovery well in the Bruhlmeyer, or Anderson, field, about six miles east of Gainesville in Cooke County, Texas.

It was reported in the May 23 issue of the *Oil and Gas Journal* that Anderson & Kerr Drilling Company, probably seeking entry into the fabulous East Texas area, had joined with the DeArman Brothers Drilling Company to form Anderson-Kerr and DeArman Inc., with offices in Houston. James L. Anderson was president; Robert S. Kerr, vice-president; and Henry J. DeArman, secretary-treasurer. The directors were R. S. Kerr, T. M. Kerr, H. J. DeArman, and Tip DeArman. Capitalized at $60,000, the new corporation had three rotary rigs. This firm apparently served as contractor on five wells, mainly along the Houston ship channel. The developers included Continental, Diadem Oil, and Hamill & Smith.[20]

The most significant project in Texas, however, was with Phillips Petroleum in Moore County. The land had originally been leased by various individuals and companies, including Gulf Production, Shell, Sinclair, Prairie Oil, and Standard of California. Phillips acquired a sizable block of about 16,500 acres by subleasing, with royalty overrides for the original

---

[19] All these documents, including Form A-1, Securities and Exchange Commission, "Registration Statement" and "Reconciliation and Tie," are found in a bound volume entitled "A&K Petroleum Company, 125,000 Shares Class A Common Stock ($5 par value)—125,000 Class B Common Stock ($1 par value)—Effective Date October 15, 1936." This was apparently the personal file of Dean Terrill.

[20] Company records contain no material relating to this company, nor do the interviews with employees. For references to the various drilling activities of Anderson & Kerr in Oklahoma, Kansas, and Texas, see *Oil and Gas Journal*, January 3, 10, 17, 31, February 14, 21, 28, March 7, 14, 21, April 18, May 9, 23, 30, June 6, 13, 27, July 4, 11, 18, August 8, 22, 29, September 12, 19, 26, October 3, 10, 31, and November 7, 14, 1935.

holder. On July 10, 1935, Phillips signed two agreements. The first was a sublease that transferred to A&K one-half of the oil and all of the gas to a depth of 3,700 feet. In return A&K would drill a well on each lease, beginning within the next 120 days, pay the override, and give Phillips 39/64th of the production until the $220,000 advanced by Phillips to drill the wells had been repaid.[21]

This property was destined to become an important gas field. Whether or not the contracts between Phillips and A&K dated July 10, August 2, and December 20, 1935, and May 15, 1936, had any connection with Kerr's work in the Oklahoma City extension fight, there can be no question about the future importance of this acquisition to A&K. The wells under these contracts would be made by Anderson & Kerr Drilling Company. Two new motorized rigs were added to the one already built, and these three, plus three cable-tool units, were sent to the Sunray-Dumas area. The company furnished bunkhouses, which moved with the rigs, but Harold Freeman, who married while working there, found a home for his bride in a remodeled garage. Phillips advanced $10,000 per well to be taken from production and a like amount for any oil that might be found. These wells, which on paper averaged $27,000 to complete, actually cost A&K only $7,000 each in cash out of pocket.[22]

By the end of 1935, Kerr and Anderson had many reasons to congratulate themselves. A&K Petroleum was established as a producing company with a respectable number of properties and output. Of the twenty-two wells Phillips had underwritten, three were completed, and work had begun on others. The sale of its class A common stock had moved moderately well. As of December 20 17,259 shares were outstanding, the property of thirty-five owners. While An-Ker, Incorporated, held the largest block (5,000), A&K could count stockholders from Illinois and Minnesota as well as Oklahoma. The largest single individual holding, 4,650 shares, was owned by C. C. Ince of Oklahoma City. Sales of oil and gas had yielded a small profit, carried over to surplus.[23] This moderate success enabled the company to hire Harold D. Jenkins, an employee of the United States Geological Survey, as

[21] The field, opened in 1926, by 1938 had some 1,498 gas wells, producing some 26 billion cubic feet daily. Lease Records Department files, "S-145 Donaldson" and "Contract file #49A"; A&K Petroleum Company, *Annual Report, 1936.*

[22] During 1935 and 1936 approximately 30 wells were drilled in the field. In 1971, 28 were still producing. At that time they had produced 276 billion cubic feet of gas and, despite the low initial purchase rate of $0.007 per mcf, had returned the company a net profit of $10,106,000. See Otto C. Barton, District Production Superintendent, to Elizabeth Ann Brenz, July 27, 1971, in Brenz files, Public Relations Department. This was the first substantial, long-lived production of any kind for the company and was, therefore, very important in its financial stability during the early years. See also interviews with George Cobb, December 7, 1972, and January 21, 1971; Dean Terrill, telephone interview, April 27, 1970; Otto Barton, July 26, 1971; J. C. Comer, June 17, 1971; J. H. Kuhlman, February 25, 1970; and Harold Freeman, April 17, 1971.

[23] A&K Petroleum Company, "Prospectus," June 4, 1935; A&K Petroleum Company, "Registration Statement"; and "Supplemental Information *re* A&K Petroleum Company Class A Common Stock."

its first geologist, and although A&K did not produce gasoline of its own, it nevertheless acquired a service station at 220 North Walker in Oklahoma City, its second. Bob's empire was growing.[24]

Bob Kerr also had other reasons for personal satisfaction. As if being in the management of four companies and running a successful election for extension of the Oklahoma City field were not enough, he found additional outlets for his energy. His friend Governor Marland had earlier appointed him to a five-man committee to study law-enforcement problems and now placed him on the Governor's Advisory Parole Board. He was also elected to the Board of Directors of the Oklahoma City Chamber of Commerce and mentioned by Senator Thomas Gore as a probable candidate for Democratic national committeeman from Oklahoma. Finally, only one hour after he joined the Kansas-Oklahoma division of the Mid-Continent Oil & Gas Association, he was elected president, a position which he held for six terms.[25] Certainly, Kerr must have believed that progress toward all of his goals was on schedule.

[24] *Kermac News*, Vol. 1 (July, 1948), p. 3; Vol. 2 (June, 1949), p. 12; *Polk's Oklahoma City Directory*, 1936; and interviews with J. H. Kuhlman and Lucille Lindsay, April 29, 1971.

[25] *Daily Oklahoman*, October 19, 1935; *Oil and Gas Journal*, Vol. 33 (October 24, 1935), p. 24; Kerr scrapbooks, 1.

This Anderson-Kerr service station was built about 1935 at the corner of Second Street and North Walker in Oklahoma City. When this picture was taken in 1940 its name was Kerr-Lynn.

Chapter 5

Transition 1936

The year 1936 was significant to the American people as the one in which judgment was passed on the New Deal. Business and finance had many emotional and some legitimate grievances. Conservatives persuaded themselves that Roosevelt was destroying the historic American pattern of laissez-faire by placing the nation's fate in the hands of eggheads and self-perpetuating bureaucrats. Liberals were surprisingly vocal in their complaints that he had been too timid. In between, Father Charles Coughlin offered "Christ's deal," Francis Townsend espoused pensions for everyone over sixty years of age, and Huey Long proposed to make "Every Man A King" with his "Share the Wealth Plan."

But the upturn in the economy had come, and everyone was feeling better. The voters emphasized this by returning heavy Democratic majorities everywhere except in Maine and Vermont. From 1935 until the last quarter of 1937 conditions steadily improved, particularly in the oil industry. The New Deal's oil codes and especially the new Interstate Oil Compact had brought sounder and more constructive limitations on production at the wells, which resulted in a better price structure and financial return. Hot oil was less important in the over-all picture; and in Oklahoma, for example, oil averaged $1.04 per barrel during the year, despite a slight rise in total production to 206,555,000 barrels.

The demand for petroleum products had increased by 11 percent, however, because of a number of factors. The biggest was the growth in the use of fuel oil for diesel engines and heating. Oil heat for homes had won public acceptance, as illustrated by an all-time high in sales of oil burners for domestic heating. The future was already taking shape in the increased sales of trucks and cars, bringing about expansion in the many areas related to their use. Filling stations with all the related services and accessories were needed by more and more Americans, who used their cars to go across town and across the country. The chain of demand for this mobilized society was unending. The more affluent and impatient took to the skies: the era of the modern airliner had begun four years earlier, and in 1936 the "Model T of aircraft," the DC-3, was introduced, thus creating yet another market for oil products.

Another significant change was the consumption of electricity in homes, farms, industries, and all immobile places of work and habitation. Power companies, using petroleum products, expanded almost yearly, offering cheap kilowatts for their power-hungry customers. For example, Oklahoma Gas and Electric Company had reduced its rates every year since 1928. Air conditioning bid to become a partner with heating for year-round comfort, especially in the South and Southwest, although its greater cost would hold up this development for another decade or so. The world had suddenly come upon a wonderful new way to do things easier, cleaner, cheaper, and more comfortably. By 1936 it could afford this new way of life.

The year was likewise a busy one for Bob Kerr and his myriad enterprises. As president of a division of the Mid-Continent Oil and Gas Association he led a vigorous campaign against discriminatory taxation in the states of his district. The number of his speaking engagements was thus greatly increased.[1] Furthermore, the new year brought a renewal of demands to drill on virtually the entire area around the Oklahoma State Capitol. By March one hundred petitions for expansion had been filed, and a special election was called for March 24. Again Kerr was in the forefront of the drive for extension.

Although this vote did not generate the excitement of the previous one, heated accusations were hurled. One Oklahoma City councilman who supported the election was charged with conflict of interest because his son worked for Phillips. He admitted that the boy, a college student, had indeed been employed during the summer by Phillips and also by Anderson & Kerr Drilling, but said that he had received the jobs as acts of friendship: "If they [the opponents] are going to bring up that sort of stuff they're certainly dirty and unfair." The *Daily Oklahoman* ran a series of pictures, usually on the front page, featuring blighted homes and schools. The climax was a photograph of a young child who had been almost decapitated by a piece of drilling equipment that crashed through his bedroom window.

The motives of the proextension advocates were likewise questioned. The Home Owners Protective League, of which Bob Kerr was a director, was denounced as "selfish" and "greedy." Kerr was attacked in a radio address by a speaker who pointed out his connection with a drilling firm and then asked, "Can you guess why he favors extension?" But, as before, Kerr and his allies

[1] *Oil and Gas Journal*, Vol. 34, January 23, 1936, p. 12; January 30, p. 188; and February 6, p. 93.

won by a sizable majority. This was accomplished chiefly by claiming that Oklahoma City was the " 'White Spot' on the National Business Map Because of Oil Development."[2]

Once more Phillips Petroleum Company benefited. And once again A&K Petroleum Company's gains were less tangible. The number of contract-drilling opportunities was increased for Anderson & Kerr Drilling, but A&K Petroleum was in no position to compete with the "big boys" for primary production sites in the newly opened areas. Dean Terrill explained:

We did not get into that [area] until kind of the tail end and in a small way because at the time when the best part was being drilled up, we didn't have the money to get into that play—the other boys, Phillips, etc.—had pretty much preempted it. So we didn't end up with too many wells there.

The crumbs A&K did get were some plots passed over by other companies because they were considered too far down the flank to be commercial and other leases which were too much trouble to consolidate. But by gambling and by piecing small bits together A&K did manage six additional wells south of the state capitol and governor's mansion by 1940.[3]

Most of the activity of the two Kerr and Anderson firms was in Moore and Cooke counties in Texas. Gainesville, in Cooke County, was attractive because of its shallow production, which could be used to finance A&K's gas wells in Moore County. Then in May, Phillips increased the acreage, hence the number of wells to be drilled, in that West Texas county. Consequently, crews were pushed hard and paid well—six dollars a day for a roughneck (with no overtime or coffee breaks). By September some fifteen gas producers were completed.

Another problem besides money surfaced in Gainesville after five holes had been drilled. It was discovered that the lease on 103 of the most promising acres was under a legal cloud. The Bruhlmeyers had owned the property for thirty-three years, but an earlier deed in 1891 had reserved half of the "Minerelles, paint-rock, etc., found or to be found on said land" for the former owner, a paint-factory operator. With the discovery of oil these heirs appeared and claimed that the term "minerelles" had reserved *all* mineral rights, including oil.[4] The case eventually ended in the courts.

The Oklahoma ventures had their misfortunes also. One of Anderson & Kerr's truck drivers had a "mystery accident" in February. In March, A&K was sued for $80,000 by the widow of a field worker killed in an explosion, which she ascribed to negligence in failing to repair a leaking gas line. Equally disturbing were the results of two wells whose progress was closely watched by the oil fraternity. The first of these, Anderson & Kerr *et al.*,

[2] *Daily Oklahoman*, January 1, 4, and March 1, 13, 19–20, 22, 25, 1936. *Oklahoma News*, February 2 and March 23, 1936.

[3] Dean Terrill interviews, November 24, 1969, and April 27, 1970.

[4] Securities and Exchange Commission, "Form A-1, Registration Statement," p. 4; "Prospectus" of 1936 stock offering; Terrill interview, November 24, 1969. After two years of litigation the Texas Supreme Court awarded the heirs a half interest.

Teeter #1 in Roger Mills County, was abandoned at 6,500 feet. The other, Anderson & Kerr *et al.*, Davis #1 in Beaver County, was described by the *Oklahoma News* as "one of the most interesting of Oklahoma's aggregation of deep tests." This well was in partnership with Bob Kerr's friend William H. Atkinson, but it, too, was abandoned after reaching 6,794 feet.[5]

The first annual report issued by A&K Petroleum—which is reproduced below in entirety—covering the period July 1, 1935, to June 30, 1936, showed a good year, however. The company held eighteen developed leases in the Oklahoma City field, and, statewide, it claimed three more in Oklahoma County, two in Logan, and one each in Pottawatomie and Pontotoc counties. Additionally, Texas provided twenty-two in Moore County and one in Cooke County. Production had been 235,770 barrels of crude, worth $254,980, and 10,313,798 thousand cubic feet (mcf) of gas, which sold for $59,654. Total assets were placed at $1,474,420; current assets at $200,774; and current liabilities at $164,782.

Total assets were increased when two large wells in which A&K had interests were added in the Oklahoma field in late June and July. By September it had five producing wells on 230 acres at Gainesville and was negotiating to buy fifteen others which Anderson & Kerr had in the same area. Altogether A&K had all or part interest in seventy oil-and-gas producers, and in fourteen months had almost doubled its monthly income. The statement of income and expenses accompanying the detailed report of assets and liabilities gives a valuable insight into A&K operations during the fiscal year ending June 30, 1936.

The expanding activities created more and more financial pressures. Anderson & Kerr Drilling needed money to carry on its exploration and contract programs, while A&K Petroleum needed additional producing properties to increase its income and to make its stock more attractive to the public. In February, A&K's executive committee had authorized payment of $125,000 to Anderson & Kerr Drilling for its interest in some oil-and-gas leases in Wheeler County, Texas, and Pontotoc County, Oklahoma. In July other properties in those areas and in Oklahoma City were also bought from the same source, but this was just a shift of funds, not a real solution to the financial problem.

This demand for money set in motion a chain of events with far-reaching implications. Bob Kerr was convinced that a new offering of public stock was the only solution, although the earlier issue in 1935, which had been handled through Phinney, had been troublesome and not entirely satisfactory. Dean Terrill was asked for his help. Terrill had done the legal work on the previous offer, and he agreed to approach Straus Securities of Chicago about an underwriting agreement to sell 125,000 of A&K Petroleum's class A

---

[5] *Capitol Hill Daily Beacon*, February 29 and March 2, 1936, and *Oklahoma News*, March 2, 1936. Almost weekly reports were carried on these wells. For first and last reports on Davis #1 see *Oil and Gas Journal*, January 2 and March 12, 1936; *Oklahoma News*, January 16 and March 10, 1936; and *Daily Oklahoman*, March 10, 1936. For Teeter #1 see *Oil and Gas Journal*, January 2 and February 20, 1936; and *Daily Oklahoman*, February 16 and March 3, 1936.

ANNUAL REPORT

of

A & K PETROLEUM COMPANY

Fiscal Year Ended June 30, 1936

◆ ◆ ◆

OFFICERS AND DIRECTORS

Robert S. Kerr, Oklahoma City ....President, Treasurer and Director

Dean Terrill, Oklahoma City.......... ....Vice-President and Director

T. W. Fentem, Oklahoma City ...... Secretary, Asst. Treasurer and Director

T. M. Kerr, Oklahoma City...Director

Frank J. Loesch, Chicago ....Diretcor

W. Earle Phinney, Chicago ....Director

Executive Offices

First National Building, Oklahoma City, Oklahoma

A & K PETROLEUM COMPANY

(A DELAWARE CORPORATION)

Statement of Income, Expenses and Surplus

JULY 1, 1935 to JUNE 30, 1936

GROSS OPERATING INCOME

Crude Oil Production and Gas Sales	$315,551.02
Steam and Compressor Sales	1,565.50
Gross Operating Income	$317,116.52
Less: Gross Production and Excise Taxes	14,366.64
Operating Income	$302,749.88

COST OF PRODUCTION—Before Depletion and Depreciation:

Production and Maintenance Expense	$ 78,262.75
Total Cost of Production	$ 78,262.75

GROSS PROFIT ON LEASE OPERATIONS: — $224,487.13

EXPENSES:

General and Administrative	$ 6,348.97
Office and Supervision Charge by Affiliate $250.00 per month	3,000.00
Taxes—Exclusive of Income Taxes	3,733.86
Legal Expense	1,266.50
Depreciation Sustained—See Note (1) below	38,989.57
Development Expense—See Note (1) below	1,893.89
Lease Rentals Paid	1,973.46
Amortization of Undeveloped Leases	4,173.55
Miscellaneous	547.21
Leases Cancelled and Expired	2,018.71
Total Expenses	$ 63,945.72

NET OPERATING INCOME—Before Depletion — $160,541.41

OTHER INCOME:

Bottom Hole Contributions	$ 7,200.00
Miscellaneous	1,428.34
Profit from Sale of Properties	20,473.65
Total Other Income	$ 29,101.99

GROSS INCOME — $189.643.40

OTHER DEDUCTIONS:

Interest Paid	$ 3,480.21
Organization and Securities Act Expense—See Note (2) below	7,147.31
Profit from Abandonment of Properties	*1,429.44
Dry Hole Contributions	325.00
Total Other Deductions	$ 9,523.08

INCOME—Before Depletion and Income Taxes — $180,120.32

* Denotes a red figure

Provision for Federal Income Taxes	$ 5,982.72
Provisions for Oklahoma State Income Taxes	3,082.10
Total Provision for Income Taxes	$ 9,064.82
Less: Restoration of Excess Prior Years Accruals	4,175.61
Net Provision for Income Taxes	$ 4,889.21
INCOME—Before Depletion. Available for distribution to "A" and "B" Stockholders under the Delaware law governing wasting assets	$175,231.11
DEPLETION SUSTAINED—Computed on a production unit method basis to return investment including present par value of capital stock. See Note (1) below	104,635.37
NET PROFIT CARRIED TO SURPLUS	$ 70,595.74
BALANCE OF SURPLUS—BEGINNING	167,155.55
Total	$237,751.29
DIVIDENDS DECLARED ON CLASS "A" COMMON	19,479.52
BALANCE OF SURPLUS - - END	$218,271.77

NOTE (1): Depletion and depreciation on the Oklahoma City properties acquired prior to June 30, 1935, have been computed for the current year on the basis of oil reserves established by Josef Faust, petroleum engineer, as of June 30, 1935, with adjustments to reflect the abandonment of producing horizons or well as a whole where necessary. This is in accordance with a letter addressed to the Company by Josef Faust and dated August 14, 1936. Depletion and depreciation on gas properties have been computed on the basis of gas reserves established by Josef Faust. Oil reserves on properties acquired during the year were established by Josef Faust as of the date of production or of acquisition.

The past policy of the Company in charging off drilling and development costs in the year incurred was changed in the current year. All development costs for the current year have been capitalized and are being recovered by charges against income on the production unit basis method.

In computing depreciation on lease equipment for the current year, an estimated salvage value of 30% was used in determining the recoverable cost of equipment on oil producing leases instead of 15% as heretofore. Estimated salvage value of 15% was used in determining the recoverable cost of equipment on gas producing properties.

NOTE (2): Commissions on stock sales included in Deferred Reorganization and Financial Expense are being amortized over a period of five years from the date of sale of the stock. Other charges therein are being amortized over a period of five years from the beginning of the current year.

A & K PETROLEUM COMPANY

(A DELAWARE CORPORATION)

Balance Sheet, June 30, 1936
ASSETS

CURRENT ASSETS:

Cash in Banks			$ 145,270.71
Accounts Receivable—Oil and Gas Sales and due from outside interest in jointly owned leases—all of which, excepting $1,789.01 were collected in July and August, 1936			35,752.20
Inventories:			
Crude Oil on Leases, valued at average sales prices of $1.126 per barrel		$ 5,474.50	
Materials and Supplies:			
Used Equipment valued at market adjusted for condition which is lower than cost	$ 653.75		
New Equipment valued at cost	13,622.28	14,276.01	19,750.53
Total Current Assets, See Note (2) below			$ 200,773.44

CONTINGENT ASSETS:

This amount is to be received by the Company from the net proceeds of the sale of oil and gas from an undivided 1/4 interest in the Volk Lease which was sold by it as at April 1, 1935. The interest from which this amount is to be received is retained by the Company until the contingent consideration, less gross production and excise taxes, has been received in full	34,589.24	
This amount is to be received by the Company out of 1/32 of the 7/8ths of the oil and/or gas and casinghead gas produced and sold from lands situated in Wheeler County, Texas. Acquired from affiliate as at April 1, 1936 at cost of $15,000.00. (See Unrecovered Cost of Oil Payment below)	$35,805.07	

LEASEHOLDS, ROYALTIES AND EQUIPMENT, at values directed to be fixed by the Board of Directors and Stockholders as at the dates acquired from affiliated companies, plus additions since at cost and less retirements and provisions for depletion, depreciation and amortization. Amounts shown do not purport to represent realizable or replacement values. See Note (1) below.

	Gross	Reserves for Depletion Depreciation and Amortization	Net
Developed Leaseholds and Producing Royalties	$ 944,799.03	215,257.84	729,541.19
Undeveloped Leaseholds and Royalties	37,698.37	5,444.17	32,254.20
Equipment	466,653.06	124,304.88	342,348.18
	$1,449,150.46	$345,006.89	$1,104,143.57

Unrecovered Cost of Oil Payment (See Contingent Assets above)		14,582.50	
Wells in Progress		51,262.67	
Salvage to be recovered from Bailey and Harrison Smith Leases—Estimated		6,877.25	1,176,865.99

DEFERRED CHARGES:

Prepaid Taxes		$ 1,169.63	
Prepaid Insurance		1,731.08	
Deferred Reorganization and Financial Expense. See Note (3) below	$101,028.02		
LESS—Reserve for Amortization	7,147.31	93,880.71	96,781.42
TOTAL ASSETS			**$1,474,420.85**

NOTE (1): Part of the leaseholds and equipment were originally acquired from affiliated companies. Values as at dates of acquisition were assigned by the Board of Directors and stockholders, which included directors of these affiliates. The properties acquired at date of organization are valued as at that date at approximately the cost in liabilities assumed and the present par value ($300,000.00) of capital stock issued therefor. The properties acquired subsequent to date of organization are valued at cost, represented by liabilities assured or cash paid. The profit to affiliates derived from the sale to this company of those properties included in the above balance sheet and including the present par value of the capital stock issued therefor was $446,568.40.

The Company originally had authorized 400,000 shares of $5 par value of which 125,000 shares were Class A Common Stock and 275,000 shares were Class B Common Stock. The authorized capital stock was increased, on April 2, 1935, to 800,000 shares of $5 par value each. 250,000 thereof being Class A Common Stock and 550,000 thereof being Class B Common Stock. 275,000 shares of Class "B" Common stock and 5,000 shares of Class "A" Common stock, each class then having a par value of $5.00 per share, were issued originally to An-Ker, Incorporated, an affiliate, in exchange for certain leaseholds and equipment, certain liabilities of the affiliate being assumed in connection with such acquisitions. On May 31, 1935, the par value of the Class "B" Common stock was reduced to $1.00 per share and at that time also the stockholders directed that the amount of $1,100,000.00 resulting from the aforementioned reduction of capital be transferred to surplus (understood to be appreciation surplus) and that the depletion on that portion of the properties which might be considered to be represented by the $1,100,000.00 so transferred be charged to such surplus and not through income. Subsequently the property account was actually reduced as at December 1, 1932 by this $1,100,000.00.

Depletion and depreciation on the Oklahoma City properties acquired prior to June 30, 1935, have been computed

LIABILITIES

CURRENT LIABILITIES:

Accounts Payable to Joint Lease Operators, Suppliers and other			$ 42,771.61
Due to Affiliated Companies—Current			79,002.15
Dividends Declared Payable to Stockholders of Record June 20, 1936		$ 10,937.50	
Less: Transferred to Affiliated Companies' Current Account		271.21	10,666.29
Accrued Taxes Payable:			
Oklahoma State Income Tax at June 30, 1934 —not assessed	$ 9,092.43		
Oklahoma State Income Tax at June 30, 1935 —not assessed	8,591.86	$ 17,684.29	
Accrued Interest on above to June 30, 1936		1,385.54	19,069.83
Reserved for Taxes Accruing June 30, 1936:			
Federal Income Tax		$ 5,982.72	
Oklahoma State Income Tax		3,082.10	
Federal Capital Stock Tax		1,500.00	
Ad Valorem, Gross Production and Excise Taxes		2,708.01	13,272.83

Total Current Liabilities .... $ 164,782.71

CONTRACTUAL OBLIGATIONS:

Original advance by Phillips Petroleum Company in amount of $220,000.00 payable from certain portions of the proceeds from the sale of oil and gas as, if and when produced from the twenty-two wells drilled in Moore County, Texas, in accordance with the terms of contracts dated July 10, August 2, December 20, 1935 and May 15, 1936. Ten of the wells are obligated to the payment of a balance of .... $ 79,238.07
seven are obligated to the payment of a balance of 69,235.96
four are obligated to the payment of a balance of 35,187.43
and one is obligated to the payment of a balance of ... 7,704.91   191,366.37

CONTINGENT LIABILITIES:

Undivided Fractional interests in certain leaseholds purchased are reserved by certain lessors or assignors and are payable only out of oil produced; these interests will be acquired by the Company as payments are completed on each property .... $ 45,242.65

CAPITAL AND SURPLUS:

Capital Stock:

Class "A" Common-Par Value $5.00 per share, callable at $5.50 per share. Convertible into Class "B" Common share for share on any call or dividend date at option of holder. Cumulative dividends payable quarterly at 35c per share per annum. Participating equally thereafter with Class "B" Common after "B" has received dividends equal to the total current dividends paid to Class "A". Preferred in liquidation, dissolution or winding up, or the sale of assets, up to $5.00 per share plus accumulated unpaid dividends.

Authorized 250,000 shares		
Issued 5000 shares to affiliate for property	$ 25,000.00	
Issued 100 shares formerly in treasurer to affiliate for cash	500.00	
Issued 119,900 shares to the public	599,500.00	$625,000.00

Class "B" Common-Par Value $1.00 per share.

Authorized 550,000 shares, of which 125,000 shares are reserved for conversion of "A" stock		
Issued 275,000 shares, all to affiliate for property		275,000.00

Total Capital Stock Issued $900,000.00

Surplus (Exhibit B) 218,271.77   1,118,271.77

TOTAL LIABILITIES $1,474,420.85

for the current year on the basis of oil reserves established by Josef Faust as of June 30, 1935, with adjustments to reflect the abandonment of producing horizons or wells as a whole where necessary. This is in accordance with a letter addressed to the Company by Josef Faust and dated August 14, 1936. Depletion and depreciation on gas properties have been computed on the basis of gas reserves established by Josef Faust. Oil reserves on properties acquired during the year were established by Josef Faust as of the date of production or of acquisition.

The past policy of the Company in charging off drilling and development costs in the year incurred was changed in the current year. All development costs for the current year have been capitalized and are being recovered by charges against income on the production unit basis method.

In computing depreciation on lease equipment for the current year, an estimated salvage value of 30% was used in determining the recoverable cost of equipment on oil producing leases instead of 15% as heretofore. Estimated salvage value of 15% was used in determining the recoverable cost of equipment on gas producing properties.

NOTE (2): Under the terms of the amended certificate of incorporation the Company is required to set aside at the end of each fiscal year an amount equal to 20% of the net profits for the fiscal year, as a sinking fund to be used for the purchase on tender or in the open market of shares of its Class "A" Common stock at a price not to exceed $5.50 per share. For the year ended June 30, 1936, this amount approximates $14.119.15. At the expiration of ninety days from the date of creation of said fund the Company may by resolution of the Board of Directors return any unexpended balance remaining in the fund to the general funds of the Company.

NOTE (3): Commissions on stock sales included in Deferred Reorganization and Financial Expense are being amortized over a period of five years from the date of sale of the stock. Other charges therein are being amortized over a period of five years from the beginning of the current year.

stock. The young lawyer succeeded in getting Straus to handle the sale, albeit under rather stringent conditions. Among these was the decision that Phinney had to go, albeit as gracefully as possible. In turn, thirty-one-year-old Dean Terrill, the witty, urbane, Harvard-trained corporation lawyer, was brought into A&K Petroleum to fill a much-needed position of legal counsel.[6]

None of this suited Jim Anderson. At the very time the partnership was on the verge of "going big time," Jim decided he wanted out. The step which might well move their companies further toward creation of a large, integrated one would also reduce the partners' personal control, as the number of outside stockholders increased. All along Anderson had asserted that his temperament was different from Bob's and that a big operation was not his goal. In truth his feelings were more involved. Most of the men who had worked for the pair from the beginning had their own ideas about why Jim wanted to leave. Pete Walton, Foley Collins, and Harold Freeman felt that the trouble began when Travis Kerr was brought in and given a 5 percent interest by each partner: "He couldn't buck all the Kerrs" or the "Kerrs could outvote him" were some of the analyses. This had probably happened with the decision to sell more stock. But Walton added another incisive observation, perhaps the most accurate: "He couldn't stand to go in debt every time they had to meet a payroll."[7]

Bob Kerr once indicated to Dean McGee that Anderson lost interest in the drilling business "because you had to beg for it." Aubrey Kerr, on the other hand, felt that their sister had kept Anderson in the company: "Bob and Jim never would have remained together if it hadn't been for Mildred." The marriage was soon to end in divorce, an event perhaps foreshadowed by his break with the business partnerships. The weakening of the personal tie strengthened Jim's feeling that the Kerrs were profiting inequitably from his knowledge and labor. He repeatedly claimed he was unable to "cotton" to anyone, even if it meant money in his pocket.[8]

At the time of the dissolution of the partnership other factors were present. Bob Kerr always had becoming a millionaire as one of his personal goals, Jim on the other hand, always said he was going to quit when he had enough money. As Mildred recalled:

Bob was more ambitious than James L. James L. could drill deeper oil wells; he knew what he was doing when he was drilling oil wells. But when the Company was about to have a $800,000 debt, James L. being older and more conservative talked with Bob and said, "Bob I don't want to be a millionaire. If you want to, lets you take

---

[6] Letter from Dean Terrill to Malvina Stephenson, June 19, 1963. In June an additional "Chicago flavor" had been added to A&K when Frank J. Loesch, a distinguished Chicago lawyer and fourth-largest stockholder with 1,500 shares, had been elected to the board of directors to replace C. H. Rives, who had died. Terrill was later called "Judge" to distinguish him from Dean McGee because Bob Kerr said two "Deans" were too confusing.

[7] Interviews with Harold Freeman, April 17, 1971; Foley D. Collins, June 11, 1971; and Quinton C. Walton, April 16, 1971.

[8] Interviews with Dean A. McGee, September 4, 1971; Aubrey Kerr, May 24, 1971; and Travis Kerr, December 16, 1969. It is interesting that the Andersons were divorced in 1938.

A 1937 picture looking north from the roof of the Oklahoma State Capitol, showing Anderson & Kerr #1 Park-o-tel. *Courtesy Western History Collections, University of Oklahoma.*

one part and I'll take one part. I'm older than you; I've gone through all these years and I'm a more nervous temperament, anyway, and I'm not as ambitious as you are."

Jim's son believed that it was his father's temperament that caused the break: He was "really kind of a loner." Boards of directors and stockholders mystified Anderson. Corporations as such and corporate management were distasteful to him and scared him. As James K. put it, "He was not one, at all, to appear before a board and to try to explain something." Jim apparently felt that Bob was moving too fast and getting in over his head. The decision to go even deeper into debt to exploit the Gainesville field was the last straw.[9]

On April 15, 1936, Jim Anderson entered an agreement with Anderson & Kerr Drilling Company to sell his 45 percent interest in An-Ker, Incorporated. The split was amicable on both sides; perhaps it was even a relief to separate finally the personal relation from the professional. Anderson never complained that the division was unfair, and Bob would later write to Jim

[9] Interviews with Mildred Kerr Anderson, January 23, 1970; and James K. Anderson, July 28, 1971.

that of the list of people to whom he was most indebted, "there is no one on it . . . more cherished in my affection, nor to whom I feel a deeper debt of gratitude than you."

The settlement consisted of "interests in certain properties, together with cash in the total amount of $400,000," which was to be paid in eight installments. The property to be divided consisted of about forty-two leases, ranging in size from 12 to 152 acres, and totaled aproximately 2,045 acres in the Gainesville field. Anderson's share was 45/100 in all but 152 acres, where his interest was one-half. His resignation was effective August 22, the same day that the contract with Straus Securities was signed. To complete the break, his position in the drilling company was filled by Travis Kerr. An-Ker's share of the Gainesville property was later assessed at $425,000, which would indicate that Anderson's part was worth $348,000. Apparently the initial cash payment of $60,000 was paid by Anderson & Kerr Drilling at the time for on June 30 the balance sheet for that company showed total assets of $1,474,420.85 and a debt to Anderson of $340,000.00.[10] The fact that Anderson & Kerr Drilling was the agency used to purchase Anderson's An-Ker stock created the anomaly of a subsidiary owning a major block of the shares in its parent company.

Anderson's departure also served to give Bob Kerr the controlling interest in the various companies which bore his name. This was possible because of the dominant role played by the holding company, An-Ker, Incorporated. As a result of Anderson's leaving and probably an employment agreement with Terrill, its shares were distributed in September, 1936, as follows:

	Percent
Robert S. Kerr	45%
Anderson & Kerr Drilling Company	37
Travis M. Kerr	10
T. W. Fentem	5
Dean Terrill	3

An-Ker owned all of the stock of its two subsidiaries, Anderson & Kerr Drilling Company and Anderson-Kerr, Incorporated. It also held 68 percent of both the A and the B stock of A&K Petroleum Company. The rest of the A&K shares were held by Anderson & Kerr Drilling and a few private individuals.

On September 3 at a special meeting of the board of directors of A&K, Bob Kerr announced two resignations: Stanley B. Catlett from the board and James L. Anderson as director, vice-president, secretary, and member of

[10] Securities and Exchange Commission, "Form A-1, Registration Statement," Exhibit I; Schedule A-7, p. 21. Of the 42 leases involved, only 10 (476 acres) were not subject to oil payments. Most of the oil payments were $75 an acre from the first 1/8th of 7/8ths of the oil and gas. Fourteen of the 42 leases were taken out in the name of Mildred Anderson, and the rest in the name of Anderson & Kerr Drilling Company.

the executive committee. The board accepted the resignations. Only the Anderson name was left in the corporate titles to mark his passing. The board then moved to other business. First, Dean Terrill was elected a director and vice-president, and T. W. Fentem was made secretary of the company and a member of the executive committee. But the major concern was ratification of recommendations made in late August by the executive committee to comply with SEC regulations and with the conditions set down by Straus that A&K procedures be brought more into line with general corporate practices.

This would mean that A&K would act in the future more like a public corporation and less informally than had previously been the case. Membership of the board was limited to seven directors, one to be designated by Straus. Five regularly scheduled meetings were to be held annually. The board's officers would have stated salaries: R. S. Kerr, $15,000; Dean Terrill, $7,500; and T. W. Fentem, $4,500. A&K also was to carry a $500,000 life-insurance policy on Bob Kerr, payable to the company, and pay a monthly fee of $250 to Anderson & Kerr Drilling for clerical and administrative services.

The board further approved payment to the drilling company of $300,000, plus 125,000 shares of class B stock for the Gainesville property. It then voted to recommend to the stockholders that A&K's stock be increased from 800,000 to 1,050,000: 250,000 of class A at $5 par and 800,000 of class B at $1 par. The August 22 contract between A&K and Straus Securities was then approved for sale of 125,000 shares of class A stock.

Straus drove a hard bargain, but one which would eventually prove beneficial to A&K. The oil company first had to pay for an investigation of its financial condition and an evaluation of the Gainesville properties. It would also have to prepare a registration statement under the Securities Act of 1933 and meet the blue-sky laws in Illinois, Indiana, Minnesota, Kentucky, Pennsylvania, New York, Ohio, and Michigan. In addition, class A stock of A&K Petroleum would be given preference and in case of liquidation redeemed at $7 a share, plus unpaid dividends. In return Straus Securities would have until September 18 to decide whether to underwrite by purchase 100,000 shares of class A at $5.55, with an option to buy 25,000 more. This initially would be offered to the public for not more than $6.50 a share. Furthermore, Straus would have a five-year option for an additional 25,000, plus up to 20,000 shares of class B at $7.

Two other conditions had to be met if the underwriting were accepted by Straus. First, Anderson & Kerr Drilling had to pay Phinney $12,500 and 2,500 shares of A&K class B to settle his claims, and Straus, in turn, would receive 22,000 shares of class B for services to the drilling company. Finally, Anderson & Kerr Drilling had to present an affidavit that its Gainesville properties had an evaluation on August 1, 1936, of not less than $425,000.

On September 17, Straus wired acceptance of the underwriting agreement. Four days later a supplemental contract gave him other important concessions. Anderson & Kerr Drilling agreed not to sell any of its property without first offering it to A&K; A&K would be offered half interest in any new property acquired by the drilling company after that date; and, finally,

Anderson & Kerr had to sell, on "mutually agreed" terms, all its assets (except capital stock of An-Ker, Inc.) at any time upon the request of A&K. [11]

The report of two geologists, W. V. Howard, of the University of Illinois, and C. H. Alexander, former general manager for Phillips Petroleum, estimated that A&K's properties exceeded $4 million in value and that the worth of the Gainesville property was between $800,000 and $1 million. By October 19, A&K had sold 100,000 shares of class A to Straus for $555,000 and had an additional 25,000 shares on the market. If all found purchasers, a total of $693,750 would be realized. The company proposed to spend $300,000 for the Gainesville acquisitions, plus $150,000 for property in Wheeler County, and $100,000 in Moore County, Texas. It was at this time that Bob Kerr proudly pasted in his scrapbook newspaper clippings announcing the sale of A&K stock which had appeared in the *Chicago Herald and Examiner* and the *Chicago American* on October 20 and 21, 1936. [12]

Needless to say, A&K moved rapidly to fulfill its obligations to Straus Securities. On October 30, J. D. Blosser and F. W. Straus were elected to the board, and the forms for new stock certificates for classes A and B were approved. In December the sinking fund, which had been established earlier for repurchase of class A stock was abolished, and its accumulation was returned to the general fund. It was agreed that henceforth directors would be paid twenty five dollars and expenses for each meeting. Straus replaced Fentem on the executive committee. A general atmosphere of success permeated the meeting, apparent when the directors voted the regular quarterly dividend of 8.75¢ for class A stock and an extra dividend of 5¢ for both A and B. In the glow of this affluence, management was authorized to seek a listing for class A common on the Chicago Stock Exchange.

The most important indication of the directors' expectations for the future was the long discussion regarding additional personnel. Specifically, they were interested in two unnamed men in the petroleum business, a geologist and an executive "then with a leading oil company." Bob Kerr announced that he and his associates were "willing to give up a substantial part of their holdings in the corporation in order to obtain for it the services and experience of these men." The board approved the opening of negotiations.

[11] S-1 Statement, Number 107, March 31, 1948, p. 10; *Annual Report of A&K Petroleum Company for Fiscal Year Ending June 30, 1936*; Oklahoma State Archives, Secretary of State, "Kerr-McGee *vs*. John Rogers," folder 3; Securities Exchange Commission, "Form A-1, Registration Statement"; Securities Exchange Commission, "Reconciliation and Tie"; A&K Petroleum Company, "Prospectus," October 15, 1936; "Supplemental Information *re* A&K Petroleum Company Class A Common Stock."

[12] Securities and Exchange Commission, "Form A-1 . . . ," exhibits E and H; "Supplemental Information . . . ," pp. 2–3; Kerr scrapbooks, 1.

Chapter 6

Kerr and Lynn
1937

The secret of the identity of the two executives was soon revealed. On January 15, 1937, the stockholders elected Robert H. Lynn as a director along with Robert S. Kerr, J. D. Blosser, F. W. Straus, T. M. Kerr, T. W. Fentem, and Dean Terrill. The following day it was announced that Lynn, vice-president in charge of land development at Phillips Petroleum, and Dean A. McGee, head of Phillips's geological department, had resigned and joined A&K Petroleum. A later acquisition was Herbert Goodpaster, an expert in production, who would provide the experience needed in that area.

The directors then elected Bob Kerr president; Lynn, executive vice-president; Terrill, vice-president and assistant secretary; and Fentem, secretary and treasurer. The new executive committee became R. S. Kerr, Straus, and Lynn. Lynn's salary was $24,000 a year although Kerr's was still $15,000; and McGee as chief geologist received $700 a month. Part of the deal in persuading the two men to move to A&K was stock in An-Ker, Inc., which made them part owners in the company: 18.90 shares for Lynn and 12.60 for McGee.

Accounts of this managerial coup vary. Rex Hawks, Kerr's close friend and associate, gave the most-repeated version: Kerr "was looking for a geologist, land-man, and production man and went to Bartlesville and told Mr. Lynn he didn't know what his salary was, but would double it, and the same to McGee, and the same to Goodpaster." Aubrey Kerr's story was that, when Jim Anderson left, Bob went to Kenneth S. ("Boots") Adams of Phillips and said that he needed a partner, and Adams suggested Lynn. Adams also reported that he recommended the three men. On the other hand, the man who should know, Dean McGee, stated that Kerr, who had known Lynn from the days of the Oklahoma City extension fights, had approached Lynn six or eight months earlier in 1936 when he knew that Anderson wanted to sell out, "and I think this is the reason that Bob Kerr made the proposals he did to the two of us to come down here, because Jim Anderson wanted to quit."[1]

Forty-year-old Bob Lynn had joined Phillips as a geologist in 1925. By 1932 he was in charge of that company's land activities in the Texas Panhandle, and the following year had become a vice-president in charge of the Land and Geological Development Department. In this capacity he had worked closely with Bob Kerr in getting the Oklahoma City zoning changed, as well as in various leases involving the two companies. It was Lynn who had worked out the deal between A&K and Phillips for the gas wells in Moore County, Texas.[2]

As the new executive officer of A&K, Lynn was viewed with mixed emotions by the other employees. Although Kerr believed that he "was the greatest thing that ever came down the pike," Dean Terrill thought that Bob Kerr's usual good judgment of men had failed in regard to Lynn. From the first Lynn was most unwelcome to Travis Kerr, Whit Fentem, and Terrill. "It was not long before all three of us heartily detested him. And we felt that he was not the man for the job from the viewpoint of the welfare of the company." Terrill, obviously no friend of Lynn's, said that he "fancied that he could direct everything, and tried to and, of course, made pretty much a failure of everything." Furthermore, he "was just a conniver and he was a little man, really, not only short but he was little in nature and character and extremely self-centered and selfish and not too far-sighted and pretty egotistical."

George Cobb, however, said that the most important decision Kerr ever made was to persuade Bob Lynn and Dean McGee to join the company, but he may have been thinking primarily of McGee. Otis Danielson, who worked under him as a roughneck, found the cigar-smoking Lynn a "likable person" and "all business," but Pete Walton believed that the crews did not like him "because he was for the company and wasn't for the working man."[3]

Dean A. McGee, on the other hand, was initially viewed by Kerr as the second man, or "sleeper," in the deal. Even so, the thirty-three-year-old McGee had impressive credentials. Born in Humboldt, Kansas, he grew up to the smell and the rhythm of the oil field. His father did various kinds of work in the industry and had even tried his hand at wildcatting, until finally

[1] Interviews with Rex Hawks, May 24, 1972, and Aubrey Kerr, April 28, 1971. Interview by Bob Leder, KTUL-TV, Tulsa, of Dean A. McGee, September 19, 1973. Transcript in Public Relations Department.

[2] Interview with Dean A. McGee, March 3, 1973; Public Relations file, "S-1 Biography, D. A. McGee"; *Oil and Gas Journal*, October 13, 1932, p. 80; January 18, 1934, p. 64; Lynn obituary, *Oklahoma City Times*, May 12, 1967.

[3] Dean Terrill to Malvina Stephenson, June 26, 1963; interviews with Dean Terrill, November 29, 1969; Quinton C. Walton, April 16, 1971; George Cobb, January 21, 1971, and December 7, 1972; Guy Swain, May 27, 1971; and G. Otis Danielson, June 1, 1971.

"he drilled one too many and went broke." Even before finishing high school McGee was convinced that he wanted to be a geologist. At the University of Kansas he concentrated on the closest major then available, mining engineering. A classmate remembered that

Dean never seemed to be a college boy. . . . he was always a college man. He was quiet about it, but he knew what he wanted and he worked for it. Dean never seemed to want leadership; he was just the sort you naturally turned to if you wanted to be sure the job got done because he followed through with things.

One of his professors, Raymond C. Moore, credited him with talent in two areas: he was able to evaluate and interpret vast amounts of data correctly, and he always liked to draw his own conclusions and "stand on his own two feet." Moore said: "He was an excellent student, not the bookworm type, but still not one I would have picked out to become a business giant. Mostly this was because he never seemed as though he would have cared about becoming important."[4]

After he graduated in 1926, Dean McGee remained at the university for a year of graduate work before joining Phillips Petroleum. As a young geologist, when such were rare in the drilling camps, he was quickly indoctrinated into the practical side of his profession. His first contact with a major discovery came in the Seminole field in 1928. J. C. Finley, who later became a vice-president of Kerr-McGee, went to work for Phillips in 1929 under the supervision of McGee. He recalled that even then the youthful McGee was a tireless worker who put in more than eight hours a day, seven days a week. Finley was also impressed by the fact that McGee's reading tastes were wide and varied, but that he devoted very little time to social life, "although there were occasions when he took a few minutes off for social activities."

McGee's first big break in the oil business came in connection with the Oklahoma City discovery. ITIO's well opened the field in December, 1928, and in 1930, Phillips sent McGee to study the area. The first wells were from the Arbuckle line, and while they were good, they were also short-lived. McGee convinced Phillips that ITIO had its wells on the top of the structure; the real production would be found in the Wilcox sand. He concluded that this was on the west flank and that it was here Phillips should take leases and drill. As C. O. Stark, a vice-president of Phillips, later said, "He had to be correct in his findings because this was a mighty big play and a lot of money and a lot of hopes were riding on it."

McGee was right. He proved beyond doubt that he could find oil, and in establishing his reputation as a geologist, he also made Phillips one of the major oil producers in Oklahoma City. In October, 1932, he and W. W. Clawson, Jr., wrote the classic description of the field in the American Association of Petroleum Geologists' *Bulletin*. By 1935, at the age of thirty-one, he was Phillips's chief geologist. It is no wonder, therefore, that Boots

[4] Typescript of "The Strata of Dean Anderson McGee," by Nora Owens, ca. 1962, in Public Relations file, "S-1 Biography of D. A. McGee."

Adams later recalled Frank Phillips was "pretty provoked with me for letting our chief geologist go to a competitor."[5]

Dean McGee himself explained how this change was effected. It was Robert Lynn, not Bob Kerr, who did the recruiting and subsequently talked him into coming to Oklahoma City. In fact, McGee met Kerr only a week or two before joining A&K and only after he had resigned at Phillips. Bob Kerr did not talk to Adams about McGee but did discuss him with Lynn. McGee himself was not a party to the conversations. Only after the arrangements had been worked out with Lynn concerning Lynn and McGee did Kerr consult Adams. By that time it was an accomplished fact that A&K had enticed away two of Phillips's top men. Dean McGee also added that his reason for accepting A&K's offer was the chance to acquire an interest in the company, thus enabling him to build an estate with means other than a salary.[6]

Geologists were highly suspect among working crews in the 1930's, but McGee quickly made himself acceptable. D. C. Lindley recalled his even temper and that he "was very comfortable to work around." E. H. ("Jeep") Harvey first met McGee at a company well in Oklahoma. It was Jeep's job to take core samples and then carry them to the geologist, who would tell the crew what to do. One night he was catching samples every five feet, which he then took to McGee, who was sleeping in his car. Harvey said, "I would take it out there and he would wake up, look at the sample, smell of it, and say, 'Drill five more feet!' " Then McGee would go back to sleep.

The less significant of the three new arrivals was Herbert Goodpaster. Although he remained with A&K for only a short time, now that the company hoped to make its mark as a producer, an experienced person in that field was a necessity. Goodpaster was a small freckled-faced man who weighed about 120 pounds. He was "friendly in every way" and was regarded as a good fellow to work for. Some old-timers recalled that "he'd get drunker than anybody."

Lynn, McGee, and Goodpaster, thus, supplied key requirements, benefiting all the various Kerr companies. At the same January board meeting in which the new officers were introduced, the directors authorized management to proceed with four wells in Oklahoma City, to lease additional acreage in Moore and Hutchinson counties in Texas, and to participate with Anderson & Kerr Drilling in two Moffat County, Colorado, ventures. They also approved the action of their officers in taking over all producing properties formerly operated by Anderson & Kerr and to pay that company $1,250 a month for office space and clerical help. Furthermore, A&K should contract with Anderson & Kerr to drill additional wells near Gainesville.

In February the board sold a half interest in the four Oklahoma City wells for approximately the cost of drilling. This money was then to be used for

[5] *Ibid.* Interviews with J. C. Finley, March 3, 1971; Dean A. McGee, September 4, 1971; and George Cobb, January 21, 1971.

[6] Interviews with Dean A. McGee, September 4, 1971, and March 3, 1973.

additional oil-and-gas leases in Hutchinson County, Texas. But more important than these transactions was the motion by Bob Kerr to change the articles of incorporation to retitle A&K Petroleum Company, the Kerlyn Oil Company. His logic was that Anderson was out and Lynn was in and the name should reflect the change. This was approved at a special stockholders' meeting called for April 12, 1937. Since An-Ker voted 373,100 shares of B stock and 2,600 shares of A stock in A&K, approval was a mere formality.

At the May meeting of the board another Bob Kerr proposal affected McGee. He was named vice-president of geology and production, but with no increase in pay over his salary as chief geologist. After this was approved, Lynn announced another step toward Kerr's dream of an integrated company: Kerlyn had purchased a quarter interest in Heiland Research Corporation of Colorado, a specialist in seismographic work, for $25,000.[7]

During all of these title and personnel changes over the months following Lynn and McGee's appointments, the need for internal and structural modifications became more and more obvious. Hardly had Dean Terrill met the dozen people in the jointly shared home office when he wrote two memorandums to the officers and directors of A&K Petroleum. One was "Relative to the Organization and Administration of the 'Legal Affairs,' " and the other, "Pertaining to the Business of our Several Corporations." In the first memorandum he stated that "to date there has been no orderly procedure in respect to the 'legal' end of our affairs." He could not handle every aspect of the law, he was hampered by the lack of a law library, and he currently was spending "a good portion" of his time on public relations. He stressed the need to centralize authority on legal matters, and proposed a study of other companies to see how their legal departments were organized.

Terrill's second memorandum dealt with the need to clarify the overlapping nature of the several corporations, especially in regard to An-Ker, Incorporated. Reports had to be made to the Securities and Exchange Commission and to the Chicago Stock Exchange in connection with the listing of A&K common stock. He would have to report the actual holdings of the Kerrs, Fentem, and Terrill and to "state further the facts in respect to the contracts of T.W.F., D.E.T., and R.H.L. (and D.M. if such be the case), in respect to further acquisitions from Anderson & Kerr Drilling Company of An-Ker, Incorporated, stock."[8] In the meantime the name A&K had been changed, and the names of Grayce Kerr, Bob's wife, and Geraldine Kerr, Travis's wife, had been added to the list of shareholders in An-Ker. Altogether it was a confused and intricate ownership structure.

The change in the name of the producing arm, from A&K Petroleum to Kerlyn Oil Company, accentuated the incongruity of the corporate struc-

---

[7] The new name was registered April 29, 1937. See Oklahoma Secretary of State, "Corporation File"; Oklahoma State Archives, Secretary of State, "Kerr-McGee *vs*. John Rogers," folder 3.

[8] Dean Terrill to Officers and Directors of A&K Petroleum Company, undated. Dean Terrell to Officers and Directors of A&K Petroleum Company, "Ownership of Stock of the Corporation and Report in that Connection to Securities & Exchange Commission and the Chicago Stock Exchange," March 4, 1937.

ture. Since An-Ker, Incorporated (the holding company) had as subsidiaries Anderson & Kerr Drilling and Anderson-Kerr, Incorporated (which was the investment and securities partnership), An-Ker was the key to any reorganization. Another complication was that Anderson & Kerr Drilling Company owned shares in its parent, An-Ker, Incorporated, as well as in Kerlyn (A&K). In addition to owning all the initial shares of A&K class B, between November 15, 1932, and June 15, 1937, An-Ker, Incorporated, acquired 2,500 more B shares and disposed of 4,750 shares of class A in transactions that cannot be documented.

In a move toward simplification and clarification, on June 15, 1937, the stockholders of An-Ker, Incorporated, agreed to a plan for its liquidation. The involved stockholders were as follows:

Stockholders	Shares
Robert S. Kerr	141
Grayce Kerr (Mrs. R. S.)	75
Travis M. Kerr	29.33
Geraldine Kerr (Mrs. T. M.)	24
T. W. Fentem	26.67
Dean Terrill	16
R. H. Lynn	18.9
D. A. McGee	12.6
Anderson & Kerr Drilling	136.5
Total	480

An-Ker now held 250 shares of Kerlyn A (valued at $6.00 each) and 277,550 of Kerlyn B ($0.80). This, plus its 2,500 shares of Anderson & Kerr Drilling (at $80.00 each) and 3 shares of Blackhawk Drilling ($100.00 each), brought the value of the assets to $423,840.

As the next step in the realignment, on June 21, Anderson & Kerr Drilling adopted its plan of liquidation. Assets included its holdings in An-Ker and 246,212 shares of Kerlyn class B and 1,800 shares of Kerlyn class A. These would be distributed to the stockholders of An-Ker since the holding company was also being dissolved. Finally, on June 28, Kerr-Lynn & Company, a copartnership which in effect became the drilling arm, was created by contributions of cash and Kerlyn Oil Company class B stock. The shares of the participants are shown in Table 6.1. In brief, An-Ker, Incorporated, and Anderson & Kerr Drilling became Kerr-Lynn & Company, just as A&K Petroleum had been replaced by Kerlyn Oil Company.

This was not considered final, for on December 11 the charter of Anderson-Kerr, Incorporated, was surrendered. This left only the question of the relationship between Kerlyn and Kerr-Lynn & Company to cause confusion. In the same month the Kerlyn board discussed a merger of the two companies, inasmuch as their close connection and identity of management made "some of their business relationships susceptible to misunderstanding by persons not fully acquainted with all of the circumstances surrounding those transactions." No final decision was reached, although

Table 6.1. Kerr-Lynn & Company, June 28, 1937

Individual	Kerlyn Class B Shares Contributed	Percent of Kerr-Lynn Stock Owned
Robert S. Kerr	153,150.10	41.048
Mrs. R. S. Kerr	81,462.66	21.834
Travis M. Kerr	31,858.52	8.539
Mrs. T. M. Kerr	26,068.98	6.987
T. W. Fentem	28,967.48	7.764
R. H. Lynn	20,527.96	5.502
Dean Terrill	17,378.99	4.658
Dean A. McGee	13,685.31	3.668
Totals	373,100.00	100.000

the members agreed that the time had come to take a step toward eventual merger.[9]

On September 24, 1937, in his second letter to the Kerlyn stockholders, which accompanied the annual report for 1936–37, Bob Kerr stated that it had been company policy to devote capital expenditures to proven areas and to stabilize income and the position of the firm by securing a diversity of production in both type and locality. Thus, it was hoped a position would be achieved "where it can not be seriously hampered by state and local regulations, price postings, or other conditions beyond our immediate control." As a result, Kerlyn's holdings were largely in three groups: Oklahoma City and Cooke and Moore counties in Texas. The first two were primarily oil and the last chiefly gas. From July 1, 1936, to June 30, 1937, seven oil wells had been completed successfully in Oklahoma City (where Harold Freeman recalled they used two motor and two steam rigs) and three oil and one gas well in the Texas Panhandle area.[10] Over all, during this period crude-oil production was 554,520 barrels—up some 321,885—and 38,791,647 thousand cubic feet of gas.[11]

This report did not, of course, cover contract drilling or dry holes. Both existed, for contract drilling grossed $883,498.53 during the year, and one documented failure was the Kerlyn Oil Company Pratt #1, Pontotoc County, which was abandoned at 2,355 feet. Also unmentioned was an

[9] "Origin of Kerr-McGee Oil Industries, Inc., stock ownership by Grayce B. Flynn," attached to a letter from S. B. Robinson to Marvin Hambrick, of Arthur Anderson & Co., dated July 5, 1966; Oklahoma Secretary of State, "Corporation File"; and interviews with S. B. Robinson, February 23, 1970, and Dean Terrill, November 24, 1969.

[10] Kerlyn Oil Company, *Annual Report for the Fiscal Year Ended June 30, 1937.*

[11] "Application of A&K Petroleum Company to List 250,000 Shares of Class A Common on the Chicago Stock Exchange—1936" in controller office; interview with R. E. Anderson, May 3, 1971; Kerlyn, *Annual Report . . . 1937*; S-1 Statement, No. 107, dated March 31, 1948, p. 10.

Kerlyn Oil Company

Table 6.2. Comparative Statement of Income, Expenses, and Surplus, 1936–37

	Year Ended June 30, 1937	Year Ended June 30, 1936
Gross operating income		
Crude-oil production and gas sales	$870,148.14	$315,551.02
Less: gross production and excise taxes	33,846.78	14,366.64
Net crude-oil production and gas sales	$836,301.36	$301,184.38
Steam and compressor sales	443.19	1,565.50
Income from services—net	22,597.50	
Gross operating income	$859,342.05	$302,749.88
Cost of production—before depletion and depreciation		
Production and maintenance expenses	190,708.31	78,262.75
Gross operating profit	$668,633.74	$224,487.13
Expenses		
General and administrative expenses	$ 53,599.57	$ 5,569.10
Office—clerical salaries, office rent, etc., charged by affiliate	9,000.00	3,000.00
Insurance and bond expense	7,989.30	547.21
Taxes exclusive of income taxes	11,134.28	3,733.86
Miscellaneous	851.79	779.87
Legal expense	7,396.09	1,266.50
Depreciation sustained	90,835.16	38,989.57
Development expense	40,402.80	1,893.89
Lease rentals paid	2,165.11	1,973.46
Amortization of undeveloped leases	24,137.04	4,173.55
Leases canceled and expired	5,966.80	2,018.71
Geological expense	7,204.53	
Total expenses	$260,682.47	$ 63,945.72
Net operating income	$407,951.27	$160,541.41
Other income		
Rental income	$ 234.05	$ 687.31
Purchase discount	1,413.80	83.40
Profit from sale of properties	109,704.32	20,523.65
Profit from collections on oil payments	5,233.71	607.63
Bottom hole contributions	....	7,200.00
Total other income	$116,585.88	$ 29,101.99
Gross income	$524,537.15	$189,643.40

82

Table 6.2. *Continued.*

	Year Ended June 30, 1937	Year Ended June 30, 1936
Other deductions		
Interest paid to affiliate	$ 1,772.68	
Interest paid—other	2,585.02	$ 3,480.21
Organization and Securities Act expense	16,074.66	7,147.31
Dry-hole contributions	250.00	325.00
Dry holes and loss from abandonment of properties	20,181.98	1,429.44*
Inventory adjustment	176.82	. . . .
Total other deductions	$ 41,041.16	$ 9,523.08
Income—before depletion and income taxes	$483,495.99	$180,120.32
Provision for income taxes		
Federal income taxes	. . . .	$ 5,982.72
Oklahoma state income taxes	. . . .	3,082.10
Total provision for income taxes	. . . .	$ 9,064.82
Less: excess prior years accruals restored	$ 2,091.53	4,175.61
Net provision for income taxes	$ 2,091.53*	$ 4,889.21
Income—before depletion available for distribution under the Delaware law governing wasting assets	$485,587.52	$175,231.11
Depletion sustained—computed on a production unit basis to return investment, including present par value of capital stock	$219,075.17	$104,635.37
Net profit to surplus	$266,512.35	$ 70,595.74
Balance of surplus—beginning	218,271.77	167,155.55
Total	$484,784.12	$237,751.29
Dividends declared		
On class A common—regular	$ 76,562.50	$ 19,479.52
On class A common—special—waiver executed by B stockholders, agreeing to the payment of this special dividend	12,500.00	
On class B common	40,000.00	
Total dividends declared	$129,062.50	$ 19,479.52
Balance of surplus—end	$355,721.62	$218,271.77

*Denotes red figure.

agreement with Phillips, dated February 11, 1937, by which Phillips acquired half interest in four blocks in Oklahoma City for an advance of $100,000 for drilling costs. In each block drilled, Phillips would pay $62,500 plus one quarter of the $100,000. In addition Phillips would also have first purchase rights on what was then A&K's share of the production. [12]

Other geographical areas were in Kerlyn's plans besides Oklahoma and Texas. J. H. ("Buster") Kuhlman and A. J. Whiting's memories of that year centered around their work on two Colorado wildcats. The project most important and influential on the future of Kerlyn, however, was one begun in late July in Arkansas. That state's oil production had been in a marked decline during 1930–36, but Phillips Petroleum and Lion Oil Refining opened a small pool in Union County in March, 1937, sparking renewed activity in the state.

Dean McGee first become interested in Arkansas while working for Phillips. Although he never mapped or recommended drilling at that time, the company had done considerable seismic work and found some production in that state. After moving to Kerlyn, McGee decided to explore in Columbia County, and Kerr-Lynn & Company began acquiring leases east of Magnolia, Arkansas. The intent was to begin drilling on September 9, and "dryhole" contributions were obtained from a number of interested parties. The test depth was set at 6,000 feet.

"Rigging up" was accompanied by an unusual air of excitement among both oilmen and natives. People in the little Arkansas cotton town saw it as potential economic salvation, and local merchants promised the crew members gifts of hats, shoes, suits of clothes, and royalty interests if they brought in a producer. The company had a larger than usual stake in a successful strike, and even Bob, Travis, and Lynn made visits to the site.

But this was McGee's personal baby, and he "sat" with it. In fact, it actually delayed his marriage to Dorothea Antoinette Swain, of Bartlesville, for six months—until June, 1938. Meanwhile, Buster Kuhlman and Henry Pryor remember breaking in their new geologist on the well. McGee slept in a bedroll in a little tin house, "the dog house," and one roughneck informed his mates that he was not going to chop wood for heat and cooking for any "so and so geologist." But he probably did, because the general consensus found McGee "jolly and he always had a smile on his face and never got upset about anything in particular."

But at times the smile must have been strained. Buster Kuhlman reminisced further concerning the mishaps which characterized the hole: "In fact, this one, I think even McGee would have given up on it a couple of times." There is some confusion about the particular rig used. Pryor believed that it was one of the new motor units, but Harold Freeman thought that it "was a crude thing—an old steam rig that been reworked and hauled from the Oklahoma City yard." All agreed, however, that there was no end of problems: location, inadequate drilling equipment, and completion dif-

[12] Lease Records file, "Contract file 25"; *Oil and Gas Journal* (August 19 and September 23, 1937).

ficulties. To make matters worse, "It rained every day once—sometimes, twice." But McGee kept his enthusiasm. Kuhlman, whose job it was to catch and prepare the samples, recalled that McGee was so eager "You had to push him away. He was trying to get those samples and he'd take a few and run. . . . I'm not sure, but I think I had him catching his own samples before it was over." The final blow came in December. After the expenditure of about $150,000, a lot of money for those days, the planned depth was reached. But there was no oil.[13]

Nothing could be done except shut down and see if more money could be raised for a deeper try. While waiting for this to develop, the crew was sent to Kansas, where apparently two wells were drilled. D. C. Lindley recalled that he was hired on November 9, 1937, to go to a rig in Plainville, Kansas, and was then sent to Ellenwood to join the Magnolia crew. Henry Pryor remembered that he went to Kansas about Thanksgiving and was there about thirty-one days. He believed that the first well there was drilled for Kerlyn. If so, it must have been unsuccessful, since no record exists. The Ellenwood well was a contract well for Stanolind Oil and Gas, and Freeman claimed that it was drilled in nine days and the crew then returned to Arkansas.[14] Bill Whiting stayed at Magnolia only during rig-up time, then went to Baggs, Wyoming, on a short contract job. It was long enough, however, for him to remember that Baggs had a population of 212 citizens, 15 roughnecks, and "lots of sheep."[15]

Meanwhile, the steady improvement of business conditions in the nation's economy suddenly reversed, and a sharp recession began late in 1937. This was reflected in the oil industry in several ways: by a decline in the consumption of all petroleum products, a lessening of exports of oil, over-production of crude and gasoline, and the excessive accumulation of crude and refined products. This last led to distress selling, which further demoralized the market until an upturn began in 1939. During 1937, Oklahoma production rose by some 22 million barrels to reach its highest peak since 1929, and although the price averaged $1.15 a barrel, the trend was steadily downward during the last quarter.

The economic downturn, the low gas prices—gas was Kerlyn's principal source of income at this time—and the Magnolia failure probably account for the legend that Kerr's empire nearly collapsed during late 1937. E. H. ("Jeep") Harvey, speaking of those days, said: "We didn't know whether the check was any good or not when we got it, but if it wasn't any good we were all in the same shape 'cause we couldn't cover the check anyway." Then when Harvey was in Kansas, Travis Kerr came up and told the crew, "If you

[13] Interviews with Dean A. McGee, September 4, 1971, March 3, 1973, May 20, 1970; J. H. Kuhlman, February 25, 1970; Harold Freeman, April 17, 1971; George Cobb, January 21, 1971; Jacob Henry Pryor, undated. Lease Records file, "S-163 Barnett 'A' "; Oil and Gas Journal, November 4 and December 16, 1937.

[14] Interviews with Jacob Henry Pryor, J. H. Kuhlman, Harold Freeman, A. J. ("Bill") Whiting, April 17, 1971; and with D. C. Lindley, June 10, 1971.

[15] A. J. Whiting interview.

fellows can get a job, you'd better do it because we're folding up." Harvey added, however: "We didn't even know where to get another job. We just didn't do anything about it."

J. Norman Baxendale and Otto Barton recalled that at times the Barnett #1 at Magnolia was the only rig drilling. It was rumored that if it were a dry hole there would be no company. Harold Freeman was more specific. He claimed that the company's credit was so bad he could not "even buy a broom on credit" from Carl Wimberly, a brother-in-law of the Kerrs, who would say, "You know, Harold, that that credit's no good." Also, according to Freeman, the superintendent, George Acuff, announced: "If you guys can find a job somewhere I recommend you go to it because we don't know whether we can pay you next payday or not." But like Jeep Harvey, Harold said "there wasn't any other work to do. We just had to stay around."[16]

Dean McGee, however, while admitting finances were tight, did not consider Barnett #1 that crucial. He recalled that when he joined the companies there was a deficit balance of around $650,000 in notes. Much of this was undoubtedly charged against the drilling branch as payment for Jim Anderson's shares. They did sink a lot of money in the Arkansas well, and "if it had failed it would have hurt but it wasn't a critical situation for the company." Thus, it was probably partly in jest that George Cobb remembered McGee as claiming. "If he had seen the balance sheet and understood the financial condition of the organization, he might not have joined this company."[17]

[16] Interviews with H. G. Kuhlman and E. H. ("Jeep") Harvey, April 15, 1971; J. Norman Baxendale, June 19, 1971; Otto Barton, July 26, 1971; and Harold Freeman.

[17] Interviews with Dean A. McGee, May 20, 1970, and September 14, 1971; George Cobb interview, January 21, 1971.

Chapter 7

Magnolia and Hard Times 1938–1939

Most Americans remember 1938 as the year Adolf Hitler dominated the world's headlines and Europe shivered in the chill of an impending nightmare. On September 30 the Munich Agreement was signed by Germany, Italy, France, and Great Britain, and a false relief was felt when Britain's Prime Minister Neville Chamberlain proclaimed that this document would bring "Peace in our Time." Nevertheless, the U.S. Navy began a billion-dollar expansion program to build a fleet which would keep the trouble across the ocean and away from American shores and lives.

The country was mainly concerned with a recession which began in the autumn of 1937 and reached into all phases of business by the first of 1938. In fact, the drab performances got even bleaker as the months went by, and the oil industry was no exception. In the petroleum world the problems of the previous year carried over, increasingly demoralizing the market and causing gasoline and crude oil to sell at distress prices. Oklahoma oil production, rising since 1935, now declined sharply, mostly because of the effort to bolster prices. Although $1.23 per barrel was the average for 1938, production was off 54 million barrels, and oil income dropped $74 million, to $209.5 million.

Of more immediate concern for most Oklahomans, however, besides the dust bowl and its effects on farm income and population, was the upcoming state election. Among the gubernatorial candidates was Leon C. ("Red") Phillips, who had Bob Kerr as an influential backer. The *Mangum Daily Star*, July 27, 1938, referred to Kerr as "one of the principal advisers and strategists." The *Daily Oklahoman*, October 26, added that Kerr would "be an important member of the inner circle of the Phillips administration." Kerr chose his man wisely: Phillips won by the largest majority ever received by any previous governor of Oklahoma.

As exciting as politics might be, the rest of the people at Kerlyn thought Barnett #1 at Magnolia, Arkansas, was more significant. During December, 1937, additional money had been raised from adjacent lease- and landholders, and drilling was resumed. Although records are scanty, it is known that an unidentified group put up $3,000, a Leon F. Russ gave $1,000, Lion Oil Refining Company pledged $1,500 if the hole was dry, and $2,000 in cash was received from Atlantic Refining Company with the proviso that it would receive 1/4 of 7/8 of any revenue up to a total of $4,000. It was indeed a patchwork of financial pieces.

In late February the long-awaited event finally occurred. J. C. Comer was on the scene and described the sight when Dean McGee checked a core sample: "His face lit up like a Christmas tree. He didn't have to tell nothing. Didn't have to tell me. He scooped up a bunch of it and smelled it. His face lit up like a Christmas tree." A few days later oil blew over the top of the derrick.

On March 5 and 6 the *Daily Oklahoman* celebrated the event in a riot of headlines: "Oil Shot Over Top of Derrick at Magnolia"; "Kerlyn Wildcat Strike in Southern Arkansas Is Sensation of the Oil Country"; "Robert S. Kerr . . . Let Out a Shout of Joy"; "Stock on the Chicago Curb Went Up a Point." On March 11, Lynn, by then on the scene at Magnolia, received a letter from Robert E. ("Bob") Anderson, who had joined the company as an attorney in the leasing department. It said, in part, "I sincerely hope you will be able to complete one of the largest wells in the Mid-Continent and that you will be able to open up a very successful and profitable field."

Oklahoma City's elation was more than matched in Arkansas. Buster Kuhlman, Harold Freeman, and Jacob Henry Pryor were on the well, and there can be little doubt that the event was one of the highlights of their long careers in the oil world. Pryor recalled that the night the well came in the crew caught oil in Coke bottles and sold it in town. Soon there were hordes of visitors. A soft-drink stand was built about a mile from the discovery and named Prosperity City. In Buster's words:

We really had a showplace down there when the well blew out; three or four hundred people and had to put up a fence to keep them out of the rig. They had a refreshment stand out there. You could buy hamburgers and cokes. Crew got coke bottles from the stand and sold that oil to the people for 50¢ a bottle as souvenirs.

Needless to say, merchants made good on their promises to give wearing apparel to all fifteen members of the crew.

The farmers were just as excited at having an oil field, and they offered the crew royalty interests. According to Freeman and Pryor, Lynn made a speech in which he told the farmers: "You're going to make all those roughnecks and drillers independent and we can't do that. We need them to help us work. Wish you'd take the royalty back and give us the equivalent money of what that royalty's worth to help set pipe in the well." All farmers

Production crew near Sunray, Texas, 1938.

agreed except Delton Baker, who reportedly "was drunk," and he said: "No, I gave it to those boys. And I like those boys down there and they're going to keep it." Pryor recalled that this royalty was later sold, and each crewman got $62.50 for his share.[1] On May 7, Bob Anderson wrote to Lynn from Magnolia, "I believe the Magnolia people think that Kerr-Lynn & Co. is the only Company that ever existed on the face of the globe to hear them talk."

It was a good well. By April 11, Kerlyn was paying an independent contractor twenty cents a barrel to haul the oil thirty-two miles to the pipeline at Eldorado, and, four days later, the allowable on the well was set at 400 barrels per day. By May 1 it had produced some 8,976 barrels. But there were problems. Bringing in the well had been costly, and equally deep and expensive offsets had to be drilled to prevent drainage. The company already owed about $600,000, much of it taxes, and the government was demanding payment. Thus management was forced to the hard decision that

[1] D. A. McGee doubts the story of Lynn's speech. See also *Oil and Gas Journal*, February 3, 10, 17; March 24; April 14, 1938. Note especially, *ibid.*, February 24, 1938, pp. 234, 236; March 10, 1938, p. 69; and March 17, 1938, p. 117.

it had to sell. Such an agreement was made with Atlantic Refining on April 27, 1938. On May 9, the partners in Kerr-Lynn & Company, transferred their interests in the Magnolia field for $200,000 in cash and a production payment of $1,000 an acre for the four hundred acres, retroactive to May 1.

If ever the urge to gamble should have been heeded, this was the time. Less than five years later Magnolia, with 116 wells, was Arkansas's largest producing reservoir, and in 1978 it was still pumping oil. In the United States there have been only fifty 100-million-barrel oil fields. Magnolia was one of them. While the $600,000 was welcome at the time, Atlantic paid a small price for Kerlyn's share of approximately 10 million barrels. The alternative had been borrowing more money on the company's equipment or on some wells being drilled east of Oklahoma City. Dean McGee could not help but question the decision to sell the Magnolia property: "If the company could have held on in that field, it would have advanced the company's progress by three to five years as it could have made $15 to 20 million from it over a period of years."[2] Attempts to justify the sale would be evident in many directors' meetings in the months to come.

There were two amusing sidelights on Magnolia. The first involved the state of Arkansas's standing offer of a $1,000 bonus for a discovery well. Kerlyn's efforts to collect were unsuccessful, even though the company hired a lawyer-politician on a split-fee basis. The second incident was a personal windfall for Bob and Travis Kerr. As Travis told it, at the time Magnolia was being drilled, he and Bob were playing poker with some oilmen from other companies. The brothers had a mutual understanding that in any game in which both participated each would cover the other's losses. The first night Travis won $1,800. The next evening—the day the well came in—seven players gathered. About 2:00 A.M. it was agreed that Bob would deal the last hand. Each player anted $50. Travis picked up two pairs and opened with $350. Four players stayed. Bob called and raised, then Travis called and raised. The process continued until Bob won a pot of $5,000 with three aces and two queens.[3]

The rest of 1938 was tame by comparison with Magnolia. The January stockholders' meeting had seen the board of directors increased to eight members, with McGee receiving the new seat. At the board meeting which followed, Travis was elected vice-president for drilling. President Kerr reported on the extensive drilling campaign of the past six months: seven new producers in the north Oklahoma City field, additional wells at Gainesville, Texas, two oil producers and one gas producer in the Texas Panhandle, and an oil strike in the Bemis pool in Ellis County, Kansas. Drilling was in progress in the so-called Fair Grounds area of Oklahoma City, in the Jessie field in Pontotoc and Coal counties, at Magnolia, and at Bemis. The Bemis

[2] For the Magnolia story see Lease Records file, "S-163 Barnett 'A,' " and interviews with R. E. Anderson, May 3, 1971; J. C. Comer, June 17, 1971; J. H. ("Buster") Kuhlman, February 25, 1970; Harold Freeman, April 17, 1971; Jacob Henry Pryor, undated; and Dean A. McGee, September 4, 1971, and March 3, 1973.

[3] Lease Records file, "S-163 Barnett 'A' " and interview with Travis M. Kerr, December 16, 1969.

field looked so good it was anticipated that a total of eight wells would be sunk there.

The February board meeting was concerned totally with Kerlyn's finances. After voting the usual 8 3/4-cent quarterly dividend on class A, the directors canceled 3,715 shares of that issue and recommended a reduction in authorized shares to 246,285. Despite the optimism of the previous month, "in line with the thoughts previously expressed as to reduction of expenditures and conservation of cash," they also decided to fire Kerlyn's publicity agent, who was receiving $150 a month. It was then debated whether to pay the auditor $5,000, with the conclusion that, "due to the present status of business generally, the Corporation should not spend more than $4,000 on these services," although it might reduce the number of reports. Since wildcatting expenses had been heavier than expected, the directors agreed that "some percentage of the funds of the Corporation must be devoted to wildcat ventures if the Corporation is to show material growth," but they were unanimous that the company should "not at this time extend itself in wildcat ventures." Management assured them that if the venture in Arkansas proved successful it would repay many times the cost of *all* wildcatting ventures during the preceding year. But the board ruled that the executive committee—R. S. Kerr, Lynn, and Straus—had to approve any expenditure of $25,000, or any wildcat of $5,000 or more.

In May the mood was much the same, despite knowledge of the sale of Barnett #1. In debating the purchase by Atlantic, Lynn told the directors that too many wells had been drilled by the industry, which now was faced with trying to avoid price cuts. He predicted that within the next three months there would be drastic cuts in production allowables and consequently a reduction in the income of Kerlyn. Kerr, always the optimist, pointed out that there would still be other opportunities to drill, *if* they could find outside finances. The board then ratified the sale of the Barnett well and all the company's leases on that structure.

Needless to say, Kerlyn's annual report for the fiscal year ending June 30 was not a happy one. Bob Kerr reminded his stockholders that the past year "commenced at approximately the same time as the most recent general business decline" so its unfortunate results should not be surprising. The reduction of allowables for natural gas and lower prices for its by-products (natural gasoline and carbon black) had sharply reduced income. Despite increased expenditures to acquire and develop producing oil properties, Kerlyn's efforts largely had been nullified by the actions of state regulatory bodies and purchasers of crude.

Worst of all were the taxes: "Our accounting department has advised us . . . that during the past year taxes . . . amounted to not less than $87,246.39, a figure equivalent to 58 per cent of the net profit," and in excess of the amount paid in total dividends on class A common. Moreover, Kerr predicted, "the trend in taxes seems still to be upward," an increasingly weighty problem which stockholders and employees might well consider a personal one. "[Every] dollar by which our taxes are increased is one dollar less which we have to pay out as dividends, to reinvest in properties, to pay our employees and to buy materials and equipment."

Kerr reported an important change in company strategy. Instead of purchase of proven reserves and producing properties, the emphasis was now on exploration for oil and gas in order to develop large new production and reserves at minimum cost. Ten such ventures had been undertaken in the past twelve months, two resulting in new fields. Since this was a better average than prevailed in the industry as a whole, it clearly demonstrated the ability of the geological department to discover new oil. One success was shallow production near Collinsville in Grayson County, Texas, which would not be expensive to develop. The other, Magnolia in Arkansas, was quite deep, and development would have been expensive: "In view of that circumstance and other considerations we sold our interests there to Atlantic Producing & Refining Company for a profit at a price payable partly in cash at the time of the sale and partly in oil when and if production is obtained from the acreage."

The figures were equally discouraging. Current assets dropped from $279,563.71 to $188,503.79; total assets, from $2,597,977.04 to $2,345,712.40; and, despite strict economy, net profit fell from $266,512 to $150,316. Although crude-oil production increased by 190,787 barrels and its value by $185,102, natural-gas output dropped by over nine billion cubic feet, with a resulting income loss of over $74,000. And then there were taxes and dry holes![4]

In August, Kerlyn's reserves were categorized. There were twenty-two leases in Oklahoma City with an estimated reserve of 1,579,739 barrels; seven other leases in the state with 148,502; eleven Cooke County, Texas, leases set at 678,441; six additional Texas oil leases with reserves of 801,874; and the Moore County, Texas, gas field had twenty-nine wells and estimated recovery potential of 239,033,429 thousand cubic feet.

The annual report and inventory did not completely satisfy the directors. At the September meeting Bob Kerr reiterated his previous explanations. Although the company had had its largest gross income during the year, the *net* had fallen for several reasons: the decrease in allowables per well for both oil and gas, the natural decline in the Gainesville field, the low prices for natural gasoline and carbon black, and the increased cost of an expanded exploratory program. This time the board was convinced and empowered management to seek outside financing.

It, therefore, must have been a bitter experience for Bob Kerr to have to bring more bad news in November. The first quarter, ended September 30, also showed reduced net profits for the same reasons, plus a drop in oil prices. But he quickly added his belief that returns would be upward in the next few months and that management was economizing in "cash outlay in every respect." When the Chicago directors wanted to know Kerlyn's plans for entering the big oil play in Illinois, he replied that the company did not plan to participate, partly because of economic conditions, but mainly because of another important project; which he did not discuss. In De-

[4] Kerlyn Oil Company, *Annual Report for the Fiscal Year Ended June 30, 1938*; S-1 Statement, No. 107, dated March 31, 1948, p. 10.

cember the directors would have heard better news had they met, for
Phillips agreed to renegotiate the contract for Moore County gas, giving
Kerlyn a better unit price.

The important project Kerr mentioned was in the Gulf of Mexico. This
news, however, was not as startling as might be expected, for other companies had already turned their attention south to the Gulf. In 1937 and
1938, for example, Pure Oil, Superior, and Humble had drilled wells in its
shallow areas. In September, 1938, "with the development of the prospecting device being worked out with the Heiland Research Corporation,"
Kerlyn had begun extensive seismographic operations in Mobile Bay.[5]
There must have been some doubt in the minds of the directors about the
feasibility of tiny Kerlyn's involvement in a venture with such great unknown risks and efforts, but this time the gambling instinct won.

In the meantime, on the world scene the political front was rapidly
becoming a battle line. Japan was on the march in China and before the end
of 1939 would be in Shanghai. Early in the year General Franco finally won
the Spanish civil war, an exceedingly cruel and bloody one, and set up a
fascist dictatorship. In March, Germany ignored the Munich Agreement
and invaded Czechoslovakia. President Roosevelt reacted with a personal
message to Hitler and Mussolini asking for assurances that some twenty
small nations would not be attacked. Hitler penned in insulting reply, and
Mussolini, first refusing to read the note, sneered at it as a "result of infantile
paralysis." In August, Hitler and Stalin announced their pact, but on September 1, the Blitzkrieg hit Poland. Two days later Britain and France
declared war on Germany, and World War II was on. The United States
reacted with the Neutrality Act of 1939.

Ironically, the world's troubles brought some economic improvement.
Recalling that costs had skyrocketed during World War I, Americans rushed
to buy at the prevailing prices. In order to meet this new surge of consumer
demand, industrial production came alive for the first time in almost a
decade. But first, the Mid-Continent oil producers had their own special
problem with which to cope. Illinois opened its producing fields to unregulated, flush production, and crude prices responded by dropping 20 to 30
percent. In a desperation move all the states in the region except Illinois
agreed to shut down their producing wells for fifteen days in an effort to
absorb the glut. Oklahoma's output continued its downward slide in 1939.
Annual production was 159,913,000 barrels, worth about $166,300,000 (a
decline of $43 million), and the state lost to Illinois its third-place rank as an
oil producer. Most oilmen probably reacted as Bob Kerr did: "Our Au-

[5] The survey indicated the possibility of a deep-seated salt dome, but the evidence was
not strong enough for a wildcat well. Lease Records file, "Contract 1197." Claude Barrow,
"Prairie Wildcatters Reach Out into Gulf," *Drilling*, November, 1947, 54; Dean A. McGee,
speech, "A Report on Exploration Progress in the Gulf of Mexico," made before the spring
meeting of the Mid-Continent District, American Petroleum Institute, Division of Production, Tulsa, Oklahoma, March 23, 1949; A. T. F. Seale, "Modern Practices in Off-Shore
Drilling," paper read before the Petroleum Mechanical Engineering Conference, New
Orleans, September 25–27, 1950; Lease Records file, "Contract file #49A."

gust . . . gross income will probably be reduced by approximately 50% of what it would have been but for the shutdowns but we feel that action to have been helpful from a long range viewpoint."

At his January, 1939, stockholders' meeting Kerr was compelled once more to explain the economic facts of life. He reiterated the reasons for the sale of the Magnolia lease but stressed that Kerlyn was continuing to develop its Rumsey lease in Ellis County, Kansas. It had completed six wells there with an average potential of 3,000 barrels per day, although production was restricted to only 18 barrels.[6] He informed them that Kerlyn also had a substantial interest in several hundred thousands of acres underlying Mobile Bay, the exploration and development of which was being carried on by Phillips Petroleum Company "at its sole cost."

There were more details at the next directors' meeting. After pointing out that Heiland Research Division was in great need of new contracts to boost its ailing balance sheet, Lynn elaborated on the Mobile Bay venture. For $3,500, Kerlyn had bought a quarter net-profit interest in three-fourths of some five or six thousand acres, without any obligation for additional expenditures. To share the risk, Phillips Petroleum had been allowed to join in the venture and was seismographing the area. Furthermore, Lynn continued, he and Kerr were investigating an Ottawa, Kansas, gas deal, while at the same time working with the state of Mississippi to get a lease on the entire Mississippi Sound, which should be awarded the following week. Kerr added that it was his belief that Kerlyn had reached the bottom of its recession. Even without an increase in allowable the company had enough new wells to enjoy an increase in production and income.

This improved outlook prompted the directors to bring up the old question of a merger with Kerr-Lynn. They instructed management to look into the possibility and to report back at the next meeting. Just what would be involved is difficult to say, because few of Kerr-Lynn's drilling-contract records have been found. It is known, however, that for the nine months ending March 31, 1938, there was a gross income of $348,164.

Some work was done for Kerlyn, but an unsigned carbon copy of a letter of April 30 indicates that Kerr-Lynn was also actively seeking other employment. This communication informed Atlantic Refining Company of Dallas that Kerr-Lynn currently had two V-8 Le Roy rigs operating in Kansas, one large Le Roy in Arkansas, another in Oklahoma, and all of its steam equipment in the Oklahoma City field. The Le Roy motors could use natural gas, gasoline, or butane as fuel. With such equipment for hire, the writer concluded, "We are most desirous of trying to work out a few drilling contracts with your company, as we like your organization and hope to do considerable business with you in the future."[7]

At the next directors' meeting the management of Kerlyn, as previously instructed, reported that Kerr-Lynn & Company was very busy, operating

---

[6] This 80-acre lease finally had a total of eight wells.

[7] Lease Records file, "S-163 Barnett 'A' "; "Prospectus for 60,000 Shares . . . April 9, 1946," p. 18.

at a profit, and that it owned some valuable properties. They recommended it should be merged with Kerlyn before it became so valuable that Kerlyn could not afford to acquire it. After a long discussion the directors voted again to delay a decision until the tax liabilities resulting from a dissolution of Kerr-Lynn could be determined.

The financial situation remained very much on everyone's mind. When the second quarter report was poor, Lynn reminded the directors that virtually all oil companies had had a bad quarter, with Illinois production being a major factor. In June, Kerr had negotiated a $75,000 loan from Liberty National Bank of Oklahoma City, and apparently the bankers criticized him for hiring so many new administrators at high salaries. Whatever the reason, Kerr defended these past actions to his own board. He pointed out that it was his purpose "in increasing the personnel of the Corporation to build an organization capable of discovering producing properties and operating them on a continuously expanding basis and . . . results to date indicate that our personnel can do that." He added that unfortunately the large increase in personnel costs roughly coincided with the decrease in the price of crude and increased allowables so that the firm's overhead was substantially larger at a time when its cash flow was falling.

As Kerr had explained to the directors, drilling made Kerr-Lynn the more fortunate of the two companies. Yet even here all was not good news. At about 11:00 P.M. on February 13, 1939, the wives and children of a number of the crewmen working on the contract well, Coline Oil Company's #1, near Marlow, Oklahoma, arrived to drive them home when the shift changed at midnight. It was a chilly night, and they took refuge in the boiler house. Suddenly one of the boilers exploded, probably because gypsum foam in the water made the boiler appear full when it was not. One of the roughnecks was killed along with the wife and daughter of the driller, and another woman and child were seriously burned. The force of the explosion was such that the dead man was blown 125 feet, and the boiler, 60 feet.[8]

But such tragedies were rare for the company. There were still contracts to be had in other Oklahoma fields, including Oklahoma City, and Harold Freeman recalled a Kerr-Lynn well near Boulder, Colorado. But the most important new connections came late in the year with entry into the Permian Basin area near Odessa, Texas. At least some of the drilling there was for Phillips on the Cowden lease. J. R. Glover believed that the well on which he worked was for Gulf, but he was positive that they had to pay $221.90 every morning to bail the roughnecks out of jail. Even if alcohol were plentiful, water was not. Buster Kuhlman recalled that since steam rigs needed a lot of water, these units were left in Oklahoma.[9]

During fiscal 1939, which, of course, included only the first six months of

---

[8] Jacob Henry Pryor identified him as John Roebuck. *Marlow* (Oklahoma) *Review*, February 16, 1939; interviews with Jacob Henry Pryor; George T. Sims, Loyal Edwards, and George Kitchel, June 17, 1971; H. G. Kuhlman and E. H. Harvey, April 15, 1971.

[9] Interviews with R. E. Anderson, J. R. Glover, June 14, 1971, Harold Freeman, and J. H. ("Buster") Kuhlman.

Kerlyn Oil Company
Table 7.1. Comparative Statement of Income and Surplus, 1938–39

	Year Ended June 30, 1939	Year Ended June 30, 1938
Gross operating income		
Crude-oil production and gas sales	$ 797,695.56	$1,083,912.38
Steam, compressor, and water sales	835.84	397.19
Profit from collections on oil payments	10,607.57	13,475.92
Income from service equipment—net	17,542.39	17,841.79
Total gross operating income	$ 826,681.36	$1,115,627.28
Operating charges		
Production and maintenance expense	$ 181,509.22	$ 273,431.31
Gross production and excise taxes	33,626.74	46,566.52
General and administrative expense	57,781.78	61,475.88
Office—clerical salaries, office rent, etc., charged by affiliate	15,000.00	15,000.00
Geological and land department expense	31,467.60	13,181.16
Taxes—exclusive of income taxes	12,618.39	16,430.36
Legal expense	5,060.18	10,866.53
Insurance and bond expense	1,448.37	14,662.12
Lease rentals paid	8,182.17	5,005.85
Miscellaneous	3,055.04	1,937.67
Total operating charges before reserves and retirements	$ 349,749.49	$ 458,557.40
Operating income before reserves and retirements	$ 476,931.87	$ 657,069.88
Other income		
Profit from sale of properties	$ 37,859.12	$ 108,533.38
Inventory adjustment	6,801.69	7,536.47
Purchase discount	704.66	2,347.08
Rental income	89.98	50.28
Total other income	$ 45,455.45	$ 118,467.21
Gross income before reserves and retirements	$ 522,387.32	$ 775,537.09

that year, Kerr-Lynn drilled twenty-nine wells, of which eighteen were straight contract and eleven were either part or totally paid for by some sort of acreage deal. The partnership earned a profit of $5,001.25 on the straight contracts but lost $111,508.44 on the interest wells. Most of the latter were probably with Kerlyn. Another factor was that the joint wells were more likely to be wildcats, hence costlier than the straight contract holes. During this period only one lease in which Kerr-Lynn had an interest was successful, hence the loss in that category. A study of drilling expenses indicated that the Le Roy "8's" cost from $2.38 to $4.73 per foot to operate and that the

Table 7.1. *Continued.*

	Year Ended June 30, 1939	Year Ended June 30, 1938
Other deductions		
Interest paid to affiliate	$ 1,759.64	$ 9,116.67
Interest paid—other	2,651.69	1,091.75
Organization and Securities Exchange Act expense	11,943.84	11,943.84
Uncollectible accounts charged off	376.64	9,284.11
Provision for income taxes		7,748.63
Total other deductions	$ 16,731.81	$ 39,185.00
Net income before reserves and retirements	$ 505,655.51	$ 736,352.09
Provision for reserves and retirements		
Depletion	$ 292,404.05	$ 343,154.05
Depreciation	101,049.75	105,913.77
Amortization of undeveloped leaseholds	27,845.37	27,709.15
Leases canceled and expired	11,554.03	4,955.92
Worthless royalties charged off	23,793.93	2,013.20
Loss from dry holes drilled	25,113.79	101,677.23
Loss from abandonment of properties	2,209.12	612.69
Total provision for reserves and retirements	$ 483,970.04	$ 586,036.01
Net income to surplus	$ 21,685.47	$ 150,316.08
Balance of surplus—earned—beginning	399,540.88	355,721.62
Total	$ 421,226.35	$ 506,037.70
Dividends declared—on class A common at the rate of 35¢ per share	$ 86,177.00	$ 86,496.82
On class B common	. . . .	20,000.00
Total dividends declared	$ 86,177.00	$ 106,496.82
Balance of surplus earned—end	$ 335,049.35	$ 399,540.88

average for the contract wells was $3.43. These holes ran from 2,865 to 6,275 feet, and the average footage per day was 218 feet.[10]

Kerr-Lynn's interest wells for the entire year 1939 can be pinpointed more exactly. There were thirteen, and six resulted in production of some kind. Oklahoma County netted one dry hole and two small oil-and-gas

[10] W. C. Bednar, "Drilling Cost Analysis," September 3, 1941, in files of drilling department. For the fiscal year 1939 contract drilling grossed $356,887.19. "Prospectus for 60,000 Shares . . . April 9, 1946," p. 18.

producers. All three in Pottawatomie County were barely commercial. Single wells in Comanche, Garvin, Garfield, Murray, Logan, and Seminole counties in Oklahoma were dry except the Garvin well, which temporarily produced gas, and the Seminole well, which tested at 160 barrels of oil per day. Outside Oklahoma a wildcat in Comanche County, Kansas, was dry and abandoned.[11]

By 1939 there were also three Kerr-Lynn service stations. The newest one was located at 1312 Westwood Boulevard in Oklahoma City.[12] A more significant departure, however, was a decision to go into the retail natural-gas business. The Franklin County Gas Company's leases, purchased on June 28, 1939, for $7,675, was unlike the Moore County field, where the principal by-product was natural gasoline and carbon black; Franklin County's reserves were "sweet" gas that could be used for heating. By later standards it was a very small operation, but it was important enough for Kansan Dean McGee to sit in on the completion of one of the six-to-seven-hundred-foot wells, which probably cost about $1.50 per foot to drill, plus $1,000 for pipe. The company had the franchise to sell gas to the municipal power plant at Ottawa and hoped eventually to supply all of eastern Kansas. Despite drilling additional wells, Kerlyn never found enough gas to make the venture economically feasible.[13]

On the other hand, the Kerlyn annual report for the fiscal year ending June 30, 1939, was even more bleak. The fact that Kerr's accompanying letter to the stockholders was dated September 29 allowed him to speculate on the future:

We learn from the history of other conflicts that all commodities necessary to carrying out of war are much higher in price while the excess demand exists. Therefore, it seems apparent that if the war actively continues for as long as a year or more and if this country is not prevented from exporting petroleum products to belligerents, the probable result will be a substantial increase in the prices of crude oil and refined products and an increase in the volume of production thereof.

The number of wells in which Kerlyn owned an interest had increased by eight to ninety-four, but the number of barrels of oil produced had declined by 163,000. Furthermore, the average price per barrel sold was only ninety cents, resulting in a low net income of $21,685 on a gross operating income of $826,681. And there were always the taxes—up 267 percent of the net profit. Total assets dropped some $122,000 to $2,224,111.63. Nevertheless, the company had maintained its exploration program and discovered new reserves equal to twice the current year's production. Although gas produc-

---

[11] References to these wells can be found in *Oil and Gas Journal*, February 16, 23; March 23; April 13, 20; May 25; June 1, 22; July 6, 13, 20; August 24; September 7; October 5; November 6; and December 2, 14, 1939.

[12] "Kerr-Lynn," *Oklahoma City Directory, 1939*; interview with Wallace Wiggs.

[13] Interviews with George Cobb, January 21, 1971, R. E. Anderson, and Dean A. McGee, May 20, 1970.

tion had fallen by almost six billion cubic feet, income from that source rose $10,000.[14]

Given the uncertainty of the period, Kerlyn's directors adopted a cautious attitude for the rest of 1939. When Bob Kerr reminded them that the new federal Wage and Hours Law reduced the work week by two hours and asked whether the company should pay its employees the same weekly wages, a decision was postponed. The same fate met a suggestion to buy the Franklin Building on West Second Street between Broadway and Robinson in Oklahoma City, at a cost of $12,000 in cash and a mortgage of $56,000. The old, cramped quarters would have to do for a while longer—at least until the future was clearer—and perhaps another Magnolia appeared.

[14] Kerlyn Oil Company, *Annual Report for the Fiscal Year Ended June 30, 1939.*

Chapter 8

War and Politics
1940–1942

By 1940 the war in Europe was the principal concern of most Americans. Russia was actively pressing its conquests in Finland and the three small Baltic states, while Germany, after its success in Denmark and Norway, turned southward into France. Mussolini also declared war on France, and that nation soon crumbled. Japan then openly allied itself with the Axis powers against Great Britain. Certainly an overwhelming majority of Americans desired the defeat of Hitler and his satellites, but they also wanted to stay out of the war. President Roosevelt, who ran for a third term that year, tried to accommodate them by his "short of war policy"—all possible aid to the democracies except a declaration of hostilities, exchanges of destroyers for bases, the first peace-time conscription act in American history, and a general strengthening of this country's armed forces. Most citizens aproved, as seen in Roosevelt's easy victory over Wendell Willkie.

While companies like Kerlyn waited to see what the year would bring, heavy industry knew its role. Its advance was largely created by America's own defense needs and a steady rise in war orders from the democratic nations. Labor too prospered. As a result of the Fair Labor Standards Act of 1938, the forty-hour work week went into effect. The first concrete effort to mesh the oil industry into the national defense program came in June, 1940, when Robert E. Wilson, the first oilman to become involved, was appointed director of the Natural Gas and Petroleum Section of the Raw Materials Division of the new National Defense Advisory Commission. Although it should have been obvious to Congress that rubber and high-test gasoline would become vital products, Wilson's strenuous efforts to stimulate the manufacture of 100-octane gasoline and synthetic rubber had little initial success. Consequently, most oil companies used these prewar months to realign their priorities in anticipation of future needs.

Oklahoma was a microcosm of the nation. Agricultural production increased, presenting an ironic situation when John Steinbeck's *The Grapes of Wrath* was awarded a Pulitzer Prize. Petroleum was Oklahoma's most important industry, but it, like others, lost workers to the armed forces. Nevertheless, some 57,000 residents worked directly in oil and gas; about 70,000 more were in allied fields—with a total payroll of upwards of $100 million. During 1940, Oklahoma's decline in oil production decelerated, but the state stayed in fourth place, behind Illinois. Prices showed improvement, averaging around $1.00 a barrel.

Bob Kerr played many roles during the year. He was reelected president of the Kansas-Oklahoma division of the Mid-Continent Oil and Gas Association (a position he had held since 1935) and successfully led the Oklahoma City fight for a bond issue to increase its water supply. Although he incurred the wrath of Governor Phillips by openly supporting a third term for President Roosevelt, Kerr was unanimously elected Democratic national committeeman from Oklahoma.[1]

Personal triumphs aside, his Kerlyn Oil Company was far from healthy, with a sick balance sheet. Plagued by debts, taxes, a shortage of capital, government restrictions, and continuing low prices for its products, management was cheered only by a slight increase in drilling activity. A January 3, 1940, contract with Phillips Petroleum brought an advance of $55,000 for a joint venture to drill certain new wells in Oklahoma City. But, on January 10, Kerlyn wrote off its investment in the Heiland Research Corporation by exchanging the 25,000 shares owned jointly with Kerr-Lynn for drilling and seismic equipment and services and for some 20,000 shares of the Heiland-owned Zodiac Oil Company. Kerlyn then bought Kerr-Lynn's half interest for 10,000 shares of class B stock. Several months later a new subsidiary, the Anchor Exploration Company, was incorporated to give Kerlyn a prospecting arm, and the equipment obtained from Heiland was immediately transferred to Anchor in exchange for shares of its common stock.[2] The dream of an integrated company was still alive.

At the January 15 stockholders' meeting, where Kerr-Lynn voted 3,050 shares of class A stock and 373,100 of class B, President Kerr was forced to report that for the four months ending October 31, 1939, the net loss had been $17,595.69. Fortunately he could then add that by the end of that year there had been an upturn, and Kerlyn could claim a surplus of some $500.00. But Dean Terrill delivered an added blow when he reported that the Texas Supreme Court had ruled against the company in the Bruhlmeyer suit (1936) involving the Gainesville field, costing Kerlyn title to one-half of the oil and gas produced by that lease.

[1] Kerr scrapbooks, 1.

[2] Oklahoma Secretary of State, "Corporation File"; Securities and Exchange Commission, "Form 8, Amendment No. 1, Amended Financial Statement of Annual Report (Form 10-K) for Fiscal Year Ended June 30, 1952, Kerr-McGee Oil Industries, Inc."

No wonder that Kerlyn's annual report for 1940 was the worst of Kerr's experience. His accompanying letter was unusually short. The good news was minimal. Although total assets had climbed $65,800, net income for the fiscal year was only $4,278.07 on a gross operating income of $871,974.06. Not surprising, the firm had made application to the Securities and Exchange Commission and the Chicago Stock Exchange to delist its class A common. Oil production amounted to 658,486 barrels, an increase of 14 percent, and nine new wells had been added, raising proven reserves by 276,174 barrels. But this had not been enough to offset the adverse factors. Certainly, Wallace Wigg's comment, "There was quite a lot of paper pushing back then to keep things going," is understandable.[3]

On the other hand, Kerr-Lynn sank thirty-six wells during the year ending June 30, 1940. Twenty-five were straight contracts, and the remaining eleven were financed by deals of varying nature. This time, however, both kinds were profitable, with the contract holes netting $8,244.95, and the interest wells, $22,552.03, on a gross of $643,993.01. The big difference was the interest ventures, where eight of eleven had been producers. During the second half of 1940 there were approximately thirty-two operations, eighteen in the Oklahoma district and fourteen in Odessa, Texas. Using both steam and rented rigs, the company made a profit in Oklahoma of about $22 per day, or $217 per hole.

For these Kerr-Lynn was reimbursed by one of the following means: (1) straight cash payments, (2) a cash consideration plus royalties, leases, or oil payments, (3) wells drilled in partnership with Kerlyn, and (4) wells sunk by Kerr-Lynn for its own account. On the cash basis, the wells for Phillips in the Oklahoma City pool proved the most profitable, while those for ITIO and Davon Matheson showed losses. Of five Stanolind wells in Seminole County only one had a net gain. The cash-plus ventures brought a profit of around $2,500, while those with Kerlyn had a loss over all. The best financial returns came when Kerr-Lynn was the sole owner. During the year it used some nine rigs, and the cost per day for its own five units ranged from $256.30 for steam down to $172.42 for motor-driven.[4]

All new Kerlyn wells during calendar 1940 were in Oklahoma or Kansas. Of these ventures in Pottawatomie (4), Logan (2), Pontotoc (2), Oklahoma (1), and Seminole (1) counties, plus Douglas County (2), in Kansas, half were dry and four were gas—a small gas pool in Pontotoc being the principal find. Nevertheless, the last half of 1940 saw a slow rise in the company's production, with Oklahoma City and Odessa, Texas, continuing as Kerlyn's main contract areas although Harold Freeman did recall being in Cut Bank, Montana. A minor internal change occurred in the drilling firm when a new numbering system was begun with the purchase of what came to be known

---

[3] Kerlyn Oil Company, *Annual Report for the Fiscal Year Ended June 30, 1940*; interview with Wallace Wiggs, August 12, 1970; *New York Times*, October 12, 1940.

[4] W. C. Bednar, "Drilling Cost Analysis," September 3, 1941; G. Otis Danielson, "Kerr-Lynn & Co. Analysis of Drilling Cost and Profit & Loss in Oklahoma District for Period March 31, 1940, to March 31, 1941," December 1, 1941; "Prospectus for 60,000 Shares . . . April 9, 1946," p. 18.

as Rig #1. Before this time they had simply called the units "old 8's," "new 8's," "old 12's," or "new 12's," depending upon the number of cylinders and the date of construction. Afterward, numbers were assigned that lasted until the equipment was junked or sold.[5] All in all 1940 had been a lackluster year for the Kerr enterprises.

For most Americans, 1941 was but a single day—December 7. But other momentous events occurred, even if pale in comparison to Pearl Harbor. President Roosevelt interpreted his reelection to signify popular approval of his "short of war" policy, and in March secured passage of the Lend-Lease Act to make America "the arsenal of democracy." Two months later came the transfer of fifty oil tankers to Britain. Conscription was extended for the duration of the emergency, and construction of a "two-ocean navy" was begun. By September the navy had orders to "shoot on sight" any German submarines. To curb the growing menace of Japan, the president began imposing embargoes on various strategic materials, such as scrap metal, and in July froze all Japanese financial assets in the United States.

These preparations for war meant not only a terrific demand for oil but also the extension of government control over the industry to an unprecedented degree. Robert E. Wilson answered for the producers when he told the Cole Committee of the House of Representatives on March 27, "The petroleum industry has been, and in my opinion will continue to be, able to supply every foreseeable demand for petroleum and its products without requiring any government funds or advance government contracts." Prices were frozen on crude and most of its products. Control of production quotas, normally a function of the states, was brought under the direction of Harold L. Ickes in his capacity as petroleum coordinator.

In the face of these conditions Kerr's report to the Kerlyn stockholders was probably typical of the reaction by any firm operating in Oklahoma:

The Management of the Company is, of course, working wholeheartedly in aid of the country's defense program. That program has created or intensified a daily increasing number of problems affecting the successful conduct of a petroleum producing business. . . . How the decrease in supplies will be allocated and to what purposes they will be devoted is as yet undecided. We are hopeful of maintaining our current rate of production and are also hopeful of creating undeveloped reserves. . . . Facing, as we are, almost daily changes in conditions, any prophesy or forecast . . . might readily be classified as idle speculation.

Almost certainly, Kerr emphasized, the future would hold drastic curtailment of supplies of tubing, rods, casing, and the like, as well as "ominous clouds of increasing taxes." For Oklahoma as a state it was good news in that oil income was up by over $12 million. The rate of decline in production had abated, and Oklahoma was back in third place among producing states.

[5] *Oil and Gas Journal*, January 11, February 1, April 4, 18, May 23, June 6, 13, 27, July 11, August 8, and December 12, 1940. Interviews with Dean A. McGee, May 20, 1970; Harold Freeman, April 17, 1971; H. G. Kuhlman and E. H. Harvey, April 15, 1971; Otis Danielson, June 1, 1971; and R. E. Anderson, May 3, 1971.

At Kerlyn the upturn was obvious. The five months ending November 30, 1940, had shown a net income of almost $64,000, while the last six months of that year gave a net of $75,949. By March 31, 1941, this reached $113,210.41, a fact so encouraging to the directors that in May they not only declared their usual 8¾-cent dividend on class A, but also added a payment of 5 cents on class B stock. At the end of the fiscal year, June 30, 1941, the company reported a net profit of $159,880.20 (second highest in the firm's history), its largest current assets, largest amount of working capital, a record tax bill, and record dividend payments of $106,577.60. Total assets, however, had fallen by some $128,000.

Production increases accounted for most of this favorable report. Oil production, at 823,393 barrels, was at its height, bringing an average of $1.17 per barrel. Although gas output was up only slightly, it contributed $28,000 in additional funds. Five new oil wells had been added from June, 1940, to June, 1941, for a total of 108, and the company had 48 gas wells.[6]

For the calendar year 1941, Kerlyn was involved in sixteen drilling ventures, nine of which produced oil or gas. Nine of the total were in Pottawatomie County, where the Cherry #1 was the discovery well in the South Maud pool, but three were dry holes and none of the oil wells was large. Four attempts in Lincoln County yielded one small oil and three gas producers, while two in Logan resulted in a gasser and a dry hole. A wildcat in Murray County was likewise unsuccessful.

The first half of 1941 was also good for Kerr-Lynn. The gross from contract drilling for this fiscal year was $929,780.95. Again, most of the work was in Oklahoma or around Odessa, Texas, with nineteen contracts in the former and thirteen in the latter by March 31. The rest of the year, however, saw a decline in activity, as government restrictions began to have their effect and, especially, predicted shortages of drilling supplies were also felt. Costs went up, and fewer contracts were available. Even Kerlyn was sinking fewer wells.[7]

All of this was reflected in the meetings of Kerlyn directors during the remainder of 1941. In September they again declared a 5-cent dividend on B stock, in addition to the usual 8¾ cents on A. Kerr-Lynn's reimbursement, for office space and the services of eighteen of its personnel, was increased from $1,250 a month to $2,000. Many discussions followed concerning the withdrawal of class A stock. The principal arguments held that this move would eliminate those dividends, allowing this money to be invested in interest-bearing securities and thereby saving income taxes on the amount currently paid for use of public money. As hard as profits were to come by, it was always painful to part with them—especially for taxes.

With the nation officially at war during 1942, all energy and concern

[6] Kerlyn Oil Company, *Annual Report for the Fiscal Year Ended June 30, 1941*; S-1 Statement, No. 107, March 31, 1948, p. 10.

[7] For notices of Kerlyn wells see *Oil and Gas Journal*, January 2, February 6, 20, 27, March 20, April 3, May 1, 8, 22, July 10, 31, October 9, 16, 30, and November 6, 27, 1941; G. Otis Danielson, "Kerr-Lynn & Co. Analysis of Drilling Cost . . ."; "Prospectus for 60,000 Shares . . . April 9, 1946," p. 18.

focused on that effort. The public mood shifted from the erratic nervousness of uncertainty to one of unified patriotism. Citizens, eager to participate on the home front if not overseas, began frenetic and concentrated work in shipyards, steel mills, uniform factories, and all production lines where the accessories of battle were manufactured. Young men and, for the first time, young women volunteered for the armed forces, intensifying the personnel problems that had started in 1941. This loss of additional thousands of employees was augmented by the scarcity of raw materials. Capital was plentiful in the form of government contracts, but the demands forced on the industrial sector by the escalating defense program strained many managerial careers to the breaking point. America was a busy place, determined to win the war, and as soon as possible.

The 1942 shortages of manpower and vital supplies hit the petroleum world hard and marked a slackened pace in operations. Oklahoma's oil production fell by 14 million barrels, and oil income by $6 million. The confusion in the oil industry was mirrored by Dean Terrill's letter to the stockholders:

In the face of the revolutionary changes presently affecting our economy and industry, it may well be that experiment and change on a sound basis, rather than rigid conformity to tradition, may be necessary in order for individual industries and business to succeed. But we know, as proud, loyal Americans, that we are going to adapt ourselves to any procedure necessary to win the war, and we, the management of your Company and proud of and loyal to it, are equally confident that we will be able to adapt our Company procedures so that the Company will survive and grow with the United States of America.

The year was a revolutionary one for Kerlyn. The January annual stockholders' meeting was cut and dried, but in February the directors decided that no dividend could be paid on class B, and management announced that the federal authorities would permit the company to drill only in its proven territories in Young County, Texas, and the Kirk area of Oklahoma, and that was all. [8] Thus prospects for increased production under current restrictions and limitations were restricted. Because of possible reductions in allowables and the natural decline in old fields, there seemed no way to avoid a fall in total output. Furthermore, the price of natural gasoline was slipping. There was nothing to do but retrench: exploration and lease purchases would have to be curtailed.

Bob Kerr was keenly aware that this was a transition period for his company and the oil industry as a whole. On December 18, 1941, just eleven days after Pearl Harbor, he had announced his decision not to stand for reelection as president of the Kansas-Oklahoma division of the Mid-

---

[8] While there was a Kirk area in Kay County, the reference is probably to a location in Pottawatomie County north of Maud. On August 12, 1941, a contract was signed with T. M. Kirk of that town to acquire leases in the area for Kerlyn, and during the winter the Kirk #1 was a producer. Lease Records file, "Contract file #37"; *Oil and Gas Journal*, November 6, 1941, and January 8, 1942.

Continent Oil and Gas Association. Instead he was on the verge of taking the long-desired plunge into politics, and the timing was of the utmost importance. The petroleum world was in neutral gear, waiting to face the challenges of a world war. With few personal or financial worries, all of Kerr's vitality and energy was straining to capture another of his goals, the governorship of Oklahoma. On March 15, 1942, he officially announced that he was a candidate for the nomination on the Democratic ticket.

The fact that Kerr was an oilman did not become an issue in the primary. Most of the attention focused on the opposition to his candidacy by Governor Phillips, the incumbent, and Kerr's support of Franklin D. Roosevelt for a third term as president of the United States. The negative effect was slight, and Kerr triumphed in the primary by some 10,427 votes. It was an exciting time for employees of the small company, and Wallace Wiggs remembers that volunteers were active in the campaign, putting up posters, calling friends, and driving voters to the polls. All of this paid off, and in November, Kerr was chosen as the twelfth governor of Oklahoma—the first native-born—by a margin of 16,111 votes.[9]

Significant developments in Kerr's business interests were also paralleling his involvement in politics. As Dean Terrill related it, the relationship between Kerr-Lynn and Kerlyn had become

a very sticky thing. It was not good public financing when you've got a corporation that is owned by the public and another company whose chief owners are the management of the corporation that is in the same business and doing a lot of business between each other, etc. It always makes for suspicion. Underwriters kept beating us over the head about this connection, and we had to get rid of the partnership.

The previous stumbling block had been the cost of the assets of Kerr-Lynn. However, the current hard times of the oil industry were an advantage. Kerlyn already had an interest in all but four of Kerr-Lynn's producing properties. The depressed market, brought about by the curtailment of drilling, made it possible to acquire all the assets at a greatly reduced cost and on very favorable terms.[10]

A week after Kerr announced his candidacy a special meeting of the board was held to discuss an agreement, dated March 21, for "Sale and Purchase of Substantially all the Tangible Assets of Kerr-Lynn & Co." The partners, who were six of the eight Kerlyn directors, proposed to sell everything except their shares of Kerlyn stock. These assets were $209,112.50 in producing leases, $1,837.50 in producing royalties, $16,500 in undeveloped leases, $13,125 in undeveloped royalties, a filling station valued at $33,750, and drilling equipment worth $162,500. In return Kerlyn would assume debts up to the amount of total assets. The major obligations were $109,399.18 owed to the Liberty National Bank of Oklahoma City, $49,265.27 to Lucey

---

[9] Kerr scrapbooks, 5, 7; interview with Wallace Wiggs.

[10] Interview with Dean Terrill, April 27, 1970; Dean Terrill, "Letter to the Stockholders" in Kerlyn Oil Company, *Annual Report for the Fiscal Year Ended June 30, 1942.*

Products, $96,092.01 to Oil Well Supply Company, $100,000 to James L. and M. M. Anderson, and $40,707.21 to Kerlyn.

Such a merger would save Kerlyn $11,307.14 in monthly expenses. Since some of its officers were also being paid by Kerr-Lynn, an adjustment was proposed to give annual salaries of $24,000 to R. H. Lynn and to R. S. Kerr, $14,400 to Travis Kerr, and $12,000 to Dean McGee. At the end of two more days of discussion the purchase was approved, effective April 1, 1942. This appeared to put Bob Kerr's business interest in order. After hearing a report on projected economies in administration, acquisitions, and operations that promised substantial savings, the Kerlyn board declared a special 2½-cent payment on class B shares, as well as the regular dividend on A.

But late in April the euphoria was shattered. Lynn announced that he wished to disassociate himself from both Kerlyn and Kerr-Lynn. During the discussion that ensued among the directors, it was pointed out that, because of curtailed operations, Lynn's services really were not vital to future plans. Besides, his salary of $24,000 would be a worthwhile saving. It was therefore agreed that it would be in the best interest of all concerned to assist his withdrawal by any steps that were reasonable and feasible. Eventually a plan was evolved by which the remaining partners would purchase Lynn's shares in Kerr-Lynn.

According to Dean McGee a written agreement had been made at the time Lynn joined Kerlyn. If he or Bob Kerr ever decided to sell his interest, the other had the right of purchase. Lynn proposed to implement this understanding, but since Kerr did not want to sell, then he, Lynn, would. His reasons for this decision were never stated publicly. Some believed that his motivation was political, Otto Barton referring to him as a "hard-headed Republican." Others thought that Lynn resented having to run the company while Kerr played in politics—that Kerr should either get out of politics or get out of the company.

Whatever the reason, Lynn should have anticipated Kerr's political plans. It had been assumed, when Kerr recruited Lynn and McGee in 1937 that he did so to bring in people competent to run the business and leave him free to devote more time to public life. There was no question that Kerr's outside involvements meant a greater workload and a heavier burden of responsibility for Lynn. Probably more important in Lynn's decision, however, was that he was heartily disliked by men who held high positions in the Kerlyn management. Some of these went so far as to consider him a traitor to the company's interest. During Lynn's tenure times had been hard for the oil industry, and for Kerlyn in particular. The chances were slight that there would be any improvement in the immediate future.[11]

At the meeting of the board in July it was announced that arrangements between management and Lynn had been executed. Lynn then tendered

[11] Interviews with Dean A. McGee, May 20, 1970, September 4, 1971, March 3, 1973; George Cobb, January 21, 1971; Otto Barton, July 26, 1971; and Dean Terrill, November 29, 1969; Dean Terrill to Malvina Stephenson, June 26, 1963, in Terrill file, Public Relations Department; Breene Kerr told Bette Brenz that Lynn thought his father should get out of oil or politics—Brenz to author.

Kerlyn Oil Company
Table 8.1. Consolidated Statement of Income and Surplus, 1940–42

	Year Ended June 30, 1942	Year Ended June 30, 1941	Year Ended June 30, 1940
Gross operating income			
Crude-oil production and gas sales	$1,079,817.57	$1,062,127.16	$ 849,541.51
Steam, compressor, and water sales	995.93	844.34	1,307.79
Drilling contracts completed	113,679.85	. . . .	. . . .
Total gross operating income	$1,194,493.35	$1,062,971.50	$ 850,849.30
Operating charges			
Cost of drilling contracts completed	$ 78,173.10	. . . .	. . . .
Natural-gas purchases for resale	8,004.72	$ 5,020.18	$ 2,453.97
Production and maintenance expense	236,545.96	246,984.13	217,086.73
Gross production taxes	55,467.48	47,847.98	35,329.03
General and administrative expense	83,399.46	54,150.84	58,548.92
Office—clerical salaries, office rent, etc., charged by affiliate	18,000.00	15,000.00	15,000.00
Geological and land department expense	28,245.34	16,003.49	30,291.85
Taxes—exclusive of income taxes	20,645.43	14,171.42	11,582.99
Legal expense	5,752.85	7,087.62	6,631.17
Insurance and bond expense—not allocated	6,294.51	6,888.82	7,596.51
Lease rentals paid	24,772.48	10,634.03	8,307.06
Miscellaneous	9,208.99	9,822.44	3,071.50
Total operating charges before reserves and retirements	$ 574,510.32	$ 433,610.95	$ 395,899.73
Less: income from service equipment—net	40,158.09	34,056.74	23,501.54
Net operating charges before reserves and retirements	$ 534,352.23	$ 399,554.21	$ 372,398.19
Operating income before reserves and retirements	$ 660,141.12	$ 663,417.29	$ 478,451.11
Other income			
Profit from sale of properties	$ 19,991.43	$ 80,377.74	$ 11,970.46
Inventory adjustment	11,208.27	12,286.46	7,254.15
Commissions received	1,016.12	2,972.28	. . . .
Miscellaneous—purchase discounts, etc.	4,208.74	2,863.78	1,594.99
Total other income	$ 36,424.56	$ 98,500.26	$ 20,819.60
Gross income before reserves and retirements	$ 696,565.68	$ 761,917.55	$ 499,270.71

Table 8.1. *Continued*

	Year Ended June 30, 1942	Year Ended June 30, 1941	Year Ended June 30, 1940
Other deductions			
Interest expense	$ 11,767.16	$ 6,465.42	$ 6,008.55
Organization and Securities Exchange Act expense	84.88	7,861.29	11,958.33
Uncollectible accounts charged off	1,008.00	7,221.35	3,093.35
Loss of producing lease interests due to failure in title	. . . .	15,510.42	. . . .
Provision for income taxes	1,963.11	30,390.04	. . . .
Total other deductions	$ 14,823.15	$ 67,448.52	$ 21,060.23
Net income before reserves and retirements	$ 681,742.53	$ 694,469.03	$ 478,210.48
Provision for reserves and retirements			
Depletion	$ 312,821.28	$ 339,258.24	$ 299.823.44
Depreciation	122,568.07	109,297.15	96,081.43
Retirement of producing oil payment costs	7,935.22	4,707.16	2,376.78
Leases canceled and expired	36,465.33	30,026.32	22,670.18
Worthless royalties charged off	167.63	400.00	5,145.74
Seismograph and exploration costs	56,177.83	26,788.51	. . . .
Loss from dry holes drilled	61,949.48	18,637.23	45,110.79
Loss from abandonment of properties	76,455.36	5,474.22	2,724.05
Total provision for reserves and retirements	$ 674,540.20	$ 534,588.83	$ 473,932.41
Net income to surplus	$ 7,202.33	$ 159,880.20	$ 4,278.07
Balance of surplus earned—beginning	266,502.72	226,747.85	335,049.35
Deductions from surplus—	$ 273,705.05	$ 386,628.05	$ 339,327.42
Dividends declared on class A common at the rate of 35¢ per share	$ 85,267.27	$ 86,077.60	$ 86,127.30
Dividends declared on class B common at the rate of 7½¢ per share	30,750.00	20,500.00	. . . .
Addition to reserve for contingency	29,726.50	13,547.73	26,452.27
Total deductions from surplus	$ 145,743.77	$ 120,125.33	$ 112,579.57
Balance of surplus earned—end	$ 127,961.28	$ 266,502.72	$ 226,747.85

his resignation as executive vice-president, member of the executive com-mittee, and director, all effective August 1. The resignations were accepted, probably without too much regret. There can be no doubt about Lynn's general ability, but there were personality conflicts, and evidence indicates that, while Lynn proved himself a good number-two man, he had shortcom-ings in the top position.

Dean McGee, the logical man to replace Lynn temporarily, was assigned the duties of Kerlyn's executive vice-president. Meanwhile, the seven remaining partners in Kerr-Lynn purchased Lynn's 20 percent share, val-ued at $250,000, retroactive to April 1, in roughly the ratio of their holdings. For example, Robert S. Kerr owned 34.26535 percent in 1941, and by this transaction he held 40.4688 percent; T. M. Kerr's share went from 6.1105 to 7.6389 percent.

On July 31, Kerr-Lynn & Company was dissolved. A new partnership, prophetically named Kerr-McGee & Co., was formed to take over Kerr-Lynn's remaining assets. The new company then sold Lynn's 9,261 shares of Kerlyn A stock to Kerlyn for $30,098.25. This, together with the earlier sale of Kerr-Lynn's tangible assets to Kerlyn, left Kerr-McGee with only the Kerlyn class B stock owned by the seven partners. By these moves Dean Terrill's objections to the existence and role of Kerr-Lynn were cleared away, and its successor would play only an insignificant role in Kerlyn activities.[12]

The Kerlyn annual report for June, 1942, reflected the increased difficul-ties of operating under wartime conditions (see Table 8.1). Although total assets grew by $238,000, net profit plummeted to $7,202.33, a drop of over $152,000—despite an average oil price of $1.21 per barrel. More signifi-cantly, working capital fell over $250,000 to a mere $5,233.12. Crude-oil production declined by 150,000 barrels, but the gas output rose some 3 billion cubic feet and its income by almost $110,000 or the report would have been worse. The newly acquired drilling capacity contributed $113,679.35 on a gross of $944,575.96. An auditor's note to the effect that Kerlyn, which owned a fourth interest, was being sued for damages because of negligence by owners of oil-and-gas properties adjacent to the Watchorn lease in Oklahoma City foreshadowed a significant development for the company.[13]

Kerlyn's record of drilling on its own behalf was equally dismal. Only seven new Oklahoma wells were spudded during the calendar year, and only one, a gas producer in Seminole County, was successful. The nine drilling rigs—seven power and two steam—acquired from Kerr-Lynn bored some 237,596 feet at some 55 locations. While most of the work was in

[12] Dean Terrill and Whit Fentem memorandum to "Partners," June 2, 1941, in T. M. Kerr file; "Origin of Kerr-McGee Oil Industries, Inc., stock ownership . . ."; interview with S. B. Robinson, February 23, 1970.

[13] Kerlyn Oil Company, *Annual Report . . . 1942; New York Times*, October 14, 1942, p. 35; S-1 Statement, No. 107, March 31, 1948; "Prospectus for 60,000 Shares . . . April 9, 1946," p. 18.

Oklahoma, chiefly in Caddo County, other contracts took them to Texas and Montana.[14]

Working capital was down to $5,000, and management's prime concern was to find more money. With wartime shortages of gasoline one decision was to sell the service stations.[15] In July, Director Straus proposed issuing debentures to buy up the class A stock. Two months later the board authorized a loan of $37,500 from Liberty National Bank of Oklahoma City, while voting also to approach the First National Bank of Chicago about refinancing the various Kerlyn obligations. With an unfavorable answer from Chicago, the decision on refinancing was deferred. Indicative of his new role, Dean McGee was moved into the inner circle with his election to the executive committee, while the five Oklahoma City directors formed an operating committee.

The year 1942 marked a decisive point in Robert Kerr's participation in Kerlyn. Although in the future he proudly wore a lapel pin which proclaimed he was a founder of the company, his role gradually decreased. All who knew Kerr well agreed that the force which drove him was not the excitement of business management. Success in business was only means to an end: money. Money, in turn, was important as a base for power and as a way of freeing him to pursue his personal goals. He apparently believed the company's future and his family's finances were secure at this time. So, tired of the drudgery of day-to-day corporate housekeeping and increasingly vulnerable to the charms of political power, he moved on to public life. It was a step which drastically altered the image and fortunes of his life, and those of the small firm which bore his name.

[14] For Kerlyn wells see *Oil and Gas Journal*, February 12; March 26, June 18, 25, July 9, and December 17, 31, 1942; Kerlyn Oil Company, "Rig Operations Fiscal Year July 1, 1942, to June 30, 1943," in Transworld file, "Rig Operations March 1940 thru [*sic*] June 1946"; S-1 Statement, No. 107, March 31, 1948, p. 14; *Kermac News*, Vol. 2 (December, 1948), p. 5.

[15] *Kermac News*, Vol. 1 (February, 1947), p. 3; interview with Lucille Landsay, April 29, 1971.

Chapter 9

Dean A. McGee
The Early Years
1943–1945

There could be no question about Dean McGee's talents as a geologist, but as a chief administrator the quiet, unassuming McGee was an unknown factor. Regardless, he had to learn quickly. He was quoted as saying: "After he [Kerr] began running for Governor, we hardly ever saw him in the office. But he kept in touch by telephone. I've spent hours on the telephone talking to him. He took part in making policy, but he never interfered in the operation of the company." On another occasion McGee said: "From the time he became Governor . . . he was never out of full-time politics. He liked to stay in touch, called daily and presided at board meetings but his contribution was more in the way of advice and counsel. I've operated the company since 1942." While outsiders described the lanky McGee as "common as an old shoe" and "a serious but friendly college professor," his employees dubbed him "Superman" and marveled at his working hours.[1]

The year 1943 was a challenge for others also. Virtually alone, Travis Kerr was responsible for acquiring the highly important drilling contracts for Kerlyn. Speaking of Bob and his entry into politics, Travis reminisced: "I didn't have him to go to Tulsa, or Bartlesville, Denver or whatnot to help get drilling contracts; it was up to me." Fortunately, contracts were plentiful for those who could furnish the manpower and the rigs.

Indeed, fortune seemed to be smiling on the Kerlyn Oil Company. It was

---

[1] *Tulsa Tribune*, March 13, 1968, p. 33; "Kerr-McGee Oil Stretches Out," *Investor's Reader*, October 7, 1964, pp. 17ff.; *Kermac News*, Vol. 1 (July, 1947), p. 3; Spring, 1955, pp. 10, 22.

announced at a special meeting of the board in early January that three wildcats had been drilled in the first week of 1943 and that all of them were producers. Blackhawk Drilling Company, bought by An-Ker, Incorporated, in 1931 for $300, was now the property of Kerr-McGee & Co., which wanted to sell it to Kerlyn. Blackhawk had been a useful drilling-labor subcontractor in the past and had assets of $47,907.94. Kerlyn decided to purchase and liquidate it. Furthermore, in line with earlier discussions, the board now felt that Kerlyn's financial position was strong enough to begin buying up its own class A stock at the rate of fifteen to sixteen thousand dollars per month.

At the January stockholders' meeting it was announced that, although Kerr had been elected governor, he still wished to remain president of Kerlyn. Not only was his request granted but also it was decided that he would receive his same salary. The seven directors were reconfirmed, and at the board meeting that followed, McGee was formally designated executive vice-president, and his new salary set at $15,000.

Undoubtedly, the most serious need which faced the directors, however, was working capital to finance the exploration program so essential to growth and expansion. This problem was unexpectedly eased by a source which had assisted most opportunely in the past: the Phillips Petroleum Company. Undoubtedly Phillips regretted the loss of McGee and wanted access to his proven talents. Furthermore, Phillips knew from past experience that Kerlyn had ability to put together workable packages. Consequently, it approached the young company with a rare, but not unheard-of proposal. Phillips would put up 75 percent of the cost for a half share in any future Kerlyn venture in which it decided to participate.

An agreement to this effect, good for up to five years, was signed by the two firms on March 31, 1943. Under this pact almost all of Kerlyn's geological, exploratory, lease acquisitions including ownership of mineral rights, and exploratory well-drilling activities were carried on for the joint and equal benefit of both parties. As a result, only 25 percent of all costs and expenses was borne by Kerlyn. If oil was discovered, the developmental and operational expenses would be shared equally. In this event Phillips also had the right to purchase, at competitive prices, the resulting production. To cash-starved Kerlyn, this was a godsend, for it had been unable to mount a real exploration program. Now it could greatly enlarge the scope of its operations.[2]

But in May, despite this agreement and a decision to make an extra dividend payment of 2¼ cents on class B stock, the board was in a more cautious mood. It decided that class A should not be bought up in the amounts previously suggested but rather the purchase limited to 2,500 shares at $4.50 each. It was also agreed to sell some 4,000 acres of oil and gas leases in Young County, Texas, to Anderson-Prichard Oil Company. And

[2] See statement by C. O. Stark, Phillips's vice-president, in typescript of Nora Owens, "The Strata of Dean Anderson McGee," in Public Relations Department files; *Mining Record*, August 16, 1956; interviews with George Cobb, January 21, 1971, and Dean A. McGee, March 3, 1973. The terms of the agreement were published in Kerr-McGee Oil Industries, Inc., *Annual Report for the Fiscal Year Ended June 30, 1949*, note "G."

once more a line of credit up to $100,000 was sought with the Liberty National Bank of Oklahoma City and mortgages executed for the same. The directors then voted to increase their own fee to $50 a meeting.

Over the nation a feeling of cautious optimism began to spread. On the war fronts, after a series of withdrawals, defeats, and stalemates, the United States and its allies were able to mount the first offensives. At home all business and labor worked overtime to support the war effort. Despite the low price of oil, governmental regulations, shortages of materials, and loss of manpower, the petroleum industry achieved its greatest production ever. By 1943, a comprehensive government-industry organization was set up to accomplish just this. Petroleum Coordinator Harold Ickes said:

This is an *oil war*. The side, which by interrupting the flow of petroleum products to the enemy, and which at the same time can supply its own tanks, its mechanized guns, its fighting ships, and its airplanes with gasoline, and lubricants, and fuel oils of the proper kind at the time required, and in the right places is the side which will eventually win this world-wide conflict.

In Oklahoma total production continued to decline as older fields neared exhaustion. However, the effort to find new oil during 1943 reversed this trend for the first time in six years. Kerlyn played a role, for, as Dean Terrill wrote the stockholders:

Despite the continued low price paid to producers for crude oil . . . the Company has responded to the pleas of the Administration to the Industry to intensify efforts toward the discovery of new oil reserves. We are presently engaged in the most extensive and intensive exploratory program which we have ever attempted, one which is probably unprecedented in scope of a company our size.

He warned, however, that the continued existence of the relatively small independent producers depended upon increasing the price of crude oil, "which has been frozen for so long," to at least balance the higher cost of labor, materials, equipment and the ever-present and ever-increasing taxes.

Despite all these problems, Kerlyn drilled the discovery well in an important new field where few people had expected one. This, McGee's first major venture as operating head, was also the first of many extraordinarily lucky events to occur over the following years. The well, which on April 25, 1943, set off the boom in Oklahoma's West Edmond field, had an eccentric, Ace Gutowsky, as the improbable hero of an even more improbable saga. Gutowsky did not believe in geology and had leased acreage in Kingfisher and Logan counties on the basis of his own homemade "doodlebug," a device described by George Cobb as looking like a radio. Ace claimed that oil would be found in the Hunton Limestone, a notoriously poor reservoir. Oil-company land men and independent promoters would not support his proposal to test his theory. It was such a poor location that he could not even secure enough geological or geophysical data to sell acreage to finance his own well.

Finally Gutowsky worked out a deal with Kerlyn. Ace supplied the derrick, casing, cement, butane, mud, $31,000 in cash plus a daily fee, and a working interest in a number of leases. Which Kerlyn official pushed this gamble is not known, but certainly the decision had McGee's concurrence. And so the drilling began. The financial shoestring was so slim that it took almost four months to reach 6,950 feet, because operations were occasionally stopped while Gutowsky looked for more money. But at that level the impossible happened. Oil flowed at the rate of 522 barrels in twenty-four hours! The "experts" were still skeptical, even those at Kerlyn who had much more to gain. Travis later laughed when recalling that on the Saturday *after* this discovery was brought in Ace offered him a lease on eighty acres just one-half mile north of the well for $400. Travis made a quick telephone call to one of Kerlyn's geologists, who told him that the lease was not worth 25 cents, much less $400. Consequently, he loaned Ace $200 as a personal favor, instead. That same lease eventually sold for $125,000.

Moreover, Kerlyn failed to exploit the offsetting acreage given it by Gutowsky as part of the agreement to drill the test well. Whether this resulted from geological skepticism or a shortage of operating capital, or both, is not clear. The fact remains that the land in question was sold back to Gutowsky for an oil payment of $750 an acre and the right to drill his wells on it. Later Kerlyn did buy a large spread on the "trend," but only after subsequent developments proved beyond question that the field was not a fluke. The U.S. Bureau of Mines annual report for 1943 listed West Edmond as the "greatest addition of new oil" for that year, and it soon ranked fourth in America's leading oil fields as a result of the greatest concentration of drilling rigs (150) in the world.

Although relatively few wells were drilled at Edmond for its own benefit, Kerlyn's contract drilling experienced a bonanza. All the old-timers vividly remember those years as the company rebuilt ancient steam rigs and bought or leased every set of tools it could find. Buster Kuhlman recalled one period when they were operating eighteen units there at one time. This went on seven days a week, sometimes twenty-four hours a day, in rain and mud. And the veteran Joe Godard claimed that manpower was so scarce he had "two roughnecks and two weevils" who had never seen a drilling rig before, and that most of Kerlyn's rigs were usually a man or two short.

During the Edmond field's heyday Kerlyn drilled more wells there than any other company, mostly by contract. While this enhanced the company's reputation as a driller and contributed to its production, it did not do much for profits because of the necessary heavy investments in equipment. Through foresight, however, Kerlyn did have a unique advantage. Since the field attracted so many old steam rigs, which put a premium on water, Kerlyn made a deal with a man who had an artesian well (two more were drilled later) to buy all of his water. This allowed Kerlyn to get contracts which otherwise might not have been available. Travis recalled that this was especially true in bidding for drilling rights against Sohio and that the "[water] well turned out to be about as profitable as the drilling."[3]

---

[3] C. C. Rister, *Oil! Titan of the Southwest*, pp. 341–42; Bette Brenz file, "West Edmond File"; interviews with Joe Godard, June 27, 1971; Travis Kerr, December 12, 1969; George

Nevertheless, the annual report for the fiscal year ending June 30, 1943, was a distinct improvement over the previous one. For one thing, net income jumped over $92,500, and working capital by $83,057.59! Most of this came from the contract drilling, which grossed $664,410.11. The oil-and-gas production and revenues actually declined, and oil sales averaged only $1.13 per barrel. The company had also operated surface parties and three seismograph crews in the Rocky Mountains, the Mid-Continent, Texas, and the south Arkansas–north Louisiana areas, and drilled wildcats in each area. All of this had been done at minimum risk through the Phillips agreement—if large strikes were found, the profit would be great, but failures would not be too large to absorb.

Specifically, Kerlyn used eleven rigs (nine owned and two rented) in the period between July 1, 1942, and June 30, 1943. Forty-nine wells were completed, with nine still in progress. Of those completed, forty were in Oklahoma; four in Young County, Texas; three in Montana; and two in Colorado. In the remaining six months of the calendar year additional rigs were bought or rented, and the geographical area of operations expanded.[4]

One more event was of significance in 1943. Kerlyn had long wished to get into East Texas and Southeast oil play. A step was taken in that direction on June 1, when a contract was made with Francis W. Scott. For a one-year period he was "Special Representative in Charge of the Southeast District," with responsibility for exploration, acquiring leases, performing exploratory drilling, and carrying on contract drilling in northeastern Texas, southern Arkansas, northern Louisiana, and a portion of western Alabama. For these services he was paid $7,500 a year and got 15 percent of any rights or interests acquired by Kerlyn. Although the contract was not renewed, Scott did acquire rights in six leases in Union and Lafayette counties in Arkansas; in Panola county, Texas; and in De Soto Parish, Louisiana.

A more significant opportunity came in October with the chance to purchase 19.50 percent, or 2,345 shares, of the capital stock of F. W. Merrick, Inc., a holder of important acreages and production in both East and West Texas. Phillips had bought 60.50 percent of the company and offered to arrange a three-year $300,000 loan at 3 percent for Kerlyn with the First National Bank of Bartlesville, Oklahoma. Harris Trust and Saving Bank of Chicago agreed to furnish $500,000 at 4 percent to complete the deal, and so the Kerlyn board authorized purchase of the property for $830,334.50. The transaction was executed on October 29, 1943, and Phillips and Kerlyn's

Cobb, January 21, 1971; Otis Danielson, June 1, 1971; Harold Freeman, April 17, 1971; and J. H. Kuhlman, February 25, 1970. Gutowsky had raised the cash from varied sources. The original drilling contract was December 8, 1942, and the sale of Kerlyn interests back to him was May 20, 1943. Lease Records file, "Contract file #15."

[4] Kerlyn Oil Company, *Annual Report for the Fiscal Year Ended June 30, 1943*; S-1 Statement, No. 107, March 31, 1948, p. 10; *New York Times*, October 7, 1943; Transworld file, "Kerlyn Oil Company Drilling Department Rig Operation Fiscal Year July 1, 1942, to June 30, 1943"; and "Kerlyn Oil Company Authorization Index of Rig Operations Fiscal Year—July 1, 1942, to June 30, 1943," in Transworld file, "Rig Operations March 1940 thru June 1946."

agents voted to liquidate F. W. Merrick, Inc., the same day.[5] This purchase brought interests in over 500 additional wells.

Although the financial condition of the oil company improved, cash flow still fell far short of management's ambitions. Consequently, during 1944 most of its energies were expended in search of additional cash and credit. Nevertheless, the February board meeting raised salaries for McGee ($20,000), T. M. Kerr ($17,400), Terrill ($12,500), and Fentem ($10,300). The directors also instructed the officers to try to purchase certain shares of class B stock which had been sold by security dealers to the general public.

But all of this was merely a prelude to the search for "big" money. Large amounts, for example, were necessary to complete the long-discussed redemption of Kerlyn's class A stock, and even more was needed to take full advantage of Phillips's financing in the enlarged exploration program. One asset which could be converted into cash was the property in the West Edmond field. Although seventeen rigs (eleven owned and six rented) were operating there, few were on Kerlyn wells. Consequently, at the May meeting of the board, after a declaration of dividends, a discussion was held on the wisdom of selling these properties versus a long-term bank loan to buy up the class A stock.

It was Magnolia all over again, and the decision was the same: on May 24 an agreement was reached with Carter Oil Company to sell Kerlyn's half interest in 15,000 acres of undeveloped property in Logan and Kingfisher counties for $1 million in cash, and an additional oil payment up to a maximum of $1 million more. This was ratified by the board on June 6, effective September 20, 1943.

Kerlyn remained active as a driller in West Edmond. Dean McGee even served as treasurer of an Oklahoma City Chamber of Commerce drive to raise funds to upgrade the roads in the field, a precedent of his future involvement in civic affairs. Between August 23, 1944, and February 28, 1945, some $46,675 was secured by prorated assessments on users. Kerlyn, which was operating fourteen rigs for Sohio, Anderson-Prichard, Sinclair, Cities Service, and Phillips, contributed $2,100 ($150 per rig) to the total.[6]

The sale to Carter Oil Company was only a temporary solution, however. Up to this time, Kerr's various companies had been able to borrow from Oklahoma banks the funds for day-to-day operations, but by 1944 Kerlyn's

[5] For Scott see Lease Records file, "Contract file #2"; the Merrick leases in Cooke, Wichita, Mitchell, Rusk, Scurry, Howard, Glasscock, Shackelford, Gregg, and Upshur counties in Texas and Carter, Stephens, and Marshall counties in Oklahoma were held 75 percent by Phillips and 25 percent by Kerlyn. Kerlyn gave Phillips a call on the oil. Lease Records file, "Contract #4." See also Securities and Exchange Commission, "Form 8, Amendment No. 1, Annual Financial Statement of Annual Report (Form 10-K) for Fiscal Year Ended June 30, 1952, Kerr-McGee Oil Industries, Inc."; S-1 Statement, No. 107, March 31, 1948, p. 15.

[6] S-1 Statement, No. 107, March 31, 1945, pp. 15–16; interview with Dean Terrill, April 27, 1970; "West Edmond Oil Field Road Improvement Fund," in Dean A. McGee's personal files. See also D. A. McGee and H. D. Jenkins, "West Edmond Oil Field, Central Oklahoma," *Bulletin of the American Association of Petroleum Geologists*, Vol. 30 (November, 1946), pp. 1797–1829.

Kerlyn Oil Company

Table 9.1. Consolidated Statement of Income and Surplus, 1942 –43

	Year Ended June 30, 1943	Year Ended June 30, 1942
Gross operating income		
Crude-oil production and gas sales	$ 935,505.93	$1,079,817.57
Steam, compressor, and water sales	1,014.86	995.93
Drilling contracts completed	664,410.11	113,679.85
Total gross operating income	$1,600,930.90	$1,194,493.35
Operating charges		
Cost of drilling contracts completed	$ 534,846.84	$ 78,173.10
Natural-gas purchases for resale	5,075.21	8,004.72
Production and maintenance expense	168,956.22	236,545.96
Gross production taxes	48,585.65	55,467.48
General and administrative expense	142,190.40	83,399.46
Office—clerical salaries, office rent, etc., charged by affiliate	. . . .	18,000.00
Geological and land department expense	40,353.69	28,245.34
Taxes—exclusive of income taxes	16,011.80	20,645.43
Legal expense	8,452.98	5,752.85
Insurance and bond expense—not allocated	6,813.09	6,294.51
Lease rentals paid	36,435.63	24,772.48
Miscellaneous	1,954.88	9,208.99
Total operating charges before reserves and retirements	$1,009,676.39	$ 574,510.32
Less: income from service equipment—net	49,277.29	40,158.09
Net operating charges before reserves and retirements	$ 960,399.10	$ 534,352.23
Operating income before reserves and retirements	$ 640,531.80	$ 660,141.12
Other income		
Profit from sale of properties	$ 54,031.82	$ 19,991.43
Inventory adjustment	6,250.57	11,208.27
Rental income	13,958.32	194.91
Miscellaneous	6,849.69	5,029.95
Total other income	$ 81,090.40	$ 36,424.56
Gross income before reserves and retirements	$ 721,622.20	$ 696,565.68

needs exceeded the lending ability of these firms. Ever since Kerr's first money-seeking trips to Chicago in the mid-1930's his ambition had been to make a financial connection with the First National Bank of Chicago. As one of the largest banking institutions in the Middle West, it was unique in its attractiveness to oil men. First was the philosophy of the bank itself; second was the presence on its staff of Hugo A. Anderson, who came to be known as the "Father of Petroleum Lending."

Table 9.1. *Continued.*

	Year Ended June 30, 1943	Year Ended June 30, 1942
Other deductions		
Interest expense	$ 12,119.59	$ 11,767.16
Provision for income taxes	23,373.13	1,963.11
Miscellaneous	585.40	1,092.88
Total other deductions	$ 36,078.12	$ 14,823.15
Net income before reserves and retirements	$ 685,544.08	$ 681,742.53
Provision for reserves and retirements		
Depletion	$ 229,687.03	$ 312,821.28
Depreciation	134,978.61	$ 122,568.07
Retirement of producing oil payment costs	4,699.72	7,935.22
Leases canceled and expired	55,412.82	36,465.33
Worthless royalties charged off	7,183.32	167.63
Seismograph and exploration costs	39,436.61	56,177.83
Loss from dry holes drilled	97,827.46	61,949.48
Loss from abandonment of properties	14,570.83	76,455.36
Total provision for reserves and retirements	$ 583,796.40	$ 674,540.20
Net income to surplus	$ 101,747.68	7,202.33
Surplus earned—beginning	$ 127,961.28	
	$ 229,708.96	
Deductions from surplus		
Dividends declared		
On class A common at rate of 35¢ per share	$ 81,022.66	
On class B common at rate of 2½¢ per share	10,233.18	
Total deductions from surplus	$ 91,255.84	
Surplus earned—end	$ 138,453.12	

The Swedish-born Anderson's place in the oil industry was noted in 1969 by the American Petroleum Institute in a citation, which read in part

You, as a young banker, realized that petroleum in the ground to the extent producible by the owner or lessee was valid collateral for bank loans. You, in great measure, have made possible the independent producer who became the backbone of the American oil industry.

This vital role was made possible by his position with the First National Bank of Chicago. For purposes of lending, the bank had a number of divisions, each headed by a vice-president who had almost unrestricted authority to make loans. Anderson joined the bank in 1901, and by 1920 he was head of Division I, with the responsibility for oil transactions, among others. Up until that time the credit of independent oilmen with commercial bankers was practically nonexistent, and loans were made for short periods and paid for out of flush production from the wells.

When conservation practices came into being, Anderson recognized the long-range potential, and set out to develop new loan-repayment policies to meet the special needs of the oil industry. Viewing reserves as inventory "on nature's shelves," he and the First National pioneered by tailoring loan arrangements to meet this particular characteristic, and some unusual and innovative plans were formulated. Soon the petroleum business was clamoring at the bank's doors, and Anderson later boasted that "we have not lost one dollar in principal or interest in these speculative projects."

Anderson has described the difficulties of being original. Bank examiners, for example, were unfamiliar with this approach to financing, and financial statements seldom revealed any justification for the credit or the true value of the supporting crude reserves. Nor could they understand the steady increase in these loans, rather than gradual repayment. The bank, on the other hand, insisted that the inventory characteristics of these borrowers were not to be compared to the traditional ones that had seasonal periods and permitted inventory liquidation and retirement of debts. In the oil industry each producing well increased inventory, and the more successful the operator the greater his need for additional credit. "It was not exceptional to have an initial loan of $250,000 to $1,000,000 develop into a credit of 20 to 40 million dollars, and when we exceeded our legal limit we shared these loans with banking and/or insurance company friends." Because of accounting principles which allowed oil companies to charge off intangibles immediately against the cost of development, "we financed companies whose actual books showed net worth in red. . . . The more successful they were, the faster the arithmetic would show . . . that they were getting deeper and deeper in the red and richer and richer in company assets."[7] Small wonder at the mystification felt by the examiners!

Hugo Anderson and his bank first became acquainted with the Oklahoma oil scene when he advanced funds to Anderson-Prichard in 1926. But it was

---

[7] Dean A. McGee, speech to the Annual Conference, Oklahoma State Chamber of Commerce, November 19, 1970, in KM/PR files. The First National Bank of Chicago maintains an archives; all bank and Anderson material, not otherwise credited, came from that source: Hugo Anderson, speech before the American Petroleum Institute, November 11, 1969, and "A Banker's View of Oil Conservation" given before the Independent Bankers' Association of Southern California, July 24, 1954. Edward E. Kulpit, assistant vice-president of Division I, generously gave me a copy of his talk "Capital for the Petroleum Industry," which gave information concerning both the bank and Anderson. Anderson is the father of Robert O. Anderson, chairman of Atlantic Richfield.

in 1944, when First National had loans totaling $455,767,000 and assets exceeding $2 billion, that Anderson made the fateful trip to Oklahoma City: he had been invited to have breakfast at the governor's mansion. Kerr "did not ask directly for credit," but Anderson had known his host for "quite a few years," having previously turned down Kerr's requests for money. Consequently, there was no doubt about what lay behind the special invitation. Indeed, a meeting, at which Dean McGee was present and the question of finances was broached directly, followed soon after the meal. Anderson was asked to share in the Harris Trust loan (arranged with Phillips's help in 1943 to buy F. W. Merrick, Inc.) and to extend future credit when Kerlyn needed it. This time Anderson agreed to take over the existing note from the Bartlesville bank—"My own philosophy was that I'd rather handle all of the financing than a part of it," but let the Harris Trust keep its $500,000 loan for the time being.

Anderson then asked Kerr the deciding question: "Are you incurably in politics?" Kerr responded with a question of his own: "Do you object to it?" To this Anderson replied, "Not at all, but we learn by experience." He then told of a very successful businessman who had also become a governor, but at the end of his term his company was bankrupt. "We don't intend to let that happen with you, Mr. Kerr, and if you will just let Dean McGee run the company and you sit by and observe what we are doing, I'll continue to go with you." Kerr later credited Anderson with his [Kerr's] being in the United States Senate as a result of this talk.

Shortly afterward Harris Trust, which always had been uncomfortable with Kerlyn's loan, turned it over to the First National Bank of Chicago when that bank wanted to increase the debt. At the time Kerlyn's total assets were only a bit above $2.5 million. Nevertheless, the First National agreed to lend over $3.5 million to make possible, among other things, the call upon its class A stock—"One of the most constructive things that we [the bank and Anderson] could have helped to bring about so far as this company was concerned."

There had been several factors which influenced Anderson to reconsider and take on this new client. The first was the fact that Kerlyn was extremely successful in getting drilling contracts. Moreover, although Anderson only met McGee in 1944, his earlier trips to Oklahoma in connection with the financing of Anderson-Prichard had revealed the role McGee played for Phillips in the Oklahoma City field. "Having this in my mind, I was tremendously interested in a certain contract Kerr-McGee [sic] had with Phillips," by which Kerlyn had the privilege of acquiring leases and drilling the first well, thereby gaining a half interest for a quarter of the cost.

But, "Bob Kerr . . . knew very well that our loans were likely predicated on what we believed Dean McGee could do for the company. . . . This agreement would be rescinded in the event of the death or disconnection of Dean McGee with the company." Anderson summarized by saying:

There is no question about his ability and the thing that has really bought me, and that I have placed most in all my discussions with him, is not only the faith in his ability but in his absolute integrity in never polishing up, coloring, or really, as a salesman, trying to make it look better than it is. . . . The man is such a humble person that when you say he is a genius, these other qualities rate, by me, higher than that element.

Thus began an association which was a continuous one. For many years the people at First National "were the money" and had final say on all of Kerlyn's major operations. Guy C. Kiddoo, who replaced Anderson as head of Division I in 1947, eventually became a director in 1957, although he had turned down earlier requests.[8]

A special July meeting of the Kerlyn board was given over to a discussion of these developments and their impact on the company. It quickly agreed to approve the A loan of $2,630,000 and the B loan of $1 million, dated July 19, 1944. Against these would be used the $1 million from Carter Oil for the West Edmond property, and a deed of trust and chattel mortgage would be issued for the rest. After declaring the last quarterly dividend of $0.35 on class A common stock, the directors were finally in a position to call for redemption, on October 1, of all outstanding shares (246,285) of this class at $7.00 each. This left the capital stock of Kerlyn consisting of 412,508 shares of the previously designated class B stock. The remainder of the First National loans paid off debts to other banks, such as the First National of Bartlesville and the Liberty National of Oklahoma City.[9]

The 1944 annual report was a pleasant change. With increased oil, gas, water, and steam sales and completed drilling contracts worth more than $2.5 million, net income and assets reached new highs. Contract drilling obviously was the biggest factor in this growth. During the fiscal year Kerlyn operated thirteen power and two steam rigs of its own and rented five power and six steam outfits. It began eighty-seven wells and completed seventy-three. Of these, fifty-five were in Oklahoma (mostly in Oklahoma County), thus helping raise the production curve there; sixteen in Montana; thirteen in Texas (all in Young County); and one each in Wyoming, South Dakota, and Colorado. Gross footage reached 451,802.[10]

The October board meeting reflected this happy state of affairs. The directors first authorized filing a "Reduction in Capital Stock," a result of the recall of class A, and then recommended that the certificate of incorporation be amended to eliminate references to A and B stock. After declaring a dividend of six cents apiece on the remaining shares, they agreed to sell oil-and-gas payment interests of $200,000 each to the H.M.S. Corporation and to the Pension Fund of the First National Bank of Chicago. When

[8] Interview with Hugo A. Anderson, September 1, 1972. On February 2, 1959, the First National Bank used its association with Kerlyn as the basis for an advertisement in *Time*. Kerlyn was identified in the advertisement as "J. Oil Company." See letter from Wallace R. Watkins of Foote, Cone & Belding, Chicago, to Ross Cummings, Kerr-McGee Public Relations Director, January 5, 1959, in Public Relations file, "General Information."

[9] Oklahoma State Archives, Secretary of State, "Kerr-McGee *vs.* John Rogers," folder 3; Kerlyn Oil Company, *Annual Report for the Fiscal Year Ended June 30, 1944.*

[10] *Annual Report, 1944*; Transworld file, "Kerlyn Oil Company Drilling Department Rig Operations Fiscal Year—July 1, 1943, to June 30, 1944."

Kerlyn Oil Company

Table 9.2. Consolidated Statement of Income and Surplus, June 30, 1944

Crude-oil production and gas, steam, and water sales		$ 952,807.21
Drilling contracts completed		2,538,039.61
Gross operating income		$3,490,846.82
Cost of sales, drilling contracts completed, and operating expenses	$2,372,071.70	
Administrative and general expense	177,619.27	
Depreciation, depletion, and amortization	444,309.46	
Dry-hole losses and abandonments	124,885.30	3,118,885.73
		$ 371,961.09
Gain from sale of properties	$ 46,715.75	
Other income	33,905.47	80,621.22
		$ 452,582.31
Interest expense		37,054.74
		$ 415,527.57
Provision for federal taxes on income		88,008.89
Net income		$ 327,518.68
Balance surplus earned—June 30, 1943		138,453.12
		$ 465,971.80
Dividend paid		99,300.99
Balance surplus earned—June 30, 1944		$ 366,670.81

McGee reported that the Cosco Refinery at Wynnewood, Oklahoma, could be bought at a reasonable figure, it was decided that the possible acquisition should be investigated.

A special stockholders' meeting in November, where Kerr-McGee & Co. voted 384,575 of the eligible shares, quickly approved the First National loans, the redemption of class A stock, and the necessary changes in the certificate of incorporation. This marked the conclusion of a notable year for Kerlyn, in which the company came of age. The fruition of the agreement with Phillips, the maturing of the drilling arm, and finally the connection with the bank in Chicago, all combined to set Dean McGee and his small company on a more certain path toward success.

The next year, 1945, brought problems of a different nature to the United States and to Kerlyn. Franklin Roosevelt's death thrust an unknown, Harry S Truman, into the presidency. The atom bomb brought Japan to the peace table, following the May surrender of Germany. Suddenly the war was over, and armies began demobilizing. It was no longer forbidden to go for long Sunday-afternoon drives and use up precious gasoline. Consumer goods were in demand as never before, and Americans rushed to compensate themselves for four years of sacrifice. The money was there to buy new cars, as well as sugar, beef, and the rationed goods so loved by all. Even the farmers continued to benefit from high wartime prices for their products because of demand from Europe and the federal government's willingness to extend credit to former allies and enemies alike.

Petroleum producers had every reason for pride and rising expectations. In fact, they had made one of America's major efforts in behalf of patriotism. This was recognized by the Army-Navy Petroleum Board in November, 1945, when it wrote of the oil industry's "superb contribution made to the victory of the United States by providing in full and on time the vast flood of petroleum products required by the Armed Forces during World War II. . . . No Government agency and no branch of American industry achieved a prouder war record."

The end of the war made a difference, however. The problem became one of conversion of all facilities back to a peacetime basis and filling the service-station tanks for civilians who were rejoicing over the end of rationing. However, the transition from war to normal production necessitated no layoffs in an industry which had been shorthanded for four years, and most companies voluntarily raised wages.

The continuing demand for petroleum products benefited Oklahoma. Its production, which had risen slightly during 1944 to 123,436,000 barrels, mounted to 139,299,000, bringing in a total of $177,050,000. Kerlyn, with continued markets for its services and products, by 1945 managed to assemble twenty-two rigs and to find and train the manpower to operate them. Furthermore, Dean McGee was about to initiate still another step toward making Kerlyn a fully integrated oil company.

January, 1945, was a hallmark for the rest of the year, and the stamp was that of Dean McGee. His mastery of the administrative duties had become more and more obvious as he also took over the role of innovator previously played by Bob Kerr. Consequently, it was no surprise when Kerr asked the board of directors to change the name of Kerlyn Oil Company to reflect McGee's position. This was readily agreed upon, and the necessary steps were started.

The directors who approved this move had been chosen earlier in the month at the annual stockholders' meeting and were the same who held the positions in 1944. This closed nature of Kerlyn continued despite the fact that sizable blocks of stock were now held by firms such as Good & Company of Chicago (17,951); Harris, Upham & Company (1,800); and individuals such as Alma J. Hintze (700) and Charles M. Spaulding (500) of Bartlesville, Oklahoma. The obvious explanation, of course, was that Kerr-McGee & Co. was still the major stockholder.

It was a time to be daring. Despite the negative results obtained in the company's first offshore venture at Mobile Bay a few years after McGee had joined the firm, on January 15, 1945, Kerlyn signed a new oil-and-gas lease with the state of Mississippi. This was 400,000 acres in the eastern half of the Mississippi Sound waters off the coast of Harrison and Jackson counties for an initial payment of $25,000. The company had to begin seismographic work within six months and could conduct exploration work on the bottom of the sound only as long as no oyster or shrimp beds, bathhouses, or other structures were disturbed. To guarantee the latter, a representative of the Mississippi Seafood Commission was assigned to monitor operations.

Dean Terrill thought that this might lead to complications. Therefore, he wrote a note to Jack Lee, head of Kerlyn's geophysical department, telling him to look up the commissioner and "explain to him in a nice way the details of the gravity meter operations . . . and so satisfy him that we won't be using any explosives or doing anything to injure the little fishes." Since Kerlyn did not want the watchdog on the boat, "Try to get rid of him in a nice way, but if any trouble develops let me know."[11] The results of this exchange are unknown.

In the meantime, a decision fateful to Kerlyn's future had been made in Chicago when the First National Bank decided to lend additional funds for acquisition of the Cosco Refinery at Wynnewood, Oklahoma. It must have been a difficult choice, for the refinery had a long and troubled history. It was one of the smallest of the state's twenty-two refineries. Construction had been started in November, 1922, by the Texas Pacific Coal and Oil Company. Completed the next June at an estimated cost of $500,000, the refinery proceeded to lose money steadily, and in 1934, Texas Pacific decided to junk the plant rather than make the effort to secure a regular oil supply.

Dismantling had already begun when J. S. Cosden, Jr., bought it. A thermal cracking unit was built, and the plant was put back into operation in December, 1936. Cosco was a family partnership, and the refinery was its only property. Once more debts and a shortage of crude forced a shutdown in late 1938, but it was reopened two years later. All during the war only the barest maintenance necessary to keep it running was supplied by the indebted family, and the plant fell into ruins. Even the topping unit was about to collapse. Employment fluctuated between two and forty, and in 1944 the Oklahoma Tax Commission threatened to close it down for failure to file processing reports over a twenty-four-month period. There were also suspicions that it was running "hot oil." Primarily an asphalt refinery (40 to 45 per cent of its yield), the little gasoline it produced was sold to unbranded distributors.

Kerlyn's management had often discussed entry into refining and marketing, and the one thing uniformly agreed on was not to go into these two phases of the oil business. Why then the sudden change of mind and interest in what contemporaries referred to as "our rusty bucket of bolts," "a tea pot," and "a miserable little old dilapidated bunch of pipes"? According to Dean Terrill, "Bob Kerr was hell bent on buying the refinery." Bob was "hipped" on asphalt. A big regional road-building program then in progress convinced Kerr that there was a lot of money to be made in asphalt and that Kerlyn should have its share. McGee and the rest of management apparently went along because it was a chance to get some knowledge and a

[11] Lease Records file, "Mississippi Sound P 165."

toehold in the business, and the investment would be minor even if they made a mistake.[12]

Ironically—in view of Terrill's negative opinions—the vehicle for the purchase was a new subsidiary named for Fentem and Terrill, the Fen-Ter Refining Company. Bob Kerr was chairman, and McGee, president. On January 25 the Kerlyn board of directors approved a loan to Fen-Ter to buy 80 percent of the refinery and to lease the remaining 20 percent from Mrs. Josh Cosden. Consequently, on February 1, Fen-Ter acquired the refinery and a small pipeline gathering system adjacent to it for $250,000.00 and a broker's commission of $4,166.66. Of course, the purchase price was only the beginning. On February 15 the Kerlyn board further authorized the purchase of ten thousand Fen-Ter shares and approved certain guarantees and indemnities on behalf of the firm.

It was now Dean McGee's job to find the special oil for the refinery, staff it, and increase production. Initially the unit had a daily throughput of around 2,000 barrels of crude and produced around 1,000 barrels of asphalt per day. The remainder was 35 percent heating fuels and the rest gasoline. Most of the crude had to be trucked in from nearby fields, and one month McGee could find only 25,000 barrels. Eventually that problem eased when Kerlyn crude was exchanged for locally produced oil.

Another handicap, and another irony, came with the company decision that no asphalt would be sold to the state of Oklahoma as long as Kerr was governor. Even more frustrating was a fact of life: expansion of asphalt production automatically means making more gasoline. The long-term result was that, in Terrill's words, "against our will we found ourselves in the damned gasoline business and that led into the marketing business." Asphalt was profitable, but at the time the other aspects were not—"so for a long time many of us wished we'd never gotten into the asphalt business."[13]

But elsewhere it was more promising. During the first two years of the Phillips agreement thirty wildcats had been completed, eight of which were producers. By June, 1945, two more neared completion in Wyoming, one of which became the discovery well in the Sheldon Dome field. Thirteen wells were ready to be drilled in Oklahoma, Colorado, Wyoming, Texas, New Mexico, and Louisiana, and thirty-seven other projects were in the geophysical stage. In short, there had been a total of seventy-one ventures under this agreement so far. Contract business was also booming. Consequently, the Kerlyn board authorized management to seek two additional loans (C and D) from the First National of Chicago for a total of $4.7 million. On May 25, Kerlyn gave the bank $8.6 million in first-mortgage notes to secure the long-term debt.[14]

[12] Interviews with Larry May, June 28, 1971; D. A. Watkins, May 5, 1971; George Cobb, December 7, 1972, and Dean Terrill, November 24, 1969.

[13] Interviews with Dean Terrill, Larry May, and D. A. Watkins. See also S-1 Statement, No. 107, March 31, 1948, p. 16; Personal Relations file, "Refinery Information"; and *Kermac News*, Vol. 1 (December, 1947), pp. 3–4; (January, 1977), pp. 6–7.

[14] Securities and Exchange Commission, "Form 10-K Annual Report for the Fiscal Year Ended June 30, 1951, Kerr-McGee Oil Industries, Inc."

Kerlyn Oil Company
Table 9.3. Consolidated Statement of Income and Surplus, June 30, 1945

Gross operating income		$6,980,476.62
Costs of products sold, drilling contracts completed,		
selling and operating expenses	$5,093,790.69	
Administrative and general expense	290,615.74	
Provision for depreciation, depletion, amortization, etc.	698,847.92	
Dry-hole losses and abandonments	349,894.31	6,433,148.66
		$ 547,327.96
Gain from sale of properties	$1,042,475.78	
Other income	62,157.07	1,104,632.85
		$1,651,960.81
Interest, discount, and loan expense	$ 122,314.96	
Bad debts	10,094.57	132,409.53
		$1,519,551.28
Provision for federal and state taxes on income		406,500.00
Net income		$1,113,051.28
Surplus earned—beginning of period		366,670.81
		$1,479,722.09
Less: Dividends paid	$ 71,883.44	
Net excess of amounts paid over the par value of class A common capital stock redeemed and converted pursuant to call (reduced by $41,604.49 arising from cancellation of certain shares acquired at less than the par value thereof and from the conversion of 2,508 shares of class A common to class B common)	403,793.51	475,676.95
Surplus earned—end of period		$1,004,045.14

The annual report of June 30, 1945, was marked by superlatives. "The Company has conducted more geological and geophysical exploration work, acquired more leased acreage, participated in the drilling of more exploratory or wildcat wells, and done more contract drilling than ever before in a like period." This allowed substantial additions to the oil-and-gas reserves. Revamping and modernization of the Wynnewood refinery was under way, and the new bank loans gave Kerlyn financial stability. Gross and net income, drilling returns, and total assets all set new records.[15]

Drilling income had again made the difference. During much of this

[15] Kerlyn Oil Company, *Annual Report for the Fiscal Year Ended June 30, 1945.*

period Kerlyn operated 20 rigs of its own (17 power and 3 steam) and rented 14 more (7 of which were steam). This increased activity was not without hazard, for one of its units was damaged and a rented one destroyed by fire. Over 200 wells were begun, and over half were completed. Nineteen came under the Phillips-Kerlyn agreement, scattered through Arkansas, Oklahoma, Texas, South Dakota, and Wyoming. Most of the major companies, including Phillips, Stanolind, Ohio, Sohio, and Carter, were represented among the contractors.[16]

Although most of the wells were drilled in Oklahoma, the Rangely boom in Colorado was just beginning. This field became the home of Kerlyn crews for many years to come. So great was the demand for personnel that, with the wartime shortage, Pete Walton recalled times when each tool pusher looked after three rigs. Eddie Baxendale, who was there at the beginning and stayed twenty years, remembered that Rangely was wide open, with lots of drinking and gambling, but no jail. Finally, to relieve this need, two posts were cemented in the ground with a chain between them to which drunks were handcuffed.

In a short time Kerlyn had over ten rigs and thirty crews (approximately 150 people) in the area, who were housed in army prefabs and trailers. The company tried to be a good citizen in this new community. The Moffat County school district quickly found itself needing a two-room schoolhouse and two or more teachers to handle the influx of new students. Kerlyn took the lead in setting up and financing this, paying about $3,000 on the cost of the building, the salary of one teacher, and twenty dollars a month toward transportation of the students. On December 12, 1945, D. W. ("Dutch") Lindsay wrote Travis Kerr: "I honestly believe that our school deal has created more good will for the Kerlyn Oil Company, in the vicinity of the camp and also in the Rangely field, than anything we could have done."[17]

At the September board meeting a special stockholder vote to change the name of Kerlyn was called for January 15, 1946. Also discussed was the need to establish a pension plan. At this time it was decided that one should be set up if it could be done on premiums of about $30,000 a year. Later this was changed to a profit-sharing plan, although it is not clear whether the limit on the spending was the cause. At any rate, the old problem of cash caused the directors to skip the quarterly dividend, and furthermore, "In view of the need to conserve cash," it was decided to see whether another company could be brought into the Mississippi Sound survey "to clear the cost of this venture." Not too surprisingly, Phillips was the one that came in, buying its half interest on January 18, 1946, with gas rights in Sherman and Moore counties in the Texas Panhandle, plus a cash payment of $21,103. This benefited Kerlyn more than Phillips, for although the western quarter of the

[16] Transworld file, "Kerlyn Oil Company Drilling Department Rig Operations Fiscal Year July 1, 1944, to June 30, 1945."

[17] Interviews with Q. C. Walton, April 16, 1971, and Eddie Baxendale, July 26, 1971; T. M. Kerr file, "Rangely School Project."

Wynnewood Refinery in 1955.

lease showed some promising structures, the two firms decided to release all claims on the entire area on April 10, 1946.[18]

In December, 1945, several significant decisions were made by Kerlyn management. Two dealt with internal matters. Experience had shown that maintenance of seismographic crews cost more than the charge for contracting such work. Consequently, it was decided to merge Anchor Exploration Company into Kerlyn (this was done on January 21, 1946). The Wynnewood refinery posed several problems and, if it was to be kept open, expert management had to be found and retail outlets obtained for its nonasphalt production. To meet this latter need, the Yellow Cab gasoline stations and Cato Oil and Grease Company were thought to be available at a cost of about $2 million. In the meantime the company built a service station at Second and Walker streets. To run the refinery, Kerlyn enticed James J. Kelly away from Allied Materials Corporation, which had a refinery at Stroud, Oklahoma, with a promise of 5 percent of the annual net profit of Fen-Ter over a three-year period and the right to purchase up to 7.5 percent of its capital stock. By successfully closing this contract on December 29, Kerlyn acquired not only a "Manager of the Refining Division" but also a future president of the corporation.

More office space for less rental charges was obtained on December 31. The eight-story Capitol Federal Savings and Loan building on the northeast corner of Robinson and Robert S. Kerr Avenue was acquired for $225,000 and a $175,000 mortgage, which was handled by the formation of Kerr-McGee Building Corporation, in which Kerlyn owned half of the common stock. Capitol Federal received five years rent-free use of the space it then occupied and an additional five-year lease with rent of $200 a month. After being remodeled, this structure became the first Kerr-McGee building.[19]

Finally, and as always, there were some financial loose ends. Discussions were opened with the First National Bank of Chicago about issuing $1 million in convertible preferred stock for buying Yellow Cab and expanding Fen-Ter's asphalt facilities. Year-end bonuses totaling $10,000 went to employees, while shareholders were rewarded with the resumption of the 5-cent quarterly dividend. On this note Dean McGee ended his third full year as president in fact, if not in title, of the soon-to-be-renamed Kerr-McGee Oil Industries, Incorporated.

[18] "Mississippi Sound P 165."

[19] Oklahoma State Archives, Secretary of State, "Kerr-McGee vs. John Rogers," folder 3; S-1 Statement, No. 107, March 31, 1948, pp. 15–16; *Kermac News*, Vol. 2 (August–September, 1949), p. 7; interview with James J. Kelly, June 26, 1971; file "KMB Fee #1," in Public Relations file, "R. E. Anderson"; and "Notice of Annual Meeting," October 2, 1961.

Morgan #1. First well drilled by James L. Anderson and Robert S. Kerr for their own account.

Wynnewood Refinery.

A modern Kerr-McGee service station.

Kerr-McGee sold gasoline under the Deep Rock brand name after 1955.

Yellow cake is produced from uranium ore in the nation's largest uranium plant, Grants, New Mexico.

Headframe for uranium mine at Ambrosia Lake, New Mexico.

Uranium miner working a drill at Ambrosia Lake, New Mexico.

Helicopters took Kerr-McGee geologists to remote places in search of uranium.

Searching for uranium in the Church Rock, New Mexico, area.

One of three gas-and-condensate collection-and-separation facilities on Block 28, Ship Shoal gas field, off the shore of Louisiana.

Rig 61 under tow from Japan to South Africa. The first rig with ability to drill while floating and having towing qualities of a ship-shaped barge.

B platform, Block 214, Ship Shoal, is typical of the company's many production facilities that dot the Gulf of Mexico.

Night view of Kerr-McGee Center opened in 1973.

Worker at the Cimarron plant.

Manufacturing complex for Searles Lake.

Loading coal produced by Jacobs Ranch strip mine in Wyoming.

A modern drill-rig floor.

Gas flares through a burner during completion testing of a new
Kerr-McGee well in the Gulf of Mexico. Rig 62 is connected by a bridge to
the main well and production platform.

Chapter 10

"1508–1526" in the Gulf of Mexico 1946–1947

Drastic changes for the American people now lay ahead, namely, acceleration in dismantling the machines of war and rapid conversion to a peacetime economy. For the petroleum industry a major development was the end of government controls in July, 1946. Crude-oil prices, which had been frozen for six years despite rising production costs, increased sharply as companies strained to meet public demand which exceeded anything in the history of the industry. More crude was produced than ever before, and pipelines ran to capacity. Crude runs to the refineries reached an all-time high, while supplies of refined products tightened throughout the country. It was mandatory that new sources of oil be found to meet the seemingly insatiable appetite for derivatives of the fossil deposits.

Chief reason for this enormous new market was the change in civilian life-style. The mechanization of farms after 1941 was revolutionary, and farm-tractor consumption of fuel increased 100 percent. More motorists were doing more driving, more airplanes were flying longer distances, railroads had four times as many diesel engines, and hundreds of thousands of homes switched to fuel oil for heating. But before the oil companies could cash in on this booming market, there was a great deal of exploration and production to be done.

In Oklahoma oil production turned down slightly, primarily from the lag in new discoveries. But the income from petroleum reached the highest point since 1938. As fast as the scarce materials used in exploration could be assembled, search and drilling crews scattered across the state. By the end

Kerr-McGee Building, 1950.

of 1946, although no major pools were discovered, there was new production in Cotton, Logan, and Garvin counties.

The administration of Governor Kerr proved to be a quiet one, with nonpartisan politics necessary because of the war, and perhaps also because of the mere sixteen-thousand-vote majority by which he had won the position. Kerr traveled extensively, creating a friendly picture of a state full of resources and good will. As the keynote speaker for the 1944 National Democratic convention, he widened his political base, and it was obvious then that any return to his company would be only until the next election. But Kerr did keep in touch and he knew the over-all progress and problems which it faced. His touch was felt in the stockholders' meetings and in the annual reports, which, as befitting a growing concern, were becoming more informative and detailed.

As would be expected from the lag in production, the Kerlyn stockholders' meeting on January 15, 1946, received some unfavorable reports: the four months from July to October of the previous year showed a loss of $35,636.10. But offsetting this was the announcement that the Phillips contract had been renewed for five more years. Then as a climax stockholders voted to change the name of Kerlyn Oil Company to Kerr-McGee Oil Industries, Incorporated. This move served to identify the new man in charge and also alleviated the confusion about an "oil company" engaging in contract drilling.[1]

At the February 11 board meeting an amendment to the articles of incorporation was proposed in order to increase the number of shares in Kerr-McGee to 1.5 million—by 60,000 of cumulative convertible preferred at $22.50 each and 1,440,000 of common. At the same time the 412,508 shares then outstanding would be split two for one. This was a first for the company. It was also in line with Dean McGee's philosophy that stock dividends should occur only when there could be a worthwhile increase in cash dividends, and then only when the money was not essential for reinvestment in the growth of the company.

A second item of business concerned a decision to buy one-third of the stock of M-B-K Drilling Company, Inc., of Tulsa, for approximately $325,000. Big Chief Drilling Company of Oklahoma City and Roeser & Pendleton, Inc., of Fort Worth, each took a third also, with Kerr-McGee the operator for all three. The M-B-K assets consisted of producing leases in the Foster and Harper pools in Ector County and the Wasson Pool in Gaines County, Texas, containing some fifty-seven producing wells, plus undrilled locations, all valued at $1,593,207. This was a great opportunity for Kerr-McGee to increase production. Furthermore, M-B-K owned ten power rigs and two and one-half steam units worth $420,631, which were needed for expanded drilling activities. On February 28, M-B-K was liquidated, and its assets were distributed among the three copurchasers. Within two years they boasted an additional twenty-one wells.[2]

April was highlighted by the move into the newly renamed Kerr-McGee Building and by the floating of the new stock issue. The April 9 prospectus

[1] The new name was registered February 18, 1946. See Oklahoma Secretary of State, "Corporation file"; Oklahoma State Archives, Secretary of State, "Kerr-McGee vs. John Rogers," folder 3.

[2] For the merger of Anchor see Oklahoma Secretary of State, "Corporation file"; for M-B-K see Lease Records files, "Contract 73," "Contract 108," and S-1 Statement, No. 107, March 31, 1948, p. 16.

announced the 60,000 shares of preferred, with an annual dividend of $1.20, available to the public for $25.00 each. With the $1,365,000 in proceeds the company hoped to reduce its debt to the First National Bank of Chicago by $600,000 and add the remainder to the general fund for refining facilities and for contract and company drilling.

As an inducement to invest, a short review of the recent history of Kerr-McGee was included. Net profits before taxes rose from $54,921 in 1942 to $1,038,239 in 1945. During the same period the company drilled 279 contract wells for 35 different customers, deriving gross revenues of $10,325,639. As of December 1, 1945, interests in 392 oil wells brought an average daily production in November of 1,660 barrels. These, together with 40 gas wells, were located in Oklahoma (44 oil and 8 gas—18 in Oklahoma City), Texas (278 oil and 32 gas—126 in East Texas), 8 in Kansas, 3 in Arkansas, and 1 in Wyoming. In the ten years since 1936 the company had produced 5,964,398 barrels of oil and 249,554,114,000 cubic feet of gas. Approximately 13.5 percent of the gas reserves, 40 percent of the oil, and 43 percent of the undeveloped properties were acquired under the agreement with Phillips. Currently 553,205 net acres were under lease or option, with Mississippi first in area, followed by Texas, Wyoming, Georgia, and Oklahoma.[3]

The successful sale of the convertibles, handled by the firm of directors Straus and Blosser, was followed by another first for Kerr-McGee. It had always been common practice for oil-field workers to provide their own transportation to the rigs and to be laid off between drilling jobs, although Anderson & Kerr Drilling and Kerr-Lynn often found make-do work for key personnel in these interims. Labor unions were unknown to Kerr-McGee and its predecessors, but with the support of the New Deal, unions showed strong growth and became very active after the war. Refinery workers were a different type from the drillers moreover, so it was not surprising that the Wynnewood employees quickly opened negotiations for membership in the International Union of Operating Engineers, AFL, and a contract was signed on May 21, 1946. This initial union covered approximately 100 of Kerr-McGee's total of 746 workers.[4]

Several months later other personnel were benefited. The board spelled out plans whereby key employees could buy company stock at conversion price (then $12.50 a share). After January 1, 1947, Kerr-McGee would pay the entire premium for $10,000 in life insurance and a monthly retirement annuity of $150 for all workers with five years of service. This new concern reflected both a maturing of the firm and a reaction to the times: during 1946 some 116 million hours were lost and 4 million workers idled by strikes. Congress's reaction to this statistic was the passage in early 1947, over President Truman's veto, of the Taft-Hartley Act.

The first half of 1946 saw other changes. A third member of the Kerr

[3] *New York Times*, March 1 and April 12, 1946; "Prospectus for 60,000 Shares Cumulative Convertible Preferred Stock $22.50 Par Value, April 9, 1946."

[4] S-1 Statement, No. 107, March 31, 1948, p. 16; "Prospectus . . . 1946."

family, Billy Bryan Kerr, joined his two older brothers at Kerr-McGee. Although he was not given a specific title, his apparent function was as a contact and public-relations man. He had been a member of the Oklahoma legislature and had a wide range of friends. The widening range of Kerr-McGee interests was also shown by the liquidation of the unprofitable Franklin County Gas Company, the purchase of an office building in Midland, Texas, and the decision to buy an airplane. A subsidiary, Kerr-McGee Skyways, Incorporated, was established to acquire a surplus C-47 with its spare parts from the federal government.

It was quite a letdown, therefore, when the annual report of June 30, 1946, showed that, although assets rose, net income declined by over $1.2 million. In his first letter to the stockholders in four years, former Governor Kerr attempted to put forth as good a picture as possible:

The balance sheet and profit and loss statement of a natural resources business enterprise do not, alone, (especially if the company in question is expending a substantial portion of its revenues in connection with the search for new reserves) truly reflect the position of such a company.

As reason for optimism Kerr cited the survey of reserves made by Raymond F. Kravis in connection with the sale of the preferred stock. Kravis's estimates, made on November, 1945, were updated to September 30, 1946, and showed a working interest of 6,535,045 barrels of oil and condensate, with an ultimate net cash realization value of $6,763,712.10, and 826,895,680,000 cubic feet of gas, valued at $14,767,937.35. If royalties, overriding royalties, and oil payments worth $706,395.57 were added, the estimate of the company's reserves had an ultimate cash realization value of $22,238,045.02. Kerr concluded:

While it is most likely that any other person who might make an evaluation of the same properties would come out with a different final result, we have tried to evaluate the Company's reserves to the best of our judgment, giving them neither an inflated nor a depressed value.[5]

The refinery, which began in 1946 under the leadership of James J. Kelly, was not the cause of the loss of income. It processed an average of 2,191 barrels of crude daily, sold products for a total of $1,398,944, with expenses of only $1,380,577. The real reasons for the drastic decline were obvious. First, oil production and income were up slightly, but gas production and income were down almost a comparable dollar amount. Second, and more important, was a sharp drop in contract-drilling revenues. Gross income from this source fell $1,702,526.18. Not only had the number of contracts fallen but also the company found its profits per well reduced by increased expenses and cutthroat competition from hundreds of small operators. (See Table 10.1).

[5] Kerr-McGee Oil Industries, Inc., *Annual Report for the Fiscal Year Ended June 30, 1946.*

During the fiscal year Kerr-McGee bought three new drilling rigs, bringing its total to twenty-two, and rented three more. Seventy-nine wells were completed, while fifteen were still in progress. Eighteen of these were under the Phillips agreement, with seven each in Oklahoma and Texas (Young County), and one each in Wyoming, Louisiana, Arkansas, and Colorado. Phillips, Gulf, California, Stanolind, Continental, and Carter furnished the largest number of contracts, but small operators were well represented.[6] The most notable discovery Kerr-McGee made for itself was the No. 1 Nabors in De Soto Parish, Louisiana, which was completed for 39 million cubic feet of gas per day to open the Spider field.

But the waters off the beaches of Louisiana presented Kerr-McGee's greatest challenge and expectation. It was an unproven idea, which as early as 1897 had been tried in California. There attempts to drill in shallow water off the ends of wharves had been made using essentially land techniques, and in 1910 and 1924 successful wells also were drilled from fixed platforms in lakes in Louisiana and Venezuela. In 1938, a noncommercial deposit was found in shallow water a mile off of Cameron Parish, Louisiana, causing that state to assert its claim to twenty-seven miles seaward from mean low tide. Three years later traces of oil were found about two miles offshore at Sabine Pass, Texas. When the state of Louisiana held its first offshore lease sale in 1945, President Harry Truman reacted by claiming all mineral deposits under the continental shelf for the federal government.[7]

The question of ownership of the submerged lands off the coastal states had first been raised in 1936, when Secretary of the Interior Harold L. Ickes claimed California's offshore oil fields for the federal government. A year later a bill was unsuccessfully introduced in Congress directing the attorney general to press that claim. It was not until 1945, however, that a suit was filed against Pacific Western Oil Company. This in turn was dropped in favor of a case then pending in the Supreme Court against the state of California. It was generally agreed that the result would affect all of the states, especially Texas and Louisiana, where most of the speculation was centered. But it was a long-delayed decision, and in the interval efforts to probe the depths continued.

The "majors" had shown little interest in going offshore. This was for several good reasons: the unique problems faced with no known technology for exploring below the surface of the waves; the millions of acres already under lease on dry land; and the many land projects already under way. These enormous holdings of the big companies meant fewer good properties available for the smaller ones, however, and they were more or less forced to look beyond the continent's perimeter. As George B. Kitchel, later Kerr-

[6] Transworld file, "Kerr-McGee Oil Industries, Inc., Drilling Department Rig Operations Fiscal Year July 1, 1945, to June 30, 1946"; random "Daily Drilling Report," also in Transworld's files.

[7] The Energy Research and Education Foundation, "A Brief History of Offshore Drilling, 1869–1955"; speech by Dean A. McGee, "A Report on Exploration Progress in the Gulf of Mexico," before the spring meeting of the Mid-Continent District of the American Petroleum Institute Division of Production, Tulsa, March 23, 1949.

In 1945, Kerr-McGee began seismographic work in the Gulf of Mexico.

McGee's vice-president for drilling, said: "I think companies like Kerr-McGee looked out there because they realized there was something there and they might be able to get it where they didn't have as good a chance of getting a real nice piece of acreage on land."

Another of Kerr-McGee's officers agreed. George Parks felt that since the Rocky Mountain area and some other prospects had not materialized, there was mounting pressure on the company to take the technological, meteorological, and environmental risks associated with exploring and developing oil-and-gas production in the Gulf. Despite the general lack of success in offshore drilling and the fact that no devices had yet been developed for use in deep water, Kerr-McGee was definitely interested in the underwater game. The projects in Mobile Bay (1938) and the Mississippi Sound (1944) never reached the point of actual drilling, but Dean McGee, in particular, kept his optimism.

There can be no doubt that it was Dean McGee who decided to tackle the seemingly insurmountable problems of exploring, drilling, and producing oil at hundreds of feet below the water. Otis Danielson said, "McGee just knew there was oil out there and as good drilling contractors we believed we could do as good a job as the next man." Robert Anderson, Kerr-McGee's land man, thought that the company's interest in drilling where others had failed was because of "McGee's conviction that if the problems of drilling in water could be solved that there were large deposits in the continental shelf area." Travis Kerr concluded: "McGee was the one principally responsible for going offshore because of his belief that just as there were [salt] domes on shore, there were domes in the Gulf," a statement confirmed by George Cobb.

Dean McGee himself explained it simply: "We decided to explore the areas where the really potential prolific production might be—salt domes—the good ones on land were gone, but we could move out in the shallow water and, in effect, get into a virgin area where we could find the real class-one type salt dome prospect." In short, the company could trade off the extra costs of working in water against a much higher opportunity for discovery. While trying to recruit F. C. Love to work for Kerr-McGee, he told Love that the greatest chance to find additional oil was in the Gulf; there was no geological reason there could not be just as much oil offshore as had been found onshore.[8]

In January, 1946, only two seismograph crews were operating off the Louisiana coast. Yet in March, Kerr-McGee began reflection seismographic work with results that looked favorable. So, at their May meeting the directors discussed the possibility of leasing in this area. Though the location in which the company was interested lay nine to eleven miles out to sea, thus involving the company in the federal-state dispute about ownership, the

[8] Interviews with George B. Kitchel, June 16, 1971; Otis Danielson, June 1, 1971; R. E. Anderson, May 3, 1971; Travis Kerr, December 16, 1969; George Cobb, January 21, 1971; George B. Parks, October 23, 1971; F. C. Love, September 2, 1971; and Dean A. McGee, September 4, 1971.

decision was made to consider a bid on some 40,000 acres in the Ship Shoal area.

Otis Danielson, assigned the responsibility for a case study, reported on August 8 that it would be an unprecedented move to drill in the proposed area. It was in open water without any protection from storms, was subject to tidal action, and was in water deeper than any heretofore explored. After talking to other companies with water-drilling experience, he concluded that to build a platform alone would cost around $200,000. Moreover, it could be erected only at certain times of the year when good weather was normally predicted. It would require fifty days to drill 11,000 feet; the water used for drilling would have to be barged in; and the boats necessary for the operation would cost about $250 a day. He estimated that the completed well, less exploration and lease charges, could total close to $351,610.

This report only served to spur Kerr-McGee to enter the sealed-bid competition, and the company became the successful bidder on its desired acreage. This was a serious commitment for the small firm. A fee of $317,000 was paid to the state of Louisiana, plus an annual rental of half that amount until such time as drilling started or the five-year lease expired. Perhaps in the euphoria of future success, the board voted raises of $10,000 for Bob Kerr, $7,500 for Travis Kerr, and $5,000 for Dean McGee.

In September, Danielson reported again on the most economical methods of drilling two test wells. He felt that his earlier estimate on building a wooden piling platform from which to drill was probably about $100,000 too low, and that little of it could be saved by salvage for future use. Instead he recommended that the pilings be constructed of steel. A cheaper base could be had by using a drilling barge, which could be rented for about $150,000, but a breakwater would be mandatory to protect it from currents, swells, and storm waves. All things considered, he recommended a conventional platform supported by the steel pilings.[9]

During the next two months this information and its implications began to penetrate Kerr-McGee's optimism about offshore work. It became management's consensus that an effort should be made to "sell portions of the Corporation's interest therein [the Gulf] in order to insure the ability of the Corporation to carry forth the development program to a successful conclusion." While not exactly a bad case of cold feet, it was definitely a sober reconsideration of the risks and expenses involved in so hazardous an attempt. Kerr-McGee did not want to find itself alone and sinking in the Gulf of Mexico.

[9] Public Relations file, "Offshore Drilling Information," has reprints of Kenneth B. Barnes and Leigh S. McCaslin, Jr., "Spectacular Gulf of Mexico Discovery," *Oil and Gas Journal*, and A. T. F. Seale, "Discovering Oil 12 Miles Offshore in the Gulf," *World Oil*, May, 1948; see also A. T. F. Seale, "Modern Practices in Off-Shore Drilling," paper presented at Petroleum Mechanical Engineering Conference, New Orleans, September 25–27, 1950; Claude Barrow, "Prairie Wildcatters Reach Out Into Gulf," *Drilling*, November, 1947, pp. 54ff. Danielson's two reports, "Report on Drilling Cost Investigation" and "Report of Investigation of Marine Rotary Drilling Methods," are in Bette Brenz file, "Discovery Well, 1947," in Public Relations Department.

Outside of this worry about its offshore gamble, Kerr-McGee showed a profit of $148,000 for the four months from July to October, 1946, as opposed to a loss during the same period in 1945, and its other projects boded well for the upcoming year. The oil business in general was good. Kansas and Oklahoma crude sold for $2.75 a barrel, the highest price since 1920. Oklahoma production increased over 7 million barrels, and oil income by almost $77 million, all without a major discovery. The national total was 1,334,196,000 barrels, with 33,646 wells completed, the largest number since 1937. But the enormous public appetite for petroleum products brought considerable talk about the United States running out of oil, and that, together with the rising costs of drilling deeper and finding fewer wells, made Kerr-McGee's proposed hunt in the Gulf more and more a reasonable undertaking.

February, 1947, brought the welcome news that the First National Bank of Chicago had made available an additional line of credit for $1.5 million to support the developmental program. Then, in recognition of Dean McGee's leadership, the board raised his salary an additional $6,000, to $31,000. Kerr was rewarded with a contribution of $50,000 for the building program of the Oklahoma City YMCA, an organization in which he had long been active.

The growing interest in the Gulf was exemplified by the presence in its waters of eighteen exploration crews. But the Gulf of Mexico was never far from their minds. In order to get as much information as possible on the proposed project before actually embarking on it, on March 4, 1947, Kerr-McGee was host to a meeting of representatives from all major oil companies which were also contemplating offshore operations. Seven companies attended Kerr-McGee's meeting to discuss "their mutual problems in connection with this huge and heretofore untried adventure." Among the more novel approaches suggested was a joint construction of islands from which drilling operations could be conducted.[10] But perhaps uppermost in their minds was the titleship case to be argued before the Supreme Court on March 13 and 14, which was expected to have a great deal of influence on actions in the Gulf.

Soon after the joint meeting some of Kerr-McGee's financial anxieties were eased. The company was, of course, operating under the Phillips agreement of March 31, 1943, which meant that Phillips had the right to choose whether or not to participate in the offshore venture. At first Phillips declined, believing that it was impossible to drill profitably in deep water. But later seismographic reports persuaded the company to reconsider, and it came in on the venture. But perhaps just as important was the decision of Stanolind Oil and Gas to join the project by taking part of Kerr-McGee's share. Under this new arrangement Phillips owned one-half, Stanolind, three-eights, and Kerr-McGee, the remaining one-eighth. Stanolind paid Kerr-McGee $300,000 and assumed three-eighths of the expenses.

In short, with one-eighth interest, Kerr-McGee became the driller and operator of the offshore properties, and its gamble was minimized by

---

[10] *Kermac News*, Vol. 1 (April, 1947), p. 1.

Phillips's and Stanolind's carrying the exploration costs. In turn Kerr-McGee agreed to drill two test wells, if possible before September 12. The west well (Block 32) would be sunk to "salt, to heaving shale, to hot flowing salt water, to any other practically impenetrable substance, to oil production in paying quantities, or to a depth of ten thousand (10,000) feet below sea level, whichever depth shall be the lesser." The east Block 28 test would be bottomed at 12,000 feet.[11]

With this heavy commitment to offshore drilling, Kerr-McGee decided at this time to bid on yet another Louisiana tract—the south half of Block 39, Rollover field, in the Vermillion area. On the way to the lease sale in Baton Rouge, Dean McGee and Chief Engineer A. T. F. ("Tom") Seale stopped at Lafayette to take a final look at the latest seismographic maps of the areas up for sale. It was at this time that McGee discovered the company's geologists had overlooked a promising formation because the structure had been divided between two separate sections of the map.

He made the decision to increase the bid on that particular block, but to do so needed a cashier's check to submit before the deadline the next day. Phillips, a partner in the bid, agreed to send the money to Baton Rouge by Western Union, where McGee could convert the form to a check. The manager of the Baton Rouge hotel at first agreed to accompany McGee to the office of Western Union to identify him. But when he casually asked how much money was involved and McGee replied $35,000, the manager reneged, saying that he knew McGee only as a guest and could not identify him for so large an amount of money.

To complicate matters further, there was a telephone strike in progress which stopped all but emergency calls from going through. Classifying this as just such an occasion, McGee managed to get a call through to Bob Kerr. At 7:30 on the very morning for the final bidding Kerr was presented with the problem of how to convert the money from the Western Union draft to a check acceptable to the state of Louisiana. His solution was a call to Louisiana Governor Jimmy Davis, who in turn contacted Western Union and vouched for McGee. Another friend stood by at the bank, holding a taxi cab for the dash to the capitol. The bid was filled out en route, and as McGee walked into the capitol door, the man collecting the bids passed by him. Kerr-McGee's new bid was dropped into the box, literally without a minute to spare. It was a successful one, by about $2,500, and only because of the increase. To make the victory even sweeter, by 1970 this structure had become a major gas producer.[12]

The problem of how to get the oil and gas which Dean McGee was so confident lay beneath the waters of the Gulf was handed to Tom Seale, his partner in the Baton Rouge adventure. It was an extremely difficult task and one that would combine the talents of his office and those of a selected

[11] Interviews with Dean A. McGee, March 3, 1973, and George Cobb, January 21, 1971; Lease Records files, "Phillips Operating Agreement, March 8, 1947," and "Stanolind Oil and Gas Company, Agreement of Purchase and Sale, Dated March 8, 1947."

[12] Interview with A. T. F. Seale, July 20, 1971.

Kerr-McGee Oil Industries Inc.

Table 10.1 Consolidated Statement of Income and Earned Surplus, 1946–47

	Year Ended June 30, 1947	Year Ended June 30, 1946
Gross operating income		
Drilling contracts completed	$4,089,613.45	3,713,489.30
Crude oil production and gas sales	1,618,920.00	1,085,063,94
Sale of refined products	2,315,129.45	1,398,944.09
Other operating income	2,652.81	8,603.87
	$8,026,315.71	6,206,101.20
Operating charges		
Cost of completed drilling contracts	$3,241,484.51	2,841,588.60
Lease operating expense	255,216.26	259,680.17
Cost of refined products and selling expense (exclusive of depreciation and general and administrative expense)	2,178,184.10	1,380,577.22
General and administrative expense	616,546.70	417,846.32
Land department expense	38,136.80	33,808.29
Geological and geophysical expense	212,663.11	216,272.36
Taxes, other than income	51,620.09	31,944.02
Lease rentals	85,197.37	61,221.92
Research expense	1,626.30	4,736.58
Depreciation (exclusive of $95,633.99 depreciation on service equipment deducted as departmental expenses)	738,457.36	564,p88.45
Depletion	224,493.99	181,268.i6
Dry-hole costs	160,789.65	182,425.41
Abandoned leaseholds and royalties	82,544.37	142,380.66
	$7,886,960.61	6,317,838.86
Less: Service department operations—net	39,498.18	45,643.40
	$7,847,462.43	6,272,195.46
	$ 178,853.28	66,094.26*
Other income		
Interest, rent and other income	$ 100,390.77	30,173.23
Gain on disposal of property	253,763.48	89,252.37
	$ 354,154.25	119,425.60
	$ 533,007.53	53,331.34

marine contractor. For the next few months, during the hot summer days of 1947, this would be an exercise in theory and experimentation, but one which had to be done successfully or the young company and McGee would suffer a severe blow.

Fortunately, other events were favorable, and for a short respite these absorbed the attention of management. Kerr-McGee bought a twelfth in-

Table 10.1 *Continued.*

	Year Ended June 30, 1947	Year Ended June 30, 1946
Other deductions		
Interest and loan expense	$ 150,543.43	148,102.91
Discounts allowed	16,120.86	9,946.38
Amortization of stock issue expense	6,439.80	1,379.56
Provision for federal income taxes		
Provision for state income taxes	15,000.00	200.00
	$ 188,104.09	159,628.85
Net income	$ 344,903.44	106,297.51*
Adjustment of operations for prior years		
Certain expenditures for seismograph exploration costs, etc., disallowed by federal tax authorities	$ 47n407.47	
Decrease provision for depreciation	16,752.70	109,532.22
Increase provision for income taxes	6,639.28*	25,000.00*
Refund of 1939 federal income taxes	2,218.51	
	$ 59,739.40	84,532.22
Balanced transferred to surplus	$ 404,642.84	21,765.29*
Surplus earned—beginning of period	545,741.30	1,004,045.14
	$ 950,384.14	982,279.85
Less: Transfer to common stock to cover shares issued in stock split-up	$	412,508.00
Dividends paid on common stock (21/2 cents a share on 817,222 shares)	20,430.58	20,430.55
Dividends paid on preferred stock	72,000.00	3,600.00
	$ 92,430.58	436,538.55
Surplus earned—end of period	$ 857,953.56	545,741.30

* Denotes red figure.

terest in 120 acres in Carter County, Oklahoma, with eight producing wells, and an exclusive "call" on all the oil for $80,000 from Kirkpatrick & Bale, Inc. The Watchorn suit, pending since 1942, began its final way through the courts. This involved the collapse of casing in an Oklahoma City well owned jointly by Watchorn Petroleum, Harrison Smith, and Kerr-McGee, which dumped mud and water into the Wilcox sand, ruining a number of adjacent wells. Their owners sued for millions of dollars, claiming "subterranean trespass." Since Kerr-McGee was the operator and Dean McGee the principal witness, the company was primarily liable for this and future suits. With prospects of enormous damage costs, the outcome of this trial was extremely significant. The case was won, however, by Watchorn's lawyer, F. C. Love, whose name was destined to become very familiar to Kerr-McGee employees in the immediate future.[13]

The "rusty bucket of bolts" refinery also came in for its share of attention. Fen-Ter acquired the remaining 20 percent interest from Mrs. Cosden for $98,420.90 and also bought the East Pauls Valley Pipeline, which supplied the refinery, from Kerr-McGee & Company for $140,000.00. In August the board was told that Fen-Ter "at last has an adequate supply of crude" and had tripled its output. An extensive renovation program had increased the number of pump stations and added new boilers, oxidizing stills, and storage facilities. The 125 employees produced gasoline, light and heavy gas oils, roofing asphalt, road oil, and asphalt (the last was even exported to Europe). Sales for fiscal 1947 amounted to $2,315,000.00 and the daily throughput averaged 2,658 barrels of crude—decided improvements over the figures for the previous year.[14]

Indirectly the refinery played an unwanted role in politics. Bob Kerr, no longer governor, was fair game for his political enemies. House Resolution #7 of the Twenty-first Oklahoma Legislature created a special investigating committee under James H. Arrington to review the activities and accomplishments of the State Highway Department during the years of Kerr's administration. While the committee's report implied that Kerr had profited through a monopoly in rock asphalt, it had to concede that in 1945 and 1946 Fen-Ter sold the Highway Department asphaltic oil at half the price it charged private contractors.[15]

The 1947 annual report mirrored these various successes; indeed, it was almost ecstatic. "The year ended June 30 . . . [has] been the most active and eventful . . . in the Company's history." More oil-and-gas reserves had been added than in any comparable period, contract drilling had recovered, the refinery was profitable, and prices received for crude-oil, natural gas, and gasoline had increased. The net result was that "the Company is currently operating with the largest net profit in its history. The manage-

[13] Lease Records file, "Contract #107"; Kerlyn Oil Company, *Annual Report for the Fiscal Year Ended June 30, 1942*, n. 5; interviews with George Cobb, December 7, 1972, and Frank C. Love.

[14] S-1 Statement, No. 107, March 31, 1948, pp. 15–16; Securities Exchange Commission, "Form 8, Amendment No. 1, Annual Financial Statement of Annual Report (Form 10-K) for Fiscal Year Ended June 30, 1952, Kerr-McGee Oil Industries, Inc."; Public Relations file, "Refinery Information," and press release, 66–60, dated October 25, 1966; and Kerr-McGee Oil Industries, Inc., *Annual Report for the Fiscal Year Ended June 30, 1951*.

[15] The rock asphalt involved not Fen-Ter but another company, Southern Rock Asphalt Co., in which it was alleged that Kerr had an interest. "Report of Special Investigating Committee" in Oklahoma State Archives file, "Investigation of Highway Commission Activities 1943–46 in Accordance with H.R. 7, 1947."

ment expects such trends to continue." The balance sheet showed this prosperity.[16]

During the entire year Kerr-McGee used twenty-six power rigs, five steam, and one rental. For its own account, it drilled fifty-four wells, twenty oil and sixteen gas producers, and twenty jointly with Phillips. Over all, 123 were completed, and were distributed as shown in Table 10.2.[17]

Table 10.2. Number of Wells Completed, 1947

Texas	60
Colorado	31
Oklahoma	27
Wyoming	16
Louisiana	6
Utah	2
Montana	1

The larger contracts involved the following companies: Gulf Oil (Texas, 44; Stanolind (Colorado and Wyoming), 20; Carter (Oklahoma, Wyoming, and Montana), 11; California (Colorado), 10; and Snowden (Texas), 4.

Since half of the gross operating income was provided by the drilling department, it is interesting to compare the rates used at this time. A folder of Travis Kerr's shows the day rates for 1947 (Tables 10.3 and 10.4).[18]

Table 10.3. Day Rates for Drilling in Oklahoma, 1947

	0–8,500 Ft.	8,500–9,500 Ft.	9,500–10,500 Ft.	Below Contract Depth, per 24 Hours
Without drill pipe and bits	$600	$650	$650	$725
With drill pipe furnished	700	750	800	625
With bits	500	. . .	625	
With bits and drill pipe	550	. . .	725	

[16] Kerr-McGee Oil Industries, Inc., *Annual Report for the Fiscal Year Ended June 30, 1947.*

[17] Transworld file, "Kerr-McGee Oil Industries, Inc., Drilling Department Rig Operations Fiscal Year—July 1, 1946, to June 30, 1947"; Kerr-McGee, *Annual Report . . . 1951.*

[18] "Drilling Department folder 7/1/46 to 11/1/47," in Travis Kerr file in Public Relations Department.

Table 10.4. Drilling Labor Rates, 1947

	Three–Five-Man Crew	Overhead Expenses
Louisiana	$192.56	
Colorado (Rangely Field)	$202.21	$109.18
Oklahoma	$204.54	$ 83.03
West Texas	$209.16	$ 93.79
Rocky Mountain Outlying District	....	$ 70.15

On June 23, 1947, the decision on the offshore land ownership was handed down by the Supreme Court. Justice Hugo Black wrote the report for the six to two majority, which decreed that California did not own the contested three-mile area. Instead, the United States had "paramount rights" there as an attribute of national sovereignty. On July 19, California petitioned for a rehearing, so the final results were still not in.[19]

The meaning of these legal maneuverings, while a dilemma to the Kerr-McGee Board, was moot if the paramount question could not be answered: Had the technological problems of oceanic drilling been solved? Besides the actual drilling there were other unique situations. How could well locations be accurately fixed without reference points? Weather forecasting was in an infant stage, and little was understood about tidal movements and ocean currents. Communication between the offshore rig and its parent facility on shore was also a new problem.

In land drilling, space and weight were no consideration, but at sea the platform had to be safe from the elements, while providing all the requirements necessary for successful and accident-free drilling, as well as housing the crews and personnel. Ideally, from the viewpoint of economy, these facilities should be portable to permit later use. Any abandoned structure, according to U.S. War Department regulations, had to be demolished down to a depth of six feet below the floor of the Gulf and the ruins salvaged. Last, but not least, the over-all cost had to be held down as much as possible, although no one could offer any reasonable estimate of what such an undertaking should cost.

A. T. F. Seale and his advisers faced all these unknown factors and came up with what they thought were suitable solutions to most of them. In a pioneering decision they concluded that a combination of a small rigid platform and a floating auxiliary tender offered the greatest possibilities, if the size and cost of the platform could be reduced enough to justify the investment in the tender. With this plan in mind Seale left in May for the Gulf to prepare for drilling the two wildcats, with spudding to take place in September. Otis Danielson, who went along to help, took the precaution of

---

[19] The best account of the tidelands' dispute is in Ernest R. Bartley, *The Tidelands Oil Controversy* (Austin, 1953), pp. 57, 137, 159–82; a condensed version can be found in the *Oil Record, 1950* (Washington, 1950), pp. 8–9.

getting weather-bureau information concerning when hurricanes were most likely to occur off the Louisiana coast.

There was not a single piece of marine equipment made specifically for offshore drilling work. Nor had anyone ever built such a platform out in eighteen feet of open water. Brown & Root Marine Operators, Inc., of Houston, Texas, was hired to perform the construction. The platform for Block 32 was 38 feet wide by 71 feet long, supported by sixteen steel pilings, each 24 inches in diameter and 140 feet long. The one for Block 28, the deeper well, was 46 by 80 feet. It took almost a month merely to drive the piles for each platform. At this point one partner threatened to withdraw, but was deterred when told that salvage value would not approximate what had already been invested.

On August 13 a drilling permit was issued by the Louisiana Department of Conservation for wells on "State Lease 754 A-1." Eleven days later drilling equipment was moved onto the two unfinished platforms, for there now began a race against time. Unless drilling were under way by September 12, a penalty of $150,000 would have to be paid. As Seale said, "The annual rental would be 'peanuts' if compared to the millions spent on leases today [1972]. But the company's financial position was far different then from what it is today." He undoubtedly was referring to management's August report to the Kerr-McGee board that it was "chronically short of working capital."

Platforms were only half the picture. Marine support was also necessary. In June, George B. Parks had been hired to handle this problem, the chief part of which would be a tender for supplies and crew quarters. Use of a vessel had the advantage that it could move from location to location and, if unsuccessful in this role, could be sold, and the platform enlarged to take over the ship's functions.

The type of ship had been determined somewhat by accident a year or so earlier, when McGee and Bob Kerr took a scenic cruise of the New Orleans harbor. There they saw some naval vessels in storage, among which were yard-freighter (YF) tenders 260 by 48 feet. McGee remembered these in 1947 and decided that one of them would serve the need, if it could be purchased.

On inquiry, Kerr-McGee was told that the yard freighters were not for sale. Thus a new search seemed imminent. Instead, Bob Kerr went to work at the game he was best suited to play. Admirals and civilians of comparable rank were invited to conferences in his hotel room. After a series of these meetings a decision was reached that the ships could be sold, and at a price of $75,000 each. Kerr triumphantly called McGee to announce his success and to ask how many he should buy. McGee gave the careful estimate of two or three. But Kerr, with his usual optimism, argued that they should buy all ten. The cautious McGee prevailed, however, and his minimum of two was purchased.

It was now up to Parks and Danielson to convert the YFs. The changes were deliberately held down so that the ships could be resold if the Gulf attempt failed. Nevertheless, at a cost of about $150,000, one was redesigned to serve as a drilling tender, with galley, crews quarters, mud and pipe storage, and other necessary space. To round out the outfitting, three air-sea rescue boats were also bought and modified to serve as crew boats, while an LCT was obtained to use as a supply vessel. Marine crews were hired for all, and Kerr-McGee could boast of its own navy of six vessels.

The pressure of the deadline was such that shortcuts had to be taken. Since the renovation of the YF was not complete, the LCT initially served in its place. And because Block 28 was merely a holding operation to meet the letter of the law, a light rotary drill was set on the platform there rather than the heavy rig which would eventually be used. The main effort was on Block 32, and Rig #16 was placed there. Finally, on September 9, a 12,000-foot test on Block 28 was spudded, and a day later, about eight miles away, drilling began on a 4,000-foot test on Block 32. The deadline had been beaten by two days.

On September 17, a week after the start of drilling, the biggest hurricane of the season moved into the area, and both platforms had to be abandoned until the skies cleared. It was the first of many such similar experiences with the capricious weather. According to Seale, "A couple of weeks earlier and that storm would have wrecked us. We would have been caught in the middle of riggin up." Once more Lady Luck had smiled on the young company.

The week of September 19 saw the resumption of drilling, and the next two weeks also passed uneventfully. Although there were some problems with keeping the barge in position, the actual drilling on Block 32 was without incident. But a sense of expectation was always present, on the rig and at the local Berwick, Louisiana, base. The company's infant magazine, *Kermac News*, graphically described the excitement which gripped everyone connected with the operation. Under the title "Picayunes" the wife of a staff member wrote of the events on Rig #16 as though she were reviewing a drama.

And high drama it was. On a platform in eighteen feet of water, ten and a half miles from the nearest land, the play reached its climax before even the cast realized what had happened. As Seale later described it, "We didn't know at first we had encountered oil. . . . The first we knew we had encountered oil sands at such a shallow depth (between 1,500 and 1,700 feet) was when oil covered the mud pits inside the barge." Instead of pumping the drilling mud back out, they were pumping out mud *and* oil. Someone informed the tool pusher, and he in turn reported to Seale. Seale listened to the complaint and told the tool pusher to get a skimmer and skim it off. The reply to this was, "Skim it off, hell! There's barrels of it."

So, on a beautiful Sunday morning, October 4, at about nine o'clock, oil was found in the Gulf of Mexico. The small company and the man who dared to predict the outcome had discovered commercial oil in the world's first well drilled in the open water. The word spread quickly, and the *Kermac News* correspondent told the story in this fashion:

Believe me, the performance at "1508 to 1526" caught the players, the Director and the critics out of costume and in the "unawares" . . . nobody expected a hit at that shallow "pitch!"

The first successful well drilled out of sight of land in 1947.

Everybody shook hands with everybody twice. . . . Congratulations came pouring in . . . [as] other radios had picked up our surprising hit and the telephone began to squeal from Houston to New Orleans. . . . Those who had been dubious about the manner in which our Play was presented extended the olive branch. . . . The newspapers gave it banner notices.

Out on the rig, celebrating was restrained. There simply was not room or facilities for more, this being before the days of air-conditioned quarters or "rec" rooms. As Seale said, "We didn't do much celebrating until we could get ashore." And there was still work to be done. At the time that the oil came in, they had only a small amount of pipe in place and were drilling a large-diameter hole. What size of casing should they use? The call to Oklahoma City was finally returned about noon, and McGee's instructions were to stop drilling and run an electric log. He then quickly flew to the well;

Kerr-McGee pioneered in the use of the fixed platform and tender for drilling offshore.

Dean A. McGee (*third from left*) aboard converted YF tender at site of first offshore well in 1947.

the log showed that they had already penetrated about three sands with one hundred feet of pay. Even with that evidence, McGee was skeptical about the log because it looked so good. He was afraid it was a fluke because the drilling had not gone as deep as he thought necessary to find oil.

Lawyer Terrill's answer was amusing, if inaccurate: they had not been drilling where they thought they were. He told it as a great joke that, while looking for flank production, they had found "a nice little pool . . . smack in the middle of the dome—flank of that dome has never been good. So by accident, Kerr-McGee found this field in a different geological age a short distance down." Although the crew had bad problems with sanding, the well was finally completed on November 14. It flowed thirty to forty barrels of 25.3-gravity oil per hour. The only problem then was the happy one of what to do with the oil. There were no tanks on the platform.

The official costs were set at $208,249 for drilling, $224,031 for the platform, and $17,950 for the derrick and superstructure—a total of

Dean A. McGee and Robert S. Kerr at the Morgan City base headquarters in Louisiana in 1947.

$450,230. The first year's production was 99,371 barrels. The current conservation practices for land wells would have permitted production of only 76 barrels per day, but Kerr-McGee argued that they could not operate at that rate. Finally the Conservation Commission decided that the great expense and extraordinary conditions under which the company had drilled warranted special consideration and so gave the well an allowable of 400 barrels.

Needless to say, the first successful well ever drilled out of sight of land got wide industry coverage. The *Oil and Gas Journal* headed its story "Spectacular Gulf of Mexico Discovery . . . Possible 100-Million-Barrel Field—10 miles at Sea," and it credited the company with having "developed a revolutionary type of drilling equipment for use in unprotected waters." It described the "revolutionary marine-drilling equipment" as a "combination platform and floating barge."

Oil (January, 1948) was even more impressed:

When the Kerr-McGee well was brought in November 14, 1947, it was recognized as one of the significant events of history, taking rank with Col. Drake's pioneer well in Pennsylvania and Cap'n Lucas' Spindletop gusher. . . . The Kerr-McGee well definitely extends the kingdom of oil into a new province that is of incalculable extent and may help assuage the all-devouring demand for gasoline and fuel oils.

Although Kerr-McGee officials recall this as one of the turning points in the company's history, they were more modest in assessing their own roles. George Cobb said, "The decision to go offshore and stay with it has been one of the major contributing factors to the financial success of Kerr-McGee and it took lots of guts." Frank Love summed it up by declaring that Kerr-McGee had "such a driving ambition to become a bigger company" that it refused to let all of the difficulties stop it from going ahead: "There was a combination of a lot of courage, but coupled with some good fortune, that the first well that the company drilled was a real good oil well. And this gave us more confidence."

What was the assessment of Dean McGee, the man who led them through all of this? Recalling that "some said it took courage; others just said we were foolish," his own evaluation, while reflecting satisfaction, was moderate:

It was one of the many "firsts" for the company. This one was indeed important to the petroleum industry because it marked the beginning of exploration of the continental shelf which now is on a worldwide basis. To drill this discovery well, the company devised new drilling concepts and equipment. It is with a great deal of pride that we note our contributions to the technology of drilling for oil and gas in oceans.[20]

[20] D. A. McGee and A. T. F. Seale, "Oil in the Gulf of Mexico," paper presented to the American Institute of Mining and Metallurgical Engineers—Petroleum Division, Dallas, October 4–6, 1948; D. A. McGee and A. T. F. Seale, "Offshore Drilling Development," paper presented at Southwestern A.P.I. Division of Production, San Antonio, April 14–16, 1948; Horst Heise, "Offshore Demands Systems Approach," *Oilweek*, June 26, 1967, pp. 42–44; Seale, "Modern Practices in Off-Shore Drilling"; "A. T. F. Seale, Profile," *Oil and Gas Journal*, April 19, 1965, pp. 191–92; Barrow, "Prairie Wildcatters," pp. 54ff.; Ron Londenberg, "Man, Oil and the Sea," *Offshore*, October, 1972, pp. 54ff.; A. T. F. Seale, "Discovering Oil 12 Miles Offshore"; Barnes and McCaslin, "Spectacular Gulf of Mexico Discovery"; *Kermac News*, Vol. 1 (November, 1947), pp. 1–3; December, 1947, pp. 1–2; April, 1949, p. 8; December, 1972, pp. 1–6; D. A. McGee, *Evolution into Total Energy: The Story of Kerr-McGee Corporation* (New York, 1971), pp. 14–15; interviews with A. T. F. Seale, February 20, 1970; George B. Parks, October 23, 1971; George Cobb, January 21, 1971; December 7, 1972; Dean Terrill, November 24, 1969; Frank C. Love, September 2, 1971; and Dean A. McGee, September 4, 1971; *New Orleans Times-Picayune*, November 18 and December 28, 1947; *New Orleans States*, December 11, 1947; and "Uranium," *Time*, July 30, 1956, p. 68.

Production platform for first offshore well as it appeared in 1977.

Chapter 11

The Year of Decisions 1948

In the fall of 1947 not only Kerr-McGee employees but also the American people as a whole were aware that they were living through historic times. Everywhere changes were taking place. The contradictory ambitions of democracy and communism were emerging through the smoke screen of distraction caused by the gigantic efforts to repair the damages of war. During 1948 these goals assumed their clearest definition when the United States employed an airlift to breach dramatically the Russian Berlin blockade. Bernard Baruch coined a national phrase when he told the Senate War Investigating Committee, "Although the war is over, we are in the midst of a cold war which is getting warmer." The nation's reaction to this "cold war" was the beginning of an A-bomb program. To bolster this, the Atomic Energy Commission (AEC) began a uranium-purchase plan, foreshadowing coming events for Kerr-McGee.

The economy seemed to be catching up with itself as the change from a war to a semipeacetime footing continued. Prices, with some exceptions, tended toward stability, suggesting that supply had materially duplicated the pace of demand. A major deviation was the petroleum industry. Despite record production and the drilling of 35,000 new wells, there was a 1947 deficit of 2,000 barrels a day—a condition which brought voluntary allocations and soaring crude prices. The United States alone was now using as much oil as the entire world had consumed in 1938. Leadership called for a 6 percent boost in production in 1948. Whether this could be accomplished depended not only upon good luck in exploration but also on whether steel manufacturers could overcome the shortage of casing and tubular goods.

At the October, 1947, meeting of the Kerr-McGee directors, the discovery well in the Gulf was the occasion for self-congratulations, but there was other pressing business. In August board members had voted the first dividend of the year, $0.03 on common stock, and now they raised it to $0.0625. To continue this progress, they decided that additional financing was needed, through either a long-term insurance company loan or an increase in indebtedness to the First National Bank of Chicago or through a combination of both. A merger with Fen-Ter was suggested for efficiency and closer corporate control, but this got only as far as agreeing, in that event, to allow James Kelly to buy stock in Kerr-McGee to offset his option for Fen-Ter stock. In November action was also deferred on redeeming the preferred stock, a move urged by financial advisers.

One positive act did take place during the closing months of 1947, however, one of great future significance to Kerr-McGee. There had long been an awareness of Bob Kerr's continuing political ambitions and plans. No one in the company or the state of Oklahoma thought he would return to the oil business as a full-time job, for it was an open secret that the United States Senate was his next goal. In fact, he was already taking the first steps to get to Washington. Kerr's preoccupation with political activities, plus the rapid expansion of Kerr-McGee, placed an increasingly burdensome strain on McGee. It was imperative that he have managerial help, so a search was begun. McGee's first choice was Frank C. Love the successful lawyer in the Watchorn case. Love knew the petroleum industry, for before going into private practice he had worked in the legal department of Shell Oil. He had also been the attorney for the insurance company that had loaned money to buy the Kerr-McGee building, and his legal firm had done some work in connection with offshore leasing deals.

Despite the fact that Love was a close friend, McGee did not believe he would come into the company. But Bob Kerr was convinced that he could persuade Love to join them. As Love later recalled, Kerr requested an appointment, at which he announced that McGee needed help and specifically wanted Love. Kerr added that he knew Love was happy where he was, but asked how much money he was making. Next Kerr inquired how much money Love would like to make. Love replied $25,000, and in Love's words, "Kerr responded, 'Well, we want to hire you to help . . . McGee run the company' and, if I had any interest in doing it, they would like to sell me some stock and pay me $30,000 a year, and would I have an interest in talking to them on that basis?"

Love did have an interest in the offer and discussed it with McGee on an overnight train ride to Dallas. McGee outlined his plans to make Kerr-McGee into a "completely integrated oil company" by tremendous expansion of oil production to match the larger gas output. McGee's conclusion was that the company's future lay in offshore fields, that the oil was there for the finding. Kerr's salesmanship and McGee's dreams convinced the naturally cautious lawyer, and so another important asset was acquired by the growing company. The modest six-foot, easy-blushing, warm-hearted diplomat brought to Kerr-McGee a talent for negotiation in legal matters and the skills of a careful student of all activities in which the company was engaged.[1]

The arrangements were completed in January, and the board appointed F. C. Love vice-president, and assistant to Executive Vice-President McGee as of March 1, with the recommendation that he also be nominated as a director. His salary was set at $30,000, and he was allowed to buy 10,000 shares of common stock. At the same time seventeen other "key" employees were given options to buy stock, illustrating the continuing use of Bob Kerr's technique to acquire and hold good people. In April, Love was duly elected a director, bringing the total to eight.

At the stockholders' meeting earlier in the year Kerr announced that the net profits for the last five months of 1947 were "by far the largest operating profit which the company has ever enjoyed." Kerr-McGee was still in a state of excitement and relishing the national attention its offshore discovery had generated. At least twenty other companies, employing some thirty exploration crews, were aggressively engaged off the Louisiana coast alone in the opening months of 1948. By year's end wells would be completed by California Oil in the Main Pass area, Humble Oil and Refining at Grand Isle, Superior Oil at Vermillion, and Barnsdall Oil at Breton Sound and Eugene Island.

Kerr-McGee had the natural advantage of a proven success, as well as the chance that Block 28 might also produce another "star." The barge and rig used on Block 32 were moved to Block 28 to complete that well down to 12,000 feet. A new rig was obtained, a second YF was converted to exploit the Block 32 find, and plans were studied for a twenty-five-mile submarine pipeline to bring in the oil.[2] A third wildcat was drilling off Cameron Parish, three miles from shore and in twenty-five feet of water, while seismographic work was being carried on off the Texas coast, although no leases had yet been acquired.

After the completion of the Block 32 well and the question of allowables had been settled, there was still a problem of logistics. As late as March it had been impossible to find an oil-cargo barge or other vessel of the correct size, draft, and capacity to meet Coast Guard requirements for operation in the open waters of the Gulf. The problem was finally solved, and the first barge placed in position on May 4, and a second on May 21. Two additional wells had been drilled from the same platform by September, and a fourth was under way. Plans called for a total of seven wells, and then an additional platform for four more wells to cover Block 32.

On Block 28 producing horizons were found at 7,600 and 8,600 feet, and major sands at 13,973. It was believed that by November an oil well with a

---

[1] Interviews with Frank C. Love, September 2, 1971, and Guy C. Kiddoo, August 12, 1971; *Kermac News*, June, 1948, p. 3.

[2] Dean A. McGee and A. T. F. Seale, "Oil in the Gulf of Mexico," paper presented to American Institute of Mining and Metallurgical Engineers—Petroleum Division, Dallas, Texas, October 4–6, 1948; *Kermac News*, December, 1947, pp. 1–2, 5.

high gas-oil ratio might be completed. The same *Kermac News* reporter happily summed it up:

Mainly, we are struggling along with the daily routine of our Hit Performance and preparing for a new and bigger (we hope) show. . . . The scenery on Stage 28 is all set except for a few minor changes and the players are well-schooled in their parts.[3]

The steel shortage plagued Kerr-McGee during this period. In April, 1948, Chairman Kerr told his board that the company had borrowed $375,000 from the First National Bank of Chicago and gone on the open market for casing and tubing. Almost $20,000 had been spent on the effort to no avail. As an option, however, he suggested a unique, if indirect, way to solve the problem. Republic Supply Company, an affiliate of the Republic Steel Company, was for sale, but not to an oil company. A group of individuals was interested in the purchase but needed guarantors, a role it proposed for Kerr-McGee. In return, the new owners would contract to sell Kerr-McGee all its requirements of steel casing and tubing at regular prices for five years. Not only did Kerr-McGee agree to participate to a maximum of $1,375,000 but Phillips Petroleum joined the plan to the amount of $4,125,000, under a similar arrangement. It proved to be a happy solution to a pressing problem.[4]

During April the decision to merge Fen-Ter and Kerr-McGee Skyways into the parent company was made, thus eliminating all subsidiaries as of July 1. The same date was set as the deadline to register a new stock offering of 200,000 shares at $15 each. The large development program was demanding additional capital in a rather urgent fashion. On June 11 the board formally authorized the sale of 300,000 shares (200,000 furnished by the company and 100,000 that were bought from the Kerrs, McGee, Terrill, and Fentem). An underwriting agreement was signed with Lehman Brothers and Straus & Blosser on June 14 for $15 per share. The S-1 registration statement indicated that the stock would be offered to the public at $18. Of the proceeds $1,448,000 was to retire short-term loans from the First National Bank of Chicago and the Liberty National Bank of Oklahoma City; the remainder was to go into the general fund.

This document also reported other interesting facts about Kerr-McGee. As of March 31, 1948, 66 percent of the undeveloped properties and 43.6 percent of the oil reserves had been acquired under the deal with Phillips for joint prospecting. Furthermore, before 1946 the company had concentrated on discovery of petroleum reserves; since that time the emphasis had been

---

[3] McGee and Seale, "Oil in the Gulf of Mexico"; A. T. F. Seale, "Discovering Oil 12 Miles Offshore in the Gulf," *World Oil*, May, 1948, unpaged reprint; *Kermac News*, July, 1948, pp. 1–2, 7.

[4] Kerr-McGee Oil Industries, Inc., *Annual Report for Fiscal Year Ended June 30, 1950*, note E; Securities and Exchange Commission, "Form 10-K Annual Report for Fiscal Year Ended June 30, 1953, Kerr-McGee Oil Industries, Inc."; Kerr-McGee, "Notice of Annual Meeting, September 28, 1956," pp. 5–6; *Tulsa World*, June 20, 1948; *Daily Oklahoman*, April 20 and October 17, 1948.

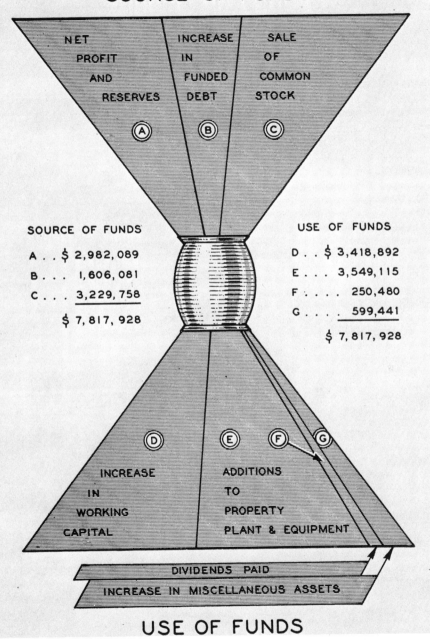

Fig. 11.1. Flow of funds, 1947–48. From Kerr-McGee Oil Industries, Inc.,
1948 Annual Report.

Kerr-McGee Oil Industries, Inc.

Table 11.1. Consolidated Statement of Income and Earned Surplus, 1948

Operating revenues	
Drilling contracts completed	$ 5,023,168.63
Sale of crude oil and gas	2,649,354.93
Sale of refined products	4,695,542.00
Other operating income (1948 includes $150,000 received from co-owners of certain oil and gas leases in excess of expenditures for development thereof)	169,992.14
	$12,538,057.70
Operating expenses	
Cost of drilling contracts completed	$ 4,066,919.81
Cost and expenses applicable to refined products sold (exclusive of depreciation and general and administrative expense)	3,891,345.70
Lease operating expense	423,958.96
General and administrative expense	777,600.00
Land department expense	41,596.62
Geological and geophysical department expense	152,155.54
Taxes, other than income taxes	90,786.80
Lease rentals expense	143,969.15
Research expense	. . . .
Depreciation (exclusive of depreciation on service equipment deducted as departmental expenses: 1948, $122,464; 1947, $95,391)	874,854.94
Depletion	305,107.15
Dry-hole costs	184,040.33
Abandoned leaseholds and royalties	127,961.70
	$11,080,296.70
Less: income from service equipment—net	104,937.95
	$10,975,358.75
	$ 1,562,698.95
Other income	
Gain on disposal of property	$ 60,187.30
Purchase discounts	45,410.39
Dividends	800.00
Interest	2,826.03
	$ 109,223.72
	$ 1,671,922.67
Income deductions	
Interest and loan expense	$ 212,324.10
Bad debts charged off	18,440.79
Cash discounts allowed	38,997.05
Amortization of stock issue expense	6,642.99
Provision for state income taxes	29,053.44
Provision for federal income taxes	. . . .
	$ 305,458.37
Net income	$ 1,366,464.30

176

Table 11.1. *Continued.*

Adjustment of operations for prior years	
Certain expenditures for seismograph exploration costs, etc.,	
disallowed by federal tax authorities	$ . . . .
Decrease provision for depreciation	207,591.38
Increase provision for income taxes	. . . .
Refund of 1939 federal income taxes	. . . .
	$ 207,591.38
Balance transferred to surplus	$ 1,574,055.68
Surplus—earned—beginning of period	857,953.56
	$ 2,432,009.24
Less: Dividends paid on Common Stock	$ 178,836.38
Dividends paid on Preferred Stock	71,643.60
	$ 250,479.98
Surplus—earned—end of period	$ 2,181,529.26

on development. Kerr-McGee had leasehold interests in 508 oil, 46 gas, and 10 gas-condensate wells. It was no longer basically an Oklahoma producer, for 376 of these wells were in Texas, 121 in Oklahoma, 7 in Kansas, 3 in Arkansas, and 1 in Wyoming. Twenty-three rotary rigs were in operation, and it had leases on 190,191 acres in Texas, Louisiana, and Oklahoma. Regional offices were located in Casper, Wyoming; Midland, Texas; and Shreveport and Morgan City, Louisiana, for the primary convenience of the forty-one different contract-drilling customers.[5]

Naturally this registration statement foreshadowed the annual report for the year ending June 30, 1948. In his letter to the stockholders Kerr reported the largest operational profit for any year in the company's history, exceeded only by the net for 1945, when the sale of properties had accounted for a large share of the total.

Assets were almost $14 million, of which $8 million was in properties. The funded debt with the First National Bank of Chicago had been increased by $1,606,080.83, resulting in a long-term debt consisting of 3¾ percent first mortgages that aggregated $9.2 million, with $4,823,576 outstanding.[6] The source and use of this and all other nonoperating funds were pictorialized,

[5] S-1 Registration Statement, January 15, 1948.

[6] Kerr-McGee Oil Industries, Inc., *Annual Report for the Fiscal Year Ended June 30, 1948*; Securities and Exchange Commission, "Financial Statements Form 1-MD—Annual Report for Fiscal Year Ended June 30, 1948." For a comparison see Dun & Bradstreet, "Kerr-McGee Analytical Report," December 21, 1948.

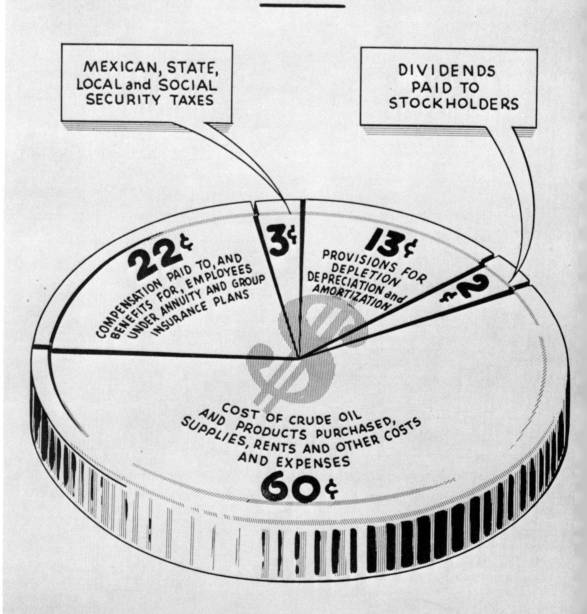

Fig. 11.2. Income expenditure, June 30, 1948. From Kerr-McGee Oil
Industries, Inc., *1948 Annual Report*.

along with a breakdown of the gross income dollar. These diagrams were an innovation for the annual report, which as a whole began to reflect the image of a growing and prosperous company.

The successful efforts in the Gulf of Mexico were also singled out, with a plea for stockholders to urge Congress to restore ownership of the offshore areas to the states, in order to facilitate their development. On land the company had been actively drilling in Moore and Sherman counties, Texas, and hoped to join these properties by year's end to a connecting line then under construction at a cost of $775,000. Over all, Kerr-McGee had been involved in sinking 104 wells in which it held an interest. Of these, 70 produced oil, 19 gas, and 15 were dry. Eight were wildcats, 2 of which were discoveries resulting directly from the efforts of its three seismographic crews. The company's gas reserves, in the Panhandle area of West Texas and De Soto Parish, Louisiana, were estimated at one trillion cubic feet, and prices ranged from 3½ to 8½ cents per thousand.

Another bright spot in this report was the Wynnewood refinery, Fen-Ter, which was merged with the parent company on July 1. The old, run-down facility had been undergoing repairs ever since its purchase in 1945, in an on-going effort to modernize and improve the facility. Capacity had been increased threefold to 7,500 barrels of crude per day, and new boilers, oxidizing stills, and product lines had been added. Among the new products were Oil Base Mud for drilling, Briquetting Asphalt, Special Wood Treating Oil, and an asphalt paint. All were marketed under the red, white, and blue Kermac trademark. As a result, annual sales at Fen-Ter had doubled to $4,698,000, and the previous year's profits rose to $546,211.27, considerably more than the initial purchase price.[7]

The drilling division, on the other hand, "consistent with the low margin of profit prevalent," had contributed relatively little net profit. Fifth in size among contract drillers, Kerr-McGee had about 575 employees in this department, including 64 in exploration, and owned 32 rotaries (2 of them steam). During the fiscal year, 162 wells were completed for a gross footage of 710,303, and 19 were still in progress. One of these, Stanolind Oil Co. No. 1 Briscoe, had reached 15,184 feet, to become the deepest producing well in the world. Of this total, 142 were contract, 31 were wholly owned by Kerr-McGee in Texas, and 9 were "interest" wells, including 3 in the Gulf.

Kerr-McGee's drilling operations were widely scattered. Greatest activity was in Texas with 82 holes; Colorado, 32; Wyoming, 26; Oklahoma, 24; Louisiana, 6 (3 in the Gulf); and Montana, 4. Contracts covered operations with seven major and six independents, the heavy users being Stanolind, Gulf, Carter, Phillips, Ohio, California, and Continental.[8] Of historical interest only, was the completion of an offset, Toge Harjo #1, to Anderson &

---

[7] For the merger see Oklahoma Secretary of State, Corporation file, and State Archives, Secretary of State, "Kerr-McGee vs. John Rogers," folder 3; *Kermac News*, December, 1947, pp. 3–4.

[8] *Kermac News*, September, 1948, pp. 1–2; December, 1948, pp. 1–2, 5; S-1 Statement, No. 107, March 31, 1948, pp. 14–15; Transworld Drilling file, "Kerr-McGee Oil Industries, Inc., Drilling Department Rig Operations Fiscal Year July 1, 1947, to June 30, 1948."

Kerr Drilling Company's first well, the Morgan #1. This must have been for sentimental reasons, for in seventeen years this well produced only 17,716 barrels of oil.

Of more importance were the contract activities in Wyoming. Q. C. Walton recalled that on one well there, because of monstrous snowstorms he did not see the ground between December and April, and that the temperature stayed below zero during the entire period. It might not have amused Walton to learn how he happened to be in Wyoming, but a humorous story reflects the inside nature of the drilling business and a human facet in what had now become a middle-sized corporation. Travis Kerr had been riding overnight on a train with a landholder from Wyoming, and to pass the time they had drinks together. Shortly afterward, this new friend called Travis to say that he had made a deal with Stanolind to advance development money for drilling fifteen wells in Elk Basin. He added, "Now Travis, I don't want any lawyers fooling with the contract. I've been with the lawyers over at Stanolind. . . . I'm sick of it. . . . If you'll write a contract on one page, I'll sign it, and you can drill all our wells in Elk Basin." Kerr-McGee did drill all his wells on the basis of that one piece of paper.[9]

It had long been the ambition of Travis Kerr to create the largest land drilling firm in the world. An opportunity to take a long stride in this direction occurred when Kerr-McGee was approached by Parker Drilling Company officials offering to sell the firm. The First National Bank of Chicago agreed to support the acquisition, and management was instructed to proceed with negotiations.

A new voice was heard for the first time, however, in dissent to the move. One of F. C. Love's first assignments had been to study Kerr-McGee and its cash flow. This exercise indicated to him that the financial future of the land-rig business was not bright, that there were too many questionable factors influencing its profitability. Consequently, he reported this belief to Dean McGee. Both men then recommended that the company turn down the Parker deal, and, furthermore, get out of the land phase of the business and concentrate on the edge it now had in offshore drilling.

To bolster this opinion, an inventory showed that much of Parker's equipment was obsolete. Although the asking price was dropped from $4 million to $3.6 million, there were still doubts about the value. Finally Bob Kerr was called in to make the decision whether to expand the drilling arm of the company or go with Love and McGee's plan to deemphasize that part. Kerr sided with Dean McGee "but didn't make a big issue of it," and Parker was not purchased. Consequently, Kerr-McGee began a gradual shift from land to offshore drilling. As this trend became evident, Travis "kind of quit running the drilling end," finding interests outside the company to fill his time.[10]

[9] Lease Records file, "S-516 Morgan"; interviews with Quinton C. ("Pete") Walton, April 16, 1971, and Travis M. Kerr, December 16, 1969.

[10] Interviews with Harold Freeman, April 17, 1971; Guy Swain, May 27, 1971; and Frank C. Love.

Besides the hiring of Love, Bob Kerr's political ambitions indirectly had other effects upon the company. In May, 1948, when he announced that he was running for the United States Senate, a Democratic rival, Mac Q. Williamson, charged that the 1945 purchase of the Wynnewood refinery had been motivated by intention to sell asphalt to the state during his term as governor. Moreover, while serving in that office, Kerr had allowed his salary to be doubled by Kerr-McGee. Now, in July following Kerr's victory by about 50,000 votes in the Democratic primary, his Republican opponent, Congressman Ross Rizley, continued the charge, claiming that a provision had been inserted into road contracts that could be met only by one producer in the state. Because of this, indirectly Rizley claimed, Fen-Ter had been able to make a profit of $146,641.32 during 1945–46.

From the beginning, Kerr's political strategy was simple. In the primary he refused to respond to personal attacks and took no stands that would alienate any faction of the badly split Democratic party. Using the theme of "a stronger America and a more prosperous Oklahoma," he attempted to "harmonize the interest of farmer and industrialist, cattlegrower and oilman" and stressed agriculture as the state's major asset with industrial growth and prosperity dependent upon it. During his time in the Senate he would develop the Arkansas, White, and Red river basins to prevent floods, retard erosion, generate cheap electricity, foster irrigation, and provide cheap transportation. This, in turn, would attract industry, create jobs, and provide recreational facilities, all at federal expense.

Kerr ignored the asphalt charges by his Republican opponent. He did, however, personally attack Rizley and his legislative record, accusing him of being a tool of the "special interests"—especially the gas industry. Kerr himself deliberately omitted appeals to the oil producers. Furthermore, Rizley's votes in Congress had shown him opposed to public power, federal aid to the Southwest, a strong military force, and a leading role for the United States in foreign affairs. Rizley spent most of his time on the defensive, and consequently made little impression on the voters concerning Kerr's past or proposed actions.[11]

In November, Robert S. Kerr, president of Kerr-McGee Oil Industries, Incorporated, became Robert S. Kerr, senator from Oklahoma. Washington was some thirteen hundred miles from Oklahoma City, and this time his political office would not be a few blocks from his corporate one. Perhaps mindful of this and of the recent campaign charges, the executive committee of Kerr-McGee decided that after January 1, 1949, Senator Kerr's salary from the company would be reduced by half.

Thus, in two different ways, and for two separate reasons, Bob and Travis Kerr's direct influence began to wane at the company which bore their name. Likewise, it was the beginning of relinquishment of family adminis-

[11] The charges were a rehash of the Oklahoma House Committee's investigation report mentioned earlier. Clippings dealing with this election are in Kerr scrapbooks, 24, 26–28, in Robert S. Kerr Collection, Western History Collections, University of Oklahoma. For a modern account of this election see Anne H. Morgan, *Robert S. Kerr: The Senate Years* (Norman, University of Oklahoma Press, 1977), pp. 24–32.

tration to outside hands and the start of a new era for Kerr-McGee Oil Industries.

Bob Kerr proudly wore in his coat lapel a button proclaiming "Kerr-McGee Founder" as he made his rounds in the United States Senate. Looking back over the past twenty years gave him ample reason for pride in this title. Instead of the two rickety rigs bought from the Dixon brothers, there were now over thirty. From a local, unknown business, his company had expanded over most of the western United States and into the Gulf of Mexico. Personnel had grown from a few dozen to over eight hundred. Six of the original men, Kerr and five field men, were still active in the firm.[12] From a contract driller to an integrated oil corporation was the synopsis of the story of Anderson & Kerr Drilling. The Midas touch of the Kerrs, Anderson, and McGee had attracted national attention, and the company's technical proficiency was soon to be carried across the world.

Kerr's move to Washington would never have been considered if he had not had supreme confidence in Dean McGee. Furthermore, it did not indicate any lessening of interest in the firm that still bore his name. Rex Hawks, a close friend and companion, recalls that Kerr always had a pocketful of change and would often stop at a pay phone to call McGee—any time he had an idea or just wanted to check on how things were going.[13] McGee remembers these telephone calls from around the nation as Kerr's means of staying in touch. Otherwise, his contribution was in the way of advice and counsel and presiding at board meetings.

Contemporaries and fellow workers have provided many accounts of how this essentially disparate pair worked together to produce a major American corporation. George Cobb summed up the relationship by saying that Kerr's contribution was his complete faith in the future and the ability of his associates to accomplish things—"It certainly wasn't the day-to-day running of the company. It wasn't the picking and hiring of the lesser executives." Guy C. Kiddoo, a director from the First National Bank of Chicago, stressed the same element: Kerr's "abiding, steady, substantial confidence in the ability of Dean McGee and his belief that the company had no way to go except up." Kiddoo found Kerr "always more optimistic than McGee in forecasting the developments ahead for the company," but "it was a happy combination of McGee having the scientific basis for finding and developing oil . . . and the Senator had the ambition to build a company."[14]

James E. Webb, director and assistant to McGee, had an interesting analogy. To Webb, McGee was an elephant hunter: "I mean he wouldn't ever go out looking for small game and he would not take his eyes off of a big

[12] The six men were Robert S. Kerr and five former drillers, some of whom dated back to the days of the Dixon brothers: General H. Johnson, Raymond A. Godard, T. L. Glover, Q. C. Walton, and Jack Tacker. *Kermac News*, February, 1949, pp. 6–7.

[13] *Daily Oklahoman*, September 23, 1962; "Kerr-McGee Oil Stretches Out," *Investor's Guide*, October 7, 1964, pp. 17–20; and interview with Rex Hawks, May 24, 1972.

[14] Interviews with George Cobb, executive vice-president, December 7, 1972, and Guy C. Kiddoo.

possibility in the way of a new discovery." The senator, however, was always thinking " 'Gee, we've got to find that herd of elephants and think what a great thing we could do with all that ivory.' " But McGee, while looking for the herd, was thinking, " 'We've got to be very careful that we don't stampede them and get trampled in the process.' "

Another director, Edwin L. Kennedy of Lehman Brothers, remarked of the relationship, "He let McGee run the company, and that wasn't exactly the Senator's way." He also felt that the

Senator sometimes became interested in an idea that was not necessarily sound. . . . It is not difficult to have new ideas but to handle those ideas in such a way and sort out the ones that will make money; there is where the art is. No man in my business experience has it to the extent that McGee has it.

Kennedy described McGee as a man of "controlled imagination," one who could direct his thoughts into only those areas that he believed would be profitable.[15]

F. C. Love likewise found this team to be unusual. Although Kerr was the major stockholder, "he never gave orders, except through McGee. How his orders were accomplished was not his concern." Furthermore, with Kerr's imagination, he was a wonderful person for McGee to talk with: "He encouraged Dean to take risks, which Dean probably otherwise would not have taken. . . . the Senator was always pushing." Love believed that this undoubtedly caused the firm to grow faster than otherwise. Since Kerr was the one with most of the money at stake, it was easier for others to go ahead and act. The right decisions, therefore, allowed McGee to develop confidence in his leadership. George Parks felt that while Kerr was alive McGee had to be the balance wheel and not let him go too far but that after Kerr was gone McGee had to become the optimistic one and push the conservatives. Guy Swain, who began as a roughneck with the company in 1938, voiced the opinion of many of the field men that McGee "probably" saved Kerr from going broke. Kerr would get so enthusiastic in his projects that he could not see how they could go wrong, but McGee was the stabilizing force.[16]

Nearer home Kerr's oldest son, Robert S. Kerr, Jr., a director, gave his views. He saw one of the secrets of the company's success in the fact that "McGee made valid decisions about ultimate objectives and then they have had the intestinal fortitude to stay with them in spite of the rather horrendous, at times, problems that would come up." Then, too, his father was "a wheeler-dealer, a gambler," and if these instincts had been given full play, it "might not necessarily have been the best for the company"—especially in later years.

The man closest to the subject offered his analysis of the successful relationship. Dean McGee said of his friend and business partner: "The

---

[15] Interviews with James E. Webb, August 12, 1971, and Edwin L. Kennedy, August 13, 1971.

[16] O. J. Scott, *The Professional: A Biography of J. B. Saunders* (New York, 1976), p. 419; interviews with Frank C. Love, George B. Parks, October 23, 1971, and Guy Swain.

Senator was always a great optimist and so far as he was concerned, opportunities were unlimited. . . . He always approached everything from the standpoint of it being something that could be done." While Kerr did not "participate from the standpoint of technology, or the day to day . . . , he furnished the leadership and gave people around him a lot of confidence in stepping out." McGee added, "Our only problem with the Senator was that he always thought we weren't moving fast enough."

To illustrate, McGee told a story which eventually was printed in several versions. After the company had designed and built a successful offshore rig, "Kerr would call and say how do they work, and I'd say they're working just fine, and he'd say, well you should have six of them instead of two." This optimism, said McGee, "is an asset every business could use." The secret of their relationship was that "we had complete confidence in each other's integrity. When he [Kerr] said 'Go ahead,' I never gave it a second thought."

When a reporter from the *New Orleans Times-Picayune* asked both men to what each attributed the success of the partnership, they both spoke simultaneously: "Kerr," said McGee. "McGee," replied Kerr.[17]

[17] Interviews with Robert S. Kerr, Jr., June 15, 1971, and Dean A. McGee, September 19, 1973; "Making Money Make Money," *Forbes*, November 1, 1963, p. 32; *Tulsa Tribune*, March 13, 1968; *Time*, July 30, 1956, p. 68; *New Orleans Times-Picayune*, December 8, 1962. 1962.

Chapter 12

Years of Struggle, Years of Promise 1949–1951

This relaxed relationship between an oil company and a United States senator was bound to have repercussions. Despite Kerr's conscientious efforts to avoid any action that could possibly be construed as beneficial to his firm by reasons of political influence, charges would still be leveled. Ironically, in view of the accusations Kerr had made against Rizley in April, 1949, the senator introduced a gas bill to limit a proposed extension of the Federal Power Commission's authority to regulate certain sales of natural gas. Opponents declared that this would allow a huge increase in the price of natural gas in nonproducing states. Pointing to the large gas reserves of Kerr-McGee, they claimed a "conflict of interest." Kerr's answer was that all of the corporation's gas was under long-term contracts at fixed prices and "would be unaffected by either an increase or decrease in the price of natural gas." Columnist Drew Pearson also added the charge that Kerr-McGee could profit from an Oklahoma highway to be financed by the Reconstruction Finance Corporation, since the senator was in a position to influence that agency to buy blacktop from his refinery.[1]

Kerr soon developed a standard, widely quoted, answer to such accusations. "Hell, if everyone abstained on grounds of personal interest, I doubt if you could get a quorum in the United States Senate on any subject." While no one was successful in proving that the company received any illegal

[1] Anne H. Morgan, *Robert S. Kerr: The Senate Years* (Norman, University of Oklahoma Press, 1977), pp. 92–93.

benefits from its association with him (his work on oil-and-gas legislation also aided his competitors), undoubtedly there were intangible rewards. Being in Washington exposed Kerr to a wide and varying range of subjects and points of view. This broadened perspective enabled him to bring new knowledge and insight to his discussions with Dean McGee. There is certainly no evidence that the company was ever seriously injured by Kerr's changed role.

In January, 1949, the stockholders reelected the two Kerrs, Fentem, McGee, Terrill, Blosser, Straus, and Love as directors. As a result of Lehman Brothers' participation in the previous year's stock sale, Edwin L. Kennedy of that firm was asked to join the board. Kennedy later explained his willingness to serve by saying, "Well, at the time I became intrigued with the possibilities of Kerr-McGee because of its management, meaning in particular Mr. Dean McGee." The board then adopted a new set of bylaws, stipulating that directors need not be stockholders, that they would receive expenses and a fixed fee, and that a majority could name a replacement to fill a vacancy on the board. The directors could also appoint the officers of the company, fix their salaries, declare dividends, and choose an executive committee consisting of two or more directors.[2]

Because of the reduced participation of Travis Kerr in the drilling department, George B. Kitchel, who had filled a similar role at Humble Oil and Refining Company for about sixteen years, was hired as general superintendent of this department, effective March 1. Twenty-five days later a new loan agreement (H) was signed for $2 million with the First National Bank of Chicago to provide funds for additional wells. Despite the continued uncertainty of the tidelands' ownership, the board had decided to proceed in the area. In May the directors learned of a slowdown in development and in drilling of exploratory wells but of an increase in production. Some gas had been found, but so far no new oil.

In contract drilling a new frontier was opened with discussion of possible deals in Kuwait and Mexico. Eighty percent of the rigs were running, and a new agreement was signed with Ohio Oil for a Gulf of Mexico well at $30 a foot (Kerr-McGee's first offshore contract). Since it was not profitable for the company to compete on land with small drillers for shallow work, it was trying to dispose of about seventeen of the smaller rigs. A special operating committee was then established by the board to review economies in operation and to control investments.

The October 29, 1949, letter to the stockholders accompanying the annual report stated that, despite increased activities, there had been "appreciably less profit on normal operations for the year." Assets rose to $18,244,270, while long-term debt reached $6,070,827. The increased number of wells in the development program had been offset by reduced allowables. Only one new oil and one new gas well had resulted from ten wildcats, but twenty-six gas producers were added by drilling in the Hugoton and Panhandle fields (see Table 12.1).

---

[2] The bylaws, since January 22, 1949, are in the corporation secretary's office. The Kennedy quotation is found in his interview dated August 13, 1971.

But the biggest disappointment occurred at the refinery, where profits dropped $533,000. While this was "consistent with the situation prevailing throughout the industry, . . . we feel justified in looking for an improvement in the refining portion of the industry."[3] In some respects the refinery's problems were evolutionary. While the amount of crude refined daily had risen slightly to 4,368 barrels, and sales to almost $400,000, cost had soared by $1 million. The basic problem lay in the refinery's principal output—heavy oil products. Most of these, aside from asphalt, were used in the generation of steam power, but that market was dying. The railroads were also switching to diesel engines, and the price of No. 6 heavy industrial fuel oil dropped in four months from $3.00 to $0.50 a barrel. The availability of cheap natural gas added to the problem. Before the year was out, therefore, steps were taken to change the emphasis of the refinery by the addition of a new vacuum distillation unit and asphalt specialty plant. With the manufacture of catalytic-based gasoline, the gasoline volume increased 50 percent, and the quality improved. Output at Wynnewood also changed to a lighter-type end product, while production of asphalt continued.[4]

Drilling success for the year was reasonable but not spectacular. With 462,694 gross acres under lease Kerr-McGee now had 248 producing leases for a gross well total of 672. Ninety-four wells were drilled for the company's account, with 43 producing oil and 35 gas—all in Hutchinson, Moore, Crane, and Sherman counties in Texas. Kerr-McGee also had interests in 17 wells: 12 in the Gulf, 2 in Wyoming, and 1 each in Colorado, Texas, and Louisiana. A total of 31 rigs were used, 4 in the Gulf, and 162 wells were completed with 6 in progress at the end of the calendar year. Of these, 120 were straight contract, involving eight major companies, with the largest numbers in Texas, Oklahoma, Wyoming, Montana, and Utah.

Activities in the Gulf again were highlighted. The well was begun for Ohio Oil in the open waters of the Gulf, and a new deep-hole record was set. Despite work stoppage by two hurricanes, the depth of 14,451 feet was reached in Block 28, Ship Shoal. By summer a new field was discovered with the Cameron Block 33 well, which was given an allowable of 540 barrels per day. Elation at these successes was tempered, however, by the introduction in Congress of an administration bill for federal control of the offshore tidelands.[5]

Although by 1949 Kerr-McGee Oil Industries had grown to a medium-sized operation, there remained evidences of its recent status as a fledgling oil company. Earl A. Berry, personnel director, still found time to write

[3] Kerr-McGee Oil Industries, Inc., *Annual Report for the Fiscal Year Ended June 30, 1949*; Securities and Exchange Commission, "Form 1-MD—Annual Report for Fiscal Year Ended June 30, 1949, Kerr-McGee Oil Industries, Inc."

[4] Interview with James J. Kelly, June 26, 1971; Public Relations file, "Refinery Information"; *Kermac News*, February, 1950, p. 2.

[5] Dean A. McGee personal file, "Kerr-McGee Oil Industries, Inc., Drilling Department Rig Operations Fiscal Year—July 1, 1948, to June 30, 1949"; *Kermac News*, February, 1949, p. 4; and August–September, 1949, p. 1.

folksy letters to new recruits. He pointed out other employees of the company with whom they might have common interests and asked how things were going for them. The new employee, on his part, could expect a wide variety of experiences before settling down to essentially one job. One example, and not an uncommon one, taken from the personnel files of that period involved Burwell G. Taylor. On June 6, 1949, Taylor joined Kerr-McGee and was sent to Morgan City, Louisiana, to gain experience as a mud engineer. In answer to a welcoming letter from Berry he replied on August 4, that his only adjustment was to the "copious rainfall and giant-sized mosquitoes."

Berry, as usual, answered all these letters with news of the home office. Typical was his reply to Taylor on September 13, 1949: "This has really been and will continue to be for a good while a busy place here—operations starting in Mexico and Arabia as you no doubt know—Hurry! hurry! hurry! Sounds like the oil industry, doesn't it." Before the year was out Taylor had served as a roustabout and as an office manager in Orange, Texas. During 1950 he worked as a junior engineer and finally moved into production at Sunray, Texas. Eventually he became vice-president of production.[6]

Berry's reference to Mexico and Arabia, and perhaps Taylor's move to Orange, Texas, concerned another company first—nondomestic drilling contracts. On June 22, an agreement was signed with American Independent Oil Company (Aminoil) for work in the Saudi-Arabia-Kuwait Neutral Zone in the Persian Gulf. The contract covered up to three years, and Kerr-McGee was guaranteed a profit of $600 a day for the first four wells drilled and $450 thereafter, plus a monthly incentive bonus for each foot of hole. Aminoil, operator for a group that included Phillips and Signal Oil, brought Kerr-McGee in because of its marine experience. It was given responsibility for the logistics of the move, the rig, and the support and marine personnel.

Again it was a rush job, for Aminoil was under a drilling deadline of January 1, 1950. McGee sent a message to all employees that this was "an extremely large and important undertaking. It is going to require the best we have in talent and resourcefulness and a lot of hard work." Kerr's senate office was asked to expedite two-year passports for twenty-eight to thirty men. An LST was acquired and converted in Orange, Texas, to first move the equipment to the Persian Gulf and then to serve as a base. Along with facilities for eighty men, the vessel also carried an LCT, two crew boats, and about ten cranes, tractors, and trucks, since there were no port facilities in the drilling area. The two-year stock of supplies included five railway carloads of frozen meat, while a special Saudi dispensation permitted the inclusion of beer, but no hard liquor. Between June 20 and August 9, when the ship sailed, Kerr-McGee spent about $1.5 million on this project.

The 10,500-mile trip by way of the Suez Canal was made in forty-five days, and the crew was ready to rig up ten days later, well under the deadline. The

---

[6] For examples see the folders of George Emery Guidry, D. L. Brown, and Burwell G. Taylor, in the Human Resources files.

initial drilling site was twelve miles inland, so the LST was anchored offshore, where it provided the living quarters and supply base for the operation. After four exploratory holes, all dry, were drilled, work was suspended in 1951, and, as previously agreed in the contract, Kerr-McGee sold the rig and its other equipment to Aminoil.[7] Thus the company's first Middle East venture could hardly have been classified as a success, although it did provide valuable experience in working abroad.

Even while all facilities were being stretched to meet the Aminoil deadline, it was announced that a contract had been signed July 14, 1949, to drill wells in southern Mexico at Las Palmas near the Yucatán Peninsula for the Mexican-American Independent Company, CIMA. To handle this project, however, management decided to create a new subsidiary, Kermac Contractors. Now that the parent firm was becoming involved in foreign operations, this move seemed wise, especially in Mexico. It would be the first time an American company had drilled there since the expropriation in 1938. Also, as a general rule, subsidiaries provide advantages in accounting, tax, and liability considerations. It is easier to account to a foreign nation for income in a limited subsidiary working there than to explain the tax situation for all the parent company's activities. Too, it had a psychological benefit, for a competitor often would rather give contracts to a subsidiary. Thus Kermac Contractors was organized as a Western Hemisphere trading company for tax purposes and also as a separate corporation in case of problems with the Mexican government.[8]

Besides the adjustment of Kermac personnel to Mexican living, the biggest problem was the logistics of getting the rigs, people, materials, and supplies to and from the operation. Kerr's Senate office in Washington again played a role in expediting passports. CIMA had a concession from PEMEX, the Mexican government company, and although CIMA was California-based, it was apparently decided to move the rigs across the Gulf of Mexico rather than down through the Panama Canal. Kermac Contractors sent two land rigs with drillers, superintendents, and mechanics across land to the Gulf and then by sea to Mexico. During the course of about two years it drilled wells at Puerto de Mexico, Tonola, and Ciudad del Carmel. A fairly respectable gas field was found, but since there was no market for gas at that time, it was shut down and remained so for many years. Again, at the end of the contract the rigs were sold to the contracting company, relieving Kermac of the job of returning them to the United States.[9]

The Ohio Company's well in the Gulf, and the Kuwait and Mexican ventures were not lucrative, however, for the July–October financial statement showed a net operating loss, before taxes, of $87,630. A Tascosa Gas

---

[7] Lease Records file, "Kuwait—General Correspondence"; Robert S. Kerr Collection, Western History Collections, University of Oklahoma, box 560, folder 7; *Kermac News*, October, 1949, pp. 1–2, 15, and Summer, 1951, p. 25; interviews with Leo P. LeBron, December 28, 1972; George B. Kitchel, June 16, 1971; and A. T. F. Seale, July 20, 1971.

[8] *Kermac News*, October, 1949, pp. 1–2; interviews with George Cobb, December 7, 1972, and Frank C. Love, September 2, 1971.

[9] Interviews with George B. Kitchel and A. T. F. Seale.

Company deal was therefore doubly welcomed. It had a farm-out on gas rights from Phillips Petroleum on 100 sections of land in Sherman and Hansford counties, Texas, and in Texas County, Oklahoma. Kerr-McGee, with a producing organization already in the area, agreed to drill and operate 100 wells for Tascosa at a stipulated service fee.[10] As the year ended, it was also negotiating with Union Oil of California to obtain an additional 19,000 acres in the Gulf Main Pass area and some cash for drilling a test well on it.

The year 1949 had not been a particularly good one for American business as a whole. During the early months there were abundant signs that the postwar momentum was slowing. The oil products shortages of 1948 were overcome, only to be replaced by ruthless, cutthroat competition. Consequently, the daily rate of crude production fell by 9 percent as regulatory agencies sought to balance supply with demand. Reduced profits were general throughout the industry, making Kerr-McGee's net of $1.2 million not too bad. It was hoped that 1950 would bring a return to a normal and healthy peacetime economy.

But in February, 1950, the prospects for earnings for the fiscal year were viewed as "meager." The reasons were refinery problems, low allowables, and the lack of immediate revenue from Gulf operations. The board of directors decided to look to the future, however. It authorized the erection of a drilling platform in the Main Pass area of the Gulf of Mexico and took steps to acquire one-half interest in 19,000 acres there from Union Oil of California.

The next month a new loan (I) for $1.5 million was negotiated with the First National Bank of Chicago for operational funds. The refinery was still losing money because of the absence of a steady supply of the low-gravity crude with which it operated. This caused loss of control over prices and often forced the refinery to pay more for its crude than similar plants had to pay. The only solution seemed to be to find new sources.

In May, therefore, the directors approved an expanded drilling program that included a second well in Carter County, Oklahoma; a well in Beaver Creek, Wyoming, to start as soon as possible; a flank test on Block 33, Ship Shoal; an offset well in the Rollover area; and a second test well in Block 27-28, Ship Shoal. Management was also interested in seeing whether Stanolind's three-eighths interest in Block 28 could be obtained by an overriding royalty agreement.

Drilling provided most of the difference between profit and loss. Total assets for the fiscal year ending June 30, 1950, fell to $17,781,938, and working capital to $257,979 (see Table 12.1). The market price for Kerr-McGee common stock fluctuated between $8.00 and $14.875 (Senator and Mrs. Kerr owned approximately 40 percent; directors and officers, 46 percent).[11] Perhaps mindful of the eyes of the 12 percent of public stock-

10 Lease Records file, "Contract #156"; interview with R. E. Anderson, March 31, 1971.

11 Kerr-McGee Oil Industries, Inc., *Annual Report for the Fiscal Year Ended June 30, 1950*; Securities and Exchange Commission, "Form 10-K Annual Report for Fiscal Year Ended June 30, 1950"; *Oil Record, 1951* (Washington, 1951), pp. 106–107.

holders, the company decided to sell the DC-3 and buy a smaller plane. The consensus, however, was that the firm had "been going through a very trying period" but that there was reason for optimism.

Even this assurance was quickly strained. In June, North Korea's violation of its treaty agreements wrenched the American people's attention to distinctly different matters. Within a week ground forces of the United States arrived to bolster the sagging lines of the Republic of Korea. By fall the North Koreans were forced back to the Yalu River before the arrival of Chinese Communist troops reversed the thrust.

Needless to say, the oil industry was vitally affected by the new war. In 1949 the United States demand for oil was down to 6,130,000 barrels a day, an amount the producers could comfortably supply and still have an adequate reserve margin. However, the war and the ensuing defense program brought a new pipe shortage and a 12 percent increase in oil consumption, taxing the industry's facilities to the utmost. Most important, for the first time foreign crude-oil imports became a significant factor, at the rate of 8.4 percent per year.

The second blow to the petroleum business came from another direction, this time from the government of the United States. On June 5, 1950, the Supreme Court handed down its decision in the offshore-ownership cases. It was a story that had begun on December 21, 1948, when the United States presented motions for permission to file complaints against Texas and Louisiana. The federal government alleged that it "was and now is the owner in fee simple of, or possessed of paramount rights in, and full dominion and power over, the land, minerals and other things underlying the Gulf of Mexico." In May, 1949, the Supreme Court granted the federal government's right to file a complaint against each of the states. Congress reacted by passing a bill proclaiming that the disputed properties belonged to the states, but President Truman vetoed it on the grounds that the issue was before the Court.

The case against Louisiana was argued on March 27, 1950, followed the next day by the one against Texas. For three months the judges deliberated. When the decision came, the verdicts in both suits essentially followed the logic of the earlier California ruling, in favor of the federal government. Petitions for rehearings were denied.

Kerr-McGee had an investment of approximately $957,950 in the Louisiana tidelands, exclusive of shore installations and marine equipment. Any federal intervention was a matter of grave concern and was so noted in the annual report's letter to the stockholders:

The Gulf of Mexico, or "Tidelands," situation continues to be a question mark in connection with the Company's activities and potentialities. To date substantial reserves have been proven and we have reason to believe that other large reserves underlie many of the tracts in which the Company has interests. . . . At the date of this writing [November 7] the Supreme Court . . . appears about to enter a final decree . . . which is to cast doubt of undetermined extent upon the Company's title to these leases; but the Management believes that opportunity for some workable arrangement will be afforded whereby the Company will participate in the development of these areas.

191

In line with this reasoning and the company's expectations, another move was made which involved Kerr-McGee even more closely in offshore drilling. A contract with Sunray to drill thirteen wells in shallow water off the Texas coast initiated a search for a cheaper, more efficient way of doing the job. A pioneer in the fixed-platform-tender drilling in the Gulf, Kerr-McGee was now about to score another first. Barnsdall Refining Company had constructed a new-style, movable platform, Breton Rig 20, measuring 11 feet by 14 by 211. It was designed by J. T. Hayward and Paul A. Wolff (who was later to join Kerr-McGee), and supposedly could drill in twenty feet of water. Barnsdall had had disappointing experiences in the Gulf and was eager to retreat to dry land. Thus it offered a package deal consisting of leases held jointly with Sunray in Breton Sound and the Breton Rig 20. At that time Kerr-McGee appraisers considered the leases a liability, since they had only two marginal oil wells and a shut-in gas well. Moreover, Phillips Petroleum flatly refused to take a share in the deal.

But Kerr-McGee wanted that rig. So in November it paid $550,000 for this barge and $100,000 for the leases. Breton Rig 20 was certainly an ugly duckling. It featured pontoons which stayed on the surface of the water while the main hull carrying the drilling rig was lowered to the floor of the Gulf. With the barge resting there, the pontoons were flooded and then also lowered for additional stability. Travis Kerr, perhaps still unhappy over the Parker deal, was obviously not impressed by the new addition, saying that it could drill in twelve to fourteen feet of water "if you hold your breath" and that even that was a gamble because of wave action. This last remark was later shown to be wrong, for while such units originally were used in protected water, Kerr-McGee gambled successfully in the open seas with its newly acquired apparatus.

Both the submersible rig and the leases were spectacular proof of McGee's Midas touch. Renamed Rig 40, the unit was in service until 1970, and by 1971 the leases were producing 8,000 barrels of oil and 50 to 60 million cubic feet of gas daily. Rig 40 not only drilled the Texas contract and most of the Breton Sound area but also set records for speed in doing so.[12]

On December 11, 1950, two decrees by the Supreme Court appeared to end the development of the oil reserves in the Gulf, however. With what was the most stunning blow of the long case, the states were ordered to give an accounting for all funds obtained after June 5, 1950, from oil operations in the submerged lands under state leases. To compound the damage, the states were also enjoined from "carrying on any activities for the purpose of taking or removing therefrom any petroleum, gas, or other valuable mineral products, except under authorization first obtained from the United States."

That same day the secretary of the interior issued a notice that persons

[12] Approval sheet, dated November 7, 1972, in Bette Brenz file, "Offshore Drilling"; Horst Heise, "Offshore Demands Systems Approach," Oilweek, June 26, 1967, pp. 42–44; Richard J. Howe, "The History and Current Status of Offshore Mobile Drilling Units," Ocean Industry, July, 1968, pp. 1–2; interviews with C. F. Miller, September 4, 1971; Paul A. Wolff, August 6, 1971; Travis M. Kerr, December 16, 1969; and George B. Parks, October 23, 1971.

Rig 40, the company's first mobile unit, became famous for its daring use in unprotected waters.

operating under state leases could continue for sixty days, subject to the payment to the United States of rentals, royalties, and other mandatory fees. Wells commenced on or before December 11, 1950, could be completed and put into production, but no new wells could be started after that date. No provision was made for exploration and geophysical operations in the Gulf or for letting new leases.

This set of orders brought on a stalemate in which not only were the questions raised by the decision left unanswered but also the much-needed production was lost. While the Korean War created a new demand for petroleum and its products, Kerr-McGee solved an old problem of its own. The ongoing modernization program at the Wynnewood refinery finally began to show results. Plant capacity was nearing 10,000 barrels a day, and two and a quarter million gallons of an improved grade of gasoline were produced monthly. In the past five years average daily crude-oil throughout had more than doubled, while sales had increased sixfold, to $6,278,000. Finally, research was developing special products that held great promise for the refinery's future.

The most promising development, however, was another agreement with Sunray. That company also had a refinery at Beckett, fifty-two miles from Wynnewood, that, because of a difference in method and end products, complemented the Kerr-McGee operation. An arrangement was made to exchange products between the two plants, and a connecting pipeline was constructed. For Kerr-McGee this meant that its operations could be more stable, needing less storage and bringing better prices. An added bonus was that it brought access to Sunray's products pipeline. It connected with the Great Lakes Pipe Line, thereby opening the Great Lakes and the Mississippi inland waterway markets for Kerr-McGee's fuel oils and gasoline.[13]

Consequently, despite the gloomy portents of the Supreme Court's decree, the company was able to take several constructive steps. An employees' royalty pool was formally established, and half of the royalties in designated tracts in Roger Mills County, Oklahoma, and Morgan County, Colorado, were made available for purchase at cost plus 10 percent. Five members of top management (excluding the senator) were also given stock options, and twenty others were awarded cash bonuses totaling $22,340.

The continuing profits from the drilling activities helped make all this possible. The Mexican and Saudi-Arabian contracts augmented the 25 rigs located in the United States, where 200 wells were being sunk. Contracts accounted for 193 of these, with Texas (chiefly for Tascosa) having 139. Other wells, including one in the Gulf, were drilled for Gulf Oil, Sun, Carter, Continental, California, and Phillips. Next in number to Texas, Kerr-McGee rigs were sinking 31 holes in Oklahoma, 13 in Wyoming, 5 in Utah, 3 in Louisiana, and 2 in Montana. At the same time 17 wells were drilled for

[13] Kerr-McGee, *Annual Report . . . 1950*; *Kermac News*, February, 1950, p. 2; interview with James J. Kelly; *Daily Oklahoman*, October 29, 1950.

the parent company: 8 in the Gulf, 7 in Texas, and 2 in Oklahoma. The year ended with a total of 251 producing leases and 684 gross wells.[14]

Trying days were ahead for all Americans. Seldom have they experienced a more unsettling year than 1951. Senator Joseph R. McCarthy began warning them that their government was riddled with Communists, that even its highest officers were part of an international conspiracy. In Korea the winter fighting had gone badly, and the military turnaround in March was largely overshadowed by the firing of General McArthur. Accusations that peace would be sought at any price came with men still dying in a "police action." Thus it seemed almost anticlimactic when a peace treaty ending World War II was signed with Japan in September, and the president officially declared the state of war with Germany at an end.

The petroleum industry had its own war. For one, demand for oil rose by 1.1 million barrels per day (a consumption rise of 10 percent), and reserve capacity dropped to a dangerous level despite new production records. The tidelands, which could have done much to ease the pressure, benefited only from debate in Congress and among the people, the meager result being a series of extensions of the original sixty-day period. Despite the claim by the chairman of Standard Oil that offshore oil production could be doubled in a year's time if the dispute over controls were settled, Gulf exploration dropped to a virtual standstill. From forty-eight geophysical crews in 1947 the total fell to a mere four in 1951, all off the coast of Texas. From twenty-six drilling rigs operating in 1946, there were only five in 1951.

For Kerr-McGee, now beginning its twentieth year as a fully incorporated firm, the tidelands situation dictated a reversal in policy, another drastic change in planning. Just as it was getting a good start in offshore drilling, that market was closed. And just as it decided that its production future lay in offshore waters, a ban was placed on new wells there. Land once more became preeminent in plans for drilling and production, but this still did not seem any more promising to McGee than it had when he first turned to the Gulf for new oil.

The closing of the offshore possibilities consequently forced the company to hunt for sources of revenue away from the oil scene. There was actually not enough cash flow from the existing enterprises to keep up with advancing costs, so a conscious decision was made to increase and to diversify into new areas. This was a far-reaching move that would bring on a period of acquisitions during the coming decade and change the entire profile of Kerr-McGee.[15]

The shift began in February, when the company purchased most of the assets of J. E. Crosbie, Inc., of Tulsa, Oklahoma. Crosbie owned producing properties in five states, chiefly in Oklahoma, the Texas Panhandle, and the Smackover field of Arkansas. For $1.6 million and oil payments totaling $3.5 million Kerr-McGee was able to enhance its daily production of oil and gas

[14] Transworld Drilling file, "Kerr-McGee Oil Industries, Inc., Drilling Department Rig Operations Fiscal Year July 1, 1949, to June 30, 1950."

[15] Interviews with George B. Kitchel, George B. Parks, and Edwin L. Kennedy.

by acquiring 322 new wells. Coincidentally, Crosbie's interest in four natural-gasoline plants was assumed, although its importance was not recognized at the time. Natural gasoline, or casinghead gas, produced at the wellhead or as a by-product of natural gas, was used as a blending agent in commercial gasoline to make it lighter and easier to burn. Kerr-McGee was the operator of three of these plants, having only a 3 percent interest in the fourth. These three processed 15.5 million cubic feet of gas daily for approximately 48,000 gallons of products. Thus Kerr-McGee became a producer of natural gasoline at a time when it knew little about the business and could not adequately predict its future profitability.[16]

An unplanned change occurred on February 9, 1951, when the popular Tom W. ("Whit") Fentem died suddenly at the age of fifty-one from a heart attack suffered in his office. The annual report of that year claimed him as one of the organizers of Kerr-McGee. He had served as the chief financial agent since 1929 and the Anderson & Kerr Drilling Company days, and "it was under his supervision that many of the company's employee benefits were put into effect, including the pension trust plan, group life insurance, and group hospitalization." A major reassignment of duties put Travis Kerr in the position of secretary. F. C. Love became treasurer, and S. B. Robinson took over as assistant to both of these officers.

In line with the policy of buying or finding more production, a number of other significant steps were taken. On March 22, an arrangement was made with Phillips Petroleum whereby that company farmed out to Kerr-McGee some 16,167 acres in Sherman and Hansford counties, Texas, and in Texas County, Oklahoma. In return Kerr-McGee drilled twenty-seven wells, paying a sliding-scale override royalty, and sold the gas produced to Phillips. On April 30, a similar deal was made for seventeen wells on 9,726 acres in the same area.[17] To help finance this undertaking in the Hugoton field, interests were sold to other parties—a practice followed whenever possible at that time. A farm-out agreement was also reached with Stanolind which allowed Kerr-McGee to drill in Saint Mary, Terrebonne, and Acadia parishes, Louisiana. Hoping to profit from recent discoveries in the Williston Basin, Kerr-McGee also acquired leases on 387,729 acres there, principally in South Dakota, and purchased from the state of Louisiana one-half interest in 21,356 acres in the Breton Sound area, adjacent to the 43,305 acres acquired from Sunray. It was believed that "most, if not all, of this Breton Sound acreage appears to be clear of the tidelands conflict." As of June 30, the company had $1,012,184 invested in offshore leases.

The 1951 annual report was definitely upbeat. An entirely new format sported glossy pages and many illustrations and sketches, as befitting the new status of Kerr-McGee Oil Industries in the oil world. In one of the sections devoted to research, it announced that the department, founded in 1949 with "three technicians to investigate problems and projects suggested by the Company's operations," could now claim a director, three chemical

[16] Kerr-McGee Oil Industries, Inc., *Annual Report for the Fiscal Year Ended June 30, 1951; Oil Record, 1957*, pp. 1110–1117; interview with J. C. Finley, March 3, 1971.
[17] Lease Records file, "Contract #174."

A Kerr-McGee gas processing plant used to separate petroleum liquids from natural gas.

engineers, one organic chemist, and two analytical chemists. Its purpose was to "originate and explore new ideas in petroleum refining and allied chemical fields . . . and to serve in a consulting capacity to other departments." Significantly, research was principally centered in the development of new or more valuable products and processes in the refining operations.[18]

This study had already helped the Wynnewood plant, as indicated by its 44 percent total of Kerr-McGee sales. Not only had throughput been increased to almost 6,000 barrels of crude per day but also sales had increased by $2.1 million. The plant was now converted into an efficient operation of adequate size to produce asphaltic products. Pipelines had been expanded to bring in the necessary crude and to exchange products with Sunray (Wynnewood was also processing and marketing asphalt from the Sunray refinery). Thirty percent of the refinery's product was asphalt, and it also turned out such specialty products as pipeline wrap, plastic cements, paint bases, roofing felts, and waterproofing compounds, among

[18] See also *Kermac News*, February, 1950, p. 12.

Table 12.1. Kerr-McGee Oil Industries, Inc.
Consolidated Statement of Income and Earned Surplus, 1949–51

	Year Ended June 30, 1951	Year Ended June 30, 1950	Year Ended June 30, 1949
Operating revenues			
Drilling contracts completed	$ 6,623,233	5,069,398	$ 5,632,316
Sale of crude oil and gas (1951 includes sale of purchased gas, $652,000; 1950 includes sale of purchased gas, $600,000; 1949 includes $470,000 received from sale of $500,000 oil payment and $207,000 sale of purchased gas)	4,144,210	3,726,241	3,961,581
Sale of refined products	8,649,666	6,278,542	5,094,371
Income from management contracts	65,161	158,135	241,882
Other income	23,597	56,190	
	$ 19,505,867	15,288,506	$ 14,930,150
Operating expenses			
Cost of drilling contracts completed	$ 4,560,380	3,860,587	$ 4,209,087
Cost and expense of refined products sold	7,864,673	6,269,370	4,914,897
Lease operating and other production expense	1,313,249	1,124,231	821,621
General and administrative expense	1,074,555	983,642	902,681
Land department expense	50,590	47,714	48,592
Geological and geophysical department expense	215,541	182,698	282,380
Taxes, other than income taxes	143,212	132,358	89,267
Lease rentals expense	232,605	189,493	223,273
Research expense	57,876	32,328	1,000
Depreciation	1,292,737	1,029,545	1,235,424
Depletion	544,734	718,528	381,196
Cost and expense of oil payment interest sold	....	....	139,432
Dry hole costs	583,199	110,471	267,407
Abandoned leaseholds and royalties	120,615	220,932	191,138
	$ 18,053,966	14,901,897	$ 13,707,395
Less: Income from service equipment—net	1,513	86,753	164,975
	$ 18,052,453	14,815,144	$ 13,542,420
	$ 1,453,414	473,362	$ 1,387,730

Other income			
Gain on disposal of property	$ 66,100	$ 84,361	$ 59,778
Purchase discounts	78,342	67,334	69,529
Dividends	....	400	800
Interest	6,533	4,981	2,959
	$ 150,975	$ 157,076	$ 133,066
	$ 1,604,389	$ 630,438	$ 1,520,796
Income deductions			
Interest and loan expense	$ 326,029	$ 282,722	$ 237,893
Bad debts charged off	390	723	1,443
Cash discounts allowed	55,753	50,214	41,307
Amortization of stock issue expense	13,172	14,577	14,577
Provision for state income taxes	1,250	2,250	6,949
Provision for federal income taxes			
Provision for Mexican income taxes	30,000	47,500	
	$ 426,594	$ 397,986	$ 302,169
Net income	$ 1,177,795	$ 232,452	$ 1,218,627
Adjustment of operations for prior years	21,592		
Additional Mexican income taxes			
Balance transferred to surplus—earned	$ 1,156,203		
Surplus—earned—beginning of period	2,977,715	3,073,042	2,181,529
	$ 4,133,918	$ 3,305,494	$ 3,400,156
Less: Dividends paid on common stock	$ 265,285	$ 263,164	$ 262,348
Dividends paid on preferred stock	59,455	64,615	64,766
	324,740	327,779	327,114
Surplus—earned—end of period	$ 3,809,178	$ 2,977,715	$ 3,073,042

HERE'S WHAT HAPPENED TO
KERR-M^cGEE'S GROSS INCOME DOLLAR

———

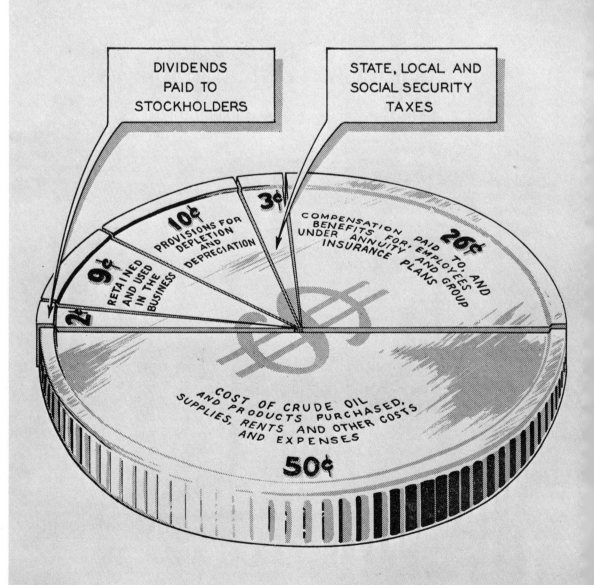

TOTAL INCOME ACCOUNTED FOR ... $1.00

Fig. 12.1. Income expenditure, June 30, 1950. From Kerr-McGee Oil Industries, Inc., *1950 Annual Report*.

others. It was a good example of the benefits derived from funds spent on research and development.

Operating revenues in each branch rose to a total of $19,505,867, a jump of $4.3 million over the previous year. The source and distribution of Kerr-McGee's income dollar was given a new graphic interpretation and showed the great improvement in the refinery's finances (Fig. 12.2). Total assets climbed to $22,935,310, and net income to $1,177,795. The only negative figures were long-term debt at $8.6 million and working capital $171,236 in the red.[19]

Kerr-McGee's rigs had kept busy, setting a new footage record of 905,000 feet. While fewer wells were drilled, the average depth increased. Although the Kuwait contract had terminated, Kermac Contractors continued to operate in Mexico. On the home front, two rigs acquired in the Cosbie purchase were combined with sets of Kerr-McGee tools and mounted on submersible barges, making a total of four of these available for use in protected or semiprotected waters "when offshore activity resumes in the Gulf of Mexico."

In January, 1951, of the twenty-six rigs under the Kerr-McGee name, ten were stacked. This total increased to eleven before business improved in March. Of the twenty-nine rigs the company owned, twenty-three were busy. Four were employed for Kerr-McGee, three each for Cities Service and Phillips, two each for CIMA, Carter, Stanolind, Tascosa Gas, and Sunray, and one each for other companies including Magnolia and Ohio. The monthly rig-location file gives a clear picture of the drilling being done by Kerr-McGee and its subsidiary, Kermac Contractors (see Fig. 12.3).

Over 190 wells were begun during 1951, and 171 were completed. A total of 54 had some company interest, producing 21 gas and 16 oil and/or gas-distillate wells. Three fields were discovered: a small gas reservoir in southern Oklahoma and oil in Stephens County (South Velma Pool), Oklahoma, and western Nebraska (the first commercial oil found in that state). Most of Kerr-McGee's drilling was in the Hugoton field, but also worked were the Crowley, Jeanerette, and Big Lake areas in Louisiana; Andrews County in Texas; and the Gulf of Mexico. More than half of the contract wells were in Texas, and Tascosa was the principal employer.[20]

As is common for all growing companies, financing was a never-ending problem for Kerr-McGee. Even though attempts were made to hold costs to a minimum by selling shares in new ventures, there was always need for money. In May, 1951, the company borrowed $500,000 from the Liberty National Bank of Oklahoma City. Throughout the year the directors discussed ways and means of obtaining a long-term loan to relieve some of the

[19] Kerr-McGee, *Annual Report . . . 1951*; Securities and Exchange Commission, "Form 10-K Annual Report for the Fiscal Year Ended June 30, 1951"; *Oil Record, 1952*, pp. 132–35.

[20] In addition to the *Annual Report* see *Kermac News*, Spring, 1951, pp. 12–13; D. A. McGee personal file, "Kerr-McGee Oil Industries, Inc., Drilling Department, Location of Rotary Rigs (by month)"; and Transworld Drilling file, "Kerr-McGee Oil Industries, Inc., Drilling Department Rig Operations Fiscal Year July 1, 1950, to June 30, 1951."

Kerr-McGee's Income Dollar

ITS SOURCE

	Total	Per $1 Received
Sale of Refined Products	$ 8,649,666	$ .443
Sale of Crude Oil and Gas	4,144,210	.212
Drilling Contracts Completed	6,623,233	.340
Other Income	88,758	.005
	$19,505,867	$1.00

ITS DISTRIBUTION

Cost of crude oil, gas and products purchased, supplies, services, rentals, interest and other expenses....	$11,839,012	
Set aside to replace cost of oil and gas reserves and plant and equipment used up in producing income (depreciation, depletion and amortization)............	2,079,066	
Direct taxes	500,747	14,418,825
The balance left for employees' wages and salaries, dividends and future use in the business		$ 5,087,042

$3,909,247 or 76.8% went for estimated wages, salaries and related insurance and benefits for employees (The portion charged against income)

$324,740 or 6.4% was paid in dividends to approximately 2500 stockholders

$853,055 or 16.8% was retained in the business

3,909,247	76.8%
324,740	6.4%
853,055	16.8%

Fig. 12.2. Income source and distribution, 1951. From Kerr-McGee Oil Industries, Inc., *1951 Annual Report*.

RIG NO.	TYPE	WELL NAME & NO.		COUNTY	STATE	OPERATOR
1	Unit-15	J. W. Brown-3	3S	Scurry	Texas	Standard Oil Co. of Texas
2	Guffey-45	Kroth	1	Sherman	Texas	Tascosa Gas Co.
3	National-75	Atwood	1	Beckham	Okla.	The Carter Oil Co.
4	National-75	McFarland	1	Yellowstone	Montana	Cities Service Oil Co.
6	National-50	Rabon Grande	15	Veracruza	Mexico	C.I.M.A.
7	National-75	V. B. Cox	2	Scurry	Texas	Imperial Production Co.
8	National-75	Red Wash Unit	13	Uintah	Utah	The California Co.
9	National-75	State Lease 700	1	Nueces	Texas	Kerr-McGee Oil Ind. Inc.
10	Oilwell-64A	Wilson Creek Unit	35	Blanco	Colorado	The California Co.
14	Wilson Giant	McKey	2	Garvin	Okla.	Magnolia Petr. Co.
16	National-100	Cont. Ld. & Fur Co.	1	Terrebonne Parish	La.	Kerr-McGee Oil Ind. Inc.
23	National-50	Burke Ranch	1	Natrona	Wyoming	The Carter Oil Co.
24	Oilwell-64A	Minnie	1	Garvin	Okla.	Kerr-McGee Oil Ind. Inc.
27	J.S.G. Spad	Guy	1	Sherman	Texas	Tascosa Gas Co.
28	National-75	Warren-18	1	Laramie	Wyoming	The California Co.
29	National-75	State Tract 352	2	Nueces	Texas	Sunray Oil Corp.
30	Oilwell-64B	Adobe	12	Ector	Texas	Phillips Petr. Co.
31	National-100	Whitlock	1	Uintah	Utah	Gulf Oil Corp.
32	National-75	Rabon Grande	7	Veracruza	Mexico	C.I.M.A.
33	Franks-5000	Stacked 11-16-51		Texas	Okla.	
34	Franks-5000	Buzzard	1	Sherman	Texas	Tascosa Gas Co.
35	Oilwell-96	State Tract 461	4	Nueces	Texas	Sunray Oil Corp.
36	J.S.G. Super Spad	Tippett "A"	16	Upton	Texas	Phillips Petr. Co.
37	Ideco 1350	Caffery	1	St. Mary Parish	La.	Kerr-McGee Oil Ind. Inc.
38	J.S.G. Super Spad	Wise	1	Midland	Texas	Kerr-McGee Oil Ind. Inc.
39	National-125	University 11-C	1	Andrews	Texas	Kerr-McGee Oil Ind. Inc.
40	Emsco J-1600	State Tract 397	1	Nueces	Texas	Sunray Oil Corp.
41	National-75	Hitchcock "A"	1	Stephens	Okla.	Phillips Petr. Co.
42	National Rev.Clutch	Red Wash Unit	14	Uintah	Utah	The California Co.

cc: D. A. McGee ✓
     T. M. Kerr
     G. B. Kitchel
     File

Fig. 12.3. Location of rotary rigs, 1951. From the private files of Dean McGee.

pressure of their indebtedness to the First National Bank of Chicago, since it was felt that the company was "sufficiently established that long term borrowed capital is feasible." In September the board debated a fifteen-year loan of $10 million, but, failing to secure it, approved the J and K loans for the same total from the Chicago bank.

On the brighter side the largest net profit in company history was anticipated for the fiscal year ending June, 1952. Consequently an extra 5-cent dividend was declared in November in addition to the usual 10 cents on the common stock, and eight employees were granted stock options. Plans were discussed concerning the possible purchase of a small refinery in Louisiana and the sinking, at a cost of approximately $900,000, of an additional twenty-four wells before April 1, 1952. Altogether, it was a typical year in the life of the young corporation, and of a middle-sized firm, in the petroleum business.

Chapter 13

The Navajo Uranium Company 1952

During 1951 the oil industry had seen all production records broken, and in the coming months of 1952 the greatest well-drilling program in its history would get under way. In a 180-degree turnabout the issue no longer was one of meeting rising demands, but rather one of overproduction. The specters became cutbacks in output, slowdowns in drilling, and competition from imported oil. Diesel motors replaced the oil burners; for example, the number of train engines using diesel fuels increased from 3,800 to 20,600 between 1945 and 1953, thus creating a severe depressive effect on sales of residual fuel oils. In 1952 the purchase of United States crude rose only 2 percent above the previous year's purchase, as compared with 12.8 percent in 1950, largely as a result of a rise in imports and a decline in the export market. To complicate the picture further, a pipe shortage resulted from another steel strike, and, as a consequence of all these factors, the total number of completed wells dropped. Although the average footage per well increased, the rate of success for wildcats was only 11 percent.

For Kerr-McGee, 1952 not only saw a continuation of the new ventures but also brought more and diverse changes. For one, Dean ("Judge") Terrill, vice-president and general counsel for fifteen years, announced in a letter dated January 28 that he was resigning his active position with the company to return to Chicago. He still planned to serve as a director, participate in the drafting of important contracts, handle special negotiations, and advise on legal questions of major concern. But his departure certainly removed one of the more colorful characters from the Oklahoma City scene.[1]

Although the position of general counsel was more restricted in the future, two new additions strengthened the company. James E. Webb, well known in Washington as director of the budget and undersecretary of state, was recruited by Senator Kerr to assist Dean McGee. Paul A. Wolff, who helped design Rig 40, was brought in to furnish technical knowledge as Kerr-McGee moved to expand its submersible holdings. The board of directors was increased to ten members, and Webb and J. H. Lollar, secretary and treasurer, were elected to fill the new positions.

Dean McGee's attitude was clear. His philosophy of management, as he told a group of Oklahoma A&M College students, was that in competition an organization can either pitch or catch. A pitching organization created its own opportunities, while a catching one waited for opportunities to be discovered by others and then bought into it. He left no doubt that he was a "pitcher."[2] He also threw curve balls, as would be seen in the coming months.

A good financial position strengthened his position. Senior management, except the senator, received pay raises during the year. Stockholders benefited also. A 10 percent stock dividend was proposed in May, followed by a 10-cent extra dividend in November, making it a record year for all concerned. The same prosperity enabled Kerr-McGee to buy another natural-gasoline plant. The Portland Gasoline Company's plant near Pampa, Texas, was purchased for $1,125,000 from none other than Baird H. Markham, the former Continental Oil official who had been so instrumental in giving Anderson & Kerr its start over twenty years earlier.[3]

All of this was explained by the company's having had the highest profits in its history. For the fiscal year ended June 30, 1952, total assets were $27,619,220, and the operating revenues and net income increased by over $5 million and $1 million, respectively. The long-term debt climbed to approximately $13.5 milliion, and included the sale of fifteen-year 5 percent notes to Mutual Life Insurance of New York ($6 million) and Northwestern Mutual Life Insurance ($4 million) that had been approved in May. Likewise, 10,000 shares of treasury stock were sold, at $29.75, to F. W. Straus, J. D. Blosser, and Lehman Brothers. The $440,000 received for equipment and supplies at the termination of the Mexican CIMA contract eased the tax bite and reduced the number of Kerr-McGee land rigs.

Another foreign venture was too recent to affect this annual statement. On February 18, a letter of agreement was signed with Antonio Iglesias, who represented the Jarahueca group that had governmental concessions in Cuba. Apparently, President Fulgencio Batista was involved through a brother-in-law in the deal. Kerr-McGee's participation was sought to help drill wells and build a refinery. A company geologist would investigate the prospects, and, if a favorable report resulted, then up to 50 percent of the Cuban rights could be earned. Most of 1952 was spent in delineating Kerr-McGee's role and in settling the terms of the financial arrangements.[4]

---

[1] *Kermac News*, Spring, 1952, p. 11.

[2] Typescript of Nora Owens, "The Strata of Dean Anderson McGee," in Public Relations files.

[3] *Daily Oklahoman*, December 30, 1952.

[4] Drilling Department file, "Cuba"; Lease Records file, "Contract 205."

Kerr-McGee Oil Industries, Inc.

Table 13.1.   Income and Income Retained for Use in the Business, June 30, 1952

Operating Revenues	
Drilling contracts completed	$ 8,688,771
Sale of crude oil and gas (includes sale of purchased gas, 1952, $676,00)	4,907,084
Sale of refined products	12,913,419
Sale of ore	84,103
Income from management contracts	694
Other income	68,143
	$26,662,214
Operating Expenses	
Cost of drilling contracts completed	$ 5,442,302
Cost and expense of refined products sold	11,507,456
Lease operating and other production expense	1,704,219
Cost and expense of ore sold	45,479
General and administrative expense	1,320,480
Land department expense	58,763
Geological and geophysical department expense	332,972
Taxes, other than income taxes	174,044
Lease rentals expense	338,606
Research expense	105,355
Depreciation	1,426,532
Depletion	607,611
Dry-hole costs	684,028
Abandoned leaseholds and royalties	165,782
Service equipment expense—net	111,197
	$24,024,826
	$ 2,637,388
Other Income	
Gain on disposal of property	$ 154,774
Purchase discounts	96,980
Dividends	1,000
Interest	12,197
	$ 264,951
	$ 2,902,339
Income Deductions	
Interest and loan expense	$ 482,340
Bad debts charged off	4,798
Cash discounts allowed	72,578
Amortization of stock issue expense	8,091
Provision for State income taxes	7,911
Provision for Federal income taxes	78,082
Provision for Mexican income taxes	13,851
	$ 667,651
Net Income	$ 2,234,688

206

Table 13.1. *Continued.*

Adjustment of operations for prior years	
Additional Mexican income taxes	
Balance Transferred to Income Retained	
for Use in the Business	$ 2,234,688
Income Retained For Use in the Business	
Beginning of period	3,809,178
	$ 6,043,866
Less: Cash dividends paid on Common Stock	$ 448,976
Cash dividends paid on Preferred Stock	44,628
Common Stock issued as Common Stock dividend	110,150
	$ 603,754
Income retained for use in the business	
End of period	$ 5,440,112

Meanwhile, sales of refined products produced 48 percent of the record income. A graphic illustration of this impact on the company's balance sheet can be seen in Figure 13.1 showing the growth from 1946 to 1952 in sales and refining of crude oil.

Next in percentage of Kerr-McGee's income dollar was the contract-drilling division, with 33 percent. During January twenty-six of the twenty-nine rigs were busy. Eleven of these were in Texas, and the rest were in Oklahoma, Utah, Mexico, Louisiana, Wyoming, Montana, and Colorado. Five were drilling for the parent company. The number of stacked units steadily decreased during the summer and, by November, offshore drilling picked up and six of Kerr-McGee's seven offshore rigs were active. The year closed with only two rigs stacked and all the offshore units in use.

During the fiscal year ending June 30, 1952, the drilling department drilled a record 1,082,821 feet of hole, with 207 wells spudded and 185 completed. Kerr-McGee had interest in 41 of these and was full owner of 17. Of these wells 37 were in Texas, while 11 were in Oklahoma, 9 were in Louisiana, and 1 was in Wyoming. This last figure in part reflected the poor prospects in the Williston Basin, an area in the center of play by the whole industry in 1951, but with generally disappointing results. Kerr-McGee had spent $214,000 in South Dakota alone on leases and seismographic work without any promising finds. So it was decided that some holdings there should be disposed of as soon as possible.

There were 149 contract wells that year, chiefly in Texas and Oklahoma. Illustrative of the changing offshore picture were the 44 operations in the Gulf off Corpus Christi, Texas, for Sinclair, Sunray, and Sun Oil com-

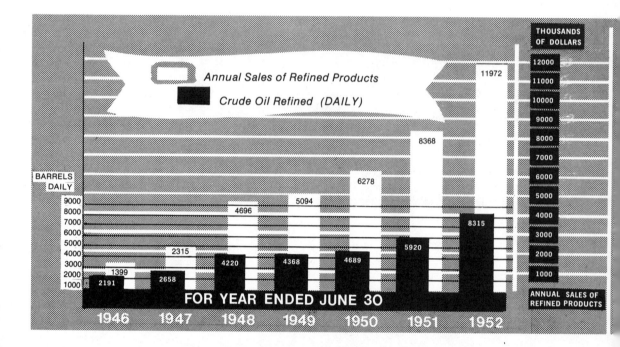

Fig. 13.1. Annual sales of refined products and crude oil refined, 1946–52.
From Kerr-McGee Oil Industries, Inc., *1952 Annual Report*.

panies.[5] The activity in the Gulf accelerated because of relaxed government restrictions.[6] In three cases of its own Kerr-McGee had been able to show the need of additional drilling for conservation needs or for evaluation of reserves in the Hog Bayou, Rollover, and Ship Shoal fields. Drilling went on also in the Breton Sound, which, although water-covered, was not involved in the tidelands dispute. Furthermore, the company continued extensive new geological work in the offshore area since it intended to develop its properties there as rapidly as controls would allow.

Included in the drilling department's successes was what was probably the first well completed with a submersible drilling barge in open water. Rig 40 proved that mobiles could be used as an exploratory as well as a developmental tool. Rig 37, on the other hand, may have brought about another first when it was used by Universal-International Studios as the locale for the motion picture *Thunder Bay*, starring Jimmy Stewart, Joanne Dru, Gilbert

[5] Transworld Drilling file, "Kerr-McGee Oil Industries, Inc., Drilling Department Rig Operations Fiscal Year July 1, 1951, to June 30, 1952"; D. A. McGee personal file, "Kerr-McGee Oil Industries, Inc., Drilling Department, Location of Rotary Rigs (by month)."

[6] Although the Senate, April 2, 1952, passed a tidelands bill favorable to the states, Kerr refused to take part in the debate and was absent on the day of the vote "to avoid the charge that he was an interested party." Anne H. Morgan, *Robert S. Kerr: The Senate Years* (Norman, University of Oklahoma Press, 1977), 274, n. 109.

Roland, and Dan Duryea, among others.[7] A bit of extra excitement and publicity resulted, to say the least.

Altogether during the fiscal year ending June 30, 1952, there were 854,497 net acres under lease, four times the 1949 figure. Since 1950 the number of producing leases, 403, had almost doubled; there were 360 more wells (1,044); and 200,000 more barrels of oil. Five successful wildcats had been drilled in the past twelve months, opening new fields or sands in Cameron, Saint Mary, and Acadia parishes in Louisiana and in Hartley and Andrews counties in Texas. The first two, both farm-outs, found significant gas fields and acquired interests for Kerr-McGee. The third, the South Crowley pool in Acadia Parish, was gas-distillate, while both wells in Texas produced oil. Forty-eight additional gas wells had been completed in established fields, and demand for this resource developed rapidly, with the sale price rising by 18 to 27 percent.[8]

Dean McGee's curve ball was thrown in May, when Kerr-McGee bought the Navajo Uranium Company. On the eighth of that month it became the first oil company to enter the search for the scarce element needed for atomic power. This move does not seem out of place or strange once the background and motivation are known; instead, it would almost be called predetermined.

Most Americans heard of uranium for the first time on August 6, 1945, when an atom bomb was dropped on Hiroshima, Japan. They were unaware that this effort had already cost over $1,681,000,000 in atomic research before the devastation was ordered by the president of the United States. With the creation of the Atomic Energy Commission (AEC) in 1946 it became a more familiar topic, especially when the federal decision was made to retain title to all nuclear materials in the country. As part of the postwar arms race, the government began stockpiling atomic bombs. In 1948, when American reserves of uranium were estimated at only 2,500 tons, the AEC announced that it would provide a market and special incentives to domestic concerns for finding and producing uranium.

The most obvious reason for Kerr-McGee's attraction to this situation was that its path was blocked both on land and on sea in the search for oil. Also, in the 1950's, acquiring companies was easier than finding raw material in the ground: it was the fastest way to accelerate growth. All these facts were reinforced by McGee's philosophy, that owning a small part of a field of interest was necessary to watch and check it properly, and to keep alert to the potentials. In other words, learning to swim was difficult without getting wet. Thus the Navajo Uranium Company, like the Wynnewood refinery, presented an opportunity to gain experience and to educate the company in a different business at a very low cost. If Kerr-McGee were ingenious and

[7] *Kermac News*, Winter, 1952, pp. 14–15, 24.

[8] Kerr-McGee Oil Industries, Inc., *Annual Report for the Fiscal Year Ended June 30, 1952*; Securities and Exchange Commission, "Form 8, Amendment No. 1, Amended Financial Statement of Annual Report (Form 10-K) for the Fiscal Year Ended June 30, 1952"; *Kermac News*, Winter, 1952, p. 21.

innovative, the venture might possibly expand into an attractive operation.[9]

The men in the decision-making process at Kerr-McGee also had their opinions about why the move into uranium was made. F. C. Love, McGee's assistant, provided further background on this. According to him, McGee had been reading about uranium and made a talk on energy before an Oklahoma City men's dinner club. He pointed out that the four sources of energy were coal, oil, gas, and uranium. After predicting an energy shortage in gas and oil, he then stated his belief that uranium was necessary to make up the deficit. Later, after the talk, McGee stopped by Love's office and said that one day the uranium business was going to be good, and the company should be following it closely. But he believed that management would not do so unless it had some kind of investment in the field—not to make money, but to hold its attention.

Dean Terrill recalled that there was little opposition within the company, just some question about whether Kerr-McGee were large enough to diversify this far afield. Board member Edwin Kennedy added that the need to increase the cash flow entered into the decision, but that from the start McGee was intrigued with the possibility of using a more scientific approach with hydrocarbon exploration techniques to find uranium reserves. Hugo Anderson, of the First National Bank of Chicago, summed it up when he stated, "As Dean McGee told me on so many occasions, . . . 'You know, Hugo, drilling for uranium is no different than drilling for oil, for gas, or for any other minerals!' "[10]

McGee, however, admitted his doubts. "Believe me we had plenty of misgivings. Uranium was a pretty wild thing." There were, nevertheless, overriding considerations. "It was clear [in 1952] that the oil business was headed for trouble, and that medium-sized companies such as ours could get pretty badly hurt." Or, as Love put it, "a company the size of Kerr-McGee has to compete. If it doesn't get the opportunities it is looking for in one area, it must direct its efforts in other directions." Although the odds were long on uranium, McGee relied on his company's demonstrable talent for finding what lay below the earth's crust. Still later, in retrospect, he discounted the extent of the gamble, although he listed the decision as one of the three most important he made. The final word came from the employees' *Kermac News*. It was simple: "We're in the energy business, and uranium is the latest type of energy."[11]

[9] D. A. McGee, "Atomic Energy and Exotic Fuels," speech before the Independent Petroleum Association of America, Phoenix, May 3, 1959; Dean A. McGee, "Supply and Demand for Uranium in Years Ahead," *Commercial and Financial Chronical*, February 13, 1969, p. 4 (684); interviews with George Cobb, December 7, 1972, and Elizabeth Zoernig, August 26, 1971.

[10] Interviews with Frank C. Love, September 2, 1971; Edwin L. Kennedy, August 13, 1971; Dean Terrill, November 24, 1969; and Hugo Anderson, September 1, 1972.

[11] *Forbes*, October 15, 1960, p. 21; Bob Leder, KTUL-TV Tulsa, interview with Dean A. McGee, September 19, 1973, in Public Relations files; interview with F. C. Love; *Kermac News*, Summer, 1952, p. 13.

The opportunity to "get their feet wet" occurred when Senator Kerr in Washington was approached with a proposition to buy the Navajo Uranium Company. As could be expected, Kerr was immediately enthusiastic and sent the agent to talk to McGee and Love. In February a consulting engineer, S. Power Warren, checked out the property in Arizona. He found three adits being operated, but the "situation at the mine at present, is simply an over-grown prospector's camp." The report was favorable enough, however, for McGee to take a personal tour of the site, accompanied by John Masters, who was then working for the AEC.

The area involved had been mined for vanadium during World War II, but that market was largely dying out. Willie Cisco, a Navajo who worked the vanadium, did some prospecting on his own and discovered uranium in a cliff face at 8,500 feet in the Lukachukai Mountains. Located on the Navajo Reservation, the strike was in Apache County, Arizona, about forty miles south of the Four Corners Area of Arizona, New Mexico, Utah, and Colorado.

In 1949, F. A. Sitton of Dove Creek, Colorado, a banker, farmer, and part-time vanadium-uranium miner, obtained the necessary documents from the Indian authorities and prospected the area. In April, 1950, he incorporated as F. A. Sitton, Inc., and during the next three months produced about 1,000 tons of high-grade ore. He next applied for and received from the AEC the exclusive rights to build a processing plant. But in January, 1951, he sold his interests for $300,000, payable out of production, to R. O. Dulaney, Jr., and the name was changed to the Navajo Uranium Company on July 18, 1951.

The Dulaneys, father and son, were the Dulaney Mining Company, which operated other uranium mines. The officers and stockholders were the younger Dulaney (president), Jack Blalock, Edmund Key III, and G. R. Kennedy (vice-president and general manager). Kennedy, a controversial figure who apparently got his position and shares as a result of the Sitton sale, was the principal contact with Kerr-McGee. "The gentleman who was handling the negotiations—I said gentleman—I'm not sure—was Buffalo Kennedy," declared Marion Bolton, later the Kerr-McGee office manager there. What Kennedy had to sell were a few shallow tunnels, a sampling plant contracted to the AEC for a dollar a year, and mining leases totaling around 1,200 acres. Since a white man was limited to holding leases on just 960 acres, some were held in the names of friendly Indians. The haphazard bookkeeping indicated that the total assets as of February 29 were $300,993.78, with net income from April 1, 1951, to February 29, 1952, of $62,734.67, based on 9,536 tons of ore.[12]

---

[12] Philip Nevill, "The Whispering Mountain," *Arizona Highways*, July, 1956, pp. 4–9; M. F. Bolton and S. B. Robinson, "A Brief History of the Shiprock Mining and Milling Operations on the Navajo Indian Reservation," in Public Relations file, "Uranium"; interviews with Frank C. Love and Marion Bolton, August 27, 1973; Dean A. McGee personal files, "Navajo Uranium Division January Through August, 1952," and "Navajo Uranium Division September Through December, 1952."

After some very complicated maneuvering, the deal making Kerr-McGee the first oil company to enter the uranium field was concluded on May 8, 1952. This latest acquisition cost Kerr-McGee approximately $50,000 in cash and the giving and assuming of ore payments of slightly less than $1 million. Thus it entered a business which was strange, not only to itself, but also to the entire petroleum industry.

In the first place, the ore of uranium did not lie in veins but in flat sedimentary rocks or in rolls, or pods, in the sandstone layers of the mountains. Deposits ranged in size from a few hundred to several thousand tons. Another unknown element was Kennedy, who had been hired for his knowledge of the industry. He became a strident voice within Kerr-McGee, and, according to McGee's long-time secretary, who was later to become the corporation's first woman officer, Elizabeth Zoernig, "Many of our men felt that it was highly out of line for Mr. McGee to keep a man around like Buffalo Kennedy. But Mr. McGee felt he had a great deal of knowledge, a great deal of know-how. He had many faults, but we learned a lot from Buffalo Kennedy in the uranium field." Dean Terrill was forced to conclude that while Kennedy "was a real promoter, he did a good job—a lot of good things."[13]

Navajo Indian Reservation, Kerr-McGee acquired a new labor force, about fifty Indians who were already working in the mines. The original leases stated that the Navajos had to be used on any job for which they could qualify, so all of the miners were Indians. As will be seen, a whole new concept of management resulted.

Marion Bolton recalled that on the day of the purchase he and Leo LeBron were called into McGee's office. "He asked how we'd like to get into the uranium business, and I think both of us asked the same question—what is uranium?" The next day the two men were on their way to find out, Leo as manager of mining operations and Bolton to run the office. There were a dozen or more small operations, but only three or four were large enough to use more than one shift. It had not been an especially profitable operation, so far. The equipment was primitive and antiquated with all of the mining done by drilling and blasting, and then shoveling the results into wheelbarrows. Mechanization and improved working conditions became an immediate priority.

Also mandatory were new sources of ore. Kerr-McGee immediately organized a Navajo Uranium Division and staffed a uranium exploration department. By October it had a dozen men and two airplanes employed in a search that extended as far north as Utah and Wyoming, where some 1,275,180 acres were leased by early 1953. Since the Arizona deposits lay high in the mountains, roads were built from the valley to the outcropping, which was then mined horizontally by going directly into the mountainside. Once underground, however, the engineers found that it was too expensive

---

[13] Interviews with Elizabeth Zoernig and Dean Terrill, November 24, 1969; *Kermac News*, Summer, 1952, p. 13. Kennedy always spelled his nickname "Bufalo."

In 1952, Kerr-McGee became the first oil company to enter the uranium field. Here Kerr and McGee visit one of the company's mines.

to "start trying to feel your way around by drilling and blasting and mining to do your exploration work."

It was also soon discovered that the ore could be mined faster than it could be found. The conventional way to outline deposits was by core drilling, and the AEC was using this method at about fifteen dollars a foot. Bolton and a friend in the seismographic business had the idea that this could be done with a "shothole" or seismograph rig. The friend agreed to drill 50,000 feet at fifty cents a foot and was hired. It soon was obvious that the absence of cores in this technique was a handicap, so Virgil Janeway, the communication superintendent from the Gulf Coast, was called in. He built what was probably the first portable logging instrument in the business—a geiger counter with a probe on a cable reel.

The secret for successful uranium mapping became the presence of many holes, because the beds were small and easily missed. Kerr-McGee's innovative approach permitted this kind of mapping, while Janeway's gadget told what was in the hole. The first 50,000 feet of tests uncovered three ore bodies, which "turned the operation from a real bleak picture" to a sunny one. They also revealed that the main reserves were not in the original mines but in the new ore bodies. The techniques developed here on the spot eventually made possible more profitable finds in New Mexico and Wyoming where the lodes were much deeper.

The ore-sampling plant which Kerr-McGee acquired in the deal used a simple process. Mainly it was a place where an operator brought his ore to be tested for moisture, uranium, and vanadium content. The AEC would buy the ore, then stockpile it to await construction of a processing plant. Since this agency was impatient to recover its money and get the processed ore, immediate pressure was put on Kerr-McGee to apply for a permit to construct such a mill. S. Power Warren again was hired, this time to advise the company on the best system of processing uranium and vanadium, and in August a contract was signed with the Colorado School of Mines Research Foundation to set up models for study of the various processes that might be used in a plant to be located at Shiprock, New Mexico, thirty-five miles east of the mines.[14]

While plans for financing the mill went on back at the home office in Oklahoma City, another sort of negotiation began in Arizona. As it turned out, it was easier to get the money from insurance companies and approval from the AEC to build the mill than to get the land for its location and the mineral claims to support it from the Navajos. No problem developed with the AEC; it had a common desire to see the plant built. In this favorable atmosphere Kerr-McGee assumed that it could easily acquire the necessary ore reserves.

But Kerr-McGee was leaving out of account its almost total lack of education in Navajo Indian ways, customs, and religion. This would play a large part in the tribal and company associations in the months and years to come. Field men, indeed executives from the home office, came to their tasks on the Navajo Reservation with all the normal assumptions and disciplines of oil-field personnel and businessmen. They had never been called upon to adjust to a radically different set of priorities in another cultural setting. Nor, for that matter, had the Navajos come to grips with their own aspirations for an industrialized tribal society. Both sides needed large measures of mutual education, and they would get it—sometimes to the point of crisis—sometimes with amusing results. To a great extent it was probably Kerr-McGee's first unique lesson in labor-management relationship, and the tribal benefits would culminate three decades later in the sophisticated councilmen under the chairmanship of the gifted Peter McDonald.

Before plans could be put into action, unfortunately, some way had to be

---

[14] Interview with Marion Bolton.

Kerr-McGee uranium mines on the Navajo Reservation.

found around the tribal restriction of a maximum of 960 acres to each lease. True, Kerr-McGee had options held by friendly Navajos, who received a monthly sum for this service from the company. But these options were not legal in the eyes of the tribe. So Kerr-McGee started working simultaneously with the Navajo Council and with the Department of the Interior to get both a mill site and recognition of the assignment by individual Navajos of their mining claims. Complicating matters further was opposition from rival companies which did not want the mill built. There were rumors that Vanadium Corporation of America led the objectors because it wanted to force the ore to its mill at Durango, Colorado. It allegedly worked through the Navajos' legal counsel and mining engineer to delay or block both proposals.

The problem with the restrictive claims proved to be the most difficult to handle, however. Marion Bolton told the story of the crucial day of bargaining between Kerr-McGee officials and the Navajos at the tribal headquarters. According to him, the company negotiators spent a frustrating day trying, through interpreters, to present its case for removing the acreage limitations from the agreement. They were obviously making little, if any, progress. Upon their return to their motel for dinner, McGee announced exasperatedly that he had decided not to build the mill. "If these [people—the white agents representing the Navajos] are the kind of people that we have to deal with, and what we are going through is what we have to go through everytime we come out here to make a deal, I just don't believe I want any part of it."

This could have been the end of the effort. But Bolton got permission to tell the chairman of the Tribal Council, Sam Ahkeah, of McGee's reaction. In the past Ahkeah had been positive about wanting the mill as a start toward industrializing the reservation, and he took personal credit for having started the negotiations. When he heard of McGee's feelings and learned that McGee blamed the white advisers rather than the Indians for the impasse, he asked for a night session with the company officials.

The request was granted, and the entire Kerr-McGee party, the tribal council, and the Navajos' attorney and engineer were present. During the lawyer's long-winded explanation of the problems from the tribal point of view, Ahkeah apparently slept soundly. But, as if on cue, he awoke at the conclusion of the speech, declaring that he had something to say. He then proceeded to deliver another address, this time in the Navajo language. There were no interpreters, so McGee and his advisers had no way of knowing what he was saying. That is, not until Ahkeah suddenly announced in English, "We are ready to vote!"

But a council member interrupted. He had something to say. Kerr-McGee officials probably held their breaths, dreading another long discourse as much as a vote. The Navajo turned to Dean McGee and said in English: "Mr. McGee, I have a question to ask before we vote on this measure."

McGee nodded his head doubtfully. The council member continued with a smile: "If we approve your building this mill, will you agree to have a barbecue?"

McGee's laugh and answer came swiftly: "Yes. If we can get this through, we'll have the biggest barbecue you've ever had!"

The tribal vote was immediate and unanimous to approve the leases and build the mill. On August 17, 1953, a contract was signed with the AEC for construction of a $3 million uranium processing plant at Shiprock to produce both uranium and vanadium. It was to use new techniques that were still under security classifications. Enlarged during construction, the finished mill had a capacity of 500 tons of ore per day and employed about 100 men, 40 percent of whom were Navajos. The financial strain on Kerr-McGee was eased by the 80 percent tax write-off for defense reasons.[15]

---

[15] *Ibid.*; Bolton and Robinson, "A Brief History of the Shiprock Mining . . . ."

In 1954, Kerr-McGee's first uranium mill was built near Shiprock, New Mexico.

The Navajos, meanwhile, educated Kerr-McGee to Indian customs in many other ways. The land management department quickly became acquainted with Navajo Dan Phillips, who received considerable income from company royalties on leases held in his name. With his first royalty monies he bought a pickup truck. Later he was killed in a traffic accident. It then became the task of Kerr-McGee's lawyers to untangle the line of inheritance for the royalty payments. Dan had been married twice and divorced according to tribal custom, but there were no records of births, marriages, or divorces. Deciding that the relationships were impossible to unravel, the lawyers handed the problem to the tribal judges. It took them a year to reach a decision.

Another custom that almost defeated the accountants working with the Social Security withholding payments was the Navajos' use of names. If a Navajo liked and admired a white man, he might adopt that name and refuse to answer to his former one. That name, however, might also be discarded later. To complicate matters further, about 10 percent of the Navajos used Begay as their last name, but not as a distinguishing one, since it simply meant "son of." Moreover, sometimes a Navajo refused to give a name at all, forcing the mine personnel to assign him one for use during employment.

Just as troublesome was the frequency of "holidays." Often only two or three men showed up for work because a sing or dance was on. At first Kerr-McGee would fire the absentees and hire replacements. Then the dance would end, and a double crew would show up for work. It was suggested that, since the mines shut down for three days every other weekend, perhaps the ceremonies and sings could be scheduled then. But this attempt failed, and a monetary incentive to work a regular schedule was tried. Miners made between $60 and $90 a week, so a paid two-week vacation was offered to those who did not miss more than three days a year because of unexcused absences. But the old customs were slow to change.

Other difficulties arose from various religious beliefs and practices. When word was spread that the "coyote man" was on the prowl, it was impossible to get a night shift at the mine, unless the workers were picked up and driven home. Nor would they enter an area where a death had occurred. Fortunately there was never a fatal accident in any of the mines. The Navajos' belief that their ancestors came back to earth in the form of animals almost caused a miners' strike when a supervisor killed a snake in the presence of a Navajo. The supervisor had to be fired.

Cultural adjustments on both sides continued long after Kerr-McGee first hired the Navajos. Fred Hohne, the superintendent of the mine, was quoted in 1956: "They're easy to train, they love machinery, and they take to jackhammers. But they have no idea of how to care for their machines. We have to be constantly on the watch, particularly with new hands, to see they do the little things like oiling and replacing worn parts." Absenteeism remained a problem: "All miners light out now and then, . . . but these Navajo seem to do it more often and for special reasons. In the spring its for planting on their farms; in the summer it's squaw dances—and is that a headache! In fall it's for roundup and sheep shearing. Only five out of every hundred Indians keep on the job long enough to qualify for their two weeks' vacation."[16]

[16] M. F. Bolton, "Random Thoughts on My Experiences on the Navajo Reservation and in Particular My Experiences with Dan Phillips," February 27, 1960, in Public Relations file, "Navajo Indians"; Nevill, "Whispering Mountains," pp. 4–9.

When the Shiprock uranium mill was opened, the Navajos were invited to share the dedication ceremonies. Here the corngrinding ceremony is performed.

But mutual accommodations came quickly. W. L. Dare, a mining engineer for the Bureau of Mines, reported in 1960 that the "tons of ore produced per man-shift" by Kerr-McGee's Navajos were higher than the average at other mines on the plateau. While at first turnover was "very high," attendance improved steadily and "by mid-1958 Kerr-McGee had a good core of reliable men averaging 3 years of service with the company." Absenteeism without prior notification also lessened as the "conscientious and hard-working miners" came to appreciate the need for reporting daily to the job. Furthermore, the "younger men . . . take a keen interest in learning, and after some experience acquire good mechanical ability."[17]

During 1956 the Shiprock operation was the subject of an illustrated story describing the physical terrain where the mines and the mill were located. At the time Kerr-McGee was working three mines at an elevation of 8,000 feet in a "spectacularly wild and beautiful country that was almost a forbidden land until it billowed up like a mushroom with the advent of the atomic age." These mines, which also contained petrified trees and dinosaur bones, were reached by a "network of roads [that] wind around the hills like string around a top. Men have dragged drills to places that look perilous for a mountain goat." Typical was Mesa No. 3, a drift-in operation with a weird pattern of rooms where the miners "really follow the ore—up and down, on slant, and in bends." After the ore was mined, it was dumped into fourteen-ton tandem trucks, which then began a trip of fifty crooked miles around and over hills and canyons on "one of the world's most tremendous jobs of bull-dozing," down to the mill.[18]

True to McGee's promise, shortly after the mill was built and in operation, Kerr-McGee planned an old-fashioned outdoor barbecue at Shiprock. A pit eight feet wide, six feet deep, and fifty feet long was dug. Wood was hauled in from Colorado, and five steers were placed over the coals on the Wednesday preceding the big event on Saturday. The whole tribe was invited, and three truckloads of soda pop, beans, and potato salad were on hand. Between four and five thousand Navajos showed up to eat and listen to speeches by their own leaders, assorted Washington dignitaries, and Senator Kerr. All agreed that it was the "biggest" barbecue they had ever seen.[19]

[17] W. L. Dare, "Uranium Mining in the Lukachukai Mountains, Apache County, Ariz., Kerr-McGee Oil Industries, Inc.," Bureau of Mines Information Circular 8011 (1961), pp. 1, 9, 18.

[18] Lewis Nordyke, "Uranium," *Explosives Engineer*, Vol. 34 (September-October, 1956), pp. 138–49.

[19] *Daily Oklahoman*, November 3 and 18, 1954; Bolton and Robinson, "A Brief History of the Shiprock Mining . . ."; interview with Marion Bolton.

Chapter 14

Expansion Years
1953–1955

Atomic energy and its unknown benefits and dangers had a definite and far-reaching effect on all of the American scene, as well as in the corporate world of Kerr-McGee. It was a shadowy challenge which redirected political thought and industrial planning, for the cold war was increasingly evident. Concerned with the threat of communism and scandal in Washington and with the ideological loss of China and Korea, the American voter turned solidly against the old-line political leaders and elected as president a popular hero, Dwight D. Eisenhower, by the greatest plurality since 1936. Who better than a general would know how to direct the awesome power so recently released from the atom? "Ike," the majority felt, would also bring peace and stand firm in the face of the communist threat. At home the budget would be balanced and the political bosses restrained from "fixing" things, while all starry-eyed radicals and crypto-communists would be thrown out of public office. In short, no president since George Washington entered office with a greater reservoir of good will upon which to draw—or with greater expectations to fulfill.

During Eisenhower's first term as president the war in Korea and the war against poliomyelitis both ended. But the appearance of the first supersonic bomber was followed by the development of the atomic submarine and hydrogen bomb, making the cold war the probable winner. Perhaps not as obvious a threat, but a dangerous one nonetheless, was the expanded and careless consumption of natural gas and petroleum products and the accompanying increase in imports of oil.

Business in general and the oil industry in particular had good reasons for optimism concerning the first Republican administration in over twenty years. One was Eisenhower's pledge to resolve the offshore controversy. Quickly Congress, with the Submerged Lands Act, assigned state ownership within the traditional three-mile limit and federal control beyond that. When the Supreme Court upheld Congress, oilmen were again free to bid competitively for offshore drilling rights, both to the states and to federal agencies.

Furthermore, in February, 1953, all price controls, except on heating oils, were removed from petroleum products. By June the price of midcontinent crude had gone from $2.57 to $2.82. This, of course, brought a corresponding rise in oil-company profits, but beneath this statistic were less favorable signs. Price wars in gasoline probably accounted for the closing of twenty refineries. Crude-oil production declined for the first time in five years; wildcats dropped for the first time in twelve. Moreover, exploration was less rewarding, resulting in only thirteen barrels of oil per foot drilled—about half the 1951 ratio.

Consequently a cloud appeared in the picture. Although the average oil company's earnings were 6.7 percent higher in 1954, production simply did not keep up with the 4.8 percent increase in consumer demand. The 13.1 percent rise in imports was followed twelve months later with a figure showing oil shipped in at the rate of 1.5 million barrels a day, out of a total demand of 3,204,891,000 barrels. Clearly indicated was the need for American companies to find and produce more oil.

The years 1953 to 1955 were pivotal not only for the United States but also for Kerr-McGee. The firm was fortieth among "Companies Ranked by Net Domestic Refinery Runs, 1953," although it was not in the top fifty-three listed under "Domestic Net Proven Crude Oil Reserves." By the end of 1954, it was sixty-ninth of ninety-six in crude reserves and fifty-ninth in value of reserves per dollar of common stock. Its net of 420 oil and 134 gas wells gave it a production that placed it sixty-first out of ninety. On the basis of capital structure it was forty-first when compared with ninety-eight other petroleum companies.[1]

To meet the challenge of growth, a number of critical decisions were made by management, often in the direction of diversification and expansion. The partners' dream of a fully integrated company moved steadily toward fulfillment, as times and events collaborated. Some moves were forced on the company; others were sought out, such as Navajo Uranium. But regardless of the incentive, there was no doubt that Kerr-McGee Oil Industries was ready to move into bigger and better things.

As 1953 dawned, the company had already mapped out its largest drilling program ever. At a cost of over $4 million, it would sink five wells in the Spider Field in Louisiana, a test hole in Wyoming, eight or more offshore wells, six wells in Borden County, Texas, and a number of wildcats. Unexpected opportunities, however, added to these and stretched the company to the limits of its resources and experience. For example, on February 6,

---

[1] *Oil Record, 1954*, pp. 153–55; *Oil Record, 1955*, pp. 102, 107.

Phillips Petroleum acquired federal leases in the Katalla-Yakataga region of southeastern Alaska, an area known for oil seeps as early as 1896 and for a producing well (from 366 feet) in 1901. Phillips contracted with Kerr-McGee to do the exploratory work, and on June 17 the latter became owner of half interest in the over 1 million acres of leases.

Kermac Contractors was to drill three test wells, and again it was a rush job, this time because of the weather. Leo LeBron, who played a key role in early Gulf developments, headed up the Kuwait expedition, and was at that time managing the uranium division, was brought in to set up the project in Alaska. Kerr-McGee was responsible during the first phase for buying and assembling the camp, transportation to the campsite, and unloading. It was five times more expensive than a usual exploration job. There was not a foot of road on the lease, which ran 120 miles along the lower coast on the Gulf of Alaska and about fifteen miles inland. Yet plans called for drilling to begin by September 1.

LeBron scouted the area and decided that the operation could be handled in a manner similar to the one in Kuwait. An LSM was loaded with equipment in Seattle, and a beach landing was made. On the west shore of Icy Bay a campsite was cleared, and the workers moved in. Whereas the construction men lived on board the ship in Kuwait, here they lived on shore and, of course, the problem was with the cold, rather than the heat. Some of the local Yakutat Indians were employed to help the regular crew.

To bring in the light supplies, an air field was built at Icy Point, which the governor of Alaska named Kerr Field. The Senator's Washington office expedited the applications to the FCC for the radio equipment, and in September the base camp was ready. The LST with the drilling rig, crew's housing, and other supplies was brought in. But already there was ice in the water, and, because the housing units could not get ashore, the drilling crew had to shiver in tents for five or six days.

Access to the drilling site was over ground that was a quagmire, in an area covered by immense pine trees and laced with river and creeks. As a result the only roads possible were corduroy ones made by paving the track with felled trees. Stretched along this highway were fences to keep out the bears. But a major effort allowed drilling finally to begin in late November, only to run into new problems. The water pressure from the mountains was so strong that it blew the drill pipe out of the hole, creating an artesian well which continued to flow, creating instead of an oil well a giant water well. The weather was so bad, according to LeBron, that because of the cold gale winds they "spent about 90 per cent of the time supporting ourselves and 10 per cent in work." Finally, the well was shut down to await better weather conditions and most of the men gratefully moved out.[2]

---

[2] Lease Records file, "Contract #229"; *Kermac News*, Summer, 1953, pp. 4–5; Fall, 1953, pp. 8–10; and Spring, 1954, pp. 8–9; Robert S. Kerr Collection, box 560, folder 1, Western History Collections, University of Oklahoma; memorandum from E. A. Berry to "Management," December 2, 1953, in Public Relations file; interviews with Leo P. LeBron, December 28, 1972, A. T. F. Seales, July 20, 1971, and George B. Kitchel, June 16, 1971.

But in February, 1954, this first well was abandoned at 4,837 feet. Back in Oklahoma City, Kerr-McGee management began to reassess its interest in Alaska. The venture was proving to be very expensive, and the risk very high. So a decision was made to sell, if possible, the greatest part of the company's share of the lease. On June 19, a second test well was spudded, but on June 30, Kerr-McGee sold three-fourths of its interest to Phillips, retaining only one-eighth of the total lease. The second test went to 10,013 feet before it too was closed down. Eventually, in 1956 a third test well was drilled about one-fourth mile south of this last effort, only to be abandoned at 12,154 feet, after shows of oil and gas of a noncommercial nature were encountered. As it would later develop, Kerr-McGee's mistake was in being on the wrong side of the mountain.[3]

December 31, 1953, saw the abandonment of another phase of the program with Phillips. The joint exploration arrangement that had been operating for about a decade came to an end. Phillips made the first move to terminate the agreement, but the disassociation came by mutual consent. This contract, probably more than any one other thing, had promoted the rapid expansion of Kerlyn during its infancy by allowing the company to mount a real exploration program. Fortunately, as Kerr-McGee it was large enough to carry that phase of its operations on its own, and both firms recognized that the advantages were lessening. Phillips had alleviated its situation in respect to development of short-term leases, and its interests now were linked more to land. Kerr-McGee, on the other hand, was firmly committed to basic exploration in offshore waters.[4]

At the same time that the Alaskan operations were getting under way, Kerr-McGee forces went into action on the other side of the world. On May 26, 1953, the company signed an agreement with Lapidoth-Israel Petroleum Co., Ltd., whereby it would furnish supervisors and skilled personnel to train crews and to operate one or more of three Lapidoth drilling rigs. Lapidoth paid travel expenses, a fixed daily fee, and a footage rate for the drilling.

Unlike Kerr-McGee's experience among the Navajos in the same year, the company was given a specific reminder that cultural and religious awareness was needed in order to operate successfully in this area. The Israelis, with a long history of which they were justifiably proud, were also correct in recognizing that an understanding and knowledge of their religion and customs were indispensable in earning an outsider's respect. Accordingly, one interesting provision in the contract with Lapidoth read: "Contractor agrees that, in conformity with advices of Operator, it will inform and instruct its employees with respect to the religion and customs of the Israeli people to the extent as from time to time may be reasonably requested by Operator."

[3] The lease was given up in 1957. Lease Records file, "Contract #229"; interview with Leo P. LeBron; *Daily Oklahoman*, March 29, 1957.

[4] Interviews with R. E. Anderson, March 31, 1971, and Dean A. McGee, March 3, 1973; "Prospectus . . . $10,000,000 4½% Convertible Subordinated Debentures."

Drilling a Kerr-McGee well in Alaska.

Reactions of Kerr-McGee workers were also interesting. Otto Barton recalled that Barney Limes was working with him when he received a message to call McGee. Barton reported Limes's end of the conversation:

"Israel? Hell no, I don't want to go to Israel!"

"When? Tomorrow?"

Limes, who had worked for Kerr-McGee since 1933, had a different version, claiming that his refusal was because he had never flown. He reported that McGee's answer was, "This is a good time for you to get started." Limes tried to prove his point when he arrived in Israel by announcing that he had not closed his eyes once during the thirty-three-hour flight.

In Israel's first attempt to find oil, the tests were run near the Dead Sea, north of Gaza, and in the southern tip of the country. It was not a happy experience for anyone concerned. George Kitchel recalled that the work was performed under "armed camp" conditions, with guards around the well and covering the transports. Limes also claimed that he had his troubles with the local crews, who worked for four days and then were off for two. According to him, they needed a day of working time to recover from the rest period.

Paul Roth's official report shed some insight on the over-all scene. "It looks like one of those East Texas promotion deals or something of that nature. I don't think they will get me enough spare parts to keep operating. . . . It does not do any good to order anything; they won't get it and then they cannot see why we have to shut down for something. . . . I hate to send in reports to you and complain all of the time, but if I did not there would not be any report to make."[5] Much to the relief of Kerr-McGee the Israeli contract continued without further incident—and without much success.

While LeBron was freezing in Alaska and Roth was fuming in Israel, the long-negotiated Cuban deal finally got under way. As in the Israeli contract, the Jarahueca group owned the equipment, and Kermac Contractors furnished skilled personnel. In this case, however, Kerr-McGee also had a six-month option of acquiring one-fourth interest in the leases. The operation had all the characters imaginable: Batista, a silent partner; 'Buffalo' Kennedy acting for Kerr-McGee; and a Cuban in charge who located wells by throwing rocks. More humor was provided by Buster Golding, who had complained of the cold while operating a rig on the Canadian border. He was sent to Cuba so fast that he had only enough time to buy a Spanish-English dictionary for two dollars.

The test well was spudded on December 21, 1953, in the central part of Cuba. It was drilled to 8,375 feet before being plugged back and completed as a producing well around 1,088. It flowed 120 barrels of oil per day through 5/8-inch choke, gravity 14.9 degrees. Although it continued to yield only

[5] *New York Times*, August 12, 1953; Lease Records file, "Contract #233"; Public Relations file, "Drilling"; *Kermac News*, Fall, 1953, p. 15; interviews with Otto Barton, July 26, 1971, O. L. ("Barney") Limes, July 12, 1970, and J. C. Comer and George Kitchel, June 17, 1971; Paul Roth, "Report on Israel Job from 3-8-54 to 3-16-54," Tel-Aviv, March 17, 1954, in T. M. Kerr file, Transworld.

about 110 barrels a day, the press heralded it as the "First Major Oil Strike in Cuba," and Senator Kerr was immediately on the telephone to Oklahoma City in quest of details. The test well looked good enough, however, for the company to exercise its option and take a quarter interest in the field. Although six more producers were quickly added, George Kitchel recalled that McGee and Love were "always worried to death that I wasn't going to be able to get the drilling department's money back that we were spending down there for labor and transportation of our people back and forth."[6]

The progress was continuous, if not spectacular. A contract as operator of the field was signed in March, 1955, and by the end of that fiscal year ten new wells were added for a total of seventeen. Remarkably, only two dry holes had been encountered. On the other hand, however, the daily production of 1,000 barrels was of such low gravity that virtually all of it was sold to sugar mills as boiler fuel.[7]

A chance to go even farther afield was turned down. Twenty years in advance of his time, a native of India carried on an extensive correspondence with Senator Kerr in an attempt to interest him in having Kerr-McGee drill in that country.[8] Although Kerr's replies have not been found, they probably indicated that that firm had all the new commitments it could currently handle. For example, Kerr-McGee had just branched out into another "foreign" operation (although not in an exotic location) that was alien to the oil business. As early as May, 1953, the board had studied a proposal to go into a mining venture with the unnamed owner of what "appears to be very large potash deposits" in New Mexico. This elicited mixed opinions, mainly unfavorable. For one, a number of the company's officials were dubious about entering the fertilizer field, the principal market for potassium chloride. Other doubts focused on the owners, which turned out to be the National Farmers Union, and the nature of the beds themselves. G. R. Kennedy reported two problems: first, the deposits had a high clay content—5 percent versus 1 percent of slime in most operating mines—and, second, the owners had "no conception of the engineering and metallurgical problems involved in this venture."[9]

What swung management around was Bob Kerr. There can be no doubt that the senator sponsored the idea and eventually also sold it to the board. His support for the project probably originated with his close personal friendship with James Patton, long-time president of the Farmers Union. The union had options on some 13,000 acres of potash leases in Eddy and Lea counties, New Mexico, upon which it hoped to base a fertilizer cooperative.

---

[6] Drilling Department file, "Cuba"; Lease Records file, "Contract 205"; interviews with George B. Kitchel, June 16, 1971, and C. F. ("Charlie") Miller, September 4, 1971; *Kermac News*, Winter, 1953, p. 10; Summer, 1954, p. 6; and Spring, 1955, pp. 4–5.

[7] Lease Records file, "Contract 205"; *Daily Oklahoman*, August 20, 1955. Their holdings were confiscated when Fidel Castro came into power.

[8] Kerr Collection, box 560, folder 10.

[9] G. R. Kennedy to D. A. McGee, August 3, 1953, in unlabeled file in McGee's personal files.

As a nonstock, nonprofit corporation, the union could not engage directly in business. Therefore, in 1942 it had created a separate entity, the National Farmers Union Service Corporation (SCORP) for this purpose. This agency held the reserves, estimated to have a value of $100 million, but were short of capital. With Kerr-McGee as a partner, it hoped to create yet another corporation to produce these leases.[10] Since all of this would involve additional financing, V. L. Mattson, director of the Colorado School of Mines Research Foundation, was hired by Kerr-McGee to investigate the project.

Edwin L. Kennedy remembered this period. It was the senator who was interested in potash: "Here is one instance in which his enthusiasm is pressed to the point where it was an important element, if not the controlling element, in the decision to do it." F. C. Love recalled that the Oklahoma City office was not overly eager about potash but that the senator "could see the need for food to feed an expanding population world-wide and had an enthusiasm for land and farming."

According to Love, McGee "studied and restudied" the project a number of times and finally "persuaded himself" that it would probably be a good business. McGee admits that he was not as enthusiastic as Kerr but claims that Kerr did not force him into the potash business. After all, as George Cobb said, Kerr-McGee was merely following through on its own concept of what a natural-resource company did: convert to use things that were found, or exploited, through geologic knowledge and background.

Hugo Anderson, of the First National Bank in Chicago, also had to be convinced. His bank had had a long relationship with companies in this field, and he believed that the area was being depleted. There was also the problem with slime slurry, or clay content, which made him think the venture probably would not be profitable. But by this time McGee was ready to go into the potash business, and Anderson reported that Dean McGee would say, "We've looked into that. We believe we can handle that," to each objection he raised. Anderson explained, "Again, having over and over again, seen him go into these different ventures, naturally we loaned the money to go into that operation."[11]

[10] On February 26, 1954, C. E. Huff, general manager of the National Farmers Union Service Corporation, wrote McGee, "The first discussions as to a possible relationship between us in the potash properties were between President [James G.] Patton and the Senator [Kerr]. It was at that time suggested that we should explore the whole field of possible operating relationships and that you should be given opportunity to meet or exceed the proposals of others." D. A. McGee personal files. *Daily Oklahoman*, October 12, 1954; *Kermac News*, Winter, 1954–55, p. 3; Public Relations news release, "76-3," January 7, 1976; John A. Crampton, *The National Farmers Union* (Lincoln, Nebr., 1965), p. 202. The Kerr Collection also contains many letters antedating the agreement that illustrates this friendship.

[11] Interviews with V. L. Mattson, November 6, 1969; Edwin L. Kennedy, August 13, 1971; F. C. Love, September 2, 1971; Dean A. McGee, September 4, 1971; George Cobb, December 7, 1972; and Hugo A. Anderson, September 1, 1972. McGee believed that the "slime" problem could be handled as it had been at the Shiprock uranium mill. D. A. McGee to Stanley Learned, Phillips Petroleum Company, November 17, 1954, in McGee's personal files.

Loans totaling $7 million in November, 1954, enabled Kerr-McGee to enter into a contract to form a company to explore for, mine, mill-treat, and refine potash and other mineral resources. On March 12, 1955, when the final agreement for the joint development of the properties was made, it was also announced that Phillips Chemical Company, a subsidiary of Phillips Petroleum, had taken half of Kerr-McGee's interest. The Farmers Union assigned all its potash leases to the new company, Farm Chemical Resources Development Corporation, and Kerr-McGee and Phillips earned their half of the stock by developing these leases. Soon after this, an extended period of core drilling began to determine the location of the mine, and research was started to find the most efficient way of producing the potash. By October foundations were laid for the buildings.[12]

These varied activities were eye-catching. Claude Barrow, *Oklahoman and Times* oil editor, wrote, "Dean A. McGee, executive vice-president of the Oklahoma City firm, . . . is a provincial-minded geologist, who likes big structures, big lease blocks and big gambles, with resulting big stakes if successful. The Kermac firm is staffed by men with similar thinking."

The "men with similar thinking" were being shuffled in a series of managerial changes. In March, 1954, the bylaws were amended to create the new title chairman of the board for Robert S. Kerr, and McGee was then moved up to the position of president. T. M. Kerr became executive vice-president and F. C. Love, vice-president in charge of operations. McGee had been running the company and making the major decisions since Bob Lynn's departure in 1942, and, as Director E. L. Kennedy said, "If a man is running a company, but doesn't have the title, give him the title; it doesn't change anything except his signature."

This was a popular move within the company. Already McGee was known as a man with a mind that assimilated facts from everywhere that he could, in turn, use for the benefit of the firm. His secretary claimed that he seldom had to look at a file a second time and that, after getting the facts, he made his judgment and then lived with it. Moreover, he never turned anything aside without a fair hearing. Outside the company J. Landis Fleming wrote of the new president: "He has no pompous airs or pretense. Quiet speaking and sincere, he attacks everything he does with a tremendous enthusiasm. . . . He is an easily approachable man. . . . He inspires and builds confidence in all who talk to him."[13]

The new title meant more than a signature change, however. McGee was now in a position to improve the subordinate structure of the firm. In June, 1954, undoubtedly feeling that Kerr-McGee was becoming too cumbersome to manage with the present administrative structure, he established a

[12] D. A. McGee personal file, "Potash 1955"; *Daily Oklahoman*, March 13, 1955; Kerr-McGee Chemical Lease Records file, "Contract 1204-33"; *Kermac News*, Summer, 1955, p. 3; interview with V. L. Mattson, November 6, 1969.

[13] Interviews with Edwin L. Kennedy and Elizabeth A. Zoernig, August 26, 1971; J. Landis Fleming, "Is Life Worth Living?" *Oklahoma City Advertiser*, December 30, 1954; *Kermac News*, Spring, 1954, p. 3.

layer of middle management by the creation of four additional vice-presidencies. J. C. Finley became vice-president in charge of exploration; J. J. Kelly, vice-president of sales; George B. Kitchel, vice-president of Gulf Coast operations; and A. T. F. Seale, vice-president of manufacturing and general engineering. Managers were appointed for two departments: W. H. Dean, drilling and J. W. Roach, manufacturing. The result was a streamlining and coordinating of functions, with better channels of communication from the top to the bottom of the organization and vice versa. Furthermore, it assured greater stability for the company in case of unanticipated loss of a member of top management.

Chairman of the Board Kerr became involved almost immediately in his fight for reelection to the United States Senate. The company which bore his name once more was made a campaign issue by his opponent for the Democratic nomination, Roy J. Turner. To refute the "untrue, malicious, and misleading statements," 512 Kerr-McGee employees took out a full-page newspaper advertisement headlined as "Truth vs. Falsehoods." The charges and their disclaimers were varied and numerous: (1) the company had extensive foreign oil production that was being imported to the detriment of Oklahoma oil; (2) the Alaskan interest and the offshore leases had been acquired by political influence; (3) the uranium holdings were a result of political pressure and "inside information" from Washington, and sales of the uranium to the government were "evil"; and (4) the Wynnewood refinery had resulted from graft and patronage during Kerr's term as governor, and the blacktop it produced was an inferior product. The loyalty of these people must have helped convince the Oklahoma voters, for Kerr was reelected to his second term as senator.[14]

The attack on the refinery, always a key target for Kerr's local political foes, showed just how well the "old bucket of bolts" was doing. A $4.5 million improvement program begun in January, 1953, expanded the plant to handle 15,000 barrels of crude a day, while the construction of a 6,500-barrel-a-day fluid-type catalytic cracking unit and a catalytic polymerization unit increased the production of high-octane gasoline. Furthermore, research work had developed a new process for upgrading asphalt products into higher-priced goods and resulted in a 1,000-barrel-a-day plant for that purpose.[15]

The closer working relationship with Sunray was also paying dividends. Through it Kerr-McGee was now able to use a new products pipeline, which tied in to the Wynnewood plant, running from southern Oklahoma to Memphis, Tennessee, giving it for the first time an outlet into eastern Oklahoma, Arkansas, and the large consuming areas served by the inland waterways. Later the two companies formed the Valley State Oils, Inc., a wholesale marketing organization for their refined products.

[14] An undated, unidentified copy of this advertisement is found in the files of Bette Brenz, Public Relations. See also, Anne H. Morgan, *Robert S. Kerr: The Senate Years* (Norman, University of Oklahoma Press, 1977), p. 108.

[15] For refining see *Daily Oklahoman*, January 21, 1953; and *Kermac News*, Spring, 1954, pp. 4–5.

All of these steps slowly led to Kerr-McGee's entrance into a new phase of the petroleum industry—retailing. There had been long and intense opposition to making this move, and the reasons for the change are interesting. J. B. Saunders, president of Triangle Refineries, credited Love with being instrumental in the move into retailing in order to get Kerr-McGee into the end-use–product business. Guy Kiddoo, of the Chicago bank, said that he was against the move, but the bank obviously did not oppose it. Dean Terrill, who fought acquiring even the Wynnewood refinery because of this very reason—that it opened the doors to the "damned gasoline business"— said that he finally decided that "if we were going to be in it, you've got to be in it bigger." McGee echoed this: "We either had to get in or get out of the refining business."

Robert S. Kerr, Jr., recalled that, although the company directors had some reservations, his father never doubted Kerr-McGee's ability to compete with the majors. Vice-President James J. Kelly, who had been a refining man from the beginning, said that the company took this step toward becoming fully integrated because it felt that it was large enough to compete—therefore the move was inevitable in the development of the firm.

Other explanations have been furnished by Love and Cobb. Love's logic ran as follows.

The most competitive, lowest price market is that for products refined and sold at the refinery gate—sales are large volume and to a limited number of customers. The refineries are simply using capacity that would be wasted and therefore sell at very low prices. You are competing with people who are selling a surplus capacity and not trying to make a profit. In 1955 Kerr-McGee was selling too much of its production into markets of that nature, so by going on and retailing gasoline to the customer, even though that market is highly competitive, the profit is better than in bulk lot sales.

In short, profits are greater in retail operations than in jobber sales and greater in jobber sales than in sales at the refinery gate.

Furthermore, diversification would enable one area to take up the slack when another was down. George Cobb emphasized this when he said the decision to go into marketing was viewed as insurance: if oil became surplus, you could turn it into gasoline and sell it. To be sure of selling it, you had to have your own branded products and your own stations, despite the fact that refining and marketing traditionally were not the most profitable parts of the industry. [16]

The vehicle was the Deep Rock Oil Corporation. Born in the Cushing, Oklahoma, oil boom before World War I, it had a distinguished career both in refining and in marketing through some 350 service stations in sixteen middle western states. In an agreement dated April 16, 1955, but effective

[16] Interviews with Dean Terrill, November 24, 1969; Robert S. Kerr, Jr., June 15, 1971; J. B. Saunders, June 9, 1971; Guy C. Kiddoo, August 12, 1971; James J. Kelly, June 26, 1971; Frank C. Love; and George Cobb.

April 1, Kerr-McGee transferred 674,880 shares of a new issue of cumulative prior convertible preferred stock ($25 par) and gave an oil payment of $3 million in exchange for $5 million in cash and assets of approximately $12 million. This latter included Deep Rock's lease of the Cushing refinery (19 million barrels capacity), 575 employees and 800 distributors, the Deep Rock trade name, its pipelines, and 347,260 net acres of undeveloped leases. The cash was especially welcome since it came at a time when investment opportunities were great.

In May it was announced that a new subsidiary, Deep Rock Oil Company, with F. C. Love as president, had been formed to operate all the refining, marketing, and pipeline activities of Kerr-McGee. All products except asphalt would be sold under the Deep Rock name.[17] With the expansion of the Wynnewood facility and the addition of the Cushing refinery, the daily rate of processed crude-oil almost doubled to 21,459 barrels, and the sale of refined products more than doubled to $16,787,000. All divisions had production increases, led by refining.

Kerr-McGee Oil Industries, Inc.
Table 14.1.   Production Record, 1953–55

	1953	1954	1955
Production			
Crude oil produced (net barrels)	1,424,649	1,723,142	1,863,441
Natural-gas sales (millions of cubic feet)	29,340	35,911	36,604
Oil-and-gas leases (net acres)	1,379,640	841,180	1,198,054
Gas Processing			
Gas liquids produced (net barrels)	579,736	950,064	966,263
Refining			
Crude oil processed (barrels)	2,936,790	2,617,780	6,127,255
Minerals			
Ore mined (tons)	21,450	22,989	24,685
Ore milled (tons)	. . . . . .	. . . . . .	40,694
U_3O_8 Concentrate sold (pounds)	. . . . . .	. . . . . .	182,705

The exploration and development arms of Kerr-McGee were spread far and wide, from Israel and Alaska to the southwestern United States. Growth was steady in all divisions of operation (see Table 14.2).

[17] Lease Records file, "Contract 290"; *Daily Oklahoman*, April 18 and May 20, 1955; *Kermac News*, Summer, 1955, p. 1; *Oil and Gas Journal*, April 18, 1955; *Petroleum Week*, May 13, 1955.

Kerr-McGee Oil Industries, Inc.

Table 14.2. Comparative Figures Showing the Growth of the Production Operation, 1951–55

	1951	1952	1953	1954	1955
Number of producing leases	354	403	420	447	466
Number of gross wells	1,013	1,044	1,093	1,112	1,120
Value of oil, distillate, and gas produced to the company's interest	$3,489,508	$4,217,235	$4,550,465	$5,914,495	$6,420,956
Value of oil, distillate, and gas produced to the company's interest and applied to oil payments	652,224	1,055,265	1,030,117	1,575,282	1,908,613
Totals	$4,141,732	$5,272,500	$5,580,582	$7,489,777	$8,329,569

Land operations accounted for the net acreage decline. Dry holes in the Williston Basin brought about a farm-out agreement, which for all purposes ended activity in South Dakota, and poor results and high expenses closed down the Alaskan attempt. Except for minor exploratory drilling in Wyoming, South Dakota, Nebraska, New Mexico, Colorado, Alaska, and Cuba, most of the company's oil-and-gas exploratory and development efforts were concentrated in three states: Louisiana, Texas, and Oklahoma. For example, in 1954 Kerr-McGee had interests in a total of 1,112 wells, more than half of which were in Texas. Oklahoma followed with 256, Arkansas with 61, Louisiana with 59 (32 offshore), and Wyoming, Indiana, Kansas, Nebraska, Cuba, Colorado, and New Mexico combined for a total of 38. A breakdown of the rig locations for June 1, 1952, shows the other companies which had contracts with the drilling department.

During the period from 1953 to 1955 discoveries were made in the Breton Sound area (Block 20, Block 21), Big Lake Field, and the Main Pass area, Louisiana; Garvin and Beaver counties, Oklahoma; Baggs Gas Field, Wyoming; Southeast Big Lake Field, Texas; and Camaguey Province, Cuba. The total number of wells drilled, along with the corresponding footage, decreased noticeably. Fewer but deeper holes were one reason, but fewer rigs also were responsible. (see Table 14.3).[18]

During this time Kerr-McGee operated a little less than 1 percent of the total number of rigs in the United States and drilled about the same percent of footage. Many of these wells, of course, were contracts. And many also were dry holes. Figure 14.1 breaks down the variety and number of each type of well in which Kerr-McGee had an interest.

Drilling during 1953 was worthy of special attention. First, the use of new

[18] Production Department file, "Summary of Gross and Net Wells as of June 30, 1954"; Transworld Drilling file, "Rig Operations July, 1951, through June, 1956"; Dean McGee personal file, "Kerr-McGee Oil Industries, Inc., Drilling Department Location of Rotary Rigs (by month)."

Table 14.3. Drilling and Exploration Operations, 1953–55

	1953	1954	1955
Feet drilled	985,537	790,707	695,992
Total wells/wells			
completed	194/181	133/123	103/90
Kerr-McGee interest	90	24	36
Rigs (average)	28	19	25
Value of rigs	$8,064,229	$9,433,818	$11,394,203

NOTE: Figures for wells completed here and in the tables below include unsuccessful, as well as successful, holes.

drilling techniques brought a major advance in mining exploration, and stratigraphic, or "slim-hole," drilling made it possible to examine subterranean structures that were inaccessible by other methods. In the waters of the Gulf especially outstanding was Kerr-McGee's use of Rig 40 in connection with work in Breton Sound. *Oil Record, 1954* hailed this use of a submersible drilling barge as "the first such exploration over large areas in deep water." During the year, Rig 40 drilled a total of 219,134 feet and completed 53 wells in the Breton Sound area. These holes were drilled at an average rate of 1,252 feet per day, and an eight-hour, six-day average of 4,058 feet per well.[19]

The versatility and durability of Rig 40 partly explained the decision to construct new offshore barges. Rig 44, fully equipped, cost just under $4 million, and Rig 45, an austere version of Rig 44, was erected on a rebuilt swamp-drilling barge. Each of these consisted of three pieces—a hull and two pontoons—and was similar in design to Rig 40, but could also drill in water depths up to forty feet. Paul Wolff recalled that "Mr. McGee, Tsu Yu, and I did 90 per cent of the work on 44 and 45."[20] A third YF tender was also added to the Kermac fleet during late 1954.

The second explanation for ordering the new rigs was the effect of the tidelands' decision. Kerr-McGee's offshore drilling picked up as twenty-four contract wells, out of its total of ninety-five, were located in the Gulf: seventeen off Corpus Christi, Texas, and seven off Louisiana. Twenty-one of the total were for Kerr-McGee and its partners.

These statistics are significant. They indicate the speedy implementation of the earlier decision to get out of land drilling as rapidly as feasible. Travis Kerr's explanation for the speedup was to the point: the company "got out of land drilling because there wasn't any money in it and there were lots of wells to be drilled in the Gulf." On land anyone could buy a rig on credit and get into the drilling business, before knowing what it took to make a profit. Offshore, however, the investment was about eight times greater. To be

[19] *Kermac News*, September, 1959, p. 2.
[20] Interview with Paul A. Wolff, August 6, 1971.

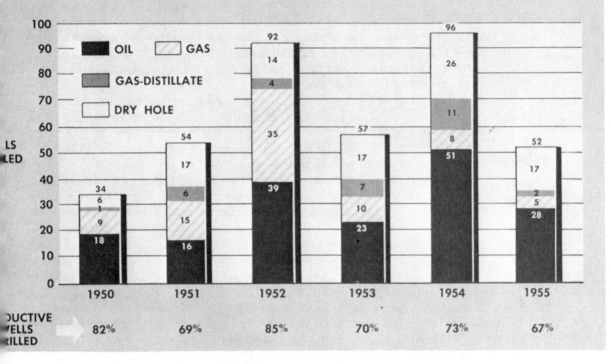

WELLS COMPLETED IN WHICH COMPANY PARTICIPATED

Fig. 14.1. Wells completed in which Kerr-McGee participated, 1950–55.
From Kerr-McGee Oil Industries, Inc., *1955 Annual Report*.

successful there required a company with stability and people with the engineering and financial background to make bids without bankrupting their firms. Offshore drilling was highly competitive, but unlike land drilling, which was plagued with fly-by-night businessmen, offshore operations were headed by men who knew what it really cost to drill in water. Here Kerr-McGee felt that it could do as good a job as any and could meet all competition.[21]

And there was competition. By 1954 twenty-three rigs belonging to other companies were operating off the coasts of Louisiana and Texas. From July 1, 1954, to August 1, 1955, about 340 holes were spudded. Eighteen oil and seventeen gas fields were found, with a success rate of 73 percent. By

[21] Interviews with Travis Kerr, December 19, 1969; G. Otis Danielson, June 1, 1971; and George Cobb.

235

August, there were fifty-two rigs in the Gulf, ten of which were mobile, and eleven more were on the way.

During this same period the average lease price per acre for offshore areas rose from $42 to $294. To meet this and the extra expense of working in the water took good bookkeeping, and Kerr-McGee did its homework well. A report in Travis Kerr's files indicated that in 1954, on a 10,000-foot well, Rig 40 cost $2,191 a day to operate. The "bare-charter" rate, where the operator furnished a minimum of materials, was figured at $4,100 a day. This was based on McGee's estimate that building a YF tender and minimum platform took about $2,665,000 and, depending on the depth at which it could operate, the price of a submersible was between $2.1 million and $2.6 million. A dry hole of 11,000 feet in 35 feet of water cost $536,000 with a tender and platform and $358,000 with a mobile unit.[22]

An embarrassing situation developed for Kerr-McGee in October, 1954. When the latest bids for offshore leases were opened, Kerr-McGee was the high bidder on eight out of twelve tracts, for a total bid of $15,014.000. Instead of elation, however, there was consternation with the discovery that in making the bids, map numbers rather than block numbers had been used. Consequently, the company ended up with tracts it had never explored and did not want. Clark Clifford, Kerr-McGee's attorney, attempted to withdraw all the bids and submit offers on the desired blocks. This was refused, and he next asked the Department of the Interior to reject all bids on the desired parcels so that Kerr-McGee could bid on them during the next sale. He especially wanted returned the slightly more than $3 million Kerr-McGee had put up as earnest money. It was finally settled, with the company getting its earnest money but losing the tracts.[23]

Despite the fact that drilling costs in the Gulf of Mexico ran about four times those on land (this is in addition to the eightfold increase in equipment cost), offshore drilling boomed. Louisiana allowed such wells to produce almost twice as much oil as equivalent wells on land. Furthermore, oil companies could control larger amounts of acreage without multiple leases and could engage in more economic spacing of their wells.[24] By 1955 the demand for offshore drilling and Kerr-McGee's commitment to this kind of contract caused the conversion of Rig 35 from a conventional inland submersible barge to a mobile platform capable of drilling in depths of water up to 35

[22] "Special Offshore Report," *World Oil*, May, 1957, pp. 118–48; Dean A. McGee, "Drilling in the Gulf of Mexico," *Offshore Drilling*, February, 1955, pp. 14ff.; George B. Parks, "The Economics of Offshore Drilling," speech at the 33d annual meeting of the Louisiana-Arkansas Division, Mid-Continent Oil & Gas Association, New Orleans, September 22, 1955.

[23] *Wall Street Journal*, October 18, 1954; *Oklahoma City Times*, October 19, 20, and 22 and November 12, 1954.

[24] Transworld Drilling file, "Rig Operations July, 1951, thru June, 1956"; Arthur W. Baum, "They Gamble on Offshore Oil," *Saturday Evening Post*, May 28, 1955, pp. 39ff.; D. A. McGee, "Point to Need for More Drilling Units," *Oil Forum*, February, 1955, pp. 52ff.

Table 14.4. Financial Highlights, 1953–55

	1953	1954	1955
Total assets	$38,646,570	$43,296,447	$67,544,562
Long-term debt	20,349,223	18,801,630	21,845,439
Working capital	9,493,769	2,307,588	13,164,290
Capital expenditures	8,161,525	12,278,119	13,219,259
Number of employees	1,210	1,245	1,325

Table 14.5. Depreciation Rates, 1955

Equipment	Percent
Drilling tools	12½
Drill pipe and drill collars	33-1/3
Automotive equipment	33-1/3
Airplanes	20
Seismic equipment	20
Refinery equipment	10
Buildings	3-1/3 to 12½
Boats and barges	20
Pipe line	10
Gasoline plants	6-2/3 to 20
Furniture and fixtures	10
Gas pipe line	5
Plant and equipment—Uranium division	10 to 50

feet. Two additional deep-water mobile platform drilling devices, capable of drilling in water depths of 65 to 70 feet (Rig 46 and Rig 47), were also started.[25]

The physical assets of Kerr-McGee increased 800 percent in gross property cost between 1946 and 1955, while the net book value of the property rose from $4.24 million to $38.73 million.[26] This large expansion in leases, plants, property, and equipment took a great amount of money to finance. A new gasoline plant at Etter, Texas, and the uranium mill at Shiprock, New Mexico, were but two of the projects covered by the sale of $10 million of 4.5

[25] *Daily Oklahoman*, July 1 and August 17 and 24, 1955; interview with Otto Barton; Kerr-McGee Oil Industries, Inc., *Annual Report for the Fiscal Year Ended June 30, 1955*, pp. 10–11.

[26] Kerr-McGee, *Annual Report . . . June 30, 1955*, p. 15.

Kerr-McGee Oil Industries, Inc.
Table 14.6. Consolidated Statement of Income, 1953–55

	Fiscal Year Ended June 30, 1955	Fiscal Year Ended June 30, 1954	Fiscal Year Ended June 30, 1953
Operating revenue			
Drilling contracts completed	$11,149,189	$ 7,844,710	$10,141,937
Sale of crude oil and gas	7,082,984	6,519,403	5,197,983
Sale of production payment interest	....	3,000,000	1,500,000
Sale of refined products	24,149,341	14,218,378	14,946,485
Sale of ore	2,702,230	642,453	483,134
Other income	111,755	146,543	69,082
	$45,200,499	$32,371,487	$32,338,621
Operating expenses			
Cost of drilling contracts completed	$ 7,829,686	$ 5,912,113	$ 6,549,695
Cost and expense of refined products sold	22,493,396	13,042,358	13,412,967
Lease operating and other production expense	2,022,131	2,078,445	1,868,522
Cost and expense of uranium division sales	1,953,471	488,609	402,643
General and administrative expense	1,987,497	1,839,255	1,635,832
Land department expense	173,989	142,046	87,384
Geological and geophysical department expense	599,112	463,038	441,365
Taxes, other than income taxes	158,705	136,923	199,505
Lease rentals expense	510,886	388,707	440,572
Research expense	120,742	101,701	102,743
Depreciation	2,327,990	1,849,941	1,746,401
Depletion	893,447	969,935	858,795
Dry-hole costs	634,038	1,168,730	957,529
Abandoned leaseholds and royalties	281,530	309,441	145,943
Service and equipment expense–net	(424,528)	174,726	138,561
Cost and expense of production payment interest sold	....	244,436	225,857
Provision for future operating expense of production payment interest sold	....	920,000	
	$41,562,092	$30,230,404	$29,214,314
	$ 3,638,407	$ 2,141,083	$ 3,124,307
Other income			
Gain on disposal of property	$ 235,257	$ 643,936	$ 293,728
Purchase discounts	85,049	132,965	116,063
Dividends	13,500	2,200	500
Interest	14,634	40,079	46,770
	$ 384,440	$ 819,180	$ 457,061
	$ 3,986,847	$ 2,960,263	$ 3,581,368

238

Kerr-McGee Oil Industries, Inc.
Table 14.6 Consolidated Statement of Income, 1953–55 (Continued)

	Fiscal Year Ended June 30, 1955	Fiscal Year Ended June 30, 1954	Fiscal Year Ended June 30, 1953
Income deductions			
Interest and loan expense	$ 1,326,057	$ 1,043,492	$ 752,953
Bad debts charged off	168,942	222,213	62,668
Cash discounts allowed	156,291	90,876	83,989
Provision for state income taxes	5,079	21,011	625
Provision for federal income taxes	18,000		
Provision for Mexican income taxes	8,101	2,912	4,099
	$ 1,682,470	$ 1,380,504	$ 912,155
Net income	$ 2,304,377	$ 1,579,759	$ 2,669,213
Adjustment of operations for prior years			
Reduce drilling-tool depreciation	. . . .	. . . .	395,643
Reduce provision for federal income taxes	. . . .	. . . .	7,867
			$ 403,510
Balance transferred to earnings retained for use in the business	$ 2,304,377	$ 1,579,759	$ 3,072,723
Earnings retained for use in business— beginning of period	6,901,191	6,470,928	4,173,386
	$ 9,205,568	$ 8,050,687	$ 7,246,109
Less: Cash dividends on common stock	835,319	759,410	746,646
Cash dividends on preferred stock	13,824	20,086	28,535
Cash dividends on prior convertible preferred stock	189,810		
Par value of common stock issued in stock split	426,522		
Provision for future operating expense of production payment sold		370,000	
	$ 1,465,475	$ 1,149,496	$ 775,181
Earnings retained for use in business—	$ 7,740,093	$ 6,901,191	$ 6,470,928

percent convertible subordinated debentures in 1953. On March 24, a special stockholders' meeting ratified an increase in company stock to 2 million shares: 1,975,000 common and 25,000 preferred. The debentures, to raise $9.75 million in cash for repayment of $4 million in short-term notes and to support capital expenditures, were handled by the Chase National Bank of New York City, and were to mature on April 1, 1968.[27]

But financial pressures quickly returned. Temporary relief was provided in March, 1954, by sale of a $3 million production payment to Murray Tool & Supply Company. A year later the amount of authorized stock was again raised to 3 million by adding 1 million common shares to provide for a four-for-three stock split.[28] This came after a large increase in assets and earnings, despite $10 million in capital expenditures the previous year. The split was noteworthy because of Dean McGee's known belief in reinvesting profits. When asked once why the stock of Kerr-McGee was split so infrequently, he answered, "When we split our stock, we would have to raise the dividends, and we have other plans for our money than paying the larger dividends."

The Deep Rock acquisition necessitated still further changes in the parent's capital structure. Another special stockholders' meeting just one month later—April, 1955—approved redemption and elimination of the cumulative convertible preferred after June 1 and an increase in total stock to 4.5 million shares (25,000 cumulative convertible, 700,000 new prior convertible, and 3,775,000 common). Deep Rock common shareholders were offered the privilege of a one-for-three stock exchange.[29]

Total assets showed a large gain over this period of time, while the working capital and long-term debt kept pace (see table 14.4).[30]

Of historical interest is a table of rates (Table 14.5) used by Kerr-McGee in determining depreciation on major items of equipment computed under the straight-line method. These rates, of course, were in addition to depletion of the quantities of recoverable oil and gas, the charge-off of the net cost of dry holes and unproductive wells, and the amortization of maintenance, repairs, and other like expenses.[31]

[27] "Prospectus Kerr-McGee Oil Industries, Inc., $10,000,000 4½% Convertible Subordinated Debentures, April 1, 1953"; Oklahoma State Archives, Secretary of State, "Kerr-McGee vs. John Rogers," folder 3.

[28] Daily Oklahoman, February 10, 1955; Kermac News, Spring, 1955, p. 7.

[29] "Prospectus Exchange Offer to Holders of Common Stock of Deep Rock . . . June 29, 1955"; Oklahoma State Archives, Secretary of State, "Kerr-McGee vs. John Rogers," folder 3.

[30] Kerr-McGee Oil Industries, Inc., Annual Report for the Fiscal Year Ended June 30, 1953; Kerr-McGee Oil Industries Inc., Annual Report for the Fiscal Year Ended June 30, 1954; Securities and Exchange Commission, "Form 10-K Annual Report for Fiscal Year Ended June 30, 1954"; Kerr-McGee, Annual Report . . . June 30, 1955; Oil Record, 1956, pp. 991–96; Securities and Exchange Commission, "Form 10-K Annual Report for Fiscal Year Ended June 30, 1955"; Kerr-McGee Oil Industries, Inc., Annual Report . . . 1959, pp. 4, 12.

[31] "A-16092 Department of Stock List New York Stock Exchange," p. 15. This document accompanied Kerr-McGee's application for listing on the New York Stock Exchange.

The consolidated statement of income (Table 14.6) reflected these reductions at the same time it showed that refined products continued to lead sales in the income column, both in amount and in percentage of increase. This was followed by drilling contracts and sales of crude oil and gas.

Perhaps a fitting conclusion to these eventful years was a tongue-in-cheek news release entitled "This Is No Bull." The story, which was widely circulated in Oklahoma newspapers, was about the purchase of a herd of prize Angus cattle:

We just wanted to steer you right on the Angus herd. Kerr-McGee Oil Industries, Inc., does *not* own any cattle. The cattle are owned by Sen. Robert S. Kerr and Dean A. McGee, two gentlemen who are identified in one way or another with Kerr-McGee Oil Industries, Inc. But the corporation is not in the cattle business. . . .
. . . we're proud that the herd will bear the name Kermac. But to be accurate in referring to ownership of the herd, fellows, don't refer to the owner as Kerr-McGee, but rather to Kerr and McGee.[32]

Not surprisingly, the wide and varying acquisitions by the company during the past few years made it possible for some to believe that Kerr-McGee had entered the cattle business.

[32] See, for example, *LeFlore County Sun*, December 8, 1955, and *Tulsa Daily World*, December 12, 1955.

Dean A. McGee (*left*) and Senator Robert S. Kerr (*center*) in 1956 at the time of the listing of the company's common stock on the New York Stock Exchange.

Chapter 15

Kerr-McGee
Comes of Age
1956

A fundamental movement in world politics accelerated soon after World War II: the liquidation of all colonial empires. More than fifty new nations eventually joined those which had formed the United Nations in 1945. The revolutions of the period from 1946 to 1965 were vastly different in character from those of the late eighteenth century, the American Revolution and the successive Latin-American wars. This time it was a revolt not only against the political control of the colonizing nation but also against the "economic imperialists" who had come to develop or exploit natural resources with native labor.

The United States granted the Philippines independence on July 4, 1946, and England, France, Spain, and the Netherlands duplicated this act in many of their colonies. Not all severance of ties was voluntary, however, and the colonial breakdown greatly lessened the worldwide power of these countries. At the beginning the United States assumed a benevolent attitude toward these nationalistic revolutions, in part because freedom was a popular idea and in part to subvert Russian influence and prevent communist takeovers. But coincident with the wars for freedom came the development of thermonuclear weapons: the H bomb, followed by guided missiles with long-range capabilities and warheads of devastating power. This gave every clash between a colony and its protector the potential of becoming a full-fledged war, with the terrifying threat of the use of atomic weapons.

Consequently, 1956 and 1957 saw an intensified uneasiness, a time of frustrating confrontations on the foreign scene, and an increasing evidence of social discontent in the United States. When Israel, France, and Great Britain invaded Egypt in response to its illegal seizure of the Suez Canal, they were forced to abort their efforts nine days later under the pressure of adverse world opinion. Likewise, the free world seethed in impotent rage over Russia's violent suppression of the Hungarian Rebellion, but then in late 1957 was forced to applaud the successful launching of Sputnik I and Sputnik II.

President Eisenhower, daily facing decisions which normally were present only in time of actual warfare, overcame personal health problems and ran for a second term, winning by a large plurality. Most areas of the United States economy were operating at record peacetime volumes, but faint signs of an approaching recession could be detected. Another cloud on the domestic scene darkened Little Rock, Arkansas, where the showdown over admission of black children to previously all-white public schools led to National Guard intervention. Within and without the country, irrevocable changes were taking place.

In the background of these political and social upheavals was the petroleum world. In the Middle East, in Asia, in Africa, in South America, this source of the world's industrial production and mechanized life-style was slowly being positioned to strike its own blow at the free world. The very abundance of oil was an encouragement to waste. Low royalties and labor costs in the countries where the oil deposits were located produced such cheap refined products that little thought was given to the ultimate consequences of turning on more lights and running more motors. Only the inconvenience caused by tankers having to detour around the blocked Suez Canal gave Europe a foretaste of its economic future.

But in the United States the situation was the opposite of deprivation. In 1957, spurred by an average price of $3.09 per barrel, the petroleum industry sank some 14,707 exploratory wells (81 percent of which were dry), utilized some 4,791 rigs, and made a gross investment in properties, plants, and equipment of $47.4 billion. Annual production from the Gulf of Mexico alone was over 16 million barrels. Oklahoma's output, the highest in twenty years, was 218,111,000 barrels, valued at $660 million. Of this, Kerr-McGee contributed 2,182,524, a yearly increase of almost 10 percent.

Acquisition rather than divestiture was a more appropriate description of the history of Kerr-McGee during this time. Unlike the nations which were losing their colonies, the company, instead, was adding new subsidiaries and new divisions, several heretofore untried by the petroleum world. These changes were revolutionary in the corporate and industrial areas, but in a creative and innovative way.

Kerr-McGee Oil Industries, Inc. could be said to have come of age on February 23, 1956, when its stock made its debut on the New York Stock Exchange (NYSE). The company had decided to take this step as a service to its stockholders and because of the greater attention it would get in the financial press. Accompanied by his directors to New York City for a special ceremony, Bob Kerr bought the first 100 shares of Kerr-McGee common stock traded on the NYSE at 46½. Before the day ended, some 5,300 shares

Kerr-McGee Oil Industries, Inc.

Table 15.1. Affiliated Companies, 1955

Name of Company and Class of Stock	Number of Shares Outstanding	Owned by the Company		
		Number of Shares	Percent of Class	Percent of Voting Stock
Deep Rock Oil Company				
Common Stock, $500 Par Value	10,000	10,000	100	100
Kermac Contractors, Inc.				
Common Stock, $100 Par Value	6,064	6,064	100	100
Valley States Oils, Inc.				
Common Stock, $1 Par Value	10,000	5,000	50	50
Kerr-McGee Building Corporation				
Preferred Stock, $100 Par Value (voting)	500	None	None	
Common Stock, $1 Par Value	5,000	2,500	50	45.4545
Republic Building Corporation				
Class A Common Stock, $100 Par Value (non-voting)	496.8235	183.3334	36.9011	—
Class B Common Stock, $100 Par Value	500	166.6666	33.33	33.33
Downtown Airpark, Inc.				
Preferred Stock, $50 Par Value (voting)	140	67	47.8751	.2460
Common Stock, $10 Par Value	27,089.25	12,430.55	45.8874	45.6515
				45.8975

sold at prices between 46¾ and 46¼, with the preferred going for 25½.[1]

On January 24, 1956, Kerr-McGee Oil Industries, Inc., had applied to the New York Stock Exchange for listing of the following:

674,880 shares of its Prior Convertible Preferred Stock, $25 par value per share (hereafter called Preferred Stock), issued and outstanding at December 9, 1955; and

1,787,439 shares of its Common Stock, $1 Par Value Per Share (hereafter called Common Stock), issued and outstanding at December 9, 1955 (including 491.3 shares represented by outstanding scrip certificates); and for authority to add to the list, upon official notice of issuance thereof,

263,173 shares of Common Stock upon conversion of the Company's 4½% Subordinated Convertible Debentures;

281,200 shares of Common Stock upon conversion of the Company's Preferred Stock; and

177,617 shares of Common Stock upon exercise of employees restricted stock options, presently in force or to be granted, making a total of 2,509,429 shares of Common Stock applied for.

[1] *Oklahoma City Times*, February 23, 1956; *Kermac News*, Spring, 1956, pp. 4–5.

Kerr-McGee Oil Industries, Inc.

Table 15.2. Summary of Consolidated Earnings, 1946–55

Fiscal Year Ended June 30

	1946	1947	1948
Total operating revenues (includes sale of production payments—1953, $1,500,000 1954, $3,000,000)	$6,197,498	$8,023,663	$12,538,058
Operating charges, excluding depletion and depreciation (includes cost and expense of production payments sold: 1953, $595,857; 1954, $1,164,436)	$5,526,838	$6,884,511	$ 9,672,933
Depletion and depreciation	573,498	741,612	1,254,976
Total operating charges	$6,100,336	$7,626,123	$10,927,909
Operating income	$ 97,162	$ 397,540	$ 1,610,149
Other income			
Profit on sale of properties	$ 89,099	$ 252,863	$ 57,405
Rental income, purchase discounts, etc.	38,777	103,043	49,036
Total other income	$ 127,876	$ 355,906	$ 106,441
	$ 225,038	$ 753,446	$ 1,716,590
Other deductions			
Other expense	$ 11,326	$ 22,561	$ 64,880
Interest expense	148,103	150,543	211,525
	$ 159,429	$ 173,104	$ 276,405
Net income before taxes on income	$ 65,609	$ 580,342	$ 1,440,185
Provision for taxes on income			
Federal income tax	$	$	$ ....
State income taxes	200	15,000	29,053
Foreign income taxes	....	....	....
	$ 200	$ 15,000	$ 29,053
Net income	$ 65,409	$ 565,342	$ 1,411,132

Since the founding of the first partnership a number of Kerr-dominated firms had played a role in the evolution of the corporation. The firms and their dates of organization are as follows:

Anderson & Kerr Drilling Company	November 5, 1930
Anderson-Kerr, Incorporated	November 5, 1930
An-Ker, Incorporated	September 15, 1931
A & K Petroleum Company	November 7, 1932
Kerlyn Oil Company	April 12, 1937
Kerr-Lynn Company	April 12, 1937
Kerr-McGee & Company	July 31, 1942
Kerr-McGee Oil Industries, Inc.	January 15, 1946

1949	1950	1951	1952	1953	1954	1955
$14,930,150	$15,288,506	$19,505,867	$26,662,214	$32,338,621	$32,371,487	$45,200,499
$11,743,007	$12,845,679	$15,977,411	$21,714,316	$26,684,612	$27,091,353	$38,340,655
1,590,786	1,972,077	2,078,176	2,313,122	2,899,702	3,139,051	3,221,437
$13,333,793	$14,817,756	$18,055,587	$24,027,438	$29,584,314	$30,230,404	$41,562,092
$ 1,596,357	$ 470,750	$ 1,450,280	$ 2,634,776	$ 2,754,307	$ 2,141,083	$ 3,638,407
$ 56,881	$ 77,940	$ 65,886	$ 143,681	$ 293,728	$ 643,936	$ 235,257
73,288	72,715	84,875	110,177	163,333	175,244	113,183
$ 130,169	150,655	$ 150,761	$ 253,858	$ 457,061	$ 819,180	$ 348,440
$ 1,726,526	$ 621,405	$ 1,601,041	$ 2,888,634	$ 3,211,368	$ 2,960,263	$ 3,986,847
$ 58,406	$ 66,986	$ 70,859	$ 90,920	$ 154,478	$ 313,089	$ 325,233
236,814	281,250	324,485	476,887	752,953	1,043,492	1,326,057
$ 295,220	$ 348,236	$ 395,344	$ 567,807	$ 907,431	$ 1,356,581	$ 1,651,290
$ 1,431,306	$ 273,169	$ 1,205,697	$ 2,320,827	$ 2,303,937	$ 1,603,682	$ 2,335,557
$	$	$	$ 70,205	$	$	$ 18,000
6,949	2,250	1,250	7,911	635	21,011	5,079
....	69,091	30,000	13,851	4,099	2,912	8,101
$ 6,949	$ 71,341	$ 31,250	$ 91,967	$ 4,734	$ 23,923	$ 31,180
$ 1,424,357	$ 201,828	$ 1,174,447	$ 2,228,860	$ 2,299,203	$ 1,579,759	$ 2,304,377

Besides the many companies in whose operations Kerr-McGee had part interest, there were six full affilliates. At the time of the application to the New York Stock Exchange they were as shown in Table 15.1.

Among the various kinds of historical data submitted was a summary of consolidated earnings for the previous ten years, 1946 to 1955. It showed a 700 percent increase in operating revenues, as well as a 15,500 percent jump in taxes (see Table 15.2).

Cash dividends on the company's stock were started on July 3, 1933, and continued as shown in Table 15.3.

The only persons listed as beneficially owning as much as 10 percent of the voting stock of the company were Robert S. Kerr, with 17.94 percent, and his wife, Grayce B. Kerr, with 10.73 percent. The common-stock holdings of

Table 15.3. Dividend Record, 1933–55

Common Stock				Cumulative Convertible Preferred Stock	
Fiscal Year Ended June 30	Per Share		Total Cash Dividend Paid	Per Share	Total Cash Dividend Paid
	A	B			
1933	$0.25				
1934	0.50				
1935	0.3875				
1936	0.40	$0.05			
1937	0.35	0.10	$129,062.50		
1938	0.35	0.05	106,496.82		
1939	0.35		86,177.00		
1940	0.35		86,127.30		
1941	0.35	0.05	106,577.60		
1942	0.35	0.075	116,017.27		
1943	0.35	0.025	91,255.84		
1944	0.525	0.11	99,300.99		
1945			71,883.44		
*1946		0.06	20,430.55	$0.60	$ 3,600.00
1947		0.025	20,430.58	1.20	72,000.00
1948		0.25	178,836.38	1.20	71,643.60
1949		0.25	262,348.00	1.20	64.766.00
1950		0.25	263,164.00	1.20	64,615.00
1951		0.25	265,285.00	1.20	59,454.90
**1952		0.4125	448,976.37	1.20	44,628.30
1953		0.60	746,646.32	1.20	28,534.80
1954		0.60	759,410.07	1.20	20,085.90
***1955		0.60	835,319.04	0.90	13,758.90
					$189,810.00

*Split 2/1: Class A common stock converted into Class B.
**Split 1/10.
***Split 4/3.
 CCPS redeemed May 31, 1955
 PCPS issued, 674,880 shares, $25 par.

Kerr-McGee Oil Industries Inc.
Table 15.4. Common Stock Owned by Directors, 1956

Name	Principal Occupation	First Fiscal Year as Director	Shares Beneficially Owned as of June 30, 1956	
			Preferred	Common
Robert S. Kerr	United States senator from Oklahoma	1933	None	309,830.0
D. A. McGee	President of the company	1938	None	147,665.0
T. M. Kerr	Executive vice-president of the company	1933	None	34,985.9
F. C. Love	General vice-president of the company	1948	None	19,933
J. H. Lollar, Jr.	Secretary-treasurer of the company	1953	None	None
Dean Terrill	Lawyer, Chicago, Illinois; assistant secretary of the company	1937	693	16,585.6
James E. Webb	Assistant to the president of the company; president of the Republic Supply Company, Oklahoma City	1953	None	500
J. D. Blosser	Investments—partner of Straus, Blosser & McDowell, Chicago	1937	None	3,684
Edwin L. Kennedy	Investments—partner of Lehman Bros., New York	1949	None	4,900
Frederick W. Straus	Investments—senior partner of Straus, Blosser & McDowell, Chicago	1937	None	17,175

Table 15.5. Annual Benefits, June 30, 1956

Name	Capacities in Which Remuneration Received	Aggregate Remuneration	Amount Set Aside or Accrued	Estimated Annual Benefits
D. A. McGee	President and director	$ 69,212.02	$5,550	$24,184
T. M. Kerr	Executive vice-president and director	43,086.00	4,832	14,476
F. C. Love	General vice-president and director	46,836.00	1,986	15,223
Robert S. Kerr	Chairman of the board of directors	32,600.02	4,139	8,460
All officers and directors as a group		371,679.31		

all directors and all officers amounted to 33.21 percent, but none of these facts were enumerated.[2] In the proxy statement for the next annual stockholders' meeting, however, the following amounts were listed:

	Shares	Percent
Robert S. Kerr	309,830.0	17.10
Grayce B. Kerr	186,850.4	10.31

Investors Mutual, Inc., was also named as owning 101,000 preferred shares, or 14.97 percent.

At the time of the listings shown in Table 15.4 the top four officers of the company received the remunerations shown in Table 15.5.[3]

Administrative changes and additions to the board of directors also were made during 1956. Travis Kerr was shifted to the newly created position of "vice-chairman of the corporation," and two of Kerr's sons were added to the board of directors, making the family representation even stronger. In the August, 1956, change General Vice-President F. C. Love became executive vice-president in Travis Kerr's old position, and L. A. Woodward was appointed administrative vice-president. Other vice-presidents continued in office were A. T. F. Seale, operations; W. M. Murray, general sales; J. J. Kelly, marketing; J. C. Finley, exploration; G. B. Kitchel, drilling contracts; R. M. Chesney, refining; J. W. Roach, crude-oil supply, pipeline and refinery mechanical services; and G. B. Parks, production and drilling operations.

In February, 1957, the board of directors was increased to twelve, adding Guy C. Kiddoo and Robert S. Kerr, Jr. Kiddoo was vice-president of the First National Bank of Chicago, which previously had declined representation on the board because of a possible conflict of interest. By now, however, Kerr-McGee had other creditors, and its loans at the First National were shared with the First National City Bank of New York.[4] At the same time the long-tenured executive committee of R. S. Kerr, D. A. McGee, and F. W. Straus was expanded to include Love and Kiddoo. Still later in the year the board was enlarged once again, this time to seat the president of Triangle Refining, J. B. Saunders, and Breene M. Kerr.

It was not merely the improved image that led to plans for a modern and enlarged headquarters. The recent acquisitions and the proposed new ones created a pressing need for more administrative space. Since 1946 three floors of the Oklahoma City First National Bank Building had been used, but they were crowded and hot from lack of air-conditioning. In April, 1956, the

---

[2] Two basic documents cover the listing of the stock: "A-16092 Department of Stock List New York Stock Exchange" and Securities and Exchange Commission, "Form 10—Application for Registration of Securities on a National Securities Exchange."

[3] Kerr-McGee Oil Industries, Inc., "Notice of Annual Meeting, September 28, 1956," pp. 3–4.

[4] Interview with Guy C. Kiddoo, August 12, 1971; "bylaws," February 28, 1957.

company, acting through the Kerr-McGee Building Corporation, obtained the old YMCA and Culbertson buildings (at 125 and 135 Northwest Second Street) and six adjacent vacant lots in Oklahoma City for approximately $420,000. The parent company made a loan of $250,000 to its subsidiary, and the rest was borrowed from the Liberty National Bank of Oklahoma City. Almost immediately a major construction and remodeling program estimated at $1.9 million was started, with completion targeted for 1958. Kerr-McGee took a twenty-year lease with the building corporation at a monthly rental of $29,152.19.[5]

But new buildings are only a single evidence of growth in a company. Kerr-McGee's self-evaluation in its application to the New York Stock Exchange gave another:

Today Kerr-McGee Oil Industries, Inc., is a fully integrated oil company. It operates in every phase of the petroleum industry from the production of oil and gas to the delivery of the finished product to its consumer. Its activities encompass exploration, production, refining, marketing of refined products, research, contract drilling and uranium mining and drilling.

A new phase in the corporate life of Kerr-McGee was about to begin.

[5] *Daily Oklahoman*, April 27, 1956, p. 1; Kerr-McGee Oil Industries, Inc., "Notice of Annual Meeting, October 2, 1961."

Original Oklahoma City plant of the Cato Oil and Grease Company in 1922.

Chapter 16

Acquisition and Diversification 1956–1957

During the years after the listing of Kerr-McGee's common stock on the New York Stock Exchange, acquisitions were made at a brisk pace. The first in 1956 involved certain assets of Johnson Oil & Refining Company, owned by Gaseteria, Inc., of Indianapolis, Indiana. A letter from F. C. Love to Gaseteria, Inc., contained a memorandum concerning the purchase of a small crude-oil refinery at Cleveland, Oklahoma; Johnson's crude oil pipeline and fleet of tank cars; all its oil, gas, and mineral interests in Oklahoma; and its inventories. Johnson would also connect its pipeline system to the one serving the Deep Rock Refinery, thirty-one miles away at Cushing. In return, Kerr-McGee paid the parent company $1,375,000 plus the value of products in the line at the time of the takeover on April 1, 1956. Before that date arrived, however, J. C. Finley notified Gaseteria that all oil leases should be assigned to Phillips Petroleum, since it had bought them for $500,000.[1]

On May 1, the Deep Rock Oil Company was liquidated and its assets merged with Kerr-McGee Oil Industries, Inc. The refinery at Cushing with its crude-oil gathering system and marketing outlets, which Kerr-McGee had been operating under lease since the Deep Rock acquisition, was then purchased from the General American Oil Company of Dallas for $3.5 million. This facility had a nominal crude capacity of 19,000 barrels a day and 800 barrels a day of finished lubricating oils. As a result of this purchase Kerr-McGee now owned three refineries with a total of more than 35,000

[1] Lease Records file, "Contract 326."

barrels per day throughput, and was also well on the way to assuring itself an adequate supply of its own branded gasoline.[2]

Then, in line with its desire to increase the number of service-station outlets, Kerr-McGee purchased half interest in Knox Incorporated, which operated stations in Texas. It also added 86 Deep Rock jobbers and 225 branded retail outlets, and the volume of branded sales increased 31 percent. A station modernization and building program was started in the northern portion of the company's marketing area.

In May, 1957, the remaining half of Knox Industries, Inc., was acquired, and what a Kerr-McGee official described as "the most drastic change in oil marketing since 1905" was launched. This was Shop 'n Gas, a scheme for selling oil products at grocery supermarket parking lots. There was to be no above-ground equipment but instead outlets at numbered parking stalls, where shopping customers were serviced by attendants on streamlined motor scooters.[3] The idea was tested at the National Food Store in Saint Louis, Missouri. It was apparently unsuccessful, for nothing more is recorded about the scheme.

The long-discussed purchase of Cato Oil and Grease Company of Oklahoma City was finally consummated on December 31, 1956. The firm had been established on September 6, 1922, by H. L. Cato, James R. Corbett, and Claude C. Huffman to manufacture lubricating oils and grease. By the time of its acquisition it had grown to the point that it employed about 100 people and produced some 500 products, including its well-known specialty greases and such exotics as nail polish, deodorants, and glass cleaners. By the agreement the owners of Cato's 1,750 outstanding shares of capital stock sold their interest for $1,250,000, partly in cash and the rest in five annual payments, and the company became a subsidiary of Kerr-McGee.[4]

The senator once more was the point of contact, and probably the prime mover, in the introduction of a new product, this time helium. The site of interest was Pinta Dome in Apache County, Arizona. Geologists had recognized the anticline before 1948, and Silas C. Brown had made a detailed geological map and assembled leases on the structure, which he turned over to C. A. Martin & Associates of Phoenix in 1948. In turn, a drilling contract with Kipling Petroleum Company led to the spudding of the first well in 1950. A large flow of gas was discovered at 1,035 feet, but since it would not burn, the well was declared worthless and allowed to blow. The U.S. Bureau of Mines ran a test that showed that it contained the unusually high helium content of 8 percent and demanded that it be shut in. There was no market for helium, however, and in 1951 Kipling drilled through the gas zone to 2,517 feet but abandoned this new well when the drill pipe stuck. There the situation remained until 1955, when the Apache Oil and Helium Corpora-

---

[2] *Daily Oklahoman*, April 28, June 6, 1956; *Kermac News*, August, 1956, pp. 8–9.

[3] This was tested at the National Food Store, Saint Louis, but was apparently unsuccessful, for nothing more is heard of the scheme. *Wall Street Journal*, June 7, 1957; *National Petroleum News*, September, 1957, pp. 96–97, 100.

[4] Lease Records file, "Contract 389"; interviews with Claude C. Huffman, July 1, 1971, and Ralph Jenks, August 17, 1972.

Cato Oil and Grease Company as it appeared in 1962.

tion took over development of the property, attempted to rework the second well, and began a third.

It is probable that Martin T. Bennett, a Washington, D.C., consulting engineer employed by the Navajos for many years, brought the prospect to the attention of Kerr. On August 22, 1956, an agreement was signed between Kerr-McGee and Apache Oil and Helium whereby the former would take over interests by assuming the latter's debts and a profits override. A memorandum of August 30 indicated that a syndicate had been formed by Kerr-McGee, Washington attorney Norman Littell, Senator Clinton P. Anderson, Bennett, and Bureau of Indian Affairs Commissioner

Glenn L. Emmons for a "joint venture" in Kerr-McGee's name. On October 1, a formal agreement was signed, with Katherine M. Littell replacing Emmons.

Kerr-McGee's interest was undoubtedly based on the purchase of helium by the government at $15.50 per thousand cubic feet, a price certain to rise because available sources were nearly exhausted. F. C. Love explained to a United Press reporter: "Kerr-McGee is in the business of exploring for and developing natural resources. Helium is a natural resource for which there is a good, and we believe expanding market. Thus the pursuit of our normal business took us into this field."[5]

The major uranium exploration program in which Kerr-McGee had been engaged since 1952, at a cost of over $100,000 per month, resulted in another significant expansion during early 1956. The potentially richest area lay in the Ambrosia Lake area of New Mexico, near Grants. This bit of geography, which *Time* magazine called "a misnamed patch of sunbaked, bone-dry limestone," had a long and varied history. One of the principal characters in its recent past was a septuagenarian religious mystic, Stella Dysart, who had spent some thirty years in a search for oil in the area. As a wildcatter she had platted a large amount of the acreage into forty-acre blocks and one-acre lots, and she even sold portions as small as one-sixteenth of an acre to people scattered all over the United States (in 1977 there were approximately 2,596 identified claimants to parts of one 640-acre section).

Then, in 1950 a Navajo sheepherder picked up some strange-looking rocks at Haystack Mountain on Santa Fe Railway land. He showed them around until they were recognized by someone who knew what uranium ore looked like. Santa Fe proceeded to open its Haystack Mountain Mine, and the Anaconda Company built a mill at Bluewater to process the ore. Shortly afterward, Anaconda made a strike of its own, the Jackpile Mine. Prospectors poured into the small railroad town in numbers reminiscent of the gold rushes, and additional small profitable finds were made.

Using Stella Dysart's drilling logs of the rock formations, a young Texan, Louis B. Lothmann, discovered a seventeen-foot seam of uranium at 360 feet on her land. A mad scramble followed to stake claims, with Kerr-McGee representatives in the middle of it. The dreams of possible fortunes made tempers run high, and claim jumping became a way of life. Massive legal problems ensued because the then current mineral law was based upon surface visibility whereas this uranium was hundreds of feet deep in the ground. Kerr-McGee officials theorized that such superficial actions as

[5] In a letter to Dean McGee, July 25, 1961, Bennett requested that his name be mentioned in future press releases, since "I am among the first outside of government who were first to realize the expanding importance of helium and I am proud of my participation in the Pinta project." Interview with Elizabeth A. Zoernig, August 26, 1971; John A. Masters, "Pinta Dome Helium Gas Reserve, Apache Co., Arizona," address to Interstate Oil Compact Commission, Phoenix, Arizona, December 5, 1960, in Public Relations file, "Helium"; "Helium is Spurring Arizona Gas Play," *Oil and Gas Journal*, Vol. 57 (March 16, 1957), pp. 78–79; Lease Records files, "Project 382 (Legal) #1 and #2," and "Project 382 (Corres.)"; interview with Otto Barton, July 26, 1971.

scooping a few surface ditches did not establish proof of subsurface mineralization, or proof of discovery. They therefore relied on core drilling to
substantiate their claims. In some instances Kerr-McGee core drillers were
actually shot at by other claimants. After long litigation the courts finally
upheld the company, and a group of the hardest-fought-over claims became
one of its best mines.[6]

Kerr-McGee obviously could not win all the claims, and it was equally
obvious that Stella Dysart and others would be involved in developing
reserves estimated at 40 million tons. Unfortunately—or fortunately for
some—Buffalo Kennedy had returned to private consulting work in December, 1955, so Marion Bolton represented Kerr-McGee at the scene. His
story was that the company sent some engineers and geologists to look over
the find since it would have to be shaft mining. If the ore was thick and of
good grade, Kerr-McGee hoped to buy the orebody.

Samples were taken to Shiprock to check their adaptability to Kerr-
McGee's process, and an effort was made to outline the ore body by drilling.
When the reports were favorable, McGee went out to New Mexico to dicker
with the owner of the option on Section 11. But the initial asking price was
$60 million for this one section. It was too much for McGee, so he ordered a
search for other good areas. This led to the purchase of part of Section 10, all
of Section 22, and, later, all of Section 17. These gave Kerr-McGee an
important interest in the deposit, and shafts were begun on the first two
sections.

For each rights' holder to build a small mill and sink adjoining shafts
would be vastly uneconomical. Kerr-McGee and two abutting property
owners decided to pool their resources into one operation, and in July, 1956,
it was announced that a new corporation, Kermac Nuclear Fuels, had been
formed by Kerr-McGee, Pacific Uranium Company, and the Anderson
Development Company to mine and mill uranium ore at Ambrosia Lake.
Kerr-McGee as the majority stockholder would staff and operate the project. The three partners also collaborated in acquiring royalty rights under
four and three-fourths additional sections that were owned by a group
known as the "Branson heirs." This was accomplished in September by
formation of the Ambrosia Lake Uranium Corporation, equally shared by
the four parties. This new company then leased the interests of the Bransons
and dedicated them to Kermac Nuclear Fuels, which became the operator
for Ambrosia Lake Uranium (section 33 Mine is located on this property).[7]
As a result of this maneuvering, Kerr-McGee could now claim ownership of
23 percent of all uranium reserves in the United States, on 22,240 acres of

[6] Minerals Lease Records file, "MP-3(a)"; "Uranium Jackpot," *Time*, September 30,
1957, pp. 88–90; interview with Dean Terrill, November 24, 1969; "The Kermac Story,"
undated publication by Kerr-McGee.

[7] Interview with Marion Bolton, August 27, 1973; *Daily Oklahoman*, July 22, 1956; *New
York Times*, July 25, 1956; *Uranium Magazine*, June, 1957, pp. 8–9; interview with George
Cobb, December 7, 1972; "G. H. C. [George Cobb] Chronology," in Public Relations file,
"Uranium."

claims, plus AEC contracts extending until 1966 with an estimated value of $300 million.

Against this backdrop the operations at Shiprock were overshadowed. Its uranium processing plant was producing at near capacity and was sufficiently valuable to support a mortgage of $3,050,000 from the First National Bank of Chicago. The 1955 price of $12.51 a pound for uranium oxide had helped shift the search from the traditional outcroppings to shallow subsurface deposits, then to deeper lodes located by the core-drilling techniques pioneered by Kerr-McGee. Besides the uranium discoveries at Ambrosia Lake in New Mexico, others were made in Utah and Wyoming. So successful were these efforts that American dependence upon Canada and the Belgian Congo was largely negated. Domestic reserves, estimated at approximately 10 million tons at the end of 1955, were revised to in excess of 30 million tons of indicated and inferred uranium-ore reserves and another 30 million of potential reserves by Jesse C. Johnson, director of the United States Atomic Energy Commission's Division of Raw Materials.[8]

But almost from the first it had been obvious that the acid-cure process being used at the Shiprock mill to produce uranium and vanadium was unsatisfactory because of high labor costs and price of acid. A metallurgical research laboratory, which moved several times between Golden and Boulder, Colorado, was established to seek a more efficient and less costly method of production. In the meantime, when the price of vanadium fell, the AEC allowed its contract to be modified to eliminate vanadium recovery.

The research paid off in a system that won a major chemical engineering award, and the new process was put into operation at the Shiprock mill. This was a continuous solvent extraction technique, commonly called raw leach, which eventually proved to be the best available for nonlimestone ore for both uranium and vanadium.[9] Its economy also allowed resumption of vanadium production in 1958.

Of long-term significance was the completion on May 3, 1957, of negotiations with the AEC for construction of a processing plant at Ambrosia Lake by Kermac Nuclear Fuels Corporation. The 3,300-ton-per-day mill, the largest in the nation, had a cost estimate of $18 million. At the same time the

[8] Kerr-McGee Oil Industries, Inc., *Annual Report for the Fiscal Year Ended June 30, 1956*, p. 6; Dean A. McGee, "Atomic Energy and Exotic Fuels," speech before the Independent Petroleum Producers Association of America, Phoenix, May 3, 1959; and Dean A. McGee, "Supply and Demand for Uranium in Years Ahead," *Commercial and Financial Chronical*, Vol. 209 (February 13, 1969), p. 4.

[9] The process is described in detail in Denver Equipment Company, *Deco Trefoil*, January–February, 1957, bulletin No. M4-B90. See also Kerr McGee, "Quarterly Report for 3 Months Ending September 30, 1957"; *Chemical Engineering*, October, 1957, pp. 148–50; *Wall Street Journal*, August 21, 1956; *Daily Oklahoman*, June 3 and October 13, 1956; "The Great Uranium Glut," *Fortune*, February, 1964, p. 108; M. F. Bolton and S. B. Robinson, "A Brief History of the Shiprock Mining and Milling Operations on the Navajo Indian Reservation," in Public Relations file, "Uranium"; and interviews with V. L. Mattson, November 6, 1969, and Marion Bolton, August 27, 1973.

Core drilling for uranium.

AEC also entered into a purchase agreement to buy 33 million pounds of processed ore (yellowcake) during the first five years of the plant's operation and 4.5 million pounds per year thereafter for the contract's duration—purchases that could gross from $300 million to $350 million.

This was an immense undertaking for Kerr-McGee as far as capital investments were concerned. To get the needed money for the mill, for property acquisitions, exploration, mining, and working capital, the partners in Kermac Nuclear agreed to contribute a total of $5 million in proportion to their stock ownership. Kerr-McGee then guaranteed a loan from the First National of Chicago and approved the sale of 78,000 shares of Kermac Nuclear Fuels to the United States Steel and Carnegie pension funds. At the end of the year Kerr-McGee stockholders were told that the financing had been completed by obtaining $31 million—$24 million from banks and $7 million from "private" funds. It was probably not a coincidence that Phillips Petroleum acquired a 20 percent working interest in some of the properties from the Ambrosia Lake Corporation about this time.[10]

In view of all this activity the following story is relevant. Ralph Jenks's account of it is that, a few months after Cato Oil and Grease had been acquired by Kerr-McGee, its cofounder and president, Claude Huffman, began wondering if "something was wrong" since he had heard nothing from Dean McGee since the purchase. Finally he decided to telephone McGee on the excuse of seeing whether any more information, papers, or such were needed. Upon hearing of Huffman's anxieties, McGee laughed and replied, "No, Claude, we have so many problems that have to be handled hour by hour that when something is going well—we leave it alone."[11]

It was indeed a busy time. In the largest acquisition to date the Triangle Refineries of Houston, Texas, was brought into the Kerr-McGee family on April 19, 1957, by an agreement for "exchange of Capital Stocks." Triangle owned some thirteen subsidiaries and was valued at slightly less than $4,995,000. Its 11,250 shares of common stock outstanding were exchanged for 85,000 common shares of Kerr-McGee, effective on May 31. Triangle was not a refiner as its name implies, but rather was one of the largest independent marketers of refined petroleum stock, selling the entire output of thirteen refineries and processing plants. With eleven river and deepwater pipeline terminals in the Middle West and South and a sizable fleet of barges, tank cars, transport trucks, and tankers, it handled approximately 20 million barrels of products annually and had sales of slightly more than $100 million.

The deal was a favorable one for both companies. For Kerr-McGee, with its increased refinery capacity and relatively weak marketing division, Triangle could solve many problems. For James B. Saunders, with the heavy responsibilities of a company too large for one man to own and operate alone, the step provided the relief he needed. In 1946, eleven years after he had founded Triangle, he attempted to sell to the Chicago Corporation and blamed Hugo Anderson of the First National Bank of Chicago for his failure to do so. In 1955 he considered going public, but was told that it would have to be over the counter, since there was not enough "romance" in a marketing company to carry it successfully on the Big Board. The advice included selling to some firm on the New York Stock Exchange.

Early in 1957 Saunders's Houston neighbor Grant Judge, head of the auditing firm of Arthur Andersen, suggested Kerr-McGee as a possibility

---

[10] Interview with Marion Bolton; Mineral Lease Records files, "MP-9(A)" and "MP-14(A)"; "The Kermac Story"; Kerr-McGee, "Interim Report for Six Months Ended December 31, 1957." In May, *Petroleum Week* credited Kerr-McGee with four "firsts" in uranium: using petroleum geology and techniques, they (1) introduced regional base mapping to show all geological data at Ambrosia Lake, (2) used commercial logging, (3) used rotary-drilled test holes, reducing the price from $3 to $5 a foot to less than $1, to define ore beds, and (4) used the solvent extraction method for processing uranium ore. "Why Kerr-McGee Leads in Uranium," *Petroleum Week*, May 10, 1957, pp. 28–31.

[11] Interview with Ralph Jenks.

The purchase of Triangle Refineries brought facilities for
wholesaling petroleum products.

and offered to act as a go-between. The negotiations began at $12 million,
which McGee considered too high. Love suggested spinning off all but the
marketing company, leaving a $6 million balance to be covered by 100,000
shares of Kerr-McGee at $60 each. Once again McGee lowered the offer, to
50,000 shares. Finally, a compromise was struck for 85,000 shares, a senior
vice-presidency and directorship for Saunders, and an option for Saunders
and some of his key employees to buy 20,000 shares of Kerr-McGee at a
favorable price. The deal was decided on April 16, twenty years to the day
after the opening of Triangle.

Although Saunders remained convinced that Kerr-McGee had been
shortsighted in not taking his whole company, management was satisfied.
Even Dean Terrill, who disliked anything that resembled refining and
marketing, agreed that Triangle was an "excellent acquisition," and Director Robert S. Kerr, Jr., believed that the Triangle acquisition made the

difference in Kerr-McGee's ability to compete in the field of marketing.[12] In August, 1957, the corporation's bylaws were changed to allow fourteen directors, and J. B. Saunders took his place, along with another son of the senator, Breene M. Kerr.[13]

The final acquisition of 1957 was a November transaction in which Kerr-McGee bought all of Gulf Refining and Gulf Oil's Oklahoma crude-oil pipeline gathering system for $1.25 million, and the Texas Pipeline and Texas Company's lines for $1 million. From the Deep Rock and Johnson mergers the company already had 1,281 miles of pipeline, which connected some 1,684 leases and handled 24,000 barrels of crude per day. But little of this was adjacent to Wynnewood, and none of it allowed surplus oil to be moved there from Cushing. The Gulf system of 1,221 miles handled 27,000 barrels daily, while the Texas line of 280 miles carried 9,000 barrels daily. Together they connected the Kerr-McGee refineries and assured Wynnewood an adequate supply of its special type of crude.

Oil-and-gas exploration and development were not slighted during the rapid expansion into other energy-related fields. During 1956 the company rigs remained in the United States, and by May the total was down to seventeen rigs, two having been sold. Seven land rigs were stacked. But in December, 1956, only four were idle, and Rig 46 had joined the offshore group to make a total of eighteen. Seven of these were in the Gulf Coast region, six in the Oklahoma-Texas division, and five in the Rocky Mountain area.[14]

Rig 46 gave Kerr-McGee another offshore-drilling first. Various factors brought this about. Although in 1956, 100 rigs had drilled a total of 446 wells offshore Louisiana, 33 off Texas, and 7 off California, it had become increasingly obvious that depth was creating a technology crisis. While tender platforms dominated shallow-water drilling, rectangular mobile units similar to Kerr-McGee's Rig 40 were used for deeper waters. These had two disadvantages, however: first, inability to withstand the wave motion in deeper water, and, second, the fact that their moving parts, the pontoons, were a handicap in operation. Millions of dollars were spent in efforts to solve the problems of wave action, soil overloading, and the danger of toppling while in descent. Most of the experiments were in the nature of a floating hull that could slide on four legs, but these were far from perfected.

For this reason Kerr-McGee had built its previous two rigs, 44 and 45, on the old pontoon system. For the next rig, however, Ingalls Shipbuilding was approached about constructing one using a new Ingalls' design. However,

---

[12] Lease Records file, "Contract 417"; *Kermac News*, May, 1957, p. 6; Otto J. Scott, *The Professional: A Biography of J. B. Saunders* (New York, 1976), pp. 301–302, 375, 384–89; interviews with J. B. Saunders, June 9, 1971; Dean Terrill, November 24, 1969, and Robert S. Kerr, Jr., June 15, 1971.

[13] *Kermac News*, March 12, 1958, pp. 1–2.

[14] Transworld Drilling file, "Rig Operations July, 1951, thru June, 1956"; Dean McGee personal file, "Kerr-McGee Oil Industries, Inc., Drilling Department Location of Rotary Rigs (by month)."

Drawing of Rig 46.

Paul A. Wolff, one of the designers of Rig 40, did not like the Ingalls approach and convinced McGee it should be rejected. In its place Wolff proposed a sketch of his own and, on the basis of that one drawing, persuaded McGee to approve it for construction.

Rig 46 was contracted for in October, 1955, and work began almost immediately. Wolff visualized his design as a "bottle-stabilized" unit that would be in a single piece, carry all of its equipment, and have no moving parts in the hull. It was characterized by four equally spaced columns, each twenty-two feet in diameter, which when flooded maintained stability in all sinking attitudes and provided sturdy drilling bases in greater depths of water. If it worked as Wolff planned, it could move from place to place with all drilling equipment aboard.

Because of the pressure of time the design was never tested in a scale model. As a result, when McGee visited the shipyard in Mississippi, a large part of the basic hull was on the way. Wolff never forgot that day. As he said, anyone who had ever brought disappointing news to McGee knew that "Mr. McGee doesn't just get blue, he *looks* a little blue. And I saw Mr. McGee look a little blue and tense-lipped and kicking a piece of gravel and sort of walking around in a circle." Approaching him, Wolff asked, "Mr. McGee, is something the matter?"

McGee's only answer was, "My God, Paul, what have you done?"

Wolff cannot remember what he said or did in response to this. In retrospect, he believed that McGee's shock resulted from having given his approval after seeing only the one sketch, plus the fact that he was not kept up to date on the progress of construction. When he first saw that 100-foot-high rig, "I think that what Mr. McGee was afraid of was that it was just too big compared to what we had in mind. And he was just completely taken by surprise." Finances, also, must have been a part of the worry. Despite the large investment the rig might not work. If somehow it did, it might not be economical to operate.

But McGee's shock did not last for long. Rig 46 did work. It was patented and later hailed as a "major contribution" and a "very important development." It became the forerunner of the semisubmersible. To the senator's delight construction on a duplicate, Rig 47, was quickly ordered.[15]

Because of Kerr-McGee's eminence in offshore drilling, as early as May, 1956, its directors were informed that management had been approached with an offer of cash for use of the plans and data on its drilling rigs. At that time it was the consensus that this should be rejected unless arrangements included Kerr-McGee's participation. But now the success of Rig 46 made the designs and data all the more valuable. An added incentive to copy the successful unit was that offshore production for all companies had climbed to 150,000 barrels per day, and 700 new wells and 27 new rigs were predicted to be offshore by the end of 1957.

On January 18, 1957, an agreement was signed with Blue Water Drilling Corporation of New Orleans, a combination of companies incorporated just eleven days earlier. Kerr-McGee was to furnish the plans and technical assistance to build a duplicate of Rig 46 at a cost of $3.5 million. In return, the company received a 5 percent interest in Blue Water in the form of stock and promissory notes for a total of $100,000.

On January 4, the *Wall Street Journal* prematurely announced another organization, Brewster-Bartle Offshore Company. To be jointly owned by

[15] Interview with Paul A. Wolff, August 6, 1971; "Special Offshore Report," *World Oil*, May, 1957, pp. 118–48; Richard J. Howe, "The History and Current Status of Offshore Mobile Drilling Units," *Ocean Industry*, July, 1968, pp. 1–24.

Rig 47 at work off the shore of Louisiana.

Kerr-McGee and Brewster-Bartle Drilling Company of Houston, it was
organized for contract drilling in the Gulf. On January 17, Kerr-McGee
entered a construction agreement with Ingalls for its Mississippi yard to
build a unit substantially the same as Rig 46 for $2,050,655, adjusted to cost
of steel and labor. But not until February 7 did Love confirm Kerr-McGee's
new partnership with Brewster-Bartle Drilling Company, which was effective upon completion of this rig. All of Kerr-McGee's rights and responsibilities concerning the new rig were assigned to Brewster-Bartle Offshore

Company in return for one-half interest in the concern and appointment of McGee, Love, and Kitchel to the board of directors.[16]

In February of the same year Kerr-McGee resumed foreign drilling, this time in South America. At a cost of approximately $2.5 million, approval was given to buy a 5.395 percent interest in two blocks in Lake Maracaibo and southern Monagas, Venezuela. Other companies involved in the project were Phillips, Sunray, Ashland, Western Natural Gas, and Canadian Atlantic Oil. Kermac Drilling Company of Venezuela, C.A., was formed in April as a new subsidiary, and it soon had contracts with Phillips and Venezuelan Sun. To meet these and its own needs, Kerr-McGee bought two new tenders and sets of drilling tools, and these, together with their auxiliary equipment, were transferred from the Gulf Coast to Lake Maracaibo, which was particularly adapted to platform-tender operations.

Other foreign contracts followed. On June 1, Champlin Oil & Refining Company, which previously had acquired a forty-year lease in the province of Bocas del Toro, Republic of Panama, signed an agreement selling Kerr-McGee a quarter interest in the lease for $300,000 and three-fourths of the operating expenses of drilling in the northwest corner of that nation. Kerr-McGee crews must have felt somewhat at home there, since most of the area was under water.[17]

On August 22, Kerr-McGee also agreed to furnish British Honduras Gulf Oil two rigs (one from Alaska) and crews to drill seven wells. This was at a charge of $1,256 a day per unit and $2 a foot for drilling. Gulf likewise had the option of purchasing the rigs at the end of the contract for $430,000 and $375,000 less depreciation. This contract was later assigned to Kermac Drilling of Venezuela, and, to meet the added responsibilities, the subsidiary was loaned $4 million by Kerr-McGee.[18]

Kerr-McGee's step up in foreign exploration was part of a national trend. Most large petroleum companies were actively seeking new sources of supply. Although the United States could no longer claim the largest oil reserves in the world, it could account for half the total consumption, and the annual demand was now up to 3,425,806,000 barrels. The gap between this and domestic production was met by foreign imports, which jumped 31,422,000 barrels, despite federal imposition of a voluntary restriction program on such crude on July 29, 1957.

Meanwhile, significant domestic discoveries were made in 1956–57, all located in or offshore Louisiana. At Ship Shoal, blocks 28, 30, and 31 accounted for three, the Main Pass Area yielded two, and Saint Martin Parish, one. These were somewhat offset by four wildcat failures in southern

---

[16] Neither of these partnerships was finalized. Blue Water's ended in April, 1966, when Kerr-McGee refused to accept the assignment of Blue Water's rights to the Santa Fe Drilling Company. On August 8, 1957, Ingalls was notified that its construction agreement was terminated, and on March 16, 1959, Kerr-McGee severed connection with Brewster-Bartle. See Transworld Drilling files, "Rig #46 Design/Blue Water" and "Rig 46 Design/Brewster-Bartle Rig"; and *Oil Record, 1957*, pp. 1110–17.

[17] Lease Records, "Contract brief." The original file, "424-1" has been destroyed.

[18] Transworld Drilling file, "B. H.-Gulf—Contract, Rigs #14 & 50."

Table 16.1. Drilling and Exploration Operations, 1956–57

	1956	1957
Feet drilled	672,263	697,975
Total wells/wells completed	102/88	107/88
Kerr-McGee interest	32	31
Rigs (average)	20	20
Value of rigs	$15,868,305	$21,621,029

Louisiana. In Alaska shows of oil and gas of a noncommercial nature caused the abandonment of that project, and while no discoveries were made in Cuba, five new producers were added for a total of fourteen.

The drilling and exploration arms had successful years, as seen in Table 16.1.

Of the thirty-two wells with Kerr-McGee interest in 1956, eighteen were in Texas, eight in Oklahoma, five offshore Louisiana, and one in Wyoming. The thirty-one company wells the next year again were principally located in Texas (nineteen), with the rest in Louisiana, Wyoming, Oklahoma, and New Mexico. Interestingly enough, Kerr-McGee had shares in a total of ninety-three new wells in 1957, making it obvious that it was contracting out most of its own land drilling.

Rig 46, the new super rig, joined the offshore group in November, 1956, followed by Rig 47 the next year, when nine rigs were offshore—five mobile and four tender-platform. Of the remaining eleven land models, six were in the Rocky Mountain division and the rest in the Oklahoma-Texas area. The offshore rigs were busy 91 percent of the year, and the land ones, over 77 percent.[19]

The 1957 production records for all divisions showed improvement over 1956 except for gas processing. But the small increases reflected the worsening depression, which struck the petroleum business particularly hard. Reduction in production was the answer given to the problem of lessening demand.[20]

Both annual reports issued in 1956 and 1957 boasted about the record sales and income for the company. Between the two years sales of products, services, etc., rose from $69,762,959 to $108,759,138. The addition to property, plant, and equipment was the largest in history, aggregating $19,710,151 for 1957, almost $2 million more than the previous year. Table 16.3 shows a breakdown of the years' highlights and other financial figures of interest.

All of this made the reports a pleasure for the stockholders to read, and they also received a share of the profits in the form of dividend checks.

[19] Kerr-McGee Oil Industries, Inc., *Annual Report, June 30th, 1957*; Transworld Drilling file, "Rig Operations July, 1956, thru June, 1961."

[20] Kerr-McGee Oil Industries, Inc., *Annual Report, June 30, 1956*; Securities and Exchange Commission, "Form 10-K Annual Report for the Fiscal Year Ended June 30, 1956"; *Annual Report, June 30th, 1957*.

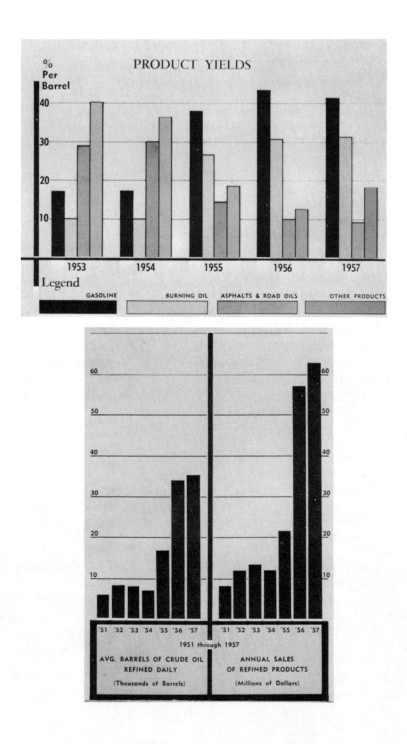

Fig. 16.1. Annual sales of refined products and crude oil refined, 1953–57.
From Kerr-McGee Oil Industries, Inc., *1957 Annual Report*.

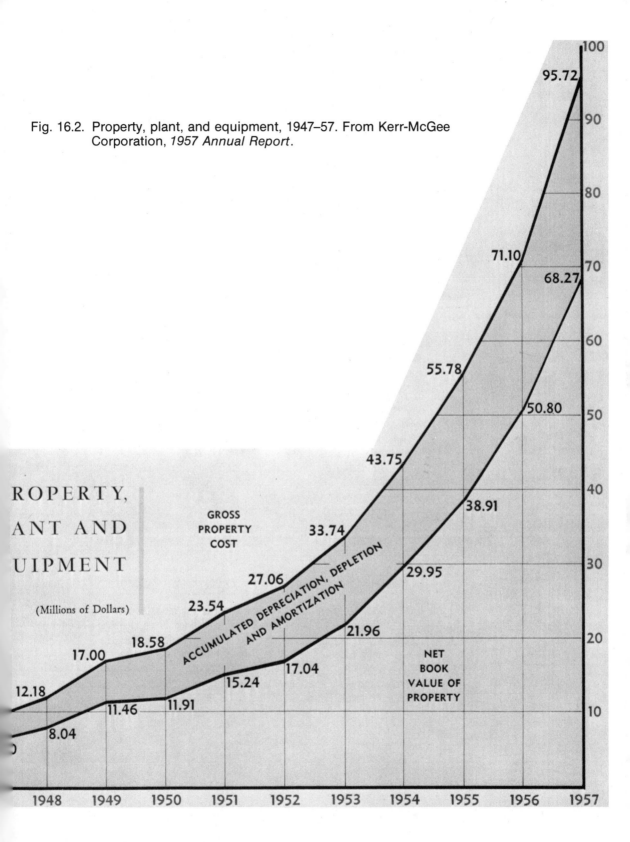

Fig. 16.2. Property, plant, and equipment, 1947–57. From Kerr-McGee Corporation, *1957 Annual Report*.

ROPERTY,

ANT AND

UIPMENT

(Millions of Dollars)

GROSS
PROPERTY
COST

ACCUMULATED DEPRECIATION, DEPLETION AND AMORTIZATION

NET
BOOK
VALUE OF
PROPERTY

95.72

71.10

68.27

55.78

50.80

43.75

38.91

33.74

29.95

27.06

23.54

21.96

18.58

17.04

17.00

15.24

12.18

11.46   11.91

8.04

1948   1949   1950   1951   1952   1953   1954   1955   1956   1957

Table 16.2. Production Record, 1956–57

	1956	1957
Production		
Crude oil produced (net barrels)	1,985,913	2,182,525
Natural-gas sales (millions of cubic feet)	38,083	39,322
Net acres of oil-and-gas-leases	1,136,666	1,640,940
Gas processing		
Gas liquids produced (net barrels)	1,217,501	1,202,852
Refining		
Crude oil processed (barrels)	12,559,290	12,844,715
Minerals		
Ore mined (tons)	30,219	40,681
Ore milled (tons)	132,831	170,558
U_3O_8 concentrate sold (lbs.)	641,848	857,381

Table 16.3. Financial Highlights, 1956–57

	1956	1957
Gross income*	$90,440,780	$109,365,121
Net income	4,679,994	6,244,648
Total assets	91,429,813	147,224,746
Cash flow from earnings	11,358,764	14,549,421
Working capital	20,047,162	37,696,954
Net properties	50,798,806	68,271,461
Capital expenditures	17,790,274	19,710,151
Long-term debt	36,847,788	44,835,897
Cash dividends	2,096,797	2,250,416
Stockholders' equity	37,202,579	72,253,211
Total taxes paid†	1,899,850	3,001,526
Number of employees	2,000	2,750

*Included income from sales and services and other income.

†This item included production and severance taxes, federal, state, and foreign taxes on income, income taxes applicable to gain on sale of properties and marketable securities, income taxes applicable to liquidation of inactive foreign subsidiary, real estate and personal property taxes, unemployment and old-age-benefit taxes, and other taxes. Did not include gasoline and oil excise taxes.

Table 16.4. Common-Stock Highlights, 1956–57

	1956	1957
Equity per share	11.22	23.33
Earnings per share	$2.16	$2.31
Cash dividends per share	$0.60	$0.80
Average yield	1.2	1.4
Number of shares outstanding	1,812,020	2,373,868
Number of stockholders	3,476	4,541
New York Stock Exchange		
High	61	75¾
Low	42⅜	38¼
Price-earnings ratio		
High	28.24	29.10
Low	19.61	14.95

Preferred stock annually paid $1.125, while the common provided the data, shown in Table 16.4.[21]

The financial condition of Kerr-McGee at the close of the 1957 fiscal year was sound with $19,850,000 cash on hand. In addition to the company generated funds, during these two years it also brought in outside financing. This was done by the sale in February, 1956, of $20 million in secured notes to Mutual Life Insurance Company and the marketing, as of June 28, 1957, of an equal amount of 5¼ percent sinking-fund debentures, due June 1, 1977. The latter was accompanied by common-stock warrants for 100,000 shares, entitling the holder to buy five shares of common stock at $80 per share for each $1,000 of the principal amount of the debentures during the period April 1, 1958, to June 30, 1964. Concurrently the company sold to the public 220,000 shares of common stock. The proceeds of these sales, after expenses, were used to retire bank loans and to replenish the general fund.

The prosperity of the firm had allowed a November, 1956, discussion of another stock split, with the board instructing McGee to take up the matter with the New York Stock Exchange. In the meantime an increased dividend to twenty cents on common stock was declared for January 1, 1957. On the same date the company called in its 4½ percent convertible subordinated debentures, all of which, with the exception of $90,000, were converted into 243,000 shares of common stock. Employee stock options for 13,150 shares of common were exercised during 1957, down from 40,202 the previous year.

On May 1, 1957, trusteed thrift and savings plans were adopted, with participation by eligible employees and the company. Of Kerr-McGee's 2,685 employees, only 507 in the refineries belonged to unions, perhaps partly explaining the creation of these additional benefits.[22]

[21] *Ibid.*

[22] "Prospectus Kerr-McGee Oil Industries, Inc., $20,000,000 5¼ Sinking Fund Debentures, due June 1, 1977, with Common Stock Purchase Warrants, 220,000 Shares Common Stock, $1 par Value," June 25, 1957.

Dean McGee and Kerr-McGee Oil Industries, Inc., were featured in a June, 1957, issue of *Forbes* that listed the many and far-flung interests of the man and the firm. The president of the company was described as "tall, tough-minded Dean A. McGee [who] is known in the oil country as a man who can smell oil in the ground." To expand his business and sell oil, he bought Triangle Refining with its marketing outlets in fifteen states, plus several other acquisitions to enlarge petroleum's role in the company's interests.

The magazine went on to recount that in 1952 McGee astonished the industry by his move into another fuel, uranium. His logic ran: "Oil and uranium strata are geological cousins . . ., so who was better set to look for it than an oilman?" As a result, five years later Kerr-McGee broke ground for a $30 million uranium mill and owned roughly 25 percent of all uranium reserves in the United States. Then, with a "reputation of being one of the best prospectors in the business," McGee got into potash. One use of potash, as everyone knew according to *Forbes*, was fertilizer. But "energy prospector McGee could have something further in mind: namely using it as a base to make a 'super fuel' for space traveling rocket ships."[23] *Forbes* evidently was learning what a lot of other people already knew: McGee's ability to look to the future and to be there ahead of it.

[23] "A Nose for Profits," *Forbes*, June 15, 1957, pp. 20–21. In 1956 Bob Kerr told a *Time* reporter that he believed he would be offered a trip to the moon in his lifetime in a rocket using Kerr-McGee fuel; "Uranium," *Time*, July 30, 1956, p. 68. But potash production had run into a snag. In April, 1956, ground had been broken for construction of "Shaft No. 1," but the work was soon terminated on the 1,623-foot hole until March 15, 1957, because of a lawsuit concerning royalties; Dean McGee personal files, "Farm Chemical Resources Dev. Cor., 1957," and an unlabeled folder dealing with potash.

Chapter 17

Recession Years 1958–1959

Not many Americans could look back on the years 1958 and 1959 with nostalgia. Chiefly it was a period of endurance, when good news on either the international or the national scene was scarce. On several occasions the "cold war" seemed on the verge of open conflagration.

Outside the "iron curtain" the forces of nationalism were creating new opportunities for the enemies of the free world. Nasser's United Arab Republic absorbed Syria and promoted a coup d'etat in Iraq in which the king and his family were killed. A similar threat hung over Jordan and Lebanon, and the latter's president appealed for outside help. While the United Nations debated the situation, the United States and Britain decided to act. On July 14, 1958, President Eisenhower ordered the Sixth Fleet to demonstrate off the coast of Palestine, and all available marines and airborne troops were landed at Beirut. Simultaneously Britain dropped 2,500 para-troops in Jordan. This display of strength saved Jordan and Lebanon, checked Nasser, and momentarily silenced the Soviet threat. But later that year Premier Khrushchev announced that if the Western powers did not get out of Berlin in six months he would turn it over to Communist East Germany. This crisis was averted, however, when the premier agreed to visit Eisenhower at Camp David to discuss a "summit meeting" between the involved powers.

Even more disturbing was evidence that the cold war, in the guise of nationalism, had spread to the Western Hemisphere. The Communist parties of Russia and China were actively taking advantage of the historic Latin distrust of the "Colossus of the North" and of the endemic economic and political unrest. One strong talking point of South American radicals was North America's alleged support of dictators. An overt warning occurred when President Eisenhower had to threaten to send in the marines to rescue Vice-President Richard Nixon and his wife during a good-will mission to Venezuela.

The most distressing events took place only ninety miles off the American coast in Cuba. In 1956 a young revolutionary fanatic, Fidel Castro, landed on the island with a tiny band of guerrillas. So hated was the cruel, corrupt Fulgencio Batista that Castro's rapidly augmented forces were able to compel Batista to flee the country on New Year's Day, 1959. Castro immediately declared himself dictator. When he visited the United States the following April, he received ovations at the leading universities and was offered liberal foreign aid by the State Department, all in the mistaken belief that he was a democratic liberator. Disillusionment set in quickly. Influenced by Che Guevara and his Communist brother, Raul, Castro decided that it would be more profitable for Cuba to become the first Russian satellite in the West. He expropriated all banks, sugar plantations, and major industries and exiled or threw into jail all who disapproved or opposed his actions.

There were scattered bright spots for Americans, however. After years of deliberations, the long-overdue admission of Alaska and Hawaii to statehood was accomplished. Population and economic pressures could no longer be ignored, and the political climate was favorable, since it appeared that one state would vote Republican and the other Democratic. Another was the diminution of the sharp economic recession that had gripped the world for two years. There was enough improvement, at least, to spark some business optimism. The petroleum industry was the bravest when it set a new dollar high in lease-sale bids for offshore Louisiana acreages.

But money so spent was truly an act of faith in the future. In 1958 the United States demand for oil had dropped by 117 million barrels. Independent producers found themselves losing in the competition with the majors, who had the ability to step up importation of cheaper foreign oil. Income fell as vicious price wars forced costs of refined products even lower than they had been in 1953. The 50 million citizens who could "drive now and pay later" by means of newly introduced gasoline credit cards became cautious, and over 200,000 primary service stations and the one million Americans employed in petroleum marketing could only hang on. Refinery runs were slashed industry-wide, production sharply curtailed, and drilling postponed. McGee said of contract drilling in February, "We will do well to keep more than three rigs running."[1]

In a speech to the Oil Analysts Group of New York on February 27, 1958, however, he accented the positive. He pointed out that in the past three years some $60 million had been invested by Kerr-McGee. It financed a very aggressive exploration division, "probably larger in relation to the size of our company than is customary in the industry," and maintained oil-

---

[1] *Kermac News*, March 12, 1958, pp. 1–2.

exploration offices in Oklahoma City, New Orleans, Midland, Amarillo, Denver, and Calgary and mineral offices in Albuquerque, Denver, Casper, and Barstow. Kerr-McGee now held 1,637,742 net acres in eighteen states, and in Alaska, Venezuela, Panama, and Cuba, with about half of these leases having been acquired in the last year and a half.

Furthermore, McGee reminded them, at one time Kerr-McGee had owned and operated thirty-five land drilling rigs. However, a planned reduction had brought this number to twelve, all but two in the United States. Its nine offshore units continued the traditions that started with Rig 16's sinking the first well out of sight of land and the company's pioneering use of submersible Rig 40 in unprotected waters. Kerr-McGee was also the first in the oil industry to mine and process uranium, and during the last three years had started a project in potash and introduced a program in boron because of an interest in solid fuels. As for oil, the current oversupply of crude and all of its products led McGee to the conclusion that "the maintenance of a strong, healthy producing domestic industry may be at stake. Maybe the time has come when crude oil prices both within and without the country need to be related to the value of products recovered and sold in competitive markets."[2]

Meanwhile, at the Oklahoma City headquarters of Kerr-McGee there was a continuing interest in sources other than oil that could bring needed income. One promising area was asphalt. It was recognized that no one agency bought, transported, and marketed asphalt comparable to the way Triangle performed the service for gasoline and fuel oils. Consequently, on January 13, 1958, a new subsidiary, General Asphalts, Inc., was created to acquire and market heavy-oil products throughout the midcentral United States. James Kelly was placed in control, while J. B. Saunders replaced him in refining and marketing. A new terminal was opened in Omaha, Nebraska, to deliver a full line of road oils and asphalts to customer tank trucks.[3]

Canada, where an office had been opened in 1957, also seemed to offer financial opportunities. On February 6, 1958, Tennessee Gas Transmission signed a farm-out agreement whereby it assigned to Kerr-McGee part of its leases in the Sylvan Lake area in the Province of Alberta, Canada, in return for Kerr-McGee's agreement to drill no less than two test wells there at its own expense. The first well, completed in March at a cost of $113,525, found gas, but had to be shut down for lack of a market. The second well was dry. Kerr-McGee had, nevertheless, earned an interest in twenty sections. A similar arrangement was made with Canadian Superior Oil of California, Ltd., and three holes were sunk. But in this case again only one of them produced gas and oil.[4]

The island of Barbados, British West Indies, was the scene of Kerr-McGee's next search for foreign production. Barbados Gulf Oil Company held a prospecting license covering the island. Kerr-McGee signed an

[2] A copy of this speech is found in the files of the Public Relations Department.

[3] This business turned out to be too local and seasonable to be profitable, and in 1962 the company was closed. Interview with James J. Kelly, June 26, 1971.

[4] Lease Records file, "Contract 497."

agreement, effective March 7, agreeing to bear half the cost, up to $400,000, of drilling a 15,000-foot test well in return for a quarter interest in 110,000 acres. Gulf would furnish the rig, and Kerr-McGee crews would operate it. The Morgan Lewis No. 1 was spudded immediately and reached its prescribed depth the following January, when it was plugged and abandoned.[5]

At this time success seemed unusually elusive. In May, McGee continued to sound a gloomy note to the directors in his explanation for a lower net income during the first three months of the year: it was the depressed market prices for petroleum products and a drop in drilling income. The number of well starts in the Gulf had dropped nearly 60 percent, with only 30 percent of the offshore rigs active. As McGee spoke, only one Kerr-McGee rig was employed. Moreover, the company had no gas contracts for blocks 28 or 32, and, even if it had, there were no pipelines connecting the wells. In fact, the only bright spot he could see in drilling was furnished by the foreign operations in Venezuela and British Honduras.

The refineries gave McGee no comfort either. The $5.5 million upgrading of the Wynnewood plant to improve crude-oil processing and asphalt blending could not add much to profits unless capacity were increased. The Cushing refinery also needed improvements that would cost four to five million dollars merely to make it competitive. The Cleveland facility was currently a drain as equipment was being added and changes made to enable it to produce a complete line of high-quality aliphatic and aromatic naphthas.

But, as McGee had told the Oil Analysts Group, Kerr-McGee was continuing to expand and improve its distribution systems, as well as its refineries, despite the depressed economics which affected marketing. The board of directors authorized Triangle to buy Bell Oil Company of Chicago, a large fuel-oil distributing firm, for not more than $1,250,000 of Triangle's long-term notes. This move, it was hoped, would assure markets for a considerable portion of Kerr-McGee's heating-oil production. Also the pipeline purchases from Gulf and Texas Pipeline were augmented by an additional 60-mile line from Pure Oil and 126 miles from Magnolia. As a result the company became Oklahoma's second-largest buyer of crude oil, approximately 70,000 barrels per day. Kerr-McGee's own refineries took about 40,000 barrels, with the rest going to Triangle for distribution. Nor was the search for new sources of domestic oil forgotten. In June the executive committee decided to enter a new geographic territory for the first time by bidding on two tracts in the Pacific Ocean offshore Santa Barbara County, California. This was for a 4.5 percent interest in a consortium which offered a total of $18,650,000 for leases three miles out to sea in water 120 feet deep.[6]

[5] This was apparently the only attempt made. On August 15, 1960, Gulf and Kerr-McGee transferred this interest to a third party, and on January 29, 1962, the government canceled the lease for failure to drill. Lease Records, "Contract brief" (original file 488-1 destroyed); *International Oilman*, August, 1958, pp. 248–49; *Kermac News*, September, 1958, pp. 3–7.

[6] *Kermac News*, August, 1958, p. 13; *ibid.*, September, 1958, p. 12. Although oil was found on one and gas on the other, the cost of the leases and their development made the California venture marginal. Interview with George B. Parks, October 23, 1971.

The annual report, dated June 30, 1958, fulfilled the gloomy forecasts predicted as the year began. Although gross income was up $28.3 million and total assets up $20 million, expenses also rose by approximately $31 million. This brought a drop in net income of $1 million and in working capital of $3 million. Long-term debt jumped $15 million, matching the change in capital expenditures, the lion's share of which went to the pipe lines, refineries, and uranium projects (see Table 17.4).

This time Dean McGee blamed excess refinery runs for the depressed prices. Nevertheless, Kerr-McGee was in a service-station building program that might require as much as $2.5 million a year for the next five years. In the drilling division the offshore equipment was only 70 percent utilized, and the land rigs even less. Six wells were shut in on Block 28 and Block 32 in the Gulf because there was no market for the gas. As a result the company was looking abroad for contracts, with prospects in Argentina, Brazil, the Persian Gulf, Venezuela, Canada, and Panama.

Mining operations had a bright spot in Shirley Basin, Wyoming, where uranium worth an estimated $20 million had been found, and plans were afoot to produce it. The helium project, on which some $155,866 had already been spent, was successfully being drilled. Searches for boron in California and Arizona were so far unsuccessful, however. In fact, the boron exploration had been curtailed because of the poor economic conditions.

There were other heartening events in drilling, however. The first well drilled in Venezuela found oil, a discovery was made in Canada, and the Rolff Lake Field was established in the Wind River Basin of Wyoming. For the first time the increased gas output provided approximately half of the company's revenue, and the sale of branded gasoline jumped 22.9 percent. At Ambrosia Lake some 75,000 tons of uranium ore were stockpiled, awaiting the imminent completion of the mill there, and at Shiprock the operations were continuing to show profit.[7]

But the oil picture was not good: Kerr-McGee had drilled a mere 67 wells during the fiscal year, and only 69 percent were producers. Since the primary business of the company was the production of oil and gas, a look at the well count gives a good historical barometer of progress. (Table 17.1).[8] Of these totals there were 440.38 net oil wells, 137 net gas, and 24.89 net gas-condensate, while the dry-hole total was 56.

Kerr-McGee and its subsidiary Kermac Drilling had a combined total of twenty-three rigs available during the fiscal year 1958. Ninety-seven wells were completed, while ten were still in progress, with eleven completions and four unfinished by Kermac's four rigs (see Fig. 4). The nineteen domestic units sank eighteen wells, including seven offshore Louisiana. Among the contract wells, twenty-nine were completed offshore Louisiana and Texas.

---

[7] Kerr-McGee Oil Industries, Inc., *Annual Report, 1958*. See also Securities and Exchange Commission, "Form 10-K Annual Report for Fiscal Year Ended June 30, 1958," and *Oil Record, 1958*, pp. 1120–28.

[8] Production Department file, "Individual Well Count as of July 1, 1958."

Table 17.1. Well Count, July 1, 1958

Location	Gross Wells			Net Wells	Dry Holes
	Oil	Gas	Gas Condensate		
Texas	499	120	346	310.40	13
Oklahoma	275	55	0	168.97	18
Arkansas	59	0	0	50.92	0
Cuba	13	0	0	3.25	0
Louisiana	30	8	37	37.21	6
				(13 shut-in)	
Indiana	7	0	0	7.00	0
New Mexico	7	0	0	4.00	2
Wyoming	7	0	18	3.41	4
Kansas	6	0	0	3.00	3
Nebraska	6	0	0	1.12	2
North Dakota	1	0	0	.50	2
Arizona	0	6	0	4.30	0
Colorado	0	5	0	3.81	2
Utah	0	0	0	0	1
South Dakota	0	0	0	0	1
Canada	0	0	0	0	1
Venezuela	0	0	0	0	1

Rig utilization was not as bad as McGee had earlier feared, for land utilization reached 64 percent and offshore, 68 (see Table 17.3).[9]

Perhaps this dreary news was offset by the July, 1958, edition of *Fortune*. After admitting that Kerr-McGee had been "mistakenly omitted" from the previous year's report, the editors of the magazine for the first time listed Kerr-McGee Oil Industries, Inc., in its prestigious list of "The 500 Largest Industrial Corporations" in the United States. The *Fortune* 500 rankings placed the company thus: sales, 342; assets, 206; net profit, 298; return on invested capital, 257; and profits as percentage of sales, 195.[10]

The continuing emphasis on foreign drilling was evident. On July 23, 1958, an agreement was signed with a Brazilian concern, Refinaria E Exploracao De Petroleo Uniao S.A., to apply jointly for a concession from the Bolivian government to explore and develop lands located in the "Brazilian Area B in Bolivia." If the grant were obtained, then Kerr-McGee would perform the drilling with Uniao paying all expenses, plus 10 percent overhead, and an overriding royalty interest. The period of the arrangement was for three to ten years.[11]

Even more important, other Latin American contracts helped offset the

[9] Transworld Drilling file, "Rig Operations July, 1956, thru June, 1961," and Dean McGee personal file, "KM Location and Availability of Rigs [by months]."

[10] July, 1958, pp. 131–42.

[11] Lease Records files, "Contract 516-1" and "Contract 516-5."

drilling decline in the United States. A major one was signed on October 10, with a Canadian corporation, L. R. Oil Development, Ltd., for five rigs and crews to work five years in developing oil-and-gas reserves in the Mendoza area of Argentina. Kerr-McGee received all transportation costs, a daily rate per unit, and a footage incentive. Then, on October 31, Phillips Petroleum hired the idle rig in British Honduras to work one scheduled well and possibly two more. This also brought a daily rate and two dollars per foot of hole.[12]

New salaries for the officers were set in November by the executive committee. McGee received $123,112; R. S. Kerr, $40,000; T. M. Kerr, $46,236; F. C. Love, $60,000; J. B. Saunders, $57,000; and J. J. Kelly, $27,500. These raises presaged management's relatively cheerful end-of-the-year report: three more wells had been brought in on Block 32, interest acquired in four additional wells in Venezuela, and the Bolivian concession approved. In anticipation of future foreign contracts, a Bahaman corporation, the Transworld Drilling Company Limited, had been established. In Canada two small producing wells and one dry hole made prospects there less attractive, and drilling was suspended. In Panama the first hole had been abandoned at 9,000 feet, while a second well, in the water, was down to 6,000 feet. If tests on it were also poor, the entire project would be scrapped.

Results were also mixed elsewhere in the company. The retail division boasted seventy-four new service stations in its new expansion program, and plans called for the addition of seventy-five a year. In mining, the completed potash shaft permitted 375 tons to be mined for laboratory testing, and the mineral rights were expanded by acquisition of additional acreages. By June 30, 1959, a total of $1,429,534.19 was spent on this venture (over $614,000 in 1958), and a patent had been obtained to cover Kerr-McGee's process. There was reason for caution, however, for potash prices were unstable.[13]

Boron exploration was canceled in Arizona and California, but lithium and beryllium leases were acquired in North Carolina. At Ambrosia Lake, New Mexico, the new uranium mill went on stream in November and surpassed expectations, with two shafts in operation and three more under construction. Work there, however, was behind schedule. According to McGee, it had become a "real tough operation," and at "one time it appeared we just might not develop this property because we feared that maybe it was just too tough for any mining system known."

The problem was the depth of the uranium mines, which went below the water table of the formation. Constantly surrounded by water at the working level, the trackless equipment bogged down. Worse yet, the large spaces, which were necessary to operate the mine, caved in from the softening effect

---

[12] Transworld Drilling files, "Argentina—Cities Service" and "Phillips—British Honduras, Rig 50"; Lease Records file, "Contract Brief—Panama." Most of the acreage in Panama was surrendered in November, 1960, and the Phillips contract was canceled in October, 1959.

[13] By June, Kerr-McGee was expressing concern over the price of potash, and this was an item on the agenda of the directors' meeting of FCRDC on July 12, 1958. Dean McGee personal file, "Farm Chemicals Resources Development Corporation."

A slusher gathering loose ore eight hundred feet below ground in a uranium mine at Ambrosia Lake, New Mexico.

Loading uranium ore at Ambrosia Lake for shipment to the processing plant near Grants, New Mexico.

of the water, and casualties began occurring. Some improvement came when the company installed mine cars on a rail track, similar to those used in mining the uranium at Shiprock. The final solution, however, was to drill from beneath the ore body and drain the water out that way, for the sandstone was fairly stable when dry. Then the ore could be mined at an upward angle, with the haulage area also serving as a trackway and drain.

But another problem, and a blow to uranium producers in general, occurred on November 24, 1958, when the AEC announced that it would not contract for new reserves after that date. Many companies immediately gave up the search. Kerr-McGee, however, in McGee's words, "did not terminate our minerals exploration program but instead diverted a part of our exploration efforts from uranium to other minerals."[14]

[14] Interview with Marion Bolton, August 27, 1973; Dean McGee, "Speech to New York Society of Security Analysts, Inc., January 19, 1961," in Public Relations file. The AEC action was later to create some controversy over the Shirley Basin deposit. For a study of labor relations at Shiprock see Arch Napier and Tom Sasaki, "The Navajo in the Machine Age," *New Mexico Business*, July, 1958.

Kerr-McGee's thirty-first year opened on a happier note. It was the first year of occupancy of the enlarged and renovated Kerr-McGee building. This complex housed all the central offices of the company, and for the first time in four years all the headquarters personnel were under one roof. The directors also received a report on the outstanding performance of the Kermac Nuclear mill, which encouraged hopes for additional revenue from that source. The Pinta Dome helium field had been fairly well defined, and its reserves were estimated to be 6 billion cubic feet of gas.

A study of the refineries showed that the Wynnewood plant should be enlarged to run 28,000 barrels per day, and $1.4 million was set as the cost. The report also recommended the sale of Deep Rock's old crude-oil unit and that Triangle should negotiate to buy Cotton Valley Solvents, Inc., and Coast Oil and Butane Company for not more than $1,125,000. The Cotton Valley acquisition would enhance Kerr-McGee's position as a supplier of industrial naphthas and solvents, since the Shreveport, Louisiana, firm had a refinery that specialized in these products, and the Kerr-McGee refinery at Cleveland, Oklahoma was almost ready for similar production.

There was also expansion in marketing. After the purchase of eighteen filling stations from H. A. Roberts, two new divisions, Knox Stations, Inc., and Rob-Lon Stations, Inc., were organized to manage the outlets that did not handle the Deep Rock brand of products. While gains in volume of branded sales were noted, prices were lower than anticipated.

The directors also learned in January, 1959, that all the submersible rigs were busy or under contract, although the deeper depths in the Gulf had idled most of the tender-types, four of them for a year. The first California well offshore Santa Barbara had been dry, but the company was drilling a 16,000-foot test well in Block 28 in the Gulf plus wells at Cameron and Jeanerette, Louisiana.

It was the foreign operations that enhanced the future. Rig 50 was in British Honduras for Phillips, Rig 14 was in Guatemala for Shell, two tender types were in Venezuela, and five rigs were in Argentina. A fifth well was spudded at Lake Maracaibo, and the Barbados well was down to 15,000 feet. Although the poor showing in Panama forced abandonment of these wells, Kerr-McGee still retained large holdings in that country.

On January 29, 1959, Kerr-McGee and Petroleum Investments (Overseas) Limited signed a drilling contract for a well in Guatemala. But the major coup came in Argentina, where the 1958 five-year-five-rig deal was already in operation. This time an agreement was signed directly with the Argentine state oil agency, Yacimientos Petroliferos Fiscales (YPF), to sink 500 wells, averaging 5,000 feet, in the Comodoro Rivadavia area of that nation. This was to be done on a per meter rate of drilling and an hourly rate for completion operations. Three more rigs were sent to Argentina to drill over a four-year period. The first shipment of equipment left the United States only hours ahead of a strike that would have made it impossible to meet the contract deadline. The first well was spudded on November 20, and by the end of the year eight rigs were operating on both of the projects in Argentina, and five wells had been completed at an average depth of 4,700 feet.[15]

Other events of 1959 underscored the far-flung interests of Kerr-McGee. The expanding activities in Latin America, and especially in Argentina, created the need for additional corporate structures. In May it was decided that the financing for the equipment for Argentina would be through a new Bahaman corporation, Amahab, Limited, which in turn would lease to Transworld Drilling Company, Limited. In August still another company, Kerr-McGee, Limited, was formed for general foreign work. Cuba, however, presented a problem. By June of that year Kerr-McGee had found it impossible to take out of Cuba its share of returns from the wells there. A Cuban law of November 23 made it doubly clear that the end of this venture was in sight, for Castro was beginning his confiscation of foreign investments. This did not deter the company from seeking new fields, as seen in its inquiry about the international laws relative to the North Sea, in particular about the extent of each nation's jurisdiction. This move foreshadowed events twenty years away.[16]

Kerr-McGee faced both good and bad news on the domestic scene. It shared some of the reflected glory when *Fortune* profiled Senator Kerr in March, 1959. Then in April the firm of Shearson, Hammill & Company, of New York City, evaluated the company thus:

. . . through the brilliant and aggressive leadership of Senator Robert S. Kerr . . . and Dean A. McGee . . . Kerr-McGee has become an exceptionally well diversified organization and a recognized leader in contract drilling, uranium development, and in seismic exploration of the Gulf Coast Tidelands. The engineering and geology staff is ranked among the most capable in the industry and the top officers of the company are now considered well-seasoned at a good depth.

Refining and distributing capabilities got a boost with the opening of a products pipeline linking the company's three refineries at Cushing, Wynnewood, and Cleveland, Oklahoma. Semirefined or finished materials could then be moved between any of the plants. In addition, Triangle's Cotton Valley Solvents refinery at Cotton Valley, Louisiana, joined the Cleveland plant in the production of aliphatic naphthas. But this achievement was somewhat tempered by an announcement in June that Kerr-McGee would reduce crude-oil purchases for the next three months by an average of 14,000 barrels a day because of a weak market and excess stocks. This was on top of the 12 percent cut already made since the beginning of the year.[17]

[15] Lease Records file, "Contract 587-5" covers Guatemala. For Argentina see "Argentine-American Cooperation Works for Kermac," *World Petroleum*, July, 1960, pp. 77ff.; *Daily Oklahoman*, April 23 and 26, 1959; *Wall Street Journal*, September 1, 1959.

[16] Breene M. Kerr to Don McBride, February 9, 1959, in Robert S. Kerr Collection, Box 560, folder #10, in Western History Collections, University of Oklahoma; Lease Records file, "Contract 205." By Resolution 1827, dated January 26, 1960, Kerr-McGee's partners' rights were confiscated, and in December the Cuban properties were written off as a loss of about $120,000.

[17] Daniel Seligman, "Senator Bob Kerr, the Oklahoma Gusher," *Fortune*, March, 1959, pp. 136–38, 179–88; Shearson, Hammill & Co., "An Analysis of Kerr-McGee Oil Industries, Inc., and Its Common Stock, April, 1959"; *Kermac News*, July, 1959, and *Daily Oklahoman*, May 16, 1959; *Wall Street Journal*, June 12, 1959.

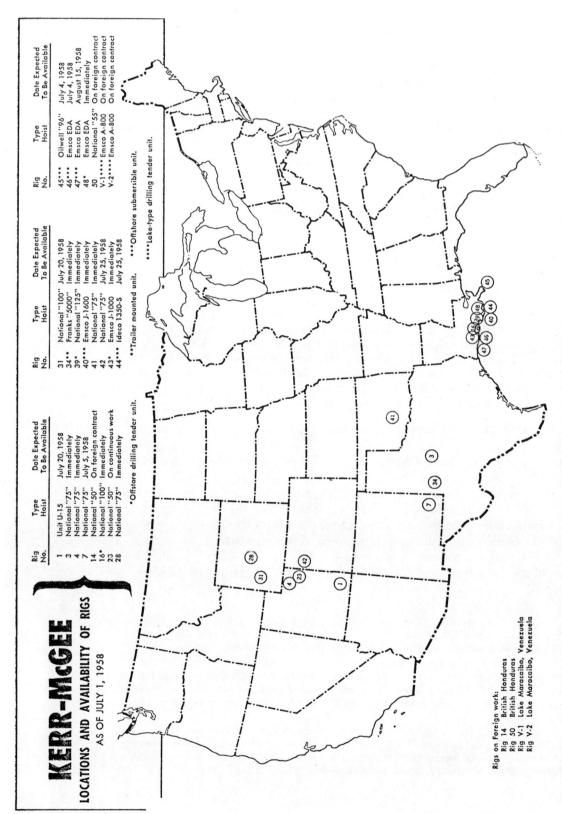

KERR-McGEE
LOCATIONS AND AVAILABILITY OF RIGS
AS OF JULY 1, 1958

Rig No.	Type Hoist	Date Expected To Be Available
1	Unit U-15	July 20, 1958
3	National "75"	Immediately
4	National "75"	Immediately
7	National "75"	July 5, 1958
14*	National "50"	On foreign contract
16*	National "100"	Immediately
23	National "50"	On continuous work
28	National "75"	Immediately

Rig No.	Type Hoist	Date Expected To Be Available
31	National "100"	July 20, 1958
34**	Franks "5000"	Immediately
39*	National "125"	Immediately
40***	Emsco J-1600	Immediately
41	National "75"	Immediately
42	National "75"	July 25, 1958
43*	Emsco J-1000	Immediately
44***	Ideco 1350-S	July 25, 1958

Rig No.	Type Hoist	Date Expected To Be Available
45***	Oilwell "96"	July 4, 1958
46***	Emsco EDA	July 4, 1958
47***	Emsco EDA	August 15, 1958
48*	Emsco EDA	Immediately
50	National "55"	On foreign contract
V-1****	Emsco A-800	On foreign contract
V-2****	Emsco A-800	On foreign contract

*Offshore drilling tender unit.
**Trailer mounted unit.
***Offshore submersible unit.
****Lake-type drilling tender unit.

Rigs on Foreign work:
Rig 14   British Honduras
Rig 50   British Honduras
Rig V-1   Lake Maracaibo, Venezuela
Rig V-2   Lake Maracaibo, Venezuela

Fig. 17.1. Locations and availability of rigs, 1958. From the private files of Dean McGee.

The annual report of June 30, 1959, showed that, although the company's position in volume sales of refined products had been maintained, product prices had been depressed. But refined products still contributed 66 percent of the gross income. The comparative production records show a steady, if slight, increase (Table 17.2).

Uranium, which received almost half of the over-all capital expenditures, showed the greatest increase, although full production was not due until 1960. The interests in four additional natural-gasoline plants showed up in the financial returns also.[18]

The reserves of oil and gas increased substantially during the year, largely through the drilling in Block 28, offshore Louisiana, and by the discovery and development of large reserves of oil underlying two of the 25,000-acre Venezuelan concessions in which Kerr-McGee owned an interest. The drilling department showed slight gains in all its operations, except for contract work (Table 17.3).

Of its completions, 46 were outside the United States, but Kerr-McGee's foreign count of net wells was still insignificant. Out of a total of 692.46 wells, Cuba had 13 (3.25 net); Canada, 2 (2.0); and Venezuela, 13 (0.7). The ten rigs of Kermac Drilling of Venezuela were involved in 24 wells in Argentina, 17 in Venezuela, 3 in British Honduras for Gulf, and 1 in Guatemala. Transworld Drilling began a single well in British Honduras for Phillips, acting as a competitor to its sister subsidiary.

The completed wells were in Venezuela, Canada, Oklahoma, Texas, Louisiana, Kansas, Arkansas, and Wyoming. Dry holes occurred in all of these but Arkansas and Wyoming, as well as in Colorado, California, North Dakota, Arizona, and Panama. The nine Gulf Coast rigs had a utilization of 44 percent; the four in the Rocky Mountain division, 69 percent; and the three in Oklahoma-Texas, only 43 percent. Six of the parent company's wells were offshore, and the largest concentration of contract work was in Utah with 27 spuds, followed by Louisiana with 18. One of these contracts was a location first: a well drilled offshore Boca Grande Key in Florida for Gulf Oil.[19]

The over-all financial picture improved, except for a drop in capital expenditures, as seen in the reports for the fiscal years ending June 30 (Table 17.4).

The increase in common-stock equity enabled the directors to discuss a stock split in November. But the decision was postponed for three to six months (see Table 17.5).

The worst news to the refining and marketing division came on August 24,

---

[18] Kerr-McGee Oil Industries, Inc., *Annual Report for the Fiscal Year Ended June 30, 1959*. See also *Oil Record, 1959*, pp. 1083–92; Securities and Exchange Commission, "Form 10-K Annual Report for Fiscal Year Ended June 30, 1959," "Past Effective Amendment No. 3 to Form S-1 Registration Statement, June 15, 1959," and "Past Effective Amendment No. 4 . . . November 23, 1959."

[19] Transworld Drilling file, "Rig Operations July, 1956, thru June, 1961," and Production Department file, "Annual Well Count as of July 1, 1959." For Florida see Lease Records file, "Contract #598."

Table 17.2. Production Record, 1958–59

	1958	1959
Production		
Crude oil produced (net barrels)	1,864,637	1,954,002
Natural-gas sales (millions of cubic feet)	43,832	49,789
Oil-and-gas leases (net acres)	1,640,237	1,595,767
Gas processing		
Gas liquids produced (net barrels)	1,262,078	1,320,142
Refining		
Crude oil processed (barrels)	13,676,550	15,513,306
Minerals		
Ore mined (tons)	54,083	265,126
Ore milled (tons)	132,115	529,260
U_3O_8 concentrate sold (lbs.)	594,251	2,318,525

Table 17.3. Drilling and Exploration Operations, 1958–59

	1958	1959
Feet drilled	807,408	879,628
Total wells/wells completed	111/97	126/107
Domestic interest	18	18
Rigs (average)	23	31
Domestic wells	76	62

1959, at 10:30 in the evening. In Oklahoma City a thirteen-year-old boy, who had just been released from a hospital after mental observation, admitted that a fire at Cato Oil & Grease was one of four he had started that night. A total of 225 firefighters and twenty pieces of equipment were used in what was described as "one of the worst [fires] in recent years." By the time the ashes had cooled, two firemen had been injured, a million-dollar loss incurred, and Cato was leveled to the ground. Only three grease kettles were not completely destroyed. An entire new plant had to be built, an office set up without any records, and a sales force kept busy with nothing to sell. The former plant and all its operations had to be reconstructed on paper to meet insurance claims and to provide a set of records. It is not surprising that 1959 was the only year in Cato's history in which it did not show a profit.[20] But it can safely be assumed that this time President Huffman got some attention from headquarters.

Table 17.4. Financial Highlights, 1958–59

	1958	1959
Gross income	$162,784,739	$174,267,477
Net income	5,378,973	5,873,330
Total assets	167,471,864	188,223,055
Cash flow from earnings	15,802,645	20,810,348
Working capital	34,717,792	33,680,666
Properties (net)	91,951,239	104,749,400
Capital expenditures	34,656,764	29,766,769
Long-term debt	60,708,479	68,914,110
Cash dividends	2,661,411	2,668,159
Stockholders' equity	75,098,784	78,785,534
Total taxes paid	1,457,198	2,969,805
Number of employees	2,981	3,411

Table 17.5. Common-Stock Highlights, 1958–59

	1958	1959
Equity per share	24.48	25.85
Earnings per share	$1.94	$2.13
Cash dividends per share	$0.80	$0.80
Average yield	1.6	1.6
Number of shares outstanding	2,378,575	2,395,611
Number of stockholders for calendar year	5,736	5,767
New York Stock Exchange		
High	60 1/4	70 3/8
Low	38	44 7/8
Price-earnings ratio		
High	30.99	33.03
Low	19.58	21.06

And there were other points of concern. After a great deal of expense and trouble Pinta Dome helium was about ready to go. The field had been outlined and set up as a multiunit operation of nine wells. Kerr-McGee and its partners controlled six of the wells and were in the process of discussing a plant to separate the helium from the gas. But a profitable market had yet to be found to buy the results of all this work.

Ironically, Shiprock uranium also faced potential marketing problems. In November, 1958, the AEC had canceled its guaranteed market and price.

[20] *Daily Oklahoman*, August 25 and 26, 1959; interviews with Charles C. Huffman, July 1, 1971, and Ralph Jenks, August 17, 1972.

By this time the federal government had invested over $19 billion in atomic energy, and thirty private companies were engaged in making concentrate from the 82.5 million tons of reserves. Other companies decided to close down their uranium operations. Kerr-McGee, however, elected to ride out the situation for the time being, since its Shiprock contract with the AEC did not expire until October 31, 1959. Senator Clinton Anderson of New Mexico, a partner of Kerr's in the Pinta Dome helium project, assisted in the successful fight that gained renewal until June 30, 1965, by pointing out the bad effects closing the mine and mill would have on the Navajos. Of the 179 employees, 125 were Navajos, and the tribal royalties averaged $17,000 a month, a sum that contributed greatly to the Navajos' well-being.[21]

Potash also caused trouble. In August, Kerr-McGee and partners discussed the type and size of the potash pilot plant. By December, however, Phillips Petroleum had become disenchanted and suggested that the operation be stretched over several years to see what happened in Canadian potash and in the fertilizer field. But a concrete-lined circular shaft fifteen feet in diameter had been completed down to the orebody at 1,695 feet, and large ore samples were being obtained to develop an efficient method of processing the ore. So the project was allowed to continue.[22]

By the end of the year the service-station program was making good progress. Two acquisitions were responsible: Peoples Oil Company, with fifty-four stations in the mid-South, and a one-half interest in Mileage Mart, Inc., with twenty-two stations in Illinois. To manage these, two more firms, Peoples Service Stations and Green Hills Oil Company, were organized, joining the two earlier subsidiaries established to handle the outlets that did not carry the Deep Rock brand.

Part of the logic for not having all the stations under one name was to avoid overt competition with corporations that were good customers for other Kerr-McGee products and services. Also, some of these outlets sold lower-priced goods, and a concerted effort was under way to upgrade the Deep Rock stations. In a program designed to increase public acceptance, the company began a training course for service-station dealers aimed at giving "high-quality driveway service." New plastic credit cards were mailed to all customers as the first step toward electronic billing of credit-card accounts, as well as to promote the sale of gasoline. These efforts must have had some effect, for in a 1960 *Kermac News* story a total of 1,200 service stations were listed under company management. Sales of Deep Rock gasoline increased by 4 percent, while the number of stations marketing Deep Rock products rose 11.1 percent.[23] Perhaps the end of the recession was in sight. At least the next year could not be much worse.

[21] For helium see Lease Records files, "Project 382 (Legal #2)," and "Project 382 (Corres.)"; Dean A. McGee, "Atomic Energy and Exotic Fuels," speech before Independent Petroleum Association of America, Phoenix, May 3, 1959; *Daily Oklahoman*, August 2, 1959.

[22] Dean McGee personal file, "Farm Chemical Resources Development Corporation."

[23] *Kermac News*, June, 1960.

Chapter 18

Recovery
1960–1961

The guarded optimism present at the end of 1959 proved justified on a limited scale during the next two years. Russia's downing of Gary Powers' U-2 spy plane just as Eisenhower and Khrushchev prepared to meet in a summit conference was a sobering note on the international scene. But on the domestic front, while inflation continued to be a problem, the unemployment rate slowly turned downward, partly in reaction to 1960 election promises of "new beginnings." Politics held the center stage much of the year as the youthful John F. Kennedy made his bid for the presidency against Vice-President Richard M. Nixon.

Oklahoma supported Nixon, and it was thought that Kerr might be vulnerable in his bid for reelection to the Senate. As in the past, his position as chairman of the board of Kerr-McGee meant that the company was an issue to be used by his opponents. B. Hayden Crawford, the Republican nominee, campaigned almost exclusively on the charge that Kerr used his Washington office to promote sales of Kerr-McGee helium and uranium to the federal government. But even the Republican-oriented *Tulsa Tribune* dismissed this as silly. Kerr was undoubtedly hurt more by his stalwart support of Kennedy, who lost in Oklahoma. But he won his Senate seat by 89,000 votes.[1]

The election of the charismatic young president and a general state of prosperity filled most Americans with a sense of tranquility. But it soon appeared obvious that most of the United States' enemies were determined

---

[1] Anne H. Morgan, *Robert S. Kerr: The Senate Years* (Norman, 1977), pp. 92–93.

to test Kennedy's inexperience in foreign affairs, and bad news poured in from abroad. Cuba was so openly hostile that on January 3, 1961, the United States formally severed diplomatic relations. On April 17, Cuban exiles, with Kennedy's backing, attempted the ill-fated Bay of Pigs invasion. In Europe, East Germany constructed the Berlin Wall, a stark warning to its citizens not to try to escape to freedom. In Africa, United Nations Secretary General Dag Hammarskjöld was killed in a mysterious plane crash while on a peace mission. The world wondered what was next.

For the petroleum industry, however, 1960 and 1961 were an improvement. Drilling activity went up, lube prices were higher, and the refining situation stabilized. The chief complaints came from producers that gasoline prices were too low and from retailers that they were unable to prevent the spasmodic price wars that brought even lower returns.

Kerr-McGee faced 1960 in an expansionist mood. A new foreign operations department was created, and on January 12 papers were signed to borrow $10 million from Chicago and New York sources to allow the company to make its largest bid ever in the Louisiana offshore lease sales. The stock split was again discussed, and once more the directors deferred it. Instead, it was decided to pay an extra 20 cents on common (a total of 40 cents) for each of the last two quarters and then to raise the quarterly dividend to thirty cents.

The February lease bids were a success as far as the company was concerned. It acquired a 64.5 percent interest in 20,000 acres in the Ship Shoal area at a net cost of $6,159,355. This acreage, which was favorably located on two large salt domes, included what was to become the important Block 214. Acquired about the same time, but of less future importance, were inland leases on 85,000 acres in the Appalachian region, believed to have a large gas potential, and a 60 percent interest in Tennessee Transmission Company's holdings in the Sylvan Lake, Canada, gas field.

Of historical note was Kerr-McGee's early desire to prospect the Atlantic coast. In February, Derwood Amonett, chief geophysicist, approached the director of the United States Geological Survey concerning the possibility of doing a marine seismic survey off the eastern coast between Cape Charles, Virginia, and Long Island, New York. The search was to be outside the three-mile limit but inside the 150-foot water-depth contour. In March a formal request was made, and a Washington attorney was hired to process it. When it became evident that the petition would have to have approvals by the various states involved, as well as the Department of Defense, the Coast Guard, and the Department of Wild Life and Fisheries, the project apparently was quietly shelved.[2]

In May the directors were told of the loss from a tornado of the new gasoline plant at Lafoon (near Stroud, Oklahoma). Refining and marketing were also having problems because of too-low product prices and too-high costs for crude. This meant that the refinery runs would probably be cut

[2] Robert S. Kerr Collection, Box 560, folder 2, Western History Collections, University of Oklahoma.

from 40,000 barrels per day to 36,000. This information probably explains
why management was instructed to consider and report back to the directors on a query concerning its interest in selling the refining and marketing system. The dissatisfaction with these areas, however, did not preclude a discussion concerning the construction of a $1 million helium extraction plant to process 2.5 million cubic feet of gas per day. It was believed that there were sufficient reserves to run such a plant for ten or twelve years.

Despite these problems the June 30 annual report was the best in the company's history. Both net income and earnings per common share reached all-time highs. Several developments were credited for this: a record volume of natural gas was matched by the record value of $8,217,934; Kermac Nuclear Fuels Corporation's uranium mill showed profit and by April had processed in excess of the contract rate of 110,000 tons per month; contract drilling improved considerably because of the foreign operations and the increased activity in the Gulf of Mexico. Still to show up in the profit column were the valuable reserves acquired by the company's oil-and-gas exploration of nonhydrocarbon natural resources. The company felt that these diversification moves broadened and enhanced the earning base.

Specifically, the balance sheet showed a rise in gross income of almost $24 million and total assets by some $15 million. The decline in capital expenditures accompanied the period of poor earnings from the previous year, as did the increase in long-term debt, but the latter also marked investments in new properties that promised future returns (see Table 18.4). Common stock earned two extra dividends between the first of the year and the annual report, bringing the fiscal-year total to $1.20. With these went the promise to review the dividend rates again in 1961, if net earnings warranted it.[3]

The exploration and development division tabulated the ratio of the gross acres of oil-and-gas leases, options, and operating rights to the net acreage as 2,665,355/1,566,679, but the quality of the discoveries made up for this decrease from 1959. These leases were spread out over the United States, Canada, Barbados, Panama, Venezuela, and Cuba. One natural-gas discovery was made in Canada. The most important new area was Ship Shoal in the Gulf, and the most important discoveries were in Block 125 offshore Louisiana, where Kerr-McGee owned 75 percent of the working interest in the well and 2,500-acre lease on which it was located.

Extension wells added thirteen producers in Lake Maracaibo and six in the Monagas field. Other significant extensions were gas completions at Sylvan Lake and nine part-interest gas wells in Beaver County, Oklahoma. The Santa Barbara, California, leases and those in Bolivia were also pursued, and the emphasis on areas with large gas potential continued to be obvious. Likewise, there were coal reserves in Oklahoma and Arkansas, lithium in North Carolina, and boron in California. Cato marketed some five hundred different types of products, and General Asphalts sold fuels in twelve states and asphalt in seventeen.

---

[3] Kerr-McGee Oil Industries, Inc., *Annual 1960 Report*.

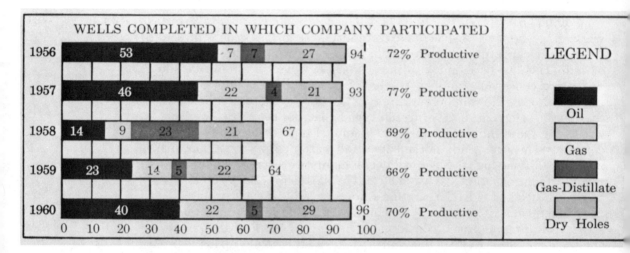

Fig. 18.1. Wells completed in which the company participated, 1956–60.
From Kerr-McGee Oil Industries, Inc., *1960 Annual Report*.

Table 18.1. Growth of the Company's Production Operation, 1956–60

	1956	1957	1958	1959	1960
Number of productive leases	495	523	542	554	583
Number of gross wells	1,195	1,258	1,266	1,304	1,436
Value of oil, distillate and gas produced					
To the company's interest	$6,618,926	$ 8,706,054	$10,344,016	$12,713,511	$14,806,339
Applied to oil payments sold	2,061,210	1,428,007	....	....	....
Total	$8,680,136	$10,134,061	$10,344,016	$12,713,511	$14,806,339
Volumes produced					
Barrels of oil and distillate produced					
To the company's interest	1,553,108	1,886,072	1,864,637	1,954,002	2,619,965
Applied to oil payments sold	432,805	296,453	....	....	....
	1,985,913	2,182,525	1,864,637	1,954,002	2,619,965
Company's net interest in natural-gas liquids produced	1,217,551	1,204,638	1,265,322	1,320,718	1,419,476
Total	3,203,464	3,387,163	3,129,959	3,274,720	4,039,441
Mcf of gas produced					
To the company's interest	29,887,534	34,004,959	43,832,129	49,788,910	53,916,291
Applied to oil payments sold	8,195,842	5,317,307	....	....	....
Total	38,083,376	39,322,266	43,832,129	49,788,910	53,916,291

Foreign drilling picked up the slack caused by the two years of domestic recession, bringing the total beyond the record 1957 figure. Kermac of Venezuela spudded seventy-eight wells in Argentina, two in Guatemala, and thirteen in Venezuela. Transworld, Ltd., worked on seventy-three in Argentina and two in British Honduras. Later in the year contracts were signed between Kermac Drilling and Guatemalan Atlantic Corporation for deepening one well and possibly drilling another. This was on the basis of a daily rental and footage charge. Finally, after extensive exploration, drilling began in Bolivia under the Uniao agreement by which Kerr-McGee received a percentage of the oil produced.[4] This was followed by contracts with Phillips and with Sun Oil for wells in Venezuela.

Although drilling made an over-all comeback, domestic land contract drilling reached a new low. Of the eighty-six domestic wells, seventeen were for the parent company and, among the contract wells, thirty-three were in Louisiana (chiefly for Continental and Gulf Oil), and twenty-six in Utah (for Standard of California). Fifteen rigs were in the United States (eight in the Gulf) with a 67 percent utilization. The four rigs in the Rocky Mountain division had a 71 percent rate of use, and the three in Texas and Oklahoma had only a 24 percent rate.[5]

In a special report to the employees *Kermac News* added more specifics to the annual report. Kerr-McGee owned and operated three thousand miles of pipeline and almost twelve hundred retail service stations. For the first time the income from natural gas was greater than that from crude oil, with Block 28, Ship Shoal, being the largest reserve. To explore these Gulf leases, Kerr-McGee owned five submersible units and three platform-tender types, with rigs 46 and 47 weighing about 6,500 tons and standing twenty-five stories tall. On the other hand, the production department operated 818 wells, 507 oil and 311 gas. More than 300 of these were in the Panhandle area of Texas and Oklahoma, and they produced about half of the company's total gas and oil. Elsewhere the firm had a small amount of oil production in Wyoming and North Dakota, two other small gas fields in the Gulf, and eight on shore in southern Louisiana.[6]

One of the domestic wells which Kerr-McGee drilled for its own interest provided an interesting story. On February 25, 1960, a well spudded on Block 125, East Cameron, was essentially a "free" well. This meant that the lease was a farm-out from another company and enough dry-hole money had been subscribed by interested parties to pay the cost of drilling. Since Kerr-McGee's crew was under a time limit, the location was not double-checked as usual. Drilling began, and when the well reached 14,006 feet, seismic tests were taken. They showed that the hole was not where it was supposed to be but was almost a mile off target. The surveyor had missed the

---

[4] Lease Records files, "Contract 587-7" and "Contract 516-2."

[5] Transworld Drilling file, "Rig Operations July, 1956, thru June, 1961"; Drilling Department file, "Annual Report, 1960"; Production Department file, "Annual Well Count as of July 1, 1960."

[6] *Kermac News*, June, 1960; see also Securities and Exchange Commission, "Form 10-K Annual Report for Fiscal Year Ended June 30, 1960."

marker buoy. The dry-hole backers refused to pay, for they claimed that the hole was not drilled where they had been told it would be. Since no production was found, Kerr-McGee did not even have a well. It was a million-dollar mistake. George Parks said: "McGee should have run us all off. There wasn't any way to sue the surveyor; he didn't have anything."

McGee did not explode but showed "terrific self control." C. M. Van Zandt recalled that it was a doubly "black day" for they also learned that some of their higher bids for offshore leases had been rejected.[7]

Even before this time McGee had become very conscious of the role of management. When the company was a small, close-knit group, there were virtually no controls and no written procedures. Management operated the business on the basis of verbal understandings and through its intimate knowledge of all the firm's activities and its people. Selection of procedures and controls was considered part of the managers' administrative responsibilities. But as the company grew, the problem became one of creating systems to provide the necessary information and direction, while at the same time retaining individual creativeness, incentive, and accountability—a goal that McGee described as "a difficult tightrope to walk."

His solution began with himself. As "those who fail to heed the changing patterns of business will eventually be absorbed by those who do," his responsibility was the profitability and development of the company. It was his task to establish policies and procedures to realize these objectives and to see that they were carried out. He had to "make sure that the Company's activities result in the corporate image that reflects the business philosophy of the Board of Directors."

Consequently he introduced a system of checks and balances: (1) no individual or unit would be in complete control of all phases of a transaction; (2) each successive level of management had a limit on its ability to authorize expenditures; (3) capital expenditures were the responsibility of executive management, who had to direct these funds into projects of maximum profit potential; (4) all applications for expenditures had to carry cost justification, pay-out data, and a summary of benefits expected.

At the top of the hierarchy was the executive committee. Bylaws adopted in February, 1960, designated membership to be five or more directors. Next in line was the principal operating group: the management committee. It was composed of representatives from the five main divisions of the company—oil and gas; marketing subsidiaries; minerals; marketing, pipeline, and refining; and corporate. It met twice a week with the president and the executive vice-president to coordinate operations and consider plans. Each division held a monthly meeting, which was attended by members of the management committee. At the middle of every month each

---

[7] Interview with George B. Parks, October 23, 1971, and C. M. Van Zandt to author, July 15, 1976. Location errors also occurred on land. R. E. Anderson (interview on May 3, 1971) recalls a case in the Texas Panhandle when the driller mistook the section-line marker for a drilling-site locator, creating an exception to the spacing rules. Fortunately the Texas Railroad Commission allowed the well to remain.

department head reported in writing to his respective supervisor, who in turn reported to the president. McGee summarized his management structure by saying: "Our only significant departure from the usual oil company set-up is the absence of decision-making committees. We have several coordinating and information-exchanging committees, but our operations are managed on an individual basis."[8]

During the rest of 1960 the emphasis was on planning. Offshore drilling was up, and, since a rig had not been built since 1956, the design of a new $4 million unit capable of operating in 170 feet of water was discussed. Advanced leasing contracts were sought for it at rates of $6,750 to $7,000 a day. It was also decided that for the time being exploration emphasis would be upon natural gas, with potash, uranium, and helium to get further study.

In potash the feasibility report had been concluded, but prospects did not look good. The problem was simple: Canada had more extensive and richer beds of potash and, if certain technological problems were solved, could flood the world market with potash at prices below United States production costs. Phillips Petroleum was already prepared to drop its share of the venture. F. C. Love recalled that he and McGee had a meeting with Farmers Union officials and expressed their fears about the Canadian supply. They added that if Kerr-McGee was in the project alone it would not commit the capital to sink the shaft and build a mill. The two firms were partners, however, and, since the union had invested a lot of money, Kerr-McGee would go along. But McGee and Love did not recommend implementation of the plan. Union officials were more optimistic. Their members were enthusiastic and would not understand dropping the project. They assured the hesitant Kerr-McGee that the union would buy a lot of potash.

The decision was made to go ahead with the joint venture. In retrospect it was a costly one. Ten years earlier the operation would have been very wise, for Carlsbad potash was highly profitable before the deep deposits in Canada became minable. Now, however, even before the shafts and mill could be completed, the Canadian problems were solved, and potash was a glut on the market. Later, when the Saskatchewan government decided to prorate production and the price went up, Kerr-McGee was able to make a modest profit in areas where it had some freight advantage.[9]

In some ways helium was simpler. Kerr-McGee controlled about 95 percent (12,409) acres of a geological structure that produced gas with the highest percentage of helium then known. In other ways it was not. The

[8] In August the board of directors was enlarged to sixteen with the election of A. T. F. Seale, operations vice-president, and Grady D. Harris, Jr., president of Fidelity National Bank, Oklahoma City. "Systems and Executive Management," speech by D. A. McGee, February 3, 1960, to the Tulsa and Oklahoma City chapters of Systems and Procedures Association, Tulsa, in Public Relations file, "S-92"; D. A. McGee, "Administrative Systems—A Management Necessity," *Management and Business Administration*, July, 1960, pp. 28ff.; bylaws, February 12 and August 6, 1960; Dean A. McGee, speech to the New York Society of Security Analysts, Inc., January 19, 1961, in Public Relations files.

[9] Interviews with F. C. Love, September 2, 1971, and George Cobb, December 7, 1972.

Helium Act of 1960 was before Congress. At issue was an amendment that would permit companies to produce and sell helium to buyers other than the government. Jack Steele, a Scripps-Howard staff writer, charged that both Senators Clinton Anderson and Kerr were guilty of conflict of interest by taking part in the debate.

Both men denied the charge, saying that they were "only trying to keep the government's nose out of 'private business.'" Senator Anderson, who presided over the Interior Committee hearings, said his 10 percent interest in Pinta Dome represented an investment of $15,000 to $20,000. Kerr dismissed the venture as "peanuts" and said that the real issue was one of private rights. Under the existing law his company had gone out and bought some leases and discovered helium, which it was willing to develop without government subsidy. "The Interior Secretary can build all the helium plants for defense he wants to. But we don't want him to be able to tell us we can't produce and sell helium because the government doesn't want anybody to compete for non-defense markets." The team of Kerr and Anderson was successful, and the purchase monopoly of the Bureau of Mines was broken. After the act passed, the directors approved construction of a $2 million plant.[10]

Problems in uranium embraced exploitation of the reserves in Shirley Basin and a further consolidation of Ambrosia Lake. More important, uranium and Kerr-McGee's involvement with it were at a crossroad. In 1960 reserves and production reached a peak. Twenty-six privately financed mills, with combined capacities of 22,000 tons of ore per day, were producing 17,000 tons of uranium a year. About six hundred domestic mines plus foreign imports more than guaranteed ample supplies of ore.

Since production had exceeded demand, the AEC moved to check the oversupply, and prices dropped by a third from 1955 to 1960. The United States nuclear stockpile of weapons was supposedly completed, and there was a moratorium on nuclear tests. The AEC's position was that it would buy only necessary uranium, and that from reserves mapped out before 1959. All purchases from Canada would end in 1962. But making the uranium producers especially unhappy was the prediction that there would be a lag of at least eight years before competitive atomic power would become available, even in the high-cost fuel areas. A Kermac Nuclear Fuel executive was quoted as saying: "We've certainly been over-optimistic in the past. But now perhaps too many people are being over-pessimistic about the future. . . . Still it does look like a matter of holding on until the late '60's."[11]

Realistically, Kerr-McGee had to hope that this view was overly dour. One-fourth of the profit reported on June 30 came from uranium. Over the past three years the company had spent $34 million on uranium development, and it had been chiefly outgo until the past year. This expenditure did

[10] On August 22, 1960, Anderson sold his interest to Kerr-McGee. Lease Records file, "Project 382 (Legal) #2."

[11] Dean A. McGee, "Supply and Demand for Uranium in Years Ahead," *Commercial and Financial Chronical*, Vol. 209 (February 13, 1969), p. 4 (684)ff.; "Uranium Runs into Trouble," *Business Week*, March 12, 1960, 177–86.

Airplanes were used to search for uranium.

Table 18.2. Capital Expenditures, 1954–60

	1954	1955	1956
Oil and gas	$5,235,730	$4,394,598	$5,121,056
Drilling and marine	2,372,831	2,522,824	5,682,975
Refining and pipeline	2,437,263	2,853,899	4,646,261
Marketing	....	260,475	877,944
Gas gathering and natural gasoline	717,879	513,912	101,087
Uranium	1,242,215	2,077,260	1,033,302
Other	272,201	596,291	327,649

bring in the greatest block of proven reserves, the biggest single processing plant, and the largest outstanding AEC contract. Consequently, in July, 1960, Kerr-McGee joined Skelly, Getty, and Tidewater Oil and took one-half interest in a new company, Petrotomics, to exploit the Shirley Basin. The next month Petrotomics signed a contract with the AEC to sell some 4 million pounds of U_3O_8 by December 31, 1966. Since the ore was only 120 feet down, it could be mined by open pit methods. Tidewater managed the facility, while Kerr-McGee did a pilot study for a 500-ton-per-day mill.[12]

Despite its contribution to profits, Ambrosia Lake was not a happy operation. The safety record was bad because of the wet sandstone and the use of contract mining. The miners were paid on the basis of production, and they tended to ignore safety precautions in order to get the maximum pay. One newspaper alleged that there had been seventeen fatalities in the area during 1960 and that a petition was circulating calling for a grand-jury investigation. Kerr-McGee and its partners spared no money in attempting to remedy these conditions, but costs did run up. To complicate an already touchy situation, Kermac Nuclear Fuels, as operator, was in a dispute over the minable ore values contributed by one of the partners, Pacific Uranium.[13]

Conditions were ripe for corporate consolidation. Both Pacific Uranium and Anderson Development were disappointed in the low revenues and profits. Both hinted a willingness to sell their interests. On November 15, 1960, Pacific agreed to merge with Kerr-McGee in return for 220,537 shares of the latter's common stock. The next day C. C. Anderson (no relation to the senator) traded his Kermac Nuclear stock for 200,000 shares in Kerr-McGee, and sold that company his part of Ambrosia Lake Uranium for

[12] "The Rock Hound [Dean McGee]," *Forbes*, October 15, 1960, p. 21; "The Great Uranium Glut," *Fortune*, February, 1964, pp. 108ff.; news release dated October 11, 1960, in Public Relations file, "Petrotomics"; *Wall Street Journal*, August 16, 1960, October 13, 1960.

[13] Letter from George H. Cobb to Porter Wharton, Jr., June 15, 1960, in Public Relations file, "Uranium"; "Notice of Special Meeting of Kerr-McGee Oil Industries, Inc., Holders of Shares . . . ," December 20, 1960.

1957	1958	1959	1960
$8,608,940	$ 5,424,396	$ 5,839,105	$12,024,769
8,193,112	2,143,933	1,647,131	817,972
1,226,494	10,059,266	2,002,843	2,319,578
640,058	1,194,778	3,358,694	4,372,808
282,556	141,443	679,267	130,195
394,091	14,969,800	15,622,380	3,803,814
364,900	723,161	617,349	1,154,086

slightly less than $1 million. Finally an additional 17,768 shares of Kerr-McGee common stock were exchanged for 78,000 of Kermac Nuclear held by the U.S. Steel and Carnegie Pension Fund. These various moves gave Kerr-McGee complete control of Kermac Nuclear and most of Ambrosia Lake Uranium, the only exception being the Branson heirs' holdings.[14]

On December 20 the stockholders formally approved the merger of Pacific Uranium by the exchange ratio of twenty shares to one of Kerr-McGee. Kerr-McGee also assumed Kermac Nuclear's long-term debt of $20 million, which was secured by an AEC contract. The same day an application was made with the New York Stock Exchange to list 478,310 additional shares of Kerr-McGee to be used in the acquisition of Kermac Nuclear's capital stock. The S-1 Registration statement covering these transactions also carried the information that, as of June 30, Kerr-McGee had 4,550 employees. Those belonging to unions included 297 at Cushing, 169 at Wynnewood, 103 in the pipeline department, and 924 at Kermac Nuclear.[15]

As previews of 1961 activities, the board was told that negotiations were under way to acquire two more uranium companies. These were located at Lakeview, Oregon, and Gunnison, Colorado. Likewise, it learned that the proposed helium plant would probably cost only $1.2 million and would produce a profit of approximately $600,000 a year. Once more, splitting the company's stock was discussed; once again, action was deferred. However, most of the officers, except Senator Kerr, were given salary increases.

Obviously Kerr-McGee viewed the new year with anticipation. In the past seven years it had invested some $168 million in capital improvements. About 35 percent of this went for oil-and-gas properties, 25 percent for refining and marketing, 14 percent on drilling, and 24 percent on uranium and other minerals (see Table 18.2).

[14] Interview with Marion Bolton, August 27, 1973; Mineral Lease Records files, "Contract #359-8 (Pac. Uran. Mines Co.)" and "Contract #359–7"; "Notice of Special Meeting . . .," December 20, 1960.

[15] "Listing Application to New York Stock Exchange, A-19369," December 20, 1960; Securities and Exchange Commission, "Post Effective Amendment No. 7 to Form S-1 Registration Statement," December 19, 1960.

Table 18.3. Common-Stock Highlights, 1960–61

	1960	1961
Equity per share	$27.36	$15.64
Earnings per share	$ 2.71	$ 2.70
Cash dividends per share	$ 1.20	$ 0.70
Average yield	2.6	1.6
Number of shares outstanding	2,405,801	6,304,478
Number of stockholders	6,075	13,194
NYSE		
High	65⅜	57⅜
Low	36⅝	38¼
Price-earnings ratio		
High	24.12	21.25
Low	13.60	14.16

The payoffs were becoming obvious. Kerr-McGee now owned 100 percent of Kermac Nuclear and 75 percent of Ambrosia Lake Uranium. January
brought the first production from Petrotomics' pit at Shirley Basin. In fact
business looked so good that the February directors' meeting, after accepting James Webb's resignation, was primarily devoted to discussions of
increasing the dividends and splitting the stock. It was agreed to increase
the first-quarter dividend from thirty to forty cents, and a two-for-one split
was recommended, with an eighty-cent annual dividend. This necessitated
a recommendation that the certificate of incorporation be amended to
increase total authorized stock to 10.7 million shares. Furthermore, management was empowered to buy the remaining capital stock of the Kerr-
McGee Building Corporation ($400,384) and the Republic Building Com-
pany ($274,849.67).

Although at that time it was too secret even to tell the directors, the AEC
recognized the significance of another Kerr-McGee first. In 1960, at Grants,
New Mexico, the company successfully used a modified rotary drilling rig to
bore a 90-inch (diameter) ventilation and escape shaft to a depth of 721 feet.
On January 5, 1961, Kerr-McGee signed a classified contract with AEC for a
"large diameter vertical hole" approximately 1,500 feet in depth at the
Nevada Test Site. The total contract price was amended on November 21 to
$324,011.05. Although the agreement was voided before conclusion, "The
termination in no way reflects any discredit upon your organization's fine
work to date, but is based solely upon scientific considerations beyond the
control of either party."[16] The company continued the technique to drill
more holes at Grants.

At this time some additional properties were acquired. Phillips Petroleum, which had no reason for special loyalty to Farmers Union, sold its

---

[16] Lease Records file, "Contract 700."

quarter interest in Farm Chemical Resources Development Corporation to Kerr-McGee for essentially the amount that Phillips had invested in it. Then, on March 27, Kermac Nuclear Fuels created an issue of 5½ percent cumulative preferred stock and exchanged 32,776 shares of it for two firms: Lakeview Mining Company, which owned a small new uranium mill in Oregon, and Gunnison Mining Company, which had a similar plant at Gunnison, Colorado. Although Lakeview lost over a million dollars in 1960, it had assets of almost $12 million. A scarcity of uranium ore was the problem with both companies, but they had good AEC contracts, and Kerr-McGee was willing to gamble on finding enough ore to make them profitable.[17]

The Petrotomics partnership, in the process of constructing a 500-ton-per-day mill in Wyoming, was soon the subject of debate. Gordon Weller, vice-president of the Uranium Institute of America, charged that the Petrotomics contract with the AEC resulted from a conflict of interest. (Some, but not Kerr-McGee, countered with the charge that Weller was opposed to development of Wyoming resources for fear it would be at the expense of Colorado uranium.) Weller claimed that in 1957 the AEC's position stated that the nation's interest did not call for expanded production of uranium concentrate. Yet in 1960 the agency signed a contract with Petrotomics for purchase of concentrates and gave permission to build the mill.

According to Weller this was a political decision. The AEC had been intimidated by Kerr, ranking member of both the Senate Finance and the Public Works committees. He also happened to be a close friend of Senator Clinton Anderson, one-time chairman of the Joint Committee on Atomic Energy. The Uranium Institute filed a written complaint with the Justice Department alleging "conspiracy and combinations between Kerr-McGee Oil Industries, Inc., and certain government officials, constituting a serious restraint of trade within the uranium industry." Kerr-McGee officials pointed out that the reserves had been developed before November, 1958, as required by the AEC. Moreover, the contract price was the lowest submitted to an Eisenhower-appointed membership of the AEC, and the company, therefore, would welcome a hearing to clarify its position. However, there was neither a congressional investigation nor a Justice Department inquiry.[18]

As anticipated, in April the stockholders approved the two-for-one stock split and the increase in capital stock to 10 million common and 700,000 prior convertible preferred. But in May it was agreed that, as of June 15, the preferred would be called in and that class of stock eliminated. At the same time McGee was given a raise retroactive to April 1, making his salary

[17] Mineral Lease Records file, "Contract #43"; Kerr-McGee Oil Industries, Inc., *1961 Annual Report*, pp. 11, 16; interview with George Cobb, December 7, 1972; *Kermac News*, May, 1961.

[18] Roberta Louise Ironside, *An Adventure Called Skelly* (New York, 1970), pp. 108–109; "Hearings Before the Subcommittee on Raw Materials of the Joint Committee on Atomic Energy," 87th Congress, 1st Session, November 15 and 16, 1961, pp. 128–42; *Wall Street Journal*, April 18, 1962; *Oklahoma City Times*, April 11, 1962.

Table 18.4. Financial Highlights, 1960–61

	1960	1961
Total gross income	$157,785,376	$175,307,376
Net income	7,287,457	17,003,125
Total assets	203,430,710	219,015,826
Cash flow from earnings	28,583,805	41,830,737
Working capital	30,065,002	33,199,726
Properties (net)	113,948,522	124,368,375
Capital expenditures	24,623,222	29,205,043
Long-term debt	67,540,877	57,935,142
Cash dividends	3,641,878	4,419,903
Stockholders' equity	82,687,084	100,501,607
Total taxes paid	40,146,197	43,940,771
Number of employees	4,557	4,838

$150,000.[19] The split was recorded in the fiscal year's financial report, as well as the increase in dividends.

The June 30 annual report was one of superlatives. Net income was at an all-time high. Long-term debt fell by almost $10 million, despite an increase in capital expenditures of almost $5 million. This happy state was the result of several conditions: a maximum year of operations at the now wholly owned Kermac Nuclear Fuels; the sale of ore mined by Petrotomics; greater volume of natural gas, including the first production from Block 28 in the Gulf; a step-up in Argentine drilling; and improved market prices for petroleum products. Even the banner year of 1960 was surpassed in the balance sheets.

In exploration and development the gross/net acreage was down to 2,630,249/1,348,505. These leases, options, and operating rights were held in the United States, Canada, Panama, and Venezuela. The company had participated in 104 wells, with a 69 percent rate of success. The first gas was delivered from the Sylvan Lake field in Canada. At the Lake Maracaibo field in Venezuela, development had been suspended and production curtailed until May because of unitization activities, but a pilot pressure-maintenance program was in effect. At the Monagas field, however, thirty-five wells were capable of commercial production, following the record completion of twenty-nine during the year. This confirmed a major low-gravity oil reserve on the concession. The finished twenty-four-inch pipeline, which ran forty-five miles from the field to the Orinoco River, allowed Kerr-McGee to schedule the marketing of this oil for September 1, 1961.

Domestic production saw the company's first seven oil wells brought in in

[19] Oklahoma State Archives, Secretary of State, "Kerr-McGee *vs.* John Rogers," folder #3.

Table 18.5. Drilling and Exploration Operations, 1960–61

	1960	1961
Feet drilled	1,519,693	1,839,385
Total wells/wells completed	252/235	414/397
Domestic interest	17	19
Domestic wells	59	83
Rigs (average)	26	30

North Dakota. The completion of six part-interest gas wells in Beaver County, Oklahoma, reflected the further development of that area, as did an additional eight new oil wells in the Panhandle field of Texas. Also of interest was the report that Kerr-McGee's participation in active water-flood, or secondary recovery, projects had increased from two in 1950 to nineteen, ten years later, with more under consideration.

Contract drilling continued to improve, owing to greater rig utilization, better prices in the Gulf of Mexico, and increased foreign activity. The two deep-water rigs, 46 and 47, had been employed 100 percent of the time, and the latter set a new world record by drilling 10,000 feet in 2 days, 2 hours, and 15 minutes. A new tender-type rig (the first in five years) joined the fleet, and construction began on a revolutionary $6.5 million offshore drilling unit. Although the 1958 contract with L. R. Oil Development was now employing only two units, the others were occupied on projects in the general area. A total of 192 foreign wells were completed during the fiscal year, versus 125 in 1960.[20] On a footage basis 1,131,254 feet were drilled, compared to 930,047 in 1960. In addition to the drilling operations, the units in Argentina effected 105 completions as opposed to only 30 during the previous year.

Four new rigs had been acquired, all of which were sent to Argentina under the YPF contract. Of Kerr-McGee's twenty-fix units, eight were offshore, where their principal customers were Gulf, Shell, Superior, Humble, Mobil, and Kerr-McGee. Seven land rigs were in the Rocky Mountain area and in Oklahoma and Texas; two in Venezuela; two in British Honduras and Guatemala; six in Argentina; and one in Bolivia. Domestic drilling began 108 wells; Kermac Drilling of Venezuela was involved with 74 in Argentina and Venezuela; Transworld Drilling, with 231 in Argentina; and Kerr-McGee Limited with 1 in Bolivia. There were 7 company-interest wells in Louisiana, 11 in Texas, and 1 in Colorado. Of the total contract wells, 59 were offshore, and 24 were in Utah. The offshore units had an

[20] Kerr-McGee, *1961 Annual Report*; Securities and Exchange Commission, "Form 10-K Annual Report for June 30, 1961" and "Post Effective Amendment Statement, October 30, 1961."

Table 18.6. Production Record, 1960–61

	1960	1961
Production		
Crude oil produced		
(net barrels)	2,619,965	2,924,337
Natural-gas sales		
(millions of cubic feet)	53,916	54,322
Oil and gas leases		
(net acres)	1,566,679	1,348,505
Gas processing		
Gas liquids produced		
(net barrels)	1,425,343	1,362,295
Refining		
Crude oil processed		
(barrels)	15,513,306	14,568,170
Minerals		
Ore mined (tons)	826,912	1,569,240
Ore milled (tons)	1,133,439	1,677,951
U_3O_8 concentrate sold		
(lbs.)	5,177,781	6,785,209

over-all utilization of 76 percent, while those in the Rocky Mountain area had 58 percent, and Oklahoma and Texas only 23 percent.[21]

Fortunately there is evidence which throws comparative light on the offshore drilling business of that time. Over all, there were approximately sixty rigs in the Gulf, compared to forty in 1958. Their crews worked twelve hours a day for seven days and then were off the same amount, earning as much for one week at sea as for two weeks on land. Platform-tender units rented from $3,800 to $4,000 a day, while Kerr-McGee's Rig 47 received about $5,300 a day for work in seventy feet of water. A company needed to make a net profit of about 10 percent to offset idle days.[22]

All four refineries operated satisfactorily, although crude oil processed dropped 2,591 barrels a day from the previous year. This was a direct result of the policy that reduced crude runs to bolster the weak prices caused by oversupply. Plans to further cut the output called for the Cushing refinery to suspend manufacture of gasoline and fuel oil, while specializing in Deep Rock lubricating oils. As a result of all these retrenchments a balance was essentially achieved between production and sales volume.

The marketing division expanded with construction of a products terminal on the Texas-Eastern Pipeline near Indianapolis, Indiana. Additional terminal sites were acquired in Missouri and Wisconsin, and work was begun

[21] Drilling Department file, "Annual Report, 1961"; Transworld Drilling file, "Rig Operations July, 1956, thru June, 1961"; *Wall Street Journal*, June 19, 1961.

[22] *Drilling* magazine interviews with George B. Kitchel for September, 1961, issue in Public Relations file, "Offshore Drilling Information."

on those in Wisconsin. All these outlets were to be supplied by direct pipeline from Kerr-McGee's Oklahoma refineries. The Deep Rock branded marketing organization was realigned into three regions, with offices in Des Moines, Oklahoma City, and Indianapolis. This spearheaded a move eastward into new areas of Illinois, Kentucky, and Indiana. There were now 1,230 service stations handling company products.

In another significant development for Kerr-McGee the nation's first privately owned helium plant at Navajo, Arizona, with sales exclusively for the commercial market, was about to go on stream. Earlier in the year the company bought the Littell interest for $58,000, and now owned 90 percent of that project. Martin T. Bennett held the remainder.

Kerr-McGee's interests in uranium were also expanded when it enlarged its holdings in Kermac Nuclear Fuels from 59 to 100 percent, and in Ambrosia Lake Uranium from 25 to 75 percent. Eventually, on December 29, 1961, the other quarter interest was acquired, although the Branson heirs retained an overriding royalty. Ambrosia Lake Uranium was liquidated, and its assets were merged into Kermac Nuclear.

The first work stoppage in the history of Kerr-McGee occurred on July 24, 1961, over working conditions at the Kermac Nuclear installation. A walkout by the hourly employees lasted until September 19, when a new contract was signed and normal work schedules were resumed. As a result quarterly earnings were predicted to be somewhat less than anticipated. It is interesting to note that this strike, not in a petroleum-related activity, perhaps could have been seen as an omen, offering a glimpse of the complications in the years ahead, which in turn were the results of the move to diversify into new and untried areas of production.

Potash was another area of consolidation. By its earlier purchase of Phillips Petroleum's interest in Farm Chemical, Kerr-McGee Oil Industries became the dominant partner in the potash undertaking. Perhaps in an effort to make this position obvious, beginning in September a series of bookkeeping moves brought about the sale by Farmers Union of its 10,000 shares of Farm Chemical stock to Kerr-McGee for $1 million; the transfer of all of Farm Chemical assets to a new company, Kermac Potash for $900,000; and finally the contribution of $900,000 by a subsidiary of Farmers Union to Kermac Potash for a share of the new partnership. Kermac Potash then executed an agreement by which Kerr-McGee became the sole operator of the potash properties.[23]

At the October stockholders' meeting it was announced that Hurricane Carla in the Gulf of Mexico had cost the company approximately $50,000 in capital losses. The same group approved the purchase of the remaining 50 percent of the shares of Kerr-McGee Building Corporation and the 66 percent of Republic Building Corporation for a total cost of $625,233.67.[24] The shares in the Kerr-McGee Building Corporation were owned by Mildred Kerr Anderson, the children of Robert S. Kerr, and Mr. and Mrs.

[23] Mineral Lease Records file, "29-09-000"; *Wall Street Journal*, September 28, 1961.
[24] Kerr-McGee Oil Industries, Inc., "Notice of Annual Meeting," October 2, 1961.

Dean McGee. The Republic Building stock was held by the children of Robert S. Kerr, Dean McGee, a daughter of Dean McGee, T. M. Kerr, and the F. C. Love family. These changes in ownership were more evidence of the gradual shift in the nature of Kerr-McGee—from a closely held, almost family, business, to a large publicly controlled corporation.

Planning continued for the future at the last board meeting of the year. Among the actions discussed was the construction of a potash mill slated to begin in April, 1962, building a vanadium plant at Soda Springs, Idaho, and completion of the Petrotomics mill. Permission was given to organize Power Oil, Inc., as a new subsidiary of Triangle Refineries; and the aforementioned liquidation of the Ambrosia Lake Uranium Company was completed. Perhaps the greatest evidence of confidence in the company's future was the directive to purchase on the open market up to 25,000 shares of Kerr-McGee common at a price up $43 a share. This was designated for use in future acquisitions of property by the company.

Chapter 19

Potash, Phosphate and Nitrogen 1962-1963

The American public did not lack for excitement in 1962, beginning with astronaut John Glenn's orbiting the earth three times. This gave the United States first place in the race into space and challenged Russia to be first on the moon. There was less cause for jubilation in other areas: the struggle of American blacks for equal rights was producing near civil war in some sections of the nation, and the unfortunate Bay of Pigs incident was hardly out of the headlines when the Cuban missile crisis brought the United States to the brink of war with Russia.

In the area of economics a more experienced President Kennedy made some progress against the problem of inflation. But business, which had viewed the president with tolerant mistrust, became generally hostile when he forced United States Steel and other companies to rescind a 3.5 percent price raise. The oil industry still suffered from the chronic problems of cheap foreign oil and unstable prices at the pump, but by June wholesale and retail gasoline prices stabilized and started upward.

The year brought increased personal recognition to Robert S. Kerr and Dean McGee. The elevation of Lyndon Johnson to the vice-presidency created a power vacuum in the Senate, which Kerr rapidly filled. He was publicly given credit for securing passage of most of Kennedy's domestic program. *Newsweek* on August 6, 1962, captioned its story on him "Oklahoma's Kerr—The Man Who Really Runs the U.S. Senate." But there were still critics who claimed that he used his new power for his own benefit. McGee, on the other hand, was not controversial, and he was approved as a member of the general advisory committee of the U.S. Arms Control and

307

Disarmament Agency, appointed a director of the Federal Reserve Bank of Kansas City, and made a civilian aide to the Secretary of the Army.

At Kerr-McGee, 1962 was the milestone in an explosive pattern of growth in assets. Many factors contributed to this expansion. The following calendar lists the most important acquisitions:

1952—Acquired Navajo Uranium Company assets
1953—Acquired Pampa, Texas, gasoline plant
       Completed Cactus gasoline plant
1954—Completed Wynnewood Refinery expansion
1955—Added Wynnewood Catalytic cracker
       Acquired certain Deep Rock assets
       Built Shiprock uranium mill
1956—Organized Kermac Nuclear Fuels Corporation
       Purchased Cushing refinery
1957—Acquired Triangle Refineries
       Acquired interests in Venezuelan leases
       Began contract drilling in Venezuela
       Offshore rigs 46 and 47 placed in service
1958—Constructed metallurgical research laboratory
       Acquired three Oklahoma pipelines
1959—Entered contract drilling in Argentina
       Completed Kermac Nuclear uranium mill
       Purchased Cotton Valley Solvents, Inc.
1960—Purchased 64.5 percent interest in 20,000-acre offshore lease
1961—Began selling gas from Block 28 reserves
       Acquired Lakeview and Gunnison mining companies
       Acquired full ownership of Kermac Nuclear Fuels

Total assets grew from $27,619,220 in 1952 to $219,015,826 in 1961.

While these were matters for self-congratulations, they were not allowed to become more than that. To start off 1962, Wallace Service Stations, Inc., was established as a new Triangle subsidiary, as were Trackside Gasoline Stations and Imperial Service Stations. Two bad guesses were cleaned up. General Asphalts was discontinued, since asphalt sales had not increased materially. Likewise, because sufficient new ore supplies had not been found for the uranium mills at Gunnison and Lakeview, they were merged into Ambrosia Lake Uranium and the Gunnison plant was closed. The effect of these moves was offset in part by completion of the Petrotomics unit in April and the first sale of yellow cake from that facility in June.

Moreover, developments at Kermac Potash were assured by a $10 million loan from Prudential Life Insurance Company and a similar amount from two banks. Engineering and construction contracts for mine shafts and a refining mill were let early in the year for this potash complex near Hobbs. By March 14 there was a total investment of $3.5 million in the undertaking. Later a management agreement was signed between Kermac Potash and Kerr-McGee by which the latter became the agent to manage the project for ten years and to continue as long as potassium ore was available in commercial quantities from the partnership's properties. In return Kermac Potash paid Kerr-McGee 5 percent of all direct costs, other than rental, royalties,

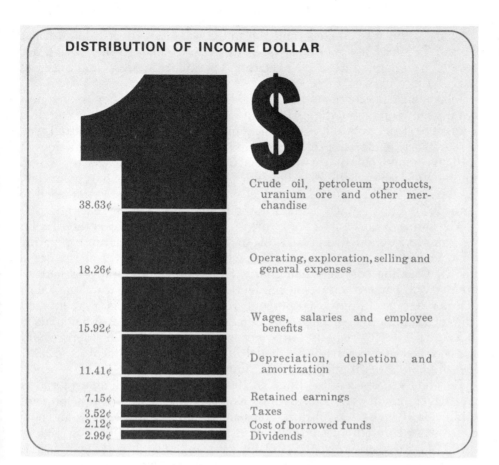

Fig. 19.1. Distribution of income dollar, 1962. From Kerr-McGee Oil Industries, Inc., *1962 Annual Report*.

and taxes, for overhead and indirect costs. Finally, effective December 31, 1962, Farm Chemical Resources Development Corporation was merged into Kermac Nuclear Fuels.[1]

The success in using a huge 90-inch bit to drill a 721-foot-deep air-vent shaft in New Mexico was a major advancement in proving big-hole drilling techniques. To exploit the commercial possibilities of this process, Big Hole

[1] Roberta Louise Ironside, *An Adventure Called Skelly* (New York, 1970), pp. 108–109; Minerals Lease files, "Contract 1204-1" and "Contract 1204-2"; Lease Records file, "Cont. #817."

Drillers, Inc., was created, and the outfit was used to drill for Kermac Potash. In March it was hired again by the AEC to sink a 64-inch shaft 2,500 feet deep on Rainier Mesa in Nevada for "scientific purposes," and Rig 4 was moved there to work the contract.[2]

Oklahoma construction was also highlighted. Work was begun on a new twenty-story office building that would incorporate the Republic Building across the street from the current headquarters. A decision to centralize all research activity led to breaking ground near Oklahoma City for a new $1 million research complex with 50,000 square feet of floor space, to be used for metallurgical, biochemical, analytical, and oil-and-gas experimentation. A completed project was an eighteen-mile pipeline from Wynnewood to Antioch Junction, which opened new supplies of crude for that refinery.

The annual report for 1962, faced with a rather flat profit year (See Tables 19.1 and 19.2), chose to emphasize a ten-year chart of financial and operating data, covering the years 1953 to 1962, which gave a good over-all picture of just how far the company had come. The number of employees had increased 500 percent; crude-oil production, 228 percent; natural-gas sales, 208 percent; gas liquids, 300 percent; refined crude oil, 600 percent; and sales of uranium concentrate, 3481 percent, from a mere 182,705 pounds in 1953 to 6,178,236 pounds ten years later.[3] In the drilling department Kerr-McGee and its subsidiaries had drilled a cumulative total of 18,752,307 feet of hole, with 10 percent of that during 1962.

For the fiscal year ending June 30, 1962, the spotlight fell on exploration and development (see Table 19.3). Kerr-McGee acquired a 52 percent interest in 10 new tracts offshore Louisiana containing 46,927 acres and now controlled, through oil-and-gas leases, options, and operating rights, 2,192,611 gross acres, or 1,077,149 net acres, in the United States, Canada, Panama, and Venezuela. During the year the company participated in the completion of 72 wells, 86 percent of which were productive. The most significant of these was the discovery of oil and gas on Block 230 of the Ship Shoal area. Altogether Kerr-McGee's 24 rigs drilled 550 wells, and 15 were still in progress in June. The domestic offshore rigs had virtually 100 percent utilization, and even the land units approached 70 percent. In foreign operations, the Bolivian contract was concluded, and that rig was sold, while in Venezuela business was so poor that the two outfits were returned to the Gulf Coast. The eight rigs in Central America and Argentina continued near full employment. The completion of the 298th well in the 500-well contract with Argentina did not indicate clear sailing, however, for YPF was having difficulty getting funds to pay its contractors. A new contract was negotiated that turned over the remaining work to Transworld Drilling at a lower cost. When the Fondizi government fell in a military coup, these contracts became a political issue.[4]

[2] Lease Records file, "Contract 752-1."

[3] Kerr-McGee Oil Industries, Inc., *1962 Annual Report*. See also Securities and Exchange Commission, "Form 10-K Annual Report for Fiscal Year Ended June 30, 1962."

[4] Dean A. McGee personal file, "Drilling Department, Operations, Rig Utilization Schedule for Month of _____"; *Kermac News*, October, 1962, carried a feature article on

The annual well count gives a good picture of Kerr-McGee's efforts in its own behalf. During the fiscal year wells had been successfully completed in Oklahoma, Louisiana, Texas, California, Colorado, Arkansas, New Mexico, and Venezuela, with dry holes in Kansas, North Dakota, Arizona, Nebraska, Wyoming, Montana, and Canada. The company had sold 109 wells, leaving a domestic and foreign total of 1,515 gross wells, or 754.07 net, of which 522.7 were oil, 143.6 gas, and 44.2 gas-condensate. They were located in Texas (48 percent), Oklahoma (24 percent), Louisiana (8 percent), Arkansas (6 percent), and abroad (2 percent).[5]

The big news in drilling in the second half of calendar 1962 was the dedication of the revolutionary Rig 54. Designed by Paul Wolff and Tsi Yu, it embodied their experience with units 46 and 47 in deeper waters. Rig 54, constructed in the shape of an equilateral triangle with three stabilizing columns, was capable of drilling in 175 feet of water. Longer than a football field (388 feet), it not only was the world's tallest floating structure (378 feet—towering over a 30-story building) but also was the only submersible unit able to drill in water that deep. It was also expensive, costing about $6,250,000. Even before its completion Mobil contracted for fourteen months of service in the Gulf. Later, taking a submersible into deeper depths proved impracticable; thus Rig 54 marked the acme of that class, "the last of the big submersibles." "Jack-ups" and semisubmersibles were to be developed for greater depths.[6]

Two units, Tender IV and Rig 55, were modernized and reactivated, while others were nearing the final design and planning stages. To service the rigs working in rougher seas at the most distant offshore operations, a new 146-foot, 1,120 horsepower workboat and two new 65-foot all-aluminum, 800-horsepower boats capable of speeds up to 30 miles per hour were added to the marine fleet.

In the processing branches of the company plans were made to bring the gas from Kerr-McGee properties on blocks 28 and 32 in the Gulf to Humphreys, Louisiana. Although the production from the seven gas-processing plants in which Kerr-McGee had interests fell somewhat because of proration and depletion of resources, it acquired additional rights in plants being constructed in Beaver County, Oklahoma, and the one near Humphreys, Louisiana.

In other divisions total sales of Deep Rock branded gasoline and heating oils increased, while sales volume through private brand outlets grew by 40 percent. Sales by Triangle again exceeded the $100 million mark. These

---

contract drilling. The Argentine problem is discussed in Raymond F. Mikesell, *Foreign Investment in the Petroleum and Mineral Industries* (Baltimore, 1971), pp. 158–59.

[5] Production Department file, "Annual Well Count as of July 1, 1962."

[6] Rig 54 was completed January 19, 1963, at New Orleans, and a working model is on display at the Smithsonian Museum in Washington, D.C. For further information see *Kermac News*, February, 1962, Summer, 1962, and February, 1977; Richard J. Howe, "The History and Current Status of Offshore Mobile Drilling Units," *Ocean Industry*, July, 1968, pp. 1–24; "Kermac Rig 54," *Offshore*, August, 1963, pp. 19–40.

Rig 54, the largest bottom-supported submersible ever built, was so large that only a part could go under a New Orleans bridge.

improvements came despite the fact that refinery runs had been reduced by some 5,000 barrels per day. In uranium the theme was consolidation of its varied interests under company control. Not only was the Lakeview mill closed but also the decision was made to dismantle the Gunnison plant and to ship it to Idaho Springs, Idaho, for incorporation in a new vanadium plant to be constructed there (see Table 19.4).

Of major significance, however, was evidence that Kerr-McGee felt itself ready to take the third step in the uranium chain. Already mining and processing uranium ores, in July it acquired the nuclear products department (key personnel, patents, and equipment) of Spencer Chemical Company and moved the operation to the Cushing refinery. The company was now in a position to produce nuclear-reactor fuel materials for use in making steam to generate electric power. "By getting into the newer applications

Rig 54 drilling in the Gulf of Mexico. A working model is in the
Smithsonian Museum, Washington, D.C.

now," an official said, "Kerr-McGee expects to be able to grow with the
industry."[7]

The year had begun with a new recognition of the political stature of Bob
Kerr, so perhaps it is not surprising that before 1962 ended critics would
attack him because of this power. Kerr, and indirectly Kerr-McGee, became
the target of Drew Pearson. The columnist's thesis was that "the Oklahoma
Democrat has never bothered to separate his business and political ties."
Pearson alleged that in 1950 Senator Kerr battled for a natural-gas bill which
would have helped his company, and currently was behind federal actions to

[7] Securities and Exchange Commission, "Post Effective Amendment No. 5 to Form S-1
Registration Statement," December 5, 1962; *Kermac News*, September, 1962; *Wall Street
Journal*, February 12 and July 5, 1962.

raise helium prices. As long as the government had been the sole supplier, Pearson claimed, it sold helium at $19 per thousand cubic feet. "Suddenly" the Interior Department raised its price to $35, allegedly as a result of a bill whose author was Senator Clinton Anderson, a partner in the Pinta Dome project until shortly before the measure was introduced. Furthermore, Senator Kerr also fought vigorously for tax concessions for oil and uranium interests and, according to Pearson, had been instrumental in keeping the depletion allowances at 27.5 percent for oil and 23 percent for uranium. When other famous targets of Pearson are recalled, Kerr could be said to have arrived.[8]

The claim by Pearson that Kerr exerted unusual power in his role as United States senator, was soon to be proved, but not in a way that the columnist could have anticipated. On January 1, 1963, the nation, and especially Oklahoma, was stunned by the unexpected death of Senator Robert S. Kerr. In a single blow the president of the United States lost one of his most able lieutenants; the Senate, its most powerful member; the oil industry, its strongest defender; and Kerr-McGee, its founder. The ripples caused by his passing spread across the nation. On January 2, oil stocks on the New York Stock Exchange declined sharply. Some analysts linked this to investors' fears for the future of depletion allowances, now without a recognized champion by reason of Kerr's death. Even as the great and small converged on Oklahoma City to pay their last respects, Kerr-McGee Oil Industries, Inc., received letters and telegrams from worried stockholders asking who would now run the company.[9]

Forbes magazine reassured investors on this question: "They really had nothing to worry about. For, although it was Kerr who founded the Company in 1929, since 1942 Kerr-McGee had actually been McGee. It was he who had run it." While Kerr was in politics, "McGee, a mild-mannered geologist-businessman, [had] used the depletion allowance which Kerr had so ably defended in the Senate to make Kerr-McGee bigger and bigger." According to *Forbes*, McGee had used the firm's depletion allowance from one natural resource to finance the development of another. The second was used to bankroll a third, and so on.[10]

This was an obvious oversimplification. Kerr-McGee did miss Kerr's interest and, above all, his unlimited optimism for the future of the company and the ability of its staff to accomplish miracles. He was not indispensable, however, as could be seen in the rapid tempo at which activities resumed once respects had been paid to its founder. At the meeting of the board on February 8, resolutions were passed memorializing the deaths of Kerr and J. H. Lollar, Jr. (a director and assistant secretary and treasurer who died on November 26, 1962). The bylaws were amended to lower the number of

---

[8] "Washington Merry-Go-Round," *Washington Post–Times Herald*, October 21, 1962. For an account of Pinta Dome and its plant see *Oil and Gas Journal* October 29, 1962, pp. 136–39.

[9] "Robert S. Kerr Memorial Issue," *Kermac News*, January, 1963; interview with J. B. Saunders, June 9, 1971.

[10] "Making Money Make Money," *Forbes*, November 1, 1963, p. 32.

directors to thirteen and to allow the presidency and chairmanship of the board to be held by one man. Dean McGee was then chosen as both chairman and president, and J. B. Saunders replaced Kerr on the executive committee. Regular business took over at that point, and the twenty-five-cent quarterly dividend was declared. The directors also approved the transfer of 20,000 shares of Farm Chemical Resources Development Corporation to Kermac Nuclear and a proposal to acquire Chicago Mill & Lumber Company by merger.[11]

Despite the sudden and unexpected death of Kerr, the company management anticipated that 1963 would find "business as usual." Nationally, it was much the same with some even hoping for an improving economic picture. The old problems, such as inflation, appeared to be yielding to government and business pressures, and a new era in foreign relations seemed at hand. The Agency of International Development (AID), the Alliance for Progress, and the Peace Corps gave signs of creating a new American image abroad, and Khrushchev apparently softened his opposition to a nuclear-test-ban treaty. Of course, the assassination of an American president was not weighed in formulating future plans.

Just as the 1950's had seen Kerr-McGee use the technique of acquisitions to build up its positions in petroleum products and in uranium, the next five years brought a major effort at achieving a significant position in the production and marketing of fertilizers. The strategy was relatively obvious after the formation of Kermac Potash. As James Kelly explained, Kerr-McGee got into the business, not because it wanted to be in marketing, but through the desire to be a basic producer of the raw materials used in fertilizer. It already had one major ingredient, nitrogen, in the natural gas it produced; potash, a second, resulted from the deal with Farmers Union; while the third, phosphate, would come with lands purchased in Florida. The processing of large amounts of potash was imminent, so a market had to be found. Kerr-McGee began looking at the possibility of acquiring marketing companies. At the time fertilizer prices were good, making the project even more desirable.

J. B. Saunders, who headed the new division, had a homelier explanation: "We felt that it was something that would not go out of style." Unfortunately, however, too many other companies could also see the advantages and went into the business. Canadian potash producers flooded the market, and fertilizer prices dropped by half. Director Robert S. Kerr, Jr., admitted that "for the short haul we were sorry about getting into fertilizer business," but Kerr-McGee was in for the long haul.[12]

At this time part of the company's history came to an end. The Shiprock plant and mines, which had provided for Kerr-McGee's entry into the uranium business, was sold on March 1, the entire facility being bought by Vanadium Corporation of America. Vanadium already had a body of ore it

---

[11] Bylaws, February 8, 1963; *Wall Street Journal*, February 11, 1963. Chicago Mill, with timberlands and manufacturing facilities, had a value of about $30 million, but the deal was called off. See *Wall Street Journal*, March 28, and May 24, 1963.

[12] Interviews with James J. Kelly, June 26, 1971; Robert S. Kerr, Jr., June 15, 1971; and J. B. Saunders.

was mining on the Navajo reservation, and Kerr-McGee felt that its own reserves in the region were not sufficient to make Shiprock worthwhile. During the ten and three-quarter years of ownership some 446,872 tons of ore were mined, containing 2,106,629 pounds of uranium and 8,940,274 pounds of vanadium. During the mill's eight and one-third years of operation 909,174 tons of ore had been processed with 4,546,348 pounds of processed uranium sold to AEC and 4,692,390 pounds of processed vanadium placed on the private market. At the height of production it had employed approximately two hundred Navajos. After the sale Kerr-McGee netted over $7 million by this venture into uranium.[13]

Shiprock was replaced by another Kerr-McGee first. Lignite, an evolutionary stage of coal, sometimes contains uranium, as Kerr-McGee had discovered in the Cave Hills and Belfield areas of North and South Dakota. The seams, twelve to twenty-four inches thick, lay under thirty to seventy feet of overburden, with each ton of lignite containing five to fifteen pounds of uranium—as compared to four to six pounds in Ambrosia Lake ore. A technique to mine these narrow beds was developed, and operations began there in late summer, 1962. A burning plant was erected near Bowman, North Dakota, to burn the lignite from several open-pit mines there, and the resulting ash was shipped to Ambrosia Lake for extraction of the uranium.[14]

Even before the Shiprock sale steps had been taken to acquire a new source of vanadium. With equipment salvaged from the Gunnison uranium mill construction was begun on a processing plant at Soda Springs, Idaho, using ferrophosphorus slag from the Monsanto Chemical Company plant nearby. Utilizing a patented roasting process, this installation produced 1.5 million pounds annually of vanadium pentoxide and ammonium metavanadate for use as a chemical catalyst and in the manufacture of high-strength steel. The unit went on stream in June, 1963, employing thirty-seven persons.[15]

In May, the directors were notified of the death of J. D. Blosser, a long-time member of the board, who had played a vital role in the initial financing of the infant A&K Petroleum Company. This was the third loss from the ranks of long-time supporters of Kerr-McGee. Yet deaths and births are often concurrent, and the completion of a million-dollar research center at Oklahoma City and the purchase of the T. J. Moss Tie Company brought new ideas and a new field of interest to the company.

T. J. Moss, without an unprofitable year since its founding in 1879, was one of the nation's largest producers of railroad crossties. Of interest to Kerr-McGee was that the firm owned some 265,000 acres of timberland,

[13] Interview with Marion Bolton, August 27, 1973; M. F. Bolton and S. B. Robinson, "A Brief History of Shiprock Mining and Milling Operations on the Navajo Indian Reservation (May 8, 1963)." Copies of this report are in L. A. Woodward notebook and "Uranium" file in Public Relations Department.

[14] Wall Street Journal, July 13, 1962; "Kermac—First to Take the Plunge," Metal Mining & Processing, March, 1965, pp. 18–23.

[15] Kermac News, June–October, 1963 [one issue]; Pocatello, Idaho, State Journal, February 28, 1964.

chiefly in Kentucky, Missouri, and Tennessee, and held mineral rights on 212,563 of them. It also had twenty-one sawmills, with an interest in eleven others, and twelve wood preserving plants. By a letter dated April 19, 1963, Dean McGee offered the Moss stockholders $8 million for their 7,611 shares. When this offer was accepted, effective July 1, the stock was assigned to a new corporation, Kermac Tie Company, which then took over the T. J. Moss name.

Many wondered about the logic of this acquisition—why was an oil and uranium company going into the wood-processing business? Even McGee admitted that it seemed to be "straying far afield." The answer, however, was simple: wood was also depletable, and Kerr-McGee acquired title to 133,000 acres of land in Missouri that lay in an area where lead and zinc had been mined for over a century—"absolutely virgin land in lead-zinc country untouched by prospectors." The company's geologists believed that the mineral prospects were worth more than the purchase price, although the timber alone would eventually repay the cost.[16]

The annual report of June 30 underscored the excellence of management at Kerr-McGee and marked the first time that Dean McGee was the lone signer of the letter to the stockholders. Although gross income declined by $1,758,000, cash flow by $700,000, and working capital by $1,449,000 net income was the highest ever. This can be explained by the decision to consolidate the healthy earnings of Triangle with the parent company. Also, economies had been achieved in all departments. For example, 255 service stations were sold and then leased back by the company. Moreover, some 98,300 shares of common stock had been repurchased, and a new seven-year bank loan refinanced some of the debts, dropping the long-term debt by $6 million.

Stockholders benefited from the increase in net earnings by the higher dividends voted during the latter part of the year.

Drilling and exploration had increases to match the financial figures. The company participated in the drilling of 80 wells, 70 percent of which were productive. Interestingly, 26 of these were offshore. Of the total number, 22 were wildcats, and 6 marked discoveries. A total of 59 gross wells gave Kerr-McGee a net addition of 17.98 wells. The largest number of the new wells was in Louisiana, Texas, and Venezuela, but Louisiana also led in dry holes.

The drilling department and the subsidiaries were now operating twenty-three rigs. Three new ones had been added, including Rig 56, a new tender-type. This brought to ten the number of units operating off the Gulf coast, including six submersibles. Of the thirteen land rigs, seven were in the United States, four in Argentina, and one each in British Honduras and Costa Rica. The home-office division undertook 92 wells, with 74 offshore,

[16] Lease Records file, "Cont. 802-1"; Public Relations file, "Moss Tie Company"; *Wall Street Journal*, May 20, 1963; *Kermac News*, June–October, 1963; "Making Money Make Money," *Forbes*, November 1, 1963, p. 32; interviews with J. B. Saunders and J. C. Finley, March 3, 1971.

Table 19.1. Financial Highlights, 1962–63

	1962	1963*
Total gross income	$167,892,014	$214,316,968
Net income	17,034,264	18,806,333
Total assets	229,092,970	233,710,908
Cash flow from earnings	41,259,296	40,558,728
Working capital	41,876,785	40,427,929
Properties (net)	130,914,120	137,331,909
Capital expenditures	29,402,849	38,360,495
Long-term debt	60,357,042	54,482,618
Cash dividends	5,025,723	5,858,500
Stockholders' equity	112,823,178	126,535,352
Total taxes paid	5,902,840	8,065,184
Number of employees	5,117	4,348

*Includes Triangle Refineries.

Table 19.2. Common-Stock Highlights, 1962–63

	1962	1963
Equity per share	$17.50	$19.33
Earnings per share	$ 2.74	$ 3.05
Cash dividends per share	$ 0.80	$ 0.95
Average yield	2.3	2.8
Number of shares outstanding	6,219,679	6,160,906
Number of stockholders	15,400	16,484
New York Stock Exchange		
High	46½	42¾
Low	24	34⅜
Price-earnings ratio		
High	16.97	14.02
Low	8.76	11.27

Table 19.3. Drilling and Exploration Operations, 1962–63

	1962	1963
Feet drilled	1,890,903	2,137,924
Total wells/wells completed	565/550	650/636
Kerr-McGee interest	72	80
Rigs (average)	24	23
Contract wells	NA	64

Table 19.4. Production Record, 1962–63

	1962	1963
Production		
Crude oil produced (net barrels)	3,166,399	3,355,182
Natural-gas sales (millions		
of cubic feet)	60,946	64,505
Oil-and-gas leases (net acres)	1,077,149	1,008,199
Gas processing		
Gas liquids produced (net barrels)	1,353,241	1,264,452
Refining		
Crude-oil processed (barrels)	12,628,796	10,906,518
Minerals		
Ore mined (tons)	1,470,455	1,394,587
Ore milled (tons)	1,409,352	1,291,401
U_3O_8 concentrate sold (lbs.)	6,472,770	5,539,351

and 64 on contract. Kermac Drilling of Venezuela completed 46 of 47; Transworld Drilling, 174 of 176; and Kerr-McGee Limited, 1. The offshore rigs were utilized approximately 97 percent of the time, but the domestic land-rig use dropped from 60 percent in January to 17 percent in December, 1963.[17]

Marketing, pipeline, and refining operations had their second-best year since 1957, although refinery output was deliberately curtailed again to meet demand. The company elected to participate in an AEC "stretchout" program, which provided for smaller purchases over a longer period of time than had originally been contracted for. This decision would guarantee uranium sales until 1971 for the Ambrosia Lake facility, but could place Petrotomics on standby in 1966 unless private markets became available. The nuclear-products equipment was ready for use, the potash mill was under construction, and an aggressive exploration for copper, lead-zinc, gold, and other minerals continued. The exterior of the new office building was 97 percent complete.[18]

Two large-diameter holes were being bored by Big Hole Drillers: one at the AEC's Nevada test site and the other a mine shaft for Kermac Potash. Even more hush-hush, if possible, than the drilling for the AEC were two holes for Deco Electronics in Pennsylvania and Virginia. The operations were isolated by fences, and the crews were ordered not to have contact with

[17] Drilling Department files, "Annual Report, 1963," and "Annual Well Count as of June 30, 1963"; Dean A. McGee personal file, "Rig Utilization Schedule for Month of_____"; and Transworld Drilling file, "Drilling Department Rig Operations Report July 1, 1962, to June 30, 1963."

[18] Kerr-McGee Oil Industries, Inc., *1963 Annual Report*. See also Securities and Exchange Commission, "Form 10-K Annual Report for Fiscal Year Ended June 30, 1963."

the public. Q. C. ("Pete") Walton, who worked on the site, doubted that anyone who knew anything about drilling believed the company was seeking oil on a ridge of the Allegheny Mountains. Furthermore, people on the adjacent highway could count the stands of pipe coming out of the hole and tell how deep it was.[19] It was later revealed that the holes were parts of a communication system for an underground command post that was deemed essential in the event of a nuclear war.

During the rest of the year there were several other developments in drilling. Design work began on a self-elevating mobile unit, later Trans-ocean I, for use in the North Sea. Also, by a letter dated July 19, 1963, Kerr-McGee joined Tidewater, Superior, Skelly, and Sunray DX companies in a proposal to the National Iranian Oil Company to make a marine seismic survey of Iranian waters. This was a prerequisite for eligibility to compete for development properties the following year, and for a 20 percent share Kerr-McGee's cost was to be $74,000.

In Argentina the old L. R. Development contract was extended until April 1, 1967, by Argentina Cities Service Development Company, which had taken over the assets of L. R. Development in 1961. In August, Transworld signed a contract with YPF to complete the remaining 100 wells on the 500-well agreement and to sink an additional 350. The original 500 were completed by October, but on November 15, the new President of Argentina, Arturo Illia, issued three decrees which canceled agreements between YPF and thirteen other oil companies, one of which was Transworld. Decree 745/63 voided Kerr-McGee's contract, ostensibly because it had been negotiated by "private invitation instead of by public tender" and because the subsequent rates were "at least 50 per cent higher than those commonly prevailing for work of this sort."[20]

In August, Kerr-McGee's board of directors amended the bylaws to read that the number of directors should be not less than three nor more than fifteen, to be determined annually by the board. Twelve directors were to be chosen at the next stockholders' meeting. The board also approved buying 275,000 shares of Kerr-McGee common stock on the New York Stock Exchange, 25,000 at large, and 100,000 from the Kerr estate. It was decided to liquidate Knox Industries, leaving Triangle with Peoples, Trackside Gasoline, Power Oil, Coast Stations, and Wallace Service Stations as wholly owned subsidiaries.

Most significant, however, were the preparations made for entry into the fertilizer business. The previous year, extensive phosphate explorations had been carried on in Florida, and leases had been acquired to provide that ingredient. At Hobbs, a man-and-materials shaft had been completed, and the $30 million mill, able to produce 1,500 tons of muriate of potash daily using a recrystallization process developed by the research laboratory, was

[19] Interviews with Quinton C. Walton, April 16, 1971, and George B. Parks, October 23, 1971.

[20] Lease Records file, "Contract 808"; Ironside, *An Adventure Called Skelly*, 96–97; *Wall Street Journal*, July 29, 1963, p. 22; and Mikesell, *Foreign Investment in the Petroleum and Mineral Industries*, pp. 158–83.

well under way. As for nitrogen, McGee explained, "We have purposely stayed out of the nitrogen business. Since we are in the oil and gas business, it would be relatively easy to produce nitrogen; but we are in no hurry to move in that direction because we can't expect to gain a competitive position that is available in potash and phosphate." Moreover, potash could be traded for nitrogen.[21]

Kerr-McGee could mine the ingredients for fertilizer, but if it were going to get into the marketing end, it needed people who knew the business and outlets. As has been shown, J. B. Saunders, whom *Farm Chemicals* described as a "bonafide marketing genius," was given the responsibility of finding the personnel and organizing that part. W. E. Jaqua, who had fertilizer experience with a West Coast chemical company, was brought in to assist him. The strategy developed was to get a few plants in as many geographical areas as possible, thus acquiring "some experience before we get too far along with our investments."

The second step came as a result of an exchange agreement dated June 19, 1963. On the following August 12, Kerr-McGee secured the 30,000 shares of Baugh Chemical Corporation, of Baltimore, by exchanging 300,000 shares of its own common stock. By this acquisition Kerr-McGee obtained a company which had been in business since 1817, producing the oldest branded fertilizer in America. In addition to the experience of the personnel Baugh had thirteen plants and seventy distribution centers. It also owned 2,000 acres of phosphate reserves in Florida, which Saunders—who was quickly named president of Baugh—said were alone worth the purchase price of the entire firm.[22]

Two other small acquisitions in November fell into the same pattern. The first was the purchase of the capital stock of the Poteau (Oklahoma) Lime Company, and, more important, the buying of Dorchester Fertilizer Company's 13,254 shares at $65 each. Thus, even before it produced a pound of potash or phosphate, Kerr-McGee was in the fertilizer business, with a marketing organization and good bases for operation in the eastern and midwestern parts of the nation. Despite these substantial outlays, the company had also brought some 600,000 shares of its own stock, half of which was used to obtain Baugh.[23]

In November the United States was stunned by the unexpected death of its chief of state when an assassin's bullet removed John F. Kennedy from the national scene and from the office of president. But again the reins of power moved into other hands, and only the emotional trauma haunted Americans during the succeeding months. Other phases of national life

[21]"Kerr-McGee New Fertilizer Giant," *Farm Chemicals* October, 1964, pages unnumbered.

[22] Lease Records file, "Contract 800-1"; *Metal Mining & Processing* (May, 1964), 65; *Wall Street Journal*, August 13, 1963; interview with J. B. Saunders. In September Jaqua became president of Baugh.

[23] Lease Records file, "Cont. #816" for Dorchester. A summary review for 1963 is found in Securities and Exchange Commission, "Post Effective Amendment No. 7 to Form S-1 Registration Statement," November 20, 1963.

adjusted rapidly to the change. Indeed, for the world of oil, Lyndon B. Johnson offered interesting speculations, his Texas background being one with which it could identify.

The year had proved that Robert S. Kerr's physical presence was not vital to the progress of Kerr-McGee. Yet there was still one area, politics, in which the senator's past continued to involve Kerr-McGee. In the campaign to fill his vacant Senate seat, surprisingly even his death did not release Kerr-McGee from involuntary participation as a campaign issue. But this time the accusations against the company had the effect of placing it on both sides of the race. In the Democratic primary an aide to former Governor J. Howard Edmondson charged that the expenses of his opponent, Fred Harris, were being underwritten by Kerr-McGee, with "over $100,000 invested in Harris' campaign in administrative assistance alone," and that Harris had the "brand of Kerr-McGee Oil Company stamped all over him." The aide continued that it was one thing for a senator to own an oil company, but "I think it's an entirely different thing for an oil company to own a United States Senator."

Then there was the other side of the fence. The Republican candidate was the former University of Oklahoma football coach Bud Wilkinson, whose weekly show had been sponsored by Kerr-McGee. The argument here ran: "For 17 years, Coach Wilkinson was on the payroll of Mr. McGee's oil company." When Edmondson himself charged that nine of Kerr's former staff members were being paid by Kerr-McGee to work against him, this was too much for Dean McGee to ignore. He publicly stated that the nine people mentioned were only part of the group of long-time Robert Kerr employees to whom he had offered positions with the company the day after the senator's death. Only six had elected to join Kerr-McGee, and two of those had soon returned to Washington. McGee added: "The other four are full-time employees of Kerr-McGee and devote their full work week to our Company's business. The others on Edmondson's list are not and never have been employees of Kerr-McGee." The charges concerning Wilkinson were not dignified by an answer.[24]

---

[24] *Daily Oklahoman*, May 21, 1964; *Tulsa Tribune*, May 21, 1964; and *Tulsa World*, May 23, 1964.

Chapter 20

Asphalt Makes Headlines 1964–1965

The spectacular deaths by violence shocked the nation in the closing days of 1963 and cast a pall that would last for years to come. A genuine fear resulted that the president's murder might well be the result of a conspiracy with foreign overtones. His assassin's slaying gave the theory credence, and a blue-ribbon panel was established to seek out the facts. But violence appeared to generate violence when the domestic civil-rights confrontations took on alarming characteristics, culminating in 1965 in the Watts riots in California and the Selma, Alabama, freedom march. The nation was further traumatized when a war, overtly backed by the Communists, broke out in Vietnam. The government's decision to support South Vietnam reminded many of the no-win Korean conflict, and angry protests erupted in the press and on college campuses.

Faced with almost daily recitals of fresh disasters, Americans sought diversions from any source. New York's misfortune in its famous blackout seemed mildly amusing for those not forced to suffer through it. But the most reassuring ego booster came from the space program. Televised scenes of American astronauts taking a walk in space seemed positive proof that the United States was ahead of the Russians there, if nowhere else. There was some hope in the economy, for, ironically, the increasing domestic disorders paralleled steady economic improvement. President Johnson optimistically stated, "We are in the midst of the greatest upsurge of economic well-being in the history of any nation."

This happy glow spread to the petroleum industry. Domestic production of oil and gas rose, and few seemed concerned that oil imports did also. By

January, 1964, Kerr-McGee was midway in the best financial year of its history. Its uranium holdings were the largest in the country, and it owned the first private helium refinery. Moreover, a major position in fertilizer was rapidly developing. The firm's wells in thirteen states and in Venezuela and Canada enjoyed good proration limits. Concentration in the Gulf of Mexico, where it held leases on 212,000 (gross) acres, paid off with major oil reserves in the Breton Sound area and a large gas pool on Block 28 of the Ship Shoal region.

Already recognized as a leading contract driller, with special experience in foreign and offshore drilling, Kerr-McGee was now preparing to enter a new frontier, the North Sea. Before January was over, Transworld Drilling and four German firms formed Transocean Drilling to seek contracts and begin construction of a new $5.5 million rig designed by Kerr-McGee for that specific area. Kerr-McGee as the parent company was the majority stockholder in this new venture.[1]

In fact, prospects looked so good that in February the regular dividend was increased by five cents a share, and the directors approved the acquisition of yet another fertilizer company. This culminated on July 1 with the purchase of Hubbard-Hall Chemical Company of Waterbury, Connecticut, through the exchange of 94,869 shares of Kerr-McGee common stock. Undoubtedly some of the optimism behind these moves derived from anticipation of successfully concluding negotiations to recover the remaining money from the Argentina 500-well contract. Another boost to the income column of the balance sheet came with the announcement that the first lignite ash from North Dakota had reached Ambrosia Lake for processing. More welcome news followed in April with the discovery of oil on Block 229, Ship Shoal; moreover, the addition of a 60-liter-per-hour liquefier at its Navajo plant made the company the only pure helium-gas producer that was also in the liquefaction and cryogenic business.[2]

Another major step was made in uranium at this time. The existing nuclear-products plant at Cushing, Oklahoma, had outgrown the available space, and it was anticipated that the markets for processed nuclear materials would increase. Consequently, plans were approved for a $1,500,000 facility on the Cimarron River north of Oklahoma City. Designed to convert enriched uranium hexafluoride (UF_6) into fuel materials such as uranium dioxide pellets ready for assembly into reactor-fuel elements, its construction was viewed by the public and management alike as a logical and farseeing, even patriotic, move. In the light of later developments, Kerr-McGee had reason for second thoughts.

But at the time there were no doubts, as attention focused on consolida-

[1] *Wall Street Journal*, January 28, 1964. In regard to uranium *Fortune* concluded that, while the firm's achievements in that industry had often been "eyed suspiciously" by other producers, they had "never been demonstrated to be due to political influence." "The Great Uranium Glut," *Fortune*, February, 1964, pp. 108ff.

[2] *Wall Street Journal*, February 17, March 31, April 20, July 1, July 8, 1964; *Kermac News*, March–April, 1964, and July, 1964.

Kerr-McGee helium liquifier plant at Navajo, Arizona.

tions and further expansions. In May and June the recently acquired Poteau Lime Company was liquidated, and a new Triangle subsidiary created. The new firm was Cloverleaf Service Stations, Inc., which was formed, according to J. B. Saunders, to avoid getting into a price war with other companies who would become alarmed if Kerr-McGee suddenly came into the area with a large number of new stations. The cash-flow situation was improved by selling Midway Foundation, Inc., a production-payment interest for $3.2 million. This might have been involved with the decision to purchase another fertilizer company. AM Chemical, of Minnesota, and its three blending plants.

The annual report for June, 1964, opened with the statement: "Your company has just concluded the most successful year in its history." It had been a year marked by solid growth in oil-and-gas production, offshore drilling, marketing, gas processing, minerals, and expansion of the firm's position in fertilizer. With the addition of Baugh Chemical and T. J. Moss, sales of products and services jumped almost $36 million, to $250,116,420; net income rose 10 percent; and cash flow reached a new high. These records were achieved despite lower earnings from Argentina and smaller sales of uranium as a result of AEC's stretch-out program. Net working capital went to $53,486,916 and total assets to $285,865,365, while long-term debt mounted by only $2,915,873 (see Table 20.3).

Other areas showed promise. Revenue from gas processing operations in the various natural-gasoline plants in which Kerr-McGee had interests was up 25 percent and would go higher when the new facility in Louisiana was completed. The program of construction and long-term leasing of modern service stations in order to control a sizable portion of its 1,324 retail gasoline outlets had been substantially achieved. The company was very sanguine concerning future demand for uranium, the vanadium plant had solved its startup problem, and the potash mill was on schedule. Acquired were important phosphate reserves in Florida and in Idaho, additional potash lands in Canada, favorable copper leases in Arizona and New Mexico, gold in Nevada, and lead and zinc in Missouri.

Some of the subsidiaries had record years. Cato had recovered so well from the fire that it reported its greatest annual sales volume. Triangle marketed in excess of 70,000 barrels of petroleum products per day, controlled about three hundred service stations in the southeastern part of the nation, and had begun expansion of its naphtha refinery to 9,000 barrels per day. Several divisions were likewise prospering. Wood products, represented by T. J. Moss, showed a profit. Although the plant-foods sector was less than a year old, it had built and put into operation five more blending units in addition to those it had bought. Additional plants would soon be constructed at selected locations in the Southwest, Midwest, and Southeast (see Table 20.2).[3]

Kerr-McGee participated in 15 foreign and 85 domestic wells. Its oldest division, contract drilling, had had a satisfactory year domestically, complet-

[3] Kerr-McGee Oil Industries, Inc., *1964 Annual Report*.

326

ing 122. In the Gulf, Rig 55 was destroyed by fire, but the remaining 9 offshore units had a 96 percent utilization. The 6 domestic land rigs, however, averaged only 25 percent utilization, although two were drilling on the AEC project. The big change was in foreign operations, where only 30 wells were completed—28 in Argentina and one each in Panama and Costa Rica. After January 1, 1964, none of the 4 rigs in Latin America had contracts, and they were either sold or brought back to the United States. Elsewhere things were more heartening. Rig 46 made the 7,000-mile trip to Africa and began operations for Nigeria Gulf Oil, and Transocean was off to a good start with its first unit soon to be commissioned, a second contracted for, and firm promises of work for both (see Table 20.5).[4]

The well count for the fiscal year sheds further light on the company's operations. Of the 77 gross successful wells (27.35 net) drilled on its account, 62 had been in the United States (46 in Louisiana), 1 in Canada, and 14 in Venezuela. Fifty-nine had produced oil, 9 gas, and 9 condensate. Total wells stood at 1,639, or a net of 779.80. Most of these were still in Texas (38.8 percent), but Louisiana had risen to 12.2 percent and Venezuela to 5.6 percent. Arizona, Colorado, Nebraska, North Dakota, and Canada were each under 1.0 per cent.[5]

Negotiations were still under way for recovery of the rest of the YPF debt. An August payment of $200,000 was viewed as evidence that Argentine authorities considered it a legitimate claim. Other foreign developments in October saw Kerr-McGee and six other companies decide to make a joint bid for a lease offshore Iran. The group name was the Persian Offshore Petroleum Company (later the Iranian Offshore Petroleum Company), of which the National Iranian Oil Company owned 50 percent and Kerr-McGee 14.2857 percent. On December 19 the group was awarded "structure F," which one oilman described as "possibly the last of the 'big elephants' in oil hunting."[6]

There were other developments of note in the United States. The purchase of AM Chemical added three new fertilizer plants, while Hubbard-Hall had fourteen installations—six fertilizer—and 250 employees. The latter acquisition also brought more diversification. Its agricultural division, which manufactured fertilizers and pesticides, accounted for over half of its sales, while its industrial division made metal cleaners, buffing compounds, deoxidizers, and liquid chlorine, among other things. Combined, this represented assets of $5.5 million, and in the past year it had net earnings of $246,000.[7]

Other logical steps led to other unusual involvements for Kerr-McGee. On the thesis that it is sometimes cheaper to buy a section of land in order to

---

[4] Dean McGee personal file, "Rig Utilization Schedule for Month of _____, 1964."

[5] Production Department file, "Well Count as of June 30, 1964."

[6] Lease Records file, "Contract 808"; *Daily Oklahoman*, December 23, 1964; *Offshore and Gulf Coast Oil Reporter*, December, 1964; and Roberta Louise Ironside, *An Adventure Called Skelly* (New York, 1970), pp. 96–97.

[7] Security and Exchange Commission, "Amendment No. 2 to Form S-1 Registration Statement," May 21, 1964.

Moss-American, a Kerr-McGee subsidiary, owns 260,000 acres of timber lands.

get one good service-station site, in 1962 the company bought 145 acres on the edge of the rapidly developing small city of Moore, Oklahoma. The problem of the extra land was solved two years later with a novel approach: platting it as the Kings Manor housing addition. As the developer, Kerr-McGee installed the streets and utilities but was not involved in any of the construction on the 478 home-sites, the 9-acre school site, or the 21 acres set apart for a shopping center.[8]

These were exciting times in the home office as new enterprises were blended with customary routines. On July 22, Dean McGee was able to write to Glen J. Talbott, vice-president of the National Farmers Union, that the contractors estimated that the potash mill would be in production by September 1, 1965, at the latest. The facility was planned to operate at half capacity for the first six months and then go on full production of 1,500 tons per day. Soon after this, Wall Street was amazed by the report that Kerr-

[8] Interview with Dean A. McGee, October 12, 1976; Oklahoma City *Guffey's Journal*, July 22, 1964; *Moore* (Oklahoma) *Monitor*, July 23, 1964, and December 9, 1965.

Poles to be creosoted at Texarkana, Texas.

McGee was talking merger with U.S. Smelting, Refining & Mining Company. For several months the discussions continued, but finally they were broken off, the speculation being that Kerr-McGee had decided that U.S. Smelting was too large and diversified for assimilation.

Receiving almost as much national publicity as this aborted merger was an addition to Kerr-McGee's college-scholarships program. The firm already offered support for children of its employees and later was to establish a scholarship at the University of Wisconsin for students enrolled in courses leading to a career in the fertilizer industry. It was the program at all-black Langston University in Oklahoma, however, which drew nationwide comment.

As has been indicated, these were years of racial strife nationally. Blacks had shifted their emphasis from school integration to demands for a share in the economic prosperity enjoyed by most white citizens. School desegregation was accomplished with relative ease in Oklahoma, and the black leadership there avoided the violence that occurred in other states. But economic inequalities in Oklahoma could no longer be ignored. Acting as a responsible citizen, Kerr-McGee made its contribution through education, with a program that annually offered four-year grants leading to a degree in business

329

Moss-American plant at Springfield, Missouri.

administration to eight students at Langston. The stated purpose was to help meet the needs for skilled black personnel in retail petroleum operations and to offer Langston graduates greater economic opportunities. Even more socially significant, Kerr-McGee coupled with the scholarships the opportunity for practical experience through summer employment with the company.[9]

Less dramatic were events within the normal sphere of business activities. In helium and uranium it was once more "good news, bad news." The good news was in the form of the laudatory article in the August 10, 1964, issue of the *Oil and Gas Journal*. It described Kerr-McGee's helium operations and a new, small discovery of that gas two miles east of Pinta

[9] For potash see Chemical Lease Records file, "National Farmers Union Service Corporation—April 1963–December 1965"; for the merger see *Wall Street Journal*, August 18, 1964; and for scholarships see *Oklahoma Journal*, August 26, 1964, and *Daily Oklahoman*, October 25, 1964.

Forest-products treatment plant at Meridian, Mississippi.

Dome on the Navajo Springs structure. The very good news was the passage of a law in August permitting for the first time private ownership of radioactive materials and establishing a "toll" system whereby the federal government would "enrich" uranium for its owners. Since this opened a private market to the uranium industry, it was of tremendous importance to Kerr-McGee. For one thing, the use of atomic power to generate electricity was practically assured; second, the company could justify construction of the Cimarron facility by the expanding markets for its fuel pellets.

Not so good were the lawsuits generated by its helium activities in Arizona. First, a group of Hopi Indians brought an unsuccessful suit in the United States District Court against Kerr-McGee to prevent drilling of any sort, on the grounds that it would destroy tribal shrines. More serious, and more costly, was an action brought by the state of Arizona over the issue of whether reasonable royalties were being paid to that government. Arizona's land commissioners canceled Kerr-McGee's leases on state-owned lands until the issue was legally settled by Kerr-McGee's loss of an appeal to the state supreme court on April 1, 1965.[10]

That the company still saw opportunities for growth in the lumber industry was demonstrated in September. On the thirtieth it purchased the American Creosoting Corporation of Louisville, Kentucky, for $3,875,000 in cash. American Creosoting had been formed in 1907, and at this time was one of the largest wood-preserving companies in the nation, with plants in seven states. Later it too was merged with Moss.

October struck Kerr-McGee with a roar. The big natural-gas discovery on Block 218, Ship Shoal, had hardly been celebrated when, on October 4, Hurricane Hilda struck the heart of Kerr-McGee operations in the Gulf off Louisiana. At the time the company had nine units working in the area, including Rig 54, the world's largest submersible. The crews and about 500 other employees were evacuated, but the rigs, worth some $25 million had to be left to ride out the fury of the storm. For two days no word was received at headquarters concerning their fate, and A. T. F. Seale admitted, "The suspense is about to get us." But fortune smiled: Rig 54 shifted about fifty feet and tilted at an angle, while another unit was moved a mile from its anchorage, yet total damage was minor.[11]

Meanwhile, the rapidity of Kerr-McGee's expansion caught the attention of *Investor's Reader*. A feature article traced the evolution of the firm and offered McGee's explanation of the company's motivation. "We think of ourselves as a natural resource company. We elected a long time ago to concentrate on materials that have to be found rather than manufactured—like petrochemicals for example." The reason was that "they are not so competitive," and natural resources "are the things I know best."[12] Despite this, however, in November, Kerr-McGee purchased five mixed-fertilizer plants, located in the Carolinas, Georgia, and Florida, from the Southern Cotton Oil Division of Hunt Food & Industries, Inc., and made plans for another acquisition in the same field.

More changes came to Kerr-McGee in the personnel area. The last member of the early management team, Travis Kerr, announced his retirement from the company and from the Board of Directors. Less and less active in recent years, he was still well liked and respected for his role during the formative period of the firm. The board did not fill his position as director and the bylaws were changed to abolish the one of vice-chairman.

Another kind of change, although unremarked, was taking place—one destined to effect Kerr-McGee's future in an emphatic way. At this time the number of its workers affiliated with unions represented only a small fraction of the total. They were primarily in refining and mining, and their activities, except for the Kermac Nuclear strike of 1961, gave the corporation little

[10] F. C. Love speech, "The Uranium Industry—1967," before National Western Mining Conference and Exhibition, Denver, February 9, 1967, in Public Relations file, "Uranium Information"; for the helium suit see *Phoenix Evening American*, January 21, 1965.

[11] Public Relations file, "Moss Tie Company"; *Wall Street Journal*, October 1, 1964.

[12] "Kerr-McGee Oil Stretches Out," *Investor's Reader*, October 7, 1964, pp. 17–20.

reason for concern. Competitive salaries, stock options, and contributions to employee retirement plans had been sufficient to hold the loyalty of most workers. However, as Kerr-McGee expanded into the lumber and fertilizer fields, it inherited additional unions and their members. For example, acquisitions in 1964 added 373 more union members. Kerr-McGee's growth, diversity, and increasing dependence upon highly skilled technicians made the company more and more attractive to union organizers, and the future would bring added pressure from this source.

The year ended on an active note with the sale of 241 service stations to Oklahoma Stations, Inc., the christening of Transocean I, and the merger, effective December 31, of Kermac Nuclear Fuels into the parent company.[13] Nor was the coming year to be much different. For Kerr-McGee, 1965 would be marked by fewer acquisitions but an increase in completion of on-the-board projects.

The January, 1965, *Kermac News* featured a story on the construction of three new offshore drilling units. Rig 50 was being built in Texas at a cost of $2.2 million. It was a self-elevating unit for use primarily in well work-overs, and completion was scheduled in seven months. A Dutch shipyard was constructing Rig 58 for $6 million, which would be the company's first rig able to drill from a floating position. Transocean II was a $6.5 million version of Transocean I. Designed for North Sea work, it was being built by a British firm.

These three units were indicative of changes occurring in the drilling business, for if Kerr-McGee were to maintain its position in the industry, it had to be able to compete at all depths and under all conditions. Tsi Yu, long-time design engineer for the company, described the problem as follows:

We are constantly competing against ourselves and others. Our aim is to come up with something new that will better meet the demands of a changing marketplace. The idea is to create a product that will sell and make money for Kerr-McGee. When we are asked to design a rig, the first thing we need to know is: Where will the new rig work? How far offshore and in what depth water will it work? How deep will it be required to probe in search of oil or gas?

And then there is the economic factor. Yu continued:

A lot of money can be spent in the design and construction of a rig. But it will not be a well-designed one unless it can make money for the company. The aim is to create a drilling unit adequate to do a prescribed job safely and economically. . . . It's like the old Chinese saying that you never judge a man until the day he dies. You don't judge a rig and its design until the last day it works. Rigs 46 and 47 were built about 1956 and are still earning money for Transworld and Kerr-McGee. They are well-designed rigs.

---

[13] Bylaws, November 8, 1964; Securities and Exchange Commission, "Post Effective Amendment No. 9 to Form S-1 Registration Statement," November 12, 1964; *Wall Street Journal*, November 3, 1964; Oklahoma Secretary of State, Corporation file.

In 1965, climatic and wave conditions in the North Sea were special challenges, demanding greater stability from the rigs and more protection for their crews. In the more temperate and placid Gulf of Mexico, exploration was now in depths beyond the capacity of any previous equipment.[14]

Most of the excitement within the company, however, focused on the Iranian venture. Kerr-McGee and its partners in the Iranian Offshore Petroleum Company (IROPCO) had won the concession by payment of a signature bonus of $40 million, a production bonus of $12 million, and a promise to pay Iranian taxes which could run up to 50 percent of profits. Kerr-McGee paid $5,714,285.71 for a one-seventh interest in the 556,128 acres. It also created Kerr-McGee Iranian Oil Company to oversee its interests in the joint structure, and, on April 27, IROPCO contracted with Kerr-McGee Limited to drill the wells for a fee of $1 million, plus $8,625 per day. Tender-Rig 55 was towed the 12,000 miles to Iran during July and August, and on September 9, its first well was spudded in the Persian Gulf about 50 miles offshore in 210 feet of water.[15]

More controversial and more profitable to Kerr-McGee than the Iranian project was another action, which passed virtually unnoticed at the time. On August 25, 1964, the company had asked permission of the Navajo Council to conduct geological and geophysical petroleum surveys on tribal lands. This approval was quickly granted, but the request for a lease ran into a delay. J. P. Ryan wrote on September 9, 1964, "I traveled to Window Rock and Gallup in an effort to determine if we could hasten the approval and issuance of the Indian lease we won at the August Navajo sale. I discovered that this process could not be interfered with, and that the Tribe would approve or disapprove our bids at such time as they chose to act and not before . . . and no one seems to know when they will get around to approving our bids."

But consent finally came. On November 27 application to drill was made, and on January 22, 1965, the Navajo #1 was spudded about fifty miles southwest of Farmington, New Mexico, in the rugged Chuska Mountains. The wildcat was drilled to a total depth of 3,864 feet before operations were suspended for about five months because of bad weather. On reactivation, two tests for oil were negative, so the hole was tested, unsuccessfully, for helium. On June 22, the well was plugged and abandoned, but it would eventually be a source of surprise and widespread debate.[16]

A federal contract, two small acquisitions, and some internal restructuring occurred before the end of the fiscal year. The new Kerr-McGee Nuclear Products Division and its fifty employees were elated by news that it had received its first contract, although the Cimarron facility was not yet completed. This $700,000 order from the AEC to produce some 80,000 pounds

[14] *Kermac News*, December, 1978, pp. 3–4.

[15] Lease Records file, "Contract 808" and "Contract 808-3"; Ironside, *An Adventure Called Skelly*, p. 97; *Oil and Gas Journal*, February 22, 1965; *Kermac News*, April, 1965; Securities and Exchange Commission, "Post Effective Amendment No. 11 to S-1 Registration Statement," October 28, 1965; and *Daily Oklahoman*, January 19, 1965.

[16] Lease Records file, "P689."

of pure thorium from thorium nitrate seemed proof that once again Kerr-McGee management had correctly assessed future developments in that energy field.

The first 1965 acquisition came in February, when Kerr-McGee offered 3,074 shares of its common stock in exchange for the 22 percent of the shares of Chem-Salts, Inc., of Georgia that were not already owned by Hubbard-Hall. A similar swap was made on March 9 when, in exchange for 3,252 shares, Kerr-McGee obtained all of the outstanding shares of Molony Fertilizer Company of South Carolina. Dean McGee was probably referring to this trade when on March 21 he announced that the company had just bought three fertilizer blending plants and was building eleven more in the South and Midwest. At the time Kerr-McGee had sixty-eight such plants in operation and expected "to be in competition in plant foods from the Rockies to the Atlantic Coast." McGee predicted that 1965 sales would reach $50 million in fertilizer and farm chemicals.[17]

Significant reorganizational changes occurred, also. American Creosoting and T. J. Moss were merged to form Moss-American, Inc. At the May board meeting the bylaws were amended to allow more than one executive vice-president, a position then held by F. C. Love. J. B. Saunders then resigned as senior vice-president and was elected to the new slot. McGee characterized this move as indicative of the emphasis upon "accelerating growth and expansion by acquisition and the development of new opportunities, both domestic and foreign."

Several more steps were taken during 1965 to change the public image of the company. The corporate symbol was redesigned in April to represent better the firm's various products and subsidiaries. It was also decided to shift the fiscal year from one that ended on June 30 to one that matched the calendar year. Last, in May, the board voted to submit at the next annual stockholders' meeting a proposal to rename the company. The logic was that the current title, Kerr-McGee Oil Industries, Inc., implied a misleading limit on the scope of its activities. The suggested new one, Kerr-McGee Corporation, eliminated this possible confusion and, in fact, left the door open for an unending number of diversifications.

Dean McGee's remark about "accelerating growth and expansion by acquisition and the development of new opportunities" needed money to implement. A breakdown of the capital expenditures for the previous years and what would be spent in 1965 shows the areas on which the company concentrated (see Table 20.1).

The June 30, 1965, annual report heralded yet another record year (see Table 20.3). Earnings increased 14 percent with sales of $300,399,770; net income rose nearly $3 million; total assets rose almost $40 million; and working capital grew by $3.5 million—all of this despite higher capital expenditures of almost $12 million, higher taxes (up by $3.5 million), and

---

[17] Lease Records file, "Cont. 881"; *Daily Oklahoman*, February 21, March 21, and April 5, 1965. The fertilizer plants were in Louisiana, Minnesota, and Iowa. *Wall Street Journal*, April 6, 1965.

Kerr-McGee Oil Industries, Inc.

Table 20.1. Capital Expenditures, 1961–65

| | Year Ended June 30 | | | | | |
	1961	1962	1963	1964	1965	Total
Oil and gas production	$ 5,869,820	$10,089,312	$ 5,015,544	$ 9,327,494	$15,121,071	$ 45,423,241
Drilling	2,245,922	3,155,503	8,047,854	6,412,343	8,717,889	28,579,511
Marketing, pipeline, and land refining	4,872,844	6,057,146	13,429,913	8,279,274	5,496,531	38,135,708
Plant food		13,879	2,767,344	8,086,586	15,206,794	26,074,603
Minerals	15,566,827	4,389,974	3,426,834	2,044,730	1,893,363	27,321,728
Other	649,630	5,696,441	5,673,006	4,199,704	3,788,381	20,007,162
Total	$29,205,043	$29,402,255	$38,360,495	$38,350,131	$50,224,029	$185,541,953

2,000 new employees. Long-term debt jumped $6,204,000 as a result of a $7 million bank loan to Transocean for rig construction and a $6.1 million loan to Kermac Potash. All divisions contributed record earnings. There was increased income from oil-and-gas production, offshore drilling, and the operations by Triangle. Uranium sales held steady, while demand for railroad ties accelerated.

There were many highlights in the report. Construction would soon bring expansion in several areas: new drilling devices would increase the total to fourteen offshore rigs, the nuclear production facility at Cimarron was about finished, and a new multimillion-dollar hydrocracker was under way at Wynnewood to update the refinery technologically. Fifty-two fertilizer plants had been built or acquired, and Kerr-McGee and its affiliates had a total of seventy-two plants in twenty-seven states east of the Rocky Mountains. Sales of gas, oil, and distillates reached a high of $24.4 million, while those of helium increased 18 percent and oil refinery throughput by 7 percent. The potash mill and mines were on schedule for fall, and production of vanadium had been increased to meet growing demand. Significant new mineral reserves had been acquired: phosphate in Florida, potash in Canada, and coal in Oklahoma and Wyoming.[18]

As of June 30, 1965, Kerr-McGee had engaged in drilling 101 development and exploratory wells in the United States, Canada, and Venezuela, with a 72 percent success ratio. Of the producing wells 25 were offshore Louisiana. The well count as of June 30 showed that 26 wildcats brought 8 discoveries. There was a total of 1,675 gross, or 790.62 net, wells, of which 551.58 were oil, 148.26 were gas, and 58.14 were condensate. Of the 73 new producers added, 45 were in the United States, 24 in Venezuela, and 4 in

[18] Kerr-McGee Oil Industries, Inc., *1965 Annual Report*. Two 10-K forms were filed, one for the year ending June 30, 1965, and one for the year ending December 31, 1965. The new corporate name appears on the later form.

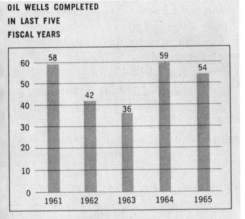

OIL WELLS COMPLETED
IN LAST FIVE
FISCAL YEARS

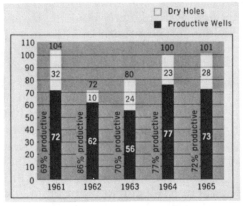

☐ Dry Holes
■ Productive Wells

WELLS COMPLETED
IN WHICH COMPANY
PARTICIPATED

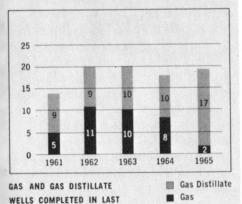

GAS AND GAS DISTILLATE
WELLS COMPLETED IN LAST
FIVE FISCAL YEARS

☐ Gas Distillate
■ Gas

Fig. 20.1. Wells completed, 1961–65, and wells completed in which company participated, 1961–65. From Kerr-McGee Oil Industries, Inc., *June 30, 1965, Annual Report*.

Canada; 54 were oil wells, and 24 were in Louisiana. The growing importance of Louisiana to the company is apparent, for Kerr-McGee had interests there in 68 wells on land and 174 offshore, although these accounted for only 13 percent of the firm's total wells. That year Louisiana also saw the largest number of dry holes—13—and an idea of the range of company drilling can be seen in the fact that dry holes were also encountered in Canada, Venezuela, Pennsylvania, and California (see Fig. 20.1).[19]

"Rig Operations" reports for the fiscal year ending June 30, 1965, have not been found, so exact figures for contract drilling are not available. Other sources, however, indicate that during this period 11 offshore devices were operated: 8 in the Gulf of Mexico, 1 off Nigeria, 1 in the German portion of the North Sea, and 1 in the Persian Gulf. Adding 8 land and 4 completion rigs brings a total of 23. Of the land units 3 worked for the Argentina–Cities

[19] Production Department file, "Annual Well Count as of June 30, 1965."

Service Development Company in Argentina, and 3 were held by Bighole Drilling for sinking large-diameter holes (see Table 20.5).

Commercial publications give an overview of the general offshore drilling picture during the year. By this time, while no two rigs were exactly alike, there were two basic types—those that were bottom-supported and those that floated. Offshore drilling was ten times more expensive than land drilling, and the price of a unit could run up to $8 million. Cost of operation in deeper waters ran as high as $10,000 a day. There were many fixed-platform rigs in the Gulf, which were worked from a supply tender. A triangular submersible barge, like Kerr-McGee's Rig 54, contained a working deck of 30,000 square feet and air-conditioned quarters for forty-four men, and was towed to the drilling area. Once there, air was released from the columnar legs and water let in, allowing the bases of the legs to sink to the ocean floor.

"Jack-up" mobile barges were also floated to the scene. There the mat was lowered for support, and the drilling tower was jacked up on four columns, the legs being adjusted for uneven ground. Ship-hulled rigs floated on the surface and were held in place with long cables and heavy anchors. Self-propelled catamarans had twin hulls, with the drill slots between them. The older, rectangular units, like Rig 45, were more restricted in depth of operation and were more difficult to tow, but they had greater stability. This particular Kerr-McGee rig set world records for the greatest number of wells drilled in the shortest time and for the highest daily footage average. Over a period of twenty months it punched down a 6,850-foot well in Block 20, Breton Sound, every nine and one-quarter days at the rate of 742 feet daily. During the preceding ten years Rig 45 had sunk 105 wells, for a cumulative footage of 901,684 feet.[20]

The last six months of 1965 marked an interim period during which the fiscal year changed to coincide with the calendar year. But no change could be noted in the company's vigorous pace of growth. In July it was announced that Kerr-McGee was ready to start mining coal in Oklahoma if a market could be found. The executive committee also approved the exchange of 29,915 shares of Kerr-McGee common for the capital stock of Potosi Tie and Lumber Company. In this deal, completed on August 16, the company acquired a firm started in Saint Louis in 1916 for the production and sale of crossties and, also, the Hobbs-Western Company, which had been bought by Potosi in 1951.[21]

Finally, after what McGee described as "a real experience for us," Argentina agreed to pay for the 500 wells drilled before 1963 and to extend the contract for 350 additional wells. This solution had been a long time in coming. In February, YPF had called for bids to drill 210 wells, and, curiously, Transworld made an unsuccessful bid, despite the fact that set-

[20] *Fortune*, February, 1965, pp. 131–35; *Offshore and Gulf Coast Oil Reporter*, March, 1965, pp. 69–72.

[21] Securities and Exchange Commission, "Post Effective Amendment No. 11 to S-1 Registration Statement," October 28, 1965; *Daily Oklahoman*, July 11, 1965.

tlement had not been reached on the earlier drilling and payment on this contract would be made in pesos. In the meantime F. C. Love made repeated negotiating trips to Buenos Aires, where even the head of YPF predicted that Transworld could win any lawsuit. At last, in October three out-of-court settlements, including Transworld's, were announced. Transworld got some $4.5 million, rumored to be about $800,000 less than its claim. Payment was by twenty-four monthly promissory notes, carrying 6.25 percent interest, through the First National City Bank of New York, beginning on June 1, 1965. Furthermore, Transworld could reexport all of its equipment, or apply for permanent residence permits, without paying import taxes.[22]

Another departure occurred in August, when Kerr-McGee added its own name to the list of branded gasolines by converting seventeen of its service stations in Oklahoma City. Other news stories announced a completion date of July, 1966, for the multimillion-dollar, 4,200-barrel-per-day hydrocracker at Wynnewood, the commissioning ceremonies for Rig 50, awarding of a contract to a subsidiary to drill the test well in Iran, and, finally, the purchase of three more fertilizer-blending plants in New Mexico and Texas from Wood Chemical Company.[23]

September was a quiet month for the company—if Hurricane Betsy is ignored. Humble Oil lost five of its twelve rigs in the Gulf, but Kerr-McGee was lucky again, with damage limited to a single derrick. Of passing interest was the notice that the company was testing a nuclear generator to operate navigational lights on one of its wellhead platforms in the Gulf. The principal news, however, was the announcement of a phosphate-mining and processing facility to be built in central Florida, near Brewster. The dragline for mining, washing, and flotation plants and a product dryer would cost about $9 million, and the facility, with a capacity of 1.5 million tons annually, was given a completion date of October, 1966.[24]

A small cloud that appeared early in 1965 had assumed threatening proportions by October. On July 22, 1965, eighteen oil companies, including Kerr-McGee, were indicted in Missouri for violation of the Sherman Antitrust Act between 1960 and 1963. Through "a continuing agreement, understanding and concerted action," it was alleged that they had submitted "collusive, non-competitive and rigged bids and price quotations" for asphalt sold to that state. Arraignment came on September 8, but before the trial date of December 20, Kerr-McGee and thirteen others changed their pleas from "not guilty" to "no contest," probably because of the small amounts involved. In November, Kerr-McGee was fined $50,000. Jack H. Mitchell, the manager of its asphalt division, received a fine of $2,000, a six

[22] *Daily Oklahoman*, July 16, 1965; *Wall Street Journal*, July 19, 1965; and Raymond F. Mikesell, *Foreign Investment in the Petroleum and Mineral Industries* (Baltimore, 1971), pp. 182–83.

[23] *Daily Oklahoman*, August 1, 15, 20, and 26, 1965; *Wall Street Journal*, August 18, 1965.

[24] Kerr-McGee press release, September 28, 1965, in Kerr-McGee Public Relations Department file; *Wall Street Journal*, September 30, 1965; *Kermac News*, October, 1965.

months' suspended sentence, and a year's probation. The company made a voluntary repayment of $91,032 to the state of Missouri for the difference between what it charged the state and private contractors.[25]

Undoubtedly influenced by the events in Missouri, the attorney general of Oklahoma began an investigation of Oklahoma's asphalt purchases for the period 1960 to 1964. On October 4, that official filed suit against Kerr-McGee and nine other companies for $30 million, including triple damages. Two days later McGee answered the charges with a statement that the complaints were "not true and have no foundation in fact." Shortly thereafter two Oklahoma paving contractors filed a similar suit in the state courts. In preliminary hearings McGee admitted that the firm had been fined by Missouri but pointed out that asphalt sales accounted for only about $5 million of the firm's annual revenues of some $350 million and that it would be idiotic to conspire for such a small sum. James J. Kelly stated that during the four-year period in question Kerr-McGee had sold only about 16 percent of its asphalt production in Oklahoma, and, considering the profits from asphalt, "It would be charitable to say they were sad." Judge Luther Eubanks, however, refused to dismiss the state's suit, saying, "It's a pretty thin case, but however slim, there are some factual elements."

McGee, in a letter dated December 2, 1965, to Martin Garber, chairman of the Oklahoma Highway Commission, stated that from January 1, 1960, through December 31, 1964, the average price to Missouri had been 10.49 cents per gallon. During that period Oklahoma had bought approximately the same volume for an average of 10.25 cents, a difference of less than one quarter of a cent. Then on January 28, 1966, in an open letter to all his Oklahoma employees, McGee charged that two aspirants for the 1966 Democratic nomination for governor had announced their candidacy based upon claims that a number of Oklahoma companies, including Kerr-McGee, had improperly set the price charged for asphalt sold in the state. McGee further claimed that, despite the facts, newspapers continued to print the charge that Oklahomans had paid three cents more per gallon for asphalt than had Missouri. He pointed out that during 1965 the company's total sales to the state of Oklahoma had amounted to only $132,586—an amount so small that "frankly it would not be missed if discontinued." During the years 1961 through 1966 Kerr-McGee's asphalt production ran between 53 million and 60.4 million gallons. Of these totals, sales in Oklahoma fluctuated between 9 million and 18.4 million gallons. Its largest percentage of the Oklahoma market was 14.29 percent in 1966, with the low being 8.1 percent in 1965.[26]

---

[25] *St. Louis Post Dispatch*, July 17 and November 19, 1965; *St. Louis Globe Democrat*, July 23, 1965. For full details of the Missouri proceedings see *Oil and Gas Journal*, August 2 and November 29, 1965.

[26] Dean McGee letter, dated January 28, 1966, in files of the Public Relations Department. See also issues of the *Daily Oklahoman* and the *Oklahoma City Times* almost daily after October 6, 1965. Production and sales figures are given in a copy of a letter dated May 5, 1970, from Jack H. Mitchell, manager, Asphalt Sales, Kerr-McGee, to Horace J. DePodwin, Tulsa, from the files of James E. Hibdon, Department of Economics, University of Oklahoma, who served as an expert witness in the case.

Table 20.2. Production Record, 1964–65

	June 30, 1964	Dec. 31, 1965
Production		
Crude oil produced (net barrels)	3,776,345	4,742,465
Natural-gas sales (millions of cubic feet)	65,827	74,698
Oil-and-gas leases (net acres)	1,167,284	967,356
Gas processing		
Gas liquids produced (net barrels)	1,331,905	1,562,511
Refining		
Crude oil processed (barrels)	12,861,143	14,144,350
Uranium		
U_3O_8 concentrate sold (lbs.)	3,652,773	3,310,418
Average price per lb.	$8.00	$8.00
Chemicals		
Plant food sold (tons)	574,526	858,796

Nevertheless, other suits would be filed, some of which would drag on for years. While they were not testifying in various courts, the company's officers spent the rest of 1965 in consolidation efforts. In October the stockholders formally voted to change the name as suggested. In November the board merged Chem-Salts into Hubbard-Hall and Potosi Tie and Hobbs Western into Moss-American, effective December 31. As of the same date Baugh Chemical became Kerr-McGee Chemical Corporation, and it was given responsibility for all fertilizer operations and farm chemicals.

A review of the calendar year 1965 shows developments in two of the older projects that are worthy of mention. By this time nuclear power had crossed the threshold of acceptance by the electric-power industry, and a total of 4,368,000 kilowatts of nuclear-generated electrical capacity was on order, almost a fourth of all electric-power generating equipment contracted that year. One effect was renewed uranium exploration. This very surge in demand perhaps indirectly sparked difficulties for Kerr-McGee at Ambrosia Lake. As noted earlier, when that unit was formed, the "Branson heirs" retained an interest. In February, 1965, they challenged Kerr-McGee's grading of ores produced from this property. Shortly afterward the Bransons sold their rights to Richard D. Bokum, who, in turn, added them to the assets of the Bokum Corporation. In August, Bokum accelerated the dispute with Kerr-McGee and denounced the company to the AEC. Finally, however, in November the two reached an agreement by which, it was hoped, the controversy was settled.[27]

[27] F. C. Love, "The Uranium Industry—1967"; Dean A. McGee, "Supply and Demand for Uranium in Years Ahead," *Commercial and Financial Chronical*, February 13, 1969, pp. 4 (684)ff.; interview with George Cobb, December 7, 1972.

Table 20.3. Financial Highlights, 1964–65

	June 30, 1964	June 30, 1965	Dec. 31, 1965
Total gross income	$253,705,994	$304,077,826	$325,216,802
Net income	20,679,162	23,516,399	25,068,302
Total assets	285,865,365	324,102,394	341,140,542
Cash flow from earnings	44,381,493	43,910,212	47,743,906
Working capital	53,486,916	56,321,016	78,567,767
Properties (net)	155,026,403	172,015,918	186,238,205
Capital expenditures	38,350,131	50,224,029	59,322,686
Long-term debt	57,398,491	63,603,389	90,198,475
Cash dividends	6,861,862	7,830,585	8,023,606
Stockholders' equity	140,763,337	161,285,878	171,561,512
Total taxes paid	11,358,038	12,560,121	11,055,895
Number of employees	5,606	7,067	7,261

The imminent production of commercial amounts of potash necessitated a decision on January 22, 1965, between Kerr-McGee and Farmers Union. They agreed not to create a sales and marketing division to sell the product; instead the two partners would become the purchasers. On April 15, Farmers Union pledged its half of the output to Tenneco Oil Company, while Kerr-McGee decided to market its share through its own sales force.

The closing days of 1965 brought other changes. The directors authorized borrowing $60 million from Prudential Insurance Company of America and sale of $6.2 million worth of phosphate lands in Florida to W. R. Grace & Co. The annual dividend was increased by 10 cents to $1.30 a year, despite the fact that the last quarter's income had risen only slightly because of higher fertilizer production costs and the effects of two hurricanes, which closed down Gulf operations for the longest consecutive period of time since the company began work there. Some good news came, however, with the discovery of copper mineralization in the Bayard area of Grant County, New Mexico, and the announcements that the potash refinery, near Hobbs, New Mexico, and the Oklahoma Cimarron facility had gone on stream.[28]

Another highlight of the year was the doubling of vanadium output to almost 700,000 pounds, at an average sales price of $1.20 per pound, and it was expected that 1 million pounds would be produced in 1966. In helium the eleven active wells at Pinta Dome and Navajo Springs yielded about 593 million cubic feet of gas, containing some 9 percent helium, in the first ten months of 1965, according to the Arizona Oil and Gas Conservation Commission—an increase of about 30 percent over 1964. With an assumed

[28] *Wall Street Journal*, October 22 and 29 and November 9, 1965; Kerr-McGee Public Relations release, "76–3 (January 7, 1976)."

Table 20.4. Common-Stock Highlights, 1964–65

	June 30, 1964	Dec. 31, 1965
Equity per share	$24.69	$26.05
Earnings per share	$ 3.24	$ 3.81
Cash dividends per share	$ 1.10	$ 1.225
Average yield	2.5	2.1
Number of shares outstanding	6,375,637	6,585,464
Number of stockholders	15,883	15,480
New York Stock Exchange		
High	$49.25	$72.12
Low	$34.00	$44.61
Price-earnings ratio		
High	15.20	18.93
Low	10.49	11.71

Table 20.5. Drilling and Exploration Operations, 1964–65

	June 30, 1964	December 31, 1965
Feet drilled	1,183,631	980,918
Total wells/wells completed	152/122	NA/89
Kerr-McGee interest	100	101
Rigs (average)	22	20
Contract drilling	NA	NA

97 percent recovery of helium, the total 1965 production was projected at about 60 million cubic feet of grade A helium.[29]

The shift of the fiscal-year base came about because most of Kerr-McGee's competitors were on a calendar-year basis. Consequently, 1965 closed with a second "mini" annual report, for June 30 through December 31 (see Table 20.3). When restated in this form, 1965 was a record year on both consolidated net income and earnings per share. Sales were $320,924,644, and the investment ratio per employee stood at $46,983.

Dividend payments to shareholders aggregated $4,109,015, or 62.5 cents per share during the last half of 1965. The remaining net income earned during this time was added to retained earnings, which now exceeded $100

[29] For potash see Mineral Lease Records file, "Contract 1204-1," "Contract 1204-33," and "National Farmers Union Service Corporation—April 1963–December 1965"; for vanadium see "S-1 Registration Statement," October 28, 1965; and for helium see *Paydirt*, January 21, 1966.

CAPITAL EXPENDITURES IN RELATION TO DEPRECIATION, DEPLETION AND AMORTIZATION

■ Capital Expenditures

▨ Depreciation, Depletion and Amortization

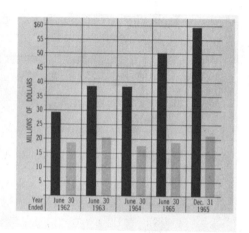

Fig. 20.2. Capital expenditures in relation to depreciation, depletion, and amortization, 1962–65. From Kerr-McGee Corporation, *December 31, 1965, Annual Report.*

DISTRIBUTION OF INCOME DOLLAR

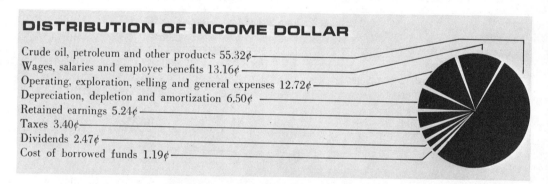

Crude oil, petroleum and other products 55.32¢

Wages, salaries and employee benefits 13.16¢

Operating, exploration, selling and general expenses 12.72¢

Depreciation, depletion and amortization 6.50¢

Retained earnings 5.24¢

Taxes 3.40¢

Dividends 2.47¢

Cost of borrowed funds 1.19¢

Fig. 20.3. Distribution of income dollar, 1965. From Kerr-McGee Corporation, *December 31, 1965, Annual Report.*

million, bringing the stockholders' total ownership interest to a new high. This regular annual reinvestment of a portion of the earnings was the principal means by which Kerr-McGee continued to grow in size and earning power. As the stockholders' equity continued to rise, so did the price of the common stock, (see Table 20.4).

The well count shows that Kerr-McGee had an interest in 81 wells during 1965. Thirty-eight of these were in Louisiana, 29 in Venezuela, 10 in New Mexico, and smaller totals in Texas, Oklahoma, Colorado, Canada, Wyoming, Nebraska, Utah, West Virginia, Iran, Montana, Arizona, and North Dakota. Thirty-one used Kerr-McGee rigs, 30 offshore Louisiana and 1 offshore Iran. The end of the year saw an interest in 811.41 net wells, an increase of 20.17 percent. In contract drilling there were offshore operations in German, Nigerian, and Iranian waters, as well as in the Gulf of Mexico. The only land operations were in Argentina, for none of the domestic land rigs were employed. During the last six months 54 wells were completed, and 11 were in process. Of the completed wells 43 were domestic—25 for Kerr-McGee and the remainder for other firms (20 for Gulf Oil, for example). Overseas Kerr-McGee Limited finished one well in Iran; Kermac Drilling, six in Argentina; Transworld Drilling Limited began four in Nigeria; and Transocean, three in the German North Sea.[30]

Developmental activities on Kerr-McGee properties in the Gulf and in Eddy County, New Mexico, had added significant new gas reserves and additional production. Company drilling had continued in Venezuela, where Kerr-McGee had an interest in 123 wells. Explorations for minerals in the United States and Canada also had progressed, with potash reserves further outlined in 390,000 acres in Canada, and additional coal lands acquired in Wyoming. At Cimarron, Oklahoma, the assembly lines were set up at the nuclear-products plant, and production had begun.

All the subsidiaries claimed a good year. Triangle marketed more than 72,000 barrels of petroleum products daily. Kerr-McGee Chemical—which had been formed from Baugh, the plant-food division of Hubbard-Hall, Molony, and the various fertilized marketing units—now had eighty-six plants, an increase of thirty-four during the calendar year. Moss-American and Hubbard-Hall (now industrial chemicals) had good years, and Cato had the highest profits in its history. The recent expansion in nonpetroleum-related activities was reflected by an increase in unionization: of 7,261 employees, 1,850, or 25.47 percent, were now members of a union.[31]

[30] Production Department files, "Well Count Detail" and "Annual Well Count as of December 31, 1965"; Transworld file, "Rig Operation Report July 1, 1965, to December 31, 1965."

[31] Kerr-McGee Corporation, *Annual Report, Year Ended December 31, 1965.*

Rig 58 has spent much of its life off the shore of Nigeria.

Chapter 21

Mineral Years
1966–1967

Ten years had passed since the listing of Kerr-McGee stock on the New York Stock Exchange. During that time the number of common stockholders quadrupled, as did their yearly cash dividend. Their equity in the company was eight times greater, raised by the eightfold increase in net earnings and sales. Price/earnings ratios were in the two-digit range, bringing the designation of "growth company" in brokers' reports.

In the *Fortune* "500" listings Kerr-McGee had achieved the rank of 213 in sales among the nation's top corporations. The ranks of various other areas were progressively more favorable than in previous years, marking the firm's progress in comparison to its peers:[1]

Assets	151
Net profit	158
Invested capital	180
Profit as a percentage of sales	122
Profit as a percentage of invested capital	139
Growth rate, 1955–65 (19.34%)	28

A Kerr-McGee Oil Industries, Inc., chart shows the over-all change in finances and operations during the ten-year period. The financial figures are restated to show the various stock splits and acquisitions, and the deviations between the drilling statistics cited and those used in the text arise from the

---

[1] "The 500 Largest U.S. Industrial Corporations," *Fortune*, July 15, 1966, pp. 238–39.

Table 21.1. Financial and Operating Data, 1956–65

Year ended:	December 31, 1965	June 30, 1965	June 30, 1964	June 30, 1963
Financial				
Sales of products, services, etc.*	$320,924,644	$300,399,770	$250,116,420	$214,316,968
Net income	$ 25,068,302	$ 23,516,399	$ 20,679,162	$ 18,806,333
Net income applicable to common stock	$ 25,068,302	$ 23,516,399	$ 20,679,162	$ 18,806,333
Shares common stock outstanding†	6,585,464	6,528,982	6,375,637	6,160,906
Net income per common share	$ 3.81	$ 3.60	$ 3.24	$ 3.05
Cash dividends on preferred stock	$ —	$ —	$ —	$ —
Cash dividends on common stock	$ 8,023,606	$ 7,830,585	$ 6,861,862	$ 5,858,500
Cash dividends per common share	$ 1.225	$ 1.20	$ 1.10	$ .95
Working capital	$ 78,567,767	$ 56,821,016	$ 53,486,916	$ 40,427,929
Long-term debt	$ 90,198,475	$ 63,603,389	$ 57,398,491	$ 54,482,618
Common stockholders' equity	$171,561,512	$161,215,878	$140,763,337	$119,095,658
Total assets	$341,140,542	$324,102,394	$285,865,365	$233,710,908
Capital expenditures	$ 59,322,686	$ 50,224,029	$ 38,350,131	$ 38,360,495
Number of employees	7,261	7,067	5,606	4,348
Number of common stockholders	15,480	16,306	15,883	16,484
Operating				
Production				
Crude oil produced—net barrels	4,742,465	4,212,314	3,776,345	3,355,382
Natural gas liquids produced—net barrels	1,562,511	1,371,863	1,331,905	1,264,452
Natural gas delivered from leases (millions of cubic feet)	66,255	65,004	61,831	58,277
Oil and gas wells completed—net interest	20.18	22.95	26.75	16.72
Drilling				
Number of drilling rigs	20	19	22	23
Number of wells drilled	89	108	152	302
Number of feet drilled	980,918	1,154,209	1,183,631	2,137,924
Refining				
Crude oil processed (barrels)	14,144,350	13,719,451	12,861,143	10,906,518
Sales				
Refined products (barrels)	29,398,000	27,446,000	26,537,000	24,488,000
Natural gas (millions of cubic feet)	74,698	72,273	65,827	64,505
U_3O_8 concentrate (lbs.)	3,310,418	3,488,119	3,652,773	5,539,351
Plant food (tons)	858,796	875,474	574,526	

*1958 through 1962 figures have been restated to make them comparable to the classification used in later periods.
†Adjusted to reflect two-for-one stock split on May 5, 1961, and net of treasury stock.

June 30, 1962	June 30, 1961	June 30, 1960	June 30, 1959	June 30, 1958	June 30, 1957	June 30, 1956
$216,671,474	$222,172,187	$194,836,665	$174,267,477	$162,784,739	$108,759,138	$89,762,959
$ 17,034,264	$ 17,003,125	$ 8,958,806	$ 5,873,330	$ 5,378,973	$ 6,244,648	$ 4,679,994
$ 17,034,264	$ 17,003,125	$ 8,199,943	$ 5,114,467	$ 4,620,110	$ 5,485,476	$ 3,920,740
6,219,679	6,304,478	5,688,212	4,791,222	4,757,150	4,747,736	3,624,040
$ 2.74	$ 2.70	$ 1.44	$ 1.07	$ .97	$ 1.16	$ 1.08
$ —	$ 552,337	$ 758,863	$ 758,863	$ 758,863	$ 759,172	$ 759,254
$ 5,025,723	$ 3,867,566	$ 2,883,015	$ 1,909,296	$ 1,902,548	$ 1,491,244	$ 1,337,543
$ .80	$ .70	$ .60	$ .40	$ .40	$ .375	$ .375
$ 41,876,785	$ 33,199,726	$ 30,065,002	$ 33,680,666	$ 34,717,792	$ 37,696,954	$20,047,162
$ 60,357,042	$ 57,935,142	$ 67,540,877	$ 68,914,110	$ 60,708,479	$ 44,835,897	$36,847,788
$108,841,825	$100,501,607	$ 65,823,834	$ 61,922,284	$ 58,235,534	$ 55,388,711	$20,330,597
$229,092,970	$219,015,826	$203,430,710	$188,223,055	$167,471,864	$147,224,746	$91,429,813
$ 29,402,255	$ 29,205,043	$ 24,623,222	$ 29,766,769	$ 34,656,764	$ 19,710,151	$17,790,274
5,117	4,838	4,557	3,411	2,981	2,750	2,000
15,446	13,194	6,075	5,767	5,736	4,541	3,476
3,166,399	2,924,337	2,619,965	1,954,002	1,864,637	2,182,525	1,985,913
1,353,241	1,362,295	1,425,343	1,320,142	1,262,078	1,202,852	1,217,501
53,578	52,758	53,916	49,789	43,832	39,322	38,083
13.55	28.19	37.79	13.70	17.08	41.97	40.18
24	26	26	24	23	21	18
263	284	201	107	97	84	88
1,890,903	1,839,385	1,519,693	879,628	807,408	697,975	672,263
12,628,796	14,568,170	15,513,306	14,697,060	13,676,550	12,844,715	12,559,290
25,364,000	25,666,000	23,740,000	23,704,000	24,618,000	14,692,000	12,637,000
60,946	54,322	53,916	49,789	43,832	39,322	38,083
6,472,770	6,785,209	5,177,781	2,318,525	594,251	857,381	641,848

349

difference in time of preparation of annual reports and the drilling department's final summaries. The assumption has been made that the department's totals are more likely to be accurate (see Table 21.1).

Forty years had passed since Bob Kerr joined the Dixon brothers in the drilling business. These years brought to fulfillment his dream of owning an integrated oil company and a diversified corporation. Although he did not live to see it, in 1966 another of his prophecies was about to come true: his prediction that man would fly in outer space. Before the end of the year ten men and two dogs orbited the earth.

Celebration of these feats was marred in the United States by a continuation of race riots and antiwar protests. On the economic scene unemployment was at its lowest level in ten years, but this good news was offset by the rising inflation, which effectively diluted much of the gains. This caused President Johnson to declare that "we cannot allow the last five years of unprecedented prosperity to be endangered and swallowed up by inflation." He warned business to curb its spending on capital improvements or face higher taxes. A proposed increase in the price of steel was once more successfully beaten down, and the Federal Reserve raised the discount rate to 4.5 percent.

Kerr-McGee did drop its capital expenditures by almost $5 million, but profits continued to rise. The Cimarron facility, which converted uranium hexafluoride into powder, pellets, or crystals, made its first shipment in January. The Iranian well, spudded in September, 1965, was completed at 7,218 feet, but unfortunately it was dry. A few days later a deeper test was begun three miles south. February brought better news when a wildcat well 100 miles north of Calgary, Canada, came in at 864 barrels per day. Rig 58 was also commissioned in Holland and soon started on its way to Nigeria to drill for Gulf Oil.

At this time the board of directors took a series of actions, some with significant future implications. After establishing a monthly fee of $100 plus an attendance payment of $300 per meeting for its members, the board authorized $7,766,866 to buy 193,000 shares of American Potash & Chemical Corporation common stock. When added to the 33,800 shares already owned, this gave Kerr-McGee control of 9.86 percent of American Potash common.[2] To a close observer this presumed more than an investment interest. Indeed, it was an indication of plans being formulated for the future.

In April the cost of additional rigs and start-up of the potash facility at Hobbs necessitated borrowing an additional $20 million of the 5 percent commitment made in 1965. The next month, however, brought warnings to company warrant holders that the fertilizer industry might be approaching overproduction. The Oklahoma asphalt suits on the other hand, were not considered likely to affect business materially.[3]

---

[2] *Kermac News*, July, 1966; Public Relations press releases for February, 1966; Lease Records file, "Contract 808"; *Wall Street Journal*, February 11, 1966.

[3] Securities and Exchange Commission, "Post Effective Amendment No. 15 to Form S-1 Registration Statement," May 24, 1966.

Just as Kerr-McGee Chemical had been created to handle fertilizer, a new wholly owned subsidiary, Transworld Drilling Company, was formed in June, 1966, to conduct domestic contract drilling in the United States. Drilling assets of Kerr-McGee Corporation were exchanged for shares in the new entity, plus a note and an "account payable." In effect this resembled the period of Anderson & Kerr Drilling Company, when the drilling arm had been a separate division, although owned by the partners. Transworld Drilling Company, Limited, responsible for foreign operations since 1959, continued in that area and retained its 51 percent of the partially owned subsidiary, Transocean Drilling Company, Limited. About this time Transocean commissioned a new rig, Transocean II, and sent it to the English North Sea to drill for Bataafse Internationale Petroleum MIJ. In July, Transworld Drilling announced construction had started on Rig 59, a $4 million self-elevating unit similar to Rig 50.

In a midyear review Dean McGee told reporters that net earnings for 1966 would probably surpass those of 1965, despite heavy start-up costs. The potash plant near Hobbs was slated to be operating at 85 percent of capacity by the end of June. Extra expenses had occurred at the Wynnewood refinery, but the hydrocracker should be completed in September. The first such unit in the state, it would make possible the production of an additional 5,000 gallons per day of high-quality gasoline and would make Wynnewood one of the most modern refineries in the Southwest. According to McGee, the company also was "continuing to emphasize offshore drilling," with $10 million earmarked for the development of leased acreage.[4]

This optimism probably accounted for the decision in August to purchase certain properties from the Louisiana estate of William C. Feazel. In addition to oil and gas producing leases involving interests in twenty-four oil, thirty gas, and sixty gas-condensate wells, Kerr-McGee acquired a half share in the Southwest–W. C. Feazel Dubach Plant in northern Louisiana. This facility produced premium and regular grades of gasoline, as well as LP gas liquids, kerosene, and gas oil.

On September 14 came the elated announcement that Kerr-McGee had finally completed a sale of uranium to the private sector, the first such sale under the 1964 law permitting private ownership of the mineral. Commonwealth Edison of Chicago contracted for a supply costing between $15 million and $20 million for deliveries beginning in 1968. Then just two weeks later Philadelphia Electric signed a $50 million contract for staggered deliveries of uranium starting also in 1968. With the AEC out of the market production of uranium had dropped. Mill capacity declined from a peak of 17,636 tons to approximately 10,000 tons, and ore reserves fell from a high of 241,000 tons to 145,000. But in 1966 the tide changed, for more than half of the new electric generating capacity was nuclear. Fuel purchases such as those announced by Kerr-McGee in September encouraged the larger

---

[4] *Wall Street Journal*, July 11 and 15, 1966.

A Transocean rig in the North Sea.

petroleum companies to enter the field and also led to an increase in uranium exploration.[5]

In November the Kerr-McGee board took several important steps. First it voted to raise the quarterly dividend to $0.35 and the annual payment to $1.40. In a reorganization move it was agreed to sell the industrial division of Hubbard-Hall and transfer ownership of Hubbard-Hall stock to Kerr-McGee Chemical. Then, as a result of the discovery of a rich deposit of phosphate on Tybee Island off the Georgia coast, the board approved acquiring of Franjo, Inc., the current owners, by an exchange of stock. This

[5] F. C. Love speech, "The Uranium Industry-1967," to National Western Mining Conference and Exhibition, Denver, February 9, 1967; Dean A. McGee, "Supply and Demand for Uranium in Years Ahead," *Commercial and Financial Chronical*, February 13, 1969, pp. 4 (684)ff.; *Wall Street Journal*, September 15 and 29, 1966.

Kerr-McGee potash mill near Hobbs, New Mexico.

was accomplished on December 20 at a cost of 24,183 shares of Kerr-McGee common.[6]

Finally, in fulfillment of an earlier prediction, the board announced implementation of its plans to mine coal in Oklahoma. Based upon reserves of metallurgical coal near Stigler, the immediate future would see shafts and coking ovens begun as the first step in a "multimillion" dollar operation. Three of a projected fifty coke ovens would be built and two mine shafts sunk. Production was predicted by December, 1968. McGee supported the project by saying, "Our company believes that Oklahoma coal now can be competitive with fossil fuels from other areas by using advanced mining methods and the low cost water transportation that will come with completion of navigation on the Arkansas River."[7] It was especially fitting that the latter should be mentioned, since the funding of the Arkansas River navigation project was one of Senator Kerr's major legislative accomplishments.

Meanwhile, the Hobbs facility, with 349 employees and a payroll of $2,464,000, completed its first full year of operation with the production of 297,739 tons of potash. But the fate of the Florida phosphate venture is seen in a letter from Porter Wharton, Jr., of Kerr-McGee, to M. R. Freeman, of London, England, on December 23: "The Engineering phase of our proposed phosphate facility in central Florida has been completed. In view of recent developments with our other phosphate projects and the current phosphate market, we have temporarily deferred the construction phase of the central Florida project." James Kelly likewise assigned poor prices as the reason that phosphate production was delayed for about five years.[8]

Kerr-McGee was still interested in Arizona as a possible oil production site as well as a source of uranium. Despite the fact that no major discovery had been made there with the failure of Navajo #1, the company continued oil-lease purchases from the Navajos during 1966, buying up over 54,000 acres, mostly in Apache County, at a cost of $884,259. As the year ended, Kerr-McGee's asphalt troubles were given additional publicity when the Iowa attorney general filed suit against it along with other oil companies.

The annual report for the calendar and now the fiscal year, however, was definitely upbeat. The year had been better than McGee predicted in July. A 6.6 percent increase in net income was another record. Sales were up by almost $20 million, to $340,761,586. Although working capital was down by $3.5 million and long-term debt up by $1 million, total assets increased $42 million. Sale of oil and gas rose by 11 percent over the record 1965, as did vanadium production and prices. Helium sales also went up 12.5 percent, and additional natural-gas processing potential was built or acquired (see Table 21.2).

[6] Securities and Exchange Commission, "Form 10-K Annual Report for the Year Ended December 31, 1966."

[7] *Daily Oklahoman*, November 23, 1966; *Wall Street Journal*, November 23, 1966; p. 15; *Kermac News*, December, 1966.

[8] For potash see Public Relations release 76-3 (January 7, 1976); for phosphate see Public Relations file, "Phosphate," and interview with James J. Kelly, June 26, 1971.

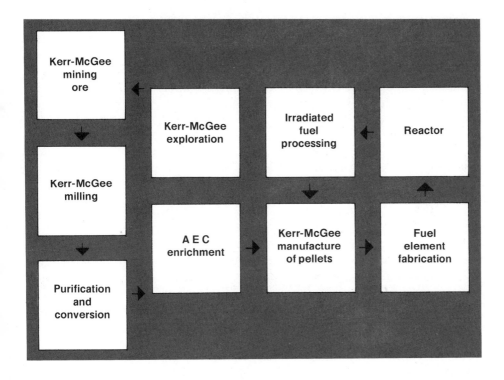

Fig. 21.1. Kerr-McGee and the nuclear fuel cycle. Adapted from
Kerr-McGee Corporation, *1967 Annual Report*.

Kerr-McGee was now active in four phases of the nuclear fuel cycle and was studying the feasibility of entering two others. As the largest domestic producer of uranium, Kerr-McGee was engaged in mining the ore and processing it to recover the concentrated uranium oxide, or yellow cake. This was then converted into a gas, uranium hexafluoride, which the AEC enriched. After this the gas was reconverted to uranium-dioxide powder and pelletized for reactor cores. When the fuel was spent, it was then reprocessed for the plutonium and the remaining uranium for reuse.

Production at the Ambrosia Lake facility near Grants, New Mexico, had been stepped up, and an addition to the five mines there was in the planning stages. In Wyoming, Petrotomics, the uranium mining and milling complex in which Kerr-McGee held a 50 percent interest, had fulfilled its AEC contract and was producing yellow cake for sale in the open market. A new uranium pit was being opened for production in 1967, when the contract for lignite ashes from North Dakota would be completed (see Table 21.5).

The other subsidiaries had an outstanding year also. Moss-American plants operated at near capacity, while Triangle furnished petroleum products in thirty states with sales reaching more than $128 million. The Transworld companies likewise had record years.[9] The 1966 total of 877,609 feet drilled made a grand total of 24,568,273 feet (see Table 21.4). Eighty-six of the wells were domestic, all offshore, of which 56 were contract wells (11 off the Texas coast), with Gulf Oil the principal employer. Nine offshore rigs were used, with the 4 idle land units being reduced to 2 by sales. Abroad there were 9 rigs: Argentina (4 idle); the Persian Gulf (1); the North Sea (2); and Angola-Nigeria (2). Transworld, Limited, was engaged with 16 wells in Nigeria and 11 in Angola; Kerr-McGee, Limited, with 2 in Iran; and Transocean with 5 in the German North Sea and 2 in the English sector.[10]

Kerr-McGee itself participated in 138 wells, of which 107 were productive. Most of these were offshore Louisiana, but onshore drilling in southern Louisiana and Texas resulted in 2 gas and 1 oil discovery. About 20 oil wells were completed in the Chaveroo Field in New Mexico, 8 in Canada, and 46 in the Campo Lamar Field in Venezuela. The annual well count shows an addition of 46.64 net wells during 1966. Of the gross, 52 were in the United States, and 40 were wildcats. Although nearly a third of Kerr-McGee's wells were located in Texas, Louisiana was rapidly overtaking Oklahoma (19.2) for second place with 18.8 percent. In Louisiana the company had an interest in 199 wells on land and 196 offshore, but, in net wells, offshore led with 88.95 to 50.68. Its interest in Venezuela was so small that, despite the large number of wells there they contributed only 8.9 percent of Kerr-McGee's total.[11]

In many respects 1967 was a continuation of 1966 for most Americans. Prosperity continued, and the number of companies with annual sales of over $1 billion jumped 33 percent. Stocks were widely touted as a hedge against the growing inflation, and some 23 million citizens shared in the boom through stock ownership (versus 8,630,000 in 1956). Oil exports went up, but so did imports. If the latter worried many people outside the petroleum industry, they were probably diverted by the mini/micro-skirt rage or by Canada's Expo 67. But not all of the news was good. The death of three American astronauts by fire, the Arab-Israeli War, and a continuation of race riots were sobering reminders of problems yet unsolved.

Kerr-McGee's year opened with a startling announcement that oil had been discovered where geologists had agreed there could be none. As noted earlier, in 1964 the company began acquiring leases in the Navajo Reservation and in early 1965 drilled and abandoned a wildcat in the Chuska Mountains. But in January, 1967, the company filed an intention to reenter the well and a month later gave notice of a producer, the first major find in Arizona.

This brought immediate repercussions. On February 21, Norman M.

[9] Kerr-McGee Corporation, *1966 Annual Report*.

[10] Transworld file, "Transworld Drilling Company and Affiliated Companies Rig Operations Report 12 Month Period Ended Dec. 31, 1966."

[11] Production Department files, "Well Count Detail" and "Annual Well Count as of Dec. 31, 1966."

Littell, legal counsel for the Navajos, immediately protested to Secretary of the Interior, Stewart Udall, claiming, "The well was brought in almost a year ago, but was sealed in and kept secret while other leasing in the area was carried on, and bids were approved by the [Navajo] Advisory Committee at lower bonus rates than could have been secured had the true facts been fully known."

The Associated Press immediately picked up Littell's accusations and gave them national coverage on the same day. Two days later the *Navajo Times* repeated the charges and asked why the tribe had not been informed of the well. It demanded to know how much leasing Kerr-McGee had done after closing the hole, and at what prices. The same day, February 23, Henry F. Pohlmann, Navajo minerals supervisor, wrote Kerr-McGee asking for the facts in the case.

George C. Hardin, Jr., prepared a digest for Dean McGee on the 24th in which he stated that Littell's charges were "a complete misstatement of fact." Kerr-McGee had drilled to a depth of 3,860 feet and bottomed in granite in 1965. Several horizons had been tested for helium without results. While the well, Navajo #1, was being drilled, "a young geologist on the well" reported a possible oil show at 2,875 feet, but the tool pusher said that it was nothing but an oily chemical being used in the drilling mud. The electric log and cuttings were analyzed, and since the cuttings consisted of minerals characteristic of igneous rocks, and "oil practically never occurs in igneous rocks," the well was abandoned. The log and the cuttings had been released to the Conservation Commission and the United States Geological Survey prior to the next lease sale on December 8, 1965. The closest lands to Navajo #1 that were offered at this sale were nine miles away.

Kerr-McGee acquired leases ten to twenty miles south of Navajo #1, and in January, 1966, drilled another well twenty miles away from it. But it too was abandoned. In trying to decide whether to sink additional wildcats to test the acreage or to drop the leases, the geology of northeastern Arizona and northwestern New Mexico was restudied. It was realized that a zone present in Navajo #1 was productive about twenty miles to the east in New Mexico. As a result the geologists decided to retest this zone in Navajo #1. A work-over rig was brought in and perforations were made from 2,860 to 2,885 feet. On January 27, 1967, the well was swabbed and showed no sign of oil. Before plugging it again, the engineer decided to acidize the zone. This produced less than a barrel an hour, but encouraged them enough to hydrofrac the zone. "Much to our surprise and delight," the well then began to produce at the rate of 24½ barrels of oil per hour. A second well was spudded one-half mile away and locations prepared for two others. "Because of the nature of the reservoir rock and the unusually low bottom hole pressure and gas-oil ratio, we still do not know what we have found. However, we have high hopes that this will develop into a large and prolific oil field."

In his letter to Pohlmann, February 28, 1967, McGee repeated these facts, stressing that before the last test had been made on Navajo #1 the closest, unleased acreage was *nine miles* away, and that all of Kerr-McGee's subsequent leases were remote from Navajo #1. This satisfied the tribal representatives, and the furor died quickly. In April, the newspapers reported that the reaction of the tribe itself was "mixed." Since by that time the two wells were producing 3,800 barrels of oil per day, and the Indians received a royalty of about 50 cents a barrel, most were "very happy," but a few wondered how this would affect "our old ways." They decided that the money should not be divided, but placed in the general tribal fund. By July, Kerr-McGee had seven wells on its 47,000 acres in what was now known as the Dineh bi Keyah field, ranging in depth from 2,800 to 3,800 feet at elevations of 6,000 to 8,700 feet. The field reservoir was estimated at 41 million barrels. By August, it was producing 12,500 barrels per day—more than the daily production of Kerr-McGee in 1966.

The field attracted international attention as a geological freak. Located on the northwestern end of the Toadlena Anticline, the producing horizon was a syenite sill of Oligocene age that had intruded lower Pennsylvanian limestones and shales. At the time of discovery the well was believed to be the first of its kind in the United States, and possibly the world. Interestingly, helium was found some 500 feet lower. By July a 32.8-mile pipeline through the mountains brought Dineh bi Keyah oil out for processing. As of March, 1968, there were sixteen producing wells with a cumulative production of 3,506,535 barrels of oil.[12]

But Dineh bi Keyah made a contribution beyond doubling the company's daily oil output. Current and long-range plans predicted the need of additional financing. A contract had been let for construction of a deisobutanizer at the Wynnewood refinery and for a sixth uranium mine at Ambrosia Lake. Therefore, in April, Kerr-McGee filed a proposal with the Securities and Exchange Commission to sell over $95 million' worth of convertible debentures. F. C. Love said of Dineh bi Keyah: "It came at a time when the Company needed to raise about $100 million and it made it possible to sell the debentures at an extremely low rate [of interest]. This was one of those fortunate things that have helped."[13]

The prospectus, dated May 19, 1967, offered $95,206,200 in 3.75 percent convertible subordinated debentures due on May 1, 1992. Priced at $100 each, they were convertible at the rate of $135 of debentures for each share of common. Kerr-McGee stockholders could buy one debenture per seven shares of common, and the proceeds were put in the company's general fund. An added inducement was the fact that dividends had been paid on the common stock each year since 1941. Consequently stock prices on the New York Stock Exchange soared.

The prospectus described other inducements. Production and sales of oil

[12] Lease Records file, "P 689"; letters, chronology, and clippings concerning the controversy are in Drilling Department files; *Navajo Times* (Window Rock, Arizona), February 23, 1967; *Arizona Republic*, May 7, 1967; *Wall Street Journal*, February 8, 1967; *Daily Oklahoman*, February 8, April 8, and July 18, 1967; *Kermac News*, August, 1967; interviews with C. F. Miller, September 4, 1971, and Otto Barton, July 26, 1971; Kerr-McGee Corporation brochure, "Dineh bi Keyah Field Apache County, Arizona," ca. March, 1968.

[13] *Wall Street Journal*, April 10 and 24 and May 22, 1967; *Daily Oklahoman*, April 22, 1967; interview with Frank C. Love, September 2, 1971.

Dineh bi Keyah, where Kerr-McGee found oil where it "shouldn't be."

and gas, including contract drilling, accounted for two-thirds of net income, and uranium for a fourth. Kerr-McGee had 848 net wells and producing leases in twelve states, Canada, and Venezuela; the wildcat discovery rate averaged almost 30 percent, as compared to an industry rate of less than 17 percent. Its three refineries had a total crude oil capacity of 50,500 barrels daily, and there were 1,600 miles of crude-oil gathering pipeline and 200 miles of products pipeline. Other assets included two wholly owned gasoline plants and interests in five others; helium reserves at Pinta Dome and Navajo Springs; and a processing plant at Navajo, Arizona. There were twenty rotary rigs, fourteen suitable for offshore drilling, and two land units which had been outfitted for large-diameter drilling in the mining industry.

In the uranium division the AEC contract expired at the end of 1970, but over $85 million in private sales had been contracted. The average price per pound for uranium concentrate over the past five years had been $7.63, with the cost of production about $5.40. The vanadium plant sold 1,383,782 pounds during 1966 at roughly $1.26 a pound. The company, in the plant food business since 1963, had bought, built, or leased twelve ammoniation and/or granulation facilities and seventy-four blending mills and had established seventeen farm centers in twenty-nine states. One bleak spot was the potash mine and mill, built at a cost of some $30 million which did not show a profit in 1966. Kerr-McGee owned additional potash leases in Canada, phosphate holdings in Florida and Georgia, some 26,000 acres of timber and twelve wood-treating plants in eleven states, and coal rights in Oklahoma. Out of 7,480 employees, 1,875—chiefly miners, refinery, forestry, and chemical workers—were union members. The company was engaged in litigation in Oklahoma and Iowa over asphalt sales, and there was a royalty dispute concerning uranium ores in one section in New Mexico.[14]

The issue was quickly subscribed, and, internally, the board authorized the listing of an additional 705,231 shares of common, issuable upon conversion of the debentures. Several other items of news may have encouraged the debenture sales. For example, in May, Rig 59 was commissioned, adding another potentially profit-making unit to the offshore fleet. And in June, rumors began spreading that Kerr-McGee and American Potash & Chemical Corporation were considering a merger. Although originally denied, the story was confirmed and on July 14 came the announcement that both companies had agreed in principle to the union. A week later the terms were set forth in a letter of agreement, which was approved by American Potash's board on July 25. Kerr-McGee's board followed suit, leaving only the votes of the two bodies of stockholders to complete the transaction.[15]

While this merger, estimated at $130 million, was going through the various steps of completion, uranium activities once more came to the forefront. As had been seen, American industry was now bullish on uranium, and producers were searching feverishly for new reserves, and

[14] "Prospectus for $95,206,200 Kerr-McGee Corporation 3¾% Convertible Subordinate Debentures, Due May 1, 1992."

[15] *Wall Street Journal*, July 12, 17, and 25, 1967; *Daily Oklahoman*, July 15, 1967.

Kerr-McGee vanadium plant, Soda Springs, Idaho.

potential users looked for guaranteed supplies. Kerr-McGee made news on three separate occasions in July. First, the company revealed talks with a number of Japanese firms concerning joint development of Kerr-McGee's uranium holdings in the Elliot Lake area of Canada. The second news item, symptomatic of the times, concerned the mad rush for reserves. Reminiscent of early days at Ambrosia Lake was the accusation by a small firm in Wyoming that Kerr-McGee was a "claim jumper." The president of American Nuclear Corporation charged that "apparently Kerr-McGee is sneaking up at night and driving in stakes." By comparison "American Nuclear," he said, "would be petty cash. Maybe that is why they think they can stomp on little David."

The conflict degenerated into the ridiculous. Both groups drilled cores around the clock, with their rigs separated by only a few yards. American Nuclear declared that Kerr-McGee was trespassing and that the point had been reached where it was prepared to "use reasonable force." A careful reading of the dispute indicates that Kerr-McGee had indeed bought the claims. But the point at issue was whether it had done enough work each year on the claims as required by law to hold them.[16]

And, finally, and perhaps predictably, at a time when Kerr-McGee controlled a fourth of American uranium resources, produced 6.6 million pounds of concentrate, and held about a fifth of the market, it decided to enter another step in the uranium cycle. In what McGee described as "a logical extension of our uranium and mining operation and . . . consistent with our objective to participate more fully in the rapidly-expanding nuclear industry," the company announced construction of a $25 million plant to convert yellow cake into uranium hexafluoride (UF_6) gas. When completed in 1970, it would be the second such plant in the United States. Kerr-McGee would then be engaged in all nuclear production phases but one, that of enriching the gas before reconversion to a solid for fuel. In October, 1967, it was announced that this plant would be constructed in Sequoyah County, Oklahoma.[17]

At the August meeting of the board, which increased the annual dividend from $1.40 to $1.50, the growing complexity of the company was discussed. This led to the decision to give administrative assistance to McGee, who had been solely responsible for the entire business since the death of Senator Kerr four years earlier. The bylaws were changed, and F. C. Love was elected to the office of president, with McGee remaining as chairman of the board and chief executive officer.[18]

Frank Criner Love, born in 1908 to a pioneer Oklahoma family, was already well established in the company. The modest six-footer had joined Kerr-McGee in 1948, bringing his prior experience as an attorney for Shell Oil and a successful record in private practice. Conscientious and diplomatic, he moved into the presidency at a propitious time. A firm believer in diversification, he said it allowed one aspect

to take up slack when another is down, but there should be a common thread that ties it together. This company always needs to be based in some fashion on the exploration for and production of natural resources, principally because top management understands that business real well and can make decisions in that area fast and accurately.

Three directors offered their appraisals of Love. According to James E.

[16] *Daily Oklahoman*, July 13, 1967, announced the beginning of the Japanese negotiations, and (on September 20, 1967) the dropping of the plan because of inability to reach agreement on costs. For the "claim jumping" charge see *Daily Oklahoman*, July 14, 1967, and *Wall Street Journal*, July 17, 1967. Interestingly, a decade later when uranium was again a hot item, charges of claim jumping were again so common that a congressional panel was investigating the situation and, especially, the work legally required to make good on claims. It heard the chairman of Fremont Energy Corporation testify that, based on 100 percent of the legal requirements, "there aren't 50 valid claims in Wyoming." *Wall Street Journal*, October 17, 1977.

[17] "Kerr-McGee Locks on to Uranium Future," *Business Week*, March 16, 1968, pp. 160–66; *Wall Street Journal*, July 28, 1967; *Daily Oklahoman*, July 28, 1967; *New York Times*, October 13, 1967.

[18] *Wall Street Journal*, August 14, 1967.

Webb, Love had the "unusual ability" to visualize how one should put business arrangements into contractual terms that would take care of everything—"both the possibility of trouble and the possibility of great unforeseen opportunity." Guy C. Kiddoo saw Love as a skilled negotiator in legal matters and as a careful student of areas in which the company was, or might be, engaged. He was also an excellent administrator and good with personnel. McGee provided the driving force, while Love presented the more conservative side.

Edwin L. Kennedy saw Love as a "careful operator," who could assist McGee in evaluating new ideas from an economic point of view and in seeing that they were "sound and tight operations."[19] This change marked a reversal of roles for McGee from the days of his teamwork with Kerr. A fourth director, Frederick W. Straus, would have been struck by this comparison, but he unfortunately died the month after Love took over the presidency. Straus was the pioneer director who played a key role in insuring the economic stability of the young company and was the last representative of the period when Bob Kerr had roamed Chicago looking for money.

In August, Kerr-McGee announced that contracts had been let for the initial shaft for a coal mine near Stigler, Oklahoma. Dean McGee later placed this decision to go into coal (along with the company's shift to offshore drilling, and its entry into the uranium field), as one of the three most important made by the firm. Love characterized the decision by saying that it was taken in order to make Kerr-McGee a total energy company and because there were then greater opportunities in coal—opportunities yet unseen by the firm's competitors. "A company the size of Kerr-McGee has to compete. If it doesn't get the opportunities it is looking for in one area, it must direct its efforts in other directions." Hence the emphasis on coal and uranium.

Some saw opportunism as the decisive factor. *Business Week* commented: "And it happens that construction of the Arkansas River Barge Canal was started the same year that Kerr-McGee acquired its first coal leases." It also queried why the company would want to create competition for its uranium business. The head of Kerr-McGee's nuclear division answered by saying, "We feel it's better to compete with ourselves as an energy company than with other producers."

Although ten years later the initial effort in coal was still unsuccessful, the company was committed. The problems were exemplified when it became evident very early that the coking aspect would not live up to expectations. The coal coked more slowly than anticipated, and the yield was not great, so that experiment was written off even as the sinking of the shaft progressed.[20]

[19] *New York Times*, August 17, 1967; interviews with Frank C. Love; James E. Webb, August 12, 1971; Guy C. Kiddoo, August 12, 1971; and Edwin L. Kennedy, August 13, 1971.

[20] *Daily Oklahoman*, August 12, 1967; interviews with Dean A. McGee (by Bob Leder, KTUL-TV, Tulsa), September 19, 1973; Frank C. Love and A. T. F. Seale, July 20, 1971; "Kerr-McGee Locks on to Uranium Future," 160–66.

The petroleum division was not downplayed by management. A new oil discovery was made offshore Louisiana on Block 214, Ship Shoal. With Canadian oil production at Clive and Pembina and gas at Sylvan Lake and Prevo, the time had come to establish a Canadian oil and gas division at Calgary. In Oklahoma the Apache Pipeline was bought, adding an additional fifty-two miles to Kerr-McGee's gathering system, and construction begun on a new $100,000 office building for the Wynnewood refinery.[21]

At the board of directors meeting in late October a number of loose ends were tied up. The certificate of incorporation was amended to authorize an increase in stock to 14 million shares in preparation for the anticipated merger with American Potash. Under this change there would be 12.5 million common and 1.5 million preferred. More specifically would be the immediate issuing of 277,450 shares of $4.50 convertible Series A preferred to be used in the swap of stock with American Potash. The board likewise approved the listing of Kerr-McGee Corporation common stock on the Toronto Stock Exchange and elected Edwin L. Kennedy as a member of the executive committee to replace Straus.

The same month McGee gave an interview to the *Wall Street Journal* in which he predicted that 1967 net earnings would top 1966's record. The future looked equally bright. The merger with American Potash would "compliment" Kerr-McGee's metal business and "justify a real technical sales staff." Furthermore, the construction of as much nuclear plant capacity had been contracted for in the first eight months of 1967 as in all of 1966. To meet this growing market, Kerr-McGee had doubled its expenditures for uranium exploration and laid the foundations for the Sequoyah uranium conversion plant to make uranium hexafluoride.[22]

In anticipation of utilization of the Sequoyah output it was announced in early November that productive capacity at Cimarron, which specialized in ceramic UO_2 and fuel pellets, would be enlarged sixfold, at a cost of $5 million to $10 million. Love explained the moves to build Sequoyah and expand Cimarron by saying that Kerr-McGee did not want to find itself in the position of having only one or two uranium buyers. So, if utilities were to become the primary market, his company had to get into the processing cycles in order to deal directly with them. This still left a major gap in Kerr-McGee's production cycle, the enrichment of hexafluoride, which was done in only three plants—all government owned. But McGee claimed: "We have visions one day of being able to build one. We've got ambitions" to erect one of the $800,000,000 complexes. But when queried on the subject a year later, he replied, "Right now it's just a glint in our eye."[23]

[21] *Daily Oklahoman*, September 13 and October 12, 1967; *Wall Street Journal*, August 23 and September 13, 1967.

[22] *Wall Street Journal*, October 12, 1967.

[23] Kerr-McGee Corporation pamphlet, "Operations of the Kerr-McGee Cimarron Nuclear Fuel Facility" (undated); *Wall Street Journal*, November 7, 1967; interview with Frank C. Love; *Daily Oklahoman*, November 7 and 12, 1967. Although federal legislation in 1975 permitted private construction of such facilities, Kerr-McGee has not undertaken to erect one.

There were also other activities on the uranium front. The Petrotomics mill's capacity was doubled to 1,000 tons of ore per day. The old open-pit mine was closed and a new location opened. The sixth mine at Ambrosia Lake started up, and the tiresome dispute over the Branson properties dragged on. The first net gain in national uranium reserves over uranium production since 1959 was achieved, with Kerr-McGee playing a role in this statistic. In October the discovery of a large deposit of uranium, possibly as large as the original Ambrosia Lake district, was made in the northeast Church Rock area of New Mexico. Forty-five miles northwest of Ambrosia Lake and sixteen miles from Gallup, Kerr-McGee's 45,000 acres of mining leases once again lay within the Navajo Reservation. At the same time a small oil and helium discovery was made in San Juan County, New Mexico, also on Indian lands. But domestic play in uranium was not enough, and Kerr-McGee Australia, Ltd., was created. In August and November it secured two, two-year prospecting permits totaling 1,963 square miles on the Eyre Peninsula in south Australia.[24]

Although 1967 saw Kerr-McGee reach a position of fifth in the vanadium industry, in other divisions results were mixed. Potash news was bad. Canadian production reached 4.6 million tons, and Kermac Potash ended 1967 with a net income deficit of $1,240,000 on sales of $4,705,000. Kerr-McGee Iranian Oil completed a second well in the Persian Gulf without the discovery of commercial oil or gas. The venture was written off by the parent company although it did not formally withdraw from the area until February, 1971. However, tender rig 55, which had done the drilling, was contracted by Kerr-McGee, Limited, to spud up to four wells in the general vicinity for Societe Irano-Italienne des Petroles (SIRIP). In Argentina, despite the unhappy past experiences, a bid was made for exploration concessions on 1,730,000 acres located offshore 100 miles southeast of Buenos Aires.[25]

The culmination of Kerr-McGee's largest merger was reached on December 27. Under terms approved by the stockholders, some 652,398 common shares and 266,502 shares of Kerr-McGee convertible preferred were exchanged at the rate of .306 shares of common and .125 of preferred for each share of American Potash & Chemical. By the swap Kerr-McGee acquired a firm that in 1966 boasted net sales of $64 million, assets of $117,719,892, and 2,100 employees. With plants in Mississippi, Nevada, Illinois, and California, the principal production facility was at Trona, California, on the edge of Searles Lake. Property here included some 13,000 acres of leased and fee lands in the lake, containing the second largest reserve of sodium borate salts in the nation. American Potash & Chemical produced—and had lengthy experience in marketing—potash, soda ash,

---

[24] *Wall Street Journal*, October 26, 1967; Mineral Lease Records files, "88-01-002" and "88-01-003"; for gas and helium discovery, see *Daily Oklahoman*, November 11, 1967.

[25] For potash see Mineral Lease Records files, "Contract 1204-1" and "29-09-000"; for the Persian Gulf see Lease Records files, "Contract 808" and "Contract 808-16"; for vanadium see *Chemical & Engineering News*, March 27, 1967, p. 28.

Table 21.2. Financial Highlights, 1966–67

	1966	1967*
Total gross income	$345,105,210	$426,905,075
Net income	$ 26,726,399	$ 34,350,444
Total assets	$383,296,755	$602,874,997
Cash flow from earnings	$ 56,425,491	$ 67,111,940
Working capital	$ 74,968,937	$181,161,050
Properties (net)	$212,350,900	$322,789,306
Capital expenditures	$ 55,471,379	$ 59,461,433
Long-term debt	$100,216,242	$215,374,692
Cash dividends	$ 8,765,095	$ 12,983,736
Stockholders' equity	$195,036,978	$279,518,647
Total taxes paid	$ 7,727,436	$ 13,413,380
Number of employees	7,480	9,223

*Includes figures for operations of American Potash & Chemical Corporation.

boron products, titanium dioxide, electro manganese, and other metal and chemical products. Thirty percent of its sales were used in paints, batteries, textile and industrial chemicals; 20 percent in paper and glass; 18 percent by domestic agriculture; and the remainder for television, electronics, and metals.[26]

Kerr-McGee was criticized for this merger because of the depressed state of potash and the low fertilizer prices. But in the minds of the administration the move was most logical. American Potash, in Kerr-McGee's view, had not taken advantage of its opportunity to grow. It was not acquired because it was profitable, but for its future growth potential. According to Director Edwin L. Kennedy, American Potash was obtained because "McGee [was] fascinated by the inherent possibilities of the great chemical reserve . . . out at Searles Lake. . . . Fascinated by the possibilities of recovering and utilizing the solids from Searles Lake." J. B. Saunders believed it was not potash but the chance to get the mineral reserves that tempted McGee, plus obtaining a sales organization which knew the fertilizer business. James J. Kelly added that American Potash had probably the greatest such natural resource in the United States, or the world. This could be produced competitively and make Kerr-McGee a worldwide marketer of sodium carbonate, sodium sulphate, borax, and potash.[27]

---

[26] *Wall Street Journal*, December 28, 1967; Kerr-McGee Corporation, "Report to Shareholders for First Three Months and Six Months Ended June 30, 1967," August 10, 1967; Kerr-McGee Corporation, "Notice of Special Meeting of Kerr-McGee Stockholders," November 27, 1967; *Kermac News*, January, 1968; Dean A. McGee, *Evolution Into Total Energy: The Story of the Kerr-McGee Corporation* (New York, Newcomen Society, 1971), p. 22.

[27] Interviews with Edwin L. Kennedy; J. B. Saunders, June 9, 1971; and James J. Kelly.

Searles Lake in the Mojave Desert, California.

The man who made the decision, Dean McGee, explained it on several occasions. He told *Forbes*, one of the critics, that potash was not the determining factor: "They are already in the type of extractive minerals and metals we would like to expand in, and they have first-rate research capabilities, something we lack." As early as the 1950's Kerr-McGee began looking for ways to reduce its dependency on the unpredictable price of crude oil, and "decided to look for ventures that would be best suited to our

Table 21.3. American Potash Sales and Net Income, 1966–67

	Sales	Net Income
Kerr-McGee only	$358,665,014	$30,159,263
American Potash only	65,168,990	4,531,481
Eliminate American Potash dividend received by Kerr-McGee	. . . .	(340,200)
Total	$423,834,004	$34,350,444

Table 21.4. Drilling and Exploration Operations, 1966–67

	1966	1967
Feet drilled	877,609	957,277
Total wells/wells completed	122/108	151/137
Kerr-McGee interest	73	82
Rigs (average)	20	21

Table 21.5. Production Record, 1966–67

	1966	1967
Production		
Crude oil produced (net barrels)	5,649,074	8,240,079
Natural-gas sales (millions of cubic feet)	81,131	72,962
Gas processing		
Gas liquids produced (net barrels)	2,154,852	2,485,100
Refining		
Crude oil processed (barrels)	16,059,117	16,772,520
Uranium		
U_3O_8 concentrate sold (lbs.)	3,306,530	3,079,538
Average price per lb.	$8.00	$8.00
Chemicals		
Plant food sold (tons)	1,002,295	1,353,897

expertise—exploration of mineral reserves—and utilize our cash flow to expand." The company started with uranium, which in 1967 was responsible for 25 percent of net profit. Enough would be made on American Potash's boron, titanium, and other minerals to offset the sagging potash business. Kerr-McGee was also going into coal because "there are few high-grade metallurgical coal seams left in the country, and industrial demand and the export market, especially Japan, look good."

To *Barron's*, Dean McGee pointed out that potash was only about 12 percent of American Potash's volume. "They are the second-largest pro-

Table 21.6. Common-Stock Highlights, 1966–67

	1966	1967*
Equity per share	$29.01	$34.51
Earnings per share	$ 4.04	$ 4.54
Cash dividends per share	$ 1.325	$ 1.45
Average yield	1.7	1.3
Number of shares outstanding	6,653,361	7,328,440
Number of stockholders	14,106	21,694
New York·Stock Exchange		
High	$87.61	$150.00
Low	$65.25	$ 80.12
Price-earnings ratio		
High	21.68	33.00
Low	16.15	17.64

*Includes figures for operations of American Potash & Chemical Corporation.

ducer of boron in the world. They have developed a process for producing titanium chloride. And then there's Searles Lake." Searles Lake was indeed the key. Its history started in 1862 when a gold prospector, John W. Searles, discovered a dry lake bed in the upper Mojave Desert region of California. Attracted by the shimmering, translucent crystals that covered the ground, he put some in his pack as he pushed on in his search for gold. He found no gold, but years later he witnessed borax being recovered from similar crystals on the Nevada border and decided that he knew of a vast borax deposit unknown to others.

In 1873 Searles and his brother organized the San Bernardino Borax Mining Company and built a plant on the northwest shore near the present-day city of Trona. The first year's production was estimated at $200,000 and was used primarily as a cleansing agent in refining gold. After Searles's death in 1898 and a subsequent drop in borax prices, his holdings passed into other hands. Interest in the lake was not renewed seriously until 1912, when commercial production of potash as well as borax was studied. In 1913 the American Trona Corporation was formed, and later a processing plant was built to meet the short supply of potash during World War I. In 1919, the production of borax was again resumed, and in 1926, American Trona became American Potash & Chemical Corporation.[28]

When the merger was approved by the stockholders of both companies, all that remained was for Kerr-McGee to wrap up the year with its annual report, restated to allow for the merger, effective December 29. As pre-

[28] "Talking Big, Acting Big," *Forbes*, December 1, 1967, p. 59; "Ore-to-Core?" *Barron's*, May 4, 1970, p. 9; L. Burr Belden and Ardis M. Walker, *Searles Lake Borax, 1862–1962* (published for the dedication of the Searles Lake Monument on November 8, 1962, by the Death Valley '49er, Inc.).

dicted, 1967 was the sixth consecutive record-breaking year, with combined sales of $423,834,004. Although capital expenditures fell, working capital almost doubled, as did long-term debt. However, the ratio between current assets and current liabilities rose to only 3.1.

American Potash contributed sales and net income data to the restated financial statement as shown in Table 21.3.

Kerr-McGee's increased income was due to continued success in finding new oil-and-gas reserves. Of paramount importance were Dineh bi Keyah and its thirteen wells and new reserves on Block 214, Ship Shoal. Transworld's offshore drilling units had a year of high utilization, being employed 91 percent of the time. Rig 59 had been added, making a total of fifteen offshore rigs with capabilities of operating in water depths of 10 to 600 feet.[29] Of the total, 104 wells were domestic—all offshore, where ten rigs were used in the Gulf. Of the completed domestic wells, 62 were under contract to such firms as Gulf and Standard Oil of Texas. Some of the wells drilled for Kerr-McGee deserve special notice because of the depths. A wildcat in the Ship Shoal area reached 15,945 feet, at a cost of $1,067,271, but was dry and so was abandoned. In the same area successful nonwildcats were drilled, to 17,500 and 18,500 feet. The first drilled 84 days and cost $1,123,250, and the second consumed 113 days and $1,638,210.

The 5 offshore rigs contracted overseas spudded 47 wells and completed all but 5. Thirty-two were sunk by Transworld, Limited, off Nigeria and Angola, 3 by Kerr-McGee, Limited, in Iran, and 7 in the German and English North Sea by Transocean. The overseas record could have been even better, but thirty-three days were lost in Nigeria because of a revolution, and four land rigs in South America were idle.[30]

The annual well count showed 1,927 gross wells, or 868.71 net. During the past year the company had participated in a gross total of 82 wells, 41 of which were wildcats, and 27 were dry holes. The largest number of wells had been in Arizona (22), with offshore Louisiana a close second (20). Other sites were located in Canada, New Mexico, Texas, Wyoming, Colorado, Oklahoma, Iran, and Venezuela—in that order. All the land wells were contracted out, with the development wells being chiefly in the Clive field in Canada, Dineh bi Keyah in Arizona, the West Welch field in Texas, and Wind River in Wyoming.[31]

Vanadium production was greater than in any previous year. But while potash production was growing and costs reduced, the sharp decline in potash prices caused a drop in anticipated income and continuation of a decision to defer construction of a phosphate mining and milling complex in Florida. Kerr-McGee Chemical had continued a program of plant modernization and improvement of distribution facilities, with an emphasis upon Kerr-McGee farm centers offering a full line of services. Cato had its most

---

[29] Kerr-McGee Corporation, *1967 Annual Report*.

[30] Transworld file, "Transworld Drilling Company and Affiliated Companies Rig Operation Report 12 Month Period Ended December 31, 1967."

[31] Production Department files, "Well Count Detail, 1967" and "Annual Well Count as of December 31, 1967."

profitable year and introduced Hi-temp Grease with Teflon. Moss-American also showed a satisfactory profit, although both sales and profits declined with reduced demands. The major uranium find at Church Rock and two additional mines under development at Ambrosia Lake enhanced the Nuclear Fuels Division. Cimarron was being expanded sixfold, and erection of a hexafluoride plant was slated for 1968. Shaft and surface construction was under way on the Choctaw coal mine, not to mention the acquisition of American Potash's reserves.

Oil and gas sales increased 20 percent, and helium returns reached new highs. The Wynnewood deisobutanizer was in operation, and the gas processing plants operated at capacity. Plans were under way to expand the facilities at Sylvan Lake, Canada, and to construct a new one near Lake Maracaibo, Venezuela. In marketing, a substantial number of new service stations were built, and Blue Velvet Motor Oil was successfully introduced. Although gasoline volume had increased 50 percent and the number of service stations 25 percent, gasoline marketing was still the weakest link, claiming only 8 percent of the Oklahoma market. Triangle continued to expand operations elsewhere, especially through its subsidiary, Cloverleaf Service Stations, Inc. By construction and acquisition it owned more than 277 stations in seven states, selling gasoline under such trade names as Imperial, Peoples, Power, Trackside, Wallace, TanKar, and Coast.[32]

As could be expected, the stockholders in Kerr-McGee and American Potash had every reason to be pleased. The future looked bright both on the New York Stock Exchange and in Oklahoma City.

[32] *1967 Annual Report.*

Chapter 22

Expansion and Litigation 1968–1969

Dean McGee had been with the company which now bore his name for thirty-one years. Having joined A&K Petroleum as its geologist, he had moved into administration and achieved the top executive position in 1963. For the past five years he had carried sole responsibility for the corporation, and these were years of dramatic growth and expansion, catching the eye and imagination of the business world.

Less well known, however, was the private and civic life of this modest man. Paralleling his corporate activities was a list of achievements almost equally remarkable—especially so in light of his reputation for spending long hours at his office desk. A devoted family man, Dean McGee not only shared the activities of his wife and two daughters but also found time for an amazing array of other commitments. His reputation was that of being a "working member" of any group with which he affiliated himself, and a glance at his four-page, single-spaced vita from that period is most impressive.

He never assigned priorities to his many obligations, other than that his family came first. But his outside involvements are easily categorized: he was a director in a number of other corporations, and he had strong interests in religion, education, research, medical science, and civic betterment. As could be expected, he was active in the Oklahoma City Chamber of Commerce, but it is perhaps surprising to find him also on the Arts Council, the Symphony Foundation, the Urban League, and YMCA and director and president of the Oklahoma State Fair and Exposition. While membership on the National Petroleum Council might be predictable, trusteeships on the boards of two universities and his presence in leadership roles on the Oklahoma-Arkansas Presbyterian Foundation, the Presbyterian Medical Center, the Oklahoma Medical Research Foundation, and the Frontiers of Science could only reflect personal interests. These numerous and varied responsibilities would certainly seem to preclude time for the ten social organizations to which he belonged.

Altogether Dean McGee combined a position as a top executive in a large company with that of a dedicated family man and responsible citizen of his city, state, and nation. Only creative drive and a strong physique, balanced by disciplined energy, can explain how he managed to perform these many roles so successfully.

But the thirty-one years with Kerr-McGee also meant that Dean McGee was in his sixty-eighth year—and, as usual in similar situations, replacement rumors were always in the background. Certainly no one could say that outside activities or age caused his business to suffer. The nationally recognized indicator of corporate success testified to his administrative ability. *Fortune's* "500" listings for 1967 ranked Kerr-McGee at 202 over-all, a rise of 30 places from the preceding year. In other categories it showed:

Assets	115
Net income	137
Invested capital	140
Net income as a percentage of sales	93

From 1957 through 1967 earnings per share rose from $1.16 to $4.53, a 14.59 percent growth rate that placed it fifty-sixth.[1]

If 1968 was a year of renewed challenge for Dean McGee, it was one of frustration for many Americans. Abroad, Russian troops brutally crushed the democratic aspirations of Czechoslovakia, while at home the Vietnam War continued to divide the citizenry and was a major factor in President Johnson's decision not to seek another presidential term. Added to this unrest were racial riots sparked by the assassination of the Reverend Martin Luther King, Jr. The revulsion over the manner of his death had scarcely waned before the nation was shocked with news of another—that of Robert F. Kennedy. It seemed that violence was becoming the way of life—and death. Economically, although the United States appeared prosperous with only 2.95 million unemployed, the balance of trade was falling, and President Johnson reacted with restrictions on foreign travel and investments and a 10 percent surcharge on federal income taxes.

For Kerr-McGee, however, the year opened on a better note with the discovery in January of another significant uranium deposit in the southern Powder River Basin of Wyoming. Then the patience with Argentina paid off. On March 5, Transworld Drilling, Limited, signed a contract with YPF to drill a total of twenty wells in the El Huemul field in the Comodora Rivadavia area within a period of 250 days. The next day Kerr-McGee of

[1] "The Fortune Directory of the 500 Largest Industrial Corporations," *Fortune*, June 15, 1968, p. 194.

Argentina, Ltd., was notified it had been awarded a permit for exploration of 1,730,000 acres in the offshore Samborombon area southeast of Buenos Aires. This carried requirements to drill a well and spend a million dollars within the first eighteen months. On June 13, a subsidiary of Allied Chemical, Union Texas (Argentina), Ltd., bought a half interest in this concession.

Other good news followed. On April 18 an agreement, effective April 1, was signed with fifteen Japanese companies—nine electric power and six mining—for a two-phase joint exploration project for uranium on 35,000 acres leased by Kerr-McGee in the Elliot Lake region of Canada. The Japanese would pay an "initial option fee" of $500,000 to share in Phase I, a general one-year survey, and $1,000,000 "additional" if they chose to participate in Phase II, a more detailed investigation of favorable areas indicated by Phase I. If commercial quantities of ore were found, the Japanese then had the option of taking half interest by paying half of the development charges.[2]

But potash continued to be bad news. Sales dropped, and deficits mounted. Over $32 million had been poured into the operation, and the March 31 balance sheet for Kermac Potash showed a long-term debt of almost $19.5 million. Consequently, on June 19, 1968, the board of directors of the National Farmers Union Development Corporation voted unanimously to sell its half interest in Kermac Potash for the sum of $5.5 million (part in cash and part in promissory notes), retroactive to March 31. Kerr-McGee assumed the outstanding loans, forgave the $948,267 owed by the Development Corporation, as well as any part of the $850,000 advanced by Kerr-McGee to fund April operations. James J. Kelly later (October 4, 1971) wrote R. S. Fulton, of the Department of Interior, "Continuing and substantial losses had exhausted the capacity of NFUDC to supply additional funds to continue operations."[3]

Thus ended a partnership which had been shaky from its inception. Even before the shafts and mill were completed, it was obvious that Canadian competition would be deadly. Farmers Union took a big loss when it sold out; Kerr-McGee, on the other hand, with such a sizable investment, had little choice but to bail out its partner and try to turn the business around. In the meantime, the potash division had to be carried financially by other parts of the company.[4]

Generally at this point in Kerr-McGee's history its press was good. The news touted the success in uranium, and *Business Week* declared that the

[2] *Daily Oklahoman*, January 23, 1968; Transworld Drilling file, "YPF—Argentine 20-Well Contract"; Lease Records file, "Cont. 1033–1." For uranium, see Mineral Lease Records file, "Contract 1267," and *Kermac News*, July, 1968. According to the *Wall Street Journal*, March 22, 1968, the discussions with the Japanese that had begun the previous year had been broken off temporarily because of Kerr-McGee's insistence that the Japanese bear the full cost of exploration and 60 percent of the development costs.

[3] Mineral Lease Records files, "Contract 1204-1" and "29-09-000"; Lease Records file, "Contract #817."

[4] Interviews with Frank C. Love, September 2, 1971, and George Cobb, December 7, 1972. Increased Kerr-McGee production, and Canadian restrictions on that nation's output, finally allowed potash to show a small profit by 1970.

company was "in the catbird seat of the uranium producing business," with 25 percent of the reserves and 33 percent of the commercial market. The move into coal was also generally applauded. *Forbes* listed the common stock as number 137 among the 200 American stocks with the largest market value (price per share times the number of outstanding shares). Kerr-McGee did not, however, make *Forbes'* list of 414 based upon growth and profitability. Most negative comments focused on the role of fertilizer and on Kerr-McGee's relative weakness in gasoline marketing: "McGee's abiding interest in exploration may have caused neglect elsewhere." While his genius in exploration was acknowledged, there was beginning to be speculation about a successor: "Notably lacking in the top-level advancement were any younger executives."[5]

Administrative changes were being made, however, even at that time. Fresh blood and experience was infused into the board of directors with the addition of three positions to the existing eleven. The three new members were Peter Colefax (former chairman of American Potash), Lloyd Austin (Security First National Bank, Los Angeles), and Earle M. Jorgenson (chairman of Earle M. Jorgenson Company), all former directors of American Potash. A major change in administrative organization came with several moves in May. The bylaws were changed to reestablish the post of vice-chairman, and J. B. Saunders was elected to that position. A new operations committee replaced the management committee, and George Cobb was named chairman. Finally a series of "group" vice-presidencies was created.

The operations committee was intended to give over-all evaluations. It looked into every project, every major expenditure, and all changes in policy. While the committee did not have a great deal of authority concerning specific budgets, its function of communication and recommendation affected the general direction of any department through coordination within the total structure.

The six group vice-presidents administered petroleum marketing, pipelines and refining, chemical marketing, drilling, oil-and-gas operations, and nuclear projects. This change was aimed at combining related activities into administratively directed groups where engineering and construction details were handled internally. All the groups relied upon the corporation for administrative services. By coordinating the various functions under a series of vice-presidents, McGee hoped to prevent administrative rigidity and provide quicker reaction when change was needed. Or, as George Cobb said, "We want to be geared for future growth and able to maximize our younger talent to the greatest exposure." *Forbes* speculated that McGee had begun testing his men for the succession in management—looking for his and Love's successors.[6]

[5] "Kerr-McGee Locks on to Uranium's Future," *Business Week*, March 16, 1968, pp. 160–66; "The Market's Judgment," *Forbes*, April 1, 1968, p. 52.

[6] *New York Times*, January 27, 1968; *Wall Street Journal*, July 11, 1968; "Plenty of Oil Yet to be Found, Says Kermac's Cobb," *Oil and Gas Journal*, July 28, 1969, p. 205; "The Energy Game," *Forbes*, October 15, 1968, p. 40.

In the meantime Kerr-McGee's decision to drill offshore continued to pay off. In May, it announced the first oil completion from Block 233, Ship Shoal, and the next month a significant oil-and-gas discovery on Block 239 in the same area. Ironically, Kerr-McGee, itself an early perpetrator of a "boner" in an offshore bid, profited from a mistake by another company. In the May 21 lease bids, Union Oil of California was high on tract 228, offshore Texas, while a combine which included Kerr-McGee came in second. After the Secretary of the Interior awarded the block to Union, it was discovered that the latter had failed to sign the bid specifications. When the award was protested, Kerr-McGee and its partners won the area.

May's big news, however, was Kerr-McGee's announcement of a $15 million building program for downtown Oklahoma City. This development, to be known as the Kerr-McGee Center, would feature a new thirty-story headquarters building. Occupying the entire block surrounded by Northwest Third Street, Robert S. Kerr Avenue, Broadway, and Robinson, the structure would be ultramodern in design, and the area was to include a park and retail shops.[7]

During June and July most company activity dealt with plans already in motion. The expansion of the Petrotomics mill was completed, and discussion soon began for another enlargement. More significant news, however, concerned coal. Two experimental coke ovens were completed in February, and arrangements were made to test their output at Lone Star Steel. In June, however, it was announced that the coking tests did not warrant construction of additional ovens. In the meantime the first shaft of the Choctaw mine had been completed at 1,420 feet, making it the deepest coal mine shaft in North America. A second was being opened, and a special school to train miners began classes. Initial production was predicted for December 1968, with full operation scheduled for 1970.[8]

July, however, brought two defeats for Kerr-McGee. In the first a federal court awarded the state of Oklahoma triple damages of $4,645,113 in a civil suit against Kerr-McGee and four other firms resulting from asphalt sales. The jury found no evidence, however, of a conspiracy. The companies involved had the option of appealing this decision, but they remained enmeshed in a suit with private contractors.[9] Several years later this case, State of Oklahoma v. Allied Materials Corporation, et al., was the subject of a doctoral dissertation. The conclusions of the presumably impartial author are significant:

Because of some market conditions peculiar to the sale of liquid asphalt to state governments, it is concluded that market performance could be expected to be the same whether firms act collusively or independently. Analysis of the State's decision to file antitrust charges suggests that firms in the industry are highly susceptible to antitrust litigation—even when they are acting independently. Analysis of the legal requirements for conviction in such actions and a historical review of similar cases

[7] *Daily Oklahoman*, May 19, 1968; *Wall Street Journal*, May 21, 1968.

[8] *Kermac News*, August–September, 1968.

[9] *Wall Street Journal*, July 29, 1968.

Headframe of Choctaw coal mine near Stigler, Oklahoma. This is the
deepest coal mine in North America.

suggest that firms in the industry face substantial risk of conviction even when their
conduct is consistent with that which an economist would expect of an
independently-acting, profit-maximizing firm.[10]

Kerr-McGee's second problem had long-range significance. It found itself
embroiled in the first of what were to become increasingly common, major
confrontations with environmentalist groups. It all began innocently enough
when Franjo, Inc., a subsidiary of Kerr-McGee, was the successful bidder
on a Georgia offshore lease. The lease brought the right to mine phosphate
from the ocean bottom near Little Tybee and Cabbage islands (which
Kerr-McGee owned) and Wilmington Island, on which it had a purchase
option. Although Kerr-McGee paid a cash bonus of $750,000 and proposed a
new industry for Georgia, a full-scale battle to stop the project quickly
developed. Because of the depression in phosphate there were claims that
Kerr-McGee was looking for something more valuable. An extreme sugges-

[10] Dale Rodney Funderburk, "Economic and Legal Implications of Liquid Asphalt Pricing
in Oklahoma, 1961–1965" (Ph.D. dissertation, Department of Economics, Oklahoma State
University, 1971).

tion was that the company's activities could set off two atomic bombs jettisoned off the Georgia coast by the Air Force in 1958.

The tourist agencies joined the chorus, charging that offshore mining would cause loss of business; and the fishing industry thought it would harm its endeavors. But most important, the environmentalists fought the venture as upsetting the entire ecological balance and destroying a national asset. The dispute was sent to the state's Mineral Leasing Committee, headed by Governor Lester Maddox, for restudy. Despite a personal visit by Dean McGee to explain the planned environmental safeguards, and a study by scientists at Georgia Tech and the University of Georgia which minimized the dangers, the debate raged for seven months. By this time, however, the question was made moot by expiration of the time limit on the lease proposal. Obviously taken aback by the passion of the objectors, McGee commented, "We have not previously had an experience quite like the one of the last few months in Georgia." J. B. Saunders was more outspoken about "the bird lovers and fish lovers and the nature lovers [who would not] let us mine."[11]

After that, the rest of the year was relatively routine. In fact, McGee's midyear speech before the New York Society of Security Analysts, Inc., was a recital of solid achievements. A total of 1,710 service stations sold Kerr-McGee petroleum products over most of the nation. Five of fifteen offshore rigs were operating overseas. Oil-and-gas production in thirteen states, plus Venezuela and Canada, daily yielded in excess of 31,000 barrels of oil and 215 mcf of natural gas. This did not include the two new fields in the Ship Shoal area which were expected to flow 12,500 additional barrels of oil per day by the end of the year. Of the twelve largest gas-producing fields offshore Louisiana, Kerr-McGee had an interest in the third largest—its 1947 discovery on Block 28, Ship Shoal—and in two other locations, for a total of three out of the twelve (a month later McGee could have added the news of another significant oil and gas discovery on Block 29). There were a million acres of leases on uranium lands in the United States, Canada, and Australia, and in 1968 some 3 million pounds of uranium would be sold to electric power companies, marking the first private sales in history.[12]

Two achievements were announced by Kerr-McGee in September. The first was a high-grade copper-ore find on its leases in the Hanover Mountain area of Grant County, New Mexico. Lying at 2,400 feet, the vein was estimated to be 100 feet thick. The second resulted from an August, 1964, change in federal law that had provided that after January 1, 1969, federal facilities would be permitted to enrich privately owned uranium hexafluoride for a service or "toll" charge. On September 4, Kerr-McGee signed the initial contract with the AEC to enrich UF_6 over a period of five years for approximately $9.4 million. The product, once treated, would be fabricated

[11] Employee release by F. C. Love, August 2, 1968, in Public Relations files; *Daily Oklahoman*, September 22, 1968; interview with J. B. Saunders, June 9, 1971.

[12] July 26, 1968, copy in Public Relations files; *Daily Oklahoman*, August 29, 1968.

by Kerr-McGee into fuel for use by Combustion Engineering in equipment for Omaha Public-Power District.[13]

Although this eliminated one block in the uranium cycle, there was still trouble in the mining phase. The dispute with the Bokum Corporation over Ambrosia Lake reached the boiling point, and on September 28, Kerr-McGee filed a declaratory judgment action in the United States District Court asking for an interpretation of the royalty provisions in its mining lease. On October 15, Bokum notified Kerr-McGee that it was canceling the 1962 lease because of alleged breaches, to which Love replied, "Kerr-McGee is of the opinion that Bokum cannot unilaterally cancel this lease contract." But Bokum then demanded payment for alleged damages and gave Kerr-McGee 180 days to remove its facilities and machinery. Moreover, it began trying to sell the disputed royalty lease to United Nuclear, petitioning the federal court to refuse jurisdiction in Kerr-McGee's suit. It would be a long and costly struggle before the matter was cleared up.[14]

Elsewhere in uranium the scene was quieter. In Australia an additional two-year exploration lease was obtained for 505 square miles in the Mount Painter area of southern Australia, after the stipulation that "while our program will be oriented toward uranium in its early stages we would like the lease to cover all minerals." Likewise, Kerr-McGee Australia, Ltd., received authority from the state of Queensland to prospect an area of approximately 758 square miles for "minerals, including gold but excluding coal, mineral oil and petroleum." The following year an additional exploration permit was granted for 2,100 acres in the state of Western Australia, but apparently it was never exercised. In the United States, Kerr-McGee announced that early in 1969 it would begin open-pit mining of its properties at Shirley Basin, Wyoming, and that the ore would be processed at the Petrotomics mill, which would be enlarged again to handle this increase.[15]

But uranium was only one of the reasons Kerr-McGee was chosen for a feature article by *Forbes*. Its stock, currently at $120, had more than tripled in price over the past five years, and its price-earnings ratio of 26 was twice as high as that of the average oil company. With a total market value of $900 million, it was almost on a par with Sinclair Oil, which was nearly three and a half times larger. Dean McGee's explanation for this favorable position was that "we were the first oil company to establish positions in all four primary fuels—oil, natural gas, coal and uranium." The move into uranium was not the result of a "grand plan," there was simply an opportunity which was recognized and taken. In coal, as in uranium, Kerr-McGee was the first oil company to move in.

[13] For copper see *Wall Street Journal*, October 1, 1968; and *Daily Oklahoman*, October 1, 1968. For uranium see *Daily Oklahoman*, September 5, 1968, and *Kermac News*, August–September, 1968.

[14] This dispute is covered in the *Wall Street Journal*, October 17, 1968.

[15] Mineral Lease Records files, "88-01-004," "88-01-005," and "88-01-001." The lease taken in Queensland in 1968 was canceled in 1969.

Part of this willingness to pioneer in diverse fields had grown out of the fact that to compete in oil on the international scale and to bid on the big overseas concessions required more money than Kerr-McGee had. According to McGee, "We've always had to walk a tight rope." But the company's payroll was "probably deeper in first-rate geological talent per dollar of company assets than any other in the energy business." Always "looking for ways to make some more money," uranium, coal, and other natural products were obvious sources. "Our idea was to find them, mine them and then process them only up to the first point where they could be sold. We didn't want to have to build up a larger marketing organization."

But as the stakes became larger in various natural resources, Love urged that Kerr-McGee's basic positions be protected by moving nearer to retail end-use markets. Thus in 1955 it had acquired a network of service stations which expanded to 1,700. Potash mining also led to establishing 170 "farm centers," providing a wide variety of services. Uranium led to a series of diversifications which now caused Kerr-McGee to dream of being the first ore-to-core uranium producer. The company had just begun in coals but was moving aggressively in mining and coking, betting on the day when gasoline could be made by adding hydrogen to coal. Until then, oil and gas remained a major interest, evidenced by the sizable new discoveries in the Ship Shoal area and at Dineh bi Keyah. *Forbes* concluded that "if any corporation is entitled to call itself an 'energy Company,' Kerr-McGee is the one."[16]

Continued commitment to its original purposes could be seen in Kerr-McGee's extensive seismic surveys off the Atlantic coast. Then, on November 25 and December 12, 1968, contracts were signed for rigs #60 and #61, both to be built by Japanese firms. Rig 60 was a four-legged, self-elevating device, which could operate in 200 feet of water, while #61, based upon a Transworld design, was ship-shaped and able to drill while floating in water up to 600 feet deep. When these were delivered, the offshore fleet would consist of eleven submersibles which rested on the bottom while drilling; one semisubmersible that could go either way; and one "floater."

The annual report again chronicled new financial highs. Sales increased by $50 million, to $473,309,048; net income by almost $5 million, and total assets by $34 million. Capital expenditures reached a new high, while long-term debt dropped $2 million (see Table 22.1).

Crude-oil and natural-gas production topped all previous years, but the amount of crude oil processed fell by 200,000 barrels. Uranium sales doubled, but plant food sales rose only slightly (see Table 22.3). In addition to the first commercial sales of uranium during 1968, the company had a backlog of orders close to $500 million. Thus, some $24 million of capital expenditures were for additional uranium mining and milling facilities. Vanadium and plant-food prices stayed low, although production was up. Sales by American Potash & Chemical were at a record level, but not

[16] "The Energy Game," pp. 32–40.

A 75,000-pound drill bit used to sink a mine shaft at Ambrosia Lake, New Mexico.

earnings. Triangle and Cato had banner years, while Moss-American's sales and earnings showed a yearly increase.[17]

The nineteen drilling rigs owned by subsidiaries showed a good year. They spudded some 203 wells and completed 188, for a cumulative footage of 1,311,790. Ten domestic units started 110 and completed 103, all offshore, with 72 as contract wells. Transworld Drilling Company, Ltd., engaged in 47 land operations in Argentina, 18 offshore Nigeria, and 11 offshore Angola. Kerr-McGee, Limited, handled 7 offshore wells in Iran, and Transocean worked 4 in the Netherlands North Sea and 6 in the English North Sea for subsidiaries of Mobil, Placid, and Union Oil (see Table 22.4).[18]

[17] Kerr-McGee Corporation, *Annual Report 1968*. A list of Kerr-McGee's eighteen subsidiaries in 1968 can be found in Securities and Exchange Commission, "Form 10-K for Fiscal Year Ended December 31, 1968."

[18] Transworld file, "Transworld Drilling Company and Affiliated Companies Rig Operations Report 12 Month Period Ended Dec. 31, 1968." For a typical 1968 contract for the Persian Gulf see Lease Records file, "Contract file 808-17."

Kerr-McGee's annual well count showed 1,985 producers, or 893.27 net. Of these 292 were in Texas, 200 in Louisiana, 170 in Oklahoma, and the remainder scattered in nine other states, Canada (19), and Venezuela (10.7). The firm had interests in 116 completed wells, almost half of which were wildcats, and 46 dry holes. More than half of the total wells had been in or offshore Louisiana, with Canada the second most active site.[19]

This banner year did not end with shouts of joy as could be expected, but incongruously with an order by the Oklahoma secretary of state for Kerr-McGee to cease all business in the state of its birth! This bombshell made newspaper headlines from coast to coast and in Alaska. At issue was a dispute started the preceding October 15, when Secretary John Rogers wrote Kerr-McGee's Assistant Secretary Carter Dudley that an official opinion had been requested from the attorney general whether Kerr-McGee could be ousted for failure to file the annual affidavits required of "foreign" companies and for not paying the required tax for doing business in Oklahoma.

Ten days later, on October 25, Rogers notified the company that an opinion had been received and Kerr-McGee must comply with the requirements. On November 13, a copy of the ruling and a deadline for compliance was mailed to Dudley. The issue then boiled down to how much tax should be paid for the issuance of Kerr-McGee stock in connection with the American Potash merger. Kerr-McGee took the position that it owed none, or at worst around $3,000. Rogers contended that over $122,000 was due. In the middle of this debate Rogers suddenly issued his ouster order on the day after Christmas. His action was loudly denounced by political officials, including Governor Dewey Bartlett, and by business leaders and chambers of commerce. In less than twenty-four hours Rogers rescinded his action, but continued to defend it, threatening to run for governor to let the people vindicate him. He claimed that technically Kerr-McGee had failed to meet the deadline, although it paid under protest by slipping a check under his office door after closing hours. Thus Kerr-McGee faced the closing hours of 1968 as a legitimate business, but the new year would open on a litigious note.[20]

The nation too was faced with unsolved problems. The chief question was how the new president, Richard Nixon, would approach the old problems of Vietnam, inflation, and school desegregation. Nixon announced the withdrawal of American troops from Vietnam and the "Vietnamization" of that conflict, but the ensuing peace talks soon stalemated. The Federal Reserve raised its interest rate to the highest point in forty years and also its discount rate, neither producing a noticeable effect on inflationary prices. Oil companies gambled some $900 million on leases on Alaska's north slope in hopes of another major find. In the states oil production did rise by 50 million barrels in 1969, but exports continued dropping and imports rising. Uncon-

[19] Production Department files, "Annual Well Count as of December 31, 1968," and "Well Count Detail."

[20] *Daily Oklahoman*, December 28 and 29, 1968; *Wall Street Journal*, December 30, 1968; "Kerr-McGee *vs.* John Rogers, Secretary of State," folder 1, Oklahoma State Archives.

Rig and casing used for a mine shaft at Ambrosia Lake, New Mexico.

cerned Americans, however, seemed more interested in Edward Kennedy's missing the bridge at Chappaquiddick.

The forty years since the founding of Anderson & Kerr Drilling Company had seen many victories over unbelievable odds by the fledgling company and its successors. Drilling in deep ocean waters and finding the elusive uranium were but two examples. When viewed in light of the past, the problems facing management in early 1969 must to some extent have seemed unreal. On January 1 the price paid by the AEC for uranium dropped; a suit was pending against Bokum and his claims at Ambrosia Lake; the Oklahoma asphalt litigation was grinding to a halt; and Secretary of State John Rogers was still to be dealt with.

Finally, there were the environmentalists and the question of what to do in Georgia. The Georgia Department of Mines estimated that Kerr-McGee owned half of a phosphate bed worth $16 billion situated on the islands and ten miles out to sea. After defeat of the offshore lease McGee declared the underwater aspect a "dead issue." In regard to the land holdings the company was "now making an economic feasibility study on mining costs." He did not, however, sound very optimistic as he pointed out that a "permit to mine . . . would still have to go through at least 15 county, state, and federal agencies. . . . Right now we're not sure where we are."[21]

But Kerr-McGee's lawyers were busy. They were pressing the Bokum suit, defending the firm against the charges of the private contractors concerning asphalt, and working with the Oklahoma attorney general for a final settlement of the state's claim. On January 15, Kerr-McGee and the other defendants agreed not to appeal the district court's decision of September, 1968, but to settle for $2.5 million, plus costs. Kerr-McGee's share of this came to $698,700.10.[22] Although this compromise became a political issue, and other suits were filed unsuccessfully against the state for accepting it, the clamor concerning asphalt would soon end. Then, on January 24, Kerr-McGee revealed that it was suing Secretary of State Rogers to recover the $122,259 paid under protest, and under the door.

As if this were not enough excitement, another merger rumor started when American Smelting & Refining Company reported in January that the two firms were holding discussions. But within two weeks Kerr-McGee announced, without explanation, that the talks had broken off. Certainly the recent confrontation with Secretary Rogers played no role in this decision, but events in March underlined how important Kerr-McGee was to the state of Oklahoma. On March 2 was announced immediate construction of a multimillion-dollar plant at Cimarron for fabrication of plutonium fuels. Then, six days later, the model for the new Kerr-McGee Center in Oklahoma City was unveiled. Plans called for bids to be taken in August, the contract awarded in September, and completion on January 1, 1972.[23]

At the first 1969 meeting of the board of directors the death of Lloyd L. Austin was noted, and James E. Webb was reappointed as a director to take his place. Of historical significance was the announcement at the same time that the last member of the Kerr family still active in the firm had resigned as vice-president of Kerr-McGee Chemical. Breene Kerr, Bob's son, left to enter a new consulting firm but would, however, continue to serve as a director.

Meanwhile, events in New Mexico were newsworthy. Two new uranium mines went into production at Ambrosia Lake, assisted by another Kerr-McGee first. This was the use of a rotary drill, with a bit weighing forty tons, by Big Hole Drillers to sink an 800-foot hole with a 15.5-foot-diameter for use as a production shaft. The job, which took four months to complete, was

---

[21] *Daily Oklahoman*, January 23, 1969.

[22] Lease Records file, "Contract 1070."

[23] *Wall Street Journal*, January 23, February 5 and 17, and March 30, 1969; *Daily Oklahoman*, January 23, February 5, 6, 8, and 14, and March 2, 8, and 29, 1969.

reported to be the "largest vertical hole ever attempted by rotary drilling methods in the Western Hemisphere."[24]

Another important oil discovery was made, this time on Block 229, Ship Shoal. But in Argentina news was not so good. Samborombon #1 was spudded on April 22 as the first test of the offshore exploration grant. It was completed on May 6, but had to be plugged and abandoned. On July 31, Kerr-McGee notified its partner, Union Texas, that after having invested some $596,000, it did not wish to make any further commitment and proposed to release all of the acreage by September 5. When Union Texas agreed to this move, the project was terminated.[25]

There was more success, however, in the Powder River Basin of Wyoming. Possessing some 300,000 acres of uranium leases there, Kerr-McGee announced that a location about fifty miles northeast of Casper would be mined by both shafts and open pits. Eventually the company planned a mill with an initial capacity of 1,000 tons per day—later to be expanded to 3,000. The first shaft would be started during the fall, and the mill would be on stream by 1971.[26]

Coal mining took a step forward with completion of the second shaft at the Choctaw mine in February. June 4 marked the first official production from the seam, and, although full production was not anticipated until 1971, by September the mine had produced some 4,000 tons, most of which was sent to various steel mills for testing. With the Arkansas River navigation project expected to be operational in 1970, hopes were high that some of the coal might be exported as far away as Japan.

During the summer the thorough reorganization of the administrative structure was completed. Four of the group vice-presidents had been appointed in January, and the remaining vacancies were filled by midyear. New divisions were created, and realignments reached down into the subsidiaries, such as Transworld and American Potash, with the intent of streamlining operations. Speculation from the outside notwithstanding, no mention was made of any planned succession to the top offices, belying any imminent changes there.

Uranium also occupied a great deal of the company's time. The Cimarron plutonium plant, the fourth in the nation, was completed, and uranium mining went on stream at Shirley Basin. The new mine, plus similar developments by other firms, promised to bring many people into this remote area. Consequently, Kerr-McGee and two other companies united efforts to build a new town at Shirley Basin, with an immediate, projected population of 2,500.

Kerr-McGee's rich oil-and-gas production areas Breton Sound and Main Pass in Louisiana bore much of the brunt of Hurricane Camille, which struck

[24] Hassell E. Hunter, "Advanced Drilling Assemblies Solve Unique Snags in Big Holes," *Oil and Gas Journal*, February 14, 1972, pp. 93–98; *Kermac News*, May–June, 1970.

[25] *Wall Street Journal*, April 1, 1969; *Daily Oklahoman*, April 1, 1969. For the Argentina venture see Oil and Gas Lease Records file, "Cont. 1033-1." The release from the Argentine government was dated December 18, 1970.

[26] *Wall Street Journal*, April 14, 1969; *Daily Oklahoman*, April 12, 1969.

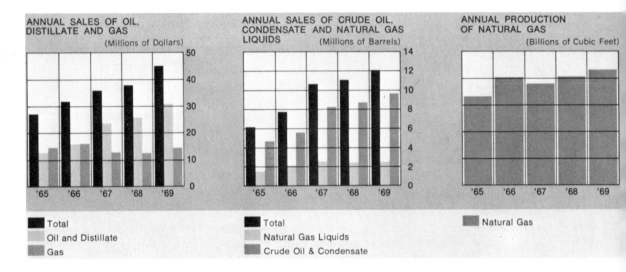

Fig. 22.1. Annual product sales, 1965–69. From Kerr-McGee Corporation, *1969 Annual Report*.

on August 17. Fortunately there was sufficient time for warning, and drilling crews and maintenance personnel were moved to safety. But the production platforms and several of the rigs had to ride out the storm. According to instruments on Rig 50, wind velocity reached 172 miles an hour. The large production platform on Block 36 was destroyed, four wells damaged, and some oil lost into the Gulf. The shutdown, destruction, and oil loss were reflected in a profit drop in the third quarter (see Fig. 22.1).[27]

During the fourth quarter, however, things improved. For one thing there was a partial victory over Secretary of State John Rogers with the ruling that Kerr-McGee owed the state only $61,127.50—roughly half of what he had claimed—and that he had to return the rest. More financially rewarding, however, was the contract signed about the same time with Metropolitan Edison of Reading, Pennsylvania. Under this agreement Kerr-McGee would furnish enriched uranium hexafluoride worth $16.7 million from its new plant at Sequoyah, with deliveries beginning in 1971.

Before the year's end several additions increased the assets column. A relatively minor acquisition was made with the purchase of International Creosoting and Construction Company of Galveston, Texas, and a new gas processing plant in which Kerr-McGee had a half interest was started in

[27] *New York Times*, August 22, 1969; *Daily Oklahoman*, October 31, 1969.

Table 22.1. Financial Highlights, 1968–69

	1968	1969
Total gross income	$477,989,697	$482,013,017
Net income	36,410,468	33,639,954
Total assets	636,917,679	667,939,872
Cash flow from earnings	84,404,067	88,401,763
Working capital	169,602,465	148,858,706
Properties (net)	365,105,431	407,879,808
Capital expenditures	79,853,064	81,159,907
Long-term debt	213,379,248	203,003,433
Cash dividends	12,216,191	12,275,724
Stockholders' equity	302,601,117	325,140,806
Total taxes paid	14,170,640	19,187,764
Number of employees	8,905	9,319

Saint Martin Parish, Louisiana, to handle gas from the Bayou Crook Chene field. At Wynnewood a new hydrofluoric alkylation unit, valued at $1.7 million, was added as part of a $4.8 million upgrading program, raising refinery capacity to 27,500 barrels per day and its labor force to 235 employees. Only in potash did the news continue bad: the Hobbs facility finished the year with a loss of $2,710,000, although sales there had increased almost $2 million.[28]

The year ended on a note of nostalgia. Morgan No. 1, Bob Kerr's first corporate well, was plugged after thirty-nine years of pumping. Located in the Konawa-Dore field in Seminole County, Oklahoma, it had produced about 130,655 barrels of oil between March, 1930, an September, 1969, and was still rated at 14 barrels per day. Somewhat ironically, its demise was caused by the need for a lake for Oklahoma Gas and Electric Company.[29]

The annual report, however, did not deal with the distant past. Production of oil and gas set records despite the disruption of Camille. Over all, the report noted the highest total sales, cash flow, and pretax earnings yet enjoyed by the company. Approximately half of the capital expenditures went for nuclear projects, and long-term indebtedness was reduced by over $10 million. Although sales reached $475,944,584, the lower price paid for uranium by the AEC and an increase of $5,107,000 in income taxes resulting from the Tax Reform Act of 1969 caused net income to drop by almost $3 million and earnings per common share to go down by $0.40 (see Table 22.2).

[28] *Kermac News* (May–June, 1970); "Kerr-McGee *vs.* John Rogers, Secretary of State"; *Daily Oklahoman*, October 16 and November 17 and 19, 1969; Mineral Lease Records file, "29-09-000."

[29] *Daily Oklahoman*, December 2, 1969.

Table 22.2 Common-Stock Highlights, 1968–69

	1968	1969
Equity per share	$ 37.49	$ 40.41
Earnings per share	$ 4.80	$ 4.40
Cash dividends per share	$ 1.50	$ 1.50
Average yield	1.2	1.5
Number of shares outstanding	7,353,308	7,374,484
Number of stockholders	19,267	18,399
New York Stock Exchange		
High	$142.50	$124.75
Low	$104.125	$ 80.625
Price-earnings ratio		
High	29.68	28.35
Low	21.69	18.32

But aside from taxes and potash the year had been good, and the future looked brighter. Branded gasoline sales reached a new high, and service stations totaled 1,835. An aggressive exploration program for uranium, copper, low-sulfur coal, and heavy minerals led to the discovery of uranium mineralization in Wyoming and South Texas, of coal in southern Illinois, and of heavy minerals in western Tennessee. American Potash had achieved a marketing high with strong demands for titanium dioxide, boron, manganese metal, soda ash, sodium chlorate, and parathions. Cato and Triangle also had record sales and earnings, and Moss-American outstripped 1968.[30]

The Transworld companies' overseas rigs were employed 94 percent of the time, and 74 percent in the domestic area. Transworld Drilling, Ltd., finished 3 land wells in Argentina and 17 offshore Angola; Kerr-McGee, Limited, accounted for 3 in Iran and 20 in Nigeria; and Transocean drilled 9 in the North Sea for Union and Mobil. Domestically, Transworld began 83 and completed 76. Of these 65 were contract, including Superior, Continental, Chevron, Mobil, Skelly, Phillips, Shell, and Gulf among the patrons. Only 8 of the 10 domestic offshore rigs were used. The two oldest units, #40 and #49, were idle, accounting for the lower utilization rate. Two land units, #16 and #31, were engaged by Big Hole in drilling the mine shaft mentioned earlier.[31]

[30] Kerr-McGee Corporation, *Annual Report 1969*; see also Securities and Exchange Commission, "Form 10-K for Fiscal Year Ended December 31, 1969."

[31] Transworld file, "Transworld Drilling Company and Affiliated Companies Rig Operations Report for the 12 Month Period Ending December 31, 1969." The three wells in Iran were drilled by Rig 55 for Société Française des Pétroles d'Iran at a day rate of $7,685; Lease Records file, "Contract 808-18."

Table 22.3. Production Record, 1968–69

	1968	1969
Production		
Crude oil produced (net barrels)	8,746,579	9,698,703
Natural-gas sales (millions of cubic feet)	77,420	83,256
Gas processing		
Gas liquids produced (net barrels)	2,410,365	2,447,532
Refining		
Crude oil processed (barrels)	16,580,517	17,275,575
Uranium		
U_3O_8 concentrate sold (lbs.)	6,811,599	4,305,593
Average price per lb.	$6.80	$5.73
Chemicals		
Plant food sold (tons)	1,467,216	1,316,450

Table 22.4. Drilling and Exploration Operations, 1968–69

	1968	1969
Feet drilled	1,311,790	1,041,529
Total wells/wells completed	203/188	138/128
Kerr-McGee interest	31	18
Rigs (average)	19	19
Contract	157	120

The annual well count shows that Kerr-McGee and its subsidiaries—
Triangle, Kerr-McGee of Argentina, and Kerr-McGee of Canada—
participated in a gross of 91 wells (40.47 net), 57 of which were wildcats. Of
the completions, 40 were in Louisiana (27 offshore) and 25 in Canada. The
remaining new wells were in Oklahoma, Texas, Argentina, New Mexico,
Wyoming, and Montana. As of December 31, Kerr-McGee had interests in
1,990 gross wells, or 892.76 net—595.60 of which were oil.[32]

As the decade of the 1960's ended, the management of Kerr-McGee could
look back with pride in its accomplishments. Time had taken its toll as death
removed three great names from its past: Robert S. Kerr, J. D. Blosser, and
F. W. Straus. But every area of interest showed dynamic growth. In the

[32] Production Department files, "Annual Well Count as of December 31, 1969" and "Well
Count Detail."

The purchase of American Potash included facilities at Henderson, Nevada, to produce sodium chlorate by an electrolytic process.

traditional roles of oil producer and contract driller the company had significantly augmented its oil-and-gas reserves, both in the United States and abroad, and its drilling arm had expanded geographically in number and sophistication of its rigs and in profitability. The refining and marketing facilities had increased in volume and kept pace with modern technology. A position of leadership was now evident in virtually all phases of the uranium industry, and its horizons now included coal and helium. Kerr-McGee had startled the financial world with its absorption of American Potash & Chemicals and with the ensuing movement into new mineral and chemical areas, at the same time creating a major wholesale and retail fertilizer division. It would be remarkable if even the experienced team of McGee and Love could project the past rate of success into the 1970's.

Manganese is also produced at the Henderson, Nevada, plant.

The Sequoyah, Ohlahoma, plant for production of uranium hexafluoride.

Chapter 23

Cimarron and Sharjah, Portents of the Future 1970–1972

Violence continued on the American scene and abroad well into the 1970's. The religious struggle in Ireland became increasingly bitter, and the ancient enemies Israel and Egypt reflected growing tension. Vietnamese peace talks entered their third year, while the entry of the United States into Cambodia sparked new outcries on college campuses. The students' deaths at Kent State University in Ohio shocked the entire country, setting off a train of accusations that echoed for over a decade. Race riots, the result of renewed conflicts over forced busing in the public schools, racked the nation, and terroristic skyjacking became so endemic that federal agents "rode shotgun" on domestic air lines.

On the political scene the right to vote was won by eighteen-year-olds, chiefly as an emotional response to the argument that if they were old enough to fight in a war they were old enough to vote. The Penn Central Railroad drifted into bankruptcy, disrupting major rail traffic in the eastern part of the United States. Because its troubles were symptomatic, the entire industry seemed headed in the same direction as that of the United States Postal Service, which Congress decided to convert into an independent agency in an attempt to end its long history of deficits. Inflation and the rising imports of foreign oil clouded the financial picture, but concern about the latter was offset somewhat by a general conviction that the North Sea was destined to become a major source of oil for the free world.

Kerr-McGee made front-page headlines in Oklahoma City on January 13, 1970, when the *Daily Oklahoman* announced that the contract had been let for construction of the company's new "center." This was a far different treatment from the reception of Anderson & Kerr Drilling Company when it slipped unnoticed into the city some forty years earlier. In fact, Kerr-McGee got a great deal of publicity during the year. Some was sad, such as the death of Travis Kerr. And sometimes it was not favorable. In March, California newspapers reported that workers at the Trona plant of American Potash were out on strike; then Pacific Engineering & Production Company filed an antitrust suit against these two companies for a sum in excess of $60 million, alleging they were monopolizing the sale of ammonium perchlorate, which was used in rocket fuel.

But there were good stories. One such piece of news on March 20 was that Kerr-McGee and Vulcan Materials Company, of Birmingham, Alabama, had "agreed in principle" to a merger, subject to approval by their respective boards. Kerr-McGee offered a stock swap of twenty-nine-hundredths share for one share of Vulcan, in what would be a $147 million transaction. Vulcan specialized in construction materials, industrial chemicals, and some metals, and the *Wall Street Journal* speculated that "mining was the common denominator." Dean McGee said that the merger would expand earnings and cash reserves and "materially assist in financing capital expenditures which would be necessary for the development of new uranium deposits in the near future." Although this was a sure indication that his company was projecting great future emphasis on its nuclear division, the plan fell through. On April 9, without explanation, Kerr-McGee suddenly declared that the merger was off.[1]

If there were any disappointment in this failure, it was quickly replaced by the spate of news concerning Kerr-McGee uranium achievements. On April 1, the company acquired the Ambrosia Lake holdings of Magna Oil Corporation of Dallas for $6.9 million in cash and notes. This acquisition included an operating mine, a stockpile, mineral leases, and equipment, and it was estimated that Kerr-McGee's productive capacity of uranium oxide would be increased by some 600,000 pounds per year. Then on April 20 came the dedication of the $25 million Sequoyah hexafluoride plant—and not a minute too soon, for on April 9 a contract worth $14.5 million had been signed with Consumers Power Company, of Jackson, Michigan, for enriched uranium hexafluoride to be delivered during the current year.[2]

It was a gala day for the company and for the state of Oklahoma. National, state, local, and company officials gathered at Sequoyah for the dedication. This was followed by a meeting of the seventeen-state Southern Interstate Nuclear Board, highlighted by an illustrious panel of speakers, who emphasized the importance of environmental protection. The dedication

---

[1] *Wall Street Journal*, March 23 and 30 and April 10, 1970; *Daily Oklahoman*, March 21, 1970. A federal district court was later to award Pacific $4.6 million in triple damages. Years later the Circuit Court of Appeals overturned that ruling, stating that Kerr-McGee had not violated antitrust laws but had engaged in "rational competitive behavior." The case was finally settled on November 28, 1977, when the Supreme Court upheld the circuit court's decision. *Daily Oklahoman*, November 29, 1977.

[2] Public Relations Department, press releases for April, 1970; *Wall Street Journal*, April 6, 7, and 9, 1970; *Daily Oklahoman*, April 9, 1970.

speaker, Chairman of the Joint Committee on Atomic Energy, Representative Chet Hollifield, hailed the Sequoyah plant as "another indication of the vision that Kerr-McGee has evidenced in leading the Nation into the nuclear age." On the other hand, Oklahoma representatives noted that the state had been thrust into national leadership by the establishment of the three uranium-related plants within its borders, and, moreover, Kerr-McGee was engaged in all but two phases of the uranium cycle: enrichment (a federal monopoly) and operation of a generating-plant reactor.[3]

Not everyone was that impressed. It should be remembered that uranium was then in a transition period. Federal purchases had ended, and only time would prove whether or not the private market, especially electric-generation capacity, could absorb the production of nuclear materials. Hardly had the applause at the dedication died when *Forbes* asked: "Why is chairman Dean A. McGee trying to beef up Kerr-McGee's uranium capacity despite a glut of the stuff?" McGee was quoted as answering, "It is only a short-term over supply." While the AEC paid only $5.86 a pound in 1969, "we've got a 53-million-pound backlog at higher commercial prices to take us through 1974. By then many nuclear plants will be coming in."

"But," replied *Forbes*, "McGee could be wrong." If so, "it would not be the first time." By acquiring American Potash, he bought into the fertilizer slump. *Forbes* concluded that while McGee, a geologist, deserved the bulk of the credit for the firm's success, "a fascination with digging can be dangerous. Last year the Company's capital expenditures, mainly for exploration, reached the $80 million mark, but continued to yield scant results."

Fortune also had other misgivings. Commenting upon the Sequoyah dedication, it pointed out that Kerr-McGee joined Allied Chemical in becoming the second private company with a plant of this type and that "the company's move at this point is something of a gamble." It speculated that Allied's plant alone could probably meet domestic demand until 1974 and noted that three similar facilities abroad were competing for American business. But Kerr-McGee did have contracts for 75 percent of the Sequoyah installation's capacity and hoped for foreign business as well.[4]

But nothing is more successful in the marketplace than success, and that came fast. In May there was the announcement of an $11 million contract to furnish enriched hexafluoride to Rochester Gas and Electric Company of New York during the year. Including the previous year's sale to Metropolitan Edison, by mid-1970, Kerr-McGee had commitments from the private market for the equivalent of more than 65.5 million pounds of uranium oxide. Friends on Wall Street rallied to its defense also. In September,

[3] *Daily Oklahoman*, April 21, 1970.

[4] James J. Kelly speech to the Grants, N.M., Chamber of Commerce, February 18, 1976, in Public Relations press release, "76#18"; "Still More Uranium," *Forbes*, May 1, 1970, p. 39; "A Big Step for an Okie Enterprise," *Fortune*, June, 1970, p. 32. In "Ore-to-Core?" *Barron's*, May 4, 1970, pp. 23, 28, gave a straightforward analysis of Kerr-McGee without judging its uranium efforts other than to say that uranium sales made up 25 percent of its earnings.

Lehman Brothers issued a report which was primarily intended to offset any pessimistic views on Kerr-McGee's future.

A security scare had brought anxious moments in May, however. A shipment of uranium by Kerr-McGee was lost while en route to Ohio, but fortunately it was found a week later—in Dallas, Texas. Nevertheless, in July the Sequoyah plant successfully made its first shipment of hexafluoride to the AEC plant at Oak Ridge, Tennessee, for enrichment. Then, in August, the initial delivery of fuel rods from the Cimarron plutonium processing facility was made to the AEC for its use in a research program at the Argonne National Laboratory. That same month a fourteen-year supply of hexafluoride was contracted to the Arkansas Power and Light Company with a value in excess of $90 million, and deliveries to begin in 1975.

Although uranium was preeminent in the company, all divisions were active. April saw completion of the new gas processing plant jointly owned with Humble Oil at Bayou Crook Chene, Saint Martin Parish, Louisiana, and the commissioning of Rig 61 in Japan. This $8.5 million drilling structure was the world's largest. In keeping with Kerr-McGee's pioneering tradition in the offshore field it was the first to possess the drill-while-floating characteristic of a semisubmersible, together with the towing traits of a ship-shaped barge. The main hull was four hundred feet long and had the configuration of a vessel with two outriggers. When in operation, the device floated on four stabilizing columns with the main hull positioned some thirty feet above the water. (Rig 60, also being built in Japan, was finished three months later.) In June, Rig 61 began a 9,000-mile trip from Japan to the coast of South Africa and two months later reached its destination. There it began work for Rand Mines, Ltd., at a rate of $40,000 per day. In August the initial oil production from eight of the projected eighteen wells on Block 229, Ship Shoal came in, at the rate of 2,000 barrels a day.[5]

The generally good financial picture enabled the board to make several moves in the economic area. The company's 4½ percent bonds, due June 1, 1971, were called in a year early, and the final payment on the Hobbs potash plant was made on March 30. Then Kerr-McGee showed its continuing faith in the fertilizer business by purchasing the Wilson & Toomer Fertilizer Company in June. Likewise, a $600,000 compaction unit was added at Hobbs, over-all production was increased to 480,580 tons, and the potash facility finally showed its first profit, $980,000.[6]

In July the last Oklahoma asphalt suit was concluded in favor of two private contracting firms and against Kerr-McGee and three other suppliers. On the grounds that the contractors had been overcharged by one cent a gallon between 1962 and 1966, the jury ordered a payment of $897,944. It was ruled however, that the alleged conspiracy was not "wrongfully, fraudulently and effectively concealed." The penalty was later re-

[5] Kerr-McGee press release of April 3, 1970; *Daily Oklahoman*, June 26 and August 6 and 23, 1970; *Kermac News*, August and November, 1970.

[6] Mineral Lease Records files, "Contract 1204-1" and "29-09-000"; Public Relations, press release, "76-3."

Uranium hexafluoride gas prepared for shipment.

duced by the judge to a total of $556,462.73, including attorney fees.
Kerr-McGee's part was $140,000 in damages. Thus ended another in a series
of suits which had their origin not in criminal intent but apparently in the
nature of the business and in human carelessness. All caused the company
embarrassment and bad publicity not only in Oklahoma but nationally.

And, finally, in September, 1970, came the welcome news that the
United States District Court had ruled Kerr-McGee's lease on the Bokum
properties was still in force. Furthermore, Kerr-McGee was in rightful
possession of the property and owed Bokum no damages. But Bokum did not
accept defeat, and the suit wound its way slowly through appeals to the
Supreme Court. Although Kerr-McGee paid in the neighborhood of a

397

million dollars for legal fees, it eventually won the case and this long-running feud was finally terminated with the purchase of the Bokum royalty rights.[7]

Better news was that the Trona strike, which had started March 18, was finally settled on July 10 with a two-year contract. Involving 615 of 850 workers in three unions and led by Harry Bridges of the longshoremen, the 115-day work stoppage saw 54 persons arrested for acts of violence and the unions fined $55,000 each for contempt of court. This settlement was offset, however, by trouble in the coal mines in Oklahoma. Kerr-McGee had spent some $7 million of a proposed $20 million in its plan to achieve production of a million tons per year. After the first six months about 40 of a projected 200 miners had an output of only 8,000 tons. There had been difficulties, however, with the unstable shale above the four-foot seam causing roof-support problems. Furthermore, the current mining machines were proving too large, and plans had to be made to try smaller ones.

To make matters worse, on July 17 some fifty people at the mine went out on strike, declaring that it was unsafe and also demanding recognition as a unit of the United Mine Workers. At first the strike was peaceful, consisting primarily of picket lines, return of Kerr-McGee credit cards, and a boycott of company products. As negotiations dragged on, however, the situation became violent, with some shooting and some dynamiting of trucks. On December 11, five months after the strike's onset, the issue was settled by a new contract.[8]

Most of the fourth quarter was given over to the program of internal reorganization. About the only exception was an announcement of "significant" copper mineralization near Patagonia, Arizona, and discussions with the Japanese partners about abandonment of the Canadian uranium project because of disappointing results. The major development, however, involved formation of Kerr-McGee Chemical. As of October 1, all chemical, fertilizer, and nonfuel mineral divisions were combined into this single subsidiary, with James J. Kelly as president. This included American Potash and Wilson & Toomer, as well as the vanadium plant. Under the arrangement Kerr-McGee Chemical had five divisions, each headed by a vice-president. Two more subsidiaries were set up to handle overseas sales of borax: Borax & Chemicals, Ltd., and Silobor S.A. (75 percent owned).[9]

Record-breaking performances had become almost routine in previous annual reports, but the 1970 version came up with a new first: sales above the half-billion-dollar mark—a 10.8 percent rise to $527,539,102—for the first time in company history. The cash flow set a new high, while net income

[7] Interview with Edwin L. Kennedy, August 13, 1971; *Wall Street Journal*, May 12, August 13 and 14, 1970; *Daily Oklahoman*, May 12 and 27, July 9, and August 13 and 22, 1970; interview with George Cobb, December 7, 1972.

[8] For Trona see *Wall Street Journal*, July 13, 1970; for the Oklahoma strike see *Daily Oklahoman*, October 11 and 12, 1970; and Public Relation's clipping file on the strike and its December 11 press release announcing the end of the strike.

[9] *New York Times*, September 23, 1970; *Daily Oklahoman*, September 23, October 8, and November 7, 1970; *Kermac News*, November, 1970.

Rig 61 on station. This rig is capable of drilling in water six hundred feet
deep.

increased 6.8 percent, and total assets by almost $68 million. Working
capital and capital expenditures fell to $124,990,410 and $79,299,754, respectively, as long-term debt grew, primarily because of purchasing the
Ambrosia Lake properties and the assets of Wilson & Toomer (see Table
23.2).

The high mark in sales came from two sources: oil-and-gas sales with the
new offshore production, and the expanded chemical operations. The 10-K
form gives further refinement. Petroleum provided 59 percent of the sales
and 76 percent of the net income; chemicals and plant foods, 27 and 21
percent, respectively. The retail fertilizer operations were handled through

Table 23.1. Kerr-McGee Corporation Capital Expenditures, 1966–70

	1966	1967	1968	1969	1970
Petroleum	$33,701,999	$23,386,999	$27,630,955	$28,224,633	$35,759,615
Chemicals and plant food	24,416,497	20,778,978	23,318,133	7,891,152	8,017,009
Uranium	2,257,216	10,097,960	21,962,298	32,925,201	27,162,245
Other	5,539,143	5,197,496	6,941,678	12,118,921	8,360,885
Total	$65,914,855	$59,461,433	$79,853,064	$81,159,907	$79,299,754

135 company-controlled outlets and 120 commission warehouses, while the products were manufactured in 13 plants. There were producing oil-and-gas leases in twelve states, plus Canada and Venezuela, amounting to 299,239 net acres. The largest amount, 31 percent, was in Louisiana and its offshore waters (see Table 23.4).

Property, plant, and equipment investments at cost showed petroleum $332.7 million; chemicals and plant food, $247; uranium, $140.8; and "other," $60.9.[10] In gas processing, Kerr-McGee completely owned two plants, had a half interest in three others, and minority interest in an additional ten. These fifteen plants had increased output by 7 percent, while helium production was up 17.1 percent. Branded gasoline sales moved into their eighteenth state with the opening of service stations in Kentucky.

A look at capital expenditures for the preceding five years shows that 1970 was down from the record highs of 1969 but that petroleum received the largest investment four of the years (See Table 23.1). Some $6 million was invested in one-half interest in 12,000 offshore acres, as development drilling in that area received the major emphasis during the year. The rising significance of uranium is seen in the fact that it replaced chemical expenditures after 1968. The backlog of contracts for uranium oxide increased to 56,115,000 pounds, and to more than 21 million kilograms of concentrate for conversion into uranium hexafluoride, justifying the need for continued expansion in this division.

The subsidiaries likewise turned in glowing reports. Cato had its third consecutive year of record sales, and Moss-American's twelve wood-preserving plants again surpassed 1969 sales and earnings. Triangle was now one of the largest wholesale marketers of refined petroleum products in the nation and continued to set new marks.[11]

The drilling subsidiaries reported a good, though not record, year. The domestic drilling was done by nine offshore units, plus two land rigs used by Big Hole, and the foreign by six offshore and two land rigs in Argentina. The Transworld Companies achieved utilization percentages of 85 for overseas rigs and 93 for domestic offshore units. They participated in 153 wells for a total of 988,987 feet, and completed 133. Of these, 90 were in the Gulf, with

[10] Securities and Exchange Commission, "Form 10-K for Year Ended December 31, 1970."

[11] Kerr-McGee Corporation, *1970 Annual Report.*

400

83 completions. There were 63 foreign wells (50 completed), all of which were offshore except for 22 in Argentina for YPF. The offshore wells were located in Trinidad, Angola, Nigeria, South Africa, Iran, and the North Sea. The drop in utilization overseas was in Iran, where only one well was drilled. All the foreign wells were contract, as were 64 of the 90 domestic wells (see Table 23.5).[12]

To augment its own reserves, Kerr-McGee looked in new areas such as off the Florida coast and in the Canadian Northwest and also participated in a total of 99 gross completions, of which 52 were wildcats and 29 were dry. Of the total, 53 were in Louisiana (43 of these were offshore, chiefly on blocks 229 and 273), 23 in Canada, and 12 in Texas (4 offshore). At the end of 1970, Kerr-McGee had interests in 2,033 gross wells, or 916.22 net. Percentage-wise, this gave 68 percent oil, 25.5 percent gas, and 0.09 percent gas condensate. In net wells per state Texas still led with 32.1 percent, followed by Louisiana (24.4), Oklahoma (18.3), and a low of 0.33 percent in Colorado. In foreign countries 3.1 percent of Kerr-McGee's net was in Canada and 1.1 percent in Venezuela.[13]

Headlines had a familiar ring in 1971. The United States continued troop withdrawals from Vietnam, 200,000 people engaged in a "March for Peace" on Washington, a new civil war broke out in Pakistan, and the Irish continued to kill each other. Surprisingly, however, the Middle East truce held. New diplomatic factors were introduced by Great Britain's withdrawal from the Persian Gulf, Nixon's trip to Peking as a result of "ping-pong" diplomacy, and the United Nation's seating of Red China.

On the domestic economic front Amtrak was created to do for the nation's railroads what the independent postal system was supposed to do for the mails. By midyear the Nixon administration struck a hard blow at the continuing problems of inflation and an unfavorable balance of trade by announcing a ninety-day freeze of wages, prices, and rents. Federal payrolls were cut by 5 percent, foreign aid was cut by 10 percent, and a 10 percent surcharge was added to all imports. Most significantly the dollar was allowed to "float," since foreign-held dollars could no longer be redeemed with gold.

Despite the decline in capital investments Kerr-McGee management remained "bullish." In January, the first of the new mines at Ambrosia Lake was opened, and, with the second shaft added later that year, the firm had a total of eight working mines. In June construction started on still another shaft in the northeast Church Rock district of New Mexico. When completed to a depth of 1,850 feet, its output would also be handled by the Ambrosia Lake mill.

The Petrotomics facility, however, was a different story. Because of its size, age, declining ore sources, and lack of efficiency, rumors were widespread that it would be shut down. Early in May the plant manager, with the

---

[12] Transworld file, "Transworld Drilling Company and Affiliated Companies Rig Operations Report for the 12 Month Period Ending December 31, 1970."

[13] Production Department files, "Annual Well Count as of December 31, 1970," and "Well Count Detail."

approval of the partners, issued a vague statement to the effect that the price of yellow cake was in a depressed state because of delays in getting new nuclear plants into operation and the increased cost of mining and milling. No decision had been made about closing, however.

The joint exploration venture with the Japanese in Canada proved unfruitful. Uranium was found, but it was too low grade for profitable production at that time. Consequently, the project was abandoned, and Kerr-McGee dropped its leases on all but about eleven square miles of the most promising acreage.

The immediate future of uranium seemed to have questionable profitability, but this was not the case with other areas in Kerr-McGee's empire. The completion of Rig 60 in Japan in March made it possible to open another part of the world for contract drilling and, even before completion, the unit had been chartered for four wells for Indonesia Gulf Oil Company. On April 1 this fifteenth offshore rig left for the northeast coast of Sumatra. Despite a severe buffeting by Typhoon Vera, it reached its destination. Rig 61, having completed its South African contract, was moved to the North Sea off Scotland. Even Rig 55, which had been idle in the Persian Gulf, won a June contract with Farsi Petroleum Company for one or more wells.[14] Kerr-McGee thus had almost half its offshore units operating in overseas waters.

The fertilizer market was also looking better. Canadian restrictions firmed the price for potash, and, consequently, the Hobbs facility had a second year in the black. This development undoubtedly influenced Kerr-McGee to begin its long-deferred entry into the phosphate field, although on a smaller scale than originally projected. In April, American Cyanamid and Kerr-McGee jointly announced the formation of a partnership, Brewster Phosphates, to mine and process phosphate rock and to produce wet-process phosphoric acid and diammonium phosphate for use in fertilizers. Kerr-McGee's share was approximately 30 percent of this new firm, which would take over Cyanamid's Haynesworth mine at Bradley, Florida, and operate Cyanamid and Kerr-McGee reserves as a unit. A toll agreement was also announced with Freeport Sulphur for half the capacity of its Louisiana phosphoric acid plant—the world's largest. Cyanamid and Kerr-McGee then would market their own shares of the products. James Kelly, as head of Kerr-McGee Chemical, said, "This partnership makes it possible for Kerr-McGee to establish a basic position in the phosphate fertilizer business and for our phosphate reserves in Florida to be mined through large, modern production facilities."[15]

There was more good news in May. A significant deep oil reserve was found on Block 52 in the Main Pass area off Louisiana, where previously there had been only shallow gas wells. This, plus the generally favorable outlook, inspired the board of directors to vote a three-for-one stock split, the first in a decade. The new annual dividend was $1.80, up from $1.50, or

[14] Lease Records file, "Contract 808-21."

[15] For Hobbs see Mineral Lease Records file, "29-09-000"; for phosphate see *Daily Oklahoman*, April 7, 1971; *Wall Street Journal*, April 7 and 8, 1971; and interview with James J. Kelly, June 26, 1971.

Dragline used to mine phosphates in Florida.

$0.60 a share on the new ones. A special stockholders' meeting in July
happily approved the motion and authorized tripling the number of shares
to 37.5 million.[16]

In July, a general rumor was confirmed by the announcement that the old
Deep Rock Refinery at Cushing, Oklahoma, would finally be closed. This
facility had been old when Kerr-McGee acquired it, and for the past several
years had been used primarily to manufacture lubricating oils. As of December 31, 1971, it ceased operation "as a result of general rising costs and

[16] *Wall Street Journal*, May 14 and 17 and July 14, 1971; *Daily Oklahoman*, July 14, 1971.

the declining production in Oklahoma of the special lube-quality oil required as a charge stock for the refinery." The refinery equipment was
auctioned off and removed in July, 1972.

Then, in October, another marginal operation, the refinery at Cleveland,
Oklahoma, was also scheduled for closing at the end of the year. It was
devoted almost entirely to production of naphthas, and the logic for its
discontinuation was the inability to get the necessary crudes. Thus decline
in the rate, and changes in the type of Oklahoma crude-oil production cost
the lives of these two old refineries.

Coal brought new excitement to headquarters, however. Kerr-McGee
claimed a "first" and fulfillment of another of Senator Kerr's dreams when on
July 22 two barges, loaded with coal from the Choctaw mine and destined for
Saint Louis, marked the first shipment of Oklahoma coal on the new Arkansas River navigation system. But the future of the mine was still not clear,
and its fate largely depended on the success of experiments then being
introduced with "longwall" mining.

The rest of the year was relatively uneventful. One of the more notable
occurrences was the August announcement that Kerr-McGee (50 percent)
and its three partners in three leases in the East Cameron area offshore
Louisiana, would drill five exploratory wells and dedicate any gas discovery
to Transcontinental Gas Pipeline Corporation, in return for a payment of
$10.5 million. The later part of that month also brought word that Rig 60 had
completed its first well offshore Sumatra and was moving to a new site.
Finally, in September, Kerr-McGee bought forty-eight Texas service stations from Kayo Oil, a subsidiary of Continental Oil.[17]

The annual report for 1971 showed that management's optimism at the
beginning of the year was justified (see Table 23.2). In fact, this had been one
of the most successful years in the company's history, with new highs in total
assets; working capital; stockholders' equity; and net income, with a 13.3
percent increase, or $1.77 per share after the split. Sales were a record of
$603,254,066. The cash flow of $101,420,773 was over the $100 million mark
for the first time and exceeded the previous high in 1970 by 17 percent (see
table 23.3).

On the other hand, long-term debt grew approximately $14 million, and
capital expenditures were cut by almost $10 million. Of the latter 42 percent
went for petroleum operations, primarily for drilling new wells in the Gulf.
Chemicals and plant foods accounted for another 20 percent, chiefly in
connection with Brewster Phosphates and plant expansion, and 21 percent
for uranium, mostly for increased mining in New Mexico and Wyoming. A
new expense and a sign of the times was over $2 million spent for programs
in pollution control and abatement.

The principal income producers were oil and gas ($59.9 million in sales),
nuclear products, minerals, wholesale marketing of petroleum derivatives,
and contract drilling. Sales of uranium oxide concentrates totaled 6.6 million
pounds, and 2.5 million kilograms were converted into uranium hexaflu-

[17] *Daily Oklahoman*, August 6 and 28 and September 3, 1971.

Brewster Phosphates plant owned by Kerr-McGee and American Cyanamid.

oride. Sale of branded gasoline reached its eighth consecutive high, and
Triangle's profits rose. Industrial chemicals benefited from better prices for
boron and other heavy chemical products, and enlarged production capacity
was achieved at the titanium dioxide and manganese plants in Hamilton,
Mississippi, and the vanadium unit at Soda Springs, Idaho. Retail plant food
and farm chemical operations showed modest improvement, but curtailment of railroad purchases caused a slight decline in Moss-American profits.
(see Table 23.4).

During 1971 exploration and development activities were concentrated in
the Gulf of Mexico, the Anadarko Basin of western Oklahoma and the Texas
Panhandle, and in Canada. The greatest success came on blocks 229 and
214, Ship Shoal, offshore Louisiana. A new departure is seen in one-half
interest in permits covering almost five million acres on Prince of Wales
Island, one of the Arctic islands.[18]

[18] Kerr-McGee Corporation, *1971 Annual Report*; Securities and Exchange Commission,
"Form 10-K for Year Ended December 31, 1971."

As has been seen, Kerr-McGee had a good year in the Gulf, but this statement does not reveal what was involved behind the scenes. The average bonus cost for offshore Louisiana in 1971 was $520 an acre, after the bidder had already spent several million dollars making surveys, drilling evaluation wells, and performing other necessary evaluations. The drilling cost per well was usually around $500,000, if no trouble were encountered. If a discovery resulted, then a drilling platform had to be constructed from which ten or more wells might be bored. This cost could run to $2 million or more. In short, before production even began, some $7 million might have been invested in capital expenditures, in addition to exploration costs. If the find were gas, then pipeline connections had to be laid to shore, where facilities to receive the gas were also necessary. Before any profit could be realized, moreover, a 16⅔ percent royalty cost had to be paid to the government as well.[19]

Against these figures Kerr-McGee subsidiaries were involved in 142 wells, of which 128 were completed, and drilled some 930,078 feet. Its foreign rigs contracted 61 holes, 52 of which were completed. All except 3 in Argentina were offshore. One was at Trinidad, 1 off Iran, 11 offshore West Africa, 16 by Nigeria, 23 in the North Sea, and 7 in Southeast Asia. The last two land rigs were sold in Argentina, leaving only those used by Big Hole to drill on dry land (see Table 23.5).

Domestically, 130 wells were spudded and 78 completed, with 61 being contracted by other firms. Kerr-McGee participated in a gross total of 105 wells, 51 of which were wildcats. Of the completions, 37 were in Louisiana, 18 in Canada, and 15 in Texas. During the year 74.25 net wells were sold, most of which were in Kansas, leaving the company a total of 859.88 net wells at the end of 1971.[20]

The presidential election year 1972 revived politicians and their promises as the various contenders argued the same old issues of the past. An attempt to murder Alabama Governor George Wallace and the "Eagleton affair" changed the race to one between George McGovern and Sargent Shriver for the Democrats versus a second term for Republicans Nixon and Agnew. A small furor developed over a break-in at the Democratic headquarters in Washington, but this generally was overlooked. Of more interest were the current events: the withdrawal of the last ground troops from Vietnam, passage by Congress of the Equal Rights Amendment, the banning of DDT, Clifford Irvin's fake biography of Howard Hughes, the antics of Martha Mitchell, and the tragic slaying of Israeli athletes at the Munich Olympics.

A "new economic policy" was announced by the Nixon administration. It aimed at stemming inflation, trimming unemployment, stimulating the domestic economy, and making American goods more competitive abroad. All was supposed to be accomplished by repeal of the excise tax on cars and

---

[19] "Newsletter," *Oil and Gas Journal*, March 8, 1971, unpaged section.

[20] Transworld file, "Transworld Drilling Company and Affiliated Companies Rig Operations Report for the 12 Month Period Ending December 31, 1971"; Production Department files, "Annual Well Count as of December 31, 1971," and "Well Count Detail."

A drawing of Rig 62, a $10.9 million mat-type self-elevating unit.

trucks, increased personal income-tax exemptions, and a 7 percent investment tax credit for business. Such were the aims of politics.

The economy did pick up, either because of or in spite of Nixon's policies. New federal agencies sought to hold the lid on wages, prices, and rents. Net growth was around 6 percent, the rate of inflation dropped to 3.8 percent, and unemployment inched downward.

At Kerr-McGee, 1972 was a year to look back into its history at the men and events which had been a part of the early company. Two significant anniversaries were celebrated. One was the twenty-fifth year since the first successful oil well was drilled in the Gulf out of sight of land, an event which established the offshore oil industry. The other marked the fiftieth year since establishment of Cato Oil and Grease, one of the company's very successful subsidiaries.

But Kerr-McGee looked back also to remember two men who had played dominant roles in its development and who would no longer be a part of its future. First was the unexplained and unsolved brutal murder in Chicago of Dean E. Terrill, whose legal genius had been responsible for so much of the early growth of the infant business. This tragedy was followed by the retirement from the board of Guy C. Kiddoo, whose presence was emblematic of the decisive support from the First National Bank of Chicago, without which the struggling young firm would not have made the transition to a large corporation. By an amendment to the bylaws Kiddoo was given the title director emeritus. George Parks was named to replace him, and James J. Kelly took the position that Terrill had held since 1936.

The future executive committee would be McGee, Webb, Kennedy, Kelly, and Parks. It would act on contracts such as the one Transworld Drilling announced in January for construction in Beaumont, Texas, of Rig 62, a $10.9 million self-elevating unit which could operate in 300 feet of water. Then, in February, in a far-reaching act the committee approved one of the largest contracts ever made in the uranium field. Westinghouse Hanford chose Kerr-McGee to fabricate 18,500 uranium-plutonium dioxide pins at a cost of $7.2 million for use in "fast-flux" experiments. A pin contained approximately 144 pellets, each pellet equivalent in energy value to one ton of coal. The pins would be used in the research and development of a liquid metal fast breeder reactor, designed to produce more fuel than it consumed.[21] This contract was executed at the Cimarron plant, and would bring problems.

Heretofore Kerr-McGee had had no success in its efforts to become an Arabian oil producer, but this was to change. The story began routinely with a March 3 contract between Transworld, Ltd., and Buttes Gas and Oil. Rig 55 was contracted to drill a series of wells located offshore Sharjah in the Arabian, or Persian, Gulf at a day rate of $9,650. This was replaced by an "Acquisition of Interest Agreement," whereby two wells would be drilled on the concession of 480,000 acres earlier granted Buttes by the ruler of Sharjah in December, 1969. In return for rebating day rates in excess of $4,300,

---

[21] Public Relations Department, "Approval file, April 1972."

Kerr-McGee earned an undivided 12.5 percent interest in the concession at the end of the first two wells. Thereafter, Kerr-McGee bore its share of all costs on any additional wells. On March 30, Buttes signed over this interest to Kerr-McGee Eastern Company, and on April 28, A-1 was spudded off the island of Abu Musa. By November it was obvious the company had a strike. The well flowed oil at the rate of 13,995 barrels per day and 30.25 million cubic feet of gas from four separate zones. Consequently, on November 22, A-2 was spudded.[22]

Meanwhile, although Rig 62 was still under construction, Transocean announced that Transocean III would be built in Germany. Able to drill in 600 feet of water, it would have the same shiplike plan used for Rig 61, then operating successfully off Spain. This $16.5 million device was slated for completion in 1973 to join Transocean's North Sea fleet. Construction of these two rigs turned out to be more fortuitous than anyone could have foreseen. An unexpected disaster struck when Rig 60 was drilling in 100 feet of water offshore Burma in the Gulf of Martaban. A high-pressure gas pocket was penetrated, eruptions occurred in the hole, and the gas ignited. Although the crew was safely evacuated, the $6.2 million rig collapsed and was lost on September 9—twenty-five years to the day after Kerr-McGee's first offshore well.

Before news of this disaster reached Oklahoma City, however, the board decided to call for redemption of its $93,783,800 in outstanding 3.75 percent convertible subordinated debentures, due May 1, 1992. By September 21, all but $60,000 of the total had been converted into Kerr-McGee common stock—a true vote of confidence. August likewise saw another shutdown, the "temporary" closing of the Choctaw coal mine. It simply was not commercially feasible and was placed on standby while studies could be carried out to solve its problems. Nevertheless, "the company will continue its coal research, acquisition, and development programs." Further evidence of this intent came with the September announcement of the formation of Mine Contractors, Inc., to handle the development and construction of new Kerr-McGee mines and facilities.[23]

In November the entire petroleum industry joined Kerr-McGee in celebrating its twenty-fifth anniversary of Louisiana "State Lease 754-A-1." Since this initial discovery in 1947, over 921,824 barrels of oil and 250 million cubic feet of gas had been drawn from this lease on the floor of the Gulf. Twenty-five years later Kerr-McGee had a total of 101,685 acres in these waters and some 261 producing wells, which contributed approximately 75 percent of its total production. The oil industry had drilled more than 15,000 offshore wells in waters claimed by the United States, and by 1972 over 400 rigs were operating off the coasts of 70 nations. An estimated $10 billion had been spent in labor, materials, and specialized equipment, and the offshore industry furnished some 17 percent of the total output of oil and 6 percent of the natural gas. Of the world's coastal nations 25 had commercial production offshore, and a dozen more claimed discoveries.

[22] Lease Records files, "Contract 808-22" and "Project 1006 (file #1)."

[23] *Wall Street Journal*, August 22, 1972.

Table 23.2. Financial Highlights, 1970–72

	1970	1971	1972
Total gross income	$530,979,722	$607,694,346	$684,674,719
Net income	35,916,975	40,688,905	50,599,374
Total assets	734,649,570	762,504,461	806,800,549
Cash flow from earnings	86,358,751	101,420,773	127,224,771
Working capital	124,990,410	159,144,145	198,247,073
Properties (net)	445,819,283	455,579,612	466,434,192
Capital expenditures	79,299,754	69,875,183	76,054,029
Long-term debt	211,448,549	225,649,896	124,426,918
Cash dividends	12,291,429	13,423,789	15,198,038
Stockholders' equity	349,191,263	378,721,735	508,226,181
Total taxes paid	22,186,156	26,437,821	31,719,280
Number of employees	9,792	9,439	9,217

Table 23.3. Common-Stock Highlights, 1970–72

	1970	1971*	1972
Equity per share	$ 43.63	$15.76	$19.76
Earnings per share	$ 4.70	$ 1.77	$ 2.14
Cash dividends per share	$ 1.50	$ 0.55	$ 0.60
Average yield	1.7	1.3	1.1
Number of shares outstanding	7,382,275	22,208,667	24,374,976
Number of stockholders	17,790	17,235	18,785
New York Stock Exchange			
High	$114.25	$49.25	$66.50
Low	$ 59.00	$31.63	$37.86
Price-earnings ratio			
High	24.30	27.82	31.00
Low	12.55	17.87	17.69

*Restated for July 21, 1971, three-for-one stock split.

Kerr-McGee's long-range planning and faith in this source of oil was shown in December, 1972, when it jointly acquired an additional 10,000 acres in federal lease sales for $13,160,000, making a total of 103,298 net acres off Louisiana and 3,226 net acres off Texas.

At the November meeting the board made some minor changes in its corporate image. An age limit of fifty-nine years was set for election as a director, and after 1977 no person over seventy could serve on the board, irrespective of prior service. The exact reason for these changes was not stated. It was also decided that the new building then nearing completion would be designated McGee Tower and that, in order to make the company's retirement plans noncontributory, the employee Thrift and Savings Plans were ended.

The annual report for 1972 again spoke in superlatives, describing "the year [as] the most outstanding in the history of the company." With a 12.7 percent increase, sales reached $679,575,614 and net income jumped by 24.4 percent. Cash flow grew by more than 25 percent, and capital expenditures by $6 million, with approximately 59 percent of this amount going for leases, drilling, and construction of new rigs. Uranium received 22 percent, principally for addition of new mines. Total assets reached $806,800,549, while long-term debt fell over $100 million.

Every department contributed to the record. A ten-year comparison shows that 1972 was a high-water mark in all but five categories: capital expenditures, number of oil and gas wells completed, number of wells drilled, total footage, and crude oil processed. Although the 13,612,348 barrels of crude processed in 1972 were below the high of 17,364,618 in 1970, refined products sales went up over 9 million. Or, to look at 1972 in another way:

Sales, 1972 (in millions)

Petroleum	$393.9
Chemicals and plant foods	218.9
Nuclear	66.5
Other	.3
Total	$679.6

Net Income, 1972 (in millions)

Petroleum	$ 40.6
Chemicals and plant foods	9.2
Nuclear	1.5
Other	−0.7
Total	$ 50.6

In marketing there were gains in bulk sales and in branded retail and wholesale operations. Mechanical and process changes at Wynnewood raised the refinery's processing capacity from 30,000 to 34,000 barrels a day. Prosperous Cato marked a top-sales year on its fiftieth anniversary. In 1922 the three cofounders had been its entire production force, and fifty years later there were about 175 employees and a plant expanded from half an acre to seventeen acres. It had also acquired the Capital Supply Company of Atlanta, Georgia, to serve as a marketing and manufacturing facility for the southeastern United States. Specializing in "space-age" greases, Cato made 75 million pounds a year with sales of over $7 million. Approximately 60

411

Table 23.4.   Production Record, 1970–72

	1970	1971	1972
Production			
Crude oil produced (net barrels)	10,146,624	11,994,700	12,392,889
Natural-gas sales (millions of cubic feet)	91,675	91,068	109,090
Gas processing			
Gas liquids produced (net barrels)	2,565,011	2,474,896	2,774,984
Refining			
Crude oil processed (barrels)	17,364,618	16,879,216	13,612,348
Uranium			
U_3O_8 concentrate sold (lbs.)	5,410,468	6,604,475	7,552,684
Average price per lb.	$6.53	$6.74	$7.13
Chemicals			
Total sold (tons)	1,967,000	2,128,000	2,951,000

percent of its business in 40 of the 50 states was custom manufacture for specific clients who marketed under their own brand. The remaining 40 percent carried the Cato brand names, which were licensed for production in Spain, Germany, and Japan.[24]

The nuclear division also had a record year. Some 6,114,642 pounds of yellow cake were produced, and 7,552,684 pounds were sold, while the Sequoyah facility converted 3,531,000 kilograms of the cake into uranium hexafluoride, with a backlog of 21 million kilograms. Significant additions to uranium reserves were also made as a result of exploration and developmental drilling in the Church Rock, East Ambrosia Lake, and Rio Puerco areas of New Mexico and the Powder River Basin of Wyoming. The Church Rock No. 1 shaft was near completion, and an initial shaft (Bill Smith mine) was under way in the Powder River Basin. It was estimated that the mining operations in Shirley Basin in connection with Petrotomics would be completed by 1973.

In chemicals and plant foods potash and phosphate sales reached record levels. But while sales increased in retail plant food and farm chemicals, income did not increase because of price ceilings. Industrial chemicals had larger volumes, as manufacturing plants operated at near full capacity. Moss-American's financial doldrums of 1971 were left behind with a 5 percent increase in sales and a 16 percent increase in net earnings. This came chiefly from increased demands for electric utility poles and an expansion in new-housing construction.[25]

[24] In addition to the Cato material in the *Annual Report*, see also *Kermac News*, September, 1972, pp. 2–5, and interviews with Claude C. Huffman, July 1, 1971, and Ralph Jenks, August 17, 1972.

[25] Kerr-McGee Corporation, *Annual Report 1972*. No mention was made that on October 22, 1972, Jack Anderson in his syndicated newspaper column charged that Kerr-McGee had exposed twenty-four employees to radioactive materials over a two-year period. The firm admitted that radioactive materials had been mishandled at one of its plants in 1970 but said that these were were "potential," not real, exposures. Another summary for 1972 is found in Security and Exchange Commission, "Form 10-K for Year Ended December 31, 1972."

Table 23.5. Drilling and Exploration Operations, 1970–72

	1970	1971	1972
Feet drilled	988,987	930,078	967,916
Total wells/wells completed	153/133	142/128	131/120
Kerr-McGee interest	26	69	48
Rigs (average)	19	17	16

The various drilling subsidiaries of Kerr-McGee were involved in 131 wells, 120 of which were completed. Of these, 46 were foreign, with Transworld Drilling Company, Ltd., responsible for 14 in the Arabian Gulf, West Africa, Southeast Asia, the North Sea, and Spain. Kerr-McGee, Limited, participated in 19 off Nigeria, and Transocean, 13 in the North Sea. Domestically, Transworld Drilling was involved in 85 wells off the Louisiana and Texas coasts, 39 of which were contracted for by outside firms. Whereas the foreign-based rigs had a 91 percent utilization, those in the Gulf were busy only 70 percent of the time.[26]

During 1972, Kerr-McGee participated in 80 gross wells, of which 42 were wildcats and 70 were completed. Of the latter, 37 were in Louisiana (23 offshore), 16 in Texas, 8 in Canada, and the remainder in Oklahoma, Montana, and Florida. During the year Kerr-McGee sold all of its interests in Nebraska, a net of 7.27 wells, leaving, as of December 31, 2,006 total, or 868.30 net, wells. Of this number 564.9 were oil, 218.6 were gas, and 84.7 produced gas condensate.[27]

Consequently, Dean McGee was able to paint a rosy picture for the Boston Petroleum Analysts. During the last fifteen years the firm's production had risen from a daily output of 8,566 barrels of oil and 120,000,000 cubic feet of gas to 41,400 barrels and 304,000,000 cubic feet, respectively. He enumerated the major areas of production as offshore wells in the Ship Shoal, Breton Sound, Eugene Island, West Cameron, and Main Pass areas off Louisiana, and the Brazos area off Texas. On land the company had some 251,000 net acres in the rich Anadarko Basin of western Oklahoma and the Texas Panhandle. In addition to a helium extraction plant it operated four natural-gasoline plants and had varying interests in ten others. It listed approximately 2,080 service stations, and fifteen pipeline and river-barge terminals.

Dean McGee told the Boston group that its Chemical Corporation boasted of sales in excess of $180 million a year and employed over 3,000 people. Over 1 million tons of chemicals, including potash, boron products, soda ash, and salt cake, were annually produced from the brine at Searles Lake.

[26] Transworld file, "Transworld Drilling Company and Affiliated Companies Rig Operations Report for the 12 Month Period Ending December 31, 1972."

[27] Production Department files, "Annual Well Count as of December 31, 1972," and "Well Count Detail."

Electrochemicals, including sodium chlorate, manganese dioxide and metal, ammonium perchlorate, titanium dioxide, and methylparathion were made at Henderson, Nevada, and Hamilton, Mississippi. Plant-food ingredients were the principal products at Hobbs, New Mexico, and Florida's Brewster plant.

In other areas McGee pointed out that a Kerr-McGee subsidiary ranked second in crosstie production, claiming twelve plants and 20 percent of the American market. The Soda Springs, Idaho, plant was a major manufacturer of vanadium pentoxide and through its patented process had the capacity for 2.8 million pounds annually. Kerr-McGee had leases on some 169,000 net acres of coal lands and was the largest domestic producer of uranium. Its mill at Ambrosia Lake was the largest in the United States. The uranium hexafluoride plant was operating at approximately 60 percent of capacity, and the Cimarron facility was reaching full potential in producing fuel pellets. Long-term debt stood at less than 20 percent of total capital. With about $200 million in working capital and a cash flow of over $100 million, the chief executive concluded that Kerr-McGee was in the strongest financial position of its history. *Petroleum News Factbook* concurred by ranking Kerr-McGee twentieth in net income and twenty-first in total assets among the top petroleum marketing firms.[28]

[28] Speech to Petroleum Analysts of Boston, April 12, 1973, in Public Relations Department files; *1973 Petroleum News Factbook*, p. 27. For more detail on vanadium, see *Kermac News*, March, 1972, pp. 3–5.

Chapter 24

The "Nation's Most 'Major' Independent Oil Company" 1973–1974

A more favorable attitude by the federal government toward the oil industry became evident in 1973. The creeping fear which had begun to permeate the offices in Washington was voiced in April, when President Nixon declared in a message to Congress, "If present trends go unchecked we could face a genuine energy crisis." The "present trends" were not so recent, having started with the era of cheap fuel and power: excessive use of electricity; careless consumption of gasoline by the nation's motorists; indifferent research into new ways to supply the power needed by the world's leading industrial nation; and last but not least lack of incentive for extensive exploration by the domestic oil companies. For them the Near East had been too easy a source of oil and too inexpensive to bother fighting the weather in the North Sea, the environmentalists in Alaska, and the Washington bureaucracy.

The president proposed to recognize these facts and to institute a solution with tax credits for new discoveries of oil, deregulation of natural gas, and conversion to other types of energy—in other words, bring about more production. By June he became more urgent as consumption rose to 17 million barrels per day while production averaged only 11 million. The formation of a new federal energy office was announced, at the same time a voluntary reduction of 5 percent in private consumption was called for, with a promise to cut federal use by 7 percent.

There was indeed a grave cause for concern. Besides the low production of crude oil in the United States, there was also a shortage of refineries, as witnessed by the closing of two of Kerr-McGee's. The oil imported from abroad contributed $4 billion to the $6.5 billion annual trade deficit, which was rising each month. The American dollar was so badly buffeted in foreign markets that it was formally devalued by 10 percent, providing a minor shock to the financial scene. But the real and covert pressure came from the Arabs. An embargo on sale of their oil by this group could bring catastrophe.

As this crisis simmered on the back burner, so to speak, another was coming to the boil on the front. Elation over the long-awaited cease-fire in Vietnam and return of the prisoners of war was quickly dampened by other events close to home. The small-time break-in at the Democratic Party's headquarters in Washington, D.C., during the presidential campaign blossomed into the front-page Watergate scandal. Eager news reporters acted as detectives in tracking down the story, trailing it to the White House itself. The Democratic Congress sat up and took notice of the misadventures of the Republican president and tabled the pending energy problems. An omen of worse to come was Vice-President Agnew's resignation because of his role in a Maryland kickback at the time he was governor of that state. The United States was about to face a traumatic period unparalleled in its history.

In Oklahoma City and at McGee Tower, the new headquarters of Kerr-McGee, 1973 was to bring numerous and far-reaching changes also. The imminent retirement of its president, F. C. Love, initiated a major managerial realignment. The system of group vice-presidents had not met its goals and was abandoned, with new corporations formed to replace the former divisions. Love retired March 1, and James J. Kelly, executive vice-president of Kerr-McGee and president of Kerr-McGee Chemical Corporation, became the new president of the parent company. W. J. F. Francis took over the chemical branch in Kelly's place. Senior management then consisted of D. A. McGee, chairman and chief executive officer; James J. Kelly, president and chief operating officer; and J. H. Barksdale, George H. Cobb, and George B. Parks, executive vice-presidents. The executive committee was McGee, Kelly, Kennedy, Parks, and Webb.[1]

Love returned to his former law firm but retained his position on Kerr-McGee's board. His successor as president indicated the direction the directors assumed the company would take in the near future. Kelly was a civil engineer and had worked for Allied Materials Corporation before coming to Kerr-McGee in 1946 as head of its infant refining division. He had quickly shown himself adept as an organizer and troubleshooter in new marketing areas and also served at various times as an executive assistant to McGee, a vice-president for corporate transportation and purchasing, a group vice-president, vice-president and president of American Potash, and president of Kerr-McGee Chemical. Thus, with the exception of exploration and drilling, he was familiar with virtually all of the company's varied activities.

The three previous presidents—Kerr, McGee, and Love—had all presented talents particularly needed for their times. Kerr was a specialist in

---

[1] *New York Times*, February 13, 1973; *Wall Street Journal*, February 13, 1973. On February 27 a Kansas asphalt suit was settled at a cost of $20,000 to Kerr-McGee.

public relations and politics, McGee was a superb explorations man, and Love possessed the skills of a conservative corporation lawyer. Kelly, characterized by the realism necessary for a successful salesman and marketeer, was also, in the words of a long-time friend, "an eternal optimist. He's always looking for ways to sell, to make a buck. It's his strong belief that businesses are run to make a profit. He's always full of ideas, always determined to make things happen and get things done." Fittingly, the revamped management team began its tenure in the imposing and distinctive new thirty-story headquarters building, which opened in June.[2]

These developments attracted attention in business circles. *Forbes* devoted a major article to the firm. The tenor was evident from the statement that the "company's biggest asset is above ground, not under it. That asset is the company's chairman, geologist Dean A. McGee." In the past McGee had carried virtually the whole weight of managing the firm, and the revampment of top executives was an effort on his part to reduce his load in every area except exploration.

Forbes also pointed out that some of the recent "mistakes" might have resulted from lack of middle-management strength. One such blunder was loss of the lead in offshore drilling, and the article quoted McGee as saying, "We lacked the courage of our convictions, and as a result paid a stiff price." Poor business during the mid-1960's cut the construction of offshore rigs down to only two, thus hampering the company's ability to secure contracts when conditions improved. Furthermore, the original plans and patents for the vital stabilizing columns on offshore rigs were sold to Blue Water only to see them become used extensively by Kerr-McGee's competitors. The first triangular rig which could either float or sit on the bottom, and also designed by Kerr-McGee, was upgraded by Sedco into a floating rig just as demand for such offshore rigs was rising. "We've kicked ourselves a number of times for that," McGee remarked wryly.

Kerr-McGee also missed a chance in the North Sea. In a 1971 lease sale, Kerr-McGee bid only $1.00 for a tract which sold for $52 million. "We didn't bid on the ones in deep water where we figured it would be too expensive to drill. So we wound up with nothing." The same thing happened off the coast of Mexico. By comparison to its action in 1947, when the energetic and imaginative Bob Kerr had to be restrained in his innovative projects, the company had become cautious and unimaginative. It felt too small to compete with the multinationals in the oceans of the world. And so, as it had abandoned land drilling in the face of heavy competition, it also retreated from offshore work. The greatest efforts and financing went into uranium mining and conversion and in exploiting the vast deposits at Searles Lake. Dean McGee, after admitting to all these questionable decisions, claimed that his new management team should make possible a return to the old vigorous initiative.[3]

All the signs were propitious to achievement of this goal. In February the

---

[2] *Kermac News*, December, 1977, pp. 2–3.

[3] "The Scarcest Resource," *Forbes*, June 15, 1973, pp. 61–62.

company's good financial performance allowed the directors to discuss calling in the Series A preferred stock, and in April a record net income was again recorded.[4] Even the May outbreak of a miners' strike at Ambrosia Lake did not dampen the corporate optimism. Recognizing the primary need for more oil-and-gas properties, the executive committee took a number of steps to secure leases. A 10 percent interest was acquired in 17,280 acres offshore Florida, and Kerr-McGee joined a group investing $59,353,250 to buy fifteen Texas offshore leases.

A chance to get into the rich production in Iran was also seized. On June 7, a drilling contract was signed between Transworld Drilling Company, Limited, and the National Iranian Gas Company for a series of wells approximately sixty miles south of Bushire, Iran, at a rate of $9,850 a day. Then on July 12, a second agreement stipulated that Transworld would provide technical assistance to a project known as "Kalingas," for all costs and $1,900 a day. Kalingas, child of an earlier contract between the National Iranian Gas Company and the International Systems and Controls Corporation, of Houston, Texas, was an onshore company responsible for developing the production, construction, and operations of a facility for liquifying gas to be transported abroad for sale. Kerr-McGee next signed an option with International Systems whereby after the first well it could acquire 5 percent in International's interest of Kalingas for 20 percent of the cost of the venture, with a preferential right to acquire up to 3 million tons of liquified gas per year. By August drilling was under way.[5]

Meanwhile, a shortage of crude oil as well as refining facilities was plaguing the United States. The closings at Cushing and Cleveland left Kerr-McGee with just the Wynnewood plant, since Triangle's Cotton Valley produced only naphthas. Moreover, the usual sources of crude were diminishing. Consequently, in June, Kerr-McGee announced that it was joining three other firms to construct the Texhoma pipeline to bring foreign and domestic crude from the Texas Gulf coast to refineries in Oklahoma and Kansas. If this project was carried to completion, Kerr-McGee planned to double the capacity at Wynnewood. Likewise, it joined other companies to begin construction of gas processing plants in Canada, Florida, and Texas.[6]

The profit potential of coal was not overlooked during this period, despite disappointments connected with the Choctaw mine in Oklahoma. Kerr-McGee signed a thirty-year contract valued at $300 million with the Arkansas Power & Light Company for Wyoming coal to be delivered beginning in 1977. In August, another coal contract with the Central Louisiana Electric Company provided for sales valued at $100 million over a thirty-year period, starting in 1978. To fulfill these commitments it was obvious that steps had to be taken soon to increase coal production.[7]

One significant move in this direction came July 30 in an agreement with

[4] *New York Times*, April 25, 1973.

[5] Lease Records files, "Contract 1441-1," "Contract 1441-3," "Contract 1441-5," and "Contract 1441-6"; *Wall Street Journal*, August 22, 1973.

[6] *Wall Street Journal*, June 13 and July 18, 1973.

[7] *Ibid.*, June 19 and August 3, 1973.

Seeking oil in the Barron Ranch Ellenburger field, Garza County, Texas.

the four owners of Jacob Land & Livestock Company. By means of a stock exchange Kerr-McGee became the owner of a 10,600-acre ranch in the Gillette area of Wyoming, with grazing rights on some 4,000 acres of National Forest Service land. The company already had adjoining property, but its main interest was access to the coal seams below the grassy sod. The land company's assets were placed at $1,145,800 and liabilities at $65,206, and, in all, Kerr-McGee swapped 17,381 shares of its common to take over real property, buildings, and the livestock. Jacob Land now became a subsidiary.

Ironically, Kerr-McGee had denied being in the cattle business during Bob Kerr's lifetime, but now it really was. By 1977, it would be running 2,500 sheep and 200 cattle on one part of the ranch, while at the same time it was strip-mining some 500 acres for coal in another portion. Only this amount would be stripped at any one time, and, as the coal was taken out, the mined area was reclaimed and returned to ranching in as good condition as before or better.[8]

At Sharjah, A-2 well was completed as a producer. With payment of $828,085 Kerr-McGee obtained its full share in the project and part of one of the most prolific wells in the world—59,500 barrels a day. A third well, B-1, was soon spudded, but success brought a rival when Occidental Petroleum claimed that the wells were an infringement on its 1969 concession from the ruler of Umm al Qaywayn. At issue was whether the offshore sea-bed boundary was three or twelve miles off the island of Abu Musa, a question which remained unanswered.[9]

In August and September significant oil finds were made in the Garza region of Texas and on Block 32 offshore Louisiana in the Ship Shoal area. Gas condensate also was found in Breton Sound, Block 45. To find even more reserves, Kerr-McGee joined eight other companies in a project to test a new method of extracting oil and gas from shale, promoted by Paraho Development Corporation.

In October the anticipated thunderbolt struck: an oil embargo by Arab nations. This artificially created shortage financially benefited firms with non-Arab overseas production, but not so Kerr-McGee which received only a minor part of its crude from Venezuela. Despite the extra profits to the international oil companies, American motorists immediately faced higher prices at the gasoline pumps, and lines waiting to "fill up the tank" were common in the larger cities. Omnipresent was the specter of enforced rationing.

Eventually the boycott developed into a worldwide political ploy. While it was increasingly evident at the gasoline stations of the free world, it was not felt immediately in the board rooms of the major oil companies. Kerr-McGee's directors were no exception in feeling prosperous, and they called in the 254,623 shares of Series A Preferred Stock and ordered a new $10 million drilling unit from a Singapore firm. Rig 63 was for use in Southeast

---

[8] Lease Records file, "Contract 1449"; *Kermac News*, January, 1977, pp. 3–5.

[9] Lease Records file, "Project 1006-1."

Asia and would replace the one lost earlier in Burma. Helping to sustain this mood was the commissioning of Transocean III and a twenty-year contract with Gulf States Utilities of Beaumont, Texas, for 50 million tons of coal for future delivery.[10]

Another step in the reorganization of Kerr-McGee took place in November with the establishment of two new subsidiaries, Kerr-McGee Coal Corporation, headed by Frank A. McPherson, and the Kerr-McGee Nuclear Corporation, led by R. T. Zitting. Each subsidiary was responsible for its own production and marketing. At a time when energy sales were low in general, another decision followed this move: to suspend operations at Petrotomics, on the basis of both the market and the availability of supplies.

A slowdown in construction of new public power projects caused the uranium market to slump to $7 a pound, and the Grants mill began operating at only 60 percent of capacity. So, when the Central Area Power Coordinating Group in Ohio placed an order for the delivery of 12 million pounds of concentrates between 1977 and 1985 at a price of $150 million, it seemed good news indeed.[11] But by 1977, it was obvious that the Ohio group had gotten a bargain.

Determination not to miss the boat again in foreign waters led to a December exploration agreement in the Irish Sea, by which Kerr-McGee could acquire 31 percent interest in any find. But most important, in the face of the refinery shortage and particularly in light of cost estimates to build a new one, the year ended with serious discussions about acquiring Southwestern Oil & Refining Company with its large modern refinery at Corpus Christi, Texas, and the Royal Petroleum Corporation of New York City, with outlets for petroleum products on the East Coast.[12]

The annual report for 1973 was another chorus of firsts. With every branch save nuclear turning in record performances, sales rose by almost $48.4 million to $727,953,282. Net income increased by 24.2 percent, total assets climbed $60 million, and working capital $6 million. In addition, earnings per common share and stockholders' equity exceeded those for any previous year. For the first time capital expenditures passed the $100 million mark, the major part again going to offshore leases and uranium exploration (see Table 24.1).

Chemicals and plant food provided 33.4 and 19.7 percent of the sales and net income, respectively; nuclear operations, 8.7 and 2.0 percent; and petroleum, 57.7 and 78.0 percent. In the last, oil-and-gas sales were up almost $1.6 million. This promised to be even higher from the new lease interests in offshore Louisiana, Texas, and Florida, and new reserves in the Ship Shoal and West Cameron areas of Louisiana, the Brazos area offshore Texas, and onshore in the Hemphill and Garza fields of Texas. More explora-

[10] *Wall Street Journal*, August 20, September 14, and October 4, 12, and 30, 1973.

[11] *Wall Street Journal*, November 12, 1973; "A Big Uranium Rush," *Business Week*, March 2, 1974, pp. 38 and 43.

[12] Lease Records file, "Contract 1457-1"; *Wall Street Journal*, December 14 and 19, 1973.

tion work was also in progress in the Williston Basin of North Dakota and the Foothills belt of Canada.

Although one gas processing plant at Cactus, Texas, was closed, the other thirteen showed a 30 percent increase in sales, and three additional units were under construction. The industry-wide shortage of crude and refinery capacity was reflected in numerous ways. Wynnewood ran at full capacity, but it was necessary to allocate gasoline and distillates. Triangle also felt adverse effects in sales volume, but not in its net income. The Texoma pipeline from Nederland, Texas, to Cushing and Wynnewood, Oklahoma, and the contemplated refinery purchase promised to improve this situation most efficiently.

Despite the slow uranium market, Kerr-McGee Nuclear had 1973 sales contracts for over $150 million and backlog orders of $518 million, this despite Petrotomics' closing and the six-month strike at Ambrosia Lake. Future plans discounted the depressed market, and a ninth mine was scheduled for Ambrosia Lake about this same time as the Church Rock mine. The first underground uranium mine at Powder River, Wyoming, was also under construction.

Chemical facilities ran at full capacity, and decontrol of fertilizer prices in October ensured even more profitability. There, expansion was the order of the day: a 500,000 ton-per-year phosphate rock production increase; a 24 percent hike in manganese dioxide and 8 percent in sodium chlorate capacity at Henderson, Nevada; while at Hamilton, Mississippi, methyl parathion was upped 61 percent, titanium dioxide capacity to 48,000 tons, and a new 4,000-ton manganese-aluminum briquette plant was added. Major improvements were slated at Trona, California, and at four fertilizer plants (see Table 24.3).

Moss-American had the best year in its history, and a sawmill expansion program was under way. In the steam-coal market serious penetration was made with long-term contracts in excess of $500 million. Research was carried on to improve all of Kerr-McGee's operations, with some $2,316,000 spent in the Oklahoma City laboratory. The $7.5 million program to extract oil and gas from shale aimed not only to provide an economic utilization of this major oil resource but also to offer environmental benefits. Uranium exploration was likewise expedited when a highly maneuverable bore-hole logging truck was designed, and four were put to work in New Mexico.[13]

The all-important drilling subsidiaries spudded 104 wells with 93 completions. Of these, 37 were in foreign waters, with Transworld Drilling, Ltd., counting for 2 each in the Persian Gulf and the North Sea and 6 in Spain. Kerr-McGee, Limited, completed 16 offshore Nigeria, and Transocean finished 8 of 11 in the North Sea. Of the 67 wells drilled domestically 19 were for the parent company, and the rest were contract work for Forest, Monsanto, Superior, Mobil, and Phillips, among others. Most of these wells were in the Louisiana Gulf area, but a dozen were off Texas. The 16 rigs

[13] Kerr-McGee Corporation, *1973 Annual Report*. See also Securities and Exchange Commission, "Form 10-K for the Fiscal Year Ended December 31, 1973."

Robert S. Kerr Park south of Kerr-McGee Center, Oklahoma City.

(including the 2 idle Big Hole units) drilled a total of 860,166 feet of hole, for a 97 percent usage abroad and 92 percent at home (see Table 24.4).[14]

Kerr-McGee and its subsidiaries took part in 105 wells for their own benefit, 45 of which were wildcats. Of those completed, 24 were dry, 28 oil, 13 gas, and 11 gas condensate. Onshore Texas (29), offshore Texas (10), offshore Louisiana (21), Canada (16), and Oklahoma (11) were major locations. Additional foreign wells were at Sharjah and in Venezuela. All of Kerr-McGee's wells in California, a total of 6.28 net, were sold, and the year ended with a company interest in 2,034 gross wells, or 881.25 net.[15]

Not shown in the annual report was Kerr-McGee's impact on the state of Oklahoma. For example, its 2,600 local employees earned $25 million, and

[14] Transworld file, "Kerr-McGee Corporation and Subsidiary Companies Rig Operations Report Twelve Months Ended December 31, 1973."

[15] Production Department files, "Annual Well Count as of December 31, 1973" and "Well Count Detail."

the company contributed $425,000 in public interest projects, $33,000 to hospitals, and $41,000 in scholarships and financial grants to Oklahoma colleges and universities. One striking and tangible evidence of Kerr-McGee's presence in Oklahoma City was the distinctive thirty-story McGee Tower in the center of the block-square Kerr-McGee Center. The complex served as corporate headquarters for the company's principal operations in the four primary energy raw materials—oil, gas, uranium, and coal—as well as industrial and agricultural chemicals, nonfuel minerals, forest products, and offshore drilling in domestic and foreign waters.

The attractive main entrance to the lobby of McGee Tower was the focal point of the plaza-level area of the center, where the four-hundred-seat Robert S. Kerr Auditorium and rental space for offices and retail stores were also located. Serving as an impressive introduction to the tower was the oval plaza, constructed of granite with parts set in a mosaic, geometric design. This was surrounded by a semicircle of fountains and was landscaped with locust and magnolia trees. Across Robert S. Kerr Avenue and directly south was a miniature park dedicated to the city as the Robert S. Kerr Park, with an amphitheater designed to entice the casual visitor or to serve as a location for planned programs of entertainment. Little could the corporate heads have guessed just how this gemlike setting would be used in the years to come.

The United States government reacted schizophrenetically to the oil crisis. On the one hand it called for higher taxes on windfall profits, while initiating "Project Independence" on the other to reduce consumption and increase production. After a confused and frustrating period for individual citizens and oilmen alike, it was obvious that the Nixon voluntary program was a failure.

And so 1974 was not destined to be remembered as a year in which Americans united and marched toward an economic victory. Instead, domestic oil production, which had peaked in 1971 at 9.5 million barrels a day, reached only 9.1 million. Although the Arab embargo ended in March, gasoline prices were up almost thirty cents a gallon, and they did not come down. Car sales dropped by two million; the bottom fell out of the housing industry; and unemployment began to rise as the recession of 1974 took hold. By the end of the year double-digit inflation was nation- and worldwide because of the increase in oil prices and shortages of food.

Grim as the economic picture was in the United States, the political one was worse. Watergate tainted the Washington scene, and congressmen darkly hinted at impeachment. The "presidential tapes" became a matter of household debate, until finally the country was subjected to watching its president resign, the first such event in its history. This was followed swiftly by two more historic firsts: the inauguration of a president not chosen in a national election and the pardon of a president faced with judicial proceedings. Despite the heroic efforts of the new chief executive, Gerald R. Ford, the 1974 congressional elections brought a Democratic landslide awash in voter anger and concern.

A grim note started 1974 off for Kerr-McGee also. On New Year's Day the company announced that the new rig, Transocean III, was irretrievably lost

Southwestern Refining Company, Inc., Corpus Christi, Texas.

in the North Sea. It had been in service for Mobil only about a week, anchored in the Beryl field one hundred miles off the Shetland Islands, when a leg collapsed. Before the rig could be towed to Norway for repairs, it capsized in rough waters and sank. Fortunately no personnel were lost, and the unit was fully insured.

One bright spot came on January 25, when Kerr-McGee made a giant stride in solving its refinery shortage. Negotiations were successfully completed to purchase Southwestern Oil & Refining Company of Corpus Christi and the Royal Petroleum Corporation of New York City. Kerr-McGee created a new subsidiary, Southwestern Refining Company, Inc., which on February 22, bought the outstanding stock of these jointly owned firms for $80 million. A payment of $23.2 million was made at the time of closing, and the remainder was tendered in 7 percent notes maturing in five equal payments. The principal assets were the much-desired 100,000 barrel-a-day refinery, at far below the price of construction of a new one, and four terminals in the New York City area which sold fuel-oil and kerosene.[16]

---

[16] Public Relations press releases of January 1 and 25, 1974; *Wall Street Journal*, January 3 and 28 and February 25, 1974; *1973 Annual Report*, p. 22. $56,800,000 was borrowed, and 71 percent of the capital stock of the new company was pledged to secure the 7 percent notes.

With this important acquisition Kerr-McGee now boasted eight principal subsidiaries:

Cato Oil and Grease Company
Kerr-McGee Chemical Corporation
Kerr-McGee Coal Corporation
Kerr-McGee Nuclear Corporation
Southwestern Refining Company, Incorporated
Transworld Drilling Company
Transworld Drilling Company, Limited
Triangle Refineries, Incorporated

The corporate vice-presidents who headed operating divisions had as their counterparts the presidents of these principal subsidiaries. These men had direct responsibility for each company's diverse activities, and the recently inaugurated management development plan emphasized promotion of capable younger executives into top operating jobs.

There was still an obvious gap in the new corporate alignment—consolidation of petroleum operations. At the February board meeting this need was discussed and a decision made to consider creation of such a subsidiary. In the meantime Southwestern would handle its refinery and the New York marketing outlets, while a new entity, Kerr-McGee Pipeline Company, was created to represent the parent in the 476-mile, 30-inch Texoma pipeline. Upon completion this line carried 640,000 barrels a day and cost about $96.5 million. Then, still planning for the future, the board adopted a company procedure to be followed in case of nuclear or atomic holocaust or war against the United States. Finally, pleased with the news that only 1,728 shares of preferred stock had been redeemed by their owners, and the rest converted into 525,914 shares of common, the directors rewarded this vote of confidence by raising the annual dividend to seventy cents.[17]

The nation's attention, however, was focused on energy, and especially on substitutes for oil. Therefore it was not surprising that advice from Kerr-McGee's chairman would be sought. His firm was the largest producer of uranium in the United States, having supplied 39,000 tons—24,000 to the AEC and 15,000 to private business—including 4.5 million pounds of yellow cake in 1973 alone. Consequently, McGee was considered an expert on this mineral, and as such he testified before the Joint Committee on Atomic Energy on February 6, 1974. It was his opinion that the nation should not dispose of its 50,000-ton stockpile of uranium oxide or lift the restrictions on the enrichment of foreign uranium for use in the United States. Such a move, he declared, would retard American exploration and delay investment in new production equipment and might lead to the same dependence on foreign uranium as that incurred with foreign oil.

On July 18, McGee returned to Washington to stress this theme. New deposits in the United States had not been put into production for the last

---

[17] Bylaws, February 8, 1974; *Kermac News*, February, 1974, p. 10.

five years because low prices had made it too risky. The recently increased returns should stimulate the industry to greater output. In the case of Kerr-McGee its exploration and mine construction budget for uranium had more than doubled since 1973. McGee therefore urged that the embargo on foreign ore be continued until it could be seen whether the developing market in this country could adequately supply the domestic need. This carried a warning, however. There was a shortage of qualified personnel at all levels in the mining industry and environmental-impact requirements were lengthening the start-up time not just for nuclear projects but for most new energy sources.[18] Dean McGee's warning in 1974 would seem to be prophetic only a few years later.

Events clearly pointed to Kerr-McGee's increased activity on the problems of energy. Rig 62, thirty-one stories tall, was commissioned in Beaumont, Texas, and was already under contract to Cities Service to drill in the Gulf. It was Kerr-McGee's fourteenth offshore rig and eighth operating in that location. Rig 63, under construction at Singapore, was scheduled for completion in November. With the start-up of the pipeline, the company was now ready to move on the expansion of Wynnewood and announced a program for a 50 percent increase in capacity—from 34,000 barrels a day to 50,000—at a cost of approximately $2.5 million. Shortly thereafter the major expansion at Trona began to add a new 1.3-million-ton soda-ash plant and expand the salt-cake facilities. This carried a price tag of $100 million and would raise output from 1 million to 2.3 million tons.[19]

In a March report to its brokerage firm, Lehman Brothers, Kerr-McGee updated its recent activities. The main area of exploration was still the Gulf of Mexico, where in the past year the company had acquired new interests in fifteen blocks offshore Texas and three offshore Florida. Seismic work was also performed off the Atlantic coast and was in preparation in the Gulf of Alaska. On land the current focus was on the Williston Basin, with 500,000 acres under lease. While 70 percent of mineral-exploration efforts were directed at uranium, copper and zinc were also stressed, and Kerr-McGee had its own ilmenite deposits in Tennessee.

Productionwise the recent Gulf discoveries were under development, and on land the Hobart Ranch field in Texas boasted fourteen consecutive gas-well completions. The Mubarek field in Sharjah had three high-capacity wells with a fourth spudded. In Iran a subsidiary was managing a confirmation drilling program for the National Iranian Gas Company, with options to participate in an onshore gas-liquidation program and to purchase part of the production. Other subsidiaries were doing well, but Triangle's growth was most impressive, with some 90,000 barrels of petroleum prod-

[18] Public Relations files, "S-102" and "S-104"; *Daily Oklahoman*, July 19, 1974.

[19] Public Relations press releases for March, 1974; Form 10-K for 1973. Two other events in March should be noted: the board voted to discontinue payment of "inside" directors, and Kerr-McGee lost a round in the monopoly suit to Pacific Engineering & Production Company, but appealed. *Wall Street Journal*, March 6, 1974.

ucts sold daily in 27 states through its 16 water and pipeline terminals and 900 independent jobbers.[20]

In this report McGee indicated a plan to step up foreign activities, and later he and Kelly stated that a "1974 decision" called for expansion of oil-and-gas exploration in "selected" overseas areas. The first new move in this direction came on March 29, 1974, in the form of a 20 percent share in an agreement with Marathon Petroleum Thailand, Ltd., among others, to buy two blocks in the Andaman Sea offshore Thailand for up to $15.2 million. This was canceled on July 1 when the bid was unsuccessful. The Iranian contract to provide technical services likewise failed to work out and was canceled. Sharjah also produced some bad news with Occidental Petroleum's suit over ownership of oil from that field.[21]

These setbacks did not, however, divert Kerr-McGee's interest from overseas. Kerr-McGee Eastern, Mapco, Inc., and Superior Oil of India entered into an assignment on August 1, 1974, whereby Kerr-McGee would acquire one-sixth share in 6.9 million acres in the Gulf of Kutch offshore India. This lay southeast of the Pakistan border, northwest of the Bombay High, and west of onshore Gujaret, where India already had production. And, on December 7, Kerr-McGee signed an agreement with three other firms to cooperate in exploring, acquiring, and developing sites suitable for production of oil and gas in an area bounded by South Korea, west to Burma, south to include Indonesia, and eastward to New Guinea and Fiji.[22]

Meanwhile Dean McGee continued to speak out on energy problems. In an April speech in Oklahoma City he pointed out that about half of the estimated discoverable oil in the United States was in public domain in Alaska and on the continental shelf. Federal regulations would hinder its recovery, causing the rate of development to be predictably slower. Furthermore, the nation lacked sufficient refineries to meet even 80 percent of domestic demand, and three to five years would be required to increase substantially the refining capacity. An additional complication was that most American refineries were constructed to handle only low-sulfur crude, and most of the new oil was not of that type.

McGee also predicted that natural-gas prices would continue to rise as supply fell short of demand. Oil-shale processing faced major problems in disposal of the waste shale solids. Although coal was abundant, a ban on surface mining would reduce productive capacity by one-half. Both mining and burning coal had environmental constraints. Coal gasification was not the answer since it required water and most coal reserves were in water-short areas. The solution might lie in use of coal or uranium-generated

---

[20] "Report of Kerr-McGee Officers to Lehman Brothers, March 16, 1974," in Public Relations file, "S-106."

[21] Dean A. McGee and James J. Kelly, "Remarks Before the N.Y. Society of Security Analysts, Inc.," October 15, 1976, in Public Relations files; Lease Records files, "Contract 1467," "Contract 1441-1," and "Project 1006-1." This was the first of a series of suits by Occidental claiming possession of a shipload of oil produced there. At the time of this writing these disputes were still in the courts.

[22] Lease Records files, "Contract P1057-1" and "Contract 1503-1."

electricity, but because of governmental policies the lead time on a new nuclear plant was about ten years. Furthermore, approximately 800 new uranium mines would have to be in production by 1985 to meet the potential demand.[23]

But despite this dismal prediction, Kerr-McGee continued expanding uranium and petroleum operations. In May it announced that the capacity of its four-year-old Sequoyah plant would be doubled to 10,000 tons, at a cost of $7 million. In petroleum a significant gas discovery was made in Wheeler County, Texas, tied in with Kerr-McGee's purchase of 44.2 percent of a new $4 million gas processing plant to be built near Canadian, Texas. Desulphurization equipment was also scheduled for installation at the Southwestern refinery to process imported sour, or high-sulphur, crude oils. This modernization would cost $32 million.

But expansion was not limited to these two fields. Rumors in May had Kerr-McGee as one of five oil companies considering construction of coal gasification plants in Wyoming. It was also confirmed that the company had exercised an option to buy 800 acres of land near Mobile, Alabama, to build a $100 million pigment facility. This involved two phases. The first was a plant to convert ilmenite into synthetic rutile. When this plant was in full production at 110,000 tons annually, it would provide the primary raw materials for the pigment plant at Hamilton, Mississippi, and later for a new 50,000-ton titanium dioxide facility at Mobile.[24]

Obviously such investments had to derive from a strong financial base. The *New York Times* of May 1, 1974, calling Kerr-McGee "the nation's 20th largest oil company," pointed out that its first quarter net income rose by 99 percent and its revenues by 61.6 percent. *Dun's Review*, in an article featuring McGee as "An Oilman's Oilman," referred to his company as the "nation's most 'major' independent oil company." It concluded that "what has given Kerr-McGee steady growth over the years is a combination of vigorous exploration of new land and new techniques and a canny sense of where and when to diversify." McGee was quoted as believing that "if the economic incentives are there, there will be discovery of both oil and gas." As an example he cited Oklahoma's gas-bearing sediments, which had been explored only to depths of 15,000 feet, while the sediments continued down to 35,000 feet. Exploiting this resource would mean much more expensive wells, since costs increased geometrically with depth. Higher prices had to be in the picture before any company would be willing to undertake exploring beyond 15,000 feet.

McGee credited his company's success with a double program: as it "has explored for and developed natural resources, so too, has it attracted and developed its human resources—innovative, imaginative, and dedicated people." It was true that most of the Kerr-McGee employees had long tenure, from the boll weevils to the executives. It was love of the industry

[23] Speech to Economics Club, April 15, 1974, in Public Relations file, "S-105."

[24] Public Relation news releases for May, 1974; *Coal Age*, May, 1974, pp. 103, 105; *Wall Street Journal*, May 2, 3, 7, and 30, 1974; *New York Times*, May 7, 1974.

and devotion to a firm that kept its ties close to the state of its origin that combined to hold these gifted people, an asset that did not show up in the balance sheets. This was no doubt part of the reason that another business publication was able to point out that Kerr-McGee was a favorite of institutional investors, with 15 percent of its common stock in their portfolios. It ranked thirteenth among the top twenty-five companies in percentage of stock so held.[25]

By mid-year the tempo slowed, and a survey of "news clips" highlighted projects already in progress. One innovation reported was development of a subsea production system, featuring a submersible work chamber. It could operate on the ocean floor and would permit completion, servicing, and production of offshore oil and gas wells in water depths to 1,500 feet. Other new stories included one in Kansas newspapers that Kerr-McGee was drilling tests for zinc and other metals near Oswego in southeast Kansas. In Georgia, meantime, it was reported that the state was negotiating to buy Little Tybee Island, one of Kerr-McGee's phosphate reserves. To the south in Florida Brewster Phosphates began construction of a new $60 million mine to double its capacity.

Prosperity continued for Kerr-McGee. Both the chairman and the president received substantial salary increases, and in August the quarterly dividend was raised to 25 cents per share. At the same meeting the board ratified financing the Texoma Pipeline, took another consolidation step by authorizing the merger of Moss-American with Kerr-McGee Chemical, and discussed a proposal to acquire General Crude. On September 1, Moss-American became the "Forest Products Division" of Kerr-McGee Chemical. Although General Crude was not obtained, Kerr-McGee did get, for less than $10,000,000, the Trona plant of Stauffer Chemical Corporation, effective October 1. This facility produced soda ash, salt cake, and borax from Searles Lake and was a natural complement to Kerr-McGee's holding in that area.[26]

In October, 1974, the Dow Jones Industrial Average dropped below 600, but Kerr-McGee continued its historic year. Third-quarter reports showed revenue up 143.9 percent, breaking the $1 billion mark for the first time. More good news came with the announcement of a contract exceeding $26 million from the Tennessee Valley Authority for converting 26.9 million pounds of uranium oxide into uranium hexafluoride. It was not all income, however, for significant capital expenditures were made. Contracts were signed for a $12 million coal-handling facility at the Jacob Ranch mine and to build Transocean IV in Hamburg, Germany, and Transworld Rig 64 in

[25] *New York Times*, May 1, 1974; "An Oilman's Oilman," *Dun's Review*, May, 1974, pp. 89–90; Dean McGee interview with Richard Karp of *Dun's* in Public Relations file, "S-100"; *Financial World*, June 19, 1974, p. 26; for another profile of the company see "Kerr-McGee: Parlays Two Steam Rigs to Billion-Dollar Company," *Pulse of Oklahoma Business*, June, 1974, pp. 17ff.

[26] For the Stauffer purchase see *Daily Oklahoman*, September 26, 1974.

Corpus Christi, Texas. Ten more lease blocks offshore Louisiana were won at a cost of $21.6 million by Kerr-McGee and its partners in November. [27]

The year was not over yet. Rig 61, which had seen service offshore Denmark, Holland, Norway, Scotland, South Africa, Spain, and Wales, was at that time working for Mobil in the Beryl field of the North Sea. Despite wind gusts of fifty to sixty miles an hour, it sank a well down to 10,457 feet in just 17 days and 10 hours, setting a record for North Sea drilling.

The final climax for 1974 was selection of Kerr-McGee as one of the five best-managed companies in the United States. *Dun's Review* had chosen it, along with AT&T, Merck & Company, R. J. Reynolds, and the Southern Railway as companies which had "best demonstrated an ability to move faster than inflation, to outpace recession, and to weather a crashing stock market." Kerr-McGee was specifically cited:

Probably no other company has planned quite so well to take advantage of the exploding energy business. Building up major stakes in oil, gas, coal, uranium, and agricultural and industrial chemicals, as well as in everything from lumber to helium, Kerr-McGee now has a commanding position astride the whole energy spectrum.

Dean McGee was cited for his goal of "developing a strong foothold in every source of energy, [bringing] Kerr-McGee to a unique position at just the right time. . . . The fact is that probably no other company has planned quite so well to take advantage of the changing energy business." McGee, in turn, was quoted as saying, "Finding things, discovering new resources, always has been and still is my first love."

McGee was also credited with having anticipated the financial bind of high interest rates. He instituted conversion of $94 million in debentures and accelerated long-term debt payments, with the result that the company's debt dropped from 37 percent of capital to just 18 percent. This allowed expansion plans to move ahead at a time when other firms were deferring their capital expenditures. Kerr-McGee spent more than $200 million during 1974 on new facilities and capital outlays, all of which came from internal cash resources. Over the past three years, consequently, holdings of undeveloped oil and gas lands in the United States had tripled, while exploration efforts had doubled. And so, the fact that most of the company's holdings were domestic separated it from the strife which plagued international oils, according to the *Dun's* experts (see Fig. 24.1).

The article went on that in uranium Kerr-McGee operated the largest ore-processing plant in the country, but Dean McGee believed that new mills would have to be built to meet prospective demand, since all of its uranium was committed through 1982. Chemicals also were a large part of the company's business, with sales of $200 million a year and still growing. Over the past two years nearly two billion tons of coal reserves had been

---

[27] Public Relations press releases for October, 1974; *New York Times*, October 30, 1974; *Wall Street Journal*, October 24 and 25, 1974; *Daily Oklahoman*, October 4, 11, 18, and 24 and November 2, 1974.

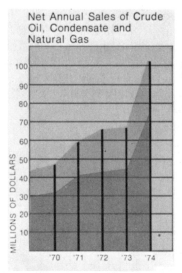

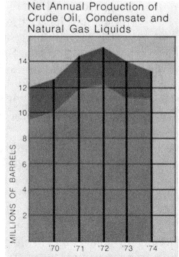

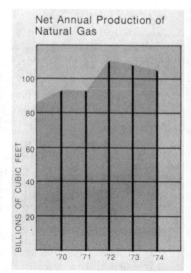

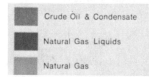

Crude Oil & Condensate

Natural Gas Liquids

Natural Gas

Fig. 24.1. Annual product sales, 1970–74.
From Kerr-McGee Corporation,
1969 Annual Report.

acquired, and signed contracts worth $500 million for coal deliveries through 1982 were on file. Copper likewise appeared in future plans.[28]

After this accolade in *Dun's* the annual report seemed anticlimactic. The company passed the one-billion-dollar milestone in both sales and assets. Sales were $1,550,349,000, up 113 percent, and assets increased by 34 percent. Net income climbed 85.3 percent, and capital expenditures doubled. On the other hand, long-term debt grew by $36 million, but the ratio of "current assets to current liabilities" fell from 2.6 to 1.7.

The 1974 sales broke down as follows:

Petroleum	$1,139,000,000
Nuclear	64,900,000
Chemicals and plant food	346,000,000
Other	400,000

In net income:

Petroleum	$ 76,700,000
Chemicals and plant food	41,900,000
Nuclear and "others"	(2,200,000)

[28] *Kermac News*, January, 1975, pp. 1, 8–11; "The Five Best-Managed Companies," *Dun's Review*, December, 1974, pp. 44ff.; Public Relations press release, "12-4-73 [*sic*]."

Table 24.1. Financial Highlights, 1973–74

	1973	1974
Total gross income	$735,365,661	$1,560,523,041
Net income	62,827,813	116,407,753
Total assets	866,671,286	1,164,431,867
Cash flow from earnings	124,975,977	192,580,365
Working capital	204,128,488	201,672,676
Properties (net)	516,323,795	650,631,052
Capital expenditures	113,041,416	227,955,524
Long-term debt	122,819,398	158,600,494
Cash dividends	15,611,335	21,253,748
Stockholders' equity	558,582,584	654,657,920
Total taxes paid	46,860,877	98,999,340
Number of employees	8,966	10,105

Table 24.2. Common-Stock Highlights, 1973–74

	1973	1974
Equity per share	$22.35	$26.17
Earnings per share	$ 2.52	$ 4.64
Cash dividends per share	$ 0.60	$ 0.85
Average yield	0.8	1.0
Number of shares outstanding	24,989,078	25,020,001
Number of stockholders	18,924	19,992
New York Stock Exchange		
High	$95.88	$92.50
Low	$52.88	$47.12
Price-earnings ratio		
High	38.00	19.93
Low	20.98	10.15

Petroleum sales escalated 171 percent, primarily as a result of acquiring the Southwestern refinery. The prices for natural-gas liquids were good also, and sales and revenue reached a new high. Kerr-McGee was operator of three natural-gasoline plants and had an interest in eleven more in the United States, Canada, and Venezuela, which produced ethane, propane, isobutane, normal butane, and natural gasoline. Cato had record sales and earnings, and Triangle's sales averaged 111,000 barrels a day. There were 1,614 filling stations carrying the Kerr-McGee or Deep Rock brand names and 349 affiliates under other names.

The Chemical Corporation enjoyed higher prices, with all operations close to 100 percent capacity, including the 390 fertilizer outlets in 33 states. Only nuclear income was far below normal because of the low prices received for 1974 deliveries under contracts entered into in 1967–68. On the

Table 24.3. Production Record, 1973–74

	1973	1974
Production		
Crude oil produced (net barrels)	11,326,297	11,192,623
Natural-gas sales (millions of cubic feet)	107,611	103,962
Gas processing		
Gas liquids produced (net barrels)	2,653,937	2,239,547
Refining		
Crude oil processed (barrels)	14,152,212	49,983,877
Uranium		
U_3O_8 concentrate sold (lbs.)	5,952,052	5,178,182
Average price per lb.	$8.13	$9.39
Chemicals		
Total sold (tons)	2,968,000	3,001,000

Table 24.4. Drilling and Exploration Operations, 1973–74

	1973	1974
Feet drilled	860,166	773,269
Total wells/wells completed	104/93	107/97
Kerr-McGee interest	21	28
Rigs (average)	16	17

other hand, these totals were increasing, and at the end of the year the backlog of uranium sales and conversion commitments was $762 million.

Production was 9,275,000 barrels of oil in the United States, 323,000 from Canada, 729,000 from Venezuela, and 749,000 from Sharjah. In natural gas 102,228 million cubic feet were produced domestically and 1,734 million cubic feet in Canada. Most of the domestic and foreign oil was exchanged for oil to be used in the company's refineries or for refined products.

Coal faced severe problems as a substitute for oil and uranium. Not only was mining difficult but litigation by the Sierra Club and other environmental groups promised future delays in the production of coal in the northern Great Plains. This and all aspects of other research were studied by Kerr-McGee's technical staff of eighty-three, and $2,375,000 was budgeted for the laboratory in Oklahoma City. Furthermore, some $8.9 million had already been spent on environmental protection, and $21 million more was projected for 1975.

In exploration and drilling 1974 was marked by the acquisition of 58,846 additional gross acres in the Gulf of Mexico. A test well was spudded offshore Florida, and gas wells were added on Block 543, West Cameron, and in the

Drilling for gas in Wheeler County, Texas.

Hemphill and Mendota fields of Texas, while more oil wells were completed in the Barron Ranch Ellenburger field of Texas.[29]

During 1974 the drilling subsidiaries had a rig-utilization rate of 90 percent domestic and 94 percent overseas. They spudded 107 wells, 97 of which were completed. Overseas Transworld Drilling, Limited, was involved in eleven wells—1 in the Persian Gulf and 10 in the North Sea; Kerr-McGee, Limited, sank 15 wells off West Africa; Transocean, 12 in the North Sea. These gave a cumulative total of 38 foreign wells, involving six rigs. The seven rigs of Transworld Drilling Company were domestically involved in 69 wells, 27 of which were for Kerr-McGee. All told, the parent company had an interest in 105 new wells, 42 of which were dry.

The greatest activity had been in Texas (40—10 offshore), Venezuela (17), Oklahoma (15), Louisiana (14—12 offshore), and Canada (12). Other locations included Sharjah, South Dakota, Wyoming, and Arizona. As of the end of the year the company had producing oil-and-gas leases in thirteen states, in Canada, Sharjah, and Venezuela. About 66 percent of the developed acreage was in Texas, Louisiana, and Oklahoma. Total wells equaled 2,055 gross or 890 net.[30]

The years 1973 and 1974 should have convinced even Kerr-McGee's most skeptical observers of the firm's continuing vitality. Mistakes of the past had been recognized, and, more important, there was evidence that the company learned from them. Greater flexibility had come with the managerial changes, and new opportunities were being seized that promised even greater profitability.

[29] Kerr-McGee Corporation, *1974 Annual Report*; Securities and Exchange Commission, "Form 10-K for Fiscal Year Ended December 31, 1974."

[30] Transworld file, "Kerr-McGee Corporation and Subsidiary Companies Rig Operations Report for Twelve Months Ended December 31, 1974"; Production Department files, "Annual Well Count as of December 31, 1974," and "Well Count Detail."

Chapter 25

Karen Silkwood 1974–1977

The annual report for 1974 noted only briefly an event which was to become a *cause célèbre* with repercussions on both the national and the international scene.[1] The locale was Kerr-McGee's Cimarron plant, near Crescent, Oklahoma, where uranium and plutonium fuel units were fabricated. The construction of plutonium fuel pins, especially, was a pioneering effort and involved an extraordinarily technical and sophisticated process. The pins had to be manufactured to extremely close tolerances by people constantly working with new techniques, and under conditions where any mistake was potentially dangerous. These workers were represented by the Oil, Chemical and Atomic Workers' International Union (OCAW). During the winter of 1972–73 OCAW led a strike which lasted some two and one-half months before a compromise was reached on the issues.

At this time a series of seemingly unrelated events was about to begin. Among the strikers in 1973 was a laboratory technician, Karen Silkwood. Six months later, in July, 1974, she was subjected to a minor degree of radioactive contamination during the course of her work. The incident was duly reported by the company to the AEC. Then, in August, Karen Silkwood was elected one of three members of the local steering committee of the union, for she was known to be a strong unionist, and the contract with Kerr-McGee came up for renegotiation in November.

---

[1] This account is based *exclusively* on secondary and public sources, since certain aspects of the case are still under litigation at the time of this writing. The principal sources used were the *Wall Street Journal*, *New York Times*, and *Daily Oklahoman*.

Manufacturing plutonium fuel pellets at the Cimarron, Oklahoma, facility.

Before that, however, on September 27, she and her fellow representatives made a trip to Washington to complain to the AEC about alleged improprieties in operations and about unsafe working conditions. One of their accusations was that Kerr-McGee had falsified some records of fuel rods by deliberately fogging the pictures which were taken as a production control. Other complaints were later formalized into thirty-nine specific charges.

Although the AEC agreed to investigate, no one apparently was too concerned about imminent danger. Kerr-McGee reported that less than 2 percent of the rods had been rejected as faulty, and on November 1 an official of Westinghouse Hanford, for whom the rods were manufactured, backed up this statement. "Our receipt inspections to date indicate that a dedicated effort is being sustained to meet our quality standards." When Kerr-McGee contacted the AEC for specific details of the charges, it received the reply that "none of the allegations was judged by the Regulatory Operations Staff to pose an immediate threat to the health and safety of Kerr-McGee employees or the general public."

In the meantime Karen Silkwood, under instructions from OCAW, was attempting to document the allegations. On November 5, the day before contract negotiations were to begin, the first of a series of bizarre occurrences took place: Miss Silkwood turned herself in for a radiation check and was once more found to be contaminated, this time from an unexplained source. She was "cleansed," only to have the same sequence of events repeated on November 6 and November 7. None of these exposures could be traced to any contact inside the plant. So, with Miss Silkwood's permission, a search was made of her Crescent apartment, and there contamination was found in the bathroom, on food in the refrigerator, and on her roommate. The apartment was sealed to await treatment by the AEC and state officials. The total quantity found was three ten-thousandths (3/10,000) of a gram.

On November 10, Karen Silkwood, her boyfriend, and her roommate were all taken to the AEC facility at Los Alamos, New Mexico, where its medical authorities tested their blood, fecal matter, urine, and lungs by various analytical procedures. Only Miss Silkwood showed (internal) contamination, and this was only one-quarter of the permissible level allowed by government standards.

On November 13, Karen Silkwood returned to Oklahoma. That same evening she set out from Crescent to drive to Oklahoma City, allegedly to give "documents" to Steve Wodka of OCAW and a reporter from the *New York Times* who awaited her there. It was a twenty-mile drive on a clear night, but she never reached the two men. En route her car left the road, which was straight and dry, and traveled for approximately 240 feet before striking a culvert. She was killed instantly.

Investigating officers of the Oklahoma Highway Patrol routinely reported it as an accident, apparently caused by the driver falling asleep. It was noted in the *Daily Oklahoman* on November 15, on page 38, and the story recalled that the victim was one of two persons exposed to radioactive plutonium during the previous week. But "authorities said it was coincidence that her death injury came a week after the exposure incident at the nuclear plant."

Because of the exposure to plutonium, however, her body was autopsied by the AEC doctors from Los Alamos. And once more they found no evidence of external contamination. They were able to determine, however, that there had been internal ingestion. Of note, also, was the fact that her blood carried a heavier-than-usual amount of a sedative, methaqualone.

Under normal circumstances this would have been listed as the tragic death of a young woman in an automobile crash. But this was not to be. For it was not a usual story. Too many melodramatic elements were present. First, a beautiful young woman, a divorced mother of three, was cut down in the prime of life. Second, she was battling on behalf of labor against a large corporation. Third, that corporation was engaged in production of a controversial product. In short, there were ingredients that variously could be interpreted as idealistic youth versus the conservative power structure, labor versus capital, female versus male chauvinism, opponents of tampering with the atom versus those willing to risk a nuclear holocaust for a profit, good versus evil, liberal versus conservative, and so on.

What cannot be ignored was the point in time. It was the year following Watergate, with all of its cover-up schemes by powerful officials in government. Watergate had been detected and exposed by a large city newspaper; here, too, as a coincidence and almost on the scene of Karen Silkwood's untimely death, was a reporter.

The second act began on November 18, when an official of the OCAW added another dimension. His suggestion was that the death of the union member, "who had raised critical safety questions about one of the two commercial plutonium factories in the United States, might not have been an accident." A private investigator hired by OCAW found evidence which suggested that her car had been struck from behind, possibly forcing it from the road. Also unaccounted for were papers reportedly documenting her charges against Kerr-McGee which she was supposed to have with her. The union called for investigations by the Department of Justice and the AEC to probe her death and the circumstances around it.

President Kelly of Kerr-McGee made a reply the same evening and stated that the implication that the company had had any part in her death was "utterly ridiculous." He voiced doubts that she carried any evidence of safety hazards or inspection falsifications, since she surely would have taken them to the AEC and not to the press.

Dean McGee also sent a telegram to the attorney general in which he denounced the OCAW claims as "wholly unfounded." He added that his company was beginning its own investigation of the charge that supervisors had occasionally ordered workers to ignore the inspection system and pass faulty materials. Once more the fact that Westinghouse had a man who also inspected and passed on the products at Cimarron was pointed out, and that the company had been pleased with the low incidence of defective materials. As for Miss Silkwood, when her contamination had been discovered she had been given a "battery of tests" and medical attention. Five days later it was determined that she was "clean," and she returned to work. The two big unanswered questions still were how she had been able to leave the Kerr-McGee compound in a contaminated state and where the plutonium had come from which had tainted her apartment and roommate.

By now the incident was front-page news. The first impulse of Kerr-McGee's management was to make public its side of the story, and a conference was called to draw up a news release. After a long discussion, however, it was decided that the subject was too complicated, too vulnerable to misinterpretation, to handle in such a statement, which by necessity would be technical and, for security reasons, incomplete. Consequently, the company chose to refuse comment on all aspects of the Silkwood "case." This became the official position for Kerr-McGee. Once this stand was taken, however, it became a two-edged sword. Some people took the silence as a tacit admission of guilt, and the way was opened for a multitude of rumors whose sources were darkly hinted at as coming from employees of the company.[2]

[2] Patrick K. Petree, Director of Public Relations, Kerr-McGee, to the author, January 21, 1977.

Checking alignment of a fabricated uranium fuel assembly at Cimarron.

On November 20, the AEC finally stated that it would investigate the allegation of falsified inspection reports on fuel rods. The same day the Justice Department responded to a telegram from the Washington representative of OCAW, who claimed there was evidence ruling out an accident in the automobile death. The department would take a "hard look" at this charge, together with such questions as how Miss Silkwood became contaminated, the inspection and safety procedures at the plant, and how plutonium got outside the compound. Kerr-McGee publicly welcomed this news.

New disclosures became a daily occurrence. OCAW charged that Kerr-McGee had had seventeen safety-hazard incidents, involving seventy-three individuals, since the Cimarron plant opened in 1970. The AEC announced the start of a formal investigation of the charge that plant records had been falsified. The report of the autopsy was publicly released and showed that Karen Silkwood had been under the influence of a sedative at the time of the wreck. The driver of the wrecker which towed the Silkwood car said that he was probably responsible for the dent in the left side of the rear bumper which the union's investigator had cited as his basic proof that she had been forced off the road. It was also revealed that Miss Silkwood had been involved in another one-car accident just two weeks before her death.

Then, in an interview with the press, the roommate speculated that Karen might have smuggled plutonium out of the plant to embarrass the company. It became evident at a later date that Miss Silkwood was not apprehensive about the contamination in her apartment, inasmuch as union official Steve Wodka testified she broke into the apartment after it was sealed to remove certain articles. The union, apparently, saw no reason not to reach an agreement on the new contract on November 26.

Then in early December spokesmen for the AEC made its report. During the week of October 28 to November 3, 1973, seven employees had been exposed to airborne plutonium; another exposure occurred during the period November 24 to December 1; and two more cases between February 10 and 16, 1974. But that agency found that in none of these incidents was there significant internal contamination. Since then Kerr-McGee had taken steps to reduce employee exposure to the radioactive material, and "there was no consideration of modifying or suspending Kerr-McGee's license, because of the corrective measures which were taken."

The Los Alamos scientists were reported as saying that Miss Silkwood's contamination had been ingested at her apartment and not at the plant, but they could not say whether this was deliberate or accidental. The high readings originally found in her urine and fecal samples, moreover, were reportedly due to material added to the samples after they left Miss Silkwood's body. Still unanswered was how the plutonium got outside the plant, but the AEC considered smuggling to be a distinct possibility.

One allegation was cleared up when a nonunion employee, who had left the company before the Silkwood incident, admitted he had touched up some photographs, but not on orders from anyone. His explanation was that he was not trained adequately to take the control pictures, and he had touched up negatives of test welds with a felt-tipped pen to avoid repeating the testing procedure.[3] Both the government and Westinghouse Hanford had full-time inspectors at the plant, thus subjecting the fuel pins to a recheck.

On December 16 five more workers were involved in fresh contamination, but under sufficiently suspicious conditions that Kerr-McGee felt there was a possibility of contrivance. The company began giving polygraph tests to the employees and announced the temporary closing of the plant until the FBI and additional investigators from the AEC could arrive. The reading public was further titillated on December 19 with release of a news story that a dozen enriched uranium pellets were found outside the guarded fence but still on plant grounds. The AEC responded that the pellets were not a health hazard, or a target for theft, because of the low level of enrichment.

This episode, however, provided a new area for speculation. An Oklahoma legislator, Representative Thomas A. Bamberger, was quoted as saying that he had information that the Cimarron facility would be closed because of "social and business pressures." He then added the shocker that he had been told by a *New York Times* reporter that sixty-six pounds of plutonium were missing from the plant. According to the newspaper, it would cost $2.5 million to shut down the unit, but the paper quoted United States Senator Henry Bellmon of Oklahoma as saying that the plant had never been profitable to the company and was being operated chiefly as a favor to the AEC. Once again Kerr-McGee had "no comment" on the rumor about permanently closing the plant. The AEC denied the story of the lost sixty-six pounds.

On Christmas Eve the union's investigator again made headlines by denying publicly that the bumper dent was made by the wrecker's retrieval of the car. Then, in a public already uneasy where plutonium was concerned, additional fears were created when the National Public Radio Network reported nationwide that from forty-four to sixty-six pounds of radioactive material, enough to make several nuclear bombs, was missing from Cimarron. For its authority the network cited a Westinghouse Electric vice-president as saying that he got this information from an AEC official. In response the AEC admitted that the plant had been closed for short intervals in March and October when inventories had shown that amounts of plutonium in excess of allowables were unaccounted for. Reinventories, however, brought the figures within acceptable limits. Any story that twenty kilograms were missing, said the AEC, was simply not true.

Here again the damage had been done before the claim was answered. No amount of correction or refutation would take away the feeling that something was indeed wrong. So, on December 30, Kerr-McGee belatedly broke its silence. In a press release President Kelly said that the missing amounts were not "anywhere near" the reported total and that the "materials described in the news stories included the material in process in the plant in pipes, pumps, tanks, glove boxes and other process equipment. . . . Therefore it can't be fully measured until the present contract is completed and

[3] *Daily Oklahoman*, December 8, 1974, gave a summary review of all known events up to that date.

the plant is closed down and thoroughly cleaned of all in-process material."

Despite a letter to the *Wall Street Journal* by the Westinghouse official that he had been incorrectly quoted, even more people rushed to get into the act. On the last day of the year Representative John D. Dingell of Michigan, chairman of the House Subcommittee on Regulatory Agencies, called for a full investigation of the Cimarron manufactory and of the AEC's role of regulation in the loss of the plutonium.

Thus 1975 began in a maze of uncertain speculations. The fact that the AEC was being replaced by two new agencies, the Energy Research and Development Administration (ERDA) and the Nuclear Regulatory Commission (NRC), was not related to the Kerr-McGee problem, but the change was interpreted by segments of the public as having been necessary because the AEC failed to do its job. Then rumors of the AEC's final report on the Cimarron plant began to leak out. A New Year's Day front-page story in the *Daily Oklahoman* was headlined: "Plutonium Exposure Didn't Occur Inside of Plant, AEC Indicates." On January 2, Kerr-McGee quietly reopened the plant, but three days later the chairman of the Oklahoma House Committee on Environmental Quality called for a hearing on the facility.

The AEC reports were formally released on January 6–7. The *New York Times*, which had been involved from the beginning and whose prestige had lent some credence to the OCAW claims, printed the initial AEC findings with the caption "AEC Can't Say How Worker Swallowed Plutonium." But on the same page with this was a story headlined "Nuclear Fuel Plant Disturbs Its Neighbors." All of the rumors about the Cimarron establishment were related, from the inconsequential fact that it was located in the tornado belt to the implication that local citizens who supported the plant were tools of Kerr-McGee.

The AEC reports made the following statements: No more than 0.0003 grams of plutonium were found to be involved with Karen Silkwood, her roommate, apartment, and car. Her body had contained less than one-half of the permissible amount deemed safe, and she had not inhaled a significant quantity. Instead she had ingested some about November 7, 1974, none of which could be traced to any plant accident. The plutonium found in her urine sample had not been there when excreted, but had been added later by an unknown person.

The AEC conceded that small amounts of plutonium had been removed from the plant, but not enough to create a health hazard. It could not be proved who took it or how it was carried out. Kerr-McGee's exposure procedures needed to be improved, but as far as the AEC was concerned that portion of the case was closed.

As to falsification of inspections and safety violations, the AEC found the following. In answer to the thirty-nine original charges brought by Karen Silkwood and her two coworkers, there were "no hazards to plant personnel or the public." Three infractions of AEC regulations were found, but these were "minor." "Some substance" was given to eighteen other charges, but none involved AEC regulations.

Although the retouching of negatives had been done "without the consent of management," there was "some evidence" of two cases of irregularities in production of fuel rods. A 2 percent rejection rate was found on the over 9,000 rods so far produced, but inspection "showed no evidence to date that the quality of the fuel rods had been compromised."

The specific violations found involved failure to keep proper records, to make a report on equipment failures within the allotted three-month period, one occasion in which an excessive amount of plutonium was allowed in one area, and one case where a small amount of plutonium was used in an illegal form. Kerr-McGee was given twenty days to submit plans to prevent any recurrences, and a special government task force was set up to monitor rod production.

On January 10, the Oklahoma Highway Patrol released its report by three specialists who had made a new study of the automobile accident. It found that Miss Silkwood's death was not the result of foul play. The nature of the dent on the rear bumper and the path of the car off the road (there was no evidence of driver reaction) ruled out any claim that she had been rammed. On the other hand, the medical examiner's evidence showed that she carried one and one-half times the "therapeutic dose" of a sedative in her blood at the time of death.

The OCAW rejected all three reports, but somewhat shifted its approach to the case. The story of the "missing documents" was again raised, and the statement that the car had not been rammed was disputed. A suggestion that Karen Silkwood had been contaminated by a second unknown party was put forth, and, although not openly charged, the union implied that perhaps Kerr-McGee was responsible in order to silence or discredit a trouble-maker. Anger was expressed at the "voluntary" polygraph tests given the employees and at the "fact" that three workers who refused to be tested, plus some leaders of the local OCAW, had been demoted and isolated in undesirable warehouse jobs. Because of this, the union planned to file suit for unfair labor practices against Kerr-McGee before the National Labor Relations Board (NLRB).

OCAW likewise secured a promise from the FBI to enter the case. This was to determine whether there had been any interference with witnesses in a government investigation, abridgment of the right to participate in union activities, or violation of the civil rights of any workers. Kerr-McGee, on the other hand, viewed the AEC reports as a vindication of its procedures. It promised immediate compliance with AEC directives and on January 18, opened the Cimarron facility to a tour by newsmen in order to show the improved safety devices and procedures.

These various reports got mixed reviews. The *New Republic* pointed out that "any scientific process loses some of its severity when moved from the research lab to the commercial factory. Mistakes happen more frequently. Workers must follow routines they don't understand or care about, and usually they get sloppy." This tendency normally did not pose a threat to life or limb, unless it involved working with plutonium. The magazine concluded, "AEC inspection files show that the Oklahoma factory is little worse than others and better than at least one." *Time* magazine's evaluation was: "It seems clear that Kerr-McGee has not been as diligent as necessary in protecting its workers from plutonium. The union has nonetheless been overzealous in its allegations of carelessness by the company. And both the AEC and its private contractors need to exercise increased vigilance in guarding the plutonium against theft or misuse by unstable or conspiratorial employees."[4]

However, new voices soon joined those wanting to make certain that Karen Silkwood would not be forgotten. On February 21, 1975, the tabloid *New Times* carried a story entitled "The Nuclear Martyr (and the strange case of the purloined plutonium papers)." In the center of the front page was a box printed in heavy black type: "The publicity surrounding the death of Karen Silkwood seems destined to elevate the young plutonium worker to virtual sainthood—and to sink the nuclear industry still further into disrepute." The second page was given over entirely to a drawing showing Miss Silkwood in a biblical-style robe ascending into heaven. Above her head, in lieu of a halo, was the nuclear symbol, while below her feet was a sketch representing a plutonium plant.

The approach of the *New Times* author was evident. The disappearance of her "documents" meant that "the country was spared—for the time being—its first full-dress nuclear scandal." As to the wreck, "Though circumstantial, the evidence of foul play is almost overwhelming." Furthermore:

The question of how someone managed to smuggle this plutonium out of the Kerr-McGee plant raises two frightening possibilities: that either security precautions designed to prevent the theft of plutonium—which is, after all, the stuff of nuclear bombs—are incredibly lax, or the radioactive material was taken from the plant to be deposited in Silkwood's apartment, with the compliance of Kerr-McGee higher-ups. Judging from its performance to date, both are conceivable.[5]

In March, *Rolling Stone* headlined its story "Malignant Giant: The Nuclear Industry's Terrible Power and How It Silenced Karen Silkwood." All the rumors in connection with the Silkwood affair were repeated. To make sure that no one was ignorant of the dangers of plutonium and the fast breeder reactor or underestimated the power and ruthlessness of the corporations involved, the story was frequently broken with other alleged guilt-by-association facts. Karen Silkwood once more ended up as a "martyr."[6]

These two papers were probably the most extreme. But others did not ignore the sensational in the search for truth. *Ms.* magazine, for example, while concluding that "there are no answers, only questions," largely nullified its stance of objectivity by the way in which the article was handled. The story was printed in startling yellow, red, and black, with a cover "blurb" which asked, "Dead Because She Knew Too Much?" A subtitle proclaimed that Silkwood's death "raises the specter of murder and a terrifying technological reality." Its heroine was a bright, outspoken woman driven

[4] Elliot Marshall, "The Karen Silkwood Case: Plutonium Scandal," *New Republic*, January 18, 1975, pp. 8–9; "The Silkwood Mystery," *Time*, January 20, 1975, pp. 47–48.

[5] Roger Rapoport, "The Nuclear Martyr," *New Times*, February 21, 1975, pp. 25–31.

[6] Howard Kohn, "Malignant Giant: The Nuclear Industry's Terrible Power . . .," *Rolling Stone*, March 27, 1975, pp. 43–46, 58–62.

446

to near hysteria by fear of plutonium hazards. Five months later, *Ms.* published a "Reply" by a Massachusetts Institute of Technology graduate student in nuclear engineering who defended the use of nuclear energy and charged that *Ms.*'s coverage had been unduly alarming.[7]

During the first half of 1975 it would have been difficult for any resident of the United States to be completely unaware of Karen Silkwood. And in addition to the American spate of articles and broadcasts, at least two British newspapers featured the investigations. ABC television highlighted the story in one of its "Reasoner Reports." A radio special called her "the unwitting catalyst in a raging controversy that challenges the ability of both the industry and the government to safely manage plutonium." Regardless of any desire to be objective, the case was tailor-made for melodrama and sensationalism. Safety issues were crucial as the nation moved toward more reliance on nuclear energy. In the Silkwood episode, per se, there were too many unresolved, and probably unresolvable, questions about her life, death, and the charges she made. Moreover, even the AEC reports could be, and were, interpreted in too many different ways.

Almost from the very beginning the entire nuclear industry shared in the attack. Carl Golstein, manager of Media Services for the Atomic Industrial Forum, a support group, defended Kerr-McGee. "The problem is that since Kerr-McGee hasn't done much talking, you're lacking an important element of the story." On the other hand, he went on, people with technical knowledge usually do not know how to operate in a political environment. By the same reasoning those who can use the political process and the media are often ignorant of the technical side. Once Kerr-McGee adopted a "no comment" posture and then abided by it for a length of time, any change in that position could be misinterpreted as panic or guilt.

While the public and press speculated, the various investigatory bodies continued to operate. In March, 1975, the Oklahoma House Environmental Quality Committee opened its hearings to the public. Kerr-McGee officials testified that the plutonium involved in the Silkwood case could not have been taken from the plant by accident. Until that incident, however, monitoring had been based to some extent on an assumption that employees could be trusted. They further claimed that changes made since that time would make it all but impossible to bypass safeguards.

The long-awaited FBI report was released on May 1. The *New York Times* headlined the story: "Foul Play Doubted by FBI in Death of Atomic Worker." The report concluded that "we have decided that there seems to be no federal violations. . . . It does appear to be an accident." The agency, however, would continue its probe of whether persons connected with the plant had gained illegal possession of the plutonium.

In some respects the opponents of plutonium's use won a partial victory. On July 31, Kerr-McGee notified its 270 employees at the Cimarron plant that reductions in the work force would begin in September and continue

---

[7] B. J. Phillips, "The Case of Karen Silkwood: The Death of a Nuclear Power Plant Worker Raises the Specter of Murder and a Terrifying Technological Reality," *Ms.*, April, 1975, pp. 59–66, and September, 1975, pp. 8–12.

through December. The reasons given were that the present contract was nearing completion and opposition from public groups had brought a halt to expansion of nuclear electrical generating plants. Hence there were no new contracts for fuel rods. Then, in October, the company announced that the plant would be put on standby in January and the remaining employees placed in other operations. If new contracts were found, the facility could be reactivated "almost immediately."

Perhaps the most incisive summary of events up to that time was given inadvertently by Robert P. Luke, manager of corporate planning and economics for Kerr-McGee. In answer to a question from the floor at Furman University's "Religion in Life" series, he replied, "Karen Silkwood is to the nuclear energy industry what the movie 'Jaws' had been to the beaches."

But closing the Cimarron plant was apparently not the full victory some wanted. The Silkwood story was not allowed to end. Labor organizations and opponents of nuclear power joined to demand reopening the case. By then all of the investigations, except for that by the NLRB, were closed. In August, 1975, the National Organization for Women (NOW) asked the Justice Department for a new study because "there is no better example of violence against women than the Silkwood case."

Despite the fact that the plutonium contract had been completed in November, 1975, and a reinventory of all equipment located most of the missing plutonium where Kelly had said it would be found, the pressures were too strong to be ignored. Toward the end of November, Senator Lee Metcalf of Montana said that his Subcommittee on Reports, Accounting, and Management would take a new look at the way the United States government had investigated the Silkwood affair. The General Accounting Office (GAO) had analyzed the previous investigations, but its reports still left some questions unanswered. Representative Jack Brooks of Texas announced that the House Government Operations Committee was also considering a review of the entire matter. Election year was at hand, and this case was definitely one in which citizens had a strong interest.

The friends of Karen Silkwood apparently were willing to await the results of these new federal probes, and the story dropped from the media until April, 1976. Early in that month Senator Metcalf announced that his committee relinquished the right to investigate her death in view of the fact that a House subcommittee would do so. The House Small Business Committee's Subcommittee on Energy and Environment, headed by Representative John D. Dingell, opened hearings during the week of April 26.[8] Among the first witnesses was Professor Karl Z. Morgan, of the Georgia Institute of Technology, who testified that in his opinion the Cimarron plant was "poorly operated from the standpoint of radiation protection" and that management

---

[8] For statements by both sides on the various issues, see *Problems in the Accounting for and Safeguarding of Special Nuclear Materials*, Hearings before the Subcommittee on Energy and Environment of the Committee on Small Business, House of Representatives 94th Cong., 2d sess. (Washington, D.C., Government Printing Office, 1977).

had shown "little concern" over long-term cancer risks. A spokesman for NRC, one of the successors of the AEC, replied, "We said there were no serious violations, but we did feel the company needed considerable improvement."

But the surprise witness, and one destined to alter the entire direction of the investigation, was a Nashville, Tennessee, newspaperwoman, Jacque Srouji. She testified that in the course of research for a book on Karen Silkwood she had obtained access to the FBI files and its work on the case. When queried how this was possible, she implied that she had a special relationship with the organization. She then announced that it was her belief Silkwood had probably contaminated herself.

Consequently, in early May, Dingell announced that the subcommittee would now seek out the links between the FBI and news persons. Srouji had since been fired by her editor on the *Tennessean* because she confessed to working for the FBI. Among the questions Dingell wanted answered was the nature of the "special relationship" between Srouji and the FBI, and whether the agency had played a "secret" role in getting her testimony before the subcommittee in hopes of heading off an investigation of the Silkwood matter. Why were there contradictions between Srouji's testimony and that of the agent she claimed gave her access to the materials? Furthermore, there were allegations, which she did not deny, that she had contacts with a Russian embassy official. And, finally, in light of the public's concern over stories that the FBI had worked to damage the reputation of national figures such as Martin Luther King, Dingell wished to question the agency's scope and purpose in compiling and maintaining files on persons opposed to the use of nuclear energy.

The FBI refused to discuss its relationship with Srouji on the grounds that its own special investigation of the matter might lead to criminal charges. Its spokesman, however, did say that he had no knowledge of any attempt to use Srouji to influence the committee or its hearings. Srouji reacted to this by speaking on National Public Radio and threatening the FBI if her reputation suffered through her connection with it. She denied she was an "informer" on the grounds that she had never been paid. Furthermore, she insisted that she had been given special access to FBI files and received news stories in return for her services.

Srouji, in her testimony, referred to the sixty pounds of missing plutonium, making it necessary for a spokesman for the Nuclear Regulatory Commission once more to announce, on June 29, that it was not aware of "any thefts, period." Moreover, the Energy Research Development Administration had recently measured the plutonium remaining at the Cimarron plant with results that agreed with Kerr-McGee's. Summer, and congressional inactivity, saw the Silkwood matter again disappear from the journals.

On November 5, at a Washington, D.C., press conference, the father of Karen Silkwood and his attorney announced that a $160,000 civil damage suit had been filed in the United States District Court in Oklahoma City. Since the statute of limitations was about to expire, the action was taken "to find out the truth," for neither the Justice Department, the FBI, nor

congressional committees had adequately probed his daughter's contamination and death. Three FBI agents and Srouji were accused of participating in
an intentional suppression of information. The top officials of Kerr-McGee
were charged with conspiracy to violate Karen Silkwood's civil rights to
organize a union and report safety hazards. They were, moreover, also guilty
of "willful negligence" in her contamination.

Almost simultaneously with the announcement of the suit Representative
Dingell said that his subcommittee would reopen hearings in December.
But in an "about face" he soon suspended the investigation indefinitely,
purportedly to avoid interference with the Silkwood suit. In reality, however, his zeal was probably dampened by other factors.

The implication by Karen Silkwood's father that the committee was inept
stung. Also worrisome were *Rolling Stone*'s allegations that his daughter had
been murdered because she had discovered a plutonium theft and smuggling ring inside the plant, and that the true facts of the case had been
concealed from the public by a massive cover-up operation involving high
federal and corporate officials. As a result, on January 12, 1977, the subcommittee's counsels sent a letter to its members stating their conclusions:

While not uncomplimentary of the subcommittee's efforts, the article distorts the
intentions and purposes of the subcommittee's work, concentrates on the sensational aspects of the Silkwood case, postulates unfounded theories and presumes to
be true a number of accusations which subcommittee counsels did not find, cannot
substantiate or do not believe to be factual.

The letter also was highly critical of federal reporting practices regarding
nuclear fuels which had led to the rumor of missing plutonium. The Justice
Department's handling of the case was also censured. As to charges that
Karen Silkwood had been murdered, "The staff could find no credible
evidence to challenge the conclusion that Silkwood died in a one-car accident." Furthermore, "Subcommittee counsels found no evidence that a
plutonium theft and smuggling ring existed at the Kerr-McGee Cimarron
plant." As for the missing documents, "The facts boil down to this: We have
no documents. We have no witnesses who can identify what documents
Silkwood had, if any, or describe their content. We have no evidence that
documents were surreptitiously taken from Silkwood's car at the accident
scene."

There was no question about her contamination. The radioactivity of her
apartment established the fact that plutonium had been diverted from the
plant and that the physical security system was deficient. But, "It is not
possible now to determine who diverted this material and why." This, the
subcommittee counsels felt, was one of the major deficiencies of the FBI
investigation. In summary, they concluded, "The Silkwood investigation of
this subcommittee ends not with a bang, but a whimper." The work,
however, had not been in vain: "Some solid, though quiet benefits were
derived." These included a revelation of the "woefully" inadequate federal
health and safety procedures concerning the processing and safeguarding of
special nuclear fuels and the exposure of "serious" flaws in accountability
and security requirements.

This apparently was enough for Representative Dingell and his subcommittee. On February 4, its majority counsel said, "I don't see the committee picking it [the investigation] up again." In Oklahoma, where dispositions were still being taken in the lawsuit, the Silkwood attorneys reacted by saying that the committee did not complete its task and had not been presented sufficient evidence to believe her death was anything but accidental: "It does not say that evidence does not exist. That's what we are looking for." Furthermore, they now suggested that the hearings may have been stopped for political reasons, with the court action being used as an easy excuse.

Throughout the rest of 1977 the case tediously inched its way through the usual legal procedures, attracting little attention outside of Oklahoma. In September it was responsible for an important legal precedent when a United States court of appeals ruled that an independent film maker who was preparing a documentary on the events surrounding the death of Karen Silkwood did not have to reveal his confidential sources of information on the subject.

There were also brief flurries of local interest occasioned by conflicts between the Silkwood attorneys and presiding Judge Luther Eubanks. The judge made several public statements concerning the "Roman holiday atmosphere." In his opinion, also, the Silkwood counsel had no case as yet—"Apparently the lawyers have taken this thing and started running with it and use the Silkwood parents as a tool." After objections by the plaintiff's attorney, Eubanks agreed to disqualify himself. The new judge, Luther Bohanon, quickly proved equally unacceptable. His reference to the case as "a suit in the clouds" and denial of some motions by the Silkwood attorney, led to the charge that this judge was "stripping us of the opportunity to prove our case."

As the year ended, the Kerr-McGee Corporation and Dean McGee each filed motions asking the court to dismiss them from the suit on the basis that no grounds had been established for the allegations against them in the "pleadings, answers to interrogatories and depositions" filed in the case. This time the decision had been made to let the public and the press know all that the company knew. "No comment" was to be replaced with an open and willing effort to cooperate. The technical side had finally learned "to play the game" and hoped to use its knowledge of the facts to help end the case.[9]

Thus a drama which played on the emotions of many Americans appeared to be slowly disappearing from the stage. For the antinuclear faction to be successful, it would need to prove that a gigantic conspiracy existed. This of necessity had to involve not only Kerr-McGee and the entire nuclear

---

[9] Judge Bohanon later removed himself and was replaced by Judge Frank G. Theis, who dismissed the two counts of alleged conspiracy involving the Kerr-McGee board of directors, its officials, the FBI, and Srouji. If the appeals are not successful, the trial will presumably address itself to an amended charge that Kerr-McGee negligently allowed radioactive materials to leave its plant and cause Karen Silkwood to be contaminated in her apartment. Meanwhile, Kerr-McGee officials met with representatives of the media to answer questions and make available to them the seventeen investigative reports dealing with the case.

industry but also the officials of several branches of Oklahoma state government, federal agencies, and even Congress itself.

Failure to prove this, however, would not mean a loss by the antinuclear forces. There can be no question that the entire nuclear-energy program in the United States suffered a setback because of the notoriety, deserved or not, engendered by the case. The truth was twofold: a private company, in a pioneering effort in nuclear engineering and production, failed to conceive of every possible contingency and, for those dangers which were recognized, had not exerted the maximum effort needed to control them. The accidents and mishandling of the radioactive materials, low degree as they had been, were highly exploited by forces beyond the judgment of the courts. Finally, the future energy supply of the United States from any and all sources became inexorably enmeshed in more and more regulations and red tape, making its outlook doubtful. In question also would be the preeminence of the nation in the industrial world.

Chapter 26

Economic Transition 1975–1976

Just as Kerr-McGee went from the satisfaction of being one of *Dun's* five best-managed companies into the frustrations of the Silkwood affair, the United States also suffered highs and lows in its affairs. The sharpest economic downturn in a generation came in 1975, psychologically aided by New York City's skidding to the edge of bankruptcy. Only massive rescue operations by city, state, and federal agencies saved the "Big Apple" from default. The two years, 1975 and 1976, saw federal efforts fail to improve unemployment and inflation by use of tax cuts, welfare programs, and creation of new agencies. Public confidence in its government continued to decline, and two attempts were made against the life of President Ford.

These were also years that brought the oil industry under almost continuous attack. When the government raised prices on petroleum products in an effort to curtail consumption, the public reacted as if there were no energy shortage, only a false appearance of one, deliberately created by the oil companies to increase their profits. The fifty-five-mile-an-hour speed limit on the nation's highways also irritated the American motorist, who saw this as another ploy to sustain the myth of an energy crisis. Politicians attacked the "obscene" windfall profits with calls to break up the larger integrated oil companies and restrict them to a single phase of the business. Another suggestion was to force them out of secondary areas such as coal and uranium. Everyone had a way to take care of Big Oil.

A direct result of these efforts was a revised tax structure. On January 1, 1975, the depletion allowance for oil and gas was removed, except for natural gas sold under a fixed contract in force by February 1, 1975. The allowance had been the subject of bitter acrimony. Opponents claiming that it favored the big companies at the taxpayers' expense, and proponents insisting that the deductions were necessary as incentives for continued exploration. The removal of the allowance, therefore, was the latest blow to the oil interests in an extended struggle. In 1969, for example, the allowance for oil and gas had been 27.5 percent, but was cut in 1974 to only 4.1 percent. Thus its final elimination did not have the impact it could have had, although Kerr-McGee estimated that it would pay approximately $5 million more in taxes in 1975.

One point was clear, however. Cancellation of the deductibles did have less significance for larger established oil companies. On the other hand, their absence could be critical to independents and smaller companies. There can be no question that part of the success and rapid expansion of Kerr-McGee had been the result of shrewd use of oil-and-gas depletion allowances. These helped provide the funds to go into uranium; uranium's allowance of 23 percent likewise helped potash; potash's allowance of 15 percent, in turn, supplied some of the funds for coal; and so on. There also were the state allowances for some of these minerals, as, for example, Oklahoma's 15 percent allowance on coal. In short, depletion could and did free necessary capital for further exploration, production, and diversification.

Other federal actions weighed heavily during these years. Of primary significance were the regulations of the Federal Energy Administration (FEA) and the laws passed to support it. Generated by Nixon's "Project Independence" to free the nation of energy dependence by 1985, in 1975 the FEA froze the price of all domestic oil produced at pre-1973 levels ("old oil") at $5.25 a barrel. "New" oil was any produced above 1972 levels, foreign or domestic. "New" oil's cost was determined by the OPEC charge of $11 a barrel plus a $2 tariff. American supplies were calculated at 62 percent old and 38 percent new; thus the average cost per barrel was approximately $8. To equalize the cost of crude to all refiners, companies with large supplies of old oil were required to make "entitlement" payments to those with above-average reliance on new oil. Thus, in essence Kerr-McGee was one of those who had to pay a premium in order to use its own resources.

Nevertheless, with Kerr-McGee's newly arrived status as a billion-dollar corporation, management was optimistic. McGee said that 1975 should be a good year, with increased earnings, "if the economy doesn't drop too much more." Capital outlays would exceed 1974's $228 million, "to accelerate its petroleum, chemical, coal and uranium discovery and development activities," although "the state of the economy and legislation affecting the petroleum industry could alter these plans."[1]

The year started off propitiously. The reports of the AEC and the Oklahoma Highway Patrol on Karen Silkwood seemed to answer the many questions raised about the accident, and for a while that subject was forgot-

---

[1] *Daily Oklahoman*, February 7, 1975.

ten. The first payoff from deep exploration in the Gulf came with a 400-barrel-per-day oil discovery on Block 28, Breton Sound, and Public Service of Oklahoma contracted for 50 million tons of coal, with delivery scheduled to start in 1978.

At headquarters plans for consolidation within the corporate structure were advanced by the creation of the long-studied Kerr-McGee Refining Corporation. This new subsidiary would handle all petroleum refining, marketing, and distribution operations as "a single, streamlined unit, allowing future planning and operations of these related activities to be accomplished in a more efficient and coordinated manner." Triangle, Southwestern, and Cato would retain their individual identities and operations, but they would be linked through their presidents' serving as vice-presidents of the refining corporation.[2]

Then, also in February, Borax & Chemicals, Ltd., of London, and Silobor SA, of France, were merged and renamed Kerr-McGee Chemicals (Europe), Limited. The new company was put in charge of the sales in Europe and Africa, while the Oklahoma City office handled the Far East, Australia, New Zealand, and Central and South America. Another part of Kerr-McGee's continuing program to make the corporate organization more responsible to changing needs and to increase efficiency was later announced on March 25. This involved a realignment of reporting responsibilities and the creation of several new corporate divisions: Public Service, Corporate Services, Human Resources, and Operational Services. The first three reported directly to McGee and the fourth to Kelly.[3]

Awareness that public relations needed more emphasis had been heightened by the Silkwood affair. Dean McGee personally visited with two groups of security analysts in February to stress the achievements and prospects of the firm. He told a San Francisco audience that exploration expenditures were up by half, and gross undeveloped acreage in the Gulf of Mexico had increased to 225,755 acres. Kerr-McGee's three new underground uranium mines would soon be in the position to ease the energy shortage if the nuclear route were taken. To the Oklahoma Society of Financial Analysts he spoke of expansions at the Wynnewood refinery to 50,000 barrels, and expressed the hope that the coal mine at Stigler, with reserves of 45,000 tons, would soon return to production. McGee mentioned the Sequoyah facility and doubling its capacity to 26 million pounds of uranium a day, but it was a news story that later gave the full explanation of the nature of the operations at Sequoyah. The story detailed the health and security provisions and stressed that "bomb material" was not being produced there since it lacked enrichment. Thus it was not worth stealing. Cimarron and its problems were never far from the minds of the Kerr-McGee officials.[4]

[2] *Wall Street Journal*, January 16, 1975; *Daily Oklahoman*, February 18, 1975; Kerr-McGee press release dated February 17, 1975.

[3] Kerr-McGee press release, "75-14"; Kerr-McGee Employee Bulletin, "75-22."

[4] Kerr-McGee press release dated February 20, 1975; *Daily Oklahoman*, February 23 and 28, 1975.

Another opportunity to enhance the company image came with the dedication of the 800-acre site of the new $100 million pigment plant in Mobile, Alabama. The rutile facility, Kerr-McGee's second, was scheduled for production in late 1976 and would also be the first to make synthetic rutile. This process used relatively plentiful ilmenite ore instead of the scarce and expensive natural rutile imported from Australia.

Other favorable notices came with the February 21 *Wall Street Journal*'s prediction that the company's first quarter sales would be up, although the rate of increase might be off some. A *New York Times* story that Kerr-McGee ranked in the top ten among stocks held by mutual funds proved that on Wall Street, as nowhere else, a good balance sheet insures a dedicated following.

The drilling department, meanwhile, continued growing, with a February 23 contract between Transworld Limited and the Gulf of Suez Petroleum Company for a one-year lease of a rig.[5] Then the next month Rig 63, commissioned in January, was completed and moved to Burma on its first assignment. Rig 67, purchased in late 1974, went into service in the Gulf of Mexico, and work on Rig 64 and Transocean IV proceeded on schedule.

But the month's best tidings came from the United States Supreme Court. Over a decade earlier Kerr-McGee had given up plans to explore off the East Coast of the United States because it could not break through the web of red tape involved. On March 17, 1975, the Court ruled unanimously that the thirteen states bordering the Atlantic did not own the oil rights, thus opening the way for the Department of the Interior to proceed with sales on the more than three million offshore acres.

April opened with reports of two new "significant" gas wells in Hemphill County, Texas, and of the completion of a new advanced gas-processing facility near Canadian, Texas. Kerr-McGee owned 42 percent, with seven partners sharing the remainder. The new plant cost $5 million and was one of seven such plants managed by Kerr-McGee. Fully automatic, it operated unattended sixteen hours a day, using a cryogenic method of separating hydrocarbon liquids from natural gas.

As this new operation was beginning, Kerr-McGee severed connections with an old friend. On April 10, the one-half interest in Petrotomics was sold to its partners, Getty and Skelly oil companies, thus ending Kerr-McGee's uranium-ore milling in the Shirley Basin. Another project died when the company and the group of Japanese utilities agreed, after several years of searching, to abandon their joint search for uranium in the Elliot Lake area of Canada. But in not so friendly a move American Electric Power Company brought suit to prevent Kerr-McGee's strip-mining a 360-acre parcel of land adjoining Jacobs Ranch. At issue was the fact that American Electric owned the surface rights while Kerr-McGee held the mineral leases.[6]

[5] Kerr-McGee press releases dated February 17 and October 10, 1975, and dedication brochure entitled "Mobile Facility"; *Wall Street Journal*, February 21, 1975; *New York Times*, February 27, 1975; Lease Records file, "Contract 808-24." The Suez contract was canceled on November 30 with payment of $1,137,465.10.

[6] *Wall Street Journal*, April 2, 1975; Kerr-McGee press releases dated April 10 and

The successful rise of his company was the subject of a *Pulse* interview with Dean McGee. According to him it was based on discovery, production, and marketing of natural resources. "What we try to do is process these resources to a point where we have multiple markets, and then we try to disengage at that point." Management stayed out of the retail market except for sales of gasoline and, to some extent, fertilizer. But generally, McGee said, "we're a wholesaler and so we try to progress to a point where we have more than a single market." His firm maintained a very active program in oil and gas, uranium, coal, and a number of natural resources, and had backlogs in those which had not been put into production.

Dean McGee discussed his company's domination in the uranium field but claimed it was still relatively small in oil and refining and just beginning in coal. Kerr-McGee preferred volume markets and those in which it was technologically competitive. It was in the titanium dioxide field simply because its superior process gave it an edge. When asked why the company continued to diversify, rather than concentrate on a few natural resources and build them up to significant market shares, McGee replied, "Well, the real name of the game is discovery, and if you can make a discovery of a natural resource, you're in business." Asked if this did not have a diluting effect on other activities, he replied that exploration caused no significant problems. When a new processing area was entered, "we take one of our top people and let him get the experience and people needed to do it."

The *Pulse* interviewer next asked McGee how he had the ability "to be in the right place at the right time." McGee credited this success to major planning moves. The first important decision had come twenty-five years before, when the money made in contract drilling was put back into diversified exploration. Through use of new equipment and techniques Kerr-McGee drilled the well which started the continental shelf development in the Gulf of Mexico. At that point, even though it was one of the larger contract drillers, the company decided to get out of land drilling and concentrate on the new area where fuels could be found—the waters of the world. Thus the land rigs were sold over a period of three or four years, and the top drillers converted into marine workers. For two or three years Kerr-McGee was the only contractor in the offshore business. During this time many extremely innovative and farsighted equipment and technique changes were developed by Kerr-McGee's own men. In another important diversification a division for uranium and other minerals was set up in 1952. By 1955 the company was into potash, with phosphates and coal following soon after.[7]

Dean McGee reiterated that Kerr-McGee had met all challenges in the

New York Times, May 18, 1975. For details of the termination on August 12, 1975, of the Japanese project, see Mineral Lease Records file, "Contract 1267."

[7] Stephen M. Dudash, "Dean McGee Discusses the Results of Long-Term Planning," *Pulse of Oklahoma Business*, April, 1975, pp. 32–35.

The Hobart Ranch cryogenic gas-processing plant near Canadian, Texas, produces 136,000 gallons of liquified gas products each day.

Bill Smith uranium mine, one of the company's most recent.

new fields of effort. Implied was the fact that it would not rest on past successes or let the Silkwood case interfere with business. In May the Board reinforced this position by approving plans for a new offering of common shares and additional notes. On May 9, Oklahoma City formally was given the beautiful 26,000-square-foot park, located across from the Kerr-McGee Center, in honor of the company's founder, Robert S. Kerr. Ironically, it was here in later years that antinuclear groups would choose to meet to memorialize the death of Karen Silkwood.

There was also a wide variety of announcements about capital improvements. First was drilling on Prince of Wales Island, Canadian Northwest Territories, where the company had one-half interest with Western De-calta, Ltd.; the $32 million modification and modernization program for Southwestern Refinery; the completed 963-foot shaft for the Bill Smith uranium mine in the Powder River Basin; a delay in opening the Jacobs Ranch Coal Mine because of a temporary injunction; and last, but far from least, groundbreaking for what Dean McGee described as the "biggest

459

single project we've ever had," a $175 million expansion program for Trona facilities to raise soda-ash production from 150,000 to 1.3 million tons a year.[8]

Success in May bids for eight more offshore leases in the Gulf of Mexico was followed by new discoveries of oil on Block 29, Breton Sound; Block 522, West Cameron; and in McKenzie County, North Dakota. These were in part responsible for *Financial World*'s characterizing Kerr-McGee as having a "wide and profitable diversification that allows the company to expand in different profit and political scenarios," thus convincing the "investors that Kerr-McGee is an ongoing energy play that is difficult to stop." The magazine pointed out that the firm had a potential moneymaker in coal, and, although nuclear operations were in the red in 1974, prices were rising to a point where they should become profitable. In short, "Kerr-McGee has been both adventurous and lucky—the kind of luck that comes from foresight."[9]

On June 24, 1975, Lehman Brothers issued a prospectus for 750,000 shares of Kerr-McGee common stock. The price was $92.50 a share, although on that date the market price was better than $95.00. This sale would realize a net of $67,087,500, and, when coupled with the simultaneous marketing of $75 million in AA notes paying 8 percent and due in 1983, the total became approximately $143,906,000. Kerr-McGee proposed to use $85.5 million for payment of short-term loans and $55,326,000 for capital expenditures.

As is customary in a document of this type, the current status of the company was summarized. Featured were the dramatic rises in capital expenditures and net income during the past five years. During 1974, Kerr-McGee had produced 9,275,000 barrels of oil in the United States, 792,000 in Venezuela, 749,000 in Sharjah, and 323,000 in Canada, for a total of 11,139,000 barrels worth $73,723,000. Foreign and domestic reserves were 67,590,195 barrels. A total of 103,962,000,000 cubic feet of gas was generated and reserves stood at 913,970,000,000 cubic feet.

Its three refineries used approximately 160,000 barrels of crude per day, most of which came from exchange of company crude and purchases. All Wynnewood products were sold through Kerr-McGee and Deep Rock stations or through independent jobbers. Southwestern marketed approximately 37 percent of its production through a subsidiary on the East Coast, 25 percent to Triangle, and the remainder to large distributors. Triangle bought approximately 75 percent of its supplies from other refiners and wholesaled to independent jobbers or marketed through its 269 stations.

Kerr-McGee owned uranium leases on 700,000 acres in Colorado, Montana, New Mexico, Texas, Wyoming, and Ontario, Canada. The principal delineated deposits were Ambrosia Lake (8 active mines and one nearing

[8] *Kermac News*, May, 1975, pp. 2–5, 12, and June, 1975, pp. 3–5; Kerr-McGee press releases on May 15 and May 30, 1975; *Daily Oklahoman*, October 5, 1975.

[9] Kerr-McGee press release, June 13, 1975; *Wall Street Journal*, June 16, 1975; "Kerr-McGee on the Move," *Financial World*, June 16, 1975, p. 16.

460

Evaporation unit to process brine from Searles Lake.

completion), Church Rock (the mine to go on stream that year), and Powder River Basin, Wyoming (the mine to be completed in early 1976). Its Ambrosia Lake mill, the nation's largest, had contracts for an annual average of 5 million pounds of uranium through 1982, and the total backlog of sales in December, 1974, was worth approximately $802 million. Kerr-McGee also had 1,231,000,000 tons of coal in in-place reserves, with sales contracts for approximately 300 million tons. Production, however, was at a standstill because of environmental court suits.

The prospectus also listed the 260,000 acres of timberland and the ten preserving plants and eleven sawmills that they supported. Another part of Kerr-McGee operations was the production and sale of seventeen chemical

461

products for industrial and agricultural uses. During 1974 two plants at Searles Lake, California, supplied 1,362,000 tons of potash, borax, soda ash, and salt cake, while at Hobbs, New Mexico, 2,762,000 tons of potash were mined and milled. The Florida partnership in Brewster Phosphates delivered another 769,827 tons of phosphate. About 20 percent of the potash and 25 percent of the phosphates were used in the company's fertilizer plants and 130 blending and granulation plants and warehouses.[10]

Despite the bad publicity from the congressional investigation of the Silkwood case, both the notes and the stock were quickly subscribed. The new owners were promptly rewarded with a record second-quarter report. Then a press release on July 1 and July 11 told of oil discoveries on Block 33, Ship Shoal, and Block 29, Breton Sound. The development of natural gas on eleven of Kerr-McGee's offshore tracts got help from an interest-free loan of $40 million from Peoples Gas Company. In return it received preferential purchase rights for any gas found there to the extent of the loan.[11]

All of this was noted when subheadlines of a feature article in *Forbes* pointed out that "Kerr-McGee has an uncanny knack for being in the right place with the right product at the right time." The opening sentences were equally laudatory: "There's a standout company in every industry, and in energy, it is Oklahoma City-headquartered Kerr-McGee. . . . In an industry where ten times earnings is a typical multiple today, Kerr-McGee's multiple is 18." Its stock commanded a premium "based both on performance and promise." Performance lay in oil, gas, and chemicals; promise, in uranium and coal. As for uranium, one analyst said: "Dean McGee was shrewder than other uranium mining company heads. He held back in the Sixties and didn't enter into too many $5-a-pound contracts. . . . Now, with the much higher volume and higher priced contracts, K-M is in position to make lots of money in the next four years." According to *Forbes* the trick was whether the company could keep its current oil and chemical earnings up until uranium and coal returns would "burgeon." The review concluded with the words of an unidentified analyst, who said, "I don't know anyone who has made money selling Dean McGee short. But I know a lot of people who have made money betting on his ability to be out front in the energy game."[12] It was obvious that the financial world did not worry about the accusations made by Karen Silkwood supporters.

Such praise was warranted. Kerr-McGee was the successful bidder on seven more Gulf leases in the sale of July 29, an event made even more significant by a gas discovery adjacent to one of these purchases, in the High Island area south of Galveston, Texas. During August it was also in negotiations with Woods Corporation of Oklahoma City about purchase of Woods's petroleum unit, but nothing resulted from these discussions.

The pace of repeated good-news reports was about to slow. First was the

[10] "Prospectus, 750,000 Shares Kerr-McGee Corporation Common Stock," June 24, 1975, and "Prospectus $75,000,000 Kerr-McGee Corporation 8% Notes Due July 1, 1983," June 25, 1975.

[11] See also *Wall Street Journal*, July 8, 14, and 17, 1975; *Kermac News*, July, 1975, p. 6.

[12] "Greening Kerr-McGee," *Forbes*, August 1, 1975, pp. 36–37.

request by Ralph Nader for the Federal Trade Commission to investigate eight industrialists. These men were thought to be in violation of the Clayton Act by serving on the boards of competing companies. One was Dean McGee, who was a member of the board of directors of General Electric. He took retirement, and both firms issued statements that they felt no competition existed between them.

Next, an expected event became a certainty when on August 21 the Venezuelan congress passed a bill to nationalize the nation's oil industry, effective December 31. It was signed into law a week later by the president of the country.[13]

These events were indications of more to come. The report for the third quarter caught some outsiders by surprise. Besides the announcement that the Cimarron nuclear plant was going on standby, the big blow was the drop in third-quarter earnings by 2.7 percent. This was a result of higher explorations expenses, lower tanker liftings of foreign crude, and a decline in refining and marketing, according to a company spokesman, who also pointed out that nine-month figures were higher than ever.

But the *Wall Street Journal* headlined a story "Kerr-McGee's Growth Image is Blurred a Bit as Analysts Study Decline in 3rd Period Net." Pointing out that the company's stock had been "a favorite of investors in energy stocks" and "has had a growth image on Wall Street," the article stated that some were now questioning "the quality of earnings, as well as the trend, and expressing new reservations about the life-span of Kerr-McGee's oil and gas reserves." Kerr-McGee, however, felt that the "future is bright" and that no unusual problems were foreseen for the fourth quarter.[14]

Meantime the company was still pioneering. The star was Transworld Rig 58. Not only had it played a key role in the first oil produced from the United Kingdom sector of the North Sea but also it was the first offshore rig converted to a floating production platform. Anchored in the Argyll field it brought the oil up to the rig floor for processing before passing it on to tankers for transport ashore. No expensive, long underseas pipelines were needed, and its floating ability eliminated the water-depth limitations of a fixed platform. A press release by Kerr-McGee quoted with pride a *New York Times* comment: "Transworld alone has mastered one of the most adverse environments oilmen have ever known—the North Sea."[15]

The annual report for 1975 once more justified "betting with" Dean McGee. Sales totaled $1,798,580,000, an increase of 16 percent, while net income rose 12.6, and earnings per share were up 10 percent. Total assets grew by $223,400,000, and while the company's tax rate jumped correspondingly from 34.3 percent to 41.2 percent, it was largely as a result of the

---

[13] Kerr-McGee press releases, August 8 and 11, 1975; *Wall Street Journal*, August 21 and 22, 1975; *Wall Street Journal*, August 21 and 22, 1975; *New York Times*, August 4, 1975; *Daily Oklahoman*, August 22 and 29, 1975.

[14] *Wall Street Journal*, November 12, 1975.

[15] *Kermac News*, December, 1975, pp. 7–9; Kerr-McGee press release, October 23, 1975. The rig could easily be reconverted for drilling.

Table 26.1. Capital Expenditures, 1971–75

	1971	1972	1973	1974	1975
Petroleum	$29,161,000	$44,229,000	$ 79,943,000	$160,664,000	$104,030,000
Chemicals and plant food	15,835,000	7,609,000	10,628,000	33,537,000	73,108,000
Nuclear	14,885,000	17,431,000	14,887,000	24,811,000	33,624,000
Other	9,994,000	6,785,000	7,583,000	8,944,000	23,972,000
Total	$69,875,000	$76,054,000	$113,041,000	$227,956,000	$234,734,000

decrease in statutory depletion. Cash flow was up 11.5 percent, and long-term debt reached 21.1 percent of total capital. Working capital increased substantially, by 43.6 percent, principally because of the record profits, increased capitalization, and long-term borrowing (see Table 26.2).

Capital expenditures for 1975 were at an all-time high. Approximately 44 percent went to petroleum and 31 to the chemical and plant-food operations. The five-year summary shows that this was a continuing trend (see Table 26.1).

At the end of 1974 the method of accounting for crude oil and refined petroleum product inventories had been changed to last in, first out (LIFO). This was done because the rapid increase in prices during the year would have resulted in a substantial inventory profit if the first-in, first-out (FIFO) method had been continued, since depleted inventories were replaced at substantially higher prices. The effect on earnings for 1974 was a decrease of over $10,029,000 or $0.40 a share.

In terms of sales and net income for 1975, petroleum provided 74 and 58 percent, respectively; chemicals and plant food, 23 and 38 percent and nuclear, 3 and 5 percent. More specifically, sales volumes in petroleum marketing and refining operations were up approximately 5 percent, while contract drilling was 59.5 percent higher. Sales volumes of industrial chemicals also increased by 38 percent, but agricultural chemicals were essentially unchanged. Balancing this were the increases in over-all costs and expenses by 16.1 percent. For example, exploration costs alone rose 68.8 percent, and expenditures related to environmental protection reached $25 million.

Refining and marketing operations had been adversely affected when OPEC (Organization of Petroleum Exporting Countries) raised crude-oil prices 10 percent, at an estimated cost to Americans of $2 billion. This was topped by the $2 import fee imposed by the United States. Regardless of this additional burden, Triangle sales averaged 123,600 barrels a day, an 11 percent increase. Helping on the marketing side was an 150,000 barrel pipeline terminal near Birmingham, Alabama, which the subsidiary acquired. Cato, on the other hand, reported only an average year, and the Forest Products Division was down in volume and earnings from 1974's record (see Table 26.4).

The chemical and plant-food subsidiary was playing a more and more important role. During the past ten years the Hobbs potash facility had

Mining potash in Kerr-McGee's mine in Hobbs, New Mexico.

grown from 349 employees and a payroll of $2,464,000 to 430 employees and a $6,028,000 payroll. By the end of 1975, Kerr-McGee had an investment of $42,663,000 in that plant alone. Especially pleasing, however, was that the export program of Kerr-McGee Chemical was its fastest-growing branch.

Other foreign projects were also showing good results. At Sharjah another well, E-1, was successfully completed, and in India the initial well, Kutch H-1, was spudded in October. Kerr-McGee's interest in the two Venezuelan fields reverted at the end of the year to the government. Lot 17, Lake Maracaibo, and Lot 9, Monagas, were lost along with minor shares in a gas-processing plant, crude-oil pipeline, and a tanker terminal. Compensation was based on $1,173,500, less 1975 depreciation, and took the form of five-year bonds bearing interest at 6 percent.[16]

As had been the case for many years, the best way to see the world was to join Kerr-McGee's contract drilling team. Since 1929 Transworld and its

[16] Kerr-McGee Corporation, *1975 Annual Report*; Securities and Exchange Commission, "Form 10-K for Fiscal Year Ended December 31, 1975."

predecessors had drilled 32,405,223 feet of hole in most of the oil fields of the world. The old tales of life in Cuba, Israel, Mexico, and South America were now topped with stories about India, Burma, Nigeria, the Arabian Gulf, and the North Sea. For example, Rig 46 had been operating offshore Nigeria for a decade under contract to Nigeria Gulf Oil. It had sunk 161 wells and drilled 1,271,793 feet of hole in a climate described as "nonstop rain." The drillers' families lived ashore in two-bedroom mobile homes and under conditions far from ideal. The tools used in the overseas ventures had changed drastically, also. Early land rigs cost a few thousand dollars; offshore units now ranged from $2 million to $25 million. In fact, the estimated replacement cost of Kerr-McGee's fleet was $233.5 million.

Contract drilling prospered in 1975. Revenues were up 59.5 percent, and utilization of the 16 rigs was 97 percent. During the year 137 wells were spudded and 123 completed. Of these 38 were in foreign waters: 3 off Southeast Asia, 16 off West Africa, and 19 in the North Sea. In the Gulf of Mexico there were 99 starts and 90 completions. Of those finished, 50 were for Kerr-McGee (one-half of which were in Breton Sound), 19 for Superior Oil, 13 for Shell, and 5 for Mobil. Foreign employers included N.A.M. (a Shell-Esso joint operation), Pennzoil Nederland, Petroland, and Amoco International (see Table 26.5).[17]

For its own account Kerr-McGee completed 120 gross wells, 73 of which were wildcats. Of the 64.9 net, 16.8 found oil, 18.1 struck gas, and 30 were dry holes. Most of the attempts were in Texas, followed by Louisiana, Oklahoma, Canada, and North Dakota. As of the end of the year the company's total stood at 1,905 gross, or 898.6 net, wells, 81.5 percent of which were located in Texas, Louisiana, and Oklahoma. Kerr-McGee stood to lose 195 wells (net 10.52) by confiscation in Venezuela, and in Arizona salt-water injections were begun at Dineh bi Keyah to halt the steady decline in production from those 19 wells.[18]

There was no less activity on the legal front. The cases involving Pacific Engineering & Production Company and Occidental Petroleum were still under litigation. Moreover, despite the 1975 expenditures for environmental protection, Kerr-McGee was faced with several such suits, while the Department of Justice was holding grand-jury investigations of the production and sale of potash. And finally, the Silkwood matter would once more demand attention.

Despite these distractions and a few prophets of doom, 1975 had been a good year for Kerr-McGee. But the annual report concluded with a prediction for 1976 that was novel in its frankness:

The year promises to be a period of lower growth in earnings, a transition from the very substantial growth of the past few years to a new period of accelerating growth

[17] Transworld file, "Kerr-McGee Corporation and Subsidiary Companies Rig Operation Report for Twelve Months Ended December 31, 1975"; *Kermac News*, August–September, 1975, pp. 3–5.

[18] Production Department files, "Annual Well Count as of December 31, 1975" and "Well Count Detail."

as a stepped-up program of oil and gas exploration and development adds to income and new projects in industrial and agricultural chemicals, coal and nuclear are completed and placed on production.

This honest appraisal of the expectations for 1976 was probably also ignored, or disbelieved, by the readers of the annual report.

As 1976 opened, in the United States expectations were high. It was the Bicentennial of the nation's founding, and it was also the year of that traditional harbinger of new beginnings—the presidential election. Prophetically, January was the busiest month in the history of the New York Stock Exchange, as 635,850,000 shares were traded. In March the Dow Jones Industrial Average hit the magic mark and an all-time high of 1,000 points. Other events, however, were ominous. March also marked the first time that the nation imported more oil than it produced. This finally spurred the federal government to cut through red tape and offer for the first time, over the strenuous objections of environmentalists, Atlantic offshore leases.

467

The growing role to be played by nature's protectors in any solution of the "energy problem" was also evidenced in seven states, where referendums to curb the use of nuclear power were voted down.

While the oil companies struggled with these problems, Americans discussed "Legionnaires' disease," Patricia Hearst, sex scandals in the House of Representatives, a potential "Korea-gate" for the Democrats, and, finally, the presidential election. It was the first since the Republican Waterloo of Watergate, and the Democrats saw a chance to win back the presidency after an eight-year hiatus. Public disenchantment with the "old faces" led to the selection of an unknown, untried southerner, James Carter, or "Jimmy," as he soon became known, to displace Gerald Ford.

A downturn in the economy during the third quarter helped. The rate of growth in the Gross National Product dropped, and higher unemployment and inflation rates hastened the trend. The Democrats won not only the presidency but also firm control of both houses of Congress.

The management of Kerr-McGee quickly let it be known that the cautious statement in the annual report was not to imply a status quo year. The first order of business was a look at the company's retirement plan for employees. In 1972 in line with the decision to make the plan a noncontributory one, the company had ended the Thrift and Savings Plan for its people. This action was at first greeted with approval, but eventually workers asked for it to be reinstated. Consequently, on January 1, 1976, a new savings-investment plan allowed employees to invest up to 10 percent of their annual base compensation in federal securities or in Kerr-McGee common stock. The company would contribute 50 percent in matching funds on the first 6 percent. Within six months, over 61 percent of the employees belonged to the plan. Their projected annual investment was $4 million, which provided not only increased financial security but also a greater involvement in their company.

Kerr-McGee management made it clear in other ways that it was "bullish" on America's future at a time when most citizens were confused by the rash of "energy problems." On January 23, McGee told the Hobbs, New Mexico, Chamber of Commerce that his optimism was based on faith that the American people would "become informed, arrive at the proper conclusions and demand that their public representatives take those actions needed to put the country back on a sound and secure base." He made it clear that in his opinion this should include a workable national plan to increase the energy supply from domestic sources, since at that time national oil production was declining at a rate of 5 percent annually, and imports made up 42 percent of total requirements.[19] His was a voice raised in futility, as future months would prove.

Meanwhile, Kerr-McGee would do its part in providing new energy. In line with the program of expanding its overseas interests, on January 7, 1976, it entered into an agreement with Buttes Resources [sic] Tunisie, Ltd., to obtain an interest in the Gulf of Hammamet. By bearing one-fourth

[19] Kerr-McGee press release, "76-12."

the cost of a test well and other expenses, Kerr-McGee got a 15 percent share in production. The well was spudded on April 15 but temporarily abandoned on July 16.[20] Illustrative of the company's increased foreign interests, separate management units were established for North American and for foreign oil-and-gas operations.

On the domestic scene the news got better. A major hurdle was overcome in getting coal into production from Jacobs Ranch when the U.S. Supreme Court stayed an injunction against the secretary of the interior. This had been aimed at preventing his endorsement of the mine plan until approval of a five-state Northern Great Plains Region environmental impact statement. Even more immediate was Kerr-McGee's announcement that the first gas deliveries were being made from Block 543, West Cameron. Discovered in 1972, the field now averaged 35 million cubic feet of gas a day from its four wells, raising the company's total daily gas deliveries to the January, 1975, level. Likewise, the 1975 discovery of the Boxcar-Butte field in North Dakota culminated in a gas-processing plant, which went into operation during the closing days of January.

Kerr-McGee's position in the financial world was shown in its ranking in *Fortune*'s 500 when its sales rank improved from 129 to 115 (see Table 26.6). According to *Fortune*, its 7.3 percent increase bettered the performance of most of the petroleum group, which had a median of 4.6 percent. The magazine characterized the poor performance of oils as follows:

Profits of the 500 fell sharply, by 13.3 percent. The group's profit problems were heavily concentrated in oil companies, which broke all sorts of records in 1974 but ran into big trouble last year. The group's earnings fell by 25 percent and accounted for more than half of the 500's overall profit decline. Elimination of the oil-depletion allowance at home, heavier taxes in most OPEC countries, and weak markets overseas were the major problems.[21]

For a time, however, Kerr-McGee was plagued by a spell of bad luck. In February the company lost another round in the protracted legal battle with Pacific Engineering. Then word was received that the first test well in the Gulf of Kutch, offshore India, was dry and had to be abandoned. On the other hand, the seventeenth drilling rig was added to the Kerr-McGee fleet with the commissioning of Rig 64 for use in the Gulf of Mexico.

Another segment of Kerr-McGee history bearing Bob Kerr's mark ended on March 24 with a letter to the working-unit owners at Pinta Dome. The company was now out of the helium business. All wells had been shut down and the plant closed. A week later the Arizona Oil and Gas Conservation Commission was notified that the facility had been decommissioned because of the low productivity of the wells.[22]

[20] Lease Records file, "Project 1082."

[21] "The Fortune Directory of the 500 Largest U.S. Industrial Corporations," *Fortune*, May, 1976, pp. 316–17, 322–23, 338; "28th Annual Report on American Industry," *Forbes*, January 1, 1976, pp. 48, 152, 162, 179, 187.

[22] Lease Records file, "Project 382 (Corres.)."

Although the stockholders had been warned, the first-quarter financial report was disappointing.[23] The House subcommittee hearings on the Silkwood matter created unwished-for notoriety. But in March and April speeches to the Grants, New Mexico, Chamber of Commerce and the Los Angeles Society of Financial Analysts President Kelly was optimistic. In Grants he said that it was his belief that the uranium industry was finally coming out of a transition period. New contracts were approaching $40 a pound and contained vital escalation clauses. Steady improvement during the next five years should make it an equal of oil, gas, and coal.

The analysts were told of predicted capital expenditures in excess of $1 billion for 1976–80. All programs in the capital forecast had attractive rates of return. A high-level petroleum exploration program would continue both domestically and abroad. Kerr-McGee refineries now had direct access to imported crude, and the market for their products was predicted to rise. Major expansions were projected for chemicals, and it was anticipated that coal would be a major new source of earnings in 1978. All in all, according to Kelly, "Kerr-McGee is entering on another exciting growth period."[24]

Almost as if to underscore these words, Transocean IV was commissioned for North Sea duty, and the largest uranium contract in Kerr-McGee's history was signed. This agreement, with Public Service Electric and Gas Company of New Jersey, called for the delivery of 20 million pounds of yellow cake in the form of uranium concentrates between 1980 and 1995. The contract was also unique in another aspect: the price depended on the one prevailing at the time of delivery, and the total could exceed $1 billion. In addition Public Service was committed to make interest-bearing advance payments equivalent to the cost of development and mining facilities, up to $115 million. The uranium would be mined from the South Powder River Basin in Wyoming and required opening two underground mines in addition to the Bill Smith mine already under construction, several open pits, and a processing facility.[25]

On May 14 the Kerr-McGee board increased the annual dividend from $1.00 to $1.25. This marked the third consecutive year, and the seventh of the last ten years, in which dividends had been raised. A week earlier an agreement in principle had been announced whereby Kerr-McGee would purchase 900,000 shares of the capital stock of Sunningdale Oils, Ltd., of Canada for $17.00 a share. After Sunningdale had disposed of its Canadian holdings, Kerr-McGee would make an offer for the rest of its shares. What the company wanted was Sunningdale's overseas properties, especially in the North Sea and off Abu Dhabi. By May 27, 925,000 shares at $17.35 had been acquired, and the same price was open for all stock tendered before October 4. The response was such that by mid-July, Kerr-McGee owned 92.3 percent. The final aggregate cost was $76,965,000, and Sunningdale

[23] Kerr-McGee press release, April 27, 1976.

[24] James J. Kelly, speech before the Los Angeles Society of Financial Analysts, April 8, 1976, in Public Relations files and digested in release "PR #34."

[25] *Kermac News*, May, 1976, p. 10; Kerr-McGee press release, "41/4-27-76"; *Wall Street Journal*, April 28, 1976.

became a new subsidiary. This purchase brought with it varying interests in the Heimdal field offshore Norway, the Brae field and two other blocks off the United Kingdom, one block in the Netherlands waters, four off Ireland, leases and production in the Abu al Bu Khoosh and the Arzanah fields in the Arabian Gulf, two licenses in the Republic of Maldives, and a concession in the Republic of Mali.[26]

This acquisition and other ventures once more necessitated new financial arrangements. An issue of sinking-fund debentures was announced, and the June 10 "Prospectus" stated that Kerr-McGee was offering $125 million in 8.5 percent debentures, due June 1, 2006, for $99.25 each. The $122,695,750 would be used for capital expenditures and long-term debt retirement. Since capital expenditures for 1976 were already budgeted in excess of $300 million, an additional $75 million would have to come from short-term bank loans if the Sunningdale acquisition were consummated in full.

In this prospectus, just one year after the previous one, Kerr-McGee presented as assets a net interest in oil-and-gas leases on 1,167,443 acres in the United States, 3,135,299 in Canada, and 205,920 in India, for a total of 4,508,662 acres. There were uranium leases on approximately 772,000 acres in the United States and Canada, and two uranium processing plants. Oil reserves were estimated at 58,783,553 barrels, 6,621,952 barrels of condensate, and 879.5 billion cubic feet of gas. It also controlled two sites in Arizona which were believed to have significant copper deposits. Likewise the company had shares in seventeen gas processing plants and owned three refineries. Almost 2,000 service stations were operating under Kerr-McGee brands or those of its subsidiaries.

Two coal mines, in addition to the Choctaw mine, were projected at a cost of approximately $35 million each. The firm had two chemical plants at Trona, California, a potash mill and mine at Hobbs, New Mexico, a 28 percent interest in Florida's Brewster Phosphates, a manganese processing plant at Henderson, Nevada, and a pigment facility at Hamilton, Mississippi, and was completing a synthetic-rutile unit at Mobile, Alabama. It also produced vanadium and owned and operated 7 fertilizer factories, 3 dry-mix plants, and 116 blending plants and warehouses. There were ten wood-preserving plants, nine sawmills, and a pallet mill. Since these assets were impressive, the response to the debenture offer was almost instantaneous. The day after the announcement virtually all these AA securities were sold.[27]

Sunningdale was only the first of the acquisitions of 1975. On June 8, Kerr-McGee announced that it had acquired the property and equipment of Bristol Silver Mines at Pioche, Nevada. Although inactive at the time, the mine had produced copper, lead, zinc, and silver. More significant, how-

---

[26] Kerr-McGee press release, May 7, 1976; *New York Times*, May 8 and July 17, 1976; *Wall Street Journal*, May 10 and June 7, 16, 1976; Lease Records files, "P 1097-1" and "P 1101-1."

[27] "Prospectus $125,000,000 Kerr-McGee Corporation 8½% Sinking Fund Debentures due June 1, 2006," June 10, 1976; *Wall Street Journal*, May 21 and June 10 and 11, 1976.

ever, was Kelly's revelation to the security analysts of Boston. Kerr-McGee had secured, subject to approval of the British and Netherlands governments, Apco Oil Limited's one-fourth interest in nine blocks in the United Kingdom sector of the North Sea and its 18 percent interest in one tract in the Dutch sector. But as these new properties were being added on one side of the world, Kerr-McGee terminated its participation in the December, 1974, "Asian Agreement" on the other for economic considerations.[28]

These latest acquisitions meant that Kerr-McGee had twenty-six leaseholdings in ten new nations, twenty-five offshore and one on land. Four were offshore Ireland, and one was in the Celtic Sea. The other fourteen were in the North Sea: ten off the United Kingdom, three off the Netherlands, and one off Norway. Besides the older production off Sharjah, the company now had a 15 percent share in the Gulf of Hammamet off Tunisia and interests in two fields in the Arabian Gulf offshore Abu Dhabi. There was an onshore concession in Mali (Central Africa), one in the Bay of Kutch, and two blocks offshore the Maldive Islands, south of India. Before the year was over, oil was discovered in Tunisia, in two blocks in the North Sea, and in two fields off Abu Dhabi. Gas was produced in the field off Norway. In short, Kerr-McGee had taken a long step toward becoming one of the "international oils."[29]

Of course, it would be some time before these acquisitions could contribute to the profit side of the ledger. When Kerr-McGee's second-quarter report was essentially "flat," Wall Street reacted rather unfavorably. Analysts were bothered by the fact that $20 million of the income had come from "spot" sales of uranium at $40 a pound, since this would later have to be made up at much lower prices. Thus the company was "borrowing from the future." With pretax net income down, some analysts reduced their estimate of projected earnings, despite Kerr-McGee's reiteration that 1976 earnings would exceed those of 1975. One market expert summed up the situation by saying, "The stock usually trades at a premium to the market, . . . but the volatility of earnings raises the question whether that kind of premium will be maintained."[30]

July, however, backed up the company's prophecy. An exploratory well in the Gulf of Hammamet tested at 1,700 barrels of oil per day. This was followed by a successful high bid on two blocks in the Baltimore Canyon area of the Outer Continental Shelf in the Atlantic Ocean in a federal lease sale on August 17. Kerr-McGee's cost totaled $6,614,000. Additionally, five more

---

[28] See D. A. McGee letter of July 29, 1976, entitled "Sunningdale Reorganization," addressed to Kerr-McGee supervisory personnel and Sunningdale directors; for Apco and Bristol see Kerr-McGee press releases for June 8 and 25 and July 19, 1976, and *Daily Oklahoman*, June 26 and July 20, 1976; for "Asian Agreement" see Lease Records file, "Contract 1503-1." By July 19 the British government had approved Kerr-McGee's purchase.

[29] "Oil and Gas Grows Over (and Under) Seas," *Kermac News*, October, 1976, pp. 6–7; *Wall Street Journal*, July 23, 1976.

[30] *Kermac News*, August, 1976, p. 12; "Kerr-McGee Spot Sale of Uranium, Weakness in Other Areas Lead to Lower Profit Estimates," *Wall Street Journal*, August 6, 1976.

blocks were acquired in the Gulf of Mexico in separate sales.[31] To manage all the company's growing resources, a change was made once more in the corporate structure, with the formation of Kerr-McGee Resources Corporation. Its purpose, according to Dean McGee, was "to consolidate into a single organization the responsibility for exploration, acquisition, evaluation and initial planning for development of Kerr-McGee's undeveloped mineral resources." Outside directors' fees were also increased from $2,400 to $3,600.

Interrupting the flow of good news was an antitrust suit brought by the attorney general of Illinois. On August 24, Kerr-McGee, along with nine other firms, was accused of influencing officials in New Mexico and Saskatchewan, Canada, to aid in monitoring potash production and prices. But it was back to happy times on September 13 with announcement of a five-year contract to supply 15 million tons of coal from the projected East Gillette, Wyoming, mine to Cajun Electric Cooperative, Inc., of Louisiana. Deliveries would begin in 1979, and the contract carried a value of $90 million, plus an escalation clause based on the price of the coal at the mine. Additional welcome news was a discovery in the Moray Firth area of the North Sea. The well, which flowed 6,066 barrels a day, was not only larger than most North Sea discoveries but also closer to shore (twelve miles from Scotland) and in relatively shallow water. Later testing indicated that the field had significant recoverable reserves.[32]

Much of this would not show up except in future balance sheets, and the third-quarter report was at hand. It showed earnings only slightly higher than those of the 1975 third quarter and nine-month earnings slightly down. For that reason the appearance of McGee and Kelly before the New York Society of Security Analysts, Inc., was watched with probably more than passing interest. McGee discussed plans for the future and the extent of the resource base to make them feasible. Over the past five years capital expenditures had doubled; sales had increased 240 percent, and net income, 285 percent. The next five years' capital expenditures were scheduled at a high level, with accent on aggressive exploration programs and development of new technology. New interests in gas and oil made the company "very optimistic" about the potential for growth in oil-and-gas production. The same was true of coal, uranium, resource chemicals, refining, marketing, and contract drilling, leading to "continued earnings growth." Significantly, to McGee the most critical problem for the future was an adequate supply of qualified personnel.

Kelly spoke on current operations and facility expansion. Domestic oil production averaged 22,400 barrels per day, slightly below 1975, but gas deliveries of 247 million feet per day were higher. Foreign production consisted of about 3,700 barrels a day from the Mubarek field offshore

---

[31] Kerr-McGee press release, July 7, 1976; *Daily Oklahoman*, July 15, 1976; *Kermac News*, July, 1976, p. 13 and September, 1976, p. 9; Kerr-McGee press release, August 20, 1976. As of late 1977 court injunctions were still delaying test of these Atlantic leases.

[32] *Daily Oklahoman*, August 25, 1976; *Wall Street Journal*, September 11, 1976; *Kermac News*, September, 1976, p. 9; Kerr-McGee "Newsline," September 23, 1976, p. 2.

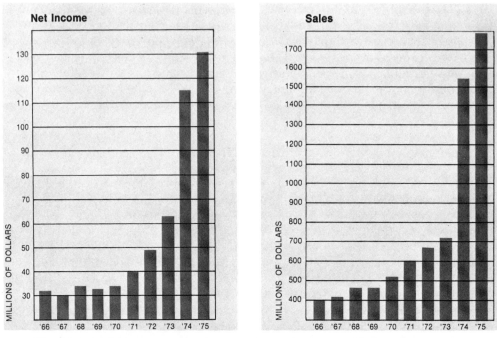

Fig. 26.1. Net income and sales, 1966–75. From Kerr-McGee Corporation, *1975 Annual Report*.

expenditures made during the year.

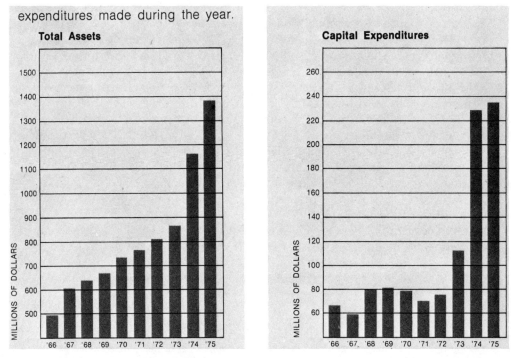

Fig. 26.2. Total assets and capital expenditures, 1966–75. From Kerr-McGee Corporation, *1975 Annual Report*.

474

Sharjah and 8,400 from Abu al Bu Khoosh offshore Abu Dhabi. Daily refining capacity stood at 181,000 barrels, and facilities to allow processing high-sulfur crude were being completed at Corpus Christi. In contract drilling only two of eighteen rigs were idle, and it was anticipated that the next five years would see an improved supply-demand balance in that business. Start-ups were under way in the expansion of Brewster Phosphates and the rutile plant at Mobile, while the $175 million expansion at Trona was on schedule for 1977–78.

Kelly enumerated further. Eight uranium mines were operating in New Mexico, with Church Rock I, on the Navajo Reservation, the newest. At Church Rock, Navajos were employed in every job category; of approximately 260 employees, 60 percent were Indians. There were plans also to mine the Rio Puerco and Roca Honda properties. Reserves in the South Powder River Basin of Wyoming were committed by contract; one mine was almost completed there, and additional ones would be opened. The Jacobs Ranch coal mine would be followed by additional operations in the area, and "Beginning about two years from now, Kerr-McGee Coal Corporation should show its first earnings, and thereafter its earnings should grow steadily."[33]

As if to underscore Kelly's words, announcement of new coal contracts followed quickly. In the later part of October agreements were reached with Houston Lighting & Power Company for delivery of 12.7 million tons of Jacobs Ranch coal between 1978 and 1980. With a price-escalation clause, the sale could exceed $80 million. This was followed in early November with a $66 million uranium transaction with Portland General Electric Company of Oregon. Some 1.6 million pounds of uranium concentrates would be delivered as uranium hexafluorides between 1983 and 1985. To top all this, a second well in the North Sea and two new discoveries offshore Louisiana made possible a December statement that Kerr-McGee's worldwide crude-oil reserves had grown during 1976 by over 16 million barrels.[34]

Fourth-quarter news was also good. Consequently, the annual report once more showed record sales and earnings, although increases were more modest than those to which stockholders had become accustomed. Higher prices in oil, gas, and nuclear products offset declines elsewhere to the degree that sales actually increased 8.7 percent to $1,955,058,000, and net income by 2.3 percent. Cash flow grew by almost $22 million, while working capital dropped by $13.5 million.

Earnings would have been even better except for the entitlements program of the Federal Energy Administration (FEA). In one month alone, Kerr-McGee was required to buy entitlements equivalent to 774,000 barrels of oil at $7.29 a barrel. That worked out to about $1.00 a share annually,

---

[33] "Remarks by Dean A. McGee and James J. Kelly Before the New York Society of Security Analysts, Inc., October 15, 1976," published by Kerr-McGee; *Wall Street Journal*, October 18, 1976.

[34] *Kermac News*, November–December, 1976, p. 11; Kerr-McGee press releases dated October 25 and November 8, 1976; *New York Times*, October 27, 1976; *Wall Street Journal*, November 11, 1976.

Table 26.2. Financial Highlights, 1975–76

	1975	1976
Total gross income	$1,807,097,000	$1,962,223,000
Net income	131,080,000	134,132,000
Total assets	1,387,882,000	1,625,595,000
Cash flow from earnings	214,892,000	236,700,000
Working capital	282,296,000	268,751,000
Properties (net)	803,153,000	1,049,539,000
Capital expenditures	234,734,000	332,642,000
Long-term debt	216,409,000	321,235,000
Cash dividends	24,415,000	30,660,000
Stockholders' equity	807,894,000	913,104,000
Total taxes paid	115,104,000	107,298,000
Number of employees	10,305	11,427

Table 26.3. Common-Stock Highlights, 1975–76

	1975	1976
Equity per share	$31.31	$35.32
Earnings per share	$ 5.15	$ 5.19
Cash dividends per share	$ 1.00	$ 1.19
Number of shares outstanding	25,805,743	25,850,323
Number of stockholders	19,300	18,961
New York Stock Exchange		
High	$95.13	$82.75
Low	$60.00	$60.13
Price-earnings ratio		
High	18.47	15.94
Low	11.65	11.58

Table 26.4. Production Record, 1975–76

	1975	1976
Production		
Crude oil produced (net barrels)	10,487,000	11,474,000
Natural-gas sales (millions of cubic feet)	86,658	89,494
Gas processing		
Gas liquids produced (net barrels)	2,245,000	2,350,000
Refining		
Crude oil processed (barrels)	55,842,000	60,212,000
Uranium		
U_3O_8 concentrate sold (lbs.)	3,638,000	4,018,000
Average price per lb.	$11.84	$19.14
Chemicals		
Total sold (tons)	3,150,000	3,246,000

Table 26.5. Drilling and Exploration Operations,
1975–76

	1975	1976
Feet drilled	984,000	934,737
Total wells/wells completed	137/123	133/116
Kerr-McGee interest	53	44
Rigs (average)	16	18

Table 26.6. Kerr-McGee's Position in
Forbes 35, *Forbes* 500, and *Fortune* 500

Forbes 35 Domestic Oils (5-Year)	1971–75	1972–76
Return on capital	14	13
Return on equity	15	16
Sales	21	19
Earnings per share	14	15
Forbes 500	1975	1976
Assets	342	319
Sales	161	161
Market value	63	79
Net profits	92	108
Dean McGee	94	148
	($379,596)	($381,750)
Fortune 500	1975	1976
Assets	121	109
Sales	115	114
Net income	63	79
Stockholders' equity	93	90
Net income as a percentage of sales	86	117

which went to the coffers of refiners who did not have access to low-cost "old" oil, as Kerr-McGee did. This undoubtedly held down the equity and earnings per share of common stock.

Petroleum provided 73 percent of the sales; chemicals and plant foods, 22 percent; and nuclear, 5 percent. In net income the respective percentages were 60, 24, and 19. Although refinery runs were up, sales were down, with Triangle's falling some 14 percent. But Kerr-McGee Chemicals had record sales, even though earnings were affected by depressed prices for fertilizer raw materials. Uranium production had declined because of a shortage of miners, but spot sales of 850,000 pounds at the current price raised the average by almost $8.00 per pound to $19.14. The backlog of uranium sales and conversion commitments stood at $1.9 billion. Some $4,311,000 was spent on research that had emphasized recovery of uranium from sources previously considered noncommercial and in development of the firm's "critical solvent deashing process" to deash and desulfur coal to make it burn cleaner.[35]

In contract drilling 133 wells had been spudded, with 116 completed for a total of 934,737 feet. Of the total, 37 were foreign, with 5 in Southeast Asia and the Arabian Gulf, 14 in the North Sea, and 18 in West Africa. With the addition of two new drilling rigs utilization dropped to 89 percent in the face of a worldwide oversupply of deep-water units. Domestically the rigs started 96 wells and finished all but 10. Of these 62 were contracted for by 16 different firms, the remainder being Kerr-McGee's. Over all, the parent company and its foreign subsidiaries participated in a gross total of 143 wells, 62 of them wildcats. Of those completed, 35 were dry and 35 produced oil, 17 gas, and 11 condensate. The domestic wells were offshore Louisiana and Texas, in Canada, Arkansas, Louisiana, Mississippi, New Mexico, North Dakota, Oklahoma, Texas, and Wyoming. Kerr-McGee Eastern completed 2 wells, 1 offshore Sharjah and 1 in the Gulf of Kutch. Wildcats were numerous, with Kerr-McGee oils (UK) Limited drilling 3; Kerr-McGee Tunisia, 1; and Sunningdale Oils, 6, the last in the Brae field, offshore Ireland, and off Abu Dhabi.[36]

The annual report once more closed with a warning that 1977, like 1976, would be a period of transition from the rapid expansion era before 1976 to the accelerating growth period projected for 1978 and the years beyond. The *Wall Street Journal* was not in a mood to look to the future, however. It was the present which counted on the New York Stock Exchange. "Kerr-McGee Corp. set some of its Wall Street followers on their ears yesterday with disclosures in its annual report. The stock fell 3½, closing at 66⅝." Accordingly, "Wall Street had been caught with its estimates up." What bothered the analysts was that the 1976 net was largely the result of spot sales of uranium and that the company's prediction for 1977 was again a year of flat earnings.[37]

On the other hand, the year had been good enough, comparatively, to move Kerr-McGee's sales rank up one step in *Fortune*'s "500" and to maintain its position in *Forbes*'s (see Table 26.6). But this time it lost in the competition with the domestic oils.[38]

[35] Kerr-McGee press release, February 11, 1977; Kerr-McGee Corporation, *1976 Annual Report*; Securities and Exchange Commission, "Form 10-K for Fiscal Year Ended December 31, 1976."

[36] Transworld Drilling files, "Kerr-McGee Corporation and Subsidiary Companies Rig Operations Report Twelve Months Ended December 31, 1976," and "Kerr-McGee Corporation and Subsidiaries Lease Development Report for Year Ended Dec. 31, 1976."

[37] *Wall Street Journal*, March 31, 1977.

[38] "The Fortune Directory of the 500 Largest U.S. Industrial Corporations," *Fortune*, May, 1977, pp. 370–71; "29th Annual Report on American Industry," *Forbes*, January 1, 1977, pp. 44, 138, 173, 180, 190; and "The Forbes 500," *ibid.*, May 15, 1977, pp. 158, 170, 178, 190, 222–23.

Chapter 27

A Year of Anniversaries 1977

President Jimmy Carter took office in January, 1977, after having won an election based on his campaign pledge to bring new faces to government and new approaches to the tiresome, continuous problems of the country. But the year was characterized more by promises than by achievements as the new administration attempted to learn the intricacies of Washington. Business also, and especially the energy companies, marked time to see just what approaches this unknown politician would bring to the chief executive's office on Pennsylvania Avenue.

The energy industry in the United States in 1977 was between the past, with its vast amounts of cheap, easily obtained oil, and the future, with its need for exploration and development of new fuels. Some in the business had already expanded into nontraditional areas, but there was still uncertainty about just where to go and how. Those who had gone into chemicals found lower earnings shadowing their annual reports, and the prospects over the next few years looked tough, somewhat similar to the earlier invasion of the fertilizer field in the 1950's.

Natural gas, on the other hand, in the traditional part of the oil industry, was getting better. President Carter's program had first envisioned $1.75 per mcf for gas in the interstate market, but, by the end of 1977, $2.00 seemed more likely. Meanwhile, a producer could charge $1.47 for new gas in the interstate market, almost three times the price only three years earlier. And when existing contracts expired on the old gas—at prices ranging from $0.20 to $0.29 per mcf—new ones of $0.53 were permissible.

Oil had settled down after the gigantic leap in price in 1973. In the Middle

East oil companies were relegated to lifting, transporting, and marketing the region's oil, sometimes at a fee larger than they made during the last years of ownership. But this arrangement did not lend itself to future profits. In the United States the three tiers in the government's pricing scheme bordered on absurd complexity. The effect of the marketplace was largely removed, taking with it the chance for greater earnings. The only hope was in the new fields opening up for production.

In coal, at last, companies began to see a return on their investments. When chemical corporations on the gas-bearing Gulf Coast began ordering coal to fuel their plants, the mineral's future seemed assured. In uranium, however, the veto by President Carter of the Clinch River breeder-reactor project effectively kept the United States out of the international race to build a nuclear power plant that manufactured plutonium fuel as it burned uranium. Instead, nuclear plants operated by splitting, or fission, of uranium atoms. But the price of uranium was up over $40 a pound, from less than $10 in 1972, making that process an expensive one indeed.

The alternative, which was mentioned in Washington, was fusion, wherein the energy came from fusing together heavy isotopes of hydrogen, plentiful and cheap from seawater. But this was something for future generations, for two decades of demonstration and pilot-plant work were needed before electricity could be produced commercially by fusion. Consequently, all short-term energy solutions came back to the old standbys: coal, gas, and oil.

The line chart on domestic oil production showed a steady decline from November 6, 1970, when it peaked at the daily average of 10,089,000 barrels. A bottom came during the week of May 6, 1977, at 7,959,000 barrels—a 21.1 percent drop. This was bad enough by itself, but it was coupled with an alarming increase in oil imports. In 1970, this had been 22.4 percent of domestic use; in 1977 it was 45 percent. This was despite the fact that 46,061 wells were drilled, 11 percent more than in 1976. The record was still 58,160, achieved in 1956.

Besides the high cost of buying foreign oil, wells drilled in the 1970's were deeper and therefore more expensive. The percentage of dry holes rose 4.5 percent, adding even more to the price. New oil from the North Sea, Mexico, and the north slope of Alaska promised some relief, and possibly some local surpluses, but for the foreseeable future OPEC still held the upper hand in determining the amount an American paid for heating his home and driving his car.

For Kerr-McGee, 1977 was one of many anniversaries marking significant steps in its history. Forty-five eventful years had passed since the establishment of A&K Petroleum Company, the vehicle upon which the integrated corporation had been constructed. On February 1, Dean McGee celebrated his fortieth year with the firm which bore his name. November 14 was the thirtieth anniversary of the completion by Kerr-McGee of the first successful offshore well in the Gulf of Mexico. It had been twenty-five years since Kerr-McGee became the first oil company to enter the infant uranium industry and twenty years since the start of uranium mining at Ambrosia Lake, New Mexico. The purchase of Triangle Refining had also been ac-

Crushing plant and storage silos at Jacobs Ranch coal mine.

complished in 1957, with potash development following five years later. Finally, the first shaft of the Choctaw Mine at Stigler, Oklahoma, had been started a decade before, in 1967.

Another anniversary was the fifty-one years since Robert S. Kerr joined James L. Anderson in the oil business as an employee of the Dixon brothers. Three years later they established their own drilling firm and began picking up some production on the side. A recapitulation of subsequent developments in this line shows the extent to which the volume, as well as the geography, expanded over these years. From the first strike in Oklahoma City, through the lost field at Magnolia, the first Gulf well, and Dineh bi Keyah in Navajoland, down to Sharjah and the North Sea, it marks an incredible journey. Despite an inability to compete there, the Oklahoma City field had contributed some 561,771 barrels of oil to Kerr-McGee. The pioneering effort in the Gulf of Mexico alone resulted in 64,192,111 barrels;

in 1977 it provided more than one-half of the firm's total oil and gas and over one-fifth of the nation's total. To date the company's most productive areas had been as follows:

Oil (Barrels)

1. Louisiana (offshore)	64,192,111
2. West Texas—Panhandle	27,779,215
3. Utah, Dineh bi Keyah	14,234,346
4. Arkansas, Smackover	9,796,526
5. Louisiana (onshore)	4,983,276
6. New Mexico, Chavaroo, and King Devonian	1,249,801

Gas Condensate (Barrels)

1. Louisiana (offshore)	25,267,749
2. Louisiana (onshore)	6,000,573
3. West Texas—Panhandle	592,831

Natural Gas (Thousand Cubic Feet)

1. Louisiana (offshore)	1,102,517,417
2. West Texas—Panhandle	658,289,110
3. Texas, Hugoton	282,663,263
4. Louisiana (onshore)	62,463,093
5. New Mexico, Indian Basin	19,332,108

And so, as Anderson & Kerr Drilling Company had done long ago, Kerr-McGee opened 1977 probing the red earth of Oklahoma for missed pockets of oil and gas. Rigs were at work in Carter, Canadian, and Grady counties, and Pittsburg County furnished a shallow gas discovery. January also brought the welcome news of a dual gas discovery on Block 34, East Cameron. This well, in which Kerr-McGee owned a 17.5 percent interest, flowed at the rate of 22 million cubic feet of gas and 240 barrels of condensate per day. Abroad, foreign potential looked so good that a new production district, headquartered in London, was organized to manage the company's European and North African oil-and-gas operations. Immediate attention focused on interests in the Brae, Moray Firth, Heimdal, and Gulf of Hammamet fields.[1]

This move proved timely, for during the first week in February word was received that the third well in the Moray Firth area, in which Kerr-McGee had a one-fourth interest, had a flow rate of 2,160 barrels a day. With three successful wells at different points on the 55,000-acre lease there was good reason to believe that an important field had been opened. Its location, in shallower water and closer to shore than any other production in the North Sea, greatly enhanced its value.[2]

In April another new domestic oil-and-gas division was created to cen-

---

[1] Kerr-McGee press release, January 20, 1977; *Kermac News*, January, 1977, p. 15.
[2] *Wall Street Journal*, February 7, 1977; *Kermac News*, February, 1977, p. 13.

tralize management of drilling, development, and production. It would likewise oversee the company's natural-gas processing plants, along with the acquisition and sale of natural gas. This restructuring was once more timely, for in May a major gas discovery was made in a deeper horizon on Block 29, Breton Sound. The well, jointly owned with Phillips, flowed at a rate of 32,298,000 cubic feet a day.[3]

The search for reserves and production continued. In June, bids were tendered for additional Gulf leases, and an agreement was reached with Creslenn Oil Company of Dallas whereby Kerr-McGee would buy Creslenn's 15 percent interest in the Moray Firth area, subject to appropriate tax rulings and the consent of the United Kingdom Department of Energy. This would make Kerr-McGee the major participant in the field with a 40 percent share. In July, Kerr-McGee and its partners were awarded three additional 5,000-acre blocks in the Gulf at a cost of approximately $15 million. More good luck came when two wells on Block 247, Vermilion, confirmed a gas discovery, and four holes on Block 261 in the same area found both oil and gas. Meanwhile, an appraisal well in the Brae Field tested at 33,121 barrels of oil. This report and the continuing success in the Beatrice Field (Moray Firth) necessitated opening an oil-and-gas production office in Aberdeen, Scotland.[4]

A new petroleum exploration division for worldwide oil-and-gas exploration was the next step in specialization of responsibility. Its range of authority was shown in the addresses of its offices: Oklahoma City, Houston, Calgary, and London. Its job was not only to find new sources but also to handle the 2,692,049 net acres of undeveloped oil-and-gas leases. Of these acres, 841,361 were in twelve states and off the shores of Texas, Louisiana, and the Atlantic Coast. The Gulf of Mexico accounted for about 82,000 of these acres; the rest were in seven foreign locations.

Already Kerr-McGee had crude-oil reserves of 47,412,000 barrels domestically and 56,133,000 foreign. The totals for natural gas were 873 billion cubic feet and 78 billion cubic feet, respectively. During 1977 exploration and developmental drilling accelerated in the province of Alberta, Canada, resulting in two oil and eight gas producers. Overseas the Beatrice Field had five wells completed, while Brae had eight with two more in progress. An additional producer came in at Mubarek (Sharjah), and, offshore Abu Dhabi, wells 21 and 22 flowed in Abu Al Bu Khoosh, and a ninth was drilling in Arzanah.[5]

The drilling division celebrated its own anniversary of being in the business for forty-nine years. The annual drilling logs and rig operations files for the earliest years were destroyed, and the first complete record dates

---

[3] Kerr-McGee press release, April 25, 1977; *Wall Street Journal*, April 29, 1977; Kerr-McGee press release, May 26, 1977; *Kermac News*, July, 1977, p. 6.

[4] Kerr-McGee press release, "#64/6-10-77"; *Kermac News*, July, 1977, p. 6; Kerr-McGee press release, "#77/7-15-77"; *Kermac News*, September, 1977, p. 6; Kerr-McGee press release. "#107/10-12-77." The Creslenn deal was not completed.

[5] Kerr-McGee press release, "#123/11-23-77"; Kerr-McGee Corporation, *1977 Annual Report*.

Table 27.1. Drilling and Exploration Operations, 1942–77

	1942	1977	Totals
Feet drilled	183,389	901,000	35,225,000 (1929–77)
Total wells/wells completed	58/49	157/137	4,659 (1942–77)
Kerr-McGee interest	25	49	
Rigs (average)	11	18	

back only to 1942, although a cumulative total was kept for the footage drilled (see Table 27.1).

During 1977 contract drilling expanded. Transocean, in which Kerr-McGee had a majority interest, announced that it had arranged for a new rig to be built in Singapore, and Transworld began construction of Rig 65. This shallow-water device, whose services were already contracted, brought the total of wholly owned rigs to nineteen. Transocean's added three majority owned. Interestingly enough, Rig 65 marked a return to the triangular shape that Kerr-McGee had pioneered so many years earlier.[6]

During 1977, Kerr-McGee subsidiaries began 153 wells and completed 137 as its 18 rigs bored a total of 901,000 feet. With a utilization factor of 96 percent, 12 of its units were in the Gulf of Mexico; 1 each offshore the United Kingdom, Nigeria, and the Arabian Gulf; and 3 off the Netherlands. In foreign waters 40 wells were begun, and 35 were completed. Transworld, Limited, contributed 4 in the Arabian Gulf; Transocean, 19 in the North Sea; and Kerr-McGee Limited, 17 off West Africa. Domestically Transworld spudded 113, of which 102 were finished. Of these 26 were off Texas and the remainder off Louisiana. Twenty-eight were Kerr-McGee's, and the rest were for such firms as Mobil, Gulf, Superior, Texaco, Continental, Sun, and Phillips.[7]

On its own account Kerr-McGee and its subsidiaries participated in a gross total of 195 wells, 93 wildcats and 102 developmental, and completed 133. Of these, 39 were dry holes, 33 found oil, 41 gas, and 20 gas condensate. Kerr-McGee spudded 174, including 43 offshore Louisiana and 5 off Texas. Onshore, Texas was the site of 51, Oklahoma 24, Canada and Louisiana 18 each, Mississippi 8, North Dakota 5, and New Mexico 2. Kerr-McGee Eastern completed a well at Sharjah; Kerr-McGee Oil (UK) Limited started 9 at Beatrice; Kerr-McGee Tunisia 3 in the Gulf of Hammamet; while Sunningdale Oils had 6 in the Brae Field and 2 off Abu Dhabi. As of December 31, there was a gross total of 2,031 domestic and foreign wells with a net total of 940.08: 576 oil, 237.09 gas, and 109.46 condensate.[8]

[6] Kerr-McGee press release, "#133/12-27-77."

[7] Transworld Drilling Company, "Kerr-McGee Corporation and Subsidiary Companies Rig Operations Twelve Months Ended December 31, 1977."

[8] Production Department, "Kerr-McGee Corporation and Subsidiaries, Lease Development Report for the Year Ended December 31, 1977."

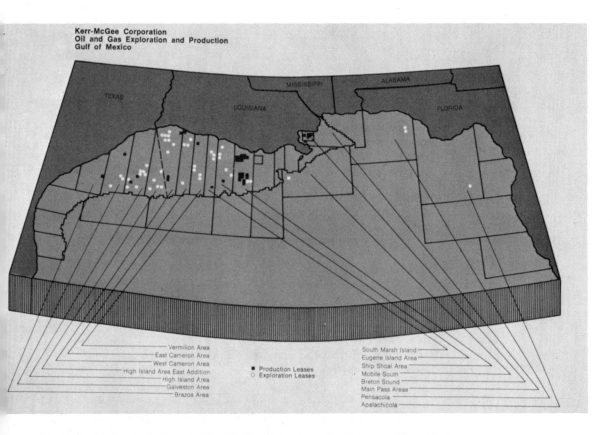

Kerr-McGee Corporation
Oil and Gas Exploration and Production
Gulf of Mexico

TEXAS

MISSISSIPPI   ALABAMA

LOUISIANA   FLORIDA

Vermilion Area
East Cameron Area
West Cameron Area
High Island Area East Addition
High Island Area
Galveston Area
Brazos Area

■ Production Leases
○ Exploration Leases

South Marsh Island
Eugene Island Area
Ship Shoal Area
Mobile South
Breton Sound
Main Pass Areas
Pensacola
Apalachicola

Fig. 27.1. Major holdings in the Gulf of Mexico, 1977. From Kerr-McGee
Corporation, *1977 Annual Report*.

Undoubtedly the highpoint of 1977 for Kerr-McGee and the small group
of thirty-year employees was being a part of the celebration acclaiming one
of the prime achievements of the petroleum industry. For their role in
bringing in the first offshore well in the Gulf of Mexico three decades earlier,
thirty of the original thirty-six men from Kerr-McGee Corporation and
Brown & Root Construction Company who had been directly involved were
feted at a banquet in New Orleans. Governor Edwin Edwards of Louisiana
expressed his state's appreciation: "We are better, the country is better for
what you did." The board of directors of the American Petroleum Institute
lauded the event: "Originating with the Kerr-McGee success in 1947,
offshore technology spawned an industry calculated to play an ever increasing role in the nation's critical energy search" and "made possible the first
successful production of oil in the offshore environment."

But mainly it was an occasion for reminiscing. To Dean McGee it was
"rewarding to know that our accomplishment sparked a giant indus-

Table 27.2. Production Record, 1936–77

	1936*	1977	Cumulative Total
Crude oil produced (net barrels)	232,635	11,195,000	170,710,000 (1931–77)
Price per barrel (North America)	$1.126	$7.97	
Natural-gas sales (millions of cubic feet)	34,320	81,000,000	2,173,000,000 (1932–77)
Price per mcf	$.007	$.877	
Gas liquids produced (net barrels)	NA	2,619,000	45,785,000 (1953–77)

*First annual report.

try. . . . In a small way, ours was kind of like the step on the moon. We were exploring a new, hostile environment." R. A. McDerby remembered the food on the makeshift barge bobbing on the water: "It was a great menu. One day we had beans and rice. The next, rice and beans." David Chauvin thought of the wages paid for the dangerous and strange work: "I made about $1.60 an hour. That was good money."

Then there were the comparisons. "When we first started you could run for hours out there and never see a light. Now they are everywhere." But prices got a lot of attention. In 1947 the 5,000-acre tract cost $25,000; in 1977 it would probably bring bids of $50 million. The Brown & Root platform, on which the stripped-down land Rig 16 was bolted, cost $230,000. Now modern production platforms could run $300 million to $400 million. Rig 16 had been worth a few thousand dollars, while its 1977 deep-sea counterpart averaged about $20 million.

The discovery well was still producing on that day of celebration, November 18, 1977. Pumping from the original platform, it had recovered a total of 1.2 million barrels of oil and more than 269 million cubic feet of gas. Over the past thirty years tens of billions of dollars had been invested in the new industry started by that well. First, there were the leases, drilling units, and production facilities. Eventually more than 350 mobile devices operated on the world's continental shelves, besides the 1,200 offshore multiple platforms and thousands of single-well structures. But it was worth it. These offshore wells cumulatively produced more than 9 million barrels of oil daily, over 16 percent of the world's total, and 29 billion cubic feet of gas, more than 20 percent of the world's daily output.[9]

Kerr-McGee's refineries were busy turning the crude oil into a variety of

[9] "Remarks by Dean A. McGee 30th Anniversary of Offshore Drilling November 18, 1977," in Public Relations files; Kerr-McGee press release, "#119/11-16-77"; *Oklahoma City Times*, November 19, 1977; *Kermac News*, November and December, 1977.

Table 27.3. Crude-Oil Processing, 1946–77

	1946*	1977	1946–77
Crude oil processed (net barrels)	771,232	60,263,000	515,904,000

*The Wynnewood refinery was purchased in February, 1945, and sales for the rest of the year were $541,200.

products at the rate of 165,105 barrels a day. From this the principal derivatives were 59,520 barrels of gasoline, 57,783 of distillate, and 27,339 of residual fuel oil, for a total of 230,497 barrels daily in refined product sales. Asphalt, the item which had lured Bob Kerr into the refining field, was holding at a current daily output of 3,800 barrels, averaging an annual sale of about 1.3 million barrels, 75 percent of which went to the paving market.[10]

The three refineries, Wynnewood, Cotton Valley, and Corpus Christi, with a combined capacity of 181,000 barrels per day, operated at above 92 percent utilization, with the exception of Cotton Valley at 57 percent. Plans were under way for a $20 million modification project at Wynnewood to increase its unleaded-gasoline-production ability to conform to new federal requirements.

The output of these refineries was merchandised through 1,633 retail stations bearing the Kerr-McGee and Deep Rock brands and through 306 outlets with other names. Triangle, celebrating its twenty years as a subsidiary of Kerr-McGee, improved sales by 14 percent. It operated twenty waterway and pipeline terminals to distribute gasoline, diesel fuels, and heating oils to its customers. Another subsidiary, Cato, had the highest return of its history as its net income rose by 48 percent.

It had been twenty-five years since Bob Kerr brought his company into the new and undeveloped field of uranium. Since then Kerr-McGee had sold about 99 million pounds of uranium and still had a backlog of $1,939,000,000 in sales and conversion commitments to be met. Now, in 1977, it was the nation's largest supplier of uranium concentrates and owner of the greatest reserves. This status had not come without problems, some of which were yet to be solved. But Frank McPherson, president of Kerr-McGee Nuclear, told a *Daily Oklahoman* reporter in January, 1977, that uranium prospects looked bright in the face of a seller's market. The product brought around $40 a pound, five times that of a decade earlier, and voters in several states had refused to allow prohibitive restrictions to be placed on new plants using atomic energy. Even if additional nuclear plants were not constructed, he believed that Kerr-McGee would not be affected for many years.[11]

[10] For asphalt see *Kermac News*, January, 1977, pp. 6–7; other material is from *1977 Annual Report*.

[11] *Daily Oklahoman*, January 2, 1977; *Kermac News*, February, 1977, p. 2.

Table 27.4. Sales of U_3O_8 Concentrate, 1955–77

	1955*	1977	1955–77
Pounds of U_3O_8 concentrate sold (lbs.)	182,705	4,576,000	100,303,740
Price per lb.	ca. $14.81	$18.09	

*Earliest date available

Reverberations from the Karen Silkwood case were being felt, however. Therefore, the presentation of an "Outstanding Performance Award" to Kerr-McGee Nuclear Fuels by Westinghouse Hanford Company must have provided officials with some pleasure. This was in recognition of its production of uranium-plutonium oxide fuel pins for the Fast Flux Test Facility under construction for ERDA.[12]

Relations with the Navajos continued on a cooperative note. In April, 1977, Kerr-McGee announced a program with the Navajo Indian Nation whereby 144 Navajos would study uranium mining at the Church Rock mine. These twelve-week courses were designed to cut at least one year from the normal time needed to advance to the highest-paying jobs in the mines.

The company continued to be active in opening new production and seeking new reserves in uranium. At Church Rock, initial development work began on a second mine, and shaft sinking was under way at the Rio Puerco property about fifty miles east of the Grants mill. The Rio Puerco installation was scheduled for initial production in 1979. In Wyoming's South Powder River Basin roads were being constructed and overburden stripped for the first surface mine, while development of the underground Bill Smith mine continued. These, plus several future pits, were planned to meet the contract requirements of Public Service Electric and Gas Company of New Jersey. One hundred miles to the west Kerr-McGee took one-half interest in 1,009 uranium claims covering 26,419 acres in the Green Mountain area, with Arizona Public Service Company and other utilities paying $10.2 million for the remainder.

The yellow cake from these sources was processed into uranium hexafluoride at the Sequoyah plant. One of two privately owned facilities in the country, this installation employed about 120 people and pumped more than $2 million annually into the economy of the small community. An expansion program, almost complete, would double its capacity from 5,000 to 10,000 tons, with a similar financial effect upon the surrounding area.[13]

[12] *Kermac News*, March, 1977, p. 4; Kerr-McGee press release, February 15, 1977. Because of obsolescence and federal policy it is probable that the Cimarron plutonium facility will be sold for salvage.

[13] Kerr-McGee Corporation, *Interim Report for the Three Months Ended March 31, 1977*; *Wall Street Journal*, May 3 and June 13, 1977; *Kermac News*, April, July, October, 1977; Kerr-McGee press release, "#113/10-24-77."

Production and delivery of nuclear products were up, with 4.6 million pounds of yellow cake and 4,578,695 kilograms of hexafluoride in 1977. But a reduction in "spot" sales at around $40.00 a pound dropped the average price received to $18.09, as compared to $19.14 in 1976. And although the early, lower-priced contracts were being renegotiated, their effects were felt.

Chemicals were the weak spot in Kerr-McGee's balance sheet in 1977. The company posted a 7.5 percent increase in sales of agricultural chemicals. But earnings declined from $54.4 million to $38 million. There were several reasons for this: lower wholesale prices for fertilizer, potash, and salt cake; start-up costs at the Lonesome mine, the 25 percent-owned phosphate mine in Hillsborough County, Florida (Brewster Phosphates); and the new $53 million synthetic-rutile plant in Mobile, Alabama. Representing approximately one-half of a more than $100 million investment there, this facility had a capacity of 110,000 tons a year of synthetic rutile for use in the company's titanium dioxide operations. It employed more than 100 workers and had a $1.8 million annual payroll. But problems with process and design modifications to meet environmental regulations would bring suspended operations in the near future, and a lengthy delay in achieving full production would begin.

To manage and oversee the Trona plant new divisions of manufacturing and marketing were created. Substantial progress had been made on the $200 million expansion program, which was the largest capital project in Kerr-McGee's history. The first unit was scheduled for completion during 1978, and the total of three units would permit production of 2,750,000 tons annually, with soda ash the principal product.

Future plans also included a southern California deep-water terminal to serve export markets and to supply East Coast bulk terminals. About 25 percent of the more than 1 million tons of chemicals from Searles Lake went to customers in Western Europe, South America, Japan and other Pacific Ocean countries. Central and South America received about 25 percent of the company's 541,000 tons of potash produced at Hobbs, New Mexico. From the mines in Florida about 521,000 tons of raw material moved through the port of Tampa to users in Western Europe, South America, and the Far East. Bob Kerr did not live to see the full growth of the program he started with potash in 1962, but in a short period of fifteen years it became a diversified chemical operation with sales to all parts of the globe.

At the end of 1977, Kerr-McGee had 35,259 acres under potassium leases between Hobbs and Carlsbad, New Mexico; 3,633 acres of phosphate lands near Lakeland, Florida; and 21,298 acres of resources at Trona, California. But historically, Kerr-McGee had never been comfortable in one phase of nonpetroleum areas, the retail market. Consequently, the decision was made to withdraw from that aspect of the fertilizer business. On December 22 the company announced that it was selling to Agrico Chemical Company its 125 blending plants and retail centers for fertilizer and other farm chemicals located primarily in the upper middle western and eastern states. The sale did not, however, include the manufacturing and marketing operations for bulk potash, phosphate rock, diammonium phosphate, and phos-

Table 27.5. Chemical Sales, 1964–77

	1964	1977	1964–77
Total chemical sales (tons)	574,526	3,597,000	31,834,091

phoric acid. Kerr-McGee would continue to sell fertilizer and plant food raw materials in bulk to the agricultural industry.[14]

The fourth member of Kerr-McGee's family of energy sources was coal. More than two decades had passed since the company initiated a program to buy coal reserves. Ten years before, the first shaft was sunk in the mine at Stigler, Oklahoma, and the first commercial production of coal was yet to be achieved. As a result of the continuing investment in coal reserves, however, Kerr-McGee owned or controlled vast reserves in Arkansas, Oklahoma, Illinois, North Dakota, Colorado, Montana, and Wyoming.

In May, 1976, James G. Randolph was made president of Kerr-McGee Coal Corporation as plans were made to exploit some of these leases. Jacobs Ranch mine, almost ready to ship coal, was scheduled to produce 14 million tons annually by 1980. Added to this would be the mines at East Gillette, Wyoming. The operation of the Choctaw mine, the first, was still in doubt, however, because of the requirements of environmental and mining permits.

Existing contracts for future deliveries called for 2.8 million tons in 1978, up to 16 million tons in 1983. This meant extensive and concentrated construction at the various locations. To help keep the miners happy at the Jacobs Ranch mine, Kerr-McGee Coal began building a 100-unit mobile home park and contributed $700,000 to help build a hard-surface road to the area. Rail lines were laid, and the overburden was stripped in anticipation of the 1978 start-up. At East Gillette No. 16, Kerr-McGee's second surface mine in Wyoming, shipments were scheduled for early 1979, while a third pit was being planned. Meanwhile, preliminary studies were under way for the No. 6 Galatia mine in Illinois. In an effort to solve the severe problems at the Choctaw mine, the long-hole drilling method for draining methane gas from the seam was being tested, since it could not be reopened without "a proven system for gas removal." This must have brought some degree of

[14] *1977 Annual Report*; Kerr-McGee Corporation, *Mobile Facility Synthetic Rutile Plant Dedication February 11, 1977*; Kerr-McGee Corporation, *Interim Reports* for three months, three and six months, and three and nine months. For sale of fertilizer interests see Kerr-McGee press release, "#132/12-22-77"; *Daily Oklahoman*, December 23, 1977; and *Kermac News*, January, 1978, p. 12. A fertilizer granulation plant at Jacksonville, Florida, was closed in March, 1978, and a pesticide facility in Baltimore, Maryland, was sold in April. *Kermac News*, April, 1978, p. 14.

relief because a new mine superintendent was later appointed, indicating that the facility might become operative soon.[15] Problems with gases were present in mines owned by other companies, as evidenced in the fact that Big Hole Drillers, which had not worked for an outside contract since 1962–64 with the AEC, sank a 76-inch ventilation shaft for United Nuclear near Gallup, New Mexico.[16]

Financially, Kerr-McGee's first-quarter report fell into the good news–bad news category. Sales were up, but net earnings fell by 5.6 percent. This was mainly because of poor showings in chemicals and an increase in income taxes from the growth of foreign crude-oil production. Two reports were issued in June; the first, a special one for the preceding twelve months, showed that income for that period exceeded the $2 billion mark. The regular second-quarter report noted a six months' record sale of $1,103,813,000.

But the third quarter brought evidence that this was atypical for the year. Net earnings were down for both the quarter and the nine months' period. Nevertheless, President Kelly told the Analysts Society of Chicago on October 13 that five years of heavy capital spending had put the corporation "in a strong position for increased profitability and long-term growth." Additionally there was a large backlog of projects based on natural-resource reserves which would provide attractive growth opportunities for the next decade or so.[17]

It was the final annual balance sheet which told the year's story. Financially, 1977 was more disappointing than had been anticipated. The fourth quarter saw sales fall by $8.2 million and net income by $8.5 million, or 24 percent. Although sales were up for the year, net income declined by 11.2 percent. Working capital dropped by $27.5 million, and the ratio of assets to liabilities from 2.0 to 1.8. Capital expenditures slid 19.1 percent.

On the positive side was an increase in stockholders' equity and in total assets. The cash flow was up $22 million, and the long-term debt dropped by an identical amount. Finally, sales officially broke the two-billion mark at $2,164,754,000. It had taken forty-two years from the incorporation of A&K

---

[15] *1977 Annual Report*; Kerr-McGee Coal Corporation, "Coal Scoop," June, 1977–January, 1978 (unpaged, issued monthly), especially June, November, December, and January issues; Kerr-McGee press releases, "#100/9-19-77" and "#12/2-17-78"; *Kermac News*, July, 1977, pp. 8–9.

[16] For a history of Big Hole see *Kermac News*, June, 1977, pp. 3–4. The largest hole by Rig 31 was a 16.5-foot-diameter hole dug at Ambrosia Lake in 1970 with a bit weighing 75,000 pounds. This method is more expensive than conventional drilling but twice as fast.

[17] Kerr-McGee Corporation, *Interim Report for the Three Months Ended March 31, 1977*; *Wall Street Journal*, May 3, 1977; Kerr-McGee Corporation, *Special Report for the Twelve Months Ended June 30, 1977*; Kerr-McGee Corporation, *Interim Report for the Three and Six Months Ended June 30, 1977*; *Wall Street Journal*, August 2 and November 1, 1977; *New York Times*, August 2, 1977; Kerr-McGee press release, "#116/10-31-77"; *Kermac News*, December, 1977, p. 12; Kerr-McGee Corporation, *Interim Report for the Three and Nine Months Ended September 30, 1977*; Kerr-McGee press release, "#108/10-12-77."

Table 27.6. Financial Highlights, 1936 and 1977

	1936*	1977
Total gross income	$ 317,116	$2,178,408,000
Net income	180,120	119,167,000
Total assets	1,474,420	1,833,301,000
Cash flow from earnings	227,560	258,646,000
Working capital	35,990	246,370,000
Properties (net)	700,785	1,209,077,000
Capital expenditures	NA	269,199,000
Long-term debt	0	299,373,000
Cash dividends	19,479	32,314,000
Stockholders' equity	1,118,272	1,002,787,000
Total taxes paid	13,273	119,668,000
Number of employees	NA	11,271

*First annual report, 1936.

Petroleum Company in 1932 for its successor, Kerr-McGee Corporation, to reach the first billion, yet the second billion came only three years later.[18]

By the same token the balance sheet of 1936 was that of a small production company, while the figures of 1977 were from a multifaceted corporation whose eighteen drilling rigs were not the least of its assets. It included figures from the twelve major subsidiaries:

Cato Oil and Grease Co.
Kerr-McGee Chemical Corporation
Kerr-McGee Coal Corporation
Kerr-McGee Nuclear Corporation
Kerr-McGee Oil (U.K.), Ltd.
Kerr-McGee Refining Corporation

Kerr-McGee Resources Corporation
Southwestern Refining Company, Inc.
Sunningdale Oils Limited
Transworld Drilling Company
Transworld Drilling Company, Ltd.
Triangle Refineries, Inc.

Additionally there were interests in such firms as Transocean, Brewster Phosphates, and many natural gasoline plants.

The 1936 executive offices had been rented rooms in the First National Building in Oklahoma City and boasted a staff of a dozen people headed by Whit Fentem and Dean Terrill. The 1977 headquarters were in the modern $20 million Kerr-McGee Center and, together with the technical center, could claim 1,800 employees. In line with the demands of the times, 43 percent of the staff was female and 13 percent from minority groups.[19] At the technical center some $4,592,000 was spent on research. Also in relation to the period $18,203,000 was spent on environmental protection. But sixteen

[18] Kerr-McGee press release, "#10/2-14-78"; *Wall Street Journal*, February 16, 1978; *Daily Oklahoman*, February 15, 1978; *1977 Annual Report*; Securities and Exchange Commission, "Form 10-K for Fiscal Year Ended December 31, 1977."

[19] Kerr-McGee press release, "#80/7-26-77."

Table 27.7. Common-stock Highlights, 1936 and 1977

	1936*	1977
Equity per share	$1.79	$138.79
Earnings per share	$ .56	$ 4.61
Cash dividends per share	$ .35	$ 1.25
Number of shares outstanding	275,000	25,854,183
Number of stockholders	35	18,700
Stock price		
High	$6.50 (OTC)	$74.50 (NYSE)
Low	$5.00 (OTC)	$45.16 (NYSE)
Price-earnings ratio		
High	11.60	16.16
Low	8.91	9.79

*First annual report, 1936.

of the Kerr-McGee facilities and plants received awards for safe operations from the National Safety Council during 1977.

Besides the employee stock plan, the common stock of the company was owned by shareholders in every state in the union plus Canada and seventy-eight other foreign countries. There were 6,623 men and 2,643 women who held certificates in their own names, while the remaining issues belonged to such diverse groups as churches, colleges, hospitals, libraries, museums, pension funds, labor unions, and professional organizations. It was a vastly enlarged group from 1936.

Kerr-McGee's performance was once more ranked by *Forbes* and *Fortune*.[20] A five-year decline to $46 by its common stock showed up in a comparable drop in *Forbes*'s market-value rank of the nation's 1,005 largest companies, a change of 550 places. Other standings were as shown in Table 27.8.

Value Line also had some interesting remarks to make about Kerr-McGee. Describing it as "a sleeping giant" because of its rich supply of resources, the investment survey suggested that the company could be a prime prospect for a takeover bid. But in 1975, just after the $140 million offering of common stock, *Value Line* had discounted a "glowing future," citing the hefty price-earnings ratio of 18.8 at that time. The 1975 prediction for performance was 3, or average, and safety, 2, above average, while the Beta or common stock fluctuation was 1, equal to that of the New York Stock Exchange.[21]

The financial record for 1966–77 gave an interesting survey of just how

[20] "30th Annual Report on American Industry," *Forbes*, January 9, 1978, pp. 44, 153, 182, 194, 213; "The Forbes 500s," *ibid.*, May 15, 1978, pp. 203, 215, 226, 234, 264, 292; "The Fortune Directory of the 500 Largest Industrial Corporations," *Fortune*, May 8, 1978, pp. 244–45.

[21] "Kerr-McGee Corporation," *Value Line*, 1975, 1978.

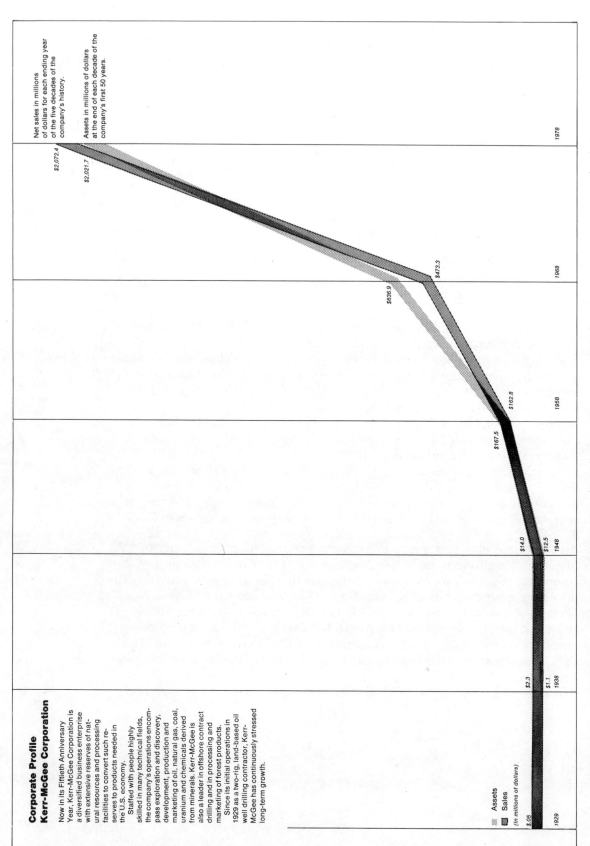

Net sales in millions
of dollars for each ending year
of the five decades of the
company's history.

Assets in millions of dollars
at the end of each decade of the
company's first 50 years.

▨ Assets
▨ Sales
(In millions of dollars)

$2,072.4
$2,021.7

$636.9
$473.3

$167.5
$162.8

$14.0
$12.5

$2.3
$1.1

$.05

1929   1938   1948   1958   1968   1978

Fig. 27.2. Sales and assets, 1929–78. From Kerr-McGee Corporation, *1978 Annual Report.*

Table 27.8. Kerr-McGee's Position in
Forbes 35, *Forbes* 500,
and *Fortune* 500

Forbes 35 Domestic Oils (5-Year)	
Return on capital	13
Return on equity	21
Sales	18
Earnings per share	14

Forbes 500	
Assets	309
Sales	160
Market value	107
Net profits	156

Fortune 500	
Assets	101
Sales	116
Net income	96
Stockholders' equity	89
Net income as percentage of sales	180
Earnings per share	134
Total return for investor	269

desirable Kerr-McGee was to a corporate suitor (see Table 27.9). One obvious fact: it would have to be a "supercompany" that attempted it.

The officials of Kerr-McGee and the members of its Board of Directors were understandably pleased with most of these results. The latter group was expanded twice during the year to a total of fifteen. New outside directors elected to the board were Glenn W. McGee, attorney of Chicago; Neil McKay, vice-chairman of the board of directors and cashier of the First National Bank of Chicago; William C. Morris, managing director, Lehman Brothers Kuhn Loeb Inc.; and Dr. Bruce C. Murray, director, Jet Propulsion Laboratory, and professor at California Institute of Technology, Pasadena, California. Fees were also increased to new levels: attendance, $500; annual, $7,200; and committee, $500, bringing the company more in line with payments by other firms.[22]

The Kerr-McGee legal staff still faced suits brought by the Silkwood family and Occidental Petroleum. It was heartened by the news that a

[22] *Wall Street Journal*, February 16 and August 9, 1977; *Kermac News*, March, 1977, p. 4, and September, 1977, p. 6.

Table 27.9. Financial and Operating Data, 1966–77

	1977	1976	1975	1974
Summary of earnings (thousands, except per share amounts)				
Sales of products, services, etc.	$2,164,754	$1,955,058	$1,798,580	$1,550,349
Operating costs and expenses	$1,942,337	$1,723,742	$1,570,089	$1,353,609
Interest expense	28,623	22,688	14,129	10,736
Total costs and expenses	$1,970,960	$1,746,430	$1,584,218	$1,364,345
	$ 193,794	$ 208,628	$ 214,362	$ 186,004
Other income	13,654	7,165	8,517	10,174
Net income before income taxes	$ 207,448	$ 215,793	$ 222,879	$ 196,178
Provision for income taxes	88,281	81,661	91,799	79,769
Net income	$ 119,167	$ 134,132	$ 131,080	$ 116,409
Net income applicable to common stock	$ 119,167	$ 134,132	$ 131,080	$ 116,409
Shares common stock outstanding at year-end	25,854	25,850	25,806	25,020
Net income per common share	$ 4.61	$ 5.19	$ 5.15	$ 4.64
Net income per common share assuming full dilution	$ 4.61	$ 5.19	$ 5.15	$ 4.64
Cash dividends paid on preferred stock	$	$	$	$ ....
Cash dividends paid on common stock	$ 32,314	$ 30,660	$ 25,415	$ 21,254
Cash dividends paid per common share	$ 1.25	$ 1.19	$ 1.00	$ .85
Financial (thousands)				
Working capital	$ 246,370	$ 273,870	$ 287,414	$ 201,673
Long-term debt	$ 299,373	$ 321,235	$ 216,409	$ 158,600
Common stockholders' equity	$1,002,787	$ 915,766	$ 810,556	$ 636,815
Total assets	$1,833,301	$1,625,595	$1,387,882	$1,164,432
Capital expenditures	$ 269,199	$ 332,642	$ 234,734	$ 227,956
Operating				
Production (net interest)				
Crude oil produced (thousands of barrels)	11,195	11,474	10,487	11,193
Natural gas liquids produced (thousands of barrels)	2,619	2,350	2,245	2,240
Natural gas sales (billions of cubic feet)	81	90	89	104
Oil and gas wells completed	40.90	20.13	34.97	22.50
Refining and marketing (thousands of barrels)				
Crude oil processed	60,263	60,212	55,842	46,984
Refined product sales (excluding commission sales)	80,255	79,388	83,693	79,201
Contract drilling (offshore operations only)				
Number of drilling rigs	18	18	16	15
Number of wells drilled	96	99	123	87
Number of feet drilled (thousands)	901	935	984	773
Chemicals				
Industrial sales (thousands of tons)	1,129	1,183	1,178	853
Agricultural sales (thousands of tons):				
Wholesale	1,514	1,040	1,109	931
Retail	922	891	817	958
Nuclear				
Deliveries of uranium (U_3O_8) (thousands of pounds)	5,425	4,018	3,638	5,178
Deliveries of uranium hexafluoride (uranium content in thousands of kilograms)	5,067	3,527	2,162	2,379
Number of employees	11,271	11,427	10,305	10,105

1973	1972	1971	1970	1969	1968	1967	1966
$727,953	$679,576	$603,254	$527,539	$475,945	$473,309	$423,494	$406,613
$632,141	$607,266	$540,783	$470,562	$428,076	$426,457	$380,379	$367,151
7,625	8,539	11,501	12,665	10,731	10,894	9,503	6,397
$639,766	$615,805	$552,284	$483,227	$438,807	$437,351	$389,882	$373,548
$ 88,187	$ 63,771	$ 50,970	$ 44,312	$ 37,138	$ 35,958	$ 33,612	$ 33,065
7,412	5,099	4,440	3,441	6,068	4,875	3,268	5,162
$ 95,599	$ 68,870	$ 55,410	$ 47,753	$ 43,206	$ 40,833	$ 36,880	$ 38,227
32,831	19,955	15,529	13,046	9,872	6,167	7,285	6,480
$ 62,768	$ 48,915	$ 39,881	$ 34,707	$ 33,334	$ 34,666	$ 29,595	$ 31,747
$ 61,897	$ 47,701	$ 38,659	$ 33,486	$ 32,114	$ 33,459	$ 28,412	$ 30,551
24,989	24,375	22,209	22,147	22,123	22,060	21,985	21,863
$ 2.52	$ 2.07	$ 1.73	$ 1.51	$ 1.45	$ 1.51	$ 1.29	$ 1.40
$ 2.51	$ 1.97	$ 1.66	$ 1.45	$ 1.39	$ 1.45	$ 1.26	$ 1.40
$ 871	$ 1,214	$ 1,222	$ 1,221	$ 1,220	$ 1,208	$ 154	$ 139
$ 14,741	$ 13,984	$ 12,201	$ 11,071	$ 11,055	$ 11,009	$ 12,830	$ 11,942
$ .60	$ .60	$ .55	$ .50	$ .50	$ .50	$ .483	$ .442
$204,128	$198,247	$159,144	$124,990	$148,859	$169,602	$177,599	$ 93,763
$122,819	$124,427	$225,650	$211,449	$203,003	$213,379	$215,375	$126,202
$540,738	$463,976	$335,440	$306,763	$283,924	$261,886	$237,075	$219,269
$866,671	$806,801	$762,504	$734,650	$667,940	$636,918	$602,875	$491,927
$113,041	$ 76,054	$ 69,875	$ 79,300	$ 81,160	$ 79,853	$ 59,461	$ 65,915
11,326	12,393	11,995	10,147	9,699	8,747	8,240	5,649
2,654	2,775	2,475	2,565	2,448	2,410	2,485	2,155
108	109	91	92	83	77	73	81
23.07	19.39	28.66	25.91	22.20	31.74	24.68	45.15
14,152	13,612	16,879	17,365	17,276	16,581	16,773	16,059
40,820	47,808	43,478	38,655	36,927	33,338	28,553	28,270
14	14	15	14	15	15	15	14
85	94	96	86	109	119	107	88
860	968	930	901	1,031	1,159	963	878
784	762	763	727	802	780	737	773
1,236	1,348	790	771	779	756	572	432
860	746	722	651	592	737	808	856
5,952	7,553	6,604	5,410	4,306	6,812	3,080	3,307
3,818	3,157	1,883	735				
8,966	9,217	9,439	9,792	9,319	8,905	9,223	9,645

federal appeals court in Denver had reversed a lower-court ruling and declared Kerr-McGee innocent of the charges brought by Pacific Engineering & Production Company regarding pricing of rocket materials. Even better was the November news that the Supreme Court had refused to review the appeals court's finding that no federal antitrust laws had been broken. In another matter Kerr-McGee and six other defendants agreed to contribute, "in varying amounts," a total of $3.2 million to settle triple-damage actions by various potash users who had charged the firms with illegal restrictions on production and price. This was to end "protracted and expensive litigation"; the defendants had already been acquitted in a criminal antitrust trial.[23]

An increase in the number of such cases may have speeded Kerr-McGee's decision to create a public-affairs division. This was done to enable the company to make more efficient and effective response to the ever-increasing volume of legislative, regulatory, and other public-policy issues. It centralized and coordinated government-contract activities formerly handled by the various operating divisions. Not only would the division keep up with current requirements and with pending and potential laws which could affect the company but also would coordinate the responses to these situations.[24] The hope was that future confrontations would be fewer.

Most of the internal reorganization of the year centered around the executive branch, however. As noted earlier, Dean McGee was celebrating his fortieth year with the company and his twenty-third as the top executive. James Kelly, who had spent thirty-two years with Kerr-McGee, reached retirement age in December. "To assure a smooth transition to new management leadership," a succession plan was formulated and then adopted. By it two new positions of vice-chairman of the board were created, and two new executive vice-presidents were authorized. The new vice-chairman positions were filled by Jere W. McKenny, vice-president of exploration, and by Frank A. McPherson, vice-president of coal and nuclear operations. Joining George B. Parks as executive vice-president were William J. F. Francis, vice-president of chemical and refining operations, and Marvin K. Hambrick, vice-president of finance. The decision was also made not to fill the presidency at this time.

Seemingly the way was now open also to name a successor to McGee. It was he who would decide the duties and responsibilities of the new officers. Rumor had it that, after being observed for an appropriate time, one would be chosen as chairman and chief executive officer, with another as president. Asked about these developments, McGee replied that he was in "the middle of phasing out." Asked how he knew this was the time to step down, he responded simply, "That's easy. My age."[25]

[23] *Daily Oklahoman*, February 17 and November 29, 1977; *Wall Street Journal*, August 22, 1977; *New York Times*, August 20, 1977.

[24] Kerr-McGee press release, "#92/8-23-77"; *Kermac News*, October, 1977, p. 6, and March, 1978, pp. 11–12.

[25] *Wall Street Journal*, August 12, 1977; *Daily Oklahoman*, August 12, 1977; Kerr-McGee press release, "#90/8-11-77"; *Kermac News*, September, 1977, p. 2; *Business Week*, January 9, 1978, p. 19.

All things being equal, it was preferred that the two top positions be filled with men forty to fifty years old in order to ensure long continuity. Also, in the early days of the company its success was often credited to the very youthfulness of its leaders. As George Cobb once said, "We had probably more guts than knowledge."

But it was more than youthful energy. McGee himself once said: "A corporation has a character. It takes on the character of the men who run it. If you know the man at the top you can tell how the people down the line are going to do business."[26] In this respect Kerr-McGee had been extremely fortunate in the men who were its chief executives. Kerr was energetic, with big dreams that extended beyond the company. He frankly admitted that it was his means to an end, a way to financial independence. His contribution, therefore, was not in the day-to-day management but rather in his ability to dream big dreams of an integrated oil company and pick good men to make all this come true. Jim Anderson's talent was his thorough knowledge of the oil field: how to drill wells efficiently, cheaply, and at a profit. Bob Lynn gave the company an expertise and experience heretofore missing at headquarters. It helped the infant concerns in their transition from a small contract-drilling company to an integrated petroleum corporation. More important, however, as unpopular as Lynn was to some people, no one ever faulted him for hiring Dean McGee.

Dean McGee first played the role of a steadying partner to Bob Kerr and his exuberant plans for expansion. This changed when McGee became the top executive, and he has since admitted that on at least two occasions Kerr-McGee was too cautious: first, when the early supremacy in offshore drilling was allowed to slip from its control, and, second, when the move into foreign oil was hindered by fear of competition with the large international companies. There can also be no doubt that Dean McGee's administrative career exemplifies his antipathy to governance by committee. Consequently, the authority to make major decisions has historically been in the hands of the very small group, the executive committee, and ultimately McGee himself.

But one characteristic has been dominant in Kerr-McGee's history, that of daring to be the first in the energy business to try the unknown and unexpected. And, usually, to do so with great success. Consequently, the new chief executive officers of the Kerr-McGee Corporation could come as a surprise to everyone.

To everyone but Dean McGee, that is.

[26] *Kermac News*, Spring, 1955, p. 10.

Appendix

Directors, Executive Committees, and Officers of the Company, 1936–77

1936

(A&K Petroleum Company)

Officers and Directors

Robert S. Kerr, President and Treasurer and Director

Dean Terrill, Vice-President and Director

T. W. Fentem, Secretary and Assistant

Treasurer and Director

T. M. Kerr, Director

Frank J. Loesch, Director

W. Earle Phinney, Director

1937

(Kerlyn Oil Company)

Board of Directors
J. D. Blosser
T. W. Fentem
Robert S. Kerr
T. M. Kerr
R. H. Lynn
F. W. Straus
Dean Terrill

Officers
Robert S. Kerr, President
R. H. Lynn, Executive Vice-President
Dean Terrill, Vice-President—General Counsel
D. A. McGee, Vice-President—Geology—Production
T. W. Fentem, Secretary and Treasurer

Executive Committee
Robert S. Kerr, Chairman
R. H. Lynn
F. W. Straus

1938–41

Board of Directors
J. D. Blosser
T. W. Fentem
Robert S. Kerr
T. M. Kerr

R. H. Lynn
D. A. McGee
F. W. Straus
Dean Terrill

Executive Committee
Robert S. Kerr, Chairman
R. H. Lynn
F. W. Straus

Officers
Robert S. Kerr, President
R. H. Lynn, Executive Vice-President
Dean Terrill, Vice-President—General Counsel
D. A. McGee, Vice-President—Geology—Production
T. M. Kerr, Vice-President—Drilling
T. W. Fentem, Secretary and Treasurer

1942–47

(Kerlyn Oil Company/Kerr-McGee Oil Industries, Inc.)

Board of Directors
J. D. Blosser
T. W. Fentem
Robert S. Kerr
T. M. Kerr

D. A. McGee
F. W. Straus
Dean Terrill

Executive Committee
Robert S. Kerr, Chairman
D. A. McGee
F. W. Straus

Officers
Robert S. Kerr, President
D. A. McGee, Executive Vice-President
Dean Terrill, Vice-President—General
 Counsel
T. M. Kerr, Vice-President—Drilling
T. W. Fentem, Secretary and Treasurer

1948–50

Board of Directors
J. D. Blosser
T. W. Fentem
Robert S. Kerr
T. M. Kerr

D. A. McGee
F. C. Love
F. W. Straus
Dean Terrill

Executive Committee
Robert S. Kerr, Chairman
D. A. McGee
F. W. Straus

Officers
Robert S. Kerr, President
D. A. McGee, Executive Vice-President
Dean Terrill, Vice-President—General
 Counsel
T. M. Kerr, Vice-President—Drilling
F. C. Love, Vice-President
T. W. Fentem, Secretary and Treasurer

1951

Board of Directors
J. D. Blosser
Edwin L. Kennedy
Robert S. Kerr
T. M. Kerr

D. A. McGee
F. C. Love
F. W. Straus
Dean Terrill

Executive Committee
Robert S. Kerr, Chairman
D. A. McGee
F. W. Straus

Officers
Robert S. Kerr, President
D. A. McGee, Executive Vice-President
T. M. Kerr, Vice-President and Secretary
F. C. Love, Vice-President and Treasurer
Dean Terrill, Vice-President—General
    Counsel

1952

Board of Directors
J. D. Blosser
Edwin L. Kennedy
Robert S. Kerr
T. M. Kerr

F. C. Love
D. A. McGee
F. W. Straus
Dean Terrill

Executive Committee
Robert S. Kerr, Chairman
D. A. McGee
F. W. Straus

Officers
Robert S. Kerr, President
D. A. McGee, Executive Vice-President
T. M. Kerr, Vice-President and Secretary
F. C. Love, Vice-President and Treasurer
S. B. Robinson, Assistant Secretary and
    Assistant Treasurer

1953–56

Board of Directors
J. D. Blosser
Edwin L. Kennedy
Robert S. Kerr
J. H. Lollar, Jr.
F. C. Love

D. A. McGee
F. W. Straus
Dean Terrill
James E. Webb

Executive Committee
Robert S. Kerr, Chairman
D. A. McGee
F. W. Straus

Officers
Robert S. Kerr, President
D. A. McGee, Executive Vice-President
T. M. Kerr, Vice-President
F. C. Love, Vice-President and Assistant
    Secretary
J. H. Lollar, Jr., Secretary and Treasurer
S. B. Robinson, Assistant Secretary and
    Assistant Treasurer

1957

Board of Directors
J. D. Blosser
Edwin L. Kennedy
Robert S. Kerr
Robert S. Kerr, Jr.
T. M. Kerr
Guy C. Kiddoo

J. H. Lollar, Jr.
F. C. Love
D. A. McGee
Frederick W. Straus
Dean Terrill
James E. Webb

Executive Committee
Robert S. Kerr, Chairman
Guy C. Kiddoo
F. C. Love
D. A. McGee
Frederick W. Straus

503

Officers

Robert S. Kerr, Chairman of the Board
D. A. McGee, President
T. M. Kerr, Vice-Chairman of the Board
F. C. Love, Executive Vice-President
J. B. Saunders, Senior Vice-President
L. A. Woodward, Administrative
Vice-President
A. T. F. Seale, Vice-President, Operations
J. C. Finley, Vice-President, Exploration
J. J. Kelly, Vice-President, Marketing
G. B. Kitchel, Vice-President, Drilling
Contracts
R. M. Chesney, Vice-President, Refining
W. M. Murray, Vice-President, General
Sales

Geo. B. Parks, Vice-President, Production
and Drilling Operations
Jack W. Roach, Vice-President, Crude Oil
Supply, Pipelines, and Refinery
Technical Services
Hubert H. Raborn, Secretary and
Treasurer
S. B. Robinson, Assistant Secretary and
Assistant Treasurer
W. O. Holdren, Assistant Secretary and
Assistant Treasurer
J. H. Lollar, Jr., Assistant Secretary and
Assistant Treasurer

1958–59

Board of Directors

J. D. Blosser
Edwin L. Kennedy
Breene M. Kerr
Robert S. Kerr
Robert S. Kerr, Jr.
T. M. Kerr
Guy C. Kiddoo

J. H. Lollar, Jr.
F. C. Love
D. A. McGee
J. B. Saunders
Frederick W. Straus
Dean Terrill
James E. Webb

Executive Committee

Robert S. Kerr, Chairman
Guy C. Kiddoo
F. C. Love
D. A. McGee
Frederick W. Straus

Officers

Robert S. Kerr, Chairman of the Board
D. A. McGee, President
T. M. Kerr, Vice-Chairman of the Board
F. C. Love, Executive Vice-President
J. B. Saunders, Senior Vice-President
L. A. Woodward, Administrative
Vice-President
A. T. F. Seale, Vice-President, Operations
Lynn Adams, Vice-President and General
Counsel
R. M. Chesney, Vice-President, Refining
W. H. Doyle, Vice-President, Branded
Marketing
J. C. Finley, Vice-President, Foreign
Exploration
J. J. Kelly, Vice-President

G. B. Kitchel, Vice-President, Drilling
Contracts
W. M. Murray, Vice-President, General
Sales
George B. Parks, Vice-President,
Production and Drilling Operations
Jack W. Roach, Vice-President, Staff
Assistant to the President
Hubert H. Raborn, Treasurer and
Assistant Secretary
S. B. Robinson, Secretary and Assistant
Treasurer
W. O. Holdren, Assistant Secretary and
Assistant Treasurer
J. H. Lollar, Jr., Assistant Secretary and
Assistant Treasurer

1960

Board of Directors

J. D. Blosser
Edwin L. Kennedy
Breene M. Kerr
Robert S. Kerr
Robert S. Kerr, Jr.
T. M. Kerr
Guy C. Kiddoo

J. H. Lollar, Jr.
F. C. Love
D. A. McGee
J. B. Saunders
Frederick W. Straus
Dean Terrill
James E. Webb

Executive Committee

Robert S. Kerr, Chairman
Guy C. Kiddoo
F. C. Love
D. A. McGee
Frederick W. Straus

Officers

Robert S. Kerr, Chairman of the Board
D. A. McGee, President
T. M. Kerr, Vice-Chairman of the Board
F. C. Love, Executive Vice-President
J. B. Saunders, Senior Vice-President
L. A. Woodward, Administrative
Vice-President
A. T. F. Seale, Vice-President, Operations
G. H. Cobb, Vice-President, Exploration
and Minerals
Lynn Adams, Vice-President and General
Counsel
R. M. Chesney, Vice-President, Refining
W. H. Doyle, Vice-President, Branded
Marketing
J. C. Finley, Vice-President, Foreign
Exploration

J. J. Kelly, Vice-President
G. B. Kitchel, Vice-President, Drilling
Contracts
W. M. Murray, Vice-President, Assistant to
Senior Vice President
George B. Parks, Vice-President,
Production and Drilling Operations
Jack W. Roach, Vice-President, Personnel
Hubert H. Raborn, Treasurer and
Assistant Secretary
S. B. Robinson, Secretary and Assistant
Treasurer
D. A. Watkins, Controller
W. O. Holdren, Assistant Secretary and
Assistant Treasurer
J. H. Lollar, Jr., Assistant Secretary and
Assistant Treasurer

1961

Board of Directors

J. D. Blosser
Grady D. Harris, Jr.
Edwin L. Kennedy
Breene M. Kerr
Robert S. Kerr
Robert S. Kerr, Jr.
T. M. Kerr
Guy C. Kiddoo

J. H. Lollar, Jr.
F. C. Love
D. A. McGee
J. B. Saunders
A. T. F. Seale
Frederick W. Straus
Dean Terrill

Executive Committee

Robert S. Kerr, Chairman
Guy C. Kiddoo
F. C. Love
D. A. McGee
Frederick W. Straus

Officers

Robert S. Kerr, Chairman of the Board
D. A. McGee, President
T. M. Kerr, Vice-Chairman of the Board
F. C. Love, Executive Vice-President
J. B. Saunders, Senior Vice-President
L. A. Woodward, Administrative
Vice-President
A. T. F. Seale, Vice-President, Operations
Lynn Adams, Vice-President and General
Counsel
R. M. Chesney, Vice-President, Refining
G. H. Cobb, Vice-President, Minerals
W. H. Doyle, Vice-President, Branded
Marketing
J. C. Finley, Vice-President, Assistant
Manager Oil & Gas Exploration
J. J. Kelly, Vice-President and Executive
Assistant to President

G. B. Kitchel, Vice President, Drilling
Contracts
W. M. Murray, Vice President and
Assistant to Senior Vice-President
George B. Parks, Vice-President, Oil &
Gas Exploration
Hubert H. Raborn, Vice-President and
General Manager, Marketing
Jack W. Roach, Vice-President, Personnel
S. B. Robinson, Secretary and Assistant
Treasurer
D. A. Watkins, Treasurer and Assistant
Secretary
P. A. Puttroff, Controller
W. O. Holdren, Assistant Secretary and
Assistant Treasurer
J. H. Lollar, Jr., Assistant Secretary and
Assistant Treasurer

1962

Board of Directors

J. D. Blosser
Grady D. Harris, Jr.
Edwin L. Kennedy
Breene M. Kerr
Robert S. Kerr
Robert S. Kerr, Jr.
T. M. Kerr
Guy C. Kiddoo
J. H. Lollar, Jr.
F. C. Love
D. A. McGee
J. B. Saunders
A. T. F. Seale
Frederick W. Straus
Dean Terrill

Executive Committee

Robert S. Kerr, Chairman
Guy C. Kiddoo
F. C. Love
D. A. McGee
Frederick W. Straus

Officers

Robert S. Kerr, Chairman of the Board
D. A. McGee, President
T. M. Kerr, Vice-Chairman of the Board
F. C. Love, Executive Vice-President
J. B. Saunders, Senior Vice-President
L. A. Woodward, Administrative Vice-President
A. T. F. Seale, Vice-President, Operations
G. H. Cobb, Vice-President, Minerals
Lynn Adams, Vice-President and General Counsel
R. M. Chesney, Vice-President, Refining
J. C. Finley, Vice-President and Assistant Manager, Oil and Gas Exploration
J. J. Kelly, Vice-President and Executive Assistant to the President

G. B. Kitchel, Vice-President, Drilling Contracts
George B. Parks, Vice-President, Oil and Gas Exploration and Production
Hubert H. Raborn, Vice-President and General Manager, Marketing
Jack W. Roach, Vice-President, Personnel
S. B. Robinson, Secretary and Assistant Treasurer
D. A. Watkins, Treasurer and Assistant Secretary
P. A. Puttroff, Controller
W. O. Holdren, Assistant Secretary and Assistant Treasurer
J. H. Lollar, Jr., Assistant Secretary and Assistant Treasurer

1963

Board of Directors

Grady D. Harris, Jr.
Edwin L. Kennedy
Breene M. Kerr
Robert S. Kerr, Jr.
T. M. Kerr
Guy C. Kiddoo
F. C. Love
D. A. McGee
J. B. Saunders
A. T. F. Seale
F. W. Straus
Dean Terrill

Executive Committee

Guy C. Kiddoo
F. C. Love
D. A. McGee
Frederick W. Straus
J. B. Saunders

Officers

D. A. McGee, President and Chairman of the Board
T. M. Kerr, Vice-Chairman of the Board
F. C. Love, Executive Vice-President
J. B. Saunders, Senior Vice-President
A. T. F. Seale, Vice-President, Oil and Gas Division
L. A. Woodward, Administrative Vice-President
G. H. Cobb, Vice-President, Minerals Division
Hubert H. Raborn, Vice-President, Marketing, Pipeline, and Refining Division
Lynn Adams, Vice-President, General Counsel, and Secretary

M. F. Bolton, Vice-President, Minerals Operations
R. M. Chesney, Vice-President, Refining
J. C. Finley, Vice-President, Oil and Gas Exploration
J. J. Kelly, Vice-President and Executive Assistant to the President
G. B. Kitchel, Vice-President, Drilling Contracts
R. M. Knox, Vice-President, Petroleum Marketing
V. L. Mattson, Vice-President, Research and Development
George B. Parks, Vice-President, Oil and Gas Operations
Jack W. Roach, Vice-President, Personnel

S. B. Robinson, Administrative Assistant
to the President, Assistant Secretary,
and Assistant Treasurer
D. A. Watkins, Treasurer and Assistant
Secretary

P. A. Puttroff, Controller
W. O. Holdren, Assistant Secretary and
Assistant Treasurer
R. D. Robins, Assistant Secretary

1964

Directors

Grady D. Harris, Jr.	F. C. Love	
Edwin L. Kennedy	D. A. McGee	
Breene M. Kerr	J. B. Saunders	
Robert S. Kerr, Jr.	A. T. F. Seale	
T. M. Kerr	F. W. Straus	
Guy C. Kiddoo	Dean Terrill	

Executive Committee
Guy C. Kiddoo
F. C. Love
D. A. McGee
J. B. Saunders
Frederick W. Straus

Officers

D. A. McGee, President and Chairman of
the Board
T. M. Kerr, Vice-Chairman of the Board
F. C. Love, Executive Vice-President
J. B. Saunders, Senior Vice-President
A. T. F. Seale, Vice-President, Operations
Division
L. A. Woodward, Administrative
Vice-President
G. H. Cobb, Vice-President, Exploration
and Research Division
Hubert H. Raborn, Vice-President,
Marketing, Pipeline, and Refining
Division
Lynn Adams, Vice-President, General
Counsel and Secretary
M. F. Bolton, Vice-President, Minerals
Operations
Edward C. Borrego, Vice-President,
International Development
R. M. Chesney, Vice-President, Refining

J. C. Finley, Vice-President, Oil and Gas
Exploration
J. J. Kelly, Vice-President and Executive
Assistant to the President
G. B. Kitchel, Vice-President, Drilling
Contracts
R. M. Knox, Vice-President, Petroleum
Marketing
V. L. Mattson, Vice-President and
Technical Adviser to the President
George B. Parks, Vice-President, Oil and
Gas Operations
Jack W. Roach, Vice-President, Personnel
S. B. Robinson, Administrative Assistant
to the President, Assistant Secretary,
and Assistant Treasurer
D. A. Watkins, Treasurer and Assistant
Secretary
P. A. Puttroff, Controller
W. O. Holdren, Assistant Secretary and
Assistant Treasurer
R. D. Robins, Assistant Secretary

1965
(June 30)

Directors

Grady D. Harris, Jr.	*F. C. Love
Edwin L. Kennedy	*D. A. McGee
Breene M. Kerr	*J. B. Saunders
Robert S. Kerr, Jr.	A. T. F. Seale
T. M. Kerr	*F. W. Straus
*Guy C. Kiddoo	Dean Terrill

*Members of Executive Committee.

Officers
D. A. McGee, President and Chairman of
the Board
F. C. Love, Executive Vice-President
J. B. Saunders, Executive Vice-President
A. T. F. Seale, Vice-President, Operations
L. A. Woodward, Financial Vice-President
George H. Cobb, Vice-President,
Exploration and Research Division
H. H. Raborn, Vice-President, Marketing,
Pipeline, and Refining Division
T. M. Kerr, Vice-President
Lynn Adams, Vice-President, General
Counsel and Secretary
M. F. Bolton, Vice-President, Plant Food
Manufacturing Division
Edward C. Borrego, Vice-President,
International Development
R. M. Chesney, Vice-President, Refining
J. C. Finley, Vice-President, Foreign
Exploration

W. E. Jaqua, Vice-President, Plant Food
Marketing Division
E. R. Jones, Vice-President, Industrial
Products Division
J. J. Kelly, Vice-President, Corporate
Transportation and Purchasing
G. B. Kitchel, Vice-President, Drilling
Contracts
R. M. Knox, Vice-President, Petroleum
Marketing
V. L. Mattson, Vice-President and
Technical Adviser to the President
George B. Parks, Vice-President, Oil and
Gas Division
Jack W. Roach, Vice-President, Personnel
S. B. Robinson, Administrative Assistant
to the President, Assistant Secretary,
and Assistant Treasurer
D. A. Watkins, Treasurer and Assistant
Secretary
P. A. Puttroff, Controller

Subsidiary Presidents
J. H. Barksdale, President, Triangle
Refineries, Inc.
Claude C. Huffman, President, Cato Oil
and Grease Co.
Meyer Levy, President, Moss-American,
Inc.

1965
(December 31)
(Kerr-McGee Corporation)

Directors
Grady D. Harris, Jr.
Edwin L. Kennedy
Breene M. Kerr
Robert S. Kerr, Jr.
T. M. Kerr
*Guy C. Kiddoo

*F. C. Love
*D. A. McGee
*J. B. Saunders
A. T. F. Seale
*F. W. Straus
Dean Terrill

*Member of Executive Committee.

Officers
D. A. McGee, President and Chairman of
the Board
F. C. Love, Executive Vice-President
J. B. Saunders, Executive Vice-President
A. T. F. Seale, Vice-President, Operations
L. A. Woodward, Financial Vice-President
George H. Cobb, Vice-President,
Exploration and Research Division
H. H. Raborn, General Vice-President
T. M. Kerr, Vice-President
Lynn Adams, Vice-President, General
Counsel and Secretary
M. F. Bolton, Vice-President, Plant Food
Manufacturing Division

Edward C. Borrego, Vice-President,
International Development
R. M. Chesney, Vice-President, Special
Projects
J. C. Finley, Vice-President, Foreign
Exploration
George C. Hardin, Jr., Vice-President,
North American Oil & Gas Exploration
J. J. Kelly, Vice-President, Corporate
Transportation and Purchasing
G. B. Kitchel, Vice-President, Drilling
Contracts
R. M. Knox, Vice-President, Marketing,
Pipeline, and Refining Division

V. L. Mattson, Vice-President and
Technical Adviser to the President
George B. Parks, Vice-President, Oil and
Gas Division
Jack W. Roach, Vice-President, Personnel
S. B. Robinson, Administrative Assistant

to the President, Assistant Secretary,
and Assistant Treasurer
D. A. Watkins, Treasurer and Assistant
Secretary
P. A. Puttroff, Controller

Chief Operating Officers of Subsidiaries
J. H. Barksdale, President, Triangle
Refineries, Inc.
Claude C. Huffman, President, Cato Oil
and Grease Co.
W. E. Jaqua, Executive Vice-President,

Kerr-McGee Chemical Corp.
E. R. Jones, President, The Hubbard-Hall
Chemical Company
Meyer Levy, President, Moss-American,
Inc.

1966

Directors
Grady D. Harris, Jr.
Edwin L. Kennedy
Breene M. Kerr
Robert S. Kerr, Jr.
T. M. Kerr
*Guy C. Kiddoo

*F. C. Love
*D. A. McGee
*J. B. Saunders
A. T. F. Seale
*F. W. Straus
Dean Terrill

*Member of the Executive Committee.

Officers
D. A. McGee, President and Chairman of
the Board
F. C. Love, Executive Vice-President
J. B. Saunders, Executive Vice-President
A. T. F. Seale, Vice-President, Operations
L. A. Woodward, Financial Vice-President
George H. Cobb, Vice-President,
Exploration and Research Division
H. H. Raborn, General Vice-President;
President, Kerr-McGee Chemical Corp.
T. M. Kerr, Vice-President
Lynn Adams, Vice-President, General
Counsel and Secretary
M. F. Bolton, Vice-President, Plant Food
Manufacturing Division
Edward C. Borrego, Vice-President,
Personnel
R. M. Chesney, Vice-President, Buildings
J. C. Finley, Vice-President, Foreign
Exploration
George C. Hardin, Jr., Vice-President,
North American Oil & Gas Exploration

J. J. Kelly, Vice-President, Corporate
Transportation and Purchasing
G. B. Kitchel, Vice-President, Drilling
Contracts
R. M. Knox, Vice-President, Marketing,
Pipeline, and Refining Division
V. L. Mattson, Vice-President and
Technical Adviser to the President
George B. Parks, Vice-President;
President, Transworld Drilling
Company
Jack W. Roach, Vice-President, Chemicals
S. B. Robinson, Administrative Assistant
to the President, Assistant Secretary,
and Assistant Treasurer
D. A. Watkins, Treasurer and Assistant
Secretary
P. A. Puttroff, Controller
William E. Heimann, Assistant Secretary
and General Attorney
R. D. Robins, Assistant Secretary and
Assistant Treasurer
Carter G. Dudley, Assistant Secretary

Chief Operating Officers of Subsidiaries
J. H. Barksdale, President, Triangle
Refineries, Inc.
Claude C. Huffman, President, Cato Oil
and Grease Co.
Meyer Levy, Chairman of the Board,

Moss-American, Inc.
George B. Parks, President, Transworld
Drilling Company
H. H. Raborn, President, Kerr-McGee
Chemical Corp.

Directors

Lloyd L. Austin
Peter Colefax
Grady D. Harris, Jr.
Earle M. Jorgensen
*Edwin L. Kennedy
Breene M. Kerr
Robert S. Kerr, Jr.

T. M. Kerr
*Guy C. Kiddoo
*F. C. Love
*D. A. McGee
*J. B. Saunders
A. T. F. Seale
Dean Terrill

*Member of Executive Committee.

Officers

D. A. McGee, Chairman of the Board and Chief Executive Officer
F. C. Love, President
J. B. Saunders, Executive Vice-President
George H. Cobb, Senior Vice-President
H. H. Raborn, Senior Vice-President
A. T. F. Seale, Senior Vice-President
L. A. Woodward, Senior Vice-President
Lynn Adams, Vice-President, General Counsel and Secretary
Edward C. Borrego, Vice-President, Personnel
R. M. Chesney, Vice-President; Vice President, Kerr-McGee Building Corporation
J. C. Finley, Vice-President; Geological Adviser
Dr. R. M. Fryar, Vice-President, Nuclear Division
George C. Hardin, Jr., Vice-President, Exploration
J. J. Kelly, Vice-President; President,

Kerr-McGee Chemical Corp.
G. B. Kitchel, Vice-President, Drilling Contracts
R. M. Knox, Vice-President, Petroleum Marketing-Refining Division
V. L. Mattson, Vice-President and Technical Adviser to the Chairman
George B. Parks, Vice-President; President, Transworld Drilling Company
Jack W. Roach, Vice-President, Chemicals
S. B. Robinson, Administrative Assistant to the Chairman, Assistant Secretary, and Assistant Treasurer
D. A. Watkins, Treasurer and Assistant Secretary
P. A. Puttroff, Controller
William E. Heimann, Assistant Secretary and General Attorney
R. D. Robins, Assistant Secretary and Assistant Treasurer
Carter G. Dudley, Assistant Secretary

Chief Operating Officers of Subsidiaries

J. H. Barksdale, President, Triangle Refineries, Inc.
Peter Colefax, Chairman of the Board, American Potash & Chemical Corporation
J. J. Kelly, President, Kerr-McGee Chemical Corp.
Meyer Levy, Chairman of the Board, Moss-American, Inc.
Leon M. Oswalt, President, Cato Oil and Grease Co.
George B. Parks, President, Transworld Drilling Company

510

Directors

Peter Colefax
Grady D. Harris, Jr.
Earle M. Jorgensen
*Edwin L. Kennedy
Breene M. Kerr
Robert S. Kerr, Jr.
T. M. Kerr

*Guy C. Kiddoo
*F. C. Love
*D. A. McGee
*J. B. Saunders
A. T. F. Seale
Dean Terrill
James E. Webb

*Member of Executive Committee.

Officers

D. A. McGee, Chairman of the Board and Chief Executive Officer
F. C. Love, President
J. B. Saunders, Vice-Chairman of the Board
George H. Cobb, Senior Vice-President
H. H. Raborn, Senior Vice-President, Finance and Administration
A. T. F. Seale, Senior Vice-President
L. A. Woodward, Senior Vice-President
Willard P. Scott, Vice-President, General Counsel and Secretary
J. H. Barksdale, Group Vice-President, Petroleum Marketing, Pipeline, and Refining Operations
Parker S. Dunn, Group Vice-President
R. M. Fryar, Group Vice-President, Nuclear Operations
James J. Kelly, Group Vice-President, Chemical Marketing Operations
C. F. Miller, Group Vice-President, Oil and Gas Operations
George B. Parks, Group Vice-President, Drilling Operations
Edward C. Borrego, Vice-President, International Development
R. M. Chesney, Vice-President

J. C. Finley, Vice-President
A. R. Gockel, Vice-President, Petroleum Marketing, Pipeline, and Refining Division
R. J. Hefler, Vice-President
G. B. Kitchel, Vice-President, Drilling Contracts
V. L. Mattson, Vice-President, Research
P. A. Puttroff, Vice-President, Personnel
Homer C. Reed, Vice-President, Engineering
Jack W. Roach, Vice-President, Hydrocarbon Development
S. B. Robinson, Administrative Assistant to the Chairman, Assistant Secretary, and Assistant Treasurer
D. A. Watkins, Treasurer and Assistant Secretary
J. D. Raunborg, Controller
William E. Heimann, General Attorney and Assistant Secretary
R. D. Robins, Assistant Secretary, Assistant Treasurer, and Tax Director
Powell O. Morgan, Assistant Treasurer, Banking and Credit
Carter G. Dudley, Assistant Secretary

Chief Operating Officers of Subsidiaries

J. H. Barksdale, President, Triangle Refineries, Inc.
Parker S. Dunn, President, American Potash & Chemical Corporation
James J. Kelly, President, Kerr-McGee Chemical Corp.
I. C. Miller, President, Moss-American, Inc.
Leon M. Oswalt, President, Cato Oil and Grease Co.
George B. Parks, President, Transworld Drilling Company

Directors
Peter Colefax
Grady D. Harris, Jr.
Earle M. Jorgensen
*Edwin L. Kennedy
Breene M. Kerr
Robert S. Kerr, Jr.
T. M. Kerr

*Guy C. Kiddoo
*F. C. Love
*D. A. McGee
*J. B. Saunders
A. T. F. Seale
Dean Terrill
James E. Webb

*Member of Executive Committee.

Officers
D. A. McGee, Chairman of the Board and
Chief Executive Officer
F. C. Love, President
J. B. Saunders, Vice-Chairman of the
Board
George H. Cobb, Senior Vice-President
H. H. Raborn, Senior Vice-President,
Finance and Administration
A. T. F. Seale, Senior Vice-President
L. A. Woodward, Senior Vice-President
Willard P. Scott, Vice-President, General
Counsel, and Secretary
J. H. Barksdale, Group Vice-President,
Petroleum Marketing, Pipeline, and
Refining Operations
Willard F. Bunker, Group Vice-President,
Exploration
Parker S. Dunn, Group Vice-President
R. M. Fryar, Group Vice-President,
Nuclear Operations
James J. Kelly, Group Vice-President,
Chemical Marketing Operations
C. F. Miller, Group Vice-President, Oil
and Gas Operations
George B. Parks, Group Vice-President,
Drilling Operations
Edward C. Borrego, Vice-President,
International Development
R. M. Chesney, Vice-President
J. C. Finley, Vice-President
A. R. Gockel, Vice-President, Petroleum

Marketing, Pipeline and Refining
Division
R. J. Hefler, Vice-President
G. B. Kitchel, Vice-President, Drilling
Contracts
Harold J. Kleen, Vice-President, Minerals
Exploration Division
Jere W. McKenny, Vice-President, Oil
and Gas Exploration Division
V. L. Mattson, Vice-President
P. A. Puttroff, Vice-President, Personnel
Homer C. Reed, Vice-President,
Technical Division
Jack W. Roach, Vice-President,
Hydrocarbon Development
J. L. Robison, Vice-President, Uranium
Mining and Milling Division
B. G. Taylor, Vice-President, Oil and Gas
Production Division
S. B. Robinson, Special Assistant to the
Chairman, Assistant Secretary and
Assistant Treasurer
D. A. Watkins, Treasurer and Assistant
Secretary
J. D. Raunborg, Controller
William E. Heimann, General Attorney
and Assistant Secretary
R. D. Robins, Assistant Secretary,
Assistant Treasurer and Tax Director
Powell O. Morgan, Assistant Treasurer,
Banking and Credit
Carter G. Dudley, Assistant Secretary

Chief Operating Officers of Subsidiaries
J. H. Barksdale, President, Triangle
Refineries, Inc.
James J. Kelly, President, American
Potash & Chemical Corporation and
Kerr-McGee Chemical Corp.
I. C. Miller, President, Moss-American,
Inc.
Leon M. Oswalt, President, Cato Oil and
Grease Co.
George B. Parks, Chairman of the Board
and Chief Executive Officer, Transworld
Drilling Company

Directors

Peter Colefax
Grady D. Harris, Jr.
Earle M. Jorgensen
*Edwin L. Kennedy
Breene M. Kerr
Robert S. Kerr, Jr.
*Guy C. Kiddoo

*F. C. Love
*D. A. McGee
*J. B. Saunders
A. T. F. Seale
Dean Terrill
James E. Webb

*Member of Executive Committee.

Officers

D. A. McGee, Chairman of the Board and Chief Executive Officer
F. C. Love, President
James J. Kelly, Executive Vice-President
George B. Parks, Executive Vice-President
J. B. Saunders, Vice-Chairman of the Board
George H. Cobb, Senior Vice-President
A. T. F. Seale, Senior Vice-President
L. A. Woodward, Senior Vice-President, Finance
Willard P. Scott, Vice-President, General Counsel and Secretary
J. H. Barksdale, Group Vice-President, Petroleum Marketing, Pipeline and Refining Operations
Willard F. Bunker, Group Vice-President, Exploration
Parker S. Dunn, Group Vice-President, Nuclear Operations
C. F. Miller, Group Vice-President, Oil and Gas Operations
Edward C. Borrego, Vice-President, International Development
R. M. Chesney, Vice-President
L. E. Craig, Vice-President, Information Services
J. C. Finley, Vice-President
A. R. Gockel, Vice-President, Petroleum Marketing, Pipeline and Refining Division

R. J. Hefler, Vice-President, Executive Assistant to Chairman
G. B. Kitchel, Vice-President, Drilling Contracts
Harold J. Kleen, Vice-President, Minerals Exploration Division
Jere W. McKenny, Vice-President, Oil and Gas Exploration Division
V. L. Mattson, Vice-President
P. A. Puttroff, Vice-President, Administration
Homer C. Reed, Vice-President, Technical Division
Jack W. Roach, Vice-President, Hydrocarbon Development
B. G. Taylor, Vice-President, Oil and Gas Production Division
D. A. Watkins, Vice-President, Treasurer, and Assistant Secretary
J. D. Raunborg, Controller
S. B. Robinson, Special Assistant to the Chairman, Assistant Secretary and Assistant Treasurer
William E. Heimann, General Attorney and Assistant Secretary
R. D. Robins, Assistant Secretary, Assistant Treasurer, and Tax Director
Powell O. Morgan, Assistant Treasurer, Banking and Credit
Carter G. Dudley, Assistant Secretary

Chief Executive Officers of Subsidiaries

J. H. Barksdale, President, Triangle Refineries, Inc.
James J. Kelly, President, Kerr-McGee Chemical Corp.
I. C. Miller, President, Moss-American, Inc.
Leon M. Oswalt, President, Cato Oil and Grease Co.
George B. Parks, Chairman of the Board, Transworld Drilling Company

513

1971

Directors
Peter Colefax
Grady D. Harris, Jr.
Earle M. Jorgensen
*Edwin L. Kennedy
Breene M. Kerr
Robert S. Kerr, Jr.
*Guy C. Kiddoo

*F. C. Love
*D. A. McGee
*J. B. Saunders
A. T. F. Seale
Dean Terrill
James E. Webb

*Member of Executive Committee.

Officers
D. A. McGee, Chairman of the Board and Chief Executive Officer
F. C. Love, President
J. B. Saunders, Vice-Chairman of the Board Until Retirement August 1, 1971
George H. Cobb, Executive Vice-President
James J. Kelly, Executive Vice-President
George B. Parks, Executive Vice-President
A. T. F. Seale, Senior Vice-President
Willard P. Scott, Vice-President, General Counsel and Secretary
J. H. Barksdale, Group Vice-President, Petroleum Marketing, Pipeline and Refining Operations
Willard F. Bunker, Group Vice-President, Exploration
Parker S. Dunn, Group Vice-President, Nuclear Operations
C. F. Miller, Group Vice-President, Oil and Gas Operations
R. M. Chesney, Vice-President
A. R. Gockel, Vice-President, Petroleum Marketing, Pipeline and Refining Division
R. J. Hefler, Vice-President, Executive Assistant to the President
G. B. Kitchel, Vice-President, Drilling Contracts

Harold J. Kleen, Vice-President, Minerals Exploration Division
Jere W. McKenny, Vice-President, Oil and Gas Exploration Division
Leon Oswalt, Vice-President, Petroleum Marketing
P. A. Puttroff, Vice-President, Administration
Homer C. Reed, Vice-President
Jack W. Roach, Vice-President, Hydrocarbon Development
B. G. Taylor, Vice-President, Oil and Gas Production Division
D. A. Watkins, Vice-President, Treasurer, and Assistant Secretary
J. D. Raunborg, Controller
S. B. Robinson, Special Assistant to the Chairman, Assistant Secretary and Assistant Treasurer
William E. Heimann, General Attorney and Assistant Secretary
R. D. Robins, Assistant Secretary, Assistant Treasurer and Tax Director
Powell O. Morgan, Assistant Treasurer, Banking and Credit
Carter G. Dudley, Assistant Secretary
Elizabeth Zoernig, Assistant Secretary

Chief Executive Officers of Subsidiaries
J. H. Barksdale, President, Triangle Refineries, Inc.
James J. Kelly, President, Kerr-McGee Chemical Corp.
I. C. Miller, President, Moss-American, Inc.
Ralph Jenks, President, Cato Oil and Grease Co.
George B. Parks, Chairman of the Board, Transworld Drilling Company

Directors

Peter Colefax
Grady D. Harris, Jr.
Earle M. Jorgensen
*James J. Kelly
*Edwin L. Kennedy
Breene M. Kerr
Robert S. Kerr, Jr.
F. C. Love

*D. A. McGee
*George B. Parks
J. B. Saunders
A. T. F. Seale
*James E. Webb
Dean Terrill
Guy C. Kiddoo

*Member of Executive Committee.

Officers

D. A. McGee, Chairman of the Board and Chief Executive Officer
James J. Kelly, President and Chief Operating Officer
J. H. Barksdale, Executive Vice-President
George H. Cobb, Executive Vice-President
George B. Parks, Executive Vice-President
Willard P. Scott, Vice-President, Finance, and Secretary
Marion F. Bolton, Vice-President, Safety and Environmental Services
R. M. Chesney, Vice-President, Operational Services
Parker S. Dunn, Vice-President, Nuclear Manufacturing
A. R. Gockel, Vice-President, Petroleum Marketing and Refining
R. J. Hefler, Vice-President, Corporate Services
William E. Heimann, Vice-President, General Counsel, and Assistant Secretary
G. B. Kitchel, Vice-President, Drilling Contracts
Harold J. Kleen, Vice-President, Minerals Exploration

Jere W. McKenny, Vice-President, Oil and Gas Exploration
C. F. Miller, Vice-President, Oil and Gas Operations
Leon Oswalt, Vice-President, Petroleum Marketing
P. A. Puttroff, Vice-President, Administration
Homer C. Reed, Vice-President, Refining Projects
B. G. Taylor, Vice-President, Oil and Gas Production
D. A. Watkins, Vice-President, Treasurer, and Assistant Secretary
R. T. Zitting, Vice-President, Minerals Operations
Carter G. Dudley, Assistant Secretary
Powell O. Morgan, Assistant Treasurer, Banking and Credit
J. D. Raunborg, Controller
R. D. Robins, Assistant Secretary, Assistant Treasurer, and Tax Director
S. B. Robinson, Special Assistant to the Chairman, Assistant Secretary, and Assistant Treasurer
Elizabeth Zoernig, Assistant Secretary

Chief Executive Officers of Subsidiaries
J. H. Barksdale, Chairman of the Board, Triangle Refineries, Inc.
Wm. J. F. Francis, President, Kerr-McGee Chemical Corp.
I. C. Miller, President, Moss-American, Inc.
Ralph Jenks, President, Cato Oil and Grease Co.
George B. Parks, Chairman of the Board, Transworld Drilling Company

1973

Directors
 Peter Colefax
 Grady D. Harris, Jr.
 Earle M. Jorgensen
 *James J. Kelly
 *Edwin L. Kennedy
 Breene M. Kerr
 Robert S. Kerr, Jr.

 F. C. Love
 *D. A. McGee
 *George B. Parks
 J. B. Saunders
 A. T. F. Seale
 *James E. Webb

*Member of Executive Committee.

Officers
 D. A. McGee, Chairman of the Board
 and Chief Executive Officer
 James J. Kelly, President and Chief
 Operating Officer
 *J. H. Barksdale, Executive
 Vice-President
 George H. Cobb, Executive
 Vice-President
 **George B. Parks, Executive
 Vice-President
 Willard P. Scott, Senior Vice-President
 and Secretary
 Marion F. Bolton, Vice-President,
 Safety and Environmental Services
 R. M. Chesney, Vice-President,
 Operational Services
 Parker S. Dunn, Vice-President,
 Nuclear Manufacturing
 A. R. Gockel, Vice-President,
 Petroleum Marketing and Refining
 M. K. Hambrick, Vice-President,
 Finance
 R. J. Hefler, Vice-President, Corporate
 Services
 William E. Heimann, Vice-President,
 General Counsel, and Assistant
 Secretary

 G. B. Kitchel, Vice-President, Drilling
 Contracts
 Harold J. Kleen, Vice-President,
 Minerals Exploration
 Jere W. McKenny, Vice-President, Oil
 and Gas Exploration
 C. F. Miller, Vice-President, Oil and
 Gas Operations
 Leon M. Oswalt, Vice-President,
 Petroleum Marketing
 P. A. Puttroff, Vice-President,
 Administration
 B. G. Taylor, Vice-President, Oil and
 Gas Production
 D. A. Watkins, Vice-President,
 Treasurer, and Assistant Secretary
 R. T. Zitting, Vice-President, Minerals
 Operations
 Carter G. Dudley, Assistant Secretary
 Powell O. Morgan, Assistant Treasurer,
 Banking and Credit
 J. D. Raunborg, Controller
 R. D. Robins, Assistant Secretary,
 Assistant Treasurer, and Tax Director
 S. B. Robinson, Special Assistant to the
 Chairman, Assistant Secretary, and
 Assistant Treasurer
 Elizabeth Zoernig, Assistant Secretary

*Also Chief Executive Officer of Triangle
Refineries, Inc. and Southwestern
Refining Company, Inc.
**Also Chief Executive Officer of The
Transworld drilling companies

Presidents of Principal Subsidiaries
Wm. J. F. Francis, Kerr-McGee Chemical
 Corp.
Ralph Jenks, Cato Oil and Grease Co.
Frank A. McPherson, Kerr-McGee Coal
 Corporation
I. C. Miller, Moss-American, Inc.

Paul D. Romano, The Transworld drilling
 companies
S. S. Seltzer, Jr., Southwestern Refining
 Company, Inc.
C. D. Tinsley, Triangle Refineries, Inc.
R. T. Zitting, Kerr-McGee Nuclear
 Corporation

Directors

Peter Colefax
Earle M. Jorgensen
*James J. Kelly
*Edwin L. Kennedy
Breene M. Kerr
Robert S. Kerr, Jr.

F. C. Love
*D. A. McGee
*George B. Parks
J. B. Saunders
A. T. F. Seale
*James E. Webb

*Member of Executive Committee.

Officers

D. A. McGee, Chairman of the Board and Chief Executive Officer

James J. Kelly, President and Chief Operating Officer

George H. Cobb, Executive Vice-President

George B. Parks, Executive Vice-President

Marion F. Bolton, Vice-President, Copper Project

R. M. Chesney, Vice-President, Operational Services

A. R. Gockel, Vice-President, Petroleum Marketing and Refining

M. K. Hambrick, Vice-President, Finance

R. J. Hefler, Vice-President, Corporate Services

William E. Heimann, Vice-President, General Counsel, and Secretary

Jere W. McKenny, Vice-President, Exploration

C. F. Miller, Vice-President, Oil and Gas Operations

Leon M. Oswalt, Vice-President, Petroleum Marketing

P. A. Puttroff, Vice-President, Administration

B. G. Taylor, Vice-President, Oil and Gas Production

D. A. Watkins, Vice-President, Treasurer and Assistant Secretary

Carter G. Dudley, Assistant Secretary

Powell O. Morgan, Assistant Treasurer, Banking and Credit

J. D. Raunborg, Controller

R. D. Robins, Assistant Secretary, Assistant Treasurer, and Tax Director

Elizabeth Zoernig, Assistant Secretary

Presidents of Principal Subsidiaries

Wm. J. F. Francis, Kerr-McGee Chemical Corporation

Ralph Jenks, Cato Oil and Grease Co.

Frank A. McPherson, Kerr-McGee Coal Corporation

Paul D. Romano, The Transworld drilling companies

S. S. Seltzer, Jr., Southwestern Refining Company, Inc.

C. D. Tinsley, Triangle Refineries, Inc.

R. T. Zitting, Kerr-McGee Nuclear Corporation

Directors

Peter Colefax
Earle M. Jorgensen
*James J. Kelly
*Edwin L. Kennedy
Breene M. Kerr
Robert S. Kerr, Jr.

F. C. Love
*D. A. McGee
*George B. Parks
J. B. Saunders
A. T. F. Seale
*James E. Webb

*Member of Executive Committee.

Officers

D. A. McGee, Chairman of the Board and
Chief Executive Officer
James J. Kelly, President and Chief
Operating Officer
George H. Cobb, Executive
Vice-President
George B. Parks, Executive
Vice-President
Marion F. Bolton, Vice-President, Copper
Projects
Wm. J. F. Francis, Vice-President,
Chemical and Refining Operations
Marvin K. Hambrick, Vice-President,
Finance
Richard J. Hefler, Vice-President, Public
Services
William E. Heimann, Vice-President,
General Counsel, and Secretary

Jere W. McKenny, Vice-President,
Exploration
Frank A. McPherson, Vice-President, Coal
and Nuclear Operations
C. F. Miller, Vice-President, Oil and Gas
Operations
P. A. Puttroff, Vice-President, Corporate
Services
B. G. Taylor, Vice-President, Foreign Oil
and Gas Production
D. A. Watkins, Vice-President, Treasurer,
and Assistant Secretary
Carter G. Dudley, Assistant Secretary
John D. Raunborg, Controller
R. D. Robins, Assistant Secretary,
Assistant Treasurer, and Tax Director
Elizabeth Zoernig, Assistant Secretary

Presidents of Principal Subsidiaries

Ralph Jenks, Cato Oil and Grease Co.
McClaran Jordan, Kerr-McGee Refining
Corporation
Frank A. McPherson, Kerr-McGee Coal
Corporation
J. L. Rainey, Kerr-McGee Chemical
Corporation
Paul D. Romano, The Transworld drilling
companies
S. S. Seltzer, Jr., Southwestern Refining
Company, Inc.
C. D. Tinsley, Triangle Refineries, Inc.
R. T. Zitting, Kerr-McGee Nuclear
Corporation

Directors
Peter Colefax
Earle M. Jorgensen
*James J. Kelly
*Edwin L. Kennedy
Breene M. Kerr
Robert S. Kerr, Jr.
F. C. Love

*D. A. McGee
*Neil McKay
*George B. Parks
J. B. Saunders
A. T. F. Seale
*James E. Webb

*Member of Executive Committee.

Officers
D. A. McGee, Chairman of the Board and Chief Executive Officer
James J. Kelly, President and Chief Operating Officer
George B. Parks, Executive Vice-President
Marion F. Bolton, Vice-President, Copper Projects
Wm. J. F. Francis, Vice-President, Chemical and Refining Operations
Marvin K. Hambrick, Vice-President, Finance
Richard J. Hefler, Vice-President, Public Services
William E. Heimann, Vice-President, General Counsel, and Secretary

Jere W. McKenny, Vice-President, Exploration
Frank A. McPherson, Vice-President, Coal and Nuclear Operations
C. F. Miller, Vice-President, Oil and Gas Operations
P. A. Puttroff, Vice-President, Corporate Services
D. A. Watkins, Vice-President, Treasurer, and Assistant Secretary
John D. Raunborg, Controller
R. D. Robins, Assistant Secretary, Assistant Treasurer and Tax Director
Carter G. Dudley, Assistant Secretary
Elizabeth Zoernig, Assistant Secretary

Principal Operating Officers of Major Subsidiaries
R. A. Freels, President, Triangle Refineries, Inc.
McClaran Jordan, President, Kerr-McGee Refining Corporation
James J. Kelly, President, Sunningdale Oils Limited
Morgan Moore, President, Kerr-McGee Nuclear Corporation
Leon M. Oswalt, Chairman, Cato Oil and Grease Co.
J. L. Rainey, President, Kerr-McGee Chemical Corporation
James G. Randolph, President, Kerr-McGee Coal Corporation
Paul D. Romano, President, The Transworld drilling companies
S. S. Seltzer, Jr., President, Southwestern Refining Company, Inc.
R. T. Zitting, President, Kerr-McGee Resources Corporation

Directors
  Peter Colefax
  Earle M. Jorgensen
  *James J. Kelly
  *Edwin L. Kennedy
  Breene M. Kerr
  Robert S. Kerr, Jr.
  Frank C. Love
  *Dean A. McGee
  Glenn W. McGee

  Neil McKay
  Jere W. McKenny
  Frank A. McPherson
  William C. Morris
  *Dr. Bruce C. Murray
  *George B. Parks
  J. B. Saunders
  A. T. F. Seale
  *James E. Webb

*Member of the Executive Committee.

Officers
  Dean A. McGee, Chairman of the Board
    and Chief Executive Officer
  Jere W. McKenny, Vice-Chairman of the
    Board
  Frank A. McPherson, Vice-Chairman of
    the Board
  George B. Parks, Executive
    Vice-President
  Wm. J. F. Francis, Executive
    Vice-President
  Marvin K. Hambrick, Executive
    Vice-President, Finance

  William E. Heimann, Vice-President,
    General Counsel and Secretary
  Charles F. Miller, Vice-President, Oil and
    Gas Operations
  Paul A. Puttroff, Vice-President,
    Corporate Services
  Richard D. Robins, Vice-President,
    Treasurer, and Assistant Secretary
  John D. Raunborg, Controller
  Carter G. Dudley, Assistant Secretary
  Thomas B. Stephens, Assistant Treasurer
  Elizabeth Zoernig, Assistant Secretary

*Principal Operating Officers of Major
  Subsidiaries*
  Ray A. Freels, President, Triangle
    Refineries, Inc.
  McClaran Jordan, President, Kerr-McGee
    Refining Corporation
  Jere W. McKenny, President,
    Sunningdale Oils Limited
  Charles F. Miller, President, Kerr-McGee
    Oil (U.K.) Limited
  Morgan Moore, President, Kerr-McGee
    Nuclear Corporation
  Leon M. Oswalt, Chairman, Cato Oil and
    Grease Co.
  James L. Rainey, President, Kerr-McGee
    Chemical Corporation
  James G. Randolph, President,
    Kerr-McGee Coal Corporation
  Paul D. Romano, President, The
    Transworld drilling companies
  Samuel S. Seltzer, Jr., President,
    Southwestern Refining Company, Inc.

Notes on Sources

In documenting this work, I have been conscious of what happened to a friend who wrote the history of another well-known oil company: after his fully documented book was published, the company then destroyed the files upon which most of his citations rested. Because of the present organization of the Kerr-McGee records it would be almost impossible for the company to open its files to outside researchers; the current system of records retention also virtually guarantees that many, perhaps most, of the sources used in this study will eventually be destroyed. For these reasons the decision was made to cite only those that have the best chance for survival and retrieval. Noncompany references that are available and have been checked for accuracy and balance against company records are the ones that have been cited. In cases of doubt both are indicated. While this is not the most desirable method, it does seem the most logical and valuable.

As indicated in the Preface, I was permitted full access to corporation records. In total these are staggering in volume, but, as would be expected, most are of such a technical nature as to have little value to a project of this sort. The following categories have proved most useful. First, and primary, were the actions of the Kerr-McGee board of directors, the annual reports, and the various kinds of information required by the Securities and Exchange Commission and the New York Stock Exchange. Next were committee reports and internal publications such as *Kermac News*. Of the files of subsidiaries and departments those of the mineral lease records and lease records departments were of the most value for specific information. The public relations department, including the materials collected by Bette Brenz, has the best accumulation of general information dealing with the company's past. Included are the tapes and transcripts of the reminiscences of sixty-one early, long-term employees, which provide much of the personal flavor and, occasionally, the only details about some of the early events. Backstopping all these were the personal files of Dean McGee, where material missing from other repositories could often be found.

Newspapers, especially those of Oklahoma City, and trade publications, such as the *Oil and Gas Journal*, yielded much valuable information, especially for the early years. The Robert S. Kerr Collection in the Western History Collections at the University of Oklahoma is rich in detail concerning Kerr's personal life and his political career but has relatively little dealing with his businesses.

Two collections of state records proved useful. First was the "corporation file" maintained by the office of the Secretary of State of Oklahoma. It contained the many reports required from the corporation, as well as the incorporation papers of the various companies established by Kerr and his successors. Some of the files of that office have been deposited in the Oklahoma State Archives. Among these one entitled "Kerr-McGee *vs.* John Rogers" gives an extensive account of the firm's corporate history in Oklahoma.

Most disappointing was that many of the companies that had extensive dealings with Kerr-McGee could furnish little additional information. Either they had destroyed their records for that period or their filing systems were such as to negate profitable use. One notable exception was the First National Bank of Chicago, which has established its own archives. Its records were unique in providing significant light on and understanding of Kerr-McGee's early financial history.

The search for obscure facts that had been lost from the corporate memory led me into dusty files in many disparate locations; however, no holdings of sufficient size or importance were discovered to warrant inclusion here.

Index

Clifford, Clark: 236
Clinch River, breeder-reactor project at: 480
Clive field: 370
Cloverleaf Service Stations, Incorporated: 326, 371
Coal: uses of, 3; reserves of, 291, 336; mining and coking of, 338, 354, 363, 371, 376, 380; land for, 345, 414; rights to, 360; emphasis on, 363; success of, 375; Kerr-McGee first in, 379; market for, 380, 418, 455, 461, 473, 479, 490–91; export of, 385; exploration for, 388, 473; problems of, 398, 434; shipment of, 404; programs for, 409; profits in, 418; strip mining for, 420; environmental restraints on, 428; plants for, 429; delivery of, 432; discovery of, 454; and depletion allowance, 454; production of, 455, 457, 471, 490; supply of, 480
Coast Oil and Butane Company: 282
Coast Stations: 320
Cobb, George H.: 76, 86, 114, 154, 169, 182, 228, 231, 375, 416, 499, 505ff.
Cold war: 171, 221, 273
Colefax, Peter: 375, 510ff.
Coline Oil Company: 95
Collins, Foley: 24, 38–39, 40, 41–42, 46, 70
Colorado, oil and gas wells in: 78, 84, 116, 122, 126, 152, 179, 187, 207, 233, 303, 311, 327, 344, 370
Colorado School of Mines Research Foundation: 214, 228
Comer, J. C.: 42, 88
Commonwealth Edison: 351
Conflict of interest: 185–86, 250, 296, 301
Conscription: 103
Conservation: 120
Consumers Power Company: 394
Continental Oil Company: 13, 28, 32, 56, 57, 404; contracts with, 179, 194, 388, 484
Contract drilling: foreign, 303; success in, 464, 466; growth in, 473; wells in, 478; expanded, 484
Coolidge, Calvin: 13
Copper: exploration for, 319, 388, 427; leases on, 326; discovery of, 342, 378, 398; delivery of, 432; production of, 471

Corbett, James R.: 254
Corpus Christi refinery: 487
Cosco Refinery, purchase of: 123, 125
Cosden, J.S., Jr.: 125
Cosden, Mrs. J.S., Jr.: 126, 160
Costa Rica, wells in: 327
Cotton Valley refinery, output of: 487
Cotton Valley solvents, Incorporated: 282f.
Coughlin, Father Charles: 61
Cowden lease: 95
"Coyote man": 218
Craig, L. E.: 513
Crawford, B. Hayden: 289
Credit cards: 288
Creslenn Oil Company: 483 and n.
Crosbie, J. E.: see J. E. Crosbie, Incorporated
Crossties, production of: 414
Crude oil: production of, 222, 380; shortages of, 418, 422; reserves of, 475; processing of, 487; see also gas, gasoline, oil

Dambold #1: 28
Dangail Oil & Gas Company: 28
Danielson, Otis: 76, 154f., 162–63
Dare, W. L.: 220
DeArman, Henry J.: 57
DeArman, Tip: 57
DeArman Brothers Drilling Company: 57
DDT, banning of: 406
Dean, W. H.: 230
Deco Electronics: 319
Deep Rock Oil Company: 133, 232, 282, 305, 433; formation of, 231–32; assets of, 240; liquidation of, 253; upgrading of stations, 288; sales of, 311; service stations for, 487
Deep Rock Refinery: 253, 403
Deisobutanizer: 358, 371
Denmark, wells in: 431
Denver Producing & Refining Company: 21f., 28, 56
Depletion allowance: 453f.
Depression: see Great Depression
Desegregation: 329, 382
Diadem Oil: 57
Diesel fuel: increased consumption of, 204; by pipeline, 487
Dineh bi Keyah: wells at, 358f., 370, 380, 466, 481; anniversary of, 481

Santa Fe Drilling Company: 266n.

Saudi-Arabia-Kuwait-Neutral-Zone: 188

Saunders, James B.: 231, 250, 260, 275, 279, 315, 321, 326, 335, 366, 375, 378

Savings-investment plan: 468

Scholarships, Kerr-McGee program of: 329

Scotland, wells in: 431, 483

Scott, Francis W.: 116

Scott, Willard P.: 511ff.

Seale, A. T. F. ("Tom"): 157, 162, 165, 230, 250, 332, 504ff.

Searles, John W.: 369

Searles Lake: 143, 367, 369, 413, 417, 430, 461f., 489

Securities Act of 1923: 73

Securities and Exchange Commission (SEC): 55, 73, 102

Seismic surveys, on Atlantic coast: 380, 427

Seltzer, Samuel S., Jr.: 516ff.

Sequoyah plant: 394, 412, 429, 455, 488

Service stations: 133, 279, 282, 288, 293, 317, 326, 327–28, 333, 339, 400; Kerr-Lynn, 60; number of, 305, 371, 378, 380, 388, 433, 487

Shaffer Oil & Refining Company: 21

Shale, oil and gas from: 420, 422, 428

Sharjah, wells at: 408, 420, 423, 427f., 434, 436, 460, 465, 472, 475, 478, 483f

Shearson, Hammill & Company: 283

Sheldon Dome field: 126

Shell Oil Company: 57, 303, 388, 466

Shelton, Reba Kerr: 8ff.

Sherman Antitrust Act: 339

Shiprock, N.M.: uranium at, 216f., 228n., 237, 240, 277, 281, 287; barbecue at, 216, 220; sale of, 315–16

Ships, for offshore drilling: 163–64, 188, 223

Ship Shoal: 139f., 155, 187, 190, 208, 266, 290f., 310, 324, 332, 364, 370, 376, 378, 380, 385, 396, 405, 413, 420, 421, 462

Shirley Basin: 296, 298, 385, 412, 456

Shop 'n Gas: 254 and n.

Shriver, Sargent: 406

Sierra Club, litigation by: 434

Signal Oil, contracts with: 188

Silkwood, Karen: contamination of, 437–52 passim; complaints of, 437; charges of, 438, 444; radiation check

of, 439; death of, 442, autopsy on, 442, as martyr, 446; foreign articles on, 447; father of, 449; reports on, 454; death of memorialized, 459

Silkwood case: 453, 455, 459, 462, 466, 470, 488, 495, 498

Silobor S.A.: 398

Silobor SA of France: 455

Silver, production of: 471

Sims, George T.: 16, 24

Sinclair Oil Company: 57, 117, 207, 379

Singapore, rigs built in: 427, 484

Sitton, F. A.: 211

Skelly Oil Company: 298, 320, 388, 456

Skyjacking: 393

Sledge, Byron: 9, 16n., 28

Smith, Bill: see Bill Smith mine

Smith, Harrison M.: 34, 53; see also Harrison Smith Oil Company

Smith # 1: 28

Snowden Oil: 161

Société Irano-Italienne des Petroles (SIRIP): 365

Soda ash, production of: 365, 388, 413, 430, 462, 489

Sodium carbonate, production of: 366

Sodium chlorate, production of: 388, 390, 422

Sodium sulphate, production of: 366

Sohio: 117, 128

South Africa, wells in: 401, 431

South America, drilling in: 266, 277ff., 282, 285, 291, 302f., 310, 320, 466; see also under individual countries

South Dakota, oil and gas wells in: 122, 128, 233, 436

Southeast Asia, wells in: 406, 413, 420–21, 466, 478

Southeast Big Lake Field: 233

Southern Interstate Nuclear Board: 394

South Maud pool: 104

Southwestern Oil & Refining Company: 425

Southwestern Refining Company, Incorporated: 425f., 455, 459f., 492

Southwest–W.C. Feazel Dubach Plant: 351

Space race: 307

Spain, drilling in: 409, 413, 422, 431

Spaulding, Charles M.: 124

Speed limit: 453

Spencer Chemical Company: 312

Spindletop Dome: 6, 169

West Cameron area, wells in: 413, 421, 434, 469
West Edmond field: 114f., 117, 122
Western Deculta, Limited: 459
Western Natural Gas: 266
Westinghouse Hanford Company: 408, 438, 488
West Virginia, oil well in: 344
West Welch field: 370
Whale, as source of energy: 3
Wharton, Porter, Jr.: 354
Whiting, A. J.: 84
Wiggs, Wallace: 42, 106
Wilcox, H. F.: see H. F. Wilcox Oil and Gas Company
"Wild Mary Sudik": 26
Wilkinson, Charles ("Bud"): 322
Williamson, Mac Q.: 181
Williston Basin: 42, 196, 207, 233, 427
Willkie, Wendell: 100
Wilson, Robert E.: 100, 103
Wilson & Toomer Fertilizer Company: 396, 398, 399–400
Wimberly, Carl: 86
Wind River field: 370
W. M. Gallagher Oil Company: 33
Wodka, Steve: 439, 442
Wolff, Paul A.: 192, 205, 263ff., 311
Wood Chemical Company: 339

Woods Corporation: 462
Woodward, L. A.: 250, 504ff.
Wooten, Elton ("Buster"): 47
World War II: 93, 100–11, 114, 123–24, 147, 171, 190, 195
Wynnewood refinery: 129, 132, 179, 181, 187, 209, 230, 351, 371, 422, 460, 487; expansion and improvement of, 197, 230, 232, 276, 282, 336, 339, 358, 364, 387, 455; pipelines for, 230, 262, 310, 422, 427
Wyoming, oil and gas wells in: 122, 126, 128, 144, 150, 152, 179f., 187, 190, 194, 207, 222, 233, 267, 277, 285, 293, 344, 370, 389, 436, 478

Yacimientos Petroliferos Fiscales (YPF): 282, 303, 310, 320, 327, 338–39, 373, 401
Yakutat Indians: 223
Yellow Cab gasoline stations: 130
Yellow cake, production of: 134, 308, 362, 402, 412, 488f.; see also uranium

Zinc: exploration for, 427, 430; production of, 471
Zitting, R. T.: 421, 515f.
Zodiac Oil Company: 101
Zoernig, Elizabeth: 212, 514ff.

DATE DUE